THE ENGLISH NAVIGATION LAWS

A SEVENTEENTH-CENTURY EXPERIMENT IN SOCIAL ENGINEERING

THE ENGLISH NAVIGATION LAWS

A SEVENTEENTH-CENTURY EXPERIMENT
IN SOCIAL ENGINEERING

BY

LAWRENCE A. HARPER

OCTAGON BOOKS

A DIVISION OF FARRAR, STRAUS AND GIROUX

New York   1973

Reprinted 1964
by special arrangement with Columbia University Press

Second Octagon printing 1973

OCTAGON BOOKS
A DIVISION OF FARRAR, STRAUS & GIROUX, INC.
19 Union Square West
New York, N. Y. 10003

LIBRARY OF CONGRESS CATALOG CARD NUMBER: 64-16382
ISBN 0-374-93667-6

Printed in U.S.A. by
NOBLE OFFSET PRINTERS, INC.
New York, N.Y. 10003

TO MY FATHER

PREFACE

THE Navigation Acts are among the most famous of English mercantile measures. Child called the Act of 1660, some decades after its enactment, the *"Charta Maritima"* of English shipping, and more than a century later Adam Smith, less iconoclastic than some of his disciples, added his praise. The subject has been discussed by many whose interests centered on broader problems, but it has never been studied for what it was, a deliberately planned attempt to regulate economic conduct along predetermined lines—or, to put it more briefly, an experiment in social engineering.

Although my ideas have undoubtedly been influenced by the right-about-face in American governmental theories since 1932, its effect has probably not been great. My interest in the subject can be traced back to ambitions awakened by the enthusiasm of Professor F. J. Teggart of the University of California for discovering how things work, and to the emphasis laid by Professor Karl Llewellyn upon the need for knowing more than the laws as they appear upon the statute books. The chief extra-documentary factors influencing my conclusions have probably been an undergraduate major in political science, a three-year course in law, and practical legal experience acquired while specializing in customs litigation.

The investigation was begun in the autumn of 1925 when I was in England. The major part of the preliminary work was done from original sources before making any extended investigation of the secondary works. This method enabled me to formulate my basic views uninfluenced by those of others, but I am fully aware of the extent of my indebtedness to such writers as Beer, Andrews, Oppenheim, Lipson, Barbour, Nef, Root, Pitman, and Shaw, whose illuminating researches have so often been used to confirm, supplement, modify, or confute my tentative theories. Unfortunately the recent books of Harrington, Judah, Hunter, Lounsbury, and Nettels, and Labaree's invaluable collection of instructions to governors were not available to lighten my original labors, but have been helpful in making the final revision. Most of all I must acknowledge my indebtedness to the editors of the Calendars of State Papers Domestic, State Papers Colonial, Treasury Books, and Treasury Papers, and most particularly to Dr. William A. Shaw, whose unrivaled knowledge of the Treasury books and papers and whose unusual ability for complete and accurate summarization have made his work invaluable.

I began, with the enthusiasm of youth, by trying to exhaust all the material on the subject. As the years passed the hopelessness of the task became more apparent, but not until 200 pounds of notes had been copied and 15,000 pages photographed. The natural result was documentary indigestion for which the only known antidote is writing and rewriting. The present version is the result of six revisions and a constant fight against the ever-present temptation to give all the details which it took so many hours to uncover.

As is explained more fully in the first chapter, the chief purpose of this work is to analyze the process of social engineering, as exemplified by the Navigation Acts, in the hope that it may throw some light upon the problems involved in our present social experiments. However, I realize that others may have different interests and may wish information on particular points of general historical concern. In so far as possible, without destroying the main continuity, all discussion of the different topics treated has been grouped together, and has been divided into four parts, the first of which deals with the origins of the laws, the second with their enforcement in England, the third with the same problem in the colonies, and the fourth with the results accomplished. Thus economic historians will be concerned primarily with Parts One and Four, administrators with Parts Two and Three, and colonial historians with Parts Three and Four.

In the first three parts the factual data have been subordinated so as not to interfere with the account of the process as a whole. Except for the necessity of tracing the early experiments, the study has concentrated upon the last half of the seventeenth century in the belief that it was wiser to focus upon the formative years than to give a more cursory sketch of a longer period. The principal contributions of this section, apart from the emphasis upon the social-engineering point of view, probably consist in the review of the mercantile background and legislative history of the Act of 1651, the outline of English customs practices, and the better perspective obtained by observing the colonial enforcement of the laws against the background of English experience merely as part of a great administrative problem in which colonial officials and smugglers alike followed examples set in the mother country.

Part Four, on results, was at first only an epilogue to an administrative study, as far as I was concerned. From year to year I changed my mind as to whether the laws were beneficial, merely ineffectual, or positively harmful. Eventually the conflicting views of the various writers who had discussed the question aroused my curiosity, and I set out to find a solution which would convince me if no one else. The method followed was to formulate a theory and then to search for facts which might tend to disprove it, and those hypotheses which did not survive the test were discarded. The procedure did not permit confining the study to the period from 1660 to 1696, since the obvious challenge to the theory that English shipping depended upon the laws was the question, how did England manage to have a merchant marine before and after the years they were in force? It therefore became necessary to pursue the history of English shipping from the days of the Armada until well into the reign of Queen Victoria. Lack of statistics for the early period forced resort to calculations and estimates, but those utilized are only the ones which withstood the various tests to which they were subjected. Literally hundreds of others were discarded because they did not seem reasonably reliable in the light of other known facts. Because of the different opinions which exist on many points it seemed best to marshal the evidence more fully than in the first three parts, but in most cases such cumulative material has been placed in footnotes which the skeptic may scan but the general reader may skip.

The habit of considering the Navigation Acts primarily in their relation to colonial history may at first cause some to wonder at the comparatively small space devoted to the plantations and to be disappointed by the failure to go more fully into the effects of the measures upon the Thirteen Colonies. Yet to have essayed any comprehensive account of American economic and political development on the same scale as that attempted for English shipping would have required many more years of detailed study of agricultural, commercial, and maritime data not yet fully analyzed. More important, such a course would have thrown the work out of proportion. After all, the Acts were English laws and the Englishmen who enacted and maintained them were chiefly concerned with their effects upon England's trade and navigation. The benefits or injuries resulting therefrom to the colonists are another story, discussed in part, at least, by my essay, "The Effect of the Navigation Acts on the Thirteen Colonies," in *The Era of the American Revolution* (New York, 1939).

Apart from a brief chart of the most important provisions of the Navigation Acts, no attempt has been made to include an appendix at this time. However, the cumulative data of a legal, administrative, or statistical nature for which there was no room here will be published in filmbook or lithoprinted form for the convenience of other research workers. Thanks to W.P.A. and N.Y.A. assistance, statistical analyses have already been made of the imports and exports in twenty of the most important colonial ports and will be available for distribution in filmbook form later this year. Attention should also be called to three books which have appeared since this volume went to press: Elizabeth E. Hoon, *The Organization of the English Customs System, 1696-1786,* for its detailed description of the English customs service; G. N. Clark, *Guide to English Commercial Statistics, 1696-1782,* for its comments on source materials; and the fourth volume of C. M. Andrews, *The Colonial Period of American History*, for information concerning all colonial phases of the Acts, especially for its discussion of the enactment of legislation after 1696 and its full account of colonial administrative institutions.

A word of explanation is due those who are accustomed to refer to the laws governing the shipping and trade of England and her colonies as the Acts of Trade. The choice of the term, Navigation Acts, has been deliberate. Although in colonial history the great control which the measures exerted over commerce suggests placing the emphasis upon their relationship to trade, this study approaches the laws from the English point of view. On that basis they are more properly described as Navigation Acts, since it was England's desire to foster her shipping which brought the original measures into being, and their success must be measured primarily by that standard. Moreover, there were many acts regulating trade, and the chief interest of this study concerns those influencing ships and seamen.

Mention should also be made of certain technical difficulties which have arisen. The distinction which has to be maintained between England and Scotland before their union complicates discussions which straddle the year 1707. To maintain the more important early distinctions, the practice has been followed of using the adjective "English" throughout, the understanding being that it is synonymous with "British" for references after 1707. Yet statistical data concerning entries and clearances and the like in England refer only to England and not to Britain unless otherwise indicated. Although the procedure obviously is illogical, it is less awkward than the others which might be followed and causes little or no confusion in practice. Similarly no attempt has been made to indicate that most of the statistics fail to correspond exactly with the calendar year to which they are attributed. They are credited to the year in which the greatest number of months fall, except in the few cases of approximately even division, such as those from June to June, where a double date has been used.

Few historical efforts are produced without the coöperation of friends and advisers, and this study is no exception. Although they should not be blamed for errors which remain, they should be credited with having detected many now removed. Special gratitude is due to Professor E. I. McCormac of the University of California, who first interested me in the subject of history; to Professor A. P. Newton of the University of London, who introduced me to the archives in England; and to Professor Evarts B. Greene, under whose guidance this work has been done, for his kindly advice and never-failing courtesy.

Professor Violet Barbour of Vassar College and Mr. F. J. Fisher of the London School of Economics have given good counsel and valuable data. Professors C. W. de Kiewiet and W. T. Root of the University of Iowa, G. H. Guttridge of the University of California, and R. B. Morris of the College of the City of New York have been so kind as to read and to criticize the manuscript in whole or in part. I am indebted to Professor C. M. Andrews not only, like all scholars in the colonial field, for his *Guides* to the sources in Britain, but also for his generosity in examining and helping to correct the volume in proof. Thanks are also rendered to the staffs of all the libraries visited, especially to B. R. Leftwich at the London Custom House, Miss Harriet Tapley at the Essex Institute, T. P. Martin at the Library of Congress, Charles Fickus of the Maryland Historical Society, R. B. Haselden at the Huntington Library, to Miss Isabel Powell, G. P. Ambrose, and Engel Sluiter for the loan of some of their notes, and to Mr. Henry Wiggins and others of the staff of Columbia University Press for many helpful suggestions and extraordinary patience which must have been sorely tried by my efforts to perfect details after the volume was set in type.

Former students who assisted include Miss Virginia Bever; Max Schumacher; Dr. Edgar Stewart, now of Albany College, Portland, Oregon; Mrs. La Wanda Cox, without whose aid the Appendix summarizing the laws might never have been completed; Miss June Sweeney, who with Mrs. Margaret v. B. Smith of the University of California Press helped in preparing the index; and Miss Margaret W. Clark, whose contributions in all phases of the work, from note-gathering to proofreading, have been greater than any prefatory note can adequately acknowledge. Above all I am deeply indebted to my father, F. F. G. Harper, both for the financial assistance which made the extended research possible and for the valuable suggestions drawn from a lifetime of experience with customs problems which so often made the data discussed more intelligible; and to my wife for her patience in crossing and recrossing the continent and the Atlantic with grips full of notes, and in suffering her house to be left in disorder for weeks on end, to say nothing of the very substantial and material aid she has given in all other respects.

L. A. H.

University of California
  Berkeley, California
    October, 1939

CONTENTS

Conclusion

Appendices

ABBREVIATIONS

Adm.	Admiralty Papers
AO	Audit Office Papers
APC	Great Britain, Acts of the Privy Council
APC Col.	Great Britain, Acts of the Privy Council Colonial
BM	British Museum
BM Add. MSS	British Museum Additional Manuscripts
BM Harl. MSS	British Museum Harleian Manuscripts
BM Lans. MSS	British Museum Lansdowne Manuscripts
BT	Board of Trade Records
CJ	Great Britain, House of Commons Journals
CO	Colonial Office Papers
CSP	Great Britain, Calendar of State Papers
CSPC	Great Britain, Calendar of State Papers, Colonial
CSPD	Great Britain, Calendar of State Papers, Domestic
CTB	Great Britain, Calendar of Treasury Books
CTBP	Great Britain, Calendar of Treasury Books and Papers
CTP	Great Britain, Calendar of Treasury Papers
CU-BUS MSS	Columbia University, School of Business Manuscripts
DNB	Dictionary of National Biography
E	Exchequer Records
GLB	Goldsmiths' Company's Library Broadsides
GL MSS	Goldsmiths' Company's Library Manuscripts
HCA	High Court of Admiralty
HMC	Great Britain, Historical Manuscripts Commission
LCB	Library of Congress Broadsides
LCH	London Custom House
LJ	Great Britain, House of Lords Journals
LTJ	Lords of Trade and Plantations Journals
Md. HS	Maryland Historical Society Manuscripts
MHSC	Massachusetts Historical Society Collections
NYCD	New York Colonial Documents
NYDH	New York, Documentary History
NYHS	New York Historical Society
NYPL	New York Public Library
PC	Privy Council Records
PHST	Pennsylvania Historical Society Transcripts
PRO	Public Record Office
SP	State Papers
T	Treasury Papers
T & SP	Tudor and Stuart Proclamations
THCM	Trinity House Court Minutes
THL	Trinity House Letters
THT	Trinity House Transactions
VCGC	Virginia, Minutes of the Council and General Court
VEJ	Virginia, Executive Journals of the Council

INTRODUCTION

I believe it will not be unacceptable to the Reader, to find some summary observations on the Act of Navigation, laid before him; because this Act is very dark and hard to be understood, and has caused great Doubt and Variety of Opinion.—Forster, *Digest of All the Laws Relating to the Customs*, p. 117.

I

HISTORY AND SOCIAL ENGINEERING

THE historian, once the most respectable of the social scientists, is at present more or less ignored while his younger brothers occupy the forefront of public attention. The man in the street is willing to let the dead past bury its dead. He wants something practical and up-to-date, takes an interest in economic reforms, and seems reconciled to a period of experimentation while our social scientists are being given the opportunity to put their theories into practice.

The historian, however, ought to have a very real contribution to make. The recent emphasis upon the theory of laissez faire has been the exception rather than the rule, and even while we adhered to it in economic matters, reformers were busy regulating the public morals. Man's earlier experiments offer plenty of data for analysis and many advantages to the investigator. Contemporary events follow one another too rapidly for a full realization of their significance, and a historical study may enable us to detect points which escape our notice in the rapid whirl of current activities and may render our judgments less biased by avoiding the contemporary controversies.

Both now and in the past, public interest has centered upon the goals to be reached. We have many "social planners" who tell us *what* is to be done, but few or no "social engineers" to explain *how* it is to be accomplished—though it is elementary that we will never attain our ends unless we can succeed in providing the means.

Use of the term "engineering" to describe the process of accomplishing deliberately planned social reforms is fraught with danger, as was Bagehot's coupling of "Physics and Politics," and the formulation of an organic theory of the State. Walter Lippmann has already complained of the analogy, pointing out that the materials with which the politician must work differ from those of the engineer, since society is not an inanimate mass of steel which can be counted upon to remain constant and to stay where placed. But there is a definite value in the concept of "social engineering" as an indivisible term, written for the sake of convenience in two words rather than one.

The engineering concept throws emphasis upon the means rather than the end. In the physical world everyone recognizes that it is not sufficient to decide what engineering projects should be undertaken; that it is fully as important to learn how they can be accomplished. If we can acquire the same point of view in dealing with social problems, we may attain greater success. It is not sufficient to dream of what ought to be. It is essential that we know how to make our dreams come true.

The process of social change is essentially one of construction. We may talk in terms of curing old ills, but what we really wish to do is to build new habits. Whatever change we strive to effect, the method is much the same. Someone must have an idea concerning the reform desired. If the reform is to be accomplished through legislative means, the idea must find its way into the statute books; it must be interpreted by the courts or other proper authorities. The administrative machinery of the government must attempt to enforce it, and sooner or later some determination must be made as to results. The details may vary somewhat if other agencies than the state are employed, and the process is, let us say, religious rather than political; but the principles involved are essentially those of social mechanics, and the application of them may well be described as social engineering.

The subject has not, of course, been altogether neglected. Lawyers, administrators, and economists have from time to time considered certain of the technical questions involved. But each has approached the problem from the point of view of his own specialty, and there is still need for a more general approach, especially for studies which will strive not merely to supply blue prints of the machinery used for certain social purposes, but to give a description of that machinery *in action*, to show the interaction of all the parts, the resistance encountered, the friction engendered, and the results accomplished.

If a historical inquiry is to be really useful, we must take great care in the methods followed. We cannot be content with too confident deductions concerning the forces that govern mankind's destinies, like those which led one very eminent historian to assert that the law of history is the law of progress, and another to decide that we are rapidly getting worse and worse and to place most of the blame upon the rise of democracy. Such sweeping conclusions about the lessons of history are too obviously influenced by other considerations, as were those of the German historian who predicted the decline of the West after the collapse of the Hohenzollern empire, only once again to have reviving hopes with the advent of Hitler.

It will do little good to recount many instances of social engineering and then to affirm or deny the merit of such activity. Until we have a better understanding of the factors involved it will be wiser to make a careful study of some one attempt in the hope that our analysis will help us to understand the fundamental problems involved in all.

It is here that the historian enters the picture. He is essentially a jack-of-all-trades, and occupies a position in the social sciences similar to that of the philosopher in the field of general knowledge. It is his task to survey the entire scene and to see it as a whole.

It goes without saying that no study of a single social experiment will suffice to establish the principles of social engineering, and the following account of the attempts England made in the seventeenth century to develop her merchant marine by legislative means is offered only as one of what it is hoped may sometime become a series. Although the purpose of the investigation is to learn how we can improve our own methods, it seems wise to let the history of the laws speak for itself and to reserve modern comparisons and applications until all evidence has been reviewed. Thus if the reader does not agree with the writer's conclusions, he has the material with which to form his own. It may be that from the deductions of one or the other or both we can profit vicariously from the experience of the past, or at least learn to avoid some of our ancestors' more obvious mistakes.

PART ONE

ORIGIN OF THE LAWS

II

THE MERCANTILE MIND

SEVENTEENTH-CENTURY England faced many of the problems which confront us today. For better or for worse, it encountered the capitalistic system, the problems of unemployment,
poor relief, monopolies, and banking. The national debt increased
by leaps and bounds, and the public credit was not merely imperiled
but actually gave way when the Exchequer stopped making payments in 1672. Relatively speaking there was the same displacement
of labor; coal was rapidly becoming a source of power; enclosures
were disturbing the agrarians; and the discovery of the New World
shifted many of the older channels of trade. International rivalry
manifested itself both in the world of trade and on the battlefield.
Nations were not afraid that there might be war; peace was considered merely a rest period between wars. Europe was free from
strife only eight years in the seventeenth century. England herself
engaged in two revolutions and nine foreign wars and was always in
fear of foreign competition, first from Spain, then Holland, and
thereafter France.[1]

The danger of war explains much that might otherwise be difficult
to understand in English mercantilism. It clears up the apparent
paradox of the adoption, by a country in which agricultural interests
predominated, of legislative programs which redounded principally

[1] The best surveys of conditions, especially in their economic aspects, are to be
found in Clark, *The Seventeenth Century;* Cunningham, *English Industry and Commerce,* Vol. II; Lipson, *Economic History,* Vols. II and III; Nef, *British Coal Industry;* and Scott, *Joint-Stock Companies,* Vol. I. For discussions of the historical and
theoretical aspects of mercantilism, the reader should consult Schmoller, *Mercantile
System;* Heckscher, *Mercantilism;* and Viner, "English Theories of Foreign Trade,"
Jour. Pol. Econ., XXXVIII, 249-301, 404-57. The account of the "mercantile mind"
given hereafter has not been compiled merely from the works of the more competent
theorists. By searching for the less carefully reasoned and more ephemeral material
contained in broadsides and similar publications, an attempt has been made to describe
the public attitude as reflected in and molded by the writings of the day.

to the merchants' advantage. The explanation lies in the correlation supposed to exist between national security, bullion, and foreign trade. War was managed "by the power of money," and it was believed that no nation could be "accounted safe, or mistress of its liberties" without an adequate supply.[2] Since England had no gold or silver of her own, she could acquire the bullion upon which the monetary system rested only by exporting more merchandise than she imported. Hence the landed gentry could be persuaded to pass legislation intended to promote a favorable balance of trade. They continually had before them, in one form or another, the warning voiced by Davenant:

Whenever we lose our trade, we must bid farewel to that wealth and strength which have hitherto enabled us to preserve our liberties, against the designs of Spain and France, . . . want of due circumspection in a point so essential to the very existence of this kingdom, may, perhaps, in less than an age, reduce us to be the prey of some conquerors, notwithstanding our large estates in land, the fertility of our soil, the richness of our product, and the convenience of our ports.[3]

Because of England's insular position, her naval force was recognized to be "the Main Body and Strength of the Nation." It in turn depended upon commerce and navigation, since ships and seamen "like Food to the Body must be dayly renewed."[4] William Potter succinctly summarized contemporary beliefs when he declared "the more Trading doth Encrease in any place, the more Ships multiply in that place . . . the more ships any Nation hath, the more strong they are at Sea."[5]

The general view was that England could protect herself, if she would. Contemporary writers declared that England's geographic situation gave her "the Preferrance of the most Valuable Trade in the World"; they proclaimed that the British Isles had better air

[2] Davenant, *Works*, V, 453. Further indication of the importance attached to bullion at that time may be found in Hodges, *The Groans of the Poor for the Want of Our Money,* and in Viner, "English Theories of Foreign Trade," *Jour. Pol. Econ.,* XXXVIII, 264-98.

[3] Davenant, *Works*, V, 455.

[4] Brewster, *Essays on Trade and Navigation*, p. 2; Yarranton, *England's Improvement*, Part I, 6-7, 37.

[5] Potter, *The Key to Wealth*, p. 77; Battie (*The Merchants Remonstrance*, p. 1) declared that "Trade is the life of a State, Manufactures are the sinews of Trade, and Money is the soule of both."

and better ports than Holland and that they were superior "in their Native Grewth and Production for Commerce; as Rich Soyl is to that which is Barren."[6] One man expressed the general belief when he wrote, "it was said of Old and grounded upon good Reason, that England was a mighty animal that would never die, unless it destroys itself."[7] Even those who believed that "all was out of joint" and that England was losing in the race for international supremacy thought of the country's supposedly desperate plight as a challenge to further endeavor. They exhorted patriots to repent of the habitual fondness for sloth that was blamed for England's being on the "brink of Ruine," to lay aside their vices, and to acquire the virtues of their arch rivals in trade, the Dutch.[8]

Each economic group, however, had its own scheme for promoting the national welfare, and there was often a clash of interests. The desires of the agriculturalist did not always coincide with those of the trader, the manufacturer, or the consumer. Merchants who banded together in chartered companies had conflicts with those who wished freedom of trade. The interests of London and of the outports were not always the same.[9] Merchants trading with Portugal and the countries within the Straits opposed opening a commerce with France for wines; importers from Italy and Turkey quarreled as to the relative merits of their trades; and the "Japaners and Joyners" raised their voices in protest against cabinetwork brought from the East Indies.[10] Even so simple a matter as the voyage of a ship might give rise to conflicts between many divergent interests. The merchants were not always owners of the vessels in which they traded; in fact, they were said to have perhaps "the least share in the Ships of England."[11] They wanted to lower freight rates, while

[6] Brewster, *Essays on Trade and Navigation*, p. 1.

[7] *The Naked Truth*, pp. 1-2.

[8] Yarranton, *England's Improvement*, Dedication; Davenant, *Works*, V, 459. See also Lipson, *Economic History*, III, 11. Jenver complained on the title-page of his *London's Blame if Not Its Shame* that "with the sluggard, we fold our hands in our bosoms and will not stretch them forth to our mouths."

[9] "J. P., Esq." (*Of Trade*, p. 130) claimed that joint-stock companies restrained trade to London, to the grievance of Exeter and Bristol. Jenver blamed the loss of the fisheries upon London, in his pamphlet, *London's Blame if Not Its Shame*.

[10] British Museum Tracts on Trade, Vol. 816 m13, Nos. 1-2, 124-26; *ibid.*, Vol. 816 m14, No. 50.

[11] Brewster, *Essays on Trade and Navigation*, pp. 88-89.

the shipowners wanted to raise them. The owners desired low wages, and the masters and men hoped for high ones.

All were united as to the need for preserving trade and shipping, but they were divided in their views about the means of effecting their ends. Many approached the problem by advocating efforts "to make trade easy and necessary, and thereby to make it our interest to trade."[12] They sought improved harbors, the development of river navigation and internal waterways, the simplification of legal procedure, better regulated insurance, and convoys in time of war.[13] Others advocated usury laws to reduce the interest rate, or plans for the recoinage of the currency, the establishment of banks, and the improvement of credit.[14]

One school of thought wished England to become a "universal merchant" and to serve as an entrepôt for the world's commerce. With this end in view William Stockton proposed that customs duties be replaced by an excise tax payable only when the goods were sold, and therefore not assessable on goods passing through England.[15] Brewster, Child, and others were willing to retain the customs duties but desired a greater rebate of the duty on imported foreign goods, which were later exported, than the moiety then allowed by law.[16] Others argued for the establishment of free ports similar to those at Venice and Leghorn,[17] and one anonymous

[12] Child, *New Discourse*, p. 160.

[13] Raleigh, "A Discourse of Seaports," *Harl. Misc.*, IV, 305-9; Yarranton, *England's Improvement*, Part I, 7; Cary, *An Essay on the State of England*, pp. 141-43; Roberts, *Treasure of Traffike*, No. 14; *A View of Some Deficiencies in the Aids of Trade*, No. 28.

[14] For suggestions regarding interest, see Child, *New Discourse*, pp. 52, 177; Barbon, *Discourse of Trade*, p. 71; Brewster, *Essays on Trade and Navigation*, p. 7; Manley, *Usury at Six Percent Examined*. For coinage and credit schemes, see Blackwell, *An Essay towards Carrying on the Present War against France*; Cary, *An Essay on the Coyn and Credit of England*; Lewis, *Proposals to Increase Trade*; Potter, *Tradesman's Jewel*; Roberts, *Treasure of Traffike*; A. V[ickaris], *An Essay for Regulating of Coyn*. For banking schemes, see Barbon, *Discourse of Trade*, pp. 27-28; Brewster, *Essays on Trade and Navigation*, pp. 6-7; Cary, *An Essay towards the Settlement of a National Credit*; "S. E.," *Touchstone of Mony and Commerce*; Lewis, *Proposals to the King and Parliament*; Yarranton, *England's Improvement*, Part I, 7, 15-23.

[15] *The Foreign Excise Considered*, pp. 27-29.

[16] Brewster, *Essays on Trade and Navigation*, pp. 36-37; Child, *New Discourse*, p. 160; Cradocke, *Wealth Discovered*, pp. 10-11.

[17] "B. W.," *Free Ports, the Nature and Necessity of Them Stated*; "Z. G.," *Excise Anatomiz'd and Trade Epitomiz'd*; Blackwell, *An Essay towards Carrying on the Present War against France*; *Considerations concerning Free Ports*.

seventeenth-century writer seemed ready for free trade when he declared:

It is the Interest of England to send their Product and Manufactory to the best Market, and from thence to bring such Commodities as they cannot purchase cheaper any where else . . . and by this natural Circulation the Nation will be enrich'd . . . .

A Free Trade makes all manner of Commodities cheap; the cheapness of Commodities impowers our People to work cheaper; the cheapness of Work encourages a Foreign Trade; and a Foreign Trade brings Wealth and People, and that alone raises the Price of Lands and Houses.

On the contrary, Prohibitions make Cloathing and every thing else dear; so that the People cannot live without they have a proportionable price for their Labour. And I conceive Prohibitions to be a principal Reason why we Cannot Trade so cheap as our Neighbours do.[18]

The contrary view was taken by those who desired to rely upon the home trade and that founded upon native staples. Carew Reynel argued:

That the more home Trade, variety of Manufactures, and Husbandries we have within our selves, the more Foreign Trade we shall have also . . . home Trade is the foundation of Foreign, and if we are full of home Commodities, every private man will be of a publick spirit to gain Transportation for them.[19]

It irked the author of *The Naked Truth* that England let traders bring "home superfluous Commodities that are purchased with our Bullion, to the hinderance of our own Native Commodities."[20] Another complained of the decrease of England's "own Growth fit for Exportation," and "the double Increase of forreign costly Goods and Commodities brought over more and more from beyond the Seas."[21] The great favorite of such writers was the wool trade, the "Golden Fleece . . . the spring of our Riches," which in 1699 supplied more than a third of England's "universal exports."[22]

Another local industry holding a peculiar fascination for contemporaries was the "great and desirable Rich Trade of Fishing."[23]

[18] *An Answer to Mr. Cary's Reply.*
[19] *The True English Interest,* pp. 35-36.
[20] *The Naked Truth,* p. 11.
[21] Haines, *Prevention of Poverty,* p. 2.
[22] *The Naked Truth,* p. 2; Davenant, *Works,* V, 460.
[23] Yarranton, *England's Improvement,* Part I, 16.

English interest in this trade was stimulated by irritation at Holland's success in procuring much of her wealth off England's own coasts. It promised a variety of employment, on land in drying and salting the fish and repairing nets and boats, and on sea both directly in fishing and indirectly in carrying the catch to the Mediterranean and in bringing back salt from France.[24] Repeated failures did not deter Parliament from renewing the efforts to promote the fisheries, always regarded in the rather florid language of Misselden as "A Mine of Gold . . . the Mine is deepe, the veines are great, the Ore is rare, the Gold is pure, the extent unlimited, the wealth unknowne, the worth invaluable."[25]

Those who favored home trades usually rated the merits of the short voyage above those of the long voyage. They countered the argument of Mun and others[26] that longer voyages employed more ships, by discussing the need for seamen. Trades pursued near at hand permitted the King to impress both men and ships "at any time for any occasion."[27] Long voyages might keep sailors away when most needed and did not increase the total supply. According to John Cary, it was the short voyages which trained seamen, "both the Imployers and the Imployed being desirous to make their first Tryals on such Voyages."[28] The voyage to Newcastle for coal was reckoned "if not the only, yet the especial Nursery and School of Seamen." Another writer declared it to be the "chiefest in employment of seamen" and "the gentlest, and most open to the landsmen," whereas ships making voyages "far out of the kingdom" were bound by their charter party to the merchant "not to carry but sufficient men, and such as know their labour, and can take their turn at the helm, top, and yard."[29] He also believed that the short trades were the most healthful, and he denounced the trade to the Indies as having been bought at "the price of blood," since it had, according to his fig-

---

[24] Misselden, *Circle of Commerce*, p. 141; Jenver, *London's Blame if Not Its Shame;* Child, *New Discourse*, pp. xxii-xxiii.

[25] *Circle of Commerce*, pp. 140-41.

[26] Mun, *England's Treasure by Forraign Trade*, p. 36; Hall, *Importance of the British Plantations*, p. 19.

[27] Hagthorpe, *England's Exchequer*, p. 8.

[28] Cary, *An Essay on the State of England*, pp. 60-61.

[29] "The Trade's Increase," *Harl. Misc.*, IV, 221.

ures, cost the lives of more than two thousand of the three thousand men engaged in it.[30]

Tradition supported the advocates of the home trade and short voyages, but potent forces were opposed to them. The lure of sudden riches fired men's imaginations. The amount of gold obtained by Spain in the New World did not diminish in the telling, and Holland was popularly supposed to have found a source of equally fabulous wealth in the East Indies. In days when tales were told of the Dutch measuring their profits by tons of gold, many more doubtless needed than heeded the contemporary dramatist's advice not to exchange the security of "competent certenties" for the dangers of "excellent uncertenties."[31] English sporting instincts were awakened by the elements of hazard and chance involved in conquering new worlds. Commerce with the Continent had, in the minds of the gentry, been tainted by the bargaining and haggling of the market, but the upper classes thought of the new trades as adventures and declared, "the stranger the country, the greater the adventure."[32]

World trade meant colonies, and colonization appealed to many classes. Patriots believed colonies could serve as a base for war with Spain. The religiously inclined thought of the Indians awaiting conversion. Philanthropists found in expansion a solution for England's surplus population. Merchants foresaw new markets, naval leaders an increase of shipping and mariners, and a new source for naval supplies. The argument was advanced that a world-wide trade, founded in part upon colonies, would be freer from interruptions in time of war than the older routes of commerce.[33]

The task of the seventeenth-century mercantilists lay in selecting the best features of all the proposals and in combining as many as possible into a workable scheme. They had no hesitancy in calling upon the government to act; they definitely believed in the virtues of legislation. In periods of depression many found fault, expressly or impliedly, with the rulers of the kingdom, their "negligent or fearful councils" and "weak laws." They declared that "Trade is

[30] *Idem.*
[31] *Eastward Hoe,* Act II, scene i, cited in Beer, *Origins,* p. 46.
[32] "The Trade's Increase," *Harl. Misc.,* IV, 218.
[33] Hall, *Importance of the British Plantations;* Davenant, *Works,* II, 2, 9, 20; V, 411-12; Beer, *Origins,* Chap. III; Beer, *Old Colonial System,* I, 16-19, 23-26, 35-38.

like a nice and coy Mistress," which one must court and pursue, that "publick spirits and wise measures" are necessary for its conquest, and that to insure its retention it must be "well fixt by a good law."[34]

But we must not think of mercantilism as a system akin to our modern schemes of social planning. Mercantile measures were primarily practical expedients, however well conceived. The cry for legislative action arose from no doctrinaire commitment to the value of legislation, similar to that held by free traders concerning its undesirability. Child, for example, approved of England's Navigation Acts, although he admitted that the Dutch had none and that he had "yet to be informed where the Dutch have missed their proper interest in trade." He defended his position by a doctrine of economic relativity, that

That which is fit for one nation to do in relation to their trade, is not fit for all; no more than the same policy is necessary to a prevailing army that are masters of the field, as to an army of less force. . . . The Dutch, by reason of their great stocks, low interest, multitude of merchants and shipping, are masters in the field of trade, and therefore have no need to build castles, fortresses, and places of retreat; such I account laws of limitation, and securing of particular trades to the natives of any kingdom.[35]

When mercantilist pamphleteers stopped to consider the point, they recognized that regulatory jurisprudence involved more problems than the enactment of a "good law." As one writer declared, "it were better to have fewer Lawes, with better Execution, than more Lawes, with more trouble and lesse use."[36] Petty recognized the correlation between the value of legislation and the possibility of making it effective when he advised his countrymen that, "as wiser Physicians tamper not excessively with their Patients," so in politics and economics the same method should be used, "rather observing and complying with the motions of nature, then contradicting it with vehement Administrations . . . for 'Naturam expellas furcâ licet usque recurrit.' "[37] Henry Robinson complained that the

[34] Davenant, *Works*, V, 453; Yarranton, *England's Improvement*, Part I, Epistle to the Reader and p. 174; "C. K.," *Some Seasonable and Modest Thoughts*, p. 5; Fortrey, *England's Interest*, pp. 37-42.
[35] *New Discourse*, pp. 106-7.
[36] Misselden, *Circle of Commerce*, p. 136.
[37] Petty, *Economic Writings*, I, 60. See also Sheridan, *A Discourse on the Rise and Power of Parliaments*, pp. 198-99.

laws were "so numerous and intricate . . . that it is not possible to know them all, much lesse keep them in memory, and avoyd the being entangled by them." He wanted to know "whether the Multiplicity of Courts of Justice do not cause a more mischievous Confusion in the World, than the Babilonian of Languages," and he hoped "That some honest publique spirited Lawyer who thoroughly understands the various Meanders, Quirks and subtilities of this over-powering Faculty would anatomize and lay open unto the Nation, how easily it is for the very best Lawes wee have to be evaded and frustrated, and the whole Formality and proceedings to be avoyded and deluded by legall fallacies and tricks."[38]

Most writers, however, were too busy advocating economic panaceas to worry about how they would be carried out. Some of the literature remained merely *ex parte* pleading, but more often the proponents of a particular idea sought to have their work attain the status of a comprehensive treatise on trade by combining various specific proposals that appealed to their fancy, the less able sometimes failing to note that one scheme would nullify another.[39]

Recognition of possible conflicts existing in social regulation between individual interest and the general welfare was usually confined to observations concerning only one-half of the problem. When considering the need for national power, the writers observed that unregulated activity would be designed to bring the greatest gain to particular persons, even at the risk of loss to the nation, "unless Authority interpose, and afford help, as there may be occasion."[40] As Brewster declared, "not only Merchants, but Seamen will Chuse, as all men naturally do, that Employment which brings Profit with least Toil and Labour."[41] Yet at other times the writers realized that, since man's actions depend upon personal motivation, individual interests must be conciliated. Thus Child argued in favor of usury laws, that no merchant would drudge in trade if the interest rate were not low enough to keep him from being tempted to turn gentleman and

[38] *Certain Considerations*, pp. ii-iii.
[39] Crosfield, *England's Glory*, Preface; Misselden, *Circle of Commerce*, p. 141; Brewster, *Essays on Trade and Navigation*, pp. i-iii; Yarranton, *England's Improvement*, Part I, Preface and pp. 193-95.
[40] "J. P. Esq.," *Of Trade*, pp. 147-48.
[41] *Essays on Trade and Navigation*, p. 77.

settle on a landed estate.[42] Another writer, opposing such laws, maintained that they would merely cause less money to be loaned.[43] "J. P., Esquire," claimed that prohibitions against the exportation of coin and bullion had never done any good, that the only remedy was to make exportation unprofitable.[44] Sir Francis Brewster declared that "no human Policy and Law can bring men into Arts with Success, and the increase of them, but by Gain, and security of enjoying it."[45]

In so far as seventeenth-century theorists attempted any reconciliation of individual interest and public welfare, it rested on the assumption that there was an ideal balance which, if attained, would secure national prosperity as well as individual advancement. To quote Brewster again: "there needs no trick to promote the true Interest of a Nation, every man will run into it; and he would be a States-man worthy of Honour that did advance the Interest of his Country above that of their Neighbours."[46] Followers of Adam Smith must not misunderstand the nature of the assumption. It did not rely upon any doctrine that the "invisible hand" of Providence would supply the necessary guidance, if only man would not interpose his puny efforts. Mercantilists probably believed as devoutly in the wisdom and omnipotence of the Deity as did Smith, but they placed less reliance upon the assumption, "the Lord will provide," than upon the proverb, "God helps those who help themselves."

[42] *New Discourse,* p. 161.
[43] Robinson, *Certain Proposals,* p. 10.
[44] *Of Trade,* pp. 9-11.
[45] *Essays on Trade and Navigation,* pp. 82-83.
[46] *Ibid.,* p. 84.

III

EARLY EXPERIMENTS

ECONOMIC regulation demands more than good intentions. It requires an appreciation of economic consequences, a comprehension of the significance of distinctions in phraseology, and an understanding of administrative difficulties not often attained by legislative bodies. Before commencing our study of seventeenth-century shipping regulations, we should endeavor to learn how the Commonwealth and Restoration Parliaments acquired their knowledge of legislative technique. It then becomes apparent that they had the benefit of centuries of earlier experiments in statutory draftsmanship.

Parliament's first effort to encourage shipping clearly indicated its inexperience.[1] The Act of 5 Ric. II, stat. 1, c. 3, which provided that none of the King's subjects should ship any merchandise going out of or coming within the realm of England except in English ships, handicapped English merchants. If enforced, it would have stopped their trade whenever an English ship was not in port, while permitting their alien competitors to trade freely. Parliament soon realized its mistake. Next year an amendatory statute provided that the rule applied only when "able and sufficient" English ships could

---

[1] Here, as is so often the case, use of the adjective "first" is somewhat arbitrary. King Alfred is said to have rewarded those of his subjects who "traveled thrice over the seas" in vessels of their own, and the Act of 42 Edw. III, c. 8, included a provision "that all the Ships of England and of Gascoigne that cometh into Gascoigne, shall be first freighted to bring Wines into England before all other." But Alfred's efforts were not those of Parliament, and the statute of Edward III is so closely connected with other regulations about buying and selling that doubts arise whether Parliament's chief interest did not lie in insuring England a satisfactory supply of wine rather than in developing her shipping (Hunter, *How England Got Its Merchant Marine*, pp. 3-13, 17-20; Oppenheim, *Administration of the Royal Navy*, pp. 7-9). But these and similar problems in the early history of English shipping should be left to others. We must confine ourselves to studying the evolution of legislative technique. For our purposes it will suffice to adopt the conventional point of departure, the reign of Richard II.

be found in the ports where the merchant dwelt.[2] Eight years later a third statute declared "That all Merchants of the Realm of England shall freight *in the said Realm* the Ships of the said Realm, and not strange Ships; so that the Owners of the said Ships take reasonable Gains for the Freight of the same."[3]

The Ricardian laws do not appear to have been of great aid to English shipping. The test of the reasonableness of rates charged by English owners presumably would be those which were charged by strangers. If so, all that the laws provided was that English merchants must ship their goods in English vessels, when it was no more expensive to do so. Parliament had merely commanded merchants to do what they naturally would do. What the shipowners needed was protection to help them meet an unfavorable competitive situation. Moreover, even if a different test of reasonableness were applied, the burden of establishing it was upon the shipowners, and their continued petitions suggest that they gained little.[4]

Although a century was to elapse before anything effective was done for English shipping, its claims were not forgotten. In Henry VI's reign, the merchants complained that the competition of Italian carracks and galleys was injuring England's naval strength and in 1439 asked that no merchant from "beyond the said Straits of Marrok"[5] be permitted to sell anything in England except Mediterranean goods. But this early proposal that each country should be confined to its own trade was not enacted into law.[6] Instead, the subsidy of 1453 provided that English merchants shipping goods in "any carrack or galley" should be assessed alien duties,[7] a provision which was

[2] 6 Ric. II, stat. 1, c. 8.
[3] 14 Ric. II, c. 6. In quotations no attempt has been made to follow the seventeenth-century usage with respect to italics. They are used in the text only for the purpose of emphasis, whether supplied by the original author or (as in the case here) by the present writer.
[4] Hunter, *How England Got Its Merchant Marine*, pp. 21-24.
[5] Marrok is a misspelling of the old French term for Morocco.
[6] Hunter, *How England Got Its Merchant Marine*, pp. 25-29. Schanz (*Englische Handelspolitik*, II, 594-95) quotes a manuscript of 4 Edw. III (1330-31) that "Galymen" were not to sell "Flaunders ware, but onlye suche ware as comythe owte of there awne natyve contre," but it lays emphasis upon the evils of forestalling rather than upon the benefits to English shipping.
[7] Hunter, *How England Got Its Merchant Marine*, p. 27.

to persist long after others had replaced the Italians as chief foreign competitors.[8] The measure apparently afforded insufficient protection, and in 1463 Edward IV's Parliament substantially reënacted the Ricardian legislation, without the second amendment limiting its operation to occasions when English merchants offered reasonable rates. This Act, however, was of only three years' duration and was not renewed.[9]

A new method of encouraging English shipping appeared during the reign of Henry VII. Whereas the earlier laws had affected only English merchants, Parliament now began to regulate aliens as well. It prohibited the importation by any person, "of what degree or condicion that he be," of any Guienne or Gascon wines or Toulouse woad unless carried in ships owned and commanded by the King's subjects and manned "for the more parte" by them.[10]

The same Act also followed along Ricardian lines by providing that "noo persone inhabited within this Rea[l]me, other then Marchauntes strangers," was to "freight nor charge within this Realme" any stranger's ship or vessel "with eny maner Merchaundisez to be caried out this Realme or Wales or to be brought into the same, yf he may have sufficient freight in Shippes or Vessellez of the deynseyns of this Rea[l]me in the same port where he shall make his freight."

The legislature's casual disregard of nice distinctions, as is so often the case, makes the exact meaning of the Act difficult to determine. At first glance it seems to regulate goods both coming into and going out of the kingdom. Yet the regulation concerns *freighting "within this Realme"* of merchandise to be carried out of or "brought into the same." Use of the phrase "to be brought into" suggests a regulation of importations, but the phrase might refer to goods shipped coastwise, "to be brought into" another part of the kingdom. Such a construction would bring all the clauses into harmony, and on logical grounds it would seem that except for wine and woad,

---

[8] For example, 1 Eliz., c. 20, viii; 12 Car. II, c. 4.

[9] 3 Edw. IV, c. 1. Hunter (*How England Got Its Merchant Marine*, pp. 30-33) declares that there was no record of enforcement and that the King himself violated the law.

[10] 4 Hen. VII, c. 10. This Act replaced and elaborated upon 1 Hen. VII, c. 8.

English ships were given preference only if freighted *within the realm*, but the officials concerned may have taken the rough-and-ready view that the laws governed all shipments—importations as well as exportations.

Despite the ambiguity of its language, Henry's Parliament can be praised for the improvement it exhibited in legislative technique. The new regulations concerning wine and woad, which applied unqualifiedly to all importations of aliens and natives alike, offered a clear-cut rule for officials to administer. Its enforcement did not depend, as had that of the Ricardian measures, upon the troublesome question whether an English vessel had been available. If wine was imported in English vessels, the importation was legal. If not, it was to be seized. The requirement that masters and the greater part of the crew be English not only helped to develop seamen; it also tended to prevent fraudulent claims that foreign vessels were English-owned. Moreover, Henry's Parliament did what its predecessors had failed to do. It made provision for exceptional cases by freeing ships from the operation of the law when driven "by tempast of Weder or enemyes" to English ports, if no goods were sold except "for vitaill or repairyng . . ., which they of necessite be compelled to make."

Some have questioned the effectiveness of the regulations because dispensations were granted, but the dispensations show that the laws were being enforced, rather than that they were inoperative. If merchants could have traded freely without special permission, they would not have gone to the trouble and expense of procuring it. Under Henry VII the dispensations were granted sparingly. In many cases the licenses restricted possible competition by being limited to ships of the country concerned, or to those of adjacent countries, and in two instances, when special permission was granted to export wool or sheep, it was specified that English ships be used.[11] Henry VIII, on the other hand, made exceptions to the law so freely that

[11] *Rerum Britannicarum*, LX, pt. 2, 355, 356, 387, 395, 424, 442, 455, 517, 518, 532; Churchill, "Dispensing Power," *Law Quar. Rev.*, XXXVII, 415. Henry VII also procured a promise from Florence in the treaty of 1490 that it would import no English wool unless brought by English subjects using English ships (Hunter, *How England Got Its Merchant Marine*, pp. 35-36; Schanz, *Englische Handelspolitik*, I, 136-37).

Parliament complained. Nevertheless, the cost of obtaining the license in itself afforded a degree of protection to English shipowners which they would otherwise have lacked.[12]

Without attempting to justify the particular wine licenses granted by Henry VIII, it is important to note that considerations of state may sometimes require modification of commercial laws. The dispensations granted by Henry VII undoubtedly helped to ease trade through the transitional period and to minimize foreign hostility. Even in Henry VIII's case, Parliament acknowledged the wisdom of trusting in the executive's discretion when it authorized the King to modify the commercial code in accordance with diplomatic necessity.[13] Henry VIII made use of the power to alleviate foreign hostility during the critical period following the destruction of the monasteries, and in 1539 freed all foreigners for the next seven years from the payment of alien duties.[14] The policy succeeded so well in relieving international tension that the next year Parliament undertook to pass a new navigation act.[15]

In addition to confirming the first two acts of Richard II and that of 4 Hen. VII, c. 10, the Act of 1540 provided that foreigners who wished the benefits of the King's proclamation freeing them from alien duties had to employ English vessels if any were available.[16] However, one of its clauses allowed the Hanse merchants to use either their own or English ships. The effects of the Act were further weakened two years later by an exception in favor of the merchants of both Spain and the Netherlands.[17] And all the provisions concerning alien shipments ceased to be of any significance after 1546,

[12] 7 Hen. VIII, c. 2; Churchill, "Dispensing Power," *Law Quar. Rev.*, XXXVII, 415-16; Williamson, *Maritime Enterprise*, pp. 209-12. Except for a few years, however, the licenses covered only a fraction of the total tunnage of wine imported (Schanz, *Englische Handelspolitik*, I, 370-71; II, 128-48).

[13] 26 Hen. VIII, c. 10; 31 Hen. VIII, c. 8; Williamson, *Maritime Enterprise*, pp. 124-25.

[14] Schanz, *Englische Handelspolitik*, II, 602-4; Williamson, *Maritime Enterprise*, pp. 126-28.

[15] Williamson, *Maritime Enterprise*, pp. 126-28, 136; Hunter, *How England Got Its Merchant Marine*, pp. 44-45. Henry's first navigation act (23 Hen. VIII, c. 7) was a temporary measure. It had confirmed earlier statutes, fixed the price of wine, and forbade its importation during the stormy season.

[16] 32 Hen. VIII, c. 14.

[17] Williamson, *Maritime Enterprise*, pp. 128-32.

when the proclamation relieving foreigners from alien duties expired and was not renewed.[18]

Nevertheless, the Act furnished a precedent which showed a considerable improvement in legislative technique. Unusual care had been taken to make the rules enforceable. Parliament attempted to protect the merchant and to eliminate disputes about the reasonableness of rates by fixing the price of freight between London and the principal trading towns of Europe. Masters of English ships about to sail were ordered to post a notice of their intended voyage in some public place in Lombard Street for the space of seven days. Provision was made for the speedy departure of ships, safe custody of goods, and due performance of engagements. In default thereof a summary hearing could be had before the admiral, his lieutenant, or his deputy. If no English ship were in port, and the alien merchant received a certificate from the Lord Admiral, his deputy, or the customer (a customs official) certifying the lack of English shipping, he might freight any foreign ship and still have the benefit of the proclamation.[19]

At first glance the interests of English shipping seem to have been forgotten during the reign of Edward VI, except for the attempt to protect fishermen by substituting legislative prohibitions against eating meat for the religious taboos which the Reformation had removed.[20] Whether because it sought French favor or because it really wished to reduce wine prices, the government permitted the subjects of all countries in amity with His Majesty to import French wines and Toulouse woad between the first of February and the first of October in vessels of any friendly country.[21] Although English vessels retained the opportunity to reach the market first with wines of the new vintage, they would have to sail during the stormy winter months which had once been considered so dangerous for navigation that all wine importations had been forbidden during that time.[22]

[18] Hunter, *How England Got Its Merchant Marine,* pp. 47-48.
[19] 32 Hen. VIII, c. 14.
[20] 2 & 3 Edw. VI, c. 19.
[21] 5 & 6 Edw. VI, c. 19; Churchill, "Dispensing Power," *Law Quar. Rev.,* XXXVII, 416; Williamson, *Maritime Enterprise,* pp. 214-15.
[22] 23 Hen. VIII, c. 7.

Nevertheless, English shipowners benefited greatly during the reign of Edward VI, and even during that of Mary, because of attempts to restrict the privileges of the Hanse. If aliens were left free to transport their goods by cheaper means, statutes which commanded English merchants to freight English vessels tended to harm the nation's trade rather than to help its shipping. Although in some cases the alien duties might have offset any such foreign advantages, commercial treaties had eliminated this element of protection in others. In fact the Hanse paid even lower duties than the English. From the English point of view the situation had been bad enough when the Hanse merchants dealt only in their own merchandise, but it became worse when they made use of their special privileges to carry on trade with other regions as well. The two Henrys had protested, and the Hanse merchants had faced popular hostility and had been harassed by minor restraints and petty impositions, but fear of Hanse naval strength had prevented any firm stand. Edward VI's government, however, revoked the privileges in 1552. Although restored under Mary, they were soon modified and continued to be limited under Elizabeth until they were finally and completely withdrawn in 1598.[23]

During Elizabeth's reign there were many experiments in shipping legislation. After repealing the earlier Acts of 5 Ric. II, stat. 1, c. 3 and 4 Hen. VII, c. 10, on the ground that they provoked foreign retaliation, her first Parliament embarked upon a new policy of levying alien duties upon all goods shipped into or out of England unless in English vessels whereof the master and the greater part of the mariners were the Queen's subjects.[24] Careful attempts were made to render the Act enforceable by limiting its operation to peace time when there was no restraint of shipping and by excepting all shipments of "Mastes (Raffe) Pitche Tarre and Corne," and certain shipments of the Merchant Adventurers, Merchants of the Staple, and Bristol merchants, but it aroused foreign resentment. King Philip forbade "all, of whatever nation they may be, to lade

[23] Schanz, *Englische Handelspolitik*, I, 182-227; II, 388-484; Williamson, *Maritime Enterprise*, pp. 35-44, 135-82; Zimmern, *Hansa Towns*, pp. 179-201, 324-53. The tables in Schanz (*op. cit.*, 86-156) show how large a proportion of the trade was conducted by foreigners, especially by the Hanse merchants.
[24] 1 Eliz., c. 13.

any English ships in any port of the Low Countries," as his father had done "in reply to some novelty of Henry VIII."[25] The retaliating measure produced results and Elizabeth's first experiment in helping shipping was not continued when it expired at the end of the next Parliament.

The same Act also attempted to increase the size of English ships by prohibiting small English vessels, known as hoyes or plates, from sailing "into or for any of the Portes beyond the seas." Although solicitude about size assumed various guises both earlier and later, the succeeding Parliament believed the particular prohibition to be too stringent and permitted such vessels to "crosse the Seas as farre as Cane in Normandye and Eastwarde as farre as Norwaye," but its successor repealed the amendment because it tended "greatly to the decay of Maryners and Shypes by the marveylous Encrease of Hoyes."[26]

The best planned and most detailed measure prior to the Interregnum was the Act of 5 Eliz., c. 5, "touching certain politic constitutions made for the maintenance of the Navy."[27] Businesslike provisions for enforcement indicated its serious intent. Unlike earlier acts, it did not merely encourage the activities of informers by allowing them a share of the penalties; it protected the public against possible abuses by limiting the time within which prosecutions could be commenced. The Lord Admiral, the Justices of the Peace, the mayors in the towns, and other appropriate authorities, were each within his jurisdiction given full power to try offenses.

Other clauses showed the many ramifications that arose from legislative attempts to develop England's maritime strength. Changes in the apprentice laws encouraged the training of fishermen, gunners, and shipwrights. The regulations concerning discipline of soldiers were extended to seamen and gunners in the royal service, but fishermen and mariners were not to be compelled to serve as soldiers.

[25] CSP Foreign (1563), pp. 608-9.

[26] 1 Eliz., c. 13; 5 Eliz., c. 5; 13 Eliz., c. 15. The measure as revived, however, was to continue only to the end of the next Parliament.

[27] As passed, the Act was to last for ten years from Michaelmas, 1564, and to the end of the next Parliament. With the exception of a few clauses which had been amended, it was continued from 1584 to the end of the reign and after by 27 Eliz., c. 11; 28 & 29 Eliz., c. 5; 31 Eliz., c. 10; 35 Eliz., c. 7; 39 & 40 Eliz., c. 18; 43 Eliz., c. 9; 1 Jac. I, c. 25; 21 & 22 Jac. I, c. 28; 3 Car. I, c. 4; 16 Car. I, c. 4.

To insure an adequate supply of flax for sails and cordage, a statute of Henry VIII[28] was revived, requiring holders of threescore acres of land fit for tillage to plant one rood, or fourth part of an acre, in flax, and the requirement was to be increased to an acre, "from the Feast of St. Michael the Arch Angel next coming."

An important innovation restricted the coastwise trade to English ships. Section six provided that all "Thinges of what kinde or nature soever" were to be forfeited if carried from one port or creek of the realm to another, "in any Bottome or Bottomes whereof any Stranger or Straungers borne then bee Owners Shipmasters or Parte Owners." Thus the master as well as the owners had to be English, but no provision was made concerning the crews—whether because it was deemed unnecessary or inadvisable cannot now be determined.[29]

English-owned shipping was given preference in the carriage of certain commodities by clauses modifying earlier legislation. When revising the section of 1 & 2 Phil. & Mar., c. 5, which permitted the exportation of corn after the price reached certain levels, Parliament stipulated that the corn must be carried in ships *owned solely* by natives.[30] The Act of 5 & 6 Edw. VI, c. 14 against regraters, forestallers, and engrossers was repealed as far as "dothe and maye concerne the byeing of Seafishe unsalted or Mudd Fishe, or any Wine Oyle or Salt, to be taken and brought in any Englishe Subjectes Shippes Crayers or other Vessell."[31] Although it had only recently been repealed by 1 Eliz., c. 10, the requirement that French wine and Toulouse woad should be imported in English vessels was revived.[32] Contemporaries were none too enthusiastic about the policy.

[28] 24 Hen. VIII, c. 4.

[29] See *infra*, p. 280, n. 26, concerning enforcement of the provision.

[30] As early as 1552 Thomas Barnabe had proposed that "neither fuel nor vittayl go out of the realm but upon English bottomes" (*Tudor Economic Documents*, II, 100). An undated special license given Lynn to export corn required that English vessels be used (HMC *Pepys*, p. 190).

[31] See also 1 Eliz., c. 18, and 13 Eliz., c. 25.

[32] Exceptions were made permitting certain ports to import limited amounts of wine in foreign vessels. The clause was carelessly drafted. It declared that wine might be imported "onely in suche Vessell and Vesselles whereof some Subjecte or Subjectes of the Quenes . . . shalbee then onely Owner or parte Owner." Parliament probably meant that vessels should be owned by one or more Englishmen, but technically construed, the statutory requirements were met if a native was a part owner, however small his share might be.

Some complained that the wine trade had failed to maintain English shipping during the reign of the two Henrys and, as Burghley later pointed out, it was in any case an unsatisfactory bulwark, since it strengthened France and drained England of specie.[33] Nevertheless France protested against the restriction, and two years later the Queen permitted importations to be made by French as well as English vessels, thereby minimizing French hostility while continuing to protect English shipping from other competitors.[34]

Parliament, however, did not revive the Ricardian statute requiring Englishmen to freight English vessels, which had likewise been repealed, since there appeared to be little chance of supporting England's navigation by such means.[35] Yet dogmatic conclusions about the right of Englishmen to freight foreign vessels during Elizabeth's reign would be ill-advised. In those early days much might be accomplished by royal command, and a full account of the law governing navigation would require a complete examination of the administrative records. Here it is possible only to note that in 1563 no one could use "any foreign vessels in the cloth or wool fleets, or in the transport of certain other merchandise";[36] that in 1565 the Merchant Adventurers felt themselves obliged to ship all their goods in English vessels;[37] and that in 1588 the Privy Council ordered English commodities to be exported only in English vessels with English masters and English crews.[38]

The Elizabethans placed greater reliance upon the fisheries as a support for England's navigation. More than half of 5 Eliz., c. 5,

[33] *Tudor Economic Documents*, II, 104-10, 124-27.
[34] CSPD (1547-80), pp. 241, 242; Churchill, "Dispensing Power," *Law Quar. Rev.*, XXXVII, 417.
[35] In 1563, English prospects were detrimentally affected in the East by the rising power of Denmark, as well as by the wars between Russia and Sweden; and in the West by the increasing sea power of the Turks, and by Venice's loss of the spice trade to Spain and Portugal, especially since Spain was prejudiced in favor of her own shipping (*Tudor Economic Documents*, II, 104-10).
[36] CSP Foreign (1563), pp. 608-9.
[37] CSP Foreign (1564-65), pp. 528-29.
[38] APC (1588), p. 3. Netherland merchants complained of their inability to carry English wares out of the realm in their own vessels, of the high customs, and of "Rigorowse lawes rigorouslye of late putt in execucion" (Schanz, *Englische Handelspolitik*, II, 379-81).

and many other measures were devoted to developing that industry both directly and indirectly. Fishermen could not be impressed for sea service except as provided by law, and then only after action by two local justices of the peace. Ancient customs were disturbed to relieve fishermen from taxation. The use of trawls was regulated to protect the propagation of fish. The interests of consumers were safeguarded by laws which regulated packing the catch and prohibited selling unwholesome fish not "seasonable nor meete for Mens meate."[39]

Most interesting of all were the attempts to develop the home market for fish. All who did not eschew meat on certain days, prescribed by law, were threatened with a £3 fine or three months' close imprisonment. The rich might be excused only by giving donations to the parish poor man's box, according to their quality, and the sick were permitted more nourishing food only if the bishop, parson, or curate approved. And even they were obliged to serve, if not to eat, a rigorously prescribed quantity of sea food. Thus the fishermen were helped at the expense of the public taste—and at the risk of religious complications, which Parliament attempted to avoid by declaring that the law was "purposely intended and ment politikely." All who contended "by Preaching Teaching Writing or open Speeche" that the eating of fish and avoiding of flesh prescribed by statute was "of any necessitee for the saving of the Soule of Man" were to be punished "as spreaders of fause Newes arr or ought to bee."[40]

Parliament made various attempts to prohibit competitive imports, which did not succeed. In 5 Eliz., c. 5, it forbade anyone to buy unsalted herrings from strangers.[41] Eight years later it prohibited foreign-caught fish, or any fish "comonly called Scottishe

[39] I Eliz., c. 17; 5 Eliz., c. 5, ii, iii, vii, xxvi; 23 Eliz., c. 7.
[40] 5 Eliz., c. 5, xi, xxiii. See also 2 & 3 Edw. VI, c. 19; 27 Eliz., c. 11; CSPD (1591-94), pp. 556-57; 1 Jac. I, c. 29; Lipson, *Economic History*, III, 117-19. Attempts were made to enforce the fish-day statutes as late as 1664 (T & SP No. 3390).
[41] Section v. The same statute required cod and ling to be imported loose or in bulk. The Act of 13 Eliz., c. 10, however, allowed Englishmen to import them in barrels ("using no Fraude or Deceipt,") for the next six years if of their own catch and carried in ships with cross sails. In order to prevent regrating, the Act of 33 Hen. VIII, c. 2 (which was continued throughout later reigns) had forbidden anyone to purchase fresh fish at sea or abroad for sale in England, with a few exceptions, although aliens were permitted to bring fish of their own catch into port and to sell them at any time.

Fishe or Flemish Fishe," from being dried on English soil for sale there.[42] By 1581 it undertook to stop all purchases of salt fish by Englishmen from foreigners, except in the case of staple fish and ling imported in English ships during the following three years. At the same time, aliens importing salted fish were obliged to pay, in addition to the regular duties, a sum equal to the duties charged in the country from which the fish was shipped.[43] Four years later the law was modified by permitting Englishmen to carry herring, staple fish, and ling into "the Northern partes" in an English ship "beinge sailed by English Mariners with crosse Sailes,"[44] and by 1597 the whole policy was abandoned. Parliament then confessed that experience showed that nine-tenths of the fish consumed was furnished by other countries which had enriched themselves, increased their navigation, and raised prices, and that England's navigation was "no whit bettered . . . nor any Marriners increased nor like to be increased."[45]

Greater success attended the effort to develop shipping by permitting the exportation of fish. Whereas earlier laws[46] had forbidden the export of fish, among other victuals, in order to insure an abundance of food for the populace, the Act of 5 Eliz., c. 5, allowed its exportation, under conditions designed to provide more seamen for the fleet. It permitted fish taken upon the seas by Englishmen to be exported by the Queen's subjects free of customs, "during the space of foure whole yeres," and thereafter during Her Majesty's pleasure, if shipped in English vessels. Parliament continued the privilege in 1571, declaring that experience had shown the Act to have been "a very good Act," one which greatly increased the navy and the number of fisherman, caused "many poore Men to be set a worke," and promised "dayly to increase the same more and more."[47] Permission was also granted aliens in 1581 to ship fish in English

[42] 13 Eliz., c. 11 (to continue six years and until the end of the next Parliament).
[43] 23 Eliz., c. 7.
[44] 27 Eliz., c. 15 (to continue five years and until the end of the next Parliament).
[45] 39 & 40 Eliz., c. 10. A bill to the same effect was passed by Parliament in 1593, but did not receive the royal assent (HMC III, App., 8).
[46] 1 & 2 Phil. & Mar., c. 5.
[47] 13 Eliz., c. 11. The continuance was to last for six years and until the end of the next Parliament, and thereafter during the Queen's pleasure. In 1584 Parliament passed a bill to continue the right of natives to export sea fish duty-free, but it did not receive the royal assent (HMC III, App., 4).

vessels, although they had to pay the usual duties.[48] In both 1571 and 1581 the requirement was added that the English vessels carrying the fish be large enough to have "crosse Sayles."

The rule that, when exported, fish be carried in English ships led to a conflict between the shipowners, represented by London Trinity House,[49] and the Yarmouth fishermen, who found it to their advantage to ship fish in Dutch vessels. The Londoners had the backing of royal authority, but the Yarmouth fishermen had great skill in devising tactics of evasion. When in 1613 the Privy Council ordered the ban against shipments in alien vessels to be enforced, the fishermen argued that they had been granted a dispensation. The Council relented to the extent of renewing it "for this time only," and Yarmouth continued to export in foreign ships. The Londoners protested, and the Council ordered the customs authorities not to accept entries of fish shipped in alien vessels, but the Yarmouth officials reported that entry had already been made. The Londoners offered to prove that the entry had been made before the ships were in port or the fish dried, salted, or casked, but the damage was done for that year. Thereafter, fish was exported in small Yarmouth vessels and transferred at sea to the larger Dutch ships, until that practice too was forbidden. The prohibitions were extended, by an order of 1631, to the exportation of fish from the western ports. Yet at the close of the period, in 1649 and 1650, we again find petitions from London, the tone of which suggests that the fishermen had had their own way throughout the intervening period.[50]

Prohibitive regulations were not the only means used to foster shipping; the psychology of rewards was likewise employed by both King and Parliament in the grant of bounties to encourage ship-

[48] 23 Eliz., c. 7. See also 39 & 40 Eliz., c. 10.

[49] The organization known as Trinity House, chartered in 1514 (*Tudor Economic Documents*, II, 90-93), was composed of shipmasters and others concerned with shipping. The London Trinity House at Deptford-sur-Strand was the acknowledged leader, although the various outports had their own separate corporations. Many of its manuscripts have been lost; those surviving have been calendared (HMC VIII, App., 235-62), but the notations are in many instances not complete enough to indicate the full significance of the document.

[50] Copies of the petitions and orders may be found in THT (1613-61), pp. 1-49; HMC VIII, App., 244, 246, 247. For a similar conflict between London shipowners and West-Coast fishermen, see Lounsbury, *British Fishery at Newfoundland*, pp. 64-71.

builders. The practice probably commenced in the middle of the fifteenth century, with the grant to John Tavener of Hull when he built the "Grace Dieu," a ship of tremendous size for that age. The reputedly parsimonious Henry VII revived the practice, and Henry VIII, Edward VI, and Elizabeth all followed suit. The award probably became a matter of right from about 1580 and took the form of rebate on the customs of the first voyage.[51] Ordinarily the bounty was reserved for ships of English build, of a type fit for His Majesty's service, and recipients were obligated not to sell their ships to foreigners without the King's permission, a requirement that could not be said to be onerous, since as early as 1181 the King had imposed similar restrictions without making any compensating grants.[52] At first the bounty definitely stimulated building, but the utility of the device diminished as the financial difficulties of the Stuarts increased. The irking delays in payment for ships used by the navy caused owners to build their vessels with less than the regulation distance between decks. They lost the bounty, but avoided the danger of having their ships impressed in war time.[53]

The grant of charters to the great trading companies offered another way to encourage shipping. In addition to the general benefits derived from whatever success the companies might have in increasing the volume of trade, English shipowners profited in some cases from clauses tending to encourage the use of English ships[54] and in others from proclamations reminding the companies whose monopolies were being protected that all subjects were expected to use English shipping.[55] Groups like the East India and Turkey merchants, who owned their own ships, found it to their advantage to employ them, and the rest seem to have refrained from violating

[51] Oppenheim, *Administration of the Royal Navy*, pp. 19, 37-38, 88-89, 107, 167-68. James I ceased paying the bounty in 1624, but Charles I revived it by proclamation in April, 1626 (*ibid.*, pp. 201, 269).

[52] Clowes, *Royal Navy*, I, 100.

[53] Oppenheim, *Administration of the Royal Navy*, pp. 269, 273-74.

[54] For example, the Act incorporating the "Merchants adventurers for the discovering of new trades" in 1566 required that they use English ships, "sailed for the most part with English Mariners" (Hakluyt, *Voyages*, III, 89-90). The charters of the Levant Company in 1592 and 1600 (Hakluyt, *Voyages*, VI, 73-92; Carr, *Select Charters*, pp. 30-42) and that of the East India Company in 1600 (Birdwood, *Register of Letters*, pp. 178-79) permitted the products they imported to be reëxported free of customs if shipped within thirteen months in English vessels.

[55] In the case of the Levant and Eastland Companies (*Infra*, pp. 35-37).

the laws for fear of giving their opponents an opportunity to attack them. The Newcastle Merchant Adventurers had in 1593 provided penalties of their own for shipping "wooll, fell, or leade" in alien vessels.[56] Although their own penalties were abolished in 1600, they claimed in 1618 that they went to great trouble to observe the laws and that when they could not find English shipping in the Netherlands, they sent the proceeds of their sales to France, at much greater expense.[57]

Similarly, English shipping benefited from the founding of English plantations, since new settlements meant new trades, and care was taken that such increased activity should benefit England. When the King made grants to explorers, he provided that they must bring back a percentage of whatever gold they discovered. When corporate enterprises established colonies, the shareholders in England wanted the colonial produce to be sent home for their own benefit.[58] There was nothing really novel in the arrangement. It was only an adaptation of the medieval idea of staple towns or ports to the new conditions of world commerce.

It must be confessed that the early experiments were a hodge-podge. It is seldom entirely clear which measures were in force or how well they were administered. It is often difficult to understand even what a particular law provided. Yet the measures must not be condemned as entirely useless. Regardless of what one may decide about their effect upon the commerce of their day, it appears that they provided a background of experience for the Commonwealth and Restoration legislation. Parliament had experimented with regulations of trade inward, outward, and coastwise, in the colonies and at home; with the size, master, crew, ownership, and cargo of ships; with the enactment of preferential tariffs, and the grant of bounties. By a process of trial and error it had gradually exhausted the possibilities, until eventually it stumbled upon a formula which was to supply protection to shipping and ease of administration.

[56] *Newcastle Merchant Adventurers*, I, 43-44.

[57] THT (1609-25), f. 49; HMC VIII, App., 238. They requested permission to ship in foreign ships, "not exceeding 20 tons in one ship," when the master could procure a certificate that no English shipping was to be had at the port of lading. Apparently their petition was granted, and the privilege continued to be enjoyed, at least until 1630 (CSPD [Addenda 1625-49], p. 393).

[58] Cunningham, *English Industry and Commerce*, II, 125; Beer, *Origins*, pp. 179-89.

IV

THE LEGISLATIVE HISTORY OF AN IDEA

THE Act of 1651 is of special interest because it provided the basic formula which, as modified by the Restoration Parliament in 1660, was destined to govern English navigation for two centuries. The older measures, although not formally repealed until 1822, were thereafter to be ignored for all practical purposes.

The abandonment of the early legislation was no sudden move. At various intervals during the preceding half century English shipowners had been seeking new safeguards. The Act of 1 Jac. I, c. 25, permitting barley and malt to be exported, required that they be carried in English ships. Two years later the Act of 3 & 4 Jac. I, c. 11, allowed the exportation of beer as well, in order to insure larger cargoes—but this time Parliament neglected to require that the shipments be made in English vessels. From 1609 to 1610 the mariners complained of "the lamentable state that our navigation is fallen into by the means of the Flemings that are daily employed." The merchants contended that English vessels cost more to freight and that to force them to use English ships was not a remedy but "a poison, for it will undo the merchant." The mariners replied that they could freight goods as cheaply as the Flemings if "considerations of state" did not prevent them from employing similar cheaply navigated vessels; that "consequently the English merchants in the same consideration of State must be enforced to their own disadvantages to freight only the English ships."[1] In 1614 Parliament considered a bill aimed directly at the Dutch flyboat, with its larger

[1] BM Lans. MSS 142, ff. 286-304; Gardiner, *Parliamentary Debates in 1610*, pp. 31-32. The agitation led to the introduction of a bill for "Shipping and mariners," which was debated in committee, but appears to have died there. No copy of the bill has been found, but some notes of Caesar (BM Lans. MSS 142, f. 293) indicate that it required Englishmen to ship in English bottoms and foreigners shipping on strangers' vessels to take an oath that they were not coloring English goods, and that it forbade wine to be transported from Bordeaux before December 1 of each year.

cargoes and smaller crews. It proposed that English shipments be confined to English-built ships and that all British ships be required to employ one seaman for every seven tons of burden.[2] When Parliament failed to act, two proclamations were issued calling for obedience to the earlier statutes.[3] But conditions did not improve. By 1620 the shipowners were so anxious for protection that they offered to pay certain new duties if the King would levy higher rates on goods imported or exported by Englishmen in foreign vessels when English ships were available. They also asked the King to forbid the exportation of coal in foreign vessels, except from the Thames or Plymouth.[4]

Although the staple on the Thames or at Plymouth does not appear to have been established as requested, the shipowners gained from the coal trade what was probably their greatest pre-Cromwellian advantage. In 1620 James I gave English vessels a preferential advantage in the export duties on coal, one which was to be continued and to stand them in good stead for more than two centuries.[5]

Another Stuart contribution to maritime regulations consisted in restricting the plantation trade, to the advantage of English shipowners. After the necessities of royal finance helped to overcome his dislike of smoking, James I, and following him, Charles I, attempted to regulate colonial trade and navigation along the lines begun by the chartered companies. Although the policy was not altogether successful nor continuously followed, the government ordered various colonial exports to be carried to England. Drawbacks were allowed for the tobacco which was reëxported; its shipment was restricted to English vessels; bonds were required that it be carried

---

[2] CJ I, 474, HMC IV, App., 119. The bill was read in the Commons, but no further proceedings were taken.

[3] T & SP No. 1160: Levant Company privileges, and 5 Ric. II, 4 Hen. VII, 32 Hen. VIII to be enforced. T & SP No. 1171: concerning the importation of French wines and the enforcement of 5 Eliz. See also APC (1615-16), p. 142.

[4] They offered 4d. on every chaldron of coals unladen in any port of England or transported in English shipping, and 6d. on every ton of goods loaded "on this side of the North Cape" to be unladen in any port of England, if the King granted their petition. The proposed duties to be charged Englishmen lading foreign vessels when English vessels were present, were "10s. per ton if lading this side of North Cape and 20s. per ton if lading to South of North Cape, and proportionably for greater distance" (THT [1609-25], f. 59b; HMC VIII, App., 239). For the history of similar proposals, see Nef, *British Coal Industry*, II, 216-18.

[5] CSPD (1619-23), p. 174; Nef, *British Coal Industry*, II, 222.

to London; and all colonial trade with foreigners was forbidden except in case of necessity.[6]

In other respects the new ideas never got beyond the discussion stage. Sir John Wolstenholme and others, who acted as referees in considering the difficulties of the Eastland Company, proposed in 1621 that a proclamation be issued "as granted to the Levant Company, prohibiting bringing in Eastern goods, except in the shipping of those countries or in English shipping,"[7] but apparently nothing came of the suggestion that ships of the country producing the goods be treated like English shipping. Although Parliament considered enacting a new measure that year, the bill was rejected upon the "question of commitment, and engrossing." The reasons given were that it would destroy the navigation of many western ports, which depended upon Dutch carriers for masts, and that it would restrain too many merchants, in addition to interfering with the reciprocal trade which existed between England and "the East Country."[8] The next year another proclamation once more called for obedience to the older statutes;[9] and the commission of 1622, which was set up to study remedies for the decay of trade, was instructed to consider "how our Laws do now stand in force for the prohibiting of Merchandize to be ymported in Forrain Bottoms, and to advise what is fitt to be done therein?"[10]

Two years later the Committee of Trade considered a proposal of the Eastland Company "That no Merchants should trade thither, but only in English Bottoms." It recommended that Parliament submit a petition to His Majesty "for accommodating these things," which was duly prepared, "read, and allowed," but apparently led to no new legislation.[11] In default thereof, royal proclamations in 1629

[6] Beer, *Origins*, pp. 189-240. See also T & SP No. 1769; APC Col. I, No. 96; Gray, *History of Agriculture in the Southern United States*, I, 246-49; Rive, "Brief History of the Regulation of Tobacco in England," *William and Mary College Quarterly*, 2d ser., IX, 1-12, 73-80; Wertenbaker, *Planters of Colonial Virginia*, pp. 68-69.

[7] CSPD (1619-23), p. 211.

[8] CJ I, 615, 642; HMC IV, App., 121; Lipson, *Economic History*, III, 120-21.

[9] T & SP No. 1333; *Acts and Ordinances of the Eastland Company*, pp. 151-53: Eastland Company privileges and 5 Ric. II, 4 Hen. VII, 32 Hen. VIII, etc., to be enforced.

[10] Rymer, *Foedera*, VII, part iv, 14.

[11] CJ I, 793, 796. The House of Lords Manuscripts contain the draft of a bill entitled an "Act for the maintenance and increase of shipping and navigation," but it concerned fishing in America (HMC IV, App., 123).

and 1630 commanded obedience to the rules governing the importation of French wines and Eastland commodities.[12] Even so the shipping industry continued in distress, and in 1634 the "poor mariners," who claimed to be injured by French and Dutch competition, asked that "no English merchandise . . . be permitted to be shipped or exported in strangers' bottoms."[13]

Although the proclamations upon which the Stuarts relied do not appear to have remedied conditions, they raise doubts as to the official interpretation of the earlier laws. The statutes mentioned were 5 Ric. II, 4 Hen. VII, 32 Hen. VIII, and 5 Eliz. The question is, could English merchants ship their goods in alien vessels if no English vessel happened to be waiting for a cargo when they were ready to make their shipments? The Tudor statutes would permit them to do so except in a few instances, but the terms of the Act of 5 Ric. II were absolute—no Englishmen could import or export except in English ships. Was the Act to be read alone, or as modified by 6 Ric. II which permitted shipments in foreign vessels if English ships were not available? It was so qualified when confirmed by the Tudor statutes, and in James I's reign the complaints of the Hull merchants suggest that the qualification still applied, since they stressed the point that foreign vessels were laden when English vessels were in port unladen. But on the other hand the proclamation of 1630 made no exceptions. It commanded that no Eastland commodities be imported or exported by the company or any one else "in other than English Bottoms."[14] All of which leads to what is probably the true answer, that there was no clear understanding of what the old navigation code actually did provide.[15]

[12] The proclamation of 1629 followed earlier laws in restricting the importation of French wines to English ships, although French vessels were also permitted to carry them "as formerly" (T & SP No. 1588; Hunter, *How England Got Its Merchant Marine*, pp. 117-18). The proclamation of 1630 ordered that the Eastland Company privileges and 5 Ric. II, 4 Hen. VII, and 32 Hen. VIII be enforced (T & SP No. 1597; *Acts and Ordinances of the Eastland Company*, pp. 153-55).

[13] CSPD (1634-35), pp. 23-24, 498.

[14] HMC VIII, App., 239. T & SP No. 1597; *Acts and Ordinances of the Eastland Company*, pp. 153-54. See also *infra*, p. 43, n. 33.

[15] In 1628 the customs officers at Newcastle misunderstood some instructions from the Lord Treasurer, and had "over strictly" interpreted the proclamation for exporting and importing in strangers' bottoms. They were ordered "to suffer the merchants of Newcastle to export and import in strangers' bottoms to and from places in amity with his Majesty" (CSPD [1628-29], p. 111).

Certainly the earlier concepts had outlived their usefulness. The regulations placed English merchants at a disadvantage as compared with aliens, because in most cases they did not apply to foreigners. If the requirement that Englishmen ship in English vessels applied only when English vessels could be had, the legislation offered opportunities for evasion, particularly when goods were imported. A merchant could declare that he had been unable to find an English ship when lading his goods abroad, and how was a customs officer to prove otherwise? Thus we would expect to find (and the available statistics support the assumption) that the rules about lading English vessels were more effective in the case of shipments from England than in the case of importations to England.[16]

As contrasted with the complex devices of earlier laws, the formula of 1651 was simple. It paid little attention to exportations and emphasized importations. It contained no qualifications about the availability of ships, which might facilitate evasions. It applied to aliens and Englishmen alike. It proclaimed the doctrine that merchandise should be brought directly from the country of production or from the port where usually first shipped, and announced that goods must be carried either in ships of the country of origin or of usual first shipment or in English ships. Salted fish of the sort "usually fished for and caught" by the English, and all fish oil, whale fins, and whalebones, had to be caught in English vessels and prepared by the people of the Commonwealth, and no goods or commodities whatsoever of Asia, Africa, or America could be imported in foreign ships.[17]

[16] The following figures are for year before 1651 (as cited *infra*, pp. 415-16):

PORTS	SHIPS ENTERED		SHIPS CLEARED	
	English	*Foreign*	*English*	*Foreign*
Newcastle	151	64	172	28
Hull	178	79	197	16
Lynn	34	18	28	3
Yarmouth	117	91	79	35
Ipswich	22	4	24	2
Southampton	64	25	57	9
Dartmouth and Exeter	108		65	4
Total	674	281	622	97

[17] *Acts and Ordinances of the Interregnum,* II, 559-62. The law applied to England, Ireland, all English islands and colonies. Unless coming from Europe, the master and most of the crew of English ships had to be English. See also *infra*, p. 48.

Although the measure can rightfully be classed as new, it still owed a debt to the past. The doctrine that each country should use its own ships was merely a modification of the contention of 1439 that Italians should compete only in the trade with Italy. Its usefulness in minimizing foreign hostility had been discovered when the Act of 1540 permitted Hanse merchants to use their own or English vessels; when Elizabeth allowed French wines to come in French as well as English vessels; and when the Eastland Company asked that trade with the Baltic be limited to English and Eastland ships.[18] Likewise the belief that English interests were best served by importing directly from the place of production had long been the logical justification for governmental activity in encouraging the great trading companies. It remained only for someone to devise a satisfactory method of combining the earlier proposals into one measure.

It is difficult to determine the origin of the new formula. As far as has been discovered, no mercantile writer advocated it prior to its adoption. The journals of the governmental committees which drafted it have been lost, and the records of parliamentary proceedings are tantalizingly brief. Nevertheless, by combining the few surviving bits of evidence with our knowledge of the general legislative process, which has remained much the same since the seventeenth century, we can gain a fairly complete picture of the steps taken, can venture some shrewd guesses concerning the identity of the Act's author, and can evaluate with reasonable accuracy the factors which influenced its enactment.

Frequent assertions to the contrary notwithstanding, there is no significance in the fact that the Act of 1651 followed the Puritan accession to power. As has been seen, there was nothing new in the idea of granting legislative protection to shipping. Sixteen fifty-one merely happened to be the year in which Parliament hit upon a satisfactory formula. In so far as the political change was of significance, its importance lay only in the readiness of new groups to experiment.

The governmental activity which led to the passage of the Act of 1651, among other measures, dates back to 1649. In December

[18] *Supra,* pp. 20, 23, 28, 36.

of that year the Council of State referred to Parliament the desires of several merchant companies, "especially those of the East India, Levant, and Eastland trade," for "some restraint to general liberty of trade."[19] Parliament in turn called upon Thomas Chaloner and Major Salwey to draft an act for the creation of a "standing Council, for Ordering and Regulating of Trade in all Parts of this Nation."[20] Although the merchants had declared that the recovery of their trade depended upon something "being done with expedition," it was not until March 16, 1650, that the Council of Trade was created.[21]

The newly created body, together with the Council of State and its Admiralty Committee, were the groups which considered commercial problems and prepared legislation for Parliament. The preceding political disturbances had left many commercial questions unsettled. In 1650 the government was busily considering the petition of the Canary merchants, the complaints against merchants trading to Tetuan, the pleas for charters from Mariners Hall, the Company of Shipwrights, and Trinity House, the problems of suppressing piracy and of supplying adequate convoys, and, by no means the least, the affairs of the colonies and of the great chartered companies.[22] Each of the groups involved had its own concerns, and not all were interested in shipping, but the conflict of forces thus aroused could not help but affect the ultimate form of the Navigation Act.

The undoubted interest of Cromwell's government in the colonies has led to the mistaken belief that a direct connection can be traced between this and the Act of 1651. If Parliament looked to colonial trade for the solution of England's shipping problems, it had expressed its intention one year earlier. The Act of 1650[23] had not been confined to punishing the "notorious Robbers and Traitors" in Barbados, Antigua, Bermuda, and Virginia by forbidding them to carry on "any maner of Commerce or Traffique with any people

[19] CSPD (1649-50), p. 462.

[20] CJ VI, 347; Stock, Proceedings and Debates, I, 214.

[21] CJ VI, 383; Stock, Proceedings and Debates, I, 215.

[22] CSPD (1650), pp. 38, 51, 59, 108, 109-10, 117, 132, 167, 183, 185, 203, 237, 238, 302, 342, 349, 428. Tetuan is on the coast of Africa near the Strait of Gibralter.

[23] Acts and Ordinances of the Interregnum, II, 425-29.

whatsoever," until they submitted to parliamentary authority. It contained another clause, designed to be permanent, which forbade all foreign ships "to come to, or Trade in, or Traffique with," any of the English colonies in America unless license had first been obtained from Parliament or the Council of State. The Act of 1651 tended rather to relax the rule of 1650. It merely put into effect in the colonies the regulations provided for trade in England. It referred only to importations and permitted European goods to be imported directly from the country of production by ships of that country.

As a matter of fact, except for the war-time measure of 1650, Parliament's attitude toward the colonies had been very conciliatory. It had attempted to draw colonial trade to the mother country by tariff concessions. Among other things it had granted a three-year exemption from English export duties to all merchandise shipped to the colonies, if the colonies would not allow their products to be exported to foreign ports except in English shipping.[24] Even in 1650 there seems to have been no thoroughgoing effort to exclude foreigners from the colonial trade. The Council of State apparently considered the Act of 1650 to be a military rather than an economic measure. The Council granted a license to two vessels of Holland and one of Hamburg to accompany the punitive expedition to Barbados, and authorized them to trade after the island was reduced to obedience.[25] It is probably true that the London merchants trading with the colonies would have liked to subordinate colonial trade to their advantage, but there is no reason for believing that the Council would blindly accept their views. Quite the contrary. On November 27, 1650, the Council denounced four propositions advanced by the merchants as "dishonourable to Council," both "in respect of matter and manner."[26]

The shipowners were not waiting for any aid from the colonial interests. They had been active in their own behalf. At least as early as 1649 they had been considering the subject of revising the regulations governing navigation, and in March, 1650, they presented a

[24] *Ibid.*, I, 912; for other such measures, see *ibid.*, I, 208, 275, 361, 571.
[25] CSPD (1651), p. 53.
[26] CSPD (1650), p. 444.

complaint to the Admiralty Committee that trade was lost to Holland "by English merchants shipping their goods in strangers' bottoms, when English ships could be had."[27] The petition, together with a proposal for regulating shipping in English and foreign ships by turns, was referred to Dr. Walker, Judge-Advocate of the Admiralty. Then followed hearings at which were present shipmasters, the Merchant Adventurers, and others trading to Holland and Zeeland. All that resulted at the time, however, seems to have been attempts to improve the system of convoying English ships. The shipmasters' petition was still pending on August 15, when the papers regarding the encouragement of English ships and mariners were ordered sent to the Council of Trade.[28] On September 13 that body

Resolved that what Comodities are most fitt to be Exported & Imported in English bottoms onely be taken into Consideracon on fryday September the 20th afternoone. Resolved that the Trinity house have Notice of theis Orders & be desired to attend the Councill.[29]

The ideas of the shipping group were undoubtedly represented by the recommendation of Trinity House, which repeated an earlier proposal on the same topic.[30] In general they were characterized by an adherence to old concepts and a wealth of detailed suggestions. English vessels were to be given a monopoly in the exportation of all sorts of English manufactures of woolen commodities, lead, tin, pewter, copperas, oils, Newcastle coal, corn of all sorts, herrings, pilchards, "Poore Jack etc.," as well as products imported from the English plantations, East India, Turkey, Italy, Spain, Biscay, or Portugal. Only English ships were to be used in importing goods of East India, Turkey, Spain, Biscay, Portugal, Italy, the Canary Islands, the English plantations, Greenland, and Muscovy. The carriage of French products, if not prohibited, and of goods from Hamburg (grain excepted) was likewise limited. A toleration was "Conceived necessary . . . for Exportinge and Ymportinge all manner of Goods in Strangers bottomes" in the trade of the Sound, Norway, Eastland, Holland, "and the provinces adiacent." Shipping

[27] *Ibid.*, p. 20.
[28] *Ibid.*, p. 288.
[29] THT (1613-61), p. 48; HMC VIII, App., 247.
[30] THT (1613-61), pp. 48-49.

to Dunkirk and Amsterdam was to "goe by Turnes as one English & one Stranger & soe Successively accordinge to there Turnes to be free both for Exportacon & Ymportacon to lade all manner of Commodities." It was also suggested that all masts and timber of all sorts "might be freely laden and imported in Strangers bottomes."[31]

Apparently the action taken by the Council of Trade followed the lines recommended, but the Council of State did not altogether approve. On October 11 it ordered the Council of Trade "to further consider that part of their report concerning the lading of goods in the Thames in English and foreign bottoms equally."[32] Thereafter further evidence of Trinity House's influence is lacking.

The long delay before the Act of 1651 was passed, and the fact that when enacted it departed radically from the proposals of Trinity House, indicate that we should look elsewhere for the group pressure behind the law. The available evidence points to the great trading companies. Except for the Merchant Adventurers, their interests lay in breaking up the entrepôt trade with the Netherlands and the Hanse towns. Some had been hard hit because their charters merely prohibited the importation of goods from the regions assigned to them and did not forbid the importation of the products of such regions from other places.[33] And even those companies protected against all importations probably preferred to invoke the prohibitions of a law passed to benefit English navigation, rather than to arouse popular complaints by insisting upon their charter rights.

One would expect the East India Company to have taken a prominent part, but the records are strangely silent. Some of the interlopers engaged in the trade to the East Indies may have pushed the legislation, but the company itself appears to have been more concerned about gaining a satisfactory settlement of its monopoly

[31] *Ibid.*, p. 49.

[32] CSPD (1650), p. 379.

[33] See charters of the Eastland Company (*Acts and Ordinances of the Eastland Company*, pp. 142-51); the East India Company (CSPC [1513-1616], No. 281); and the Levant Company (Epstein, *The Levant Company*, pp. 153-210). The proclamations enforcing their monopolies sometimes referred to the *importation of merchandise* such as pepper or whale fins (T & SP Nos. 1087, 1149, 1726). The proclamations of 1622 and 1629 prohibiting the importation of Eastland commodities except by freemen of that company were confined to goods "brought from any of the forraine parts or regions wherein the sayd Company have used to trade" (*Acts and Ordinances of the Eastland Company*, pp. 151-55).

rights.[34] Once the measure was passed, however, the company used it to good advantage.[35]

The Eastland Company was undoubtedly concerned with the measure. Although it had opposed regulation in 1615, it had become convinced of its desirability by 1624, if not before.[36] Its interest in shipping restrictions apparently continued, and in 1651 certain Eastland merchants who resided at Danzig were advocating that the carriage of Eastland commodities be restricted to English ships.[37] Once passed, the law appears to have benefited the company, and it vigorously opposed a proposal to modify the regulations.[38]

There is even more direct evidence of the influence exerted by the Levant Company. In December, 1650 (at about the same time that Trinity House drops from the scene), the Levant Company ordered the preparation of a petition explaining the "prejudice likely to befall the Commonwealth [and most particularly the Levant Company] by the Importations of Turkey Goods from Holland." Although the entry in the Court Minutes of the company states that the petition was prepared at the request of the Council of Trade,

[34] William Love, who took the chair while the Act was under consideration in the House (Stock, *Proceedings and Debates*, I, 223-24), belonged to a company of interlopers trading to the East Indies (Scott, *Joint-Stock Companies*, I, 247). Maurice Thompson, who has been suggested as having had an influence on the passage of the Act (*infra*, p. 46, n. 46), although a member of the company, was the most active of the men agitating for a regulated trade, as opposed to the company's monopoly (*Cal. Ct. Min. East India Co.* [1650-54], pp. 340, 353, 357-60, 364). G. N. Clark suggests that the East India traders were behind the Act ("The Navigation Act of 1651," *History*, n.s., VII, 285). But the East India Company's petitions in the years preceding the Act (*Cal. Ct. Min. East India Co.* [1645-49], pp. 93, 109-10, 176-78, 187-89, 209, 276-77, 365-67; [1650-54], pp. 2, 49, 143) make no mention of anything resembling it, and in the decade following its passage there are only two references to the statute in the company's Court Minutes. One raised the question of what means should be used to obtain fine spices that could no longer come from Holland (*ibid.* [1650-54], p. 133), and the other involved an evasion of the Act by the company itself (*ibid.* [1660-63], p. 8).

[35] The Exchequer records show that practically one-fourth of the seizures for 1652, 1653, 1655, 1656, and 1659 involved East India goods. Decisions are noted for only about one-half the cases. In those involving East India commodities, 19 percent resulted in forfeitures, 38 percent were compounded, and only 43 percent were released; whereas in other cases only 8 percent resulted in forfeitures, only 22 percent were compounded, and 70 percent were released (Exchequer, KR Memo Rolls).

[36] CJ I, 793; APC (1615-16), p. 142; CSPD (1619-23), p. 211; Lipson, *Economic History*, III, 120 n.; *supra*, pp. 36-37.

[37] CSPD (1651), pp. 273-74.

[38] *Acts and Ordinances of the Eastland Company*, p. 76. See also *infra*, pp. 71, 72, 95.

it adds that the Council's order was occasioned by "some intimation" of the evils caused by such importations, an intimation which
probably came from traders to the Levant. The entry suggests that
the Council "thinke of some remedy," but the form of statement
doubtless merely followed the customary phraseology.[39] The petition drawn up by the company (and now unfortunately lost) probably did suggest a remedy, in addition to stating grievances. Certainly later letters, discussing the dangers of Dutch competition at
Smyrna, show that the company expected its position to be improved by "a settlement at home."[40]

As far as can be determined, the immediate antecedents of the
measure presented to Parliament date back to April, 1651. According to Thomas Violet, a mercantile enthusiast of the day, the Council
of Trade on April 4 made a report to the Council of State regarding
the "restraint of goods of forraign growth, to be imported in forraign bottoms," upon which the Navigation Act was said to be
based.[41] Records of the Council of State's proceedings do not directly
corroborate Violet's assertion, but an entry of March 31, 1651,
states that the propositions offered by Major Salwey for the advancement of trade were to be read "next Wednesday."[42] What they were
we have no means of discovering at present. Apparently they required
alterations, because Violet tells us that another report was presented
on July 31.[43] This one was apparently satisfactory, since Lord Commissioner Whitelocke reported the proposed bill to the House of
Commons on August 5.[44]

There the measure again received very careful consideration. It
was read for the second time on the nineteenth, and referred to a
committee of the whole House, which was to discuss it every Thurs-
day. Beginning on the twenty-first, William Love took the chair
instead of the speaker, and on August 21 and 28 and September 4,

[39] SP 105/151, pp. 96, 98. See also SP 105/109, No. 108; SP 105/143, pp. 326, 349,
368, 412; SP 105/144, pp. 21-22, 55-56; CSPD (1649-50), pp. 11-12; Epstein, *The
Levant Company*, pp. 150-51.
[40] CSPD (1651), pp. 290-91.
[41] Violet, *Briefe Observations of Whatte Hath Beene Acted at the Council of Trade
20 Aug. 1650 to Last Dec. 1651*, p. 178.
[42] CSPD (1651), p. 119.
[43] *Supra*, n. 41.
[44] CJ VI, 617; Stock, *Proceedings and Debates*, I, 223.

11, and 18, the House discussed the bill. On September 26 Dennis
Bond, reporting for the Committee of the Whole, proposed amendments which were accepted, and the amended bill was ordered to
be engrossed and was finally passed on October 9. On that date other
provisos were proposed, but none was added, the only alteration
being a slight change in the date on which the clause touching the
fisheries should become effective. Thereupon, "the said Act, so
amended, being put to the Question, passed: And ordered to be
forthwith printed and published," and the sergeant at arms attending Parliament was enjoined to proclaim the Act "with the sound
of trumpet, and beat of drum."[45]

Although many writers have claimed the credit for their heroes,
and Thomas Violet claimed it for himself, surviving records fail to
identify the author of the Act.[46] In default of conclusive evidence,
it seems reasonable to assume that the creator of the successful
formula would have maintained a close relationship with it throughout its legislative evolution. If this premise is accepted, Major Salwey
and Oliver St. John present the best claims for fame.

Major Salwey had had the most nearly continuous contact with
commercial problems during the period under review. As one of
those who brought in the bill creating a Council of Trade, it was he
who reported to the Council of State, on March 31, certain propositions for the advancement of trade which probably formed the basis
of the Act.[47] Moreover, he seems to have earned the gratitude of

---

[45] CJ VII, 2, 4-19, 21, 27; Stock, *Proceedings and Debates*, I, 223-25.
[46] Violet, *Briefe Observations*, p. 178. G. N. Clark ("The Navigation Act of 1651,"
History, n.s. VII, 284), citing the opinions of certain contemporary Dutchmen, suggests that Maurice Thompson and James Drax had much to do with the law's enactment. Thompson and Drax were interested in the East and West Indies and were
intimate with Cromwell, but there is little direct evidence of their activities. Cromwell,
whose name has often been mentioned, probably had little to do with the measure
because of the multiplicity of his other activities (Cunningham, *English Industry and
Commerce*, II, 210), and if Roger Coke can be trusted (*Discourse of Trade*, p. 22),
he disapproved of the measure. Other possible sponsors of the Act include Thomas
Chaloner, a member of the Council of Trade, the Council of State, and the Admiralty
Committee, who kept in close touch with commercial questions (CJ VI, 383, 426, 478;
CSPD [1650], pp. 5, 18, 423; Stock, *Proceedings and Debates*, I, 216, 219); William
Love, who served as chairman when Parliament debated the bill in committee (CJ
VII, 4-19; Stock, *op. cit.*, I, 223-24); and Dennis Bond, who served on the Committee
for the Act and reported the amendments from the Committee of the Whole (CJ VII,
21; Stock, *op. cit.*, I, 224).
[47] CSPD (1651), p. 119.

two of the groups interested in the measure. He was proposed as minister to Sweden, an appointment about which Eastland interests had much to say. He declined, but later was sent as ambassador to Turkey, upon the recommendation of the Levant Company.[48]

If the report of March 31 did not contain the formula, but followed previous proposals for adapting old concepts to existing needs, the case for St. John is strong. Although a member of the Council of State, he had attended few of its meetings before his mission to Holland, and none when the various proposals about shipping were being considered.[49] His very disassociation from the earlier schemes corroborates the testimony of Clarendon and Ludlow that he was responsible for the measure enacted.[50] A correlation is possible between the date of his return from Holland and that of the appearance of the new concept. The speed with which results were accomplished becomes significant. The measure that had been pending twenty-one months before St. John showed interest in it, became law within fifteen weeks thereafter. Moreover, the structure of the Act strengthens his claims. It is characterized by a theoretical approach to problems of commerce, an attempt to evolve comprehensive formulae, a clarity of statement, and a disregard of the complexities of trade or practical considerations of administrability, which might be expected from a Chief Justice of the Common Pleas who had had a legal rather than a mercantile or administrative training.

We must remember, however, that despite the tendency to credit legislative achievements to individuals, no measure can truly be attributed to a single person. The original proposal is considered by committees, which refer it to the various economic groups and administrative authorities interested. When eventually the committee presents its draft of the proposal to Parliament, it is subjected to further changes as a result of petitions, parliamentary debates, and

---

[48] SP 105/144, pp. 95, 124, 125; SP 105/151, pp. 163, 166, 167, 183, 208, 211, 213, 216, 219; DNB. The correspondence of Major Salwey is calendared (HMC X, App. IV, 410-15), but the calendar throws no light upon the enactment of the statutes.
[49] See tables of attendance, following the prefaces in CSPD, for 1649-50, 1650, 1651.
[50] Ludlow, *Memoirs*, I, 267; Clarendon, *History of the Rebellion*, VII, 30. Child can be quoted to the same effect (Andrews, *The Colonial Period*, IV, 43 n.).

amendments. When enacted it is the product not of one but of many minds.

The Act of 1651 as it appears upon the statute books affords an excellent illustration of the point. The first four provisions set forth with unusual clarity the idea behind the legislation in its primitive state.[51] In section five, older ideas apparently prevailed in the retention of the requirement that salt fish be exported only in English ships. Next, exceptions were made to the new rules, permitting Levant and East India merchants to import their merchandise from certain ports other than those of the country of production.[52] Another clause allowed merchants to bring products of the Portuguese and Spanish colonies from their mother countries, the only places from which such commodities could be procured. Someone feared that the old Elizabethan prohibition against aliens engaging in the English coast trade might be overlooked, and an additional provision reiterated the earlier restrictions. "Lastly," another exception was made to permit the importation of the then much-desired bullion, regardless of the origin of the gold or the nationality of the ship carrying it. Ships taken by way of reprisal or as prizes were also freed from the ordinary rules. And still another proviso permitted, under due administrative safeguards, the importation of silk and silk wares if bought with the proceeds of English commodities, and brought overland from Italy, to be shipped "in English Vessels from Ostend, Newport, Rotterdam, Middleburgh, Amsterdam or any Ports thereabouts."

The influence that the general temper of the times exerts upon legislative bodies requires that we do not overlook the element of hostility to the Dutch. As the Masters of Trinity House later remarked, the Act "was made when there was Inclinacon to have warrs with the Dutch."[53] England had political as well as commercial grievances. The English had not forgotten the affair at Amboyna, the murder of their ambassador by royalist refugees in Holland, the insulting refusal to receive his successor, and the pro-Stuart

[51] *Supra*, p. 38.

[52] Later, when asking to have the exemption removed, the Levant Company declared that it had originally been inserted for the company's benefit (CO 388/10, H1).

[53] THT (1613-61), p. 167.

sympathies of the House of Orange. The failure of Oliver St. John's embassy caused that individual at least to be extremely wrathful against the Dutch and, according to reports, intent upon punishing them by economic means.[54]

The terms of the law were obviously designed to cripple the carrying and entrepôt trade of the Dutch. It was international gossip that such was the aim and to some extent the result.[55] Moreover, the same month that the Council of State was completing its consideration of the bill presented to Parliament, that body wrote to the Lord General telling him of its desire "to forbid the importation of any goods into Scotland by the Dutch" as soon as it could be done without inconvenience to the army.[56] And finally the pamphlet, *Advocate,* written to explain and defend the Act, openly stated that it was designed to drive the Hollanders from those trades which they had been preëmpting to the prejudice of the English.

Much of the discussion about the Act has concerned the question whether its enactment was motivated by national interest or corporate selfishness. The multiplicity of factors involved permits only one answer, that both contributed. The interests of shipping and the complaints of trading companies furnished the impetus, and national antagonism toward the Dutch prepared the way. The point which should be emphasized, however, does not concern the motives for action but the concepts employed. We must remember that proposals submitted by Trinity House called for a patchwork enactment in which shipping would have been regulated in minute detail, trade by trade or commodity by commodity. Parliament chose to disregard this expert advice and to proceed on more comprehensive principles. But, as we shall see, experience was to show that Parliament was wrong: that a legislature, unlike a sculptor, cannot fashion its masterpiece from a single block of marble, but, like a worker in mosaics, must patiently produce its pattern bit by bit.

[54] CSPD (1650), pp. 126, 219; Cobbett, *Parliamentary History,* III, 1312, 1362, 1363-65; Ludlow, *Memoirs,* I, 266-67.
[55] CSP Venetian (1647-52), pp. 230-31, 234; (1653-54), p. 103; Thurloe, *State Papers,* III, 494.
[56] CSPD (1651), p. 300.

V

PARLIAMENT AND THE ACTS

RESTORATION statesmen owed a great debt to their immediate predecessors. The Act of 1651 not only provided most of their fundamental concepts; its administration had also indicated what alterations, modifications, and supplements were required. The easy generalizations of contemporary observers have caused some to believe that, once enacted, the Act was quietly forgotten, but administrative evidence and judicial records demonstrate the law's vitality.[1] Equally important, they disclose the technical defects in certain clauses of the Commonwealth measure which made revision inevitable.

Favorable administrative conditions in England had facilitated the enforcement of the rule that goods be imported directly. The officials who collected customs duties were available to seize merchandise imported illegally, and if they failed, special agents of the chartered companies might act instead. The offense was easily established. A ship's papers showed where it had laden its cargo; their accuracy might be confirmed by passengers or by reports from abroad. Commercial knowledge established where imports had been grown, produced, or manufactured. Many petitions and orders show that merchants believed it dangerous to ignore the rule without official sanction,[2] and the Exchequer records reveal a constant ad-

[1] Roger Coke stated that "Old Oliver held the Act but coldly" (*Discourse of Trade*, p. 22). In 1660 Trinity House was not satisfied that the law "tended to the Advantage of the English Navigation, unlesse it had been more Exactly pformed" (THT [1613-61], p. 167). On the other hand, certain correspondence indicates that the laws irritated the Dutch sufficiently to be an important contributing cause of the war of 1652 (CSP Venetian [1647-52], pp. 231, 234; [1653-54], p. 103). A letter from the Hague in 1655 states that the Acts of 1650 and 1651 caused shipping at Amsterdam to decline by 300 ships (Thurloe, *State Papers*, III, 494). See also newspaper reports cited by Clark, "The Navigation Act of 1651," *History*, n.s., VII, 284.

[2] The Council of State was chary of making exceptions. Dispensations were necessary at first for individuals taken by surprise (CSPD [1651-52], pp. 334, 341, 367, 396,

ministrative pressure to prevent violations, more than forty seizures having been made each year for this offense alone.[3]

On the other hand, there was no practical method of enforcing the rule that European goods be imported only in English ships or in ships of the country producing them. Records in the Court of Exchequer fail to disclose any seizures, and the testimony of the Masters of Trinity House and of the Customs Commissioners corroborates the conclusion that this phase of the law was a failure.[4] No provision had been made for a system of registering ships, nor had the lawmakers required English ships in the European trades to have English masters and crews. If a master falsely swore that his vessel was English-owned, the authorities were helpless.[5] The vessel itself could not disclose the nationality of its owners.

As far as the colonial clauses were concerned, experience showed the need for enforcement provisions. Except for a clause commanding the Admiralty to seize violators, the Act had relied upon the activity of informers, who were promised a moiety of forfeitures.[6] The navy seized about sixty foreign vessels for trading with the colonies, but its activities were sporadic,[7] and the number of vessels taken in its occasional raids indicates the extent of disobedience rather than the success of the laws. Contemporary observers, officials in England, and diplomatic representatives abroad all reported violations. Even official reports from the colonies show that foreigners were welcomed. In Virginia and Barbados the terms under which the colonies surrendered to the Commonwealth furnished grounds for arguing that they were entitled to "have as great freedom of

476, 496, 551, 557, 558, 560, 569), and for the importation of naval stores during the Dutch War (CSPD [1652-53], p. 442). See CSPD (1655-56), pp. 12, 26, 27, for a rather harsh refusal of a merchant's petition to bring home in any vessel available some goods stranded in Spain after war had been declared with her.

[3] Exchequer, KR Memo Rolls for 1651/2-1653/4, 1655, 1656, 1659, *passim*. The numerous releases upon payment of a small fine, or because the Attorney General refused to prosecute, do not show that the law was nullified. Failure to prosecute may often have resulted from equitable considerations, and acceptance of small sums in composition, in order to avoid the costs and hazards of trial, is common practice in revenue administration even today.

[4] THT (1613-61), p. 167; CSPD (1658-59), pp. 7-10.
[5] CSPD (1658-59), pp. 7-10.
[6] *Acts and Ordinances of the Interregnum*, II, 559.
[7] Beer, *Origins*, pp. 388-99.

trade as ever." In New England the authorities then, as later, were indulging in dreams of legislative autonomy and declined to recognize laws made "without the consent or allowance of authoritie heere established."[8]

Although a revision of the Act would have occurred regardless of the Restoration, the change in government probably hastened it. In 1658 the Customs Commissioners had proposed that the European clauses be rendered enforceable by requiring English ships in the European trade to be manned by Englishmen,[9] but, as is so often the case with administrative reforms, other events sidetracked the proposal. The return of Charles II and the refusal of his government to recognize any of its predecessor's statutes, forced Parliament to reëxamine the measures of the Interregnum. The records do not disclose what struggles over questions of policy ensued between such groups as the Merchant Adventurers of Newcastle, whose trade with the Netherlands had caused them to be antagonistic to the Act,[10] and the owners and masters of ships, who petitioned that before Parliament adjourned something effectual be done to prevent further losses to English shipping.[11] But the results show that in

[8] *Ibid.*, pp. 363, 386, 396-98; Bruce, *Economic History of Virginia*, I, 350-54; II, 310-11; Gray, *History of Agriculture in the Southern United States*, I, 249-50.

[9] CSPD (1658-59), pp. 7-10. In 1657 a temporary revision of the Act permitted the exportation of fish in any ships during the Spanish War, so that trade with the enemy would absorb the fish that "will stink on our hands else" (Stock, *Proceedings and Debates*, I, 239, 242, citing *Diary of Thomas Burton*, I, 296; II, 164-65; *Acts and Ordinances of the Interregnum*, II, 1099).

[10] Some of their vessels had been seized shortly after the passage of the Act, for importing entrepôt goods from Holland. Consequently they made efforts "for the disinableing or nulling of the late acte," and on March 17, 1651/2, prepared a petition to Parliament that they might "enjoy such ancient libertyes and fredomes in their trade for the Low Cuntryes and elsewhere" as they and their predecessors had formerly had, "they employing shipps according as the said acte provides" (*Newcastle Merchant Adventurers*, I, 169-79). Clark ("The Navigation Act of 1651," *History*, n.s., VII, 285) states that the City of London also petitioned against the Act.

[11] They declared that 2,000 ships had been lost in a very few years, because of the great employment of foreign-built shipping and foreign seamen (HMC VII, App., 141). When consulted by the committee in charge of the bill, the Masters of Trinity House were unwilling to determine that the "Act or prtended Act" of 1651 had benefited English navigation "unlesse it had been more Exactly pformed." They recommended that two-thirds of the crews and the masters of English-owned foreign-built ships be required to be English. They also discussed the possible advantages of a retaliatory duty of 5 shillings a ton upon French vessels, but their real enthusiasm seemed to be reserved for their recommendations that the fisheries be encouraged and better protected; that "fish days" and a political Lent be established; that aliens fishing off

the course of its deliberations Parliament must have paid much more attention to administrative questions in 1660 than it had in 1651.

Revision once begun, continued, and subsequent acts illustrate the expansive nature of legislative processes. The experimental law of 1651 had been confined to eleven clauses. Its successor in 1660 possessed nineteen,[12] and that measure's equally important corollary, the Act of Frauds of 1662, contained thirty-five.[13] Nor was that all. Almost periodically Parliament passed new measures for the benefit of one group or another, or to improve the working of the laws already enacted.[14]

In 1660 the principal change in policy concerned provisions relating to importations from Europe. Briefly stated, in the Act of 1651 restriction was the rule with certain exceptions; in the Act of 1660 exceptions dominated the rule, the carriage of commodities being unrestricted unless specifically enumerated. European products might be imported in any ship from any place, except that certain enumerated articles must be brought either in an English ship or, if alien duties were paid, in a ship of the country producing them.[15] The specified goods constitute a somewhat impressive list, including as they did, all Russian goods, as well as masts, timber, boards, foreign salt, pitch, tar, rosin, hemp or flax, raisins, figs, prunes, olive oils, corn or grain, sugar, potashes, wines, vinegar, and spirits called aqua vitae, or brandy-wine, together with currants and Turkish goods. But calculated from the London import figures for 1663 and 1669, they composed only slightly more than 50 percent of Europe's trade with England in weight and less than 50 percent in value.[16]

Various factors must be considered in explaining the selection

Britain's coasts be required to preserve their catch in some of His Majesty's ports; and that the export of fish be limited to English ships. They also advocated maintaining the quality of the wool manufactures, excluding foreigners from the plantations, and permitting foreigners to purchase sea coals, lead, and tin only at London and then only after all Englishmen had been served and full duties had been paid (THT [1613-61], pp. 162, 166-67).

[12] 12 Car. II, c. 18.
[13] 14 Car. II, c. 11.
[14] *Infra*, pp. 58-62, 387-414. See also Table of Statutes cited.
[15] Or in ships of the port of usual first shipment (section viii).
[16] The percentage by weight (56 percent) is necessarily an approximation because some goods are entered in terms of yards or other measures. The percentage by value is 44 percent (BM Add MSS 36785).

of the commodities enumerated. The bulky character of most suggests a legislative response to pleas of Trinity House that the carriage of commodities like grain and corn be confined to English shipping. Traditional policy may have been the reason for enumerating wines; the desire not to be dependent upon others for national necessities explains the inclusion of naval stores. The wishes of the various groups who desired protection, the Turkey, Muscovy, Eastland, Spanish, and Portuguese merchants, are clearly reflected. The enumerated list included nearly all their importations. But the merchants in the cross-Channel trades had no such interest, and only fractional amounts, ranging in value from a fifth to a twenty-fifth of the trade with Holland, Flanders, Germany, and France, were affected by the Act.[17]

European commodities were not required to be brought directly from the country of origin by the Act of 1660. It is true that section four reads:

. . . noe Goods . . . that are of forraigne growth . . . and which are to be brought into England Ireland Wales, the Islands of Guernsey and Jersey or Towne of Berwicke upon Tweede in English built shiping, or other shiping belonging to some of the aforesaid places, and navigated by English Mariners *as abovesaid*, shall be shiped . . . from any other place or Places . . . but onely from those of their Growth . . . or from those Ports where the said Goods . . . usually have beene first shiped for transportation and from none other.

Nevertheless, the law officers and the courts held that the provision referred only to importations from Asia, Africa, and America, for it used the words "as abovesaid," and the section regulating European importations *followed* instead of *preceded*.[18]

In view of the apparent inclusiveness of section four, the ruling was probably a great shock to the Eastland, Levant, and other merchants interested in eliminating indirect importations by way of Holland. They soon obtained the desired protection, however. In 1662 the Act of Frauds declared:

[17] As before, the calculations are based upon London's trade in 1663 and 1669 (BM Add MSS 36785).

[18] BM Add MSS 36109, ff. 84r, 208, 217-18, 220; *Index Vectigalium*, p. 35; Reeves, *Law of Shipping and Navigation*, p. 158; Forster, *Digest of Laws relating to the Customs*, pp. 126-29.

That no sort of Wines (other than Rhenish) no sort of Spicery Grocery Tobacco Potashes Pitch Tar Salt Rozen Deale Boards Fir Timber or Olive Oyle shall be imported into England Wales or Berwick from the Netherlands or Germany upon any pretence whatsoever in any sort of Ships or Vessels whatsoever upon penalty of the losse of all the said Goods as alsoe of the Ships and Furniture.[19]

The manner of accomplishment was more involved, but the result was less burdensome to trade. It had been obviously absurd to force a master, anxious to complete his lading, to inquire too closely into the national origin of all the component parts of his cargo. The products enumerated in 1662 by the Act of Frauds were for the most part not grown or produced in Holland or Germany. They included nearly all, if not all, the goods for which English merchants most desired protection from the competition of Dutch and Hanseatic entrepôts. By sacrificing the earlier law's neatness of statement, the Acts of 1660 and 1662 escaped its nuisance element and evolved a workable rule.

The enforcement problems previously experienced were decreased by requiring that foreign-built ships be registered and that all English ships subject to the law's regulations have a master and three-quarters of the crew who were English or Irish. Foreign vessels importing the enumerated goods were required not only to be owned by people of the country producing them, but also to have been built there and to have masters and three-quarters of their crews people of that country. The first rule was obviously advantageous to English seamen, as was another clause that no abatements granted by the Book of Rates on certain goods carried in English-built shipping were to be allowed unless the ships were properly manned.[20] An English judge later suggested that the rule concerning foreign vessels contained a Machiavellian touch, since some countries, like Russia, which could build their own ships, had few seamen; and others, like France, which had seamen, had few ships of their own build.[21] But the history of the Act of 1651 indicates that the predominant, if not the only reason for the requirement was to identify vessels more easily.

---

[19] 14 Car. II, c. 11, xxiii.
[20] See 12 Car. II, c. 4, for the Book of Rates.
[21] Chief Baron Parker. See Reeves, *Law of Shipping and Navigation*, pp. 187-88.

The Act of 1660 did not require English ships to be English-built, except when importing Turkish goods, despite the fact that as far back as 1614 there had been agitation to confine English shipments to English-built vessels, and that in 1660 the shipping interests had complained of the great employment of foreign-built shipping.[22] Strangely enough, when the Act of Frauds finally did provide that ships not of English build and not duly registered before October 1, 1662, should be deemed alien vessels, neither Trinity House nor the Company of Shipwrights appears to have originated the measure. They were consulted only after the initiative had been taken by the customs authorities, whose primary interest probably lay in utilizing the objective test of English build rather than in having to rely upon the allegations of possible offenders when determining the English character of a vessel.[23] Thus a matter of administrative convenience led to a provision destined to be of the utmost substantive importance.

Unlike its predecessor, the Act of 1660 did not require fish to be exported in English ships, but continued the freedom of exportation which the Commonwealth had permitted during the war with Spain. It also allowed the importation of certain foreign-caught fish and whale products if "double alien customs" were paid. A new provision levied a duty of five shillings per ton on French ships in retaliation for the French duty of fifty sous per ton on English ships. The exemptions allowed by the Act of 1651 for Levant and East India commodities, as well as for bullion and prize goods, were repeated, new provisos were added for Scottish corn, salt, and fish, and for seal oil of Russia, while the coast trade was closed to alien ships as before.

Although the general provisions regulating goods coming to England from Asia, Africa, and America remained substantially the same, important changes occurred in those dealing with the colonies. The principal changes in the Act, as originally drafted, concerned more efficient enforcement. The old rule that only ships owned, commanded, and manned as required for trade with Europe could trade

[22] *Supra,* pp. 34-35, 52. The Act also required that shippers availing themselves of the exception in favor of East India goods from the south of the Cape of Good Hope bring them in English-built shipping. See *infra,* p. 360, for favors granted English-built ships by other measures and for the status of foreign-built, English-owned ships.
[23] THT (1613-61), pp. 162, 166.

with the plantations was reënacted, but efforts were made to insure obedience. All admirals "and other commanders at sea" were authorized "and strictly required" to bring in as prizes all ships violating the laws. Governors, "before their entrance into their government," were to take a solemn oath to do their utmost to enforce the Act. Another provision, suggested by the London Trinity House, prohibited aliens from exercising "the trade or occupation of a merchant or factor" in any of His Majesty's plantations.[24]

After the bill had been engrossed, a new provision of great importance was added. Clause eighteen returned to the earlier Stuart policy of requiring certain staple colonial products to be carried to England.[25] Under penalty of forfeiture no sugar, tobacco, cotton-wool, indigo, ginger, fustic, or other dyeing woad, "of the Growth, Production, or Manufacture, of any English Plantations" were to be carried elsewhere than to England, or to another plantation.[26] Any persons shipping the articles listed were required to give bond that they would comply with the law. Thus commenced a new era in the regulation of navigation, an era in which the interests of English merchants obtained an even greater ascendency in legislation.

Comparatively little mystery attaches to the question of who guided the legislative development of the Navigation Act of 1660 and its immediate successors. John Shaw took the lead, ably seconded by Sir George Downing.[27] Shaw, a competent financier, later to become one of the Customs Farmers, was the one who brought the bill before Parliament in 1660, and after its enactment he was appointed to the newly created post of Surveyor of the Act.[28] It was Downing,

---

[24] *Ibid.*, p. 162.

[25] CJ VIII, 151; Stock, *Proceedings and Debates*, I, 278-79. For earlier measures, see *supra*, pp. 35-36; Beer, *Origins*, pp. 400-2.

[26] The *Commons Journals* (VIII, 151) lists ". . . Tobacco, Cotton, Wool." The *Statutes of the Realm* (V, 249) list ". . . Tobaccho Cotton Wool," enumerations which would suggest that both cotton and wool were mentioned separately; but it is well established that a hyphen was intended and that the only commodity listed was "cotton-wool" (25 Car. II, c. 7; 10 Gul. III, c. 16; 6 Geo. III, c. 49; Labaree, *Royal Instructions*, II, 767, 772).

[27] CJ VIII, 120, 142, 151, 153; Stock, *Proceedings and Debates*, I, 277, 278, 281. Forster declares that a Mr. Dickenson, Commissioner of Customs, 1684-87, "is reckoned to have drawn the Navigation Act" (*Digest of Laws relating to the Customs*, p. 117).

[28] For Shaw's administrative activities consult indexes of CTB, Vols. I-VIII, and see *infra*, pp. 78-79, 80, 82.

however, who was most prominent in guiding the bill through Parliament. Although formerly Cromwell's Scoutmaster General, Downing had made his peace with the royalists and as secretary to the Treasury, Commissioner of the Customs, and ambassador to Holland, as well as member of Parliament, was destined to assume a prominent rôle in guiding England's economic destinies. His first connection with shipping regulations appears to have been in 1656, when, on behalf of the Committee of Trade, he asked permission to bring in an act licensing the export of fish. Thereafter, until his death in 1684, his name appears in connection with all the important acts concerning navigation, especially with those concerning the plantations in America, where he had resided in his younger days.[29]

The Restoration records are more complete than those of the Commonwealth, and it is possible to demonstrate for that period what we can merely infer for earlier years. The laws were referred from group to group before being finally enacted. The Farmers or Commissioners of the Customs, Committees for Trade and Plantations, officials of the Treasury or Admiralty, and law officers of the Crown were prominent among the experts who participated. Financiers, merchants, shipowners, and even farmers offered their suggestions. Petitions were read within the legislative chamber, and pamphlet wars raged without.[30]

The variety of statutes and provisions regulating trade and navigation precludes a discussion of all of them. A system of preferential rates gave rewards to those who entrusted to English ships the carriage of articles, such as beer, coal, corn, drugs, ostrich wool, fish, iron, spicery, wrought silk, and whale fins.[31] Other measures

[29] CJ VII, 456; VIII, 104, 142, 467-68, 496; IX, 158, 275; Stock, *Proceedings and Debates*, I, 238, 241-42, 277-78, 311, 314, 362, 399; Beer, *Old Colonial System*, I, 9-11. See also Beresford, *Godfather of Downing Street.*

[30] Stock, *Proceedings and Debates, passim*. For typical pamphlet literature, see Library of Congress Broadsides and the collections of the Goldsmith, Seligman, and Huntington Libraries.

[31] Various conditions and limitations were usually specified. See 12 Car. II, c. 4; 15 Car. II, c. 7, x, xi; 9 Anne, c. 6, v. (coal); 1 Gul. & Mar., c. 12, ii (corn); 12 Car. II, c. 4 (drugs); 11 Geo. I, c. 7 (ostrich wool); 12 Car. II, c. 4, v; 25 Car. II, c. 6, iii (fish); 12 Car. II, c. 4, ii; 9 Gul. III, c. 23, v; 8 Geo. I, c. 15, xv-xviii (spicery); 12 Car. II, c. 4; 11 Gul. III, c. 10, x (wrought silk); 12 Car. II, c. 4; 10 Geo. I, c. 16, i; 12 Geo. I, c. 26, vii (whale fins); 2 Gul. & Mar., sess. 2, c. 4, i

encouraged the construction of "ships of force" in the foreign trade by rebating one-tenth of the customs duties charged on the first two voyages.[32] The Act of 1 Jac. II, c. 18 laid a discriminatory tax on foreign-built ships in the coast trade, even when they were English-owned. Many valiant but futile efforts were made to recover the fisheries from the Dutch.[33] Still other measures will be mentioned from time to time, but at present it must suffice to discuss the legislative history of the Acts of 1663, 1673, and 1696 only.

The parliamentary history of the Staple Act of 1663 stands as a monument to legislative capacity for combining diverse and unrelated topics, and serves as a stumblingblock to those who claim that the old colonial system was well-balanced and impartially designed for the good of the empire as a whole. Early in 1663 Parliament interested itself in preparing a sumptuary law and in preventing encroachments on trade by Jews, Frenchmen, and other foreigners. The committee appointed on February 26 to prepare bills to accomplish these ends reported that the kingdom would benefit if no European commodities were carried into the plantations "but from England, and in Shipping belonging to the People of England, whereof the Master, and Two Third Parts of the Mariners at least, are English." That the primary interest of the committee was in restricting trade is indicated by its ignorance of the more rigorous restrictions which already governed the manning of ships sailing to the colonies. On the second reading of the proposed bill, a committee headed by Sir George Downing was empowered "to sever the Matters in the Bill; and to bring in distinct Bills upon such several Matters of the Bill as they shall find necessary; and also to consider of a Clause to be inserted in this Bill; or else to prepare and bring in a Bill to inhibit Butchers from Selling of live fat Cattle." On May 30 and thereafter the committee's amendments were discussed, as well as such matters as the sheep and cattle trade, how to

---

(iron); 12 Car. II, c. 4; 22 & 23 Car. II, c. 13 (beer). Foreign wool could be exported only if carried in English shipping (12 Car. II, c. 4). See also *infra*, pp. 277-78, 360, 387-414.

[32] 14 Car. II, c. 11, xxxiv; 22 & 23 Car. II, c. 11, xii. The rebate was extended to the first 3 voyages by 5 & 6 Gul. & Mar., c. 24.

[33] On this subject, see Elder, *Royal Fishery Companies*; Lipson, *Economic History*, III, 147-53.

supply the plantations with horses and coal, and the duties to be laid upon fish. By the time the bill finally received the approval of the two Houses and the royal assent, thereby binding the colonists to purchase nearly all their European goods in England, much more had been heard of the interests of English groups than of those of the empire as a whole.[34]

Little need be said about the Act of 1673, but it is necessary to correct a somewhat widespread misapprehension. Although the Act assessed duties on the enumerated commodities when shipped from one plantation to another, its importance lay in the provision for the appointment by English authority of a staff of officials who might enforce the restrictions on colonial trade. The measure was enacted at a time when Parliament was petitioning the Crown to enforce the laws, and resulted from a motion to consider ways and means "for securing and improving the Plantation-Trade to Virginia, and other Places."[35] As the Customs Commissioners, who were charged with collecting the duties, stated, the law "was intended not so much to raise a revenue to the Crown as to prevent an unlimited trade then in practice of carrying tobacco to another [Plantation] and conveying it thence into divers parts of Europe."[36]

The Act of 1696 manifested the increased legislative interest in commerce produced by unfavorable conditions of trade during the last decade of the seventeenth century. *Inter alia*, Parliament was considering the wearing of East India silks and calicoes, the wool trade, the garbling of spices, the establishing of duties on wine, vinegar, tobacco, and other commodities, and the trade in Negroes from Africa. In December, 1694, and January, 1695, the merchants and traders of Bristol and Liverpool had complained of ships going from the plantations to Scotland and Ireland, "to the great Prejudice of their Majesties Revenue," and (though not expressed) to the greater loss of profits which the aforesaid merchants had hoped to monopolize.[37] Colonial officials, particularly Edward Randolph, the northern surveyor general of customs, had complained of defects

[34] CJ VIII, 441, 447-48, 467-68, 480, 494, 495, 496, 502, 532; LJ XI, 541, 568-69, 571, 578-79; Stock, *Proceedings and Debates*, I, 309-20. See also *infra*, p. 401.
[35] 25 Car. II, c. 7; CJ IX, 252, 273; Stock, *Proceedings and Debates*, I, 398-99.
[36] CTB IX, 1504, 1965-66.
[37] CJ XI, 188, 195; Stock, *Proceedings and Debates*, II, 104, 106.

in the laws, and reforms were obviously destined to come in time.[38] The impetus of immediate parliamentary action came from mercantile fears and excitement, caused by the establishment of the Darien Company as a center for Scottish trade with the West Indies. A committee report of December 20, 1695, recommended four measures for frustrating the Scottish enterprise, among them being a proposal that the Commissioners of the Customs attend Parliament to give an account whether, as the law then stood, there was sufficient power in the proprietary colonies to collect the King's duties there and "to prevent the Inconveniencies" which might arise because of Scottish activities.[39]

Credit for the passage of the Act of 1696 has been given to Randolph, who was in England at the time. He undoubtedly did his best to obtain its passage, although as finally adopted it did not accord with all his views.[40] Preparation of the bill was begun by the Customs Commissioners at least as early as January 8, and was "in Mr. Attorney's hands in order to be presented to the Parliament" by the sixteenth. Leave was given to bring it in on the twenty-third, and it was brought in by Mr. Chadwick (a Commissioner of the Customs) on the twenty-seventh.[41] Beginning on February 12, it was subjected to a month's discussion in the Commons. During that time petitions for modification in detail were read and various amendments made, three being offered from the floor of the House in addition to those proposed by the Committee of the Whole. When the bill reached the House of Lords in March, that body went into the subject carefully. It called Randolph before it and sought from the Lord Chief Justice of the Court of King's Bench "an account of the several laws now in force concerning the plantation trade, and whether those laws interfere one with the other, and how they consist with the clauses herewith sent."[42] On the twenty-eighth the bill was passed with several amendments and provisos, which the House accepted on the thirty-first and to which it

---

[38] CSPC (1693-96), No. 2198; CTB VIII, 506-7.
[39] LJ XV, 618-19; Stock, *Proceedings and Debates*, II, 143-44.
[40] Jacobsen, *Blathwayt*, pp. 296-97; Toppan, *Randolph*, II, 145.
[41] CJ XI, 409, 415; Stock, *Proceedings and Debates*, II, 148, 151-52, 155.
[42] LJ XV, 714, 916; Stock, *Proceedings and Debates*, II, 168-69.

added another of its own that was agreed to by the Lords on the same day. Whereupon both Houses turned their attention to the preparation of an act intended to restrain the wearing of East India silks and calicoes;[43] and so continued the parliamentary processes of mercantilism.

[43] CJ XI, 539-40; LJ XV, 720, 722-23; Stock, *Proceedings and Debates*, II, 171-73.

VI

THE LAW AT THE WATERSIDE

THE work of Parliament was done, but the acts on the statute books were not the law applied at the waterside. Much remained to be accomplished. Terms had to be construed, conflicting provisions reconciled, involved sections reduced to simple statements, and modifications made to meet exceptional circumstances. The history of the Navigation Acts shows the fallacy of the theory that lawmaking is a matter for legislatures and not the concern of administrators.

Theoretically statutes were construed by the courts, but practically judicial decisions had little general effect. In the seventeenth century the court records were not easily accessible. It cost Lord Chief Baron Somers £700 to unearth the precedents which guided his opinion in the *Banker's Case* in 1699.[1] Administrative officials had only vague recollections of what judicial rulings had been made. Published reports were few; less than ten decisions involving offenses against the laws of trade were included in reports published prior to 1770.[2] Most decisions depended upon their own particular facts, and afforded no precedents of general influence. Also the merchants hesitated to raise legal issues in court, since their merchandise was forfeit if they failed to sustain their points.

Administrative influence predominated in determining the law. The Privy Council itself passed upon the most important questions, and others were determined by the Lords of the Treasury, acting upon the advice of the Commissioners of the Customs. Debatable points were referred to His Majesty's Attorney General and the Solicitor General, whose opinions were carefully preserved and quoted, but even these legal experts were influenced by administrative

---

[1] Price, *Treatise on the Law of the Exchequer*, p. xi.
[2] Reeves, *Law of Shipping and Navigation*, pp. 4-5.

adjudications. As they themselves declared, it was "not reasonable to disturb the merchants" unless clearly necessary,[3] and practice was "a good interpreter of all Acts which are generally penned or not very clear and particular in the letter of it."[4] Moreover, it was under administrative direction that the involved clauses of parliamentary statutes were reduced to the simple statements appearing in the official handbooks. Rightfully or wrongfully, such statements were to govern the trade of England. In the great majority of cases, questions were settled at the waterside by actions of humble underlings, to whom the law was what their handbook of instructions said it was.

Many difficulties beset the task of construing the Acts. Even such simple words as "build," "importation," "country," and "manufacture" required definition. How extensive did the repairs on a wrecked foreign vessel have to be before it could legally be classed as English-built, rather than as a foreign ship rebuilt? Were ships driven to port by contrary winds importing merchandise? For purposes of the Navigation Act, did Courland, after its conquest by Sweden, remain Russian territory as it had been when the Act was passed, or did it become part of Sweden? Did the separation of molasses from sugar constitute a process of manufacturing, so that each could be imported as a manufacture of the country in which the separation occurred?

Patchwork construction added to the complexities of interpretation. Mention has already been made of the different lists of enumerated commodities: those articles which had to be carried in English vessels or in ships of the country producing them, those which could not be imported from Germany or the Netherlands, those colonial products which must be exported only to England, and those goods which could not be carried from colony to colony without the payment of plantation duties.[5] In some cases the lists would correspond, but in others discrepancies would occur to the great inconvenience of administrators, merchants, and historians.

There were also many different classifications of English shipping.

[3] BM Add MSS 36109, f. 218.
[4] *Ibid.*, ff. 91-92.
[5] For details, see *infra*, pp. 387-414.

At the top of the hierarchy stood English-built and English-owned vessels, which, if of certain size and naval strength, were entitled to special rebates in duties. Next came English-built and English-owned ships not of the favored size, and thereafter foreign-built ships, English-owned and registered prior to October 1, 1662, or else made free either for all trades or for certain specified purposes. There were also prize ships, foreign-built and English-owned, sometimes made free for all purposes and sometimes not.[6] Least favored were the foreign-built, English-owned vessels, not made free. Plantation build and English build, like colonial ownership and English ownership, seem for all practical purposes to have been accepted as synonymous terms; although, interpreted technically, the Act of 1660 would have excluded English-built ships owned by colonists from privileges granted colonial-built and colonial-owned vessels. In all cases the privileges accorded the different classes of shipping varied, depending upon whether the master and three-quarters of the crew were English.[7]

The possible combinations and permutations of various phases of the law were increased by the number of areas under the King's rule, possessing different legal status. In Asia there were the factories of the East India Company; in Africa, Tangier and the posts of the African Company; in America, the royal and the charter colonies; in Europe, England, Ireland, Wales, the islands of Guernsey and Jersey, the town of Berwick upon Tweed, Scotland, and the Isle of Man. Among the European group, Scotland and the Isle of Man were usually treated as separate from England, unless specifically mentioned. Of the remainder, at times only some were enumerated when only some were meant, but there were also instances in which only some were mentioned when the reference was to all.

Many of the problems arose from the inherent complexities of the situations for which Parliament was legislating, but sheer carelessness intensified the difficulties. For example, when mentioning England's colonial possessions, section one of the Act of 1660 referred to "any land, islands, plantations or territories to His Majesty

[6] 19 & 20 Car. II, c. 3; BM Add MSS 36109, f. 32.
[7] See *infra*, pp. 387-414, especially pp. 388-89.

belonging or in his possession, or which hereafter may belong to, or be in the possession of His Majesty, his heirs and successors in Asia, Africa or America." Sections three and eleven made the same enumeration except for the omission of future possessions. Section seven varied it to "lands, islands, *dominions,* and territories"; and sections seventeen, eighteen, and nineteen referred only to English plantations or English plantations in Asia, Africa, or America. Later laws sometimes followed one, sometimes another of these models, and sometimes added variations of their own, thereby causing considerable trouble to those interpreting the statutes, because of the rule that "when different expressions are used in the same act of Parliament it cannot be believed but that different things are meant."[8]

The Act of 1696, however, shows that this rule of construction could not always be applied. Earlier laws had resulted in a hodgepodge of regulations. They permitted foreign-built, English-owned ships to carry goods *from* the plantations, but required English-built vessels to transport European goods *to* the plantations; they allowed English-owned vessels of any build to trade between the plantations, and demanded that plantation-owned vessels be plantation-built. The Act of 1696 attempted, in section two, to eliminate such absurd distinctions by providing that no goods could be imported into or exported out of, or carried from one port to another port in the plantations, in any vessel "but what is or shall be of the built of England, or of the built of Ireland, or the said colonies or plantations, and wholly owned by the people thereof, or any of them, and navigated with the master and three-quarters of the mariners of said places only." It would seem that build, ownership, master, and mariners of ships were subject to the same requirement, that all must be of England, Ireland, the colonies, or any of them and no other places. But section seventeen, governing the registration of vessels, mentioned not only England, Ireland, and the plantations, but also Wales, Berwick, Guernsey and Jersey. Another discrepancy occurred with the mention, in section two, of plantations in Asia, Africa, and America; and in section seventeen, of only those in America. And thus even in a statute intended to settle doubts about the meaning

[8] Reeves, *Law of Shipping and Navigation,* pp. 106-10.

of previous acts, Parliament managed to provide new legal conundrums.

Adherence to strict rules of construction sometimes led to conclusions that were absurd in operation, while bolder attempts to follow Parliament's intent might do violence to common sense. The rule that the geography of Europe, for purposes of the Navigation Act, should be determined by the political status in 1660, followed logically from the fact that the first task of interpretation was to discover the legislative intent.[9] Parliament obviously knew only of conditions existing when it enacted the law. Nevertheless, in succeeding years the rule prevented England's customs officials from recognizing facts of political geography accepted by her diplomats. On the other hand, in interpreting the Act of Frauds, a logical absurdity resulted from the bold attempt made to reconcile the intent of Parliament with its language. It was generally agreed that by the Act of Frauds Parliament had merely wished to prevent Holland and the Hanse towns from serving as entrepôts and not to prevent them from sending goods of their own growth, production, or manufacture to England. Yet the law declared that, among other commodities, no sort of pitch and no sort of timber should be imported from them. In order that England might obtain the white pitch and the fir timber they produced, the law officers of the Crown were forced solemnly to declare that white pitch was no sort of pitch and fir timber no sort of timber.[10]

On the whole, a happy medium was preserved between adherence to the strict letter of the law and that liberality which one of His Majesty's counsel declared to be permissible in expounding acts made for the encouragement of trade.[11] Reason and public policy were invoked in interpreting some obscure passages in the Book of Rates. The lesser of two duties was assessed because collection of the higher rate would practically have prohibited the trade and have opposed the public policy of encouraging English shipping.[12] English goods returned from abroad were ordinarily not considered to be imported, but none of the goods prohibited to come from

[9] BM Add MSS 36109, f. 221r; Reeves, *Law of Shipping and Navigation*, p. 190.
[10] BM Add MSS 36109, ff. 118, 134r.
[11] *Ibid.*, ff. 91-92.
[12] *Ibid.*, f. 127.

Holland could be brought back, even if they had originally been sent there from England. Parliament had forbidden such goods to be imported "upon any pretence whatsoever," and certain rulings adhered to the strict letter of the law.[13] On the other hand, although the Act prohibiting French goods made no allowance for vessels driven ashore by stress of weather, an exception was "understood to be expressed by that equity which is allowed in interpreting."[14] It did not, however, extend to ships acting in bad faith, and a ship driven into England with French goods could be seized, upon proof that the master had intended to violate the law in Ireland.[15]

Whatever changes legal rulings might have made in the statutes, they nevertheless, in theory, followed the law as enacted by Parliament. Dispensations, however, were deliberate changes in the legislative code, made by administrative action. They were of two sorts: minor modifications by letters patent in favor of particular individuals or groups, and major changes announced to the public at large by proclamations posted at the Custom House, "as is usuall to be done in matters of publique concern."[16]

The most important and far-reaching dispensations were occasioned by catastrophes. During the Second and Third Dutch Wars, the Acts were suspended in order that English merchants might bring home their goods from foreign ports with less likelihood of capture, the merchants having claimed that they would be at a disadvantage compared with their Dutch competitors unless they could ship their goods in war time as the property of aliens in alien ships.[17] Also modifications of the peace-time requirements for crews were permitted during wars, because manning the fleet left fewer seamen for the merchant marine.[18]

The great London fire of 1666 led first to the grant of individual licenses to import timber, brick, tile, iron, paint, and glass for rebuilding the city, the Navigation Acts notwithstanding; and as the scarcity of materials and the high prices continued, the Acts

[13] 14 Car. II, c. 11, xxiii; BM Add MSS 36109, ff. 100r-101, 103r; CTB VIII, 395. Cf. BM Add MSS 36109, f. 117 for an opposing decision.
[14] BM Add MSS 36109, f. 131. [15] *Idem.* [16] CTB IV, 98.
[17] PC 2/58, pp. 56, 247; PC 2/59, pp. 113, 124-25; CTB X, 585.
[18] PC 2/63, pp. 184, 237-38; APC Col. I, No. 937; see also *infra*, p. 390.

were suspended for a whole year, beginning March, 1668, in so far as they affected the importation of timber, brick, and tile.[19] Peace-time requirements were frequently waived to increase the supply of naval stores in war time, and special licenses permitted their importation under conditions not ordinarily legal.[20] England's need for spices caused another divergence from the ordinary rules. The English had to obtain nutmegs, cinnamon, cloves, and mace from Holland, or go without.[21] The Navigation Acts also gave way to the interests of the English dyers, who desired "gum seneca" from the river Senegal in Africa, whence sanders wood had been permitted to come by special license in early years, but further exemptions were prevented by groups dealing in competing dyewoods.[22]

Political as well as economic considerations led Charles II to attempt to gain the friendship of the four great Hanse towns of Hamburg, Bremen, Lübeck, and Danzig, by granting dispensations in their favor.[23] The Duke of Courland would have received special favors but for the objections of colonial officials.[24] In the unfavorable Treaty of Breda closing the Second Dutch War, England promised not to construe the Act of Frauds as prohibiting her from importing from Holland products of Dutch or of German growth.[25] During the same war, attempts to persuade the Dutch to leave their homes for England had led the government to promise that their ships would be counted as English-built and they themselves naturalized, promises which were partly performed, despite native jealousies and fears that the aliens might

[19] PC 2/59, pp. 155, 177, 192-93; PC 2/60, p. 232; CSPD (1666-67), p. 170; (1667-68), pp. 295-96.
[20] T & SP, No. 3414; PC 2/59, pp. 124-25.
[21] CTB I, 421, 432; CSPD (1661-62), p. 597. Note the number of seizures released: PC 2/56, p. 257; CTB I, 171-72, 309, 432, 452, 463, 464, 467.
[22] PC 2/57, p. 65; PC 2/62, p. 352; PC 2/68, p. 372; PC 2/70, p. 269; CTB I, 441; V, 238, 455, 652, 660, 734, 750; VI, 546; VII, 1425, 1447, 1496.
[23] The earliest dispensations were revoked in 1662, but they were soon renewed, at least in part, and a memorial of 1709 indicates that some were still in effect at that time (PC 2/56, pp. 402, 549; PC 2/57, pp. 54, 72, 79; PC 2/61, p. 377; CO 388/12, K63; SP.82/10, ff. 10-11, 70-71, 88-89, 114, 138; SP 82/11, f. 95; SP 82/12, ff. 166-67, 228-29; SP Holland 167, ff. 140-41; T & SP, Nos. 3363, 3418, 3458, 3489; CSPD [1663-64], pp. 530, 534, 543, 590; [1668-69], p. 358). See also infra, pp. 307-8, 407.
[24] PC 2/70, pp. 111-13; APC Col. II, No. 138; CTB VII, 1032-35.
[25] Reeves, Law of Shipping and Navigation, pp. 164-65.

engage in the plantation trade or compete with English masters and crews.[26]

Conflicting economic policies caused other modifications. The provisions of the laws designed to develop fishing conflicted with the necessities of the East India trade, which, it was claimed, required Norwegian fish because English fish would not withstand the great heat encountered on the voyage.[27] Plans to establish a Virginian fishery were threatened until a dispensation permitted it to receive salt directly from Europe, despite the rule that European goods be shipped via England.[28]

Other provisions of the Acts were dispensed with for the encouragement of a "composition trade" at Dover, which had first been established in Charles I's reign and had then proved to be beneficial to the revenue. Goods might be imported there from anywhere, but were to be exported only in English shipping, and no ships going to or coming from any of the English plantations were to be admitted "in any Kind, into the liberty of this trade, but to proceed as according to law already settled." The ruling permitted Dover to act as a free port for the transshipment of goods and the preparation of composite cargoes. His Majesty's revenue was to be benefited by an ad valorem duty of one percent on the goods imported, and one-fourth of one percent on those exported, with the exception of a few articles which were to be assessed as formerly. The Council of Trade had recommended, before the dispensation was granted in 1661, that it continue for only three years, and the grant was limited as suggested.[29] The Dover merchants petitioned again in 1670 that the town be made a free

---

[26] PC 2/63, p. 259; T & SP, No. S2361. Similar concessions were granted to the French Protestants seeking a refuge from the religious persecutions of Louis XIV (PC 2/71, pp. 251, 437, 454; PC 2/73, p. 188; CTB VIII, 315-16, 1402, 1431; IX, 126, 198).

[27] PC 2/61, pp. 161-62.

[28] PC 2/72, pp. 515, 538; APC Col. II, No. 241. For similar exemptions granted other colonies by statute, see infra, p. 401.

[29] PC 2/55, pp. 44-45, 216, 221, 245-47, 272-74, 302; CSPD (1660-61), p. 531; (1661-62), pp. 19-20; CTB I, 44, 117, 245-47, 250; Ogg, England in the Reign of Charles II, I, 234-35. In the case of Portuguese, Rhenish, and French wines, the duty seems to have been raised instead of continuing "as formerly" (CTB I, 250; BM Add MSS 25115, ff. 133-40).

port, but this time the Privy Council decided against them.[30] A somewhat similar project was proposed at Plymouth by special agreement with Sweden, but even less is known about it.[31]

Executive authority did not altogether disregard the interests of consumers. The obvious effect of many of the dispensations already discussed was to keep down prices, and the possibility that other exemptions might be made probably had the same tendency. In 1663 the Privy Council permitted 150 tons of Russian potash to be imported from Holland, upon the complaint of the London Company of Soap Makers that several rich men had bought up all the potash and most of the soap in London. Governmental interest in consumers, however, should not be overemphasized. Even in the incident mentioned, the Council carefully provided that the order "be not made a Precedent for others who are not in the like Condition."[32] And the Eastland Company took care that it should not be extended. In 1676 a "caveat" was lodged in the Treasury Books that no person should receive a license to import potashes from Holland, Hamburg, Dunkirk, etc., contrary to the Navigation Act, until a representative of that company should have had a chance to be heard.[33]

Most prolific of the exceptions were those of minor importance. Extensions of dispensations were sought for the benefit of ships which, by reason of storms, capture as prizes, or contrary winds, arrived too late to come within the terms of general exemptions[34]; and in one instance, for a ship that arrived a day too soon.[35] Con-

[30] The Treasury was in favor of the proposal, and at least two merchants imported goods believing the matter to have been settled. The failure to act favorably may have been due to opposition on the part of the worsted weavers of Norwich and Norfolk, who were scheduled to appear before the Privy Council (PC 2/62, p. 195; PC 2/64, pp. 261, 438; CTB IV, 233, 245, 532, 582, 596).

[31] CTB III, 1353; VII, 182, 185, 220. When considering the Dover grant, the Council of Trade had recommended that "if but one place be allowed for the composition, Dover is the best place . . . but if more than one, Plymouth or Portsmouth for the west, Harwich or Newcastle for the east, and Deptford for gross goods, would be more fitting places" (CSPD [1661-62], p. 531).

[32] PC 2/56, pp. 44, 113, 148; CSPD (1661-62), p. 629; CTB I, 435. In this case it should also be noted that the merchants had shipped their potash from Russia in Dutch ships to Holland in 1661, before they knew of the restraint on its importation from that country.

[33] CTB V, 398.

[34] PC 2/69, pp. 419, 464; CTB VII, 356-57, 402.

[35] PC 2/63, p. 120; CTB X, 1238.

siderable leniency was shown in cases of misfortune. Exceptions were made to permit merchants to secure payments of "desperate debts" by capturing ships or goods contrary to law.[36] When English privateersmen wrongfully captured neutral ships, fairness and spoiling wines demanded that the ships be permitted to discharge their cargoes in the port to which they had been so unwillingly brought.[37] A vessel owned by Shilling Terry was made free in recognition of his gallant services "in the last Dutch war,"[38] and so was one belonging to Captain Riches Utber, in order that he might be gainfully employed until the next war.[39] The laws gave way again when the Queen wished her tea and the King desired fresh lobsters, the triviality of each occasion appearing to have been more than offset by the political prestige of the person involved.[40]

Exceptions to the laws were not made without arousing controversies. A "Commonwealth man" complained of the war-time dispensation: "it should have been done by privately warning the merchants, for it looked as though we feared the Dutch."[41] Farmers of the customs complained of the loss of customs which dispensations occasioned.[42] The Eastland, African, East India, and Greenland Companies protested against exemptions granted others from the laws which had, at least in part, been made for their own benefit.[43] In one instance a bitter controversy arose between two groups, each wishing dispensations. One wanted permission to use boats built in Holland to import "fresh cod, quick eels, lobsters, and fresh river fish." The other desired to develop such fisheries in

[36] PC 2/62, p. 6; PC 2/63, p. 120; CSPD (1663-64), p. 668; (1671), p. 451; CTB III, 1147.

[37] PC 2/73, p. 383; CTB III, 143, 282, 285; IX, 506.

[38] PC 2/67, p. 50.

[39] PC 2/61, p. 225; CSPD (1665-66), p. 165.

[40] CTB VIII, 405-6, 1056-57, 1194-95; IX, 836. Similar dispensations were made for the Duke of Lauderdale, who wanted some herring (CTB III, 1331); various ambassadors desiring wine (CTB I, 155, 362, 447); the royal architect (CTB I, 443); the Duke of York (CTB I, 143); the Earl of Montagu (CTP [1557-1696], p. 469); and William Blathwayt, Secretary at War (CTP [1557-1696], p. 467).

[41] CSPD (1664-65), pp. 246-47.

[42] PC 2/61, p. 97; PC 2/64, p. 121.

[43] PC 2/63, p. 346; PC 2/68, pp. 186, 507; PC 2/69, pp. 189-90, 431; CTB IV, 618-19; VI, 164, 641; VII, 20-21, 1425, 1447, 1496; VIII, 490, 499; IX, 314, 328.

England, and sought authority to bring over forty Dutch families to teach the English the Dutch way of fishing.[44]

The constitutional questions provoked by royal dispensations suspending parliamentary statutes were not fully determined during Charles II's reign. Some questions were raised about the legal validity of the special privileges granted the Hanse towns,[45] and the Privy Council itself questioned its right to admit the Scots to freedom of trade in defiance of parliamentary exclusions, although its misgivings may have served merely as a convenient excuse for failure to act.[46] Yet in the great emergencies such as arose during wars, or after the Fire, the Council showed no hesitation in acting. Even in matters of minor concern, law officers seem to have had no doubts about the King's right to set aside laws of Parliament. Their concern was with matters of form, that grants of freedom to ships should be under the Great Seal, rather than the Sign Manual.[47]

The failure of James II's attempt to defy a parliamentary desire for religious intolerance caused rulers after the Glorious Revolution to refrain from dispensing with statutes of the realm. Freedom to ships, war-time dispensations, permission to import spices, and other exceptions were made, after 1688, by Act of Parliament, rather than by order of the King or Privy Council.[48] Despite the obvious cumbersomeness of procedure, the new method had certain advantages. Far fewer ships were made free, thus insuring greater protection to shipbuilders.[49] And those in whose favor exemptions were made received greater privileges. A parliamentary grant of freedom remained valid during the life of the ship,

[44] PC 2/71, p. 346; PC 2/72, pp. 556, 563, 571; CTB VII, 1371; VIII, 405-6, 1056-57, 1194-95; see also CTB VIII, 1567, 1576.
[45] PC 2/57, pp. 54, 72, 79; PC 2/61, p. 377; CSPD (1661-62), p. 629; (1663-64), pp. 530, 534-35, 590.
[46] PC 2/55, pp. 427-28, 453-55. See also PC 2/56, p. 145; CSPD (1663-64), p. 253; (1664-65), pp. 65, 95.
[47] BM Add MSS 36109, f. 31.
[48] 5 & 6 Gul. & Mar., c. 16 provided for a war-time supply of saltpeter. See Reeves, *Law of Shipping and Navigation*, pp. 259-61, for a discussion of parliamentary action on making ships free. Permissions for spice importation were granted in 1 Gul. & Mar., sess. 2, c. 6, v and 6 & 7 Gul. & Mar., c. 7, ii.
[49] Reeves (*Law of Shipping and Navigation*, pp. 259-61) states that there were only twenty-six instances from 1689 to 1710 and none thereafter.

whereas royal grants, although usually renewed, had legal validity only during the lifetime of the monarch making them.[50]

The complete story of executive relationship to legislation does not lie in the account of changes wrought by dispensations. A full account demands consideration of the question, how well was the law enforced? Although there was a change in legal theories concerning the right of the King to excuse offenses in advance, no question was raised as to his right to pardon offenders by releasing goods from seizure after the violation occurred. The line of demarcation, however, was not always very clear. Dispensations permitting everybody to import timber were closely akin to licenses given individuals. Licenses often differed only slightly from pardons. Instead of waiting for permission to act contrary to law, seventeenth-century hustlers imported their merchandise and then sought relief from seizure.[51] They were obliged by this method to pay tribute to the informers who had seized the merchandise, and ran the risk that the government might insist upon observance of the laws; but they got their goods sooner by acting first and pleading afterwards.

The release of seizures was not the only constitutional method available to the sovereign for the practical nullification of statutes; there remained failure to enforce the laws. Modifications thus effected might result from deliberately planned oversights,[52] or merely from unwitting failures to detect violations and apprehend offenders. In either case the consequence was the same. Therefore we must turn from the parliamentary origin of the laws to their administrative enforcement, if we wish to understand the rules which actually governed the course of trade.

[50] BM Add MSS 36109, ff. 102r-103; CTB VIII, 435, 436, 447.
[51] PC 2/57, pp. 239-40; PC 2/61, p. 243; PC 2/74, pp. 85, 160; CTB I, 171, 444; V, 238, 652; IX, 784, 825, 864, 872; CTP (1557-1696), pp. 131, 132.
[52] See for example, *infra*, p. 79.

PART TWO

ENFORCEMENT IN ENGLAND

VII

THE ADMINISTRATIVE HERITAGE

EW, if any, laws stand alone, and certainly the Navigation
Acts did not. Their enforcement depended upon administrative regulations inherited from the past, and upon customs officers
originally appointed for other purposes. To learn how they were
made effective, one must be familiar with the officials and the regulations for collecting the customs revenue, and one must always
remember that neither the customs machinery nor its adaptation
to mercantile purposes was entirely the product of logical planning. Both represented a historical evolution in which considerations
of national finance, the interference of political favoritism, and other
elements extraneous to administrative efficiency, as well as mere
delays of inertia, frequently obstructed orderly developments.

Originally the customs officers were subordinates of the Lord
Treasurer. They usually held office by virtue of his warrant, until
the practice of granting such posts by royal letters patent developed in later years. The customer, who made the collections, and
the comptroller, who served as a check upon his activities, were
the first appointed and were followed by searchers, surveyors,
and waiters, in the order named.[1]

Soon the financial necessities of impecunious kings added another set of officials and led to decentralized control. Some rulers
sought to anticipate the customs revenue by leasing it to financiers
who would pay in advance. Their deputies made the collections,
and the function of the original officials became merely that of a
royal check upon the activities of others. Sometimes the farmers, as
these lessees were known, did not have sufficient capital to purchase

---

[1] Gras, *Early English Customs System*, pp. 95-100; Newton, "The Great Farm,"
RHS Trans., 4th series, I, 130; Atton and Holland, *The King's Customs*, I, 30. An
establishment to collect customs appears to date back to 1275, and may have been
anticipated in part by King John.

all the customs revenues even of a single port, and the different duties were farmed to different individuals.[2]

The resulting inefficiency led Elizabeth's government to plan the purchase of existing farms. Although financial necessities and the lack of trustworthy agents with administrative ability kept the government from eliminating the farms entirely, it did succeed in strengthening the royal power in several ports and in unifying the customs administration. The Great Farm of 1605, which was destined to serve as a model for later grants, included the customs and subsidies on all goods carried into or out of all ports of England and Wales, except such as had already been otherwise granted by various petty farms.[3] But it was not until the Interregnum that farms were abolished. Parliament then entrusted the customs to a commission of five,[4] an arrangement which continued until the return of Charles II, despite some discussion in 1657 about creating a new farm.[5]

At the Restoration, financial exigencies again interrupted the evolution from farmer to government control.[6] The Treasury was empty, and the King owed numberless debts, both personal and public. Not the least of these was £250,000 due those who had farmed the customs during his father's reign, a debt which Charles agreed to assume if the creditors would loan him an additional £150,000, "to be paid in within a month."[7]

From the administrative point of view, the new farms were not an unmixed evil. The Treasury showed good sense in the men it appointed to Charles II's first farm.[8] Four had been farmers under Charles I,[9] two also held other customs posts,[10] and the

---

[2] Newton, "The Great Farm," *RHS Trans.*, 4th series, I, 130, 133.

[3] *Ibid.*, pp. 132-34, 136-39, 148-55; Dietz, "Elizabethan Customs Administration," *Eng. Hist. Rev.*, XLV, 35-57.

[4] *Acts and Ordinances of the Interregnum*, II, 1268.

[5] CSPD (1657-58), p. 94.

[6] For an account of the financial situation, see Shaw, *The Beginnings of the National Debt*, and his Introductions to the *Calendar of Treasury Books*, Vols. I-VIII.

[7] PC 2/55, pp. 207-8. For further advances requested, see CTB I, 436, 449; III, 866, 875.

[8] The farmers were Sir Job Harby, Sir John Wolstenholme, Sir John Jacob, Sir Nicholas Crispe, Sir John Harrison, and Sir John Shaw (CTB I, 431-32).

[9] Harby, Jacob, Crispe, and Harrison. PC 2/55, pp. 207-8; CSPD (1663-64), p. 639; CTB I, 132.

[10] Harby also participated in collecting the imposition on coal (CSPD [1660-61],

personal experience of one was supported by a family interest in customs administration extending back to the Great Farm of 1605.[11] For the most part the farmers kept the task of collecting the duties under their control and were active in its administration.[12] In 1664 one of them was authorized "to take a view in the various ports" of the customs management, to report "neglects, frauds, and abuses," and to suggest rules for the future. They also initiated, at their own expense, the practice of appointing agents resident in the plantations to report violations of the Navigation Acts.[13] The second group of farmers prepared an excellent handbook of customs administration for the use of the English service.[14] In short, the spice of private profit stimulated efficiency.

Yet private administration of the laws caused complications. The farmers' interests did not extend to the higher phases of mercantilism. They had contracted to pay a certain rent, presuming that certain laws would continue. When unforeseen circumstances required the various executive modifications that have already been described,[15] the farmers believed themselves entitled to "defalcations," lessening the contracted amount due the King.[16] Even in matters of routine, their interests might run counter to those of the nation. In administering the duty of five shillings per ton on French vessels, experience had shown that more revenue would be forthcoming if it was not computed according to the extreme gauge of the ship. Otherwise vessels would attempt to stop at unguarded spots along the coast and to avoid the duty altogether. To protect their revenue, the farmers modified their demands and disregarded Parliament's intent that the duty should serve to offset a similar tax laid by France on English ships.[17] When the question arose whether the same duty should be levied on a Dutch prize

---

pp. 44, 181, 433; CTB I, 541, 583). Sir John Shaw held the office of Surveyor, Collector and Receiver of the Navigation Act and that of Collector of Customs Inward at London, coincident with his post as Customs Farmer (CTB I, 232; III, 199; IV, 610).

[11] Sir John Wolstenholme. Newton, "The Great Farm," *RHS Trans.*, 4th series, I, 153. See also CSPD (1619-23), pp. 111, 157, 211; CTB I, 226, 304, 431, 574.

[12] The various petty farms were separately administered. See *infra*, pp. 83-85.

[13] CTB I, 606; CSPC (1669-74), No. 104.

[14] *Index Vectigalium.*   [15] *Supra*, pp. 68-73.

[16] CSPD (1668-69), p. 196; CTB II, 361.   [17] CTB VIII, 1817.

recaptured from the French,[18] or on French vessels whose masters claimed to have been driven ashore by stress of weather,[19] the answer should have been determined by policies of state and of international relations, rather than by considerations of private profit.

Moreover, the farms did not solve the financial problems of the government. The farmers of 1660 were continually harassed by requests for advances,[20] and when the revenue fell below anticipations because of the decline in trade caused by the Plague, the Fire of London, and the Dutch War, they asked for defalcations.[21] In the farm of 1667, rich men replaced all except two of the older group, who happened to be sufficiently wealthy to continue.[22] The new farmers succeeded in meeting the demands of the Treasury for some time, but eventually its continual requests exhausted their resources and forced the government to seek loans elsewhere.[23] Finally, they too sought defalcations. At the end of their farm, the Treasury was trying, on the one hand, to resist their demands for defalcations; and on the other, to find another group sufficiently rich and venturesome to advance more money. Lord St. John and his colleagues were willing to assume the risk, but inability to raise an advance payment of £250,000 saved them from their folly. The negotiations were almost completed when the Treasury suddenly announced that there would be no new farm, and in 1671 control of the customs revenue once more returned to commissioners, where it was thereafter destined to remain.[24]

The penniless government found new methods of spending its revenue before it was received, methods that did not interfere, as

[18] PC 2/64, p. 438.

[19] PC 2/62, pp. 407, 420; PC 2/63, pp. 12-13; CTB III, 9.

[20] CTB I, 436; II, 82, 87-88, 115-16.

[21] CTB II, 236, 463; III, 114-16.

[22] The new farmers were Millington, Turner, Vyner, and Alderman Backwell, a prominent London goldsmith; and the two former farmers were Wolstenholme and Shaw (BM Harl. MSS 6013, p. 57; CTB III, 190; CSPD [1667], p. 151).

[23] CTB II, 80, 469-70, 492. In 1670 the Customs Farmers failed to furnish £6,500 for the Earl of Sandwich and £15,000 for the navy (CTB III, 83). The government turned to the goldsmiths, who made loans at high rates of interest (CTB II, 87, 470; III, xxxvi, 413, 471, 477, 648, 759, 1323). Instead of loaning more during 1670 and 1671, the Customs Farmers appear to have been at least partly successful in collecting the interest on the money already loaned (CTB III, 655).

[24] CTB III, 491, 796, 819, 1126, 1127, 1172, 1414; IV, 236, 360-61.

had the farms, with the orderly operation of the governmental machine. Individuals who loaned money with the customs as a guarantee for repayment were sometimes appointed to posts in which they could keep their eyes on their security. Thus Thomas Fox was granted the office of "Receiver General and Cashier of Customs and subsidies, new impositions, Four and a Half per cent Duty and Coinage Duty," it being provided that as he "has lent and hereafter may lend to the King several considerable sums . . . said Fox shall not be removed from said office (save for fraud or misfeasance) until he be fully paid all such his loan money with the interest of the same."[25] At the end of the century, specified duties were definitely pledged for the repayment of certain public loans.[26]

These methods enabled the government both to anticipate the revenue and to administer the laws as public policy directed, comparatively free from the conflict of private interests. But in other respects the government was not so successful in freeing itself from past mistakes.

Administrative positions tended to survive long after any excuse for their existence had disappeared. The original posts of customers, comptrollers, searchers, surveyors, and waiters continued. Although the usefulness of these functionaries as checks upon the farmers had ceased when the Treasury undertook to administer the revenue, they remained to burden trade with demands for fees. Moreover, such officers were administratively undesirable, since the positions were granted by the King's letters patent under the Great Seal,[27] a form of appointment which gave the patentee rights in his office as firmly vested as a property right in a landed estate. Although Parliament, as early as the reign of Richard II, had forbidden officers to have any estate in their offices even for a term of years,[28] and although in 1668 the Treasury had declared all grants for customs places "are now during pleasure,"[29] individuals continued to secure posts for life or even in reversion, notwithstanding the law "in this

---

[25] CTB IX, 21, 403. See also 6 & 7 Gul. & Mar., c. 3, lxxxiv.
[26] A statement, showing how the various statutes pledged the customs, can be found in CU-BUS MSS D.430.6942.G792113.
[27] Newton, "The Great Farm," *RHS Trans.*, 4th series, I, 130.
[28] 14 Ric. II, c. 10; 17 Ric. II, c. 5.
[29] CTB II, 308; see also CSPD (1661-62), p. 613.

particular instance."[30] Thus "patent" officers who misbehaved could not be removed until their grants had been canceled by legal process.[31]

Strangely enough, the sole office created especially for enforcing the Navigation Act of 1660 was granted by letters patent. The post of Surveyor of the Navigation Act, later to be known by the more elaborate title, Surveyor, Collector and Receiver of the Moneys and Forfeitures Payable by the Act, was principally concerned with the registry and build of ships, and was granted to Sir John Shaw and Joseph Ashe with a salary of £100 per annum and £500 from the forfeitures for the breach of the Act.[32] It is also interesting to note that when the grant terminated, on the death of Charles II, the office ceased to be awarded by patent. Thereafter it was held merely by virtue of a Treasury warrant, terminable without legal procedure at the pleasure of the Lord Treasurer, and the annual salary was reduced to £60.[33]

The customs service was not so successful in ridding itself of other patent appointments. At first, efforts were directed to learning "how far the patent officers may be serviceable and useful" in performing the duties of commissioners' deputies, without additional salary.[34] The Treasury apparently became convinced that political

[30] CTB III, 848. See also CTB I, 413. There is a three-page memorandum from the Signet book of offices granted in reversion from May, 1667, to Sept., 1669 (CSPD [1668-69], p. 510).

[31] They might, however, be suspended from office. See the case of Cadwallader Jones (CTB II, 65, 364, 367, 402, 444, 509; III, 417, 424, 479, 562, 597).

[32] CSPD (1660-61), p. 524. A warrant of April 3, 1661, permitted Sir John Shaw to execute the office by self or deputy, and stated that he was the only person intended for the office, despite Ashe's inclusion in the patent (CTB I, 232). In the following cases, Shaw alone is mentioned: CSPD (1660-61), pp. 306, 359, 523; CTB I, 87, 244. Salaries were paid jointly, however, in 1661, 1666, 1669, and 1674 (CSPD [1661-62], p. 48; CTB I, 725; III, 221, 271, 897; IV, 610). Ashe's executors continued to collect his salary as late as 1687 (CTB VIII, 1404, 1517, 1524). Mention should also be made of the authority granted Frances Carpenter in 1677 to make seizures under the Navigation Act for six months (CTB V, 818).

[33] CTB VIII, 1253, 1286, 1404; IX, 7, 145, 478.

[34] CTB IV, 233. Various methods of economizing were used. Patent officers performed the duties of commissioners' deputies in collecting duties at Dover and acting as landwaiters in London and Bristol, without additional pay (CTB V, 198; VI, 26, 98; CTP [1557-1696], p. 451). In 1679 the Treasury ordered that as the office of customer became vacant, the collector of the port was to succeed therein, and all grants in the future must be for pleasure rather than life (CTB VI, 28).

favorites could not be made useful, and changed its policy to insist that competent deputies be appointed. In 1690 it went so far as to require, as a condition of continuing Oliver Lyme in office, that he refrain from performing the duties for which he was paid and that he entrust them entirely to an approved deputy.[35] The most direct and effective solution of the patent evil, of course, would have been to refrain from making more appointments at the expiration of those already in existence. But such heroic measures were too much to expect in an age ever on the outlook for posts for favorites, and patent officers continued to handicap administrative efficiency and to burden trade until considerably after the American Revolution.[36]

Various "petty farms" of the minor branches of the revenue proved to be another troublesome survival. Unlike the great farms of the principal revenues, which had been made for national purposes, they were granted for various personal considerations or to pay the King's private debts. The beneficiaries were a mixed group ranging from the Earl of Kinnoul to Mistress Nell Gwyn and the King's coachman,[37] and the farms consisted of a jumble of duties, including those on unwrought wood, glass, earthen and stonewares, oranges, citrons, lemons and pomegranates, alum, spices, logwood, exported sea coal, exported lamperns, imported salt, potashes, barilla, smalt, "saffers," and coach horses, as well as butlerage and purveyage of wine, the Irish revenue, and the duty of five shillings a ton on French ships.[38] Little or nothing escaped the onslaughts of favorites and courtiers or of the more worthy claimants to whom

[35] CTP (1557-1696), p. 126. 1 Hen. IV, c. 13; 4 Hen. IV, c. 20; 13 Hen. IV, c. 5 had long forbidden the use of deputies and patent officers. However, the need for such officers in large ports was recognized by 1 Eliz., c. 11, vii; and by 1687 more than twenty-four clerks were employed to perform the duties of three of the patent officers in London (CTB VIII, 1359), and in 1689 the power to act by deputy was considered customary (CTB IX, 148-49). Deputies for the more important offices were to be approved by the Treasury (CTB VII, 48, 125; VIII, 654; CTP [1557-1696], p. 465), but patent landwaiters seem to have gained the power to deputize others (CTB VI, 117-18; VIII, 2158).
[36] See Atton and Holland, The King's Customs, I, 362-65, for an account of the burdens thus put upon trade.
[37] CTB III, 1041; IV, 210; V, 106; VII, 1110, 1308; VIII, 230, 452; X, 860, 895-96; CTP (1557-1696), p. 382.
[38] For the history of these farms, see CTB, passim. In CSPD (1668-69), p. 79, an entry indicated that the farmers themselves sublet the customs on Scottish goods.

the King was personally indebted.[39] Despite legal rulings "that penal statutes cannot be farmed,"[40] the fines and forfeitures on prohibited and uncustomed goods were leased at one time.[41] But this grant was soon canceled, compensation being offered those who surrendered their interest willingly and jail being ordered for the obdurate.[42]

The process by which the Treasury sought first to reform and then to eliminate the petty farms was painfully slow.[43] It took more than two years to force the various patentees to enroll their grants in the Exchequer.[44] Occasional threats of seizure were supplemented by harassing tactics, when the Treasury ordered that the petty farmers make no use of the King's officers, or of his weights and scales or storehouses, and that they refrain from meddling with seizures and giving deputations which did not relate to their own farms.[45] In 1672 the "wood farmers" injudiciously antagonized the all-powerful Privy Council, which thereupon ordered that the Treasury "doe Inquire into these small Farmes, and consider whether it may not be fit to reassume them into his Maj^{tys} hands."[46] In November of the same year the Treasury determined to notify all the petty customs farmers of its intent to take in their farms, but consideration of the matter dragged. The Treasury accumulated a book of data about the small branches of the revenue, but it remained in My Lord Treasurer's closet while vested interests continued.[47]

[39] The revenues on silk, Rhenish wine, and lobsters, and the tax on aliens, somehow escaped, although farms were sought (CTB I, 217, 219; V, 122, 262; VII, 1457; CTP [1557-1696], pp. 229, 264-65, 274, 439).

[40] CTB III, 157.

[41] These grants were made to the Earl of Berkshire, the Earl of Bristol, and Mr. Bridge (CSPD [1665-66], p. 71; CTB III, 364, 365; IV, 207, 211, 423, 426, 433). It should be noted that by Privy Seal these fines and forfeitures were granted to the Privy Purse (CSPD [1664-65], p. 581; CTB III, 364).

[42] CSPD (1665-66), p. 71; CTB IV, 211.

[43] The Treasury had not favored the system of petty farms. In 1665 the then Lord Treasurer, in a report on a duty on Scottish salt, stated, "I am in my judgment no friend to minute farms" (CTB I, 666-67).

[44] CTB II, 221, 226, 334, 452; III, 144, 148-49.

[45] CTB III, 1094, 1197, 1291. The farmers sometimes resisted the Treasury, as in the case of the farmers of the duty on exported coals, who exhibited their defiance by refusing to show their books (CTB III, 985).

[46] PC 2/63, p. 269.

[47] CTB III, 948, 1111; IV, 298, 311, 315; V, 29. However, the King's officers of the customs were to be instructed to take charge of the collection of duties at the expiration of the existing wood farm, in spite of any other grants (CTB II, 92).

Victory over the farms did not come until James II's reign, and even then it was not complete. Charles II's death had, as a matter of law, automatically terminated the parliamentary grant of any duties which were not part of the hereditary revenue of the Crown, and all farms of such revenues ended—whether or not the term of years specified in the grant had expired.[48] In most cases, however, the government seemed to recognize a moral obligation and did not take full advantage of its legal rights. The rights of patentees were seldom if ever disregarded. The recognition granted Nell Gwyn's patent claim to the logwood farm[49] and the Widow Jackson's equity in the proceeds of the customs of smalt, barilla, and potashes for which her husband had been the sublessee,[50] merely illustrate the general rule. In the case of both, however, the concession was financial, rather than administrative. Although the proceeds eventually reached the ladies, the duties were collected by the Treasury's appointees,[51] a policy of centralization in accord with the Treasury's earlier efforts. But shortly thereafter, failure to make similar administrative reservations, when renewing another grant,[52] showed that consistency was not a seventeenth-century virtue.

Troublesome as may have been the tendency of posts to persist long after the excuse for their existence had disappeared, the administrative heritage was not an unmixed evil. In the field of administrative regulations, previous experience proved invaluable. From feudal days to the present, the secret of administering a revenue or regulatory system has remained the same. In so far as possible, methods must be devised to relieve the authorities of the need for proving violations and to throw the task of demonstrating compliance with the law upon the individual.

The baneful results of doing otherwise were early brought home to customs officials. The rules had once provided that if no officer

[48] CTB I, 227-28; VIII, 221, 306.
[49] CTB V, 106; VII, 1110; VIII, 263, 601.
[50] CTB VIII, 496; IX, 1228, 1242, 1429; X, 895-96; CTP (1557-1696), pp. 212, 378, 382-83.
[51] This was true while Mr. Jackson (also called Johnson) was alive (BM Harl. MSS 6013, f. 25). The Earl of Yarmouth's farm of unwrought wood, glass, and oranges was also collected by the Treasury officials after 1685 (CTB VIII, 221, 446-47, 1884).
[52] CTB VIII, 306, 1460, 1500; IX, 2.

demanded duty within twenty-four hours of coming into port, the master of a ship was entitled to unload his cargo without payment. A game of hide and seek ensued. Masters sailing along the coast sought to mislead the officer on the shore into believing that they were destined for a neighboring port. While the officer hastened there, the ship would wait for nightfall, or until he was out of sight, and then alter its course for some comparatively uninhabited creek or harbor, where the master might legally escape the payment of duties if the officer took too long to find him.[53]

The authorities soon learned that they could avoid pursuing ships by making the masters come to them. As early as 1275 the English coast was divided into ports, and later subdivided into member ports and creeks, to which ships must go, and any unlading elsewhere was for that reason alone subject to penalties.[54] Later regulations provided that certain merchandise could be transported only through specified towns, and carriers taking such articles as wool by fresh water or the arms of the sea had to give bonds not to carry them elsewhere.[55] Disputes as to the market value of merchandise were avoided by establishing a "book of rates," which fixed the values to be used in calculating the ad valorem customs duties.[56] Best of all, from the officials' point of view, was the bonding requirement. When utilized, it forced those engaged in regulated trades, upon penalty of losing the sum specified in their bond, to furnish satisfactory proof that they had obeyed the rules, and thus relieved the officials from the task of supplying legal proof of violations.[57]

Administrative regulations were not confined to penalizing the prohibited act. Insurers were forbidden to guarantee smugglers against loss. Masters and mariners were not only to abstain from violations, they were to refrain from becoming objects of suspicion. Ships were forbidden to hover off the seacoasts or to delay more than three days in sailing from Gravesend to London. Otherwise

[53] Leftwich, "The Early London Customs Service," *P.L.A. Monthly*, Sept. 1928, pp. 340-41.
[54] Gras, *Early English Customs System*, p. 105.
[55] Hen. V, stat. 2, c. 6; 15 Hen. VI, c. 8; 14 Ric. II, c. 7 (repealed by 15 Ric. II, c. 8); 21 Ric. II, c. 17; 27 Edw. III, stat. 2, c. 15.
[56] Gras, *Early English Customs System*, pp. 122-29.
[57] For illustrations of the care taken to prevent opportunities for fraud in canceling the bonds, see *Rules and Orders of the Court of the Exchequer*, pp. 57-64.

innocent actions were penalized, because they might lead to violations. Brandy could not be imported in containers of less than sixty
gallons nor tobacco in casks weighing less than two hundred pounds.
Ships of small burden were forbidden to carry frequently smuggled
commodities, because of the ease with which such vessels might slip
up shallow, uninhabited creeks and avoid the authorities. And wool,
the exportation of which was forbidden, could not legally be taken
within fifteen miles of the seacoast unless registered. Neither alamodes nor spices could be imported until notice had been given and
license obtained, and fine Italian, Sicilian, and Neapolitan thrown
silk had to be brought to Their Majesties' London Custom House,
"wheresoever landed."[58]

Some of the administrative devices thus utilized for the purposes
of mercantilism were the products of the feudal era and the "ancient
practice touching real estate." Sometimes they were adapted to
commercial conditions by administrative modifications, as in the
method of appraising merchandise, but upon other occasions they
were changed by statutes like the Act of Henry VIII which altered
the older rules concerning obligations on bonds.[59] In other instances
new methods of procedure were evolved by the tedious process of
trial and error. Many of the most useful administrative provisions
were collected and reënacted in the Act of Frauds of Elizabeth[60]
and that of Charles II,[61] but even more were scattered throughout
the statutes of the realm and judicial and administrative records. All
had the same general purpose; the effort was to free the customs staff
from the necessity of proving the evil intent and the overt acts
usually required to convict of crime, and to reduce the task merely
to one of discovering goods unladen or shipped without accompanying documents to prove that they had been duly declared.

In the field of rules, as in the realm of officialdom, many regula-

---

[58] 4 Gul. & Mar., c. 15 (insurance); 14 Car. II, c. 11 (hovering); 4 Gul. & Mar.,
c. 5, vi (brandy); 10 Gul. III, c. 10, xxvi (tobacco); 12 & 13 Gul. III, c. 11, xvi (ships
of small burden); 1 Gul. & Mar., c. 32, i; 9 Gul. III, c. 40, iii-vi (wool); 4 Gul. &
Mar., c. 5, xii (spices and alamodes); 5 Gul. & Mar., c. 3 (thrown silk).

[59] 33 Hen. VIII, c. 39; CO 388/5, A 10; Gilbert, *Treatise on the Court of Exchequer*,
pp. 96-102; Price, *Treatise on the Law of the Exchequer*, pp. 29-35; Brown, *Practice
of His Majestie's Court of Exchequer*, pp. 3-4.

[60] 1 Eliz., c. 11.

[61] 14 Car. II, c. 11.

tions persisted long after occasion for their existence had disappeared. Sheer inertia attended to that. Yet obsolete regulations proved to be a much less troublesome heritage than superfluous officials. Administrative provisions had no friends at court to clamor for their continuance, if they could not demonstrate their own utility. The customs needed to retain only those rules which continued to be of service; those rendered out of date by changed conditions could be forgotten.

VIII

METHODS OF ENFORCEMENT

THE detailed nature of the administrative regulations may best be observed by studying the machinery of enforcement. Seventeenth-century customs routine proves that the idea of checks and balances was not merely a theoretical notion. Eighteenth-century political philosophers could find many pertinent examples in pre-existing administrative practices.

The master of a ship coming to England was obliged by law to make proper entry of his vessel and its cargo publicly in the Custom House, immediately upon arrival. He was to furnish the collector with a written list of the packages carried, showing the marks, numbers, and names of the merchants, as well as the quantity and description of the goods belonging to each. He was also required to answer upon oath all questions which might be asked of him concerning the ship and cargo, in what port the cargo had been laden, where the ship had been built, how it was manned, and who had been its master during the entire voyage. If any of the enumerated goods were imported from the colonies, he must present evidence that the required bond had been given. If the master failed to make a complete and accurate report, his ship and its lading were subject to seizure. After the master had declared his cargo, the merchants could make a bill of entry for their goods. The collector estimated the duty, and a warrant was signed by him and countersigned by the comptroller and surveyor, to permit the unloading of the goods.[1]

From the time a ship first came into port, which in London meant when it arrived at Gravesend, tidesmen were put aboard to search it, and no person was permitted to go ashore until he also had been searched. The tidesmen took special care to discover prohibited

---

[1] 14 Car. II, c. 11; 25 Car. II, c. 7; "Rules and Regulations Made by Elizabeth" in "B.Y.," *Modern Practice of the Court of Exchequer*, pp. 417-26.

and hidden goods and prepared a dated and numbered list of all articles aboard, which they checked whenever a package was put into the lighter. They then accompanied the lighter to the quay, where other officers, known as "landwaiters," received it and gave the tidesmen a certificate of receipt, discharging them from further responsibility if the goods unladen corresponded with the list they had prepared.[2]

The landwaiter's duties, however, had only begun. It was his concern to unpack, search thoroughly, and weigh all the goods, to make certain that no prohibited articles were concealed and that all the merchandise had been properly declared—a task often requiring exact knowledge of the subtle flavors of wine and the various qualities of cloth. If any goods were discovered that had not been accounted for, such articles were sent to the King's storehouse for an additional inspection. When the landwaiter or warehouseman had finished his inspection, the goods were ready to be delivered and were released to the merchant, if in the meantime he had paid, or had arranged with the collector to pay, the duty and had procured from him a warrant for the goods' discharge.[3]

The procedure upon exportation was much the same as that followed upon importation, the principal differences being that the functions of the landwaiters were exercised by officers known as searchers and that the warrants were referred to as "cockets."[4]

Although the report of the landwaiter served as a check on the tidesman, and vice versa, other officials were appointed with supervisory powers. In the larger ports, a surveyor and comptroller were provided as checks on the collector. The tidesmen were supervised by a tidesurveyor; the landwaiters had a surveyor of their own; and the searchers were watched over by a head-searcher. In addition, the Commissioners residing in London could supervise activities there for themselves, and it was also customary either for them or

---

[2] 14 Car. II, c. 11; BM Add MSS 4761, ff. 104-5; CTB VII, 275-77. In smaller places the boatmen, "when not employed in the boat," acted as tidesmen (CTB VII, 1325).

[3] 14 Car. II, c. 11; BM Add MSS 4761, ff. 104, 109, 113; CTB VI, 260; VII, 276-77.

[4] BM Add MSS 4761, f. 114; "B.Y.," *Modern Practice of the Court of Exchequer,* p. 411.

for a surveyor general to make periodic inspection tours of the outports, in order to detect frauds and to discover remedies.[5]

A further safeguard was provided by the voluminous records that the officers were obliged to keep. The tidesman was supposed to carry a pocketbook with numbered pages, in which to enter not only the time at which he went on duty and the time at which he left, but also a notation of all goods he discharged and of the warrant authorizing such action. The tidesurveyor kept a similar register of the "names of all inward bound ships, their masters' names, burthen, qualities and ladings and a like register of the names of the tidesmen that are boarded upon them, with the time when they were sent to Gravesend, when boarded and when cleared, an account of all the watchmen, to what stations they are each night appointed and what ships or goods are under their charge." The same official also kept a record of the collectors' warrants, which showed the goods to be unloaded, and the tidesman's receipts from the landwaiters. The landwaiters kept similar detailed records, with numbered pages, and their surveyors kept the lighter bills upon which the landwaiters had endorsed the tidesman's name, the date, and the quantity of the goods. The surveyor of the warehouse also had a record arranged to correspond with those of the landwaiters, so that he might readily give an account of what goods were still in his custody, as well as those that had been discharged. In addition, the collector and the comptroller each kept a copy of the bills of entry, the bills of evaluation, the customs bills, and the warrants to unload and discharge.[6]

By this elaborate system of records, which were periodically to be turned over for checking and comparison to an officer known as the "jerquer," it was intended that frauds and discrepancies might be rendered impossible. The tidesurveyor and the surveyor of the landwaiters might check the actions of their subordinates; by comparing lighterage bills and certificates of receipt, the collector and the jerquer could supervise the activities of their colleagues, and the visiting inspectors might check the work of all.[7]

[5] BM Add MSS 4761, ff. 105, 112; CTB VII, 276; VIII, 857; *infra*, p. 141.
[6] BM Add MSS 4761, ff. 100, 104-6, 108, 113; CTB VII, 276; VIII, 857; "B.Y.," *Modern Practice of the Court of Exchequer*, pp. 417-20.
[7] BM Add MSS 4761, ff. 100, 104-6, 108, 113; CTB VII, 276; VIII, 857; "B.Y.," *Modern Practice of the Court of Exchequer*, pp. 417-26.

Enforcement activities were by no means confined to the ports established by law. Officers were stationed along the seashore to prevent ships from unlading at unauthorized places. When one of them saw a ship, he was to note both its name and the hour he first viewed it, and to ride along the coast, keeping it in sight until it reached port or passed under the surveillance of another riding officer. The watch extended beyond the seacoast to the roads inland, where landcarriagemen were stationed to detect such smuggled goods as might have reached the shore.[8] Nor were customs activities confined to the land. Except in times of war or unusual danger, sections of the seacoast were patrolled by customs smacks, which sometimes appear to have been built especially for the service, and one of which was "reported the nimblest sailor in England."[9] In the sixties and eighties at least, the commanders of these boats held commissions from the Lord High Admiral, as well as from the Treasury.[10] Sometimes, especially during wars, these predecessors of the revenue cruisers were replaced or supplemented by naval vessels.[11] Occasionally, in the interests of economy, they were replaced by smaller vessels, as at Dover, when a shallop costing from £100 to £200 was replaced by a boat "which may be managed by two or three hands," with two persons as boatman and tidesman at £20 per annum each, and an allowance for an extraordinary man on occasion.[12]

The navy was not the only government service which aided the customs. On occasions the army lent its dragoons, and the governors of forts at seaport towns were directed to assist. The sheriff extended but little aid, and that only as he performed his ex-officio functions in the trial of seizures.[13] That important individual, the justice of the peace, who administered so many of the affairs of the realm, had comparatively little to do with the customs. Nevertheless, he was supposed to furnish general assistance, to issue search warrants in certain cases, to commit to jail offenders who abused the customs

[8] BM Add MSS 4761, f. 100; CTB III, 949; VIII, 1838-39. See also CTB V, 245; IX, 490; CTP (1557-1696), pp. 381, 383.
[9] CTB IV, 866; V, 785; CSPD (1665-66), p. 492.
[10] CTB I, 169; VII, 841, 875.
[11] 10 Gul. III, c. 16, xvi; PC 2/69, pp. 628, 660, 667; APC Col. II, 45; CTB I, 277; VII, 710, 716; IX, 658.
[12] CTB V, 652. See also CTB IX, 658, 708.
[13] PC 2/69, p. 373; CTB I, 627; II, 439-40; VII, 280, 605; CSPD (1661-62), p. 139.

officers, and in the eighteenth century two or more justices were authorized to try various seizures involving specified commodities.[14] Occasionally the aid of mayors in the outports was invoked. Records show that they were requested to coöperate in obtaining information from masters of vessels coming from overseas, to aid in settling controversies about fees, to suppress riots, and to report concerning suspected frauds.[15] In short, the customs authorities did not have to act alone; they had the aid of nearly all officialdom.

The network of enforcement extended abroad. In Holland, especially in the river Maas and the port of Rotterdam, an effort was made to examine the "cocketts and other dispatches from the several ports of England," which masters were supposed to have for plantation goods enumerated in the Acts. Most of the time the work appears to have been entrusted to the consul, but an entry in 1693 tells of a Rotterdam merchant, Mr. Abraham Kick, having been appointed to that duty.[16] A special correspondent was maintained in Scotland, at the cost of £30 per annum, to report on violations which might occur there,[17] and consular reports indicate that elsewhere English representatives were active.[18] The consul at Genoa informed his English superiors, even before the arrival of the ship itself, that a vessel was expected there from Barbados contrary to the laws of trade.[19]

The mere detection of fraud was helpful; the name, build, and burden of the ship might be given His Majesty's men-of-war so as to assure its seizure wherever found, or the offending ship might be punished upon its return to England.[20] Moreover, it was apparently possible, when enforcing the mercantile measures of the seventeenth century, for one government to obtain the active coöperation of those countries which were benefited by the violations they aided in punishing. England had, at great trouble to the Privy Council, aided in enforcing the Portuguese laws regulating trade to Brazil against certain ships which had come to England.[21] Similarly the English

[14] 14 Car. II, c. 11; 14 Car. II, c. 13; Hoon, English Customs System, pp. 186, 277, 280.
[15] PC 2/61, p. 378; PC 2/67, pp. 65, 153; CTB I, 654; II, 439-40, 590; IV, 271.
[16] T 1/22, No. 40; CTP (1557-1696), p. 297.
[17] CTB V, 1000.
[18] For additional cases, see CTB VIII, 199, 235, 769, 898.
[19] CTB VIII, 971.
[20] T 27/7, pp. 288-89; CTB VII, 1049.
[21] PC 2/55, pp. 369, 373, 443, 570; CTB I, 158.

government told its consuls in Genoa, Amsterdam, and Rotterdam to seek the assistance of the local authorities in arresting vessels there.[22] Nothing in the order to the consuls indicates that the requests to be made of the foreign governments were deemed unwarranted; and in fact we know of seizures being made of the "Hannah" at Hamburg, the "Black Greyhound" at Altona, and an unnamed Irish ship in Terveer.[23]

A study of the costs of extraterritorial enforcement throws much light upon the problems involved. Mr. Kennedy, who seized the ship at Terveer, was instructed to send it with the least possible charge to England for trial, but the account of expenditures he submitted, showed the difficulties in the way of economy. There was a reward given to the official who searched the ship for letters; there were port dues, fees paid officers, charges for provisions which had been required, payments for bringing the ship to England, and the expenses of sending home the needful proofs and witnesses.[24] A less costly procedure was to promise immunity from further prosecution if the owner or master would pay a composition or fine equal to the full customs duty payable in England, "reckoned as if the tobacco had been imported into England and not shipped out again."[25] And despite its earlier determination to exact the full penalty of the law, this was the method the government followed in the cases of the "Hannah" and the "Black Greyhound"—after it had received Mr. Kennedy's statement of expenses.[26]

But enforcement abroad, even by the way of composition, was expensive. Mr. Skelton, the envoy to Hamburg, reported that "the President of Altona in the King of Denmark's dominions where the seizure was first made deserves a gratuity of £5 for his assistance," and Skelton himself, having waived his property rights in the forfeiture, expected some benefits from the £150 composition paid by the master of the ship he seized. The Lord Treasurer agreed, and £50 was paid to Skelton "as a reward for his pains."[27] Whatever the cost, it was probably more than offset by the consequent discourage-

[22] CTB VII, 1119; VIII, 982.
[23] CTB VII, 1049, 1180, 1342.
[24] T 27/7, pp. 245, 288-89, 311, 350; T 53/4, pp. 403-4; CTB VII, 965, 1049, 1086, 1130, 1135.
[25] CTB VII, 1049, 1342.   [26] Ibid., VII, 1180, 1343.   [27] Ibid., VII, 1049, 1343.

ment to smuggling; tenaciously pursued, the policy would have meant that there was no port or haven in which an illegal trader could be free from the wrath of outraged English mercantilism.

The records of enforcement activities abroad are irritatingly incomplete, but enough have survived to indicate the watchfulness of official or unofficial agencies. As we have seen, various consuls in Genoa, the Netherlands, Germany, and Zante were alert to detect violations. In Aleppo the Levant Company's agents made it their concern to inquire into violations of the Navigation Laws; those who sent goods by French caravans and ships and later transferred them to English ships not only violated the laws of the realm but also defrauded the company of its duties.[28] The Eastland Company had its deputy at Danzig, and doubtless there were representatives of it and other companies elsewhere, ready to act when the invocation of national policy would, as it so often did, benefit corporate monopolies.[29]

Even individual assistance was forthcoming, if private gain were promised. John Baptist Seth, who had been forced to leave the kingdom by reason of the Test Act and who had been in the Custom House in Flanders, prayed for some place in the customs service, that he might be an agent in redressing the "numerous practices not conducing to his Majesty's interest" which he had there observed.[30] The case of the yacht "Kitchen" shows that sometimes, when a master's bad reputation caused fear that the cargo might be shifted into coasters "or privately stolen ashore," a tidesman was placed aboard the vessel to remain with it until its return, thereby helping to insure that the goods were actually unladen beyond the seas.[31] When it was suspected that French wines were being imported from San Sebastian under the guise of being Spanish, two officers were sent "to take knowledge of the wine there & its growth."[32] In 1682 a correspondence was carried on with Calais about the practice whereby the same vessels passed in France for French and in England for English, and thus avoided the duties imposed by each country upon the vessels of the other.[33] Seven years later, despite

[28] CSPD (1660-61), p. 592.
[29] CSPD (1671), p. 485.
[30] CTB VIII, 1463.

[31] CTB, VI, 409.
[32] CTP (1557-1696), pp. 492, 540, 543.
[33] CTB VII, 547.

the outbreak of war, the Customs Commissioners "were daily receiving" from France reports concerning ships which had "by art and violence" left England and gone there contrary to the King's orders.[34]

If somehow the would-be smuggler should escape the customs officer, there were at the water front in England many local officers and others who, although not directly interested in enforcing the Navigation Acts, were nevertheless, in the ordinary exercise of their own duties, likely to be in a position to observe possible violations. Like the customs officials, the excise officers in search of brandy and other excisable liquors could and did enter and search ships.[35] The watermen of the River Thames were enjoined by their oath not to "take goods to or out of ships to impairment of customs," and not to conceal any offenses, but to report them to the Lord Treasurer or the customs officials;[36] and the wharfingers were required to keep their books open for inspection, so that uncustomed goods might be detected.[37] In London there was the city garbler, who inspected imports of galls and spices; the receiver of the coal duty for the church of St. Paul; and collectors of the duty for the relief of orphans and other creditors of the city.[38] The collection of some of these duties might be delegated to the customs establishment, as was the ancient right of the Lieutenant of the Tower to receive from every ship bringing wine into the River two gallons from before and two from behind the mast.[39] Other receivers took charge of their own collections, the officers of the waterbailage, for example, having a seat in the Custom House itself.[40]

Official and semiofficial activities were supplemented by agents for the various chartered companies which invoked and helped to enforce the "several Acts of Parliament." Among others, the Bermuda and East India Companies and the bone-lace makers had special agents to search for and seize prohibited goods.[41] A London

[34] CTP (1557-1696), p. 34.
[35] CTB VII, 761; VIII, 11, 139; IX, 1673.
[36] PC 2/56, p. 312.   [37] CTB I, 200.
[38] 5 & 6 Gul. & Mar., c. 10; CTP (1557-1696), p. 462.
[39] CTB VIII, 1827-28.
[40] CTB VI, 27. A representative of the Canary Company likewise had a place in the Custom House (CTB I, 662; Skeel, "The Canary Company," Eng. Hist. Rev., XXXI, 535).
[41] CTB I, 550; II, 512; III, 184, 432, 575; VIII, 98, 511-12.

dyer reported frauds in paying customs for dyeing stuffs, and the Hudson's Bay Company petitioned that the importation of furs from Holland and France be prohibited, since it was to the damage of the company and contrary to the laws of the realm.[42] The Canary Company complained that its charter rights were nullified "by the officers of His Majesty's Customs, who, contrary to the Act of Navigation and His Majesty's Royal Proclamation," permitted the importation of Canary wines. Investigation disclosed fraudulent activities on the part of certain underofficials, and led to orders to the customs staff that the laws be obeyed and enforced, and that the company's taster be permitted to taste wines suspected or known to be Canary wines.[43]

Attempts were also made to enlist the services of the public at large by offering informers a moiety of the proceeds of forfeitures arising out of violations.[44] Thus the interest of the populace as a whole, as well as the activity of those specially charged with enforcement, was stimulated by motives of pecuniary self-interest. It would seem that the volunteer assistants thus obtained, together with the administrative cordons of officialdom, would have provided a network of enforcement authorities so closely interlaced that no illegal trade could exist; but before we draw conclusions it will be well to consider the character of the people whose activities were to be regulated. Perhaps what human ingenuity could devise, human ingenuity could find a way to circumvent.

[42] PC 2/55, p. 632; CTB VIII, 1817.
[43] PC 2/59, pp. 203, 342, 411-12, 418-19.
[44] 12 Car. II, c. 18; 14 Car. II, c. 11.

IX

THE HUMAN FACTOR

IN GOVERNMENT as in mechanics there is no guarantee that machinery will operate according to the specifications described in blue prints. In addition to the possibility of structural defects, the human factor must always be taken into account. Thus in the case of the laws governing trade and navigation, when there was sufficient desire to evade the machinery of enforcement some one could usually find a way. Brandies might be entered in the name of "persons who are very poor and not the proper owners thereof," so that when His Majesty's officer came to collect the duty, he would have no valuables on which to levy it.[1] False casks might be used; vessels might lie in the river and discharge their most valuable goods before coming to port; French vessels lying off the coast might evade the duty of five shillings a ton by discharging their lading into smaller boats of English ownership.[2] Worse still, officers might be corrupted, intimidated, or even murdered.[3] Whether resistance to the laws assumed such forms depended, of course, upon the attitude of the people and the character of the officers.

The offense of smuggling, or, as it was once more accurately described, "stealing the King's customs," seems to be one of those crimes that attract many otherwise respectable members of the community. The modern girl who puts on extra pairs of silk stockings in order to escape customs duties is a typical illustration of this psychological phenomenon, and an excellent seventeenth-century example is afforded by the righteous Puritan traders who complained of a certain informer's immorality because he went snooping around to discover smuggled goods on Sunday, instead of going to church

[1] CTB III, 809.
[2] CTB I, 199-200, 279, 364-65.
[3] In addition to discussion in text, see Harper, *The Smugglers*; Teignmouth and Harper, *The Smugglers, passim.*

like a respectable Christian.[4] The churches themselves were used upon occasion to conceal smuggled goods, and the clergy do not seem to have been unduly concerned about the crime. Parson Woodforde, for one, confessed to his diary that he sat up one night to await an "honest smuggler with some gin."[5]

High duties upon importations were a comparatively recent innovation in English fiscal policy, to which the trading community had not yet become reconciled. The furor which greeted the customs duties exacted by the first two Stuarts centered on constitutional issues, but general economic distaste for such taxes undoubtedly had much to do with its origin. The objections to the excise, under Cromwell, and to the increased taxes, during Charles II's reign, disclose an unreadiness to pay taxes, regardless of who imposed them.[6] Moreover, the way in which duties were laid, made them especially hard to bear. Although theoretically the basis of customs duties was a levy of one shilling in the pound, the valuation on which this 5-percent rate was calculated was not the market price, but a predetermined figure set forth in the Book of Rates. Sometimes the legal valuation might accord with that fixed by competitive conditions, but more usually it did not, and often it was excessively high.[7] From the merchant's point of view, matters became worse and worse as the financial needs of the Crown led to the imposition of duty upon duty, until eventually the original assessment, the subsidy of tonnage and poundage, formed but a slight fraction of the total collected.[8] Traders might have felt guilty when evading the ancient subsidy, since it had had time to become a part of the mercantile code of morality; but new duties were added with a rapidity that

[4] BM Stowe MSS 746, f. 45.
[5] Harper, *The Smugglers*, pp. 81-83; Woodforde, *Diary*, I, 282.
[6] The dissatisfaction is clearly expressed in the literature of the time. See, for example, Cradocke, *Wealth Discovered*; Roberts, *Treasure of Traffike*, p. 44, *et seq.*; Cary, *An Essay on the State of England*, Dedication.
[7] "J. P. Esq.," *Of Trade*, pp. 146-47. Beer (*Old Colonial System*, I, 130) states that the valuation in the Book of Rates for tobacco was from ten to twenty times higher than the price paid in America.
[8] To aid in the calculation of such duties, the sums charged by virtue of the different laws were listed in separate columns, in such guides to the customs as those of Carkesse. The minor part played by the original assessment of tunnage and poundage in revenue calculations is clearly shown in such statements of the source of customs income as appear in CU-BUS MSS D.430.6942.G792113.

afforded little opportunity for them to acquire a hold on the public conscience.

The question of obedience to the mercantile code was usually one of expediency—the relation between the advantages of violation and the risks of evasion. Unfortunately for enforcement, an additional risk or two meant little or nothing to the seamen and traders of the era. They were necessarily a hardy lot. All knew that the sea would take its toll; for those who escaped, the pirates furnished a threat. Privateering in war time would result in loss of cargo at least; capture by the Algerines meant a horrible slavery from which release was as likely to come by death as by ransom; and an encounter with the freebooters of the Spanish Main often resulted in the vanquished's walking the plank. Even when a vessel was safely anchored in port, disease or pestilence might demand its tribute and if ship and crew escaped other dangers, there remained the necessity of keeping a weather eye open to avoid the press master and his gang.[9]

As compared with the ordinary perils of commerce, the risks involved in violating the mercantile code were slight. For the most part the penalties consisted merely of fines, or forfeiture of the prohibited or uncustomed goods and of the smuggler's ship,[10] except in instances of physical violence, which were punished by physical restraint.[11] Otherwise, imprisonment was the punishment for only a few offenses, such as allowing men who were not lords, "true and notable Merchants," or King's soldiers to go overseas without license,[12] and permitting the illegal exportation of horses,[13] leather, tallow, or rawhides,[14] which were believed to be vital to England. The most savage of all the statutes were those designed to protect the English woolen industry. One of Elizabeth's Parliaments provided that anyone carrying sheep or lambs out of England was to lose all his goods, to suffer one year's imprisonment, and at the end

[9] See account of difficulties of the ship "Adventure" of Bristol (E134, 22 Car. II, Mich. 43).
[10] For list of penalties, see BM Stowe MSS 322, f. 24.
[11] 14 Car. II, c. 11, vi.
[12] 5 Ric. II, stat. I, c. 2; *Index Vectigalium*, p. 17.
[13] 1 Edw. VI, c. 5; 1 Eliz., c. 7; *Index Vectigalium*, p. 12.
[14] 18 Eliz., c. 9; *Index Vectigalium*, pp. 12-13.

THE HUMAN FACTOR

of the term to have his left hand cut off in some market town on market day.[15] A statute of Charles II made the offense a felony punishable by death and similarly penalized the transportation of wool.[16] But these harsh measures were seldom if ever put into effect. It became an unwritten rule of "owling" (as the illegal exportation of wool was known) for the officers to content themselves with the forfeiture of the wool seized when they managed to surprise the owlers.[17] The owlers saved their necks, the officers avoided a struggle, and the law of Parliament bowed to the unwritten code of expediency thus established.

Parliament attempted to deplete the ranks of the smugglers by enacting statutes of pardon and indemnity which granted forgiveness for past transgressions, in the hope that offenders would forsake their evil ways and settle down to respectability.[18] Although it was possibly unsound in principle to condone wrongdoing, it was advantageous in practice; once the smugglers had joined the law-abiding element of the mercantile community, their interest lay in eliminating illicit activities, a task for which their personal experience furnished a knowledge of the tricks of the trade.

The government realized that it was fully as important to make it possible for the well-intentioned merchant to continue in his law-abiding habits as it was to punish the wrongdoer. The Privy Council, therefore, mitigated the alien duties which, by burdening legal trade, had tended to throw it "into the hands of those who are not fair traders,"[19] and the administrative statutes contained provisions intended to prevent enforcement activities from being unduly burdensome. Searchers at Gravesend could not, "without just and reasonable cause," detain any ship "above three tydes," nor searchers elsewhere "above one tide." Officers were to be in attendance in

---

[15] 8 Eliz., c. 3, v; *Index Vectigalium*, pp. 12-13.

[16] 14 Car. II, c. 18.

[17] The accounts of the Treasury solicitors give no indication of the capital penalty having been exacted, but do show that fines were collected (AO 3/1101). See also Harper, *The Smugglers*, pp. 12-23, and entries in CTB for 1680-1700 referring to the activities of William Carter and Henry Baker. See also Trevers, *An Essay to the Restoring of Our Decayed Trade, Wherein Is Described the Smugglers, Lawyers, and Officers Frauds, etc.*, which deals principally with the wool trade.

[18] 6 & 7 Gul. & Mar. c. 20. For legal problems arising under the pardon of 1717, see BM Add MSS 8832, pp. 313-16.

[19] CTB VIII, 530.

the Custom House from nine to twelve and from two to four for the dispatch of business. Merchants were to be received in turn; no one was to be delayed nor to be charged a larger gratuity or fee than those established by Parliament. In London, merchants were entitled to lade or unlade their goods at any lawful quay between the Tower and London Bridge, from sunrise to sunset in winter and from six in the morning to six at night in the summer, and the officials were required to be available. A merchant might "break bulk" in any port by unlading part of the ship's cargo and paying duty only on the goods landed. Allowances were made for such wine as had leaked, abatements granted for such as turned to vinegar. Adjustments were likewise authorized for tobacco or other goods damaged by salt water.[20] When goods were lost at sea, an equal amount could be exported customs free. When vessels were driven ashore by tempest, the master could sell such part of the cargo as was necessary to enable his ship to continue the voyage. And the law provided that no owner was to lose his ship "for a small thing uncustomed," of which he was ignorant.[21]

Similarly, the authorities were willing to overlook minor violations if a strict insistence upon the letter of the law would run counter to popular conceptions of common fairness. Thus when the ship "Concord" came to port carrying a few bottles of French wine and brandy for the ship's company, when some poor mariners imported small parcels which in some way did not meet the requirements of the law, or when a merchant inadvertently entered in his own name goods which should have been entered as those of aliens and should have paid six shillings and ninepence additional duty, the Lords of the Treasury wisely determined to have the seizure proceedings quashed.[22] Often the immateriality of the violation demonstrated that the offense was inadvertent and technical rather than intentional, but the importer's good faith might be established by other circumstances, such as appeared in the case of Christopher Mosyer. A young merchant of good reputation, he usually dealt in linens and wine, but imported some red wool on one occasion when

[20] 12 Car. II, c. 4, i, viii-xi, xiii, xviii-xix, xxii, xxiv; *Index Vectigalium*, pp. 26-27.
[21] 28 Edw. III, c. 13; 38 Edw. III, c. 8; 20 Ric. II, c. 4; *Index Vectigalium*, p. 26.
[22] CTB VII, 104; VIII, 1701; IX, 1155.

an opportunity presented itself for him to make a favorable purchase in France. He had examined the Book of Rates and found that red wool was listed as being free of duty; yet he failed to note that the wool had been produced in the Spanish West Indies, and not in France, and that the Navigation Act of 1660 required such wool to come directly from those islands or from Spain. His ship was seized, but was ordered released by the Privy Council, on the grounds that the young man's good faith was evident throughout and was made doubly clear by virtue of the goods having been publicly laid on the ship, "free for anyone to make stay thereof."[23]

Such modifications of the laws were not so much a matter of charity as of necessity. Traders who tried to comply with the law, only to lose their ships and goods because of technicalities, would soon cease trying. Smuggling would seem to be a better means of circumventing technical rules and unreasonable officials. Something had to be done to avoid antagonizing the honest merchant who might be merely the victim of circumstances, and thus we frequently find the notation that a seizure was released, the petitioner being a "fair trader."[24]

Not only did enforcement of the laws depend upon the temper and obedience of the populace; it also depended upon the character and diligence of the administrative officers. Unfortunately an abundance of evidence, both circumstantial and direct, demonstrates that the caliber of the customs personnel was not always of the highest. Judged by standards of probable efficiency in the service, many of the applications for office are merely ludicrous. They become depressing reading, however, when one remembers that the applicants were alleging reasons that contemporary opinion apparently held to be grounds for appointment—ancestors slain in the service of His Majesty, staunch adherence to the Church of England, high recommendation from an alderman, or tenure of a particular office within the same family for about fourscore years.[25] One applicant rested his plea upon the claim that experience as a smuggler had given him knowledge of all the creeks and coves where smugglers traded,

[23] PC 2/57, pp. 318, 330.
[24] *Idem*; CTB V, 733-34; VIII, 515.
[25] CTB III, 948; VI, 36; VII, 267; VIII, 309; CTP (1557-1696), p. 66.

as well as all the intrigues and frauds practiced upon land and sea.[26]

Earnest efforts were made to improve the personnel of the customs staff. The Commissioners fully appreciated the necessity of officials being capable and not merely well meaning. In their report to the Treasury concerning one Robert Crompton, who had considerable political support when applying for a landsurveyor's post, they stated that, while he might, "upon reasonable experience," make a good official of the customs, he was not as yet eligible for the post for which he was applying. They declared that the surveyor was required "not only to be a judge for the King in matters of the nicest nature, but also to be guide and instructor of inferior officers," and consequently that it was "absolutely necessary to be beforehand expert and knowing in the rules of the customes and the distinction of comoditys (which is by noe meanes to be obteyned but by time)."[27]

The Commissioners made a serious attempt to establish within the service a system of promotion as a reward for ability and diligence. At least as early as 1685 it was determined that no new appointments were to be made to any position higher than that of tidewaiter; presentments for higher posts were to be made from the established officers in the next lower rank, chosen "according to merit." In selecting new men to fill the places of persons thus advanced, care was to be taken that they possessed the requisite qualifications, and "that they be free from debt and incumbrances of the world and under such habits and circumstances of life that the salary or pay will be a competent and congruous subsistence to them." As stated by Treasurer Rochester, in adopting the regulations, they were designed to conduce "to a faithful and industrious management of the Customs by letting the officers see that their honesty and diligence will be rewarded with preferment and the contrary punished with neglect and dismission and to prevent the discouragement to them by their seeing their own experienced merits and abilities

---

[26] CTB VIII, 2000. Additional illustrations of personnel problems appear in the Treasury records, many of which have been collected by Dorothy C. Cummins in an unpublished thesis, "The English Customs Administration under the Stuarts," in the University of California Library.

[27] CTP (1557-1696), p. 235.

slighted and superseded by new persons, not so well qualified, stepping in before them."[28]

An earnest effort was made to follow the rules and to improve upon them. At the end of the seventeenth century, the Commissioners added another requirement for presentation to office. They ceased presenting any candidate for an office of higher status than that of tidesman unless he had been instructed at the waterside for six months. Thereafter, an applicant for the position of collector, surveyor, or landwaiter was personally examined by the Commissioners as to the qualifications necessary for the position. If successful, the surveyor of the port at which he wished to serve gave him a further examination to determine his fitness for the office in that port, and only thereafter was he supposed to be presented to the Treasury Lords as a suitable candidate.[29] At an even earlier date Treasury officials had requested applicants to take an examination to prove their physical and mental fitness.[30] Such tests were apparently required to keep out applicants like the seventy-four-year-old Robert Harwar and the insane Henry Hene.[31]

In addition to attempting to raise the qualifications of those entering the service, the Customs Commissioners tried to protect the honesty of those already in it, an effort which raised questions of policy about salaries. Although the returns from fees in some offices were so valuable that Henry Allen paid £900 for the post of King's waiter in London and Edmund Page £1,300 for that of searcher at the same port, the success or failure of administrative enforcement depended primarily upon the honesty and efficiency of the rank and file, and their salary and share in the fees were usually in keeping with their humble position.[32] The Commissioners realized that when salaries were too small no official could attend to his duties and live

[28] CTB VIII, 52.
[29] CTP (1697-1701/2), pp. 560-61.
[30] CTB VII, 1521; VIII, 2115.
[31] CTB V, 1094; VII, 252.
[32] CSPD (1660-61), p. 70. See also CTB VIII, 465. For fees paid for passing customers' accounts and handling port books, see CTP (1557-1696), p. 338. For reference to monthly amounts received for fees by various officers at the Treasury, see *ibid.*, p. 567. Moreover, even the humblest probably received some of the "presents" which custom allowed seventeenth-century officials to accept. For examples, see Bryant, *Samuel Pepys: The Years of Peril*, p. 59; Evans, "Emoluments of the Principal Secretaries of State," *Eng. Hist. Rev.*, XXXV, 519-20; Jacobsen, *Blathwayt*, pp. 459-62.

honestly, and that when poor men were in underpaid customs offices they would be overly tempted to accept bribes, to steal goods from the King, to extort exorbitant fees, or to "do anything for a little money."[33] Thus when determining the salary of the winetaster, the Commissioners considered how much discretion had to be entrusted to him in the matter of making allowances and "how great a leak" it would prove to the revenue if he did not perform his duty faithfully. Subsequently, they recommended that his salary be raised from £60 to £100 per annum, although in the interests of economy they added that when not engaged in tasting wines he might be employed in inspecting linens, "he having special experience in the knowledge of linens."[34]

The Commissioners were also ready to protect whatever salaries were paid, and managed in most years to have the salaries of officers who received less than £60 per annum exempted from taxation and the money already collected by virtue of the Poll Acts or other tax measures repaid.[35] The Treasury, however, wanted to be sure that it received its money's worth and ordered the Commissioners "to make a strict inspection whether the King receives any advantage by the divers increases of salaries."[36]

A pension system of sorts was also developed. The posts of watchman and "noontender" were positions designed for older men, and it appears to have been a common practice to maintain infirm or superannuated deputies in part from the salaries of their successors.[37] In 1729 there was a charity fund, from which one Richard Blackwell was paid £25 for his long and faithful service as collector. Some time later a fund was established to provide pensions for the subordinate officers of the customs by deducting sixpence per pound from the salaries of all officers who received less than £60 a year,

[33] CTB VII, 146.
[34] CTB X, 849. See also CTB VII, 1310. The most complete statement of salaries paid to the different officials appears in the lists in Customs 18. Entries may also be found in CTB. Salaries might run as low as £5 for waiters and tidesmen, while the tidesman at Mumble in 1675 received only £2 per annum. However, collectors received from £60 to £400, and Richard Montgomery, the receiver general and cashier of the customs, was paid £1,000 a year.
[35] CTP (1557-1696), pp. 109, 134, 142, 171, 533; (1697-1701/2), p. 188; but see *ibid.* (1557-1696), p. 124.
[36] CTB VII, 859.
[37] CTB VIII, 1278; X, 1150; CTP (1557-1696), p. 142; (1697-1701/2), p. 179.

except watchmen and noontenders; but this praiseworthy enterprise, unfortunately, soon showed a deficit because of the great number of aged officers thus supported.[38]

Attempts were also made to keep officials up to the mark. Customers, collectors, or comptrollers who were convicted of stealing the King's custom were to forfeit treble the value of the customs of which the King had been defrauded. Any officer making a false certificate of the landing of goods was to lose his employment, forfeit £50, and endure a year's imprisonment, while offenders who did not hold office were let off more lightly. A similar distinction was made in punishing for bribery. The official bribed was forever after to be incapable of holding any office under His Majesty and was to forfeit £100, whereas the merchant who gave the bribe was to forfeit only £50.[39] Informers taking any reward, or compounding without the consent of one of His Majesty's courts at Westminster, were to be denied the right to sue or to be plaintiffs or informers in any suit or information, civil or penal, to lose £10 English money, and to stand for two hours in the pillory in some market town next adjoining,[40] by no means a nominal punishment, the hatred of informers and the habit of throwing stones being what they were.

Sometimes the web of malpractices became so tangled that offenders escaped their just deserts, despite the efforts to punish wrongdoing. One John Rowe, gentleman, was promised a reward because he had been instrumental in discovering tobacco frauds, but before he received it he was detected in accepting £10 as a bribe for allowing a merchant to enter cocoa as indigo. If his superiors punished him as he deserved, they would discredit his character and impair the value of his testimony when prosecuting the more important tobacco case. So despite his offense, they allowed him to continue in office, at least for the time being.[41]

Official morality being what it was, officers sometimes directed their ingenuity to circumventing rather than to enforcing the rules. Two landwaiters made no entries in their books until they learned of an impending visit from the surveyor general, and then they hired

[38] CTBP (1729-30), p. 137; (1742-45), pp. 498-99.
[39] 14 Car. II, c. 11; Index Vectigalium, pp. 17, 19.
[40] 18 Eliz., c. 5; Index Vectigalium, p. 18.
[41] CTB IX, 1938; CTP (1557-1696), p. 275.

a "scrivoner" who spent the night copying those which had been kept by their friend, the comptroller, thus destroying the effectiveness of the provision for duplicating posts and records.[42] Another failure of the system of checks and balances occurred in London, where the under-searchers eliminated the possibility of the head-searcher interfering with their misdeeds by purchasing the post and giving it to one who held it in trust for them.[43]

Yet as soon as one means of enforcing the law proved to be imperfect, another device was added or substituted in its stead. Although the Commissioners might not have sufficient proof of fraudulent conduct to warrant dismissing or suspending officers, strong suspicion of illegal activities, or even of "too great familiarity with the merchants," might cause officers to be moved from one port to another, thereby breaking up "their measures and correspondences, without which any ill-practices could hardly be executed."[44] Among other means of insuring an official's responsibility for his actions, the Commissioners arranged a scheme of bonding, and a special officer was appointed to investigate the various certifications of securities, to discover which were insufficient or defective.[45]

In short, the moral of this chapter, if chapters can have morals, is that any true understanding of the actual interactions of legislation and society must involve consideration of the inescapable human factor. The process of law enforcement, in the seventeenth century at least, was a game wherein administrators and smugglers were constantly struggling to checkmate one another. As in chess, the success or failure of the contenders depended upon their skill, the pertinacity with which they sought solutions to the problems that arose, and their success in discovering counters to the moves of their opponents.

[42] T 64/139, pp. 1-12.
[43] CTB VI, 463-66; IX, 452. Apparently the head-searcher's office was a perennial source of difficulty (CTB I, 171; VIII, 1204, 1258).
[44] CTP (1557-1696), p. 346.
[45] CTB IV, 746; V, 346.

X

THE COURTS AND THE LAW

THE struggle for enforcement reached its climax in the courts. It was there that offenders paid the penalty or finally escaped. There, as elsewhere, a carefully planned code of procedure endeavored to insure that the guilty be punished and the innocent be absolved. Laymen are likely to scoff at the niceties of legal form and to cry "red tape," but they must remember that rules are needed to safeguard the judicial process against the perversions which always threaten to corrupt it.

By the terms of the Navigation Acts, legal proceedings to condemn seizures made thereunder could be brought in any of His Majesty's courts of record "by Bill Information Plaint or other Action wherin noe Essoigne Protection or Wager in Law shall be allowed."[1] Nevertheless, in England the chief, if not exclusive, reliance was placed upon only two, the vice-admiralty courts and the Court of Exchequer.

Use of the vice-admiralty courts was open to possible objection on the theory that they were not courts of record, but the fact remains that they were used. Their familiarity with procedure *in rem*, the opportunities they offered to take testimony by deposition, and the advantages they possessed in dealing with seizures made upon the high seas or abroad, offered reasons for using them. Since the first two characteristics were shared with the Court of Exchequer, which was the generally preferred court, the greater part of their work in England with relation to the Navigation Acts concerned offenses committed overseas, in Europe, or in Ireland. Strangely enough, in view of arguments to arise in the colonies, the fact that Exchequer

[1] 12 Car. II, c. 18, iii. An essoigne was an excuse for not appearing in court at the proper time, such as being on a pilgrimage.

cases were decided by juries, and admiralty cases without them, appears to have been immaterial.[2]

Many reasons existed for using the Court of Exchequer. It was the historic court of the King's revenue. It was the court in which all cases involving revenue officers were to be tried; suits initiated elsewhere might be transferred to it by an officer pleading this privilege. Long experience in collecting feudal revenues had led the Court to develop prerogative processes which were both swift and severe. Armed with a writ issued from one of its offices, a plaintiff or his bailiff might pursue the defendant from county to county without seeking the new warrants of authority that other courts required, and customs officials might make searches under the general authority conferred by its writs of assistance. All its writs had authority in Wales and the Duchy of Lancaster, places otherwise exempt from legal processes of His Majesty's courts at Westminster, and they might legally profane even the sanctity of the Sabbath. On the other hand, the court had power to mitigate the law's severity when extenuating circumstances arose. Moreover, the same judges who acted in revenue matters served as a court of common law and also sat in equity proceedings, in which capacity they could and did grant "English bills" that enabled the parties to take testimony by deposition.[3]

Although in medieval days the Lord Treasurer and the Chancellor of the Exchequer were accounted judicial officers of the court, by the seventeenth century the judges of the court, for most purposes, were the Lord Chief Baron, three Puisne Barons, and the Cursitor Baron.[4] Ordinary legal business, such as the issuance of process and the trial and judgment of cases, was left to the Barons; but on such administrative questions as whether or not forfeitures should be compounded, the action of the Barons was merely formal, the actual decision

[2] For a discussion of the nature and practice of the English Admiralty Court, see Crump, *Colonial Admiralty Jurisdiction*, pp. 1-23.

[3] BM Harl. MSS 1383, *passim;* BM Harl. MSS 3278, f. 13; Burton, *Practice of the Office of the Pleas*, II, 398-401, 474; Fanshaw, *Practice of the Exchequer Court*, pp. 48-49, 136-50; Fowler, *Practice of the Court of Exchequer in Proceedings in Equity*, I, 1-61; Price, *Treatise on the Law of the Exchequer*, pp. viii, 46; Price, *Attorney's Practice in the Exchequer of Pleas*, p. 349; *Practice in the Office of Pleas*, pp. 5-6; 14 Car. II, c. 11, iv; Hoon, *English Customs System*, pp. 272-73.

[4] Puisne Barons were judges of inferior rank; the Cursitor Baron did not sit in the trial of cases, but concerned himself with administrative matters.

usually being made by the Treasury on the advice of the Commissioners of the Customs.[5]

Proceedings for violations of the Navigation Acts or customs laws could be brought either against the smuggler or against the offending ship and its illegal cargo, by actions *in personam* against the person involved or *in rem* against the thing concerned. Common law courts ordinarily confine actions *in rem* to questions concerning the ownership of land, but the Exchequer had from ancient times used the method to give the King title to treasure-trove, wrecks, waifs, and strays, since there were no obvious owners against whom suit could be brought,[6] and the same technique proved valuable in customs seizures because the authorities could more often lay their hands upon smuggled merchandise than upon the smugglers.

The first step, when proceeding *in rem*, was to have the goods appraised, following which two proclamations were issued. One called upon those interested in the goods to show cause why they should not remain forfeit, and the other invited bidders to make an offer of more than the appraised value. If a bidder made such an offer, he was "charged with the said Goods" after their final condemnation and "obliged to take them away with all their Faults," unless the proceedings had been so long delayed that the goods had decreased in value, in which case the court might in its discretion excuse the bidder. One-half the amount bid was to be paid into the Exchequer and the other half to the officer making the seizure. If there was no bidder, the officer was charged with half the appraised value, upon payment of which the goods were delivered to him or his assigns, by virtue of an order from the Customs Commissioners.[7]

The procedure was geared to permit a summary disposal of the seized articles, if the owner did not bestir himself. The goods stood condemned without further trial, unless someone appeared to claim them within eight days after the proclamation, in the case of London seizures, and within fourteen days in the case of seizures made in the counties. The claimant's problem was to disprove the allegations in the information, which had been filed at the same time the writ of

---

[5] See CTB, *passim.*
[6] Blackstone, *Commentaries*, III, 262.
[7] "B.Y.," *Modern Practice of the Court of Exchequer*, pp. 139-43, 148-49.

appraisement had been issued. After giving security to pay costs, he was allowed due time for pleading. When the pleadings of the parties had joined in issue, one alleging " 'tis," and the other " 'tisn't," the record was made up for trial. But for good cause shown and due notice given, either party could procure postponement of trial, and postponements frequently occurred, whether because it was necessary to take the testimony of witnesses abroad or merely because a jury had failed to answer the sheriff's summons.[8] In case of too great delay, the defendant often was given a writ of delivery for his goods, provided he gave security by recognizance to answer for the value, especially if the goods were perishable and oath was made that they were decaying. Although judgment was rendered by the Barons of the Exchequer sitting in Westminster, the trial might, when necessary, be held by the judges going through the counties on commissions of *nisi prius*.[9] After the trial and verdict by the jury, a statement of what had happened, known as the *postea*, was engrossed on the back of the record and returned to the Exchequer. If an application to arrest judgment was not filed within four days, judgment was entered on the roll after the *postea*, and the case was concluded.[10]

If the claimant was unwilling to risk a trial, he might take out a license to compound with the officer making the seizure. In practice many, if not most, were unwilling "to hazard the Event of a Trial," and officers often assented to compromises, which were usually advantageous because of the saving in fees and the increased certainty of return. To prevent collusion, no compositions were permitted without licenses, which were to be signed by one of the Barons and recorded. When the composition was agreed upon, the officer had to give oath as to the amount received, which could not be less than a third of the value of the goods. The arrangement then had to be approved by the Lord Chief Baron, one other of the Barons, and the Attorney General. Thereafter the claimant paid the King's share of the composition into the Receipt of the Exchequer and was entitled to a writ of delivery for his goods.[11]

[8] See, for example, the case of the "Sara and Elizabeth" of Amsterdam (E 159/491/43).
[9] To hold courts for the trial of civil cases with the presence and aid of a jury.
[10] "B.Y.," *Modern Practice of the Court of Exchequer*, pp. 147-48.
[11] *Ibid.*, pp. 132-35, 148.

The proceedings did not need to be brought against the smuggled goods; they might be brought against the smuggler, although the usual penalty was a fine or forfeiture rather than imprisonment. In such cases, as in actions *in rem*, the solicitor of customs directed proceedings, and informations, which were prepared by an attorney in the King's Remembrancer's office, were not drawn up unless the informer furnished an affidavit attesting to the truth of his charges. The defendant was taken into custody by the sheriff on a writ of *capias*, but he could secure his release by giving the sheriff bail for the amount endorsed on the back of the writ, commonly one-third of the penalty, to insure that he would appear in court. When he appeared, the bail given the sheriff was released, but other bail was required to satisfy "whatever shall be adjudged to them on a trial to be had thereon," and such bail had to be guaranteed by two persons of "Substance and Ability" approved by the customs solicitor. Refusal to give bail availed the defendant nothing; he was served in jail with a copy of the information, and one term thereafter, judgment was entered by default. If bail was given and the informer prevailed, prosecution was commenced against the bailors unless the defendant paid the penalty or surrendered himself as prisoner, in which case execution was taken against "his Goods and Chattels, Lands and Tenements," and he remained in durance until satisfaction was given. In other respects the procedure followed in pleading, bringing on the trial, compounding, etc., was practically the same as in prosecutions *in rem*.[12]

The obvious counter for a smuggler whose merchandise had been seized was to bring another suit against the seizer, since taking property without justification is an offense in itself.[13] Although customs officials might eventually be protected by a "writ of privilege" from the Court of Exchequer, or the other courts concerned might deny the suit, the defense of such actions was troublesome and expensive. William Kirkby, who had seized and secured the condemnation of some parcels of Scottish linen in the Exchequer, had four actions brought against him in the Court of Common Pleas "with intent to

[12] *Ibid.*, pp. 284-89.
[13] See the petition of a constable thus threatened for seizure of gold and pistoles (PC 2/55, p. 195). See also a complaint of the Eastland Company that its official had been arrested for doing his duty (PC 2/56, p. 164).

vex him with charges," a plan that succeeded to the extent of £78 18s. The smugglers lost the suit, and Kirkby obtained a verdict for costs "against each of said four prosecutors," but for only £9 10s. each, or £38 in all. Even then he could "obtain no benefit of those judgments," as all the prosecutors lived in Glasgow, so that he had to seek a partial reimbursement from the Treasury, all of which cost time and fees.[14] No writs of *replevin*[15] were supposed to be brought against the King, but on a number of occasions they were brought against the officer who seized the goods,[16] and in any event he might be harassed in other ways. One customs officer prosecuted an owler and was ruined in revenge by the offender and his son. He then prosecuted the son for perjury, but retaliatory justice being of little help, the officer petitioned that the prosecution be stayed when the father offered recompense for the damage done.[17] Sometimes the illicit traders did not wait until seizure was made. It was said to be the practice of certain ill-disposed merchants, wharfingers, and "a sort of people called smucklers" to have customs officers arrested on trumped-up charges, and then to bring in their goods illegally.[18]

Although the theory of the informer system, like that of any similar *qui tam* proceeding,[19] was that the informer's financial interest would insure his prosecuting the seizures he made, in practice it opened too many avenues of evasion if unsupervised. Informers might be prevailed upon not to prosecute the seizure, or at least to proceed in a half-hearted manner. The first to inform possessed a vested interest in the seizure and a claim prior to all others. Since the law gave the informer one-half of the forfeiture, he obviously could help offenders if, after bringing suit, he delayed in prosecuting it. Thus it is small wonder that the Treasury contemplated canceling the patent of Mr. Low, "clerk of the seizures for the Act of Naviga-

[14] CTB V, 959.
[15] A form of action to regain possession of personal chattels which had been taken from the plaintiff unlawfully.
[16] PC 2/56, p. 371; CTB III, 668-69, 1111 (cases involving excise and hearth money). In the case of some goods seized by the alnagers at Peterborough, the officials concerned were taken into custody for granting the writ (CTB IV, 205).
[17] CTB IX, 1735-36, 1793.
[18] PC 2/55, p. 401; CTB I, 297; VIII, 625.
[19] An action which gives part of the penalty imposed to the one who brings the suit.

tion," of whom it was reported, "he makes many seizures but prosecutes none."[20]

Under an unsupervised informer system, it might be cheaper to smuggle goods and have them condemned than to import them in a legal manner. No customs duties were collected on goods seized for the King's use,[21] whereas those on goods regularly imported were often very high.[22] Merchandise subject to a 100-percent tax might be seized by a member of the smuggling ring and the offense compounded at two-thirds of the value, one-half of which would be due the conspirator making the seizure. Thus by the process of seizure and forfeiture, the ring might safely import goods at one-third of the regular rate. The merchandise might, of course, be appraised at more than its foreign value and the appraisement include the duty in whole or in part. But the practice was to underappraise, and the protection afforded by the bidding was sometimes more apparent than real. One official report complains that "commonly . . . the goods are appraised at under values and dispersed where the seizer thinks fit, leaving the King's part to be sought after, which in truth comes to little or nothing."[23]

The King's interest in enforcing the laws was such that his legal officers had a well-established right to direct the conduct of such *qui tam* proceedings, but the exercise of that right depended upon there being officers available for the purpose. The Attorney General, who was nominally responsible, obviously required aid. In 1661 John Rushworth, of Lincoln's Inn, was engaged to attend the King's Attorney General "in all cases and things relating to His Majesty's Revenue in the Exchequer."[24] There was also a solicitor of the Treasury whose duty it was "to attend said Treasurer," and to defend and prosecute all actions and suits relating to the revenue, as he might be directed from time to time.[25] In practice, however, he was more concerned with the granting of patents and the settling of accounts than with seizures, although he did take part in suits con-

---

[20] CTB III, 38.   [21] T 1/41, No. 24.
[22] Under the Acts of 1660 and 1685, the total duty on colonial tobacco was 5d. and that on foreign tobacco 1s. per pound, while the price of tobacco in Virginia averaged about 1½d. per pound (Beer, *Old Colonial System*, I, 161, 168n.). For other duties, see Lipson, *Economic History*, III, 141-42.
[23] CTB IX, 264-65.   [24] CTB I, 215-16.   [25] CTB V, 1307.

cerning forgery, riots, or other customs violence, the transportation of wool, and illicit trade with France.[26]

The officials having the most intimate contact with customs seizures were the register of seizures and the solicitor of the customs. The register, whose office was said to have been created in Elizabeth's reign, originally acted as customs solicitor as well, but merely served as a check on the solicitor after that official's appointment in 1671.[27] Nevertheless, the post's continued usefulness was attested by its inclusion as part of the many and varied schemes of reform which were proposed. The post of solicitor was created so that someone might watch after the King's interests and frustrate the efforts of those informers who failed to prosecute seizures effectively or in some other way sought to evade the law.[28] It probably was a part-time occupation at first, but in 1686 one Richard Hutchinson was granted a salary of £500 per annum upon an agreement to apply himself wholly to the service and to maintain an able assistant, "breeding up a young person under him for the King's service."[29] By the eighteenth century the business of the office had so increased that two posts were created, one for the northern and the other for the southern ports of England.[30]

In addition, a special agent concerned himself with the returns from seizures which were assigned to the Privy Purse, "it being no part of public money." His task was to insure that the fines and forfeitures were actually received by that account.[31] And in 1683 one William Aldworth was granted by letters patent (provided that the grant "interfere not with the right of any auditor already constituted") the office of auditor "of all such casual revenue as shall arise to the Crown by reason of any penal laws and of such other accounts as shall be referred to him from time to time by the Treasury Lords."[32] In addition, the office of Inspector of Prosecutions was created in 1686 by a Treasury warrant and granted to John Pearse,

[26] AO 1/2311, Roll 6; 1/2312, Rolls 8, 9, 10, 11; 1/2313, Rolls 14, 16; 1/2314, Rolls 17, 18, 19.

[27] CSPD (1661-62), p. 277; CTB II, 297, 336, 523, 572.

[28] See *supra*, pp. 114-15. The first solicitor, Richard Prowse, was appointed in 1671 (CTB III, 935).

[29] CTB VIII, 1313.   [30] LCH Minutes (1696-1758) on solicitors.

[31] CTB IV, 459, 460.   [32] CTB VII, 861.

a London merchant, for one year, "to take care that informations concerning uncustomed and prohibited goods be effectually prosecuted and the fines and recoveries duly brought to the King's account: he to be obliged to leave off his present trade and to give sufficient security."[33] Pearse continued in office until 1689, when he lost his post to a Mr. Hosier.[34] He was paid a fee of one shilling per pound, but the Crown benefited to the extent of about £4,500 during his second year in office.[35]

The policy of creating new officials to cure old ills gave rise to still other evils; the matter of expense in prosecuting seizures became serious. The age was one in which there were fees to be paid to nearly everyone for almost everything. Under the practice then flourishing, His Majesty's Solicitor of the Treasury paid fees to His Majesty's Attorney General when the former consulted the latter on business of the Crown. There were fees to court officials, dinners in Guildhall for witnesses, and even carriage fares to be paid.[36] It cost £277 and some shillings to collect a debt due His Majesty, £213 17s. 2d. of which were paid by His Majesty to his own Attorney and Solicitor General as their charges.[37] During 1696 the total payments and allowances to the Treasury solicitor, including his salary of £200, were £6,682 15s.[38] In 1693 it cost £275 18s. to punish some rioters.[39] In 1697-98 the prosecution of owlers in Sussex cost £1,008 4s. 5d.; in 1700 the expense for suing out a commission for trying pirates in America amounted to £1,207 9s. 4d.[40]

The matter of fees directly affected the enforcement of the Navigation Acts. Since the rule was that the informer should pay the charges from his moiety of the seizure, the expenses of the suit often left him little profit, and sometimes the recovery did not even equal the charges.[41] Nathaniel Spencer spent £106 1s. 2d. in the prosecution of a seizure of rye under the Act of Frauds, and his moiety produced but £66 13s. 4d.[42] In his case, and in a number of others,

[33] CTB VIII, 764, 1179.   [34] CTB IX, 206.
[35] CTB VIII, 1998, 2033; IX, 7.   [36] AO 1/2311, Rolls 5, 6; 1/2312, Roll 8.
[37] AO 1/2314, Roll 17.   [38] Idem.
[39] AO 1/2314, Roll 19.   [40] AO 3/1101, Roll 38.
[41] Statements of the costs in almost one hundred admiralty trials concerning illegal trade between Ireland and America (infra, p. 261) show that informers seldom made great profits from their activities (HCA, Instance Papers 12).
[42] CTB VII, 414.

the Treasury aided in the payment of prosecution costs, but the officer seldom if ever had an advance guarantee of reimbursement.[43] Certain smugglers in Bristol found a means of utilizing the situation to their advantage and to the embarrassment of an honest official who was proving troublesome. They imported illegally small parcels of inconsiderable value in such a way that the offense would attract the officer's attention. Whenever he made the seizure he was forced to bear the expenses of prosecuting it, and when he failed to do so, the smugglers reported him to his superiors for neglect of duty.[44]

Various modifications of the ancient formalities of the Exchequer practice were required for the smoother working of mercantilism. According to the ancient rule, whenever a charge appeared upon the rolls of the Exchequer a corresponding discharge had to be noted. Officers making seizures became "chargeable with the King's moiety according to the appraisement unless discharged."[45] When goods, the sale of which was totally prohibited, were seized, they were destroyed instead of being sold, and if the agent of the Privy Purse had not been given authority to take part in the Exchequer procedure, "by levying of tallies and throwing down the same for discharge of the officer," he would have been forced to pay one-half of the value of goods from which he received no benefit.[46] Other modifications had to be made when seizures involved goods of little value. Two customs surveyors, who had seized certain pieces of Dutch linen, duly entered into a composition arrangement with the offender by which they were entitled to £50, only to discover that "the ordinary way of payment by Privy Seal out of the Exchequer" was "so chargeable that so small a sum would not bear it."[47] One of the remedies for this situation, and the one used for the relief of the surveyors, was to have the Attorney General enter a *nolle prosequi* to the information in the Exchequer, which signified to the court that for reasons best known to himself the Attorney General declined to proceed further in the matter.[48]

Another method was to accept the Treasurer's warrant as a discharge, instead of requiring complete compliance with the older

[43] CTB I, 399, 407; V, 388; VII, 414, 1312; IX, 319.
[44] Culliford's report on frauds, T 64/139, pp. 16-17.
[45] CTB IV, 578.　　　　　　　　[46] CTB IV, 460.
[47] CTB I, 457.　　　　　　　　[48] CTB IV, 578; VIII, 850.

feudal forms.[49] Even this process was too burdensome for seizures the customs of which did not exceed forty shillings,[50] and the proceedings therein were removed entirely from the complications of Exchequer routine. The Commissioners of the Customs were authorized to compound such seizures for nonpayment of the customs and to relieve the offenders from further liability. The sum given in composition was paid to the receivers of London port, and by them to the cashier general of the customs, and thus kept outside the expensive Exchequer process. Concession was made to administrative formalism in the matter of records, however, and the collectors, the comptroller, the surveyor, and the surveyor general were required to enter such sums "in their books of account to be transmitted from time to time into the Exchequer."[51]

It would have been dangerous to simplify routine too much. Compositions which might have to be permitted in the case of small seizures would have been unwise in the case of greater offenses. An official report in 1689 explained how names were "put in for the owner of the goods that cannot be heard of whereby the King is deceived of his part or else the goods are demised in the hands of some pauper, who knows nothing thereof or is unable to bear any loss."[52] A good illustration of how the King might be left with an empty legal victory is afforded by the case of the ship "Recovery." After the vessel had been seized for unlading in Ireland, it was claimed by Henry Bowen, merchant, and William Estwick, mariner, and released upon their entering into a bond, with one Mr. Browne as surety, to pay its appraised value if judgment went against the ship. By the time a verdict was returned for the King, Bowen and Estwick were not to be found, and Mr. Browne, the only remaining surety, insisted that as servant to the Lord Privy Seal he was exempt from suit, a claim which necessitated a request from the Treasury to the Lord he served, that "if he be privileged, as he insists, please leave him liable so that the King may have the benefit of the law against him."[53]

Of all administrative devices, the bonding requirement would

[49] CTB III, 522; VIII, 2068.
[50] CTB III, 1154, 1156.
[51] CTB IV, 752.
[52] CTB IX, 265.
[53] CTB VI, 196-97.

seem to present the fewest difficulties for the judicial machinery. If the trader could demonstrate his compliance with the law according to the terms of the bond, he was released from his obligation; otherwise his bond was forfeit. During medieval times the Exchequer had developed many processes to force a King's debtor to appear before the court. If he did not respond to the first writ, which was known as a *distringas*, it was followed by others, an *alias distringas*, a *plures*, and a *capias*, in the order named, until he did appear. If none of these compelled obedience, the recalcitrant might be outlawed. His lands and goods were then forfeit unless, as was usually the case, the outlawry was reversed after he finally made his appearance. Under certain circumstances, when the account owed the King appeared on the Rolls of the Pipe,[54] it was possible to issue the prerogative process known as the Long Writ, which ruthlessly combined in the one writ the processes of *fieri facias, capias,* and *extent.* The first authorized the sheriff to seize the defendant's goods and chattels, and the rents and profits of his lands, the second to take the defendant himself into custody, and the third to seize not only his person and goods but also his lands.[55]

The bonding requirement, however, was less self-operative than at first appears. The old feudal forms, which had sufficed for a period when most wealth took the form of landed estates, required considerable modification before they were suitable to commercial conditions. Property had begun to assume many forms which were easily concealed. Formerly a surety could not escape his obligation, both because he could not hide his land and because the King had acquired a lien on it from the time the bond was signed, but in the commercial era, if an obligor on a bond concealed all his intangible wealth or transferred it to another and then sailed overseas, the King was left with many theoretically valid legal rights that could not be enforced in practice. It was necessary to speed up the leisurely processes which had served satisfactorily under more static conditions.[56]

The Statute of 33 Hen. VIII, c. 39 made it possible to expedite action. Thereafter bonds given to customs collectors were a lien

---

[54] These were early records, containing the account of the King's profits, etc.

[55] Gilbert, *Treatise on the Court of Exchequer,* pp. 122-26.

[56] BM Harl. MSS 6343; Gilbert, *Treatise on the Court of Exchequer,* pp. 88-94.

upon the obligor's estate from the time they were received by the collector, whereas formerly they had constituted a lien only when they had become a matter of court record by being sued upon. The statute also gave the King liberal rights in suits upon such bonds. He was entitled to recover costs and damages and to charge "the Issue in Tail and the Heir who hath the Land of the gift of his Ancestors." More important still, he could execute his rights immediately.[57] There were, however, many problems still to be met. The various rules governing the writs were as technical as they were multitudinous. One example should suffice to illustrate the point. The rule in executing the writ of *fieri facias*[58] was that the sheriff might not even unlatch the outer door of the defendant's home without permission, but that once inside he could, if necessary, forcibly break down any or all of the inner doors.[59] Insistence upon such refinement in procedural distinctions offered equally nice questions for the law officers of the Crown.

Many other practical problems arose before it was possible to put the bonds in suit. Details of the procedure in taking and keeping the bonds varied from time to time, but its essential features may be summarized as follows: The bonds were given to the King's officers when the customs were in farm, in the presence of, and by the approbation of, the officer of the Farmers, who received a copy. Bonds were to be returned to the Exchequer periodically, at first once a year, later every six months, and eventually each quarter. Elaborate rules were made in the Exchequer for the comparison of bonds with the certificates which purported to show that the merchant had complied with the terms of his bond. The statements in the certificates were also checked against the customers' books at the ports concerned. The Customs Farmers or the Customs Commissioners were at liberty to inspect the bonds; the court was to be provided with full information about each of them; and all processes sent out on any port bonds were to be signed by the King's Remembrancer and one of the attorneys or sworn clerks of the office, who were not to permit any judgment of discharge to be entered until

---

[57] Brown, *Practice of His Majestie's Court of Exchequer*, pp. 3-4; Gilbert, *Treatise on the Court of Exchequer*, pp. 122-26; Price, *Treatise on the Law of the Exchequer*, pp. 29-30.

[58] See *supra*, p. 120.   [59] Bouvier, *Law Dictionary*, pp. 412-13.

the court was informed. In addition, when bonds were put in suit, they were to be entered in a public book, which was to be open in the office for anyone to view, and the Attorney General was to be attended

wherewith to the end he may either join issue or confess. If he confess any plea, the Court is to be acquainted therewith before any judgment be entered on such confession.

The customers of the various ports were to return their port books, according to the former order, and any fee was to be paid into the King's Remembrancer's office. If they omitted to make such return, process was to be issued against them.[60]

The rules seem unduly elaborate for so simple a matter as the handling of bonds, but sad experience had demonstrated the necessity of careful attention to detail. The customs records show that administering the bonding scheme provided a perennial problem. A letter of March, 1684, to Henry Fanshaw, the keeper of the port books, shows the state into which unattended bonds might fall. It complained that the bonds were "kept in such disorder that it requires long time to search before many of them can be found."[61] Fanshaw replied by asking for "a better settlement of salary for himself and for his clerks who are two years in arrear," and by telling of the irregularities and frauds relating to the coast trade with which he had to contend. He claimed that 173 of the King's bonds were not sent to the Exchequer by the officers of the outports, and declared that his office had improved conditions, "the defects being not nigh so numerous as they were," the books formerly returned by the customs officials "containing 699 and these last but 211."[62]

Administrative errors seriously inconvenienced trade. In 1669 the merchants trading from port to port with coal complained that the certificates, which ought to have been filed with their bonds and to have served to discharge them, were often not where they belonged, "by which means their bonds are often returned into the Exchequer although they returned certificates: which creates trouble and charge to them."[63] When the Great Farms of the Customs were in existence, there was conflict between the officers of the King and those of the

[60] CTB III, 796; IV, 38; VI, 117-18, 457-58; VII, 1415.
[61] CTB VII, 1075.   [62] Ibid., VII, 1384.   [63] CTB III, 283.

Farmers as to the respective rights of each in watching over the bonds.[64] The disputes continued with the petty farmers, especially those concerned with the coal duties, and led eventually to the creation of a new office, that of solicitor of the coast bonds.[65]

There were other problems, however, which, although they might be simplified, could not be solved by mere routine management. The best of officials might be tricked. In 1671 Butler Buggins, a clerk and attorney in the Exchequer, prayed for and received His Majesty's pardon for the misdemeanor of delivering a bond that discharged a port cocket, which he had been induced to allow by the fraud of Rawlins and Reynes, although the condition had not been fulfilled.[66] Exceptional circumstances were bound to arise that would require the system to be adjusted to the exigencies of the occasion. Contrary winds and stress of weather might drive vessels carrying coal from Newcastle to London off their course to foreign ports, and consequently the Customs Commissioners were authorized to release the bond, when the situation warranted it, upon payment of the customs due for coal carried abroad.[67] Special problems might arise even when bonds were forfeited. The case of Henry Stancombe, a Bristol grocer, is in point. He lost a large part of his wealth when tobacco, that he had sent to Ireland illegally, was seized and sold, thus leaving him unable to meet the bond for the duties which he owed. Although he could have been consigned to debtors' prison, such action would have furnished an empty satisfaction to a poverty-stricken Treasury, and consequently the Commissioners were instructed not to sue upon the bond, but to obtain what Stancombe was able to pay.[68]

In short, judicial procedure, like other phases of administration, requires careful regulation. Formalism and attention to minutiae may be irksome, but experience showed that detailed regulations were necessary, so that "the mischiefs that have been in these matters" might be "in a great measure remedied."[69] Despite centuries of experience, the Court of Exchequer failed to provide a self-operative administrative mechanism, even in the matter of bonds, the simplest and most effective of the devices upon which the enforcement of the Navigation Acts depended.

[64] CTB III, 796.   [65] CTB IX, 345.   [66] CTB III, 965, 980, 1151.
[67] CTB IV, 384-85, 499.   [68] CTB X, 435, 698, 761, 1007.   [69] CTB VIII, 966.

XI

MY LORDS AND ADMINISTRATION

SINCE neither the Acts of Parliament, nor the legislative, administrative, and judicial devices designed to enforce them, were self-operative, it becomes our task to inquire whose was the controlling hand that provided guidance and direction. Who was to determine when legal rules should be tempered with equity? Who was to keep each part of the administrative machine geared to the point of greatest efficiency, and who was to eliminate the friction which arose when the parts did not work together smoothly, when the naval guard boat challenged the right of the customs officers to ply the water front at night, or when the Customs Farmers presumed to libel one of His Majesty's own men-of-war?[1]

The ultimate administrative power in England, in the seventeenth century, was vested in His Majesty, the King. All tales of royal debauchery notwithstanding, Charles II and James II maintained a personal relationship to the government. In addition to engaging in diplomatic intrigues, financial controversies, and religious squabbles, both kings reserved enough time from their amorous dalliances to busy themselves with governmental details concerning trade, plantations, and the customs revenue. The minutes of the Privy Council and of the Councils for Trade and Plantations show that Their Majesties were frequent attendants, and the diarist John Evelyn declared that when he was a member of the Council for Plantations, it moved its lodgings to Whitehall so that the King might more easily hear its debates.[2] William III, likewise, was no passive spectator. It was he who ordered a change in the practice of appointment to office previously followed by the Commissioners of the Customs, and

[1] PC 2/59, p. 423; CTB VIII, 1155.
[2] Evelyn, *Diary*, II, 263; Andrews, *Committees and Councils*, p. 98. Charles II also played a part in the arrangements which led to the farm of the customs in 1667 (CTB II, 48, 52).

in at least two instances concerning executive clemency, he reversed the recommendations of his subordinates.[3]

It is difficult, nevertheless, to determine the actual effect of royal interference. Versatile but easy-going, Charles II was inclined to please whenever possible, a tendency which led to inconsistencies. He declared it to be his pleasure that John Evelyn be made Clerk of the Bills or Tickets in the Custom House at London, but the warrant for the appointment shows that the position went to Sir Andrew King.[4] He ruled that no posts be granted in reversion and then ordered that the Treasury Lords break the rule, "saying that he had made this promise [to grant the post] before that he had taken the other resolution."[5] As Samuel Pepys confided to his diary, after satisfying Charles II that the navy was not running the kingdom into debt, "his satisfaction is nothing worth, it being easily got, and easily removed."[6]

Royal control was also handicapped by the spasmodic character of its exercise, and the various boards and departments sometimes fared better than their weaker legal position warranted. Although in theory obliged to recognize the royal command, these underlings had the great practical advantage afforded by the last word. It was they who actually installed new officials or enforced new policies, and the records suggest that now and then royal commands which did not meet their approval were quietly filed away, as effectively vetoed by the pigeonhole process as if overruled by warrant of law.[7]

Whatever may have been the sovereign's powers, it is clear that for the most part they soon became departmentalized. At first the great officers of state were few enough to form a group of personal advisers, known, by virtue of its size, as the Privy Council; but by the Restoration, the expansive nature of governmental institutions had deprived the Council of any claim to the adjective "privy." Nevertheless, its power was then firmly established, and its historical

---

[3] CTB IX, 50, 582; CTP (1557-1696), pp. 68, 79, 94.
[4] CTB I, 2, 5, 28.   [5] *Ibid.*, I, 4-5.   [6] *Diary*, VIII, 214.
[7] Francis Smethwicke was first granted a post in 1669, which he never actually received. In 1673 the King, in Council, "having particular knowledge of the petitioner and his merit," was pleased to recommend him to the Treasury. The latter apparently failed to take any action, because more than six years later the same person again received His Majesty's recommendation "for such speedy relief as is consistent with His Majesty's service" (PC 2/64, p. 155; PC 2/68, p. 353).

relation to the Crown, together with its growing parliamentary connections, managed to keep it the center of administrative control. Acts might be performed, and were performed, by the governmental heads without a meeting of the Council, but in matters of great importance official distaste for assuming individual responsibility practically assured that the Council would be summoned.[8]

Commercial regulations occupied much of the Council's time. Mention has already been made of the dispensations granted by Order in Council because of national emergencies such as fire, plague, or war, and the exigencies of trades like those in spice, timber, and dyewood.[9] In administrative matters it protected revenue officers from local interference, established wharves, and found a location for the London Custom House.[10] It heard petitions of various companies, from the humble watermen and energetic shipwrights to the wealthy lords and merchants of the Royal African, Turkey, East India, Eastland, and Canary Companies.[11] It considered international bargains with Venice about the currant trade, with Algiers about piracy, and with the Hanse towns about privileges.[12] In managing the colonies, it heard complaints and judicial appeals, reviewed legislation, appointed officials, and directed policy.[13] Of course its activities were not confined to problems directly or indirectly related to the Navigation Acts. The questions it considered ranged from foreign affairs, war, ordnance, and policies in Ireland to minor grievances of unimportant individuals. Should Hans Kroeger receive his freight money?[14] Might the trading fishmongers be licensed to import foreign fish?[15] Could Edward Tassell be mayor of Lynn and customs surveyor at one and the same time?[16]

There was apparently no limit to the triviality of the queries which might be propounded. Many of the applications were referred to

---

[8] Barbour, *Arlington*, p. 110.   [9] *Supra*, pp. 68-69.
[10] PC 2/56, pp. 533, 559, 560, 571, 577, 591, 600, 610, 616; PC 2/60, pp. 252, 261; PC 2/61, p. 257 *et seq.*; PC 2/59, p. 150.
[11] PC 2/64, pp. 2, 286, 321 (Watermen); PC 2/75, pp. 209-16 (Shipwrights); PC 2/69, pp. 478, 481 (Royal African Company); PC 2/56, pp. 401, 409 (Eastland Company); PC 2/59, pp. 476, 555 (Canary Company); PC 2/69, pp. 313, 342-43, 346, 413 (East India and Turkey Company quarrel).
[12] PC 2/64, p. 69; PC 2/56, pp. 27, 402.   [13] *Infra*, pp. 199-203, 220-24.
[14] PC 2/56, pp. 98, 383, 397-98, 400, 404, 415, 655, 695.
[15] PC 2/71, p. 384.   [16] PC 2/69, p. 334.

other authorities and could have been presented to them originally, but the only relief afforded the Privy Council from such petitions was the practical consideration that it cost the petitioner less in fees to apply directly to subordinate officials. However, if a petitioner became too insistent, the Council was not without recourse when its patience gave way. One mariner who had troubled it for a long time "with insolent demeanour and vexatious applicacons upon pretences of injury by him suffered" remained unsatisfied with the relief granted him, and as the Council believed that he had received all "the dispensacôn of that Justice, which his cause could merit," it sent him to the Fleet prison until he begged pardon for his "over-importuning."[17]

The multitude of its tasks forced the Council to reduce its activities, wherever possible, to a routine management. Certain problems became almost standing orders for the various months. In war time, for example, the rule was to start discussing in August the numbers of seamen to be permitted to leave on the different trades, because the best time for sailing was about the twentieth of October, and the intervening time was required by the various committees concerned to consult with the Custom House, the Admiralty, and other offices involved.[18] When the Privy Council itself heard a case, the parties to the controversy were permitted to appear before it and to be heard by counsel. When deemed necessary, ample time was given to prepare cases, one respondent—probably much to his opponent's disgust—being allowed six months' time to answer.[19] If there was discussion among the members of the Council, an order of 1668 provided that "the old Rule is ever strictly to be observed, that the youngest Councell͏ʳ do begin, and not to speake a second time without leave first obteyned." The same rules indicate the constant effort to attain systematic uniformity:

Nothing is hereafter to be resolved in Councill, till the matter . . . have received the Opinion of some Committee, . . . Nothing be referred to any Committee, untill it have been first read at the Board, except in Forraine

[17] PC 2/57, pp. 83, 181.
[18] The system and rules of procedure worked out may be studied in Professor Turner's two-volume work, *The Privy Council of England in the Seventeenth and Eighteenth Centuries.* See also E. Southwell's memorandum (BM Add MSS 34349, f. 14).
[19] PC 2/66, p. 493; APC Col. I, No. 1237.

Affaires. . . . No Order of Councill be henceforth any time issued out by the Clerks of the Councill till the same have been first perused by the Reporter of each Committee respectively.[20]

The rule to refer all petitions to the proper persons and places "in order to a full information of the fact by reports" had, according to one of the clerks, been found advantageous because very few requests were "of that nature as to allow of a final determination at the first reading (unless they are rejected)." Petitions relating to the Custom House and revenue were generally referred to the Treasury; those relating to complaints about maritime matters and the sailing of ships, to the Admiralty; anything relative to the plantations or new proposals about trade, to the Council of Trade; and points of law and questions whether seizures should be released by the entry of a *nolle prosequi*, to the "Attorney General or Solicitor General or both." No reference was necessary in cases where property was concerned, "for there the law must decide it."[21]

The mechanism of reference insured greater wisdom in judgment, but it presented difficulties of its own in the form of delays and costs. There were many desks upon which a petition might become lost in the successive steps of its journey from Council to Treasury to Customs Commissioners, and back again from Commissioners to Treasury to Council, unless a solicitor were retained to see that it was not covered by petitions of others whose agents were more insistent. The process was cumbersome and costly, even for the most simple requests. In 1693 Lord Inchiquin wished that a ship carrying his horses to Ireland might be permitted to sail, notwithstanding the embargo. The petition was read before the Council and referred to the Admiralty, a routine procedure, but one which involved fees for the copying of the petition and the accompanying order of reference. The Admiralty reported favorably, the report was read in Council and approved. Thereupon an order for the ship to sail was made out in duplicate. One copy went to the Admiralty, which granted the ship protection for her men; the other was sent to the Treasury, which signified its pleasure to the Commissioners of the Customs "that they should notify the same to the officer of the Customs at

---

[20] BM Egerton MSS 2543, f. 205; Andrews, *Committees and Councils*, pp. 88-90.
[21] BM Add MSS 34349, ff. 19-20.

Bristoll." By the time the various fees were paid, it had cost £13 10s. to obtain permission to do something to which no one objected.[22]

The Councilors had been convinced by sad experience that, despite its delays, the process of reference was advantageous. On certain occasions they were too anxious to please and acted without sufficient investigation, only to discover, after they had heard the other side of the story, that the petitions thus approved conflicted with previous grants.[23] Soon after the passage of the Navigation Act of 1660, "some merchants trading for New England" argued that, inasmuch as New England produced lumber and similar bulky commodities which could not bear the cost of transshipment by way of England, they should be permitted to carry goods laden in New England directly to market, provided only that the return therefrom be brought back to England. The Council granted the New Englanders' request. Some years later the question was referred to the Attorney General. It then appeared that, since New England products were not among the enumerated commodities listed in the Act, the request had been unnecessary, and that the dispensation, which covered *all commodities laden* in New England, had been useful merely to excuse the shipment of tobacco from Massachusetts.[24] Such episodes doubtless helped to emphasize the dangers attendant upon attempts to apply rules of "fireside justice" to problems that had escaped the confines of the family hearth.

Wise judgment and speedy determination of questions might have been attained by reference with power to act. Much time and expense would have been saved in handling Lord Inchiquin's petition if the Council had instructed the Admiralty to issue all necessary orders for the ship's dispatch, but such delegation of power

[22] BM Add MSS 34350, f. 7r.

[23] Peremptory orders were issued in 1661 for the customs authorities to aid Walter Rought in seizing the ship "Hope of Lübeck," but the Council found itself in an embarrassing position when the Dutch ambassador intervened and showed that the ship had been unladen by violence and that the customs authorities had already determined that there was no reason for detaining the ship (PC 2/55, pp. 439, 462, 505-6; CSPD [1661-62], p. 139).

[24] APC Col. I, Nos. 504, 990. Note, however, that Governor Berkeley in Virginia made the same mistake of believing that the Act of 1660 regulated all colonial exports instead of merely those enumerated. He complained that the colonists could not "carry a pipe-stave or a barrel of corn to any place in Europe out of the King's dominions" (Hunter, *How England Got Its Merchant Marine*, p. 171).

was the exception rather than the rule.[25] The excitement over the proper relationship between King and Parliament caused both to overlook the advantages of this procedure. Parliament had not yet reduced the kingship to a useful figurehead by absorbing its powers in a parliamentary ministry and was suspicious of "small and irregular cabinets," special committees, and other devices which, although of value, might serve to conceal responsibility. As was shown by the Act of Settlement in 1701, which required each Councilor to sign the resolutions he approved, Parliament wanted the Privy Council to regain its former functions and the Councilors to be held individually responsible. The Councilors likewise avoided delegations of power. Their fear of being blamed for another's erroneous decision in matters of consequence led to habits of caution which prevented their expediting the settlement of details. The doctrine that the King could do no wrong had been shaken by Charles I's execution, while belief in the fallibility of ministers increased as Parliament repeatedly criticized or punished them for their own or others' sins of omission, commission, or prevision.[26]

Whatever the explanation, fear of delegating power existed, and affected even the formation of committees in the Privy Council. Although the committee created to consider problems of trade and navigation had a continuous existence after 1660, despite three or more reorganizations, it was in reality a committee of the whole. After 1668, if not before, any Privy Councilor who wished could attend any of its meetings.[27] The committee system was apparently intended to meet the necessity for action, and the permission granted all to attend was designed as a protection against the charge of secrecy. Inconsistencies in dividing work might be immaterial, but insistence upon action by the Council was not. The Council's committees had no executive power and were expected to, and did, report back to the Council as a whole. Even if their recommendations were

[25] An exception was made for a ship desiring to sail to New England (BM Add MSS, 34350, f. 8).

[26] *Infra*, pp. 146-47.

[27] Andrews (*Committees and Councils*, pp. 88-90) and Bieber (*Lords of Trade*, p. 48) show that more members attended than the number named. Dickerson in his *American Colonial Government* (pp. 84-85) claims that despite entries under various names in the register, there was but one committee, the Committee of the Whole, whose actions were entered under various titles as inspiration moved the clerk.

approved as a matter of routine, which was usually the case, more time was consumed and more fees incurred. In short, the Privy Council's committee system managed to delay the conclusion of issues, but failed to solve the problem of reference.

Most problems of law enforcement, by virtue of their technical nature, are best left to the consideration of specialists. By the latter half of the seventeenth century, there were a number of governmental agencies concerned with varying phases of problems that the Navigation Acts presented. The Attorney General and the Solicitor General and sometimes even My Lords, the Justices, were consulted on the more important questions concerning patents, instructions, and the interpretation of the laws, despite the fact that the various commissions and departments usually had legal staffs of their own.[28] The chief connection of the two principal Secretaries of State with the Navigation Acts during the seventeenth century was their concern with international controversies that might arise because of such legislation, the information about illicit trade supplied to them by the consuls abroad, and their relationship to the government of the colonies.[29] The Admiralty obviously had many contacts with England's navigation.[30] In addition to its war-time duties of defending the coast and providing convoys, it attempted to keep statistics of England's shipping so that it might know the number of men available for impressment; it granted passes to protect English ships from the privateers of other nations and from the Algerine pirates, and furnished frigates, sloops, and other vessels to stamp out illegal trade in England and in the colonies.[31] The Lord High Admiral was also the one from whom, in part at least, the colonial admiralty jurisdiction was derived.[32]

More important than any of these officials was the succession of committees, councils or boards for trade, for plantations, or for trade and plantations, which were appointed to inquire into "the present condition of Our respective Plantations" and "examine what

---

[28] See, for examples, CSPC (1675-76), No. 987; (1681-85), Nos. 92, 122, 1286; APC Col. I, No. 1119; II, Nos. 5, 288, 320.
[29] *Supra*, pp. 93-95.
[30] Andrews' *Guide* (II, 1-65) gives a good general introduction to the subject.
[31] Adm. 1/3863; Adm. 2/3, pp. 377-78; Adm. 2/1748, pp. 34, 107; PRO Index 10666.
[32] Crump, *Colonial Admiralty Jurisdiction*, p. 35.

Trades are or may prove hurtfull, or are or may be made beneficiall to our Kingdom of England, and by what ways and means the profitable and advantageous Trades may be more improved and extended and such as are hurtfull and prejudiciall rectifyed or discouraged."[33] In accordance with the prevailing economic theory of the time, the interests of trade and of plantations were considered together, although not consolidated in the hands of a single board until 1672.[34] The paramount interest of these councils, when first created, was commerce, but their most absorbing duty soon became colonial administration.[35]

All the councils came into direct contact with the Navigation Act. The Council of State submitted the Act of 1651 to Parliament;[36] its standing committee for trade dealt, among other matters, with the law's operation;[37] and the Committee of 1655 included among its recommendations "giving license for transporting fish in foreign bottoms."[38] The Council of Trade of 1660 was instructed to concern itself with the enforcement of the Navigation Act and with "all matters relatinge to Navigation, & to the increase, & the Security thereof"; and the Council for Foreign Plantations was required once

---

[33] The Board of Trade was also to settle on work for the poor, to make them "Usefull to the Publick." Smith (*Board of Trade*, pp. 16-17) states that John Locke, one of the first commissioners, prepared an interesting "Representation on the Employment of the Poor," dated 1695 (p. 363 of the Board of Trade report on "Agencies and Methods for Dealing with the Unemployed," 1893), and that the Minute Book of the Board for 1697 contains a number of entries with regard to the subject. Andrews (*The Colonial Period*, IV, 301 n.) calls attention to the Board's activities in this field in 1700. For a copy of its instructions see Basye, *Lords Commissioners of Trade*, p. 3 et seq.; NYCD IV, 145-48. For accounts of its predecessors, see Andrews, *Committees and Councils*, and Bieber, *Lords of Trade*.

[34] They were not separated thereafter until 1782 (Andrews, *Committees and Councils*, p. 9).

[35] Smith, *Board of Trade*, pp. 15-17. The debate in Parliament, which led to the creation of the Board of Trade in 1696, made no mention of colonial administration, but shortly after the Board's creation, it devoted three times as much attention to the colonies as it did to trade in general (Dickerson, *American Colonial Government*, p. 24 n.; Smith, *op. cit.*, p. 19). Nevertheless, its duties concerning trade were extensive, including such subjects as foreign customs duties, especially the Sound dues, the African trade and the Royal African Company, and commercial treaties for which instructions must be drawn up and envoys sent. The earlier Council for Trade and Plantations had had much the same experience, and devoted more of its time to colonial affairs than it did to trade (Andrews, *Committees and Councils*, p. 133 et seq.).

[36] CJ VI, 617; Stock, *Proceedings and Debates*, I, 223.

[37] Andrews, *Committees and Councils*, pp. 33-34.

[38] *Ibid.*, p. 42.

every year to obtain an account from the governors of the plantations "of every Shipp Tradeing there and its ladeing and whither consigned and what the proceeds of that place have beene in the late years; that thereby the intrinsick value and the true condicon of each part of the whole may be thoroughly understood."[39] When considering the question of making Dover a free port, the Council of Trade of 1660 resolved that the Navigation Act should be kept inviolable.[40] The Select Council of Trade of 1668 considered dispensations from the operation of the Act of 1660 and the execution of the laws in the colonies, reporting against the permission granted for seven years to the Dutch to employ three ships a year in the trade from Holland to New York, and in favor of accepting the Customs Farmers' offer to appoint and maintain agents in the colonies.[41] Likewise, the Council for the Plantations of 1670 and the Council for Trade and Plantations for 1672 were to see that the Navigation Acts were enforced;[42] and the Lords of Trade of 1675 frequently investigated violations and considered difficult cases of interpretation.[43]

Because of the relationship between these councils and colonial administration, detailed discussion of their work can best be deferred until considering enforcement in America. Here we need only mention that, whatever may have been their official titles, they were vested with inquisitorial rather than executive power,[44] and their relationships with other agencies of the government were seldom clearly defined. Consequently they tended to limit their activities to discussion and soon acquired the habit of reporting only on the matters referred to them.[45]

The everyday activities of business could not have been conducted under such an inefficient system; and fortunately for English traders, no attempt was made to do so in England. The councils

---

[39] *Ibid.*, pp. 69-74.
[40] BM Add MSS 25115, ff. 138-40; CTB I, 245-47, 250. See also *supra*, pp. 70-71.
[41] APC Col. I, Nos. 730, 809, 812, 826, 850, 852; CSPC (1661-68), Nos. 947, 1613, 1874, 1884; Andrews, *Committees and Councils*, pp. 94-95; Bieber, *Lords of Trade*, p. 19.
[42] Andrews, *Committees and Councils*, pp. 100, 109.
[43] Bieber, *Lords of Trade*, p. 24.
[44] Andrews, *Committees and Councils*, pp. 48, 112; Bieber, *Lords of Trade*, p. 82.
[45] Basye, *Lords Commissioners of Trade*, p. 20.

or boards which functioned in so unsatisfactory a manner were not concerned with established rules and regulations—except in the plantations. They were engaged in advisory work, the determination of new policies. Failure on their part to accomplish results did not mean that the wheels of government and of trade ceased to revolve; it merely meant that the established order continued unaltered.

XII

THE CONTROL OF ENFORCEMENT

T HE actual administration of the navigation system, like that of the customs revenue, rested with the Lords of the Treasury and their subordinates, the Commissioners of the Customs. Theirs was the task of preparing rules and regulations, of supervising officers of enforcement, and of determining questions of administrative discretion. Unlike the Board of Trade, the Treasury was not handicapped by the necessity of going to the Privy Council for authority to act upon the ordinary problems of administration. During the King's pleasure, the Treasury possessed power to maintain and administer the customs establishment, and even to compound those violations of the revenue and mercantile codes which in its judgment were best excused.[1]

The post at the head of the Treasury was no place for a mere courtier, and the desperate state of the kingdom's finances kept the office from becoming only a favorite's reward. The contemporary diarists, John Evelyn, Samuel Pepys, Andrew Marvell, and Bishop Burnet, followed with a critical eye the grants of the white wand that symbolized the treasurership, and their verdict on the whole was favorable. Charles II's first Lord Treasurer, Southampton, was an elderly gentleman. Although he probably did not possess a brilliant mind, his honesty was unimpeachable and his industry in office was believed to have hastened his death.[2] Pepys hailed appointment of the commission which succeeded him as "the happiest thing

[1] A list of the Lords High Treasurers from the accession of Henry VII can be found in Great Britain, PRO, *Deputy Keeper's Report on Public Records,* App., pp. 61-70, 25th report.

[2] CTB I, Shaw's Introduction, p. xx; Beresford, *Godfather of Downing Street,* pp. 209, 214. The East India Company attempted to curry favor with Southampton, despite his well-known objections to receiving any indirect profit from his post, by providing a present of East India commodities, to the value of £100, for "the Earl of Southhampton's lady" (*Cal. Ct. Min. East India Co.* [1660-63], p. 137).

that hath appeared to me for the good of the nation since the King come in."[3] Its most famous member was the renowned George Monck, Duke of Albemarle and king-maker in his own right, and with others Lord Proprietor of Carolina, one whose prestige was such that after the Great Fire of 1666 he could, "in his quiet sober way," bring back confidence and order by laying aside all business and minding the City.[4] Among the others was a parson's son, Thomas Clifford, who, as sole Treasurer, eventually replaced the commission. Although he was known as the creature of Arlington, the Machiavelli of the day, Pepys and Evelyn agreed that he was "a man of virtue, and comely, and good parts enough," one who came into his place "with a great grace, though with a great skip over the heads of a great many."[5] The high standard thus set was on the whole rather well maintained by later occupants of the post.[6]

Whatever may be one's opinion of the merits of individual treasurers, the businesslike organization of the Treasury's activities cannot fail to impress. Centuries of experience, experiment, and tradition, acquired in the early days when the Treasury's identity was merged into that of the medieval Exchequer, had molded a system which, despite all its archaic features, did function. As Andrews has well said, "of all the departments constituting the British system from 1660 to 1783, none was so imperious and dictatorial and none so intimately connected with the routine of government as was the Treasury."[7]

It took great care to insure that all matters within its jurisdic-

---

[3] *Diary*, VI, 313.   [4] *Ibid.*, V, 406.

[5] *Ibid.*, VI, 273; Evelyn, *Diary*, II, 213, 294-95. Of the other members of the commission, the brilliant if not always steadfast Lord Ashley, later Earl of Shaftesbury, had had experience as Chancellor of the Exchequer (see article on Sir Anthony Ashley Cooper, in DNB); Sir William Coventry, former Secretary of State, although tactless, was thoroughly honest, and was characterized by Bishop Burnet as "a man of the finest and the best temper that belonged to the Court" (Burnet, *History of My Own Time*, I, 265; Pepys, *Diary*, II, 357, 372); and Sir John Duncomb, former Master of the Ordnance, although rather scoffed at by Marvell:

> "All men admir'd, he to that pitch could fly.
> Powder ne'er blew man up so soon, so high;"

was described by Burnet as "a judicious man, but very haughty, and apt to raise enemies" (Marvell, *Works*, III, 391; Burnet, *op. cit.*, I, 265).

[6] Compare *supra*, this chapter, n. 1, with CTB and DNB. See also Gill, "The Treasury, 1660-1714," *Eng. Hist. Rev.*, XLVI, 600-22.

[7] *Guide*, II, 139.

tion should pass through its hands. At its request, His Majesty's orders were given to the Secretaries of State that they sign nothing relating to the customs or "aught else of the revenue; but that all such matters begin in the Treasury, and so go hence to His Majesty for signature."[8] The Lord Keeper of the Great Seal, the Attorney General, the Customs Farmers, and the Customs Commissioners were all, in one respect or another, asked to coöperate, so that the Treasury Lords would be advised of all matters within their concern.[9] The varied character of the precautions taken to forestall irresponsible administrative action may seem somewhat surprising, but instances which occurred indicate that they were not superfluous.

The Treasury was also interested in devising a routine which would minimize, even if it could not completely avert, the inconsistencies which sometimes characterized the Privy Council's actions. Its administrative success depended to a great extent upon the systematic organization of its records and the efficiency with which its secretarial staff functioned. The Earl of Southampton, when Lord Treasurer, tried to do much of the work himself, and the various papers bear endorsements indicating his decisions.[10] But the real organization of the work of the department dates from the secretaryship of George Downing, "a business active man" who valued himself "upon having of things do well under his hand."[11] Not the least of his services consisted in establishing a system of records which his successors continued. First of all, there was a minute book in which the matters considered and the decisions reached were concisely set forth, in a form which permitted ready reference. Supplementing it was an orderly series of entry books, in which were copied the records of the King's warrants, of issues of moneys upon warrants signed by the Treasury Lords, of Irish affairs, of Crown leases, of customs, and of the various other matters with which the Treasury dealt.[12]

With the Commission of 1667, the work of the Treasury Lords

[8] CTB II, 114; VII, 708-9.
[9] CTB II, 187, 191, 298, 519; III, 1048.
[10] CTB I, passim.
[11] The characterization is that of Pepys (Diary, VI, 320).
[12] Shaw, Introductions to the Calendar of Treasury Books, I, III, and to the Calendar of Treasury Books and Papers (1729-30); BM Add MSS 30219, ff. 15-17. See also Beresford, Godfather of Downing Street, pp. 216-17.

themselves assumed dignity and a businesslike character. On May 30, 1667, "the ordinary times for my Lords' meeting" were fixed to be at 3 P.M. on Tuesdays and Thursdays, and at 8 A.M. on Wednesdays and Fridays.[13] The manner of their meetings met Pepys' approval: "I do like the way of these lords, that they admit nobody to use many words, nor do they spend many words themselves, but in great state do hear what they see necessary, and say little themselves, but bid withdraw." The brevity was, of course, commendable, and the taciturnity permitted them, like others, to entrust problems to their able staff.[14]

The staff handling customs matters was headed first by the Customs Farmers and later by the Commissioners of the Customs. The Treasury Lords realized the necessity of seeking expert advice. They resolved, shortly after the appointment of the Commissioners of the Customs, that when any matter relating to the customs was being considered the Commissioners were to be acquainted with it before it was presented to the Lord Treasurers for their consideration.[15] The Treasury could, of course, grant petitions without reference, but fortunately seldom did. Such instances as occur concern almost routine matters, such as the ordering of "due appraisement of ten baskets and one fatt of foreign hats."[16]

The usual procedure was for a reference to be made, with instructions "to consider this matter and report to my Lords on it,"[17] whereupon My Lords ordinarily accepted the report both as to facts and as to policy. Sometimes the reference might leave the handling of the case to the Commissioners, but would outline the policy which was to govern it.[18] Occasionally the order of reference was hortatory in tone: the selling of customs places was to stop;[19] the wishes of an informer who desired to have his name remain unknown were to be respected by the Commissioners when they discoursed with him and proceeded upon his information;[20] they were to give orders "that no officer of the Customs shall presume on any pretence

[13] CTB II, 3. On Jan. 29, 1668/9, it was provided that "Tuesdays only [were] to be petition days" (CTB III, 16).
[14] Pepys, Diary, VI, 329-30; Beresford, Godfather of Downing Street, pp. 217-19.
[15] CTB IV, 189.   [16] CTB I, 34; III, 1097; IV, 189.
[17] CTB X, 213-14.   [18] T 51/1, p. 246; CTB I, 33-34; III, 968.
[19] CTB IX, 50, 254.   [20] CTB VI, 552-53.

whatsoever to visit, search or so much as touch any of his Majesty's mails or pacquets to or from any place or country whatsoever under pain of losing their place"—an order which bears all the earmarks of having originated with an outraged Privy Council.[21]

On the other hand, the Treasury did at times delegate power with authority to act. The Commissioners were allowed to use their discretion in granting extraordinary commissions for seizing any uncustomed and prohibited goods.[22] They were also empowered to determine whether to remit duty or to prosecute bonds on ships driven off their course by storms, and discretion was granted them "to prosecute or not in cases of seizure of wines and tobacco and to take bonds or deposits for landing any quantity of tobacco."[23]

The Customs Commissioners were not unduly subservient to the Lords of the Treasury. In many, if not most, matters concerning the various phases of administration, they took the initiative and proposed rules and projects which were acted upon by their superiors.[24] Despite the fact that the Treasury Lords were an essential part of the system, the Customs Commissioners were undoubtedly the keystone of the arch of administration.

When their opinions differed from those expressed by their superiors, they did not hesitate to voice their dissent. In 1689 they objected vigorously to the dismissal of two of their appointees, arguing that it "occasions much discouragement, and might tend greatly to the prejudice of Their Majesties' service, by setting them [the customs officials] loose from their duty, and their dependence on the Board, whose business it had always been to instruct and direct, as well as to punish and correct them [their subordinates], by suspension, dismission, or otherwise." They maintained that "a due knowledge and choice of the officers is one of the most essential parts of the duty of this Commission in the management of the customs"; that all commissions prior to 1671 had the "power of constituting as well as dismissing the officers, . . . and the Commissioners of Excise still retain the same authority," and that, "though this Commission obtained warrants from the Lords of the Treasury for the constitution of deputed officers, yet the general course had been

[21] CTB VIII, 1809.
[23] CTB IV, 384-85; VI, 24-25.
[22] Ibid., VIII, 139. See also CTB III, 968.
[24] CTP (1557-1696), pp. 59-60.

not to grant such warrants but upon the presentment or approbation of this Board." Nevertheless, when the Lords maintained their earlier stand against the officials in question, the Customs Commissioners could do nothing but acquiesce.[25] In most instances, however, their reports were minuted, "agreed."[26]

The powers of the Customs Commissioners were granted them under authority of the Great Seal of England. They were instructed to collect the subsidies and imposts in England and Wales and the duty of 4.5 percent in the West Indies, to nominate inferior officers for appointment or dismissal by warrant from the Treasury, and to take security for their good behavior. Likewise, under Treasury warrant, they could authorize the receiver general and the collectors in the outports to expend customs money for incidentals. They were to supervise the importation of goods which paid duty under the various farms and to administer the Acts in encouragement of shipping, to board and search vessels by day or night, and to search warehouses and similar buildings by day. Authority was given them to allow portage bills to shipmasters, as rewards for reporting their cargoes correctly, and to compound petty seizures. They were empowered to administer oaths on customs matters; and admiralty officers, justices, sheriffs, and other officials were directed to assist them.[27]

In 1671 there were six Commissioners, each receiving a salary of £2,000 per annum. Thereafter, the number varied, usually being from five to eight; but their commission of January 8, 1675, lowered the annual salary to £1,200, and it was lowered again on August 10, 1694, to £1,000, and remained at that figure until at least the middle of the next century. The Commission had a secretary, clerks, and one or more solicitors of its own.[28] After 1678 one of the Treas-

[25] CTP (1557-1696), pp. 527-28. In the case of William Culliford, however, the Treasury favored his appointment to the post of surveyor general, while the Commissioners opposed it. The matter was warmly debated, but the Commissioners finally prevailed, the Treasury creating another post for Culliford who appears to have been a more than usually competent official (CTB XI, 33, 37, 44, 264, 298; *infra*, p. 143). For another example, see CTP (1557-1696), p. 476.

[26] See, for example, CTB III, 968; IV, 186; VIII, 1394; IX, 318; CTP (1557-1696), pp. 43-44, 386, 462.

[27] Atton and Holland, *The King's Customs*, I, 104, 146.

[28] A list of the Commissioners may be found in Hardy, *Chronological List*. For notes on their activities, see CSPC, CTB, CTP, and DNB. The Commission's secretary

ury messengers was appointed to aid the Commissioners and their officers in making searches on land or water at any time lawful under the Act of Frauds, and to arrest any person disturbing them.[29] In addition, the Commissioners could and did call upon the experts who formed the customs staff, the advice of the "most knowing and ancient" officers of London being valued most highly.[30]

The Commissioners' regular post was at the bench at the head of the Long Room of the Custom House at London.[31] When the volume of customs business became too great for the regular officials to handle, the Commissioners attended to the signing of cockets, and thus eliminated heavy loss on the part of the merchants.[32] Sometimes they gave personal attention to Treasury orders concerning adjustments to be made upon decayed wines—a frequently controverted subject.[33] And on rare occasions the Treasury Lords ordered the Commissioners to inspect the baggage of some ambassador or person of note before it was transported.[34] During the latter years of the seventeenth century, one of the Commissioners went "on circuit," visiting the various outports.[35]

The scope of the Commissioners' activities can best be realized by studying the variety of subjects referred to them for consideration. Should William Beeke, "in regard his 60 years age and infirmities," be excepted from the order that all landwaiters in London port be sent in turn to some outport, to attend the King's business there?[36] Was it wise to accept the offer of Gerrard Andrews, a King's waiter in London port, to surrender his place if he were acquitted of the information against him?[37] Could Gervas Scroope properly perform his duty in the Custom House at the same time that he was a commissioned officer in the army?[38] Was James Blackburne unfit to be a surveyor at Plymouth because his father was a merchant?[39]

is referred to in CSPD (1661-62), p. 452; CTB III, 1131; IX, 18; for the clerk, see CTB IV, 285; some references to the solicitor are found in CTB III, 935; VII, 1493; VIII, 1293, 1313; X, 1179; and *supra*, p. 116.
[29] CTB V, 1035.   [30] CTB VIII, 1.
[31] Atton and Holland, *The King's Customs*, I, 148.
[32] CTP (1720-28), p. 266; Atton and Holland, *The King's Customs*, I, 200.
[33] CTB VIII, 315.   [37] CTB VII, 1032.
[34] CTB VI, 493; VIII, 414.   [38] CTB VIII, 242.
[35] CTB VII, 983, 986, 991, 1133; VIII, 634.   [39] CTB VI, 392.
[36] CTB VI, 809.

What weight should be given to the accusation of neglect of duty made by one customs officer against another "that had married his mother-in-law"?[40]

Contemporary comments concerning the Commissioners' merits do not paint an altogether adequate picture. The diarists usually ignored such humble underlings, and administrative records tended to emphasize the exceptional, since those satisfied with public servants usually say nothing, while those having a grievance record their complaints. Pamphleteers disliking the customs duties contended that the Commissioners were naught but highly salaried parasites. Merchants whose importations did not pass quickly enough through the customs complained that they were taking too many holidays.[41] Higher governmental authorities, who permitted even holy offices to be sold and exchanged, feared that the Commissioners' practice of taking turns to make nominations for vacant customs posts led to the sale of such places.[42] Writers have cited the charges to demonstrate the Commissioners' poor character, but they might equally well have contended that the complaints indicate that the Commissioners were men of sufficient force to have made enemies.

Judged by other tests, the Commissioners were men of merit. Of the thirty-six who acted as Customs Commissioners between 1672 and 1700, twenty-three had been or were members of Parliament; four had been diplomats; two had served as secretary to the Treasury. All had occupied government posts of varying importance, twenty of which were closely related to the Treasury, such as Revenue Commissioner in Ireland and Commissioner of Excise. One of the Commissioners had been Sheriff of London and another, Lord Mayor. Three were destined for promotion to the position of Lord of the Treasury, one was to become Secretary of War and Lord of the Admiralty.[43]

At least six of the Commissioners had risen from the ranks of the

[40] CTB VIII, 258. See CTB I, 19-49, for other problems referred to the Commissioners.
[41] CTP (1720-28), p. 266.
[42] The King himself ordered that persons presented by the Commissioners for places should be agreed upon by a majority of the Board, and that no particular commissioner should have "a nomination by turn" (CTB IX, 50, 582; CTP [1557-1696], p. 68).
[43] This information was compiled by Wilma B. Meyer in an unpublished thesis, "The English Commissioners of the Customs," in the University of California Library.

customs service, of whom William Culliford presents the most interesting example. For some time he had held the post of register of seizures and had also been delegated to make a special survey of the outports in the eighties.[44] In the latter half of that decade, he was Commissioner of the Revenue in Ireland and later a Commissioner of the Customs in England.[45] When, as a result of a revision of the Commission, he was left without official position, he sought a post, and in 1696 received that of the newly created Inspector General of the Exports and Imports,[46] and in 1701 he was again appointed to the English Commission.[47]

The best testimonial of the Commissioners' abilities, however, lies in the record of common sense and good judgment they left behind them. They took a reasonable view of technical offenses and did not hesitate to declare that, although the law provided for the loss of the ship and its tackle and lading if it were manned by a crew less than three-quarters English, it was unduly harsh to execute the penalty for a breach not exceeding the fraction of a man.[48] Their reports on economic policies were sound. They recognized that trade flourishes best when least restrained. The truth of the statement, however, in no wise blinded them to the equal truth that monopolies usually benefited the monopolizers. Thus we find them recommending the disallowance of colonial laws which placed restraints upon English trade, and at the same time arguing for the enforcement of restrictive measures designed by England for the benefit of her own merchants.[49]

They were not doctrinaire theorists and did not hesitate to risk the charge of inconsistency if common sense required. Although they had been relentless opponents of the policy of making foreign-built ships as free to trade as if they had been constructed in England, they argued for a renewal of these naturalizations when the death of Charles II terminated them. Despite their hostility to the original grants, they recognized that the influx of foreign merchantmen into the English marine was an accomplished fact, and that a sudden

[44] CTB VI, 475, 702; VII, 84.
[45] CTB VIII, 313, 1681, 1689.
[46] CTP (1557-1696), pp. 527-28. See also CTB XI, 298.
[47] *Supra*, p. 140, nn. 25, 28.
[48] CTB X, 346.
[49] CSPC (1681-85), Nos. 3, 318.

reversal of policy would bring about untold hardships to English commerce.[50]

Their judgment in administration was equally sound. Their policies would furnish a topic worthy of study in itself, and might startle those who believe that the insistence upon high wages, pension systems, and the development of personnel morale are modern innovations.[51]

No account of the control of enforcement would be complete which failed to stress the work of the "ancient and experienced officers" who formed the permanent staff, and especially that of its most important member, the secretary. The importance of the post of secretary to the Treasury Lords is illustrated by the bankers' fear at the appointment of the energetic Sir George Downing, who was supposed to be their enemy.[52] The Journal of the Board of Trade shows that that body's secretary determined what matters were to be brought before it "in such method, time, and place" as he might judge "to be for the convenience and dispatch of business," unless otherwise directed by his superiors.[53] An instance from the customs service discloses the multifarious details that might be intrusted to the secretary's care. The Customs Commissioners' secretary, for example, drew up the "Establishment of Offic[rs] for [the] whole Kingdom and all their instructions," which truly was, as he declared, "a work of great variety and Labour."[54]

Continuity in administration was supplied by the long tenure of the various secretaries. John Sansom "spent the best of his years," from the close of the last farm in 1672 until after the Glorious Revolution of 1688, as secretary, although most of the time in a position subordinate to Robert Bertie. Sansom's "ability, industry and fidelity in the affairs of our Customs" was attested by long experience, according to the royal warrant which in 1684 finally granted him the title of secretary in his own right, but nevertheless reserved £300 of the £400 salary for placeman Bertie, "of the Honorable Family of Earl Lyndsey."[55]

[50] CTB VIII, 447.   [51] Supra, pp. 103-108.
[52] Pepys, Diary, VI, 321; Beresford, Godfather of Downing Street, p. 206.
[53] CO 391/64, f. 295; Basye, Lords Commissioners of Trade, pp. 15-16. Under the Board of Trade, this office tended to become an inheritance of the Popple family.
[54] T 1/32, f. 76.   [55] CTB VII, 1306.

Some may object that the foregoing analysis of factors influencing the laws has neglected the part played by those outside the administrative circle. That outsiders were free with their suggestions is obvious from the numerous proposals which flooded the government; that their proposals were sometimes accepted seems to be illustrated in the case of Martin Noell and Thomas Povey; but that they were more often rejected finds ample illustration in the lack of consideration paid to the proposals of Thomas Violet[56] and others too numerous to mention. Noell and Povey were probably largely responsible for the creation of the Council of Trade during the time of Lord Protector Cromwell, and its revival in another form by the King after the Restoration. But Noell and Povey were made members of the councils which they helped to create and thus soon lost their amateur standing.[57]

There are various reasons for discounting the influence of nonprofessional elements in administrative matters. Their proposals often labored under the handicap of impracticability,[58] and in any case they found it difficult to obtain a hearing. As a contemporary complained:

Tis the practice of thins in this nature, to refer men to those in whose Province such matters ly. Now how can it be agreable for men to aprove that wch condemns themselves, at least in theire owne judgent, however they may be of the Greatest Integrity and Honour.[59]

Whatever the explanation, it seems clear that nonprofessional ideas played a comparatively slight part in developing the laws of trade. Conceding that the Act of Cromwell's time may have had an amateur origin, the original idea, as expressed in all its logical nicety in 1651, survived less than a decade. As we have seen, when it was reënacted in the Act of 1660, modifications caused it to conform much more nearly to the ideas of Trinity House and other administrative agencies from which one might have expected the theory to have originated.[60] Certainly the influence of the professional hand is evident throughout the various laws which were added, and thus the

[56] For one of Violet's proposals and its reception, see CTB I, 178.
[57] Andrews, *Committees and Councils*, pp. 68-71, 77.
[58] CTP (1557-1696), pp. 61-62. [60] *Supra*, pp. 42-58.
[59] BM Add MSS 4761, f. 171.

ideas of outsiders were eventually bent to the will of those whose business it was to attend to such matters. No matter how brilliant an idea might have been, it had to be tested by men of experience and perfected by the laborious toil of many others.

It is usual to underestimate the work of humble underlings and to attribute great deeds to great names, because of the important offices listed among their titles. The habit is encouraged by the close correlation which frequently appears between administrative innovations and changes in political leadership, and by the tendency of some administrators to become merely mechanical followers of stereotyped procedure. Yet new administrative ideas usually are a matter of gradual growth, the result of repeated proposals from the permanent staff. Reforms are irksomely delayed until a new superior combines political influence with the persuasiveness to overcome inertia, the courage to resist vested interests, the canniness to foresee pitfalls that would lead to disaster, and a freshness and enthusiasm enabling him to persevere. By the very nature of their position, politicians who acquire control of the administration do not usually possess sufficient technical knowledge to investigate the facts and master the details involved in inaugurating a new policy. At best, problems of government are none too simple, and in the seventeenth century foreign intrigues, ministerial maneuvering, royal mistresses, financial embarrassments, religious prejudices, and parliamentary politics did their bit in adding complications.

The difficulties of their position are such that one cannot begrudge political leaders their readiness to assume full credit for all their subordinates' successes, if they are willing to accept blame when failure ensues. But seventeenth-century courtiers did not hesitate to shift opprobrium for mistakes to more humble, if less blameworthy, shoulders. Although the fault was probably its own, the Privy Council showed no disposition to relieve the Commissioner of the Navy of the blame for the Dutch raid at Chatham. Their attitude was indicated by Lord Arlington, who said, "if he was not guilty, the world would think them all guilty," and if he should be hanged "much of the staine will be wip'd off of the Gouverment which lyes heavily upon it."[61] That being the attitude of My Lords,

[61] Quotations from Barbour, *Arlington*, p. 109.

fairness demands that the credit due their subordinates be properly emphasized.

It is, of course, impossible to determine with mathematical exactitude the relative importance of administrators and titular heads in enforcing the Navigation Acts, but the evidence suggests that His Majesty, the Privy Council, and the Lords of Trade, by whatever name known, played the lesser rôles while the Treasury, the Commissioners of the Customs, and their subordinates performed the greater part of the work. The latter refrained from the injudicious shortcuts which led the Privy Council into pitfalls when it tried to be too obliging. Inaction on their part formed a qualified sort of veto which, as has been seen, might sometimes be exercised even against the royal commands. Moreover, the many memorials from them or from their underlings, proposing ways whereby administrative methods might be improved, contain suggestions which might easily run over the line dividing matters of method from those of general policy, as is clearly seen in the case of the Act of Frauds. The limitation of English registry to ships of English build was a matter of administrative convenience, but its far-reaching effects upon the development of English shipbuilding entitle it also to be placed in the front rank among measures of policy.

PART THREE

ENFORCEMENT IN THE COLONIES

XIII

ADMINISTRATION OUTSIDE THE REALM

DIFFICULT as were the problems of administration in England, the difficulties increased when efforts were made to enforce the laws outside the realm, whether in the near-by islands or in the transatlantic colonies. Even in England it had been difficult to adapt administrative machinery, originally created for local purposes, to the task of enforcing national measures. In one county a constable joined some rioters in rescuing wool which had been seized; in Cornwall a justice of the peace protected some smuggled wine; and in the Scilly Islands the commander in chief seized the customs which had been collected there.[1] The legal distinctions that English jurisprudence drew between the kingdom of England and other areas belonging to the English king interposed barriers to the free flow of imperial authority which charter grants sometimes intensified. Seventeenth-century administrators, like present-day radio technicians, found that their problems of remote control arose not so much from the mere physical distance to be covered as from the interference likely to be encountered.

In view of recent discussions of the historical rights of Parliament outside the realm, it is interesting to note that there was comparatively little debate in the seventeenth century about the powers of Parliament.[2] The question was not so much whether Parliament could pass, as whether Parliament *had* passed, laws binding the inhabitants of the neighboring isles and the plantations. When a law was enacted, the inhabitants who resisted it concentrated their attention upon evading its effects rather than upon denying its validity. Consequently, in our discussion we need not consider the precedents

[1] PC 2/58, p. 351; PC 2/69, p. 567; PC 2/71, p. 107; CTB VII, 478; VIII, 853; IX, 1699; CTP (1557-1696), pp. 33, 78.
[2] McIlwain, *The American Revolution;* Schuyler, *Parliament and the British Empire.*

or metaphysics of constitutional law, except in so far as they affect questions of administrative technique.

The Irish customs officials, from the Commissioners to the most humble waiter, lacked a whole-hearted interest in enforcing the Navigation Acts, although obligated by the terms of their appointment to do so. As had been the case in England, the customs machinery, being created for local purposes, centered on Irish interests and failed to function as effectively as the English service in enforcing English mercantilism, although its administrative organization and practices were the same. The failure may be attributed in part to the great confusion in the laws relating to the Irish plantation trade, but probably it was in greater measure due to the interest of Irish officials in increased customs and additional fees, which may have tempted them to encourage the plantation trade, rather than to prohibit it as the English laws required. Effective enforcement awaited the appointment of special English officials or commissions charged with making seizures and with keeping accounts of ships coming from the plantations "on any account or pretense whatsoever."[3]

Problems arising in the Channel Islands show how the existence of political subdivisions could complicate enforcement. When questions concerning their right to trade with the American plantations, and later with France, were resolved against them, the islanders, like others of their day, resorted to smuggling. They relied primarily upon the opportunities offered by their geographic location for a surreptitious trade in French goods and in drawback-paid tobacco,[4] but they were also aided by legal technicalities which often interfered with administrative efficiency. At first the theory that no customs officials could be established in Jersey and Guernsey threw the task of enforcement solely upon the governor.[5] This method was unsatisfactory, and the Customs Commissioners eventually procured the appointment of an English-commissioned register, to reside on

[3] CTB IX, 1079. For other references on enforcement in Ireland, see BM Add MSS 4761, ff. 93-125; PC 2/70, p. 85; HCA, Instance Papers 12; CTB III, 1280; IV, 35; V, 781, 1046, 1350; VI, 94, 543; VII, 551, 617.

[4] PC 2/74, p. 330; CTB VI, 210, 221, 546; VIII, 1638; CTP (1557-1696), p. 429; CTBP (1729-30), pp. 116, 132.

[5] PC 2/65, p. 160; APC Col. I, No. 1068; CO 389/3, p. 59; CTB III, 978; V, 1353.

the island.[6] The islanders were handicapped in their assertion of ancient rights by their desire for increased trading privileges with England.[7] When their charter was revised upon the accession of James II, the right of English customs officials to reside in the island was recognized, and the register was supplemented by two riding surveyors and such boatmen as were needed (the cost "not to exceed £25").[8] Other questions soon arose concerning the right of the English officials to search ships and houses and to examine the inhabitants under oath.[9] Still later the Jerseymen contended that English laws were not obligatory in their island until registered in the local court, a point which was determined against them.[10] But the English authorities did concede that the processes of the Exchequer did not extend to the Channel Islands, and goods seized there had to be sent to England instead of being kept in the nearest King's warehouse, as was done when seizures were made within the realm.[11]

The Isle of Man offers a thoroughgoing example of how much confusion the factor of charter rights could interject into the orderly processes of customs administration.[12] The privileges of autonomy granted the island's owner were so all-inclusive and advantageous that he endeavored to maintain them regardless of the commercial pressure which English displeasure brought to bear against the islanders. A series of charters and acts of Parliament, dating back to 7 Hen. IV, had granted the Isle to the Earl of Derby "in the most general and comprehensive terms," with a general saving clause expressly barring all rights of the Crown, and permitted the pro-

[6] CTB VI, 161, 303, 415, 546, 674, 690. See also CTB XII, 300.

[7] CTB VIII, 836, 1056, 1265. Under the Navigation Acts, Jersey goods could come to England freely; foreign goods from Jersey had to pay duty. Jersey vessels of foreign build paid duty, as did such ships in the English coastwise trade (CTB X, 701, 765-66). For purposes of the embargo in 1696, trade to the Channel Islands was ruled to be coast trade (BM Add MSS 28019, f. 377).

[8] CTB VIII, 1056, 1265, 1475; CTP (1557-1696), p. 101. Similar officers were established in Guernsey. See also PC 2/71, p. 107; CTB VI, 563; VII, 942; VIII, 1475; IX, 531-32; X, 1188-89, 1207. The Treasury Lords had taken pains to obtain a clause in the first appointee's letter of authority, requiring all officers in the islands to assist him (PC 2/69, p. 567).

[9] CTB VIII, 1638, 1831; X, 418.

[10] Schuyler, Parliament and the British Empire, pp. 14-15. Subsequent actions of the government reiterated this position.

[11] BM Add MSS 30189, ff. 528-29.

[12] By comparison, Massachusetts was a model of obedience (infra, pp. 251-53).

prietor to claim exemption from all laws of Parliament which did
not mention the island, as well as the right to control the enforcement of those statutes which did.[13]

Situated in the Irish Sea, almost equidistant from England, Ireland, and Scotland, the Isle of Man afforded a convenient entrepôt
for prohibited merchandise, only forty miles removed from its intended but illegal destination. Smuggling vessels could leave the
Isle's ports, carrying fictitious documents to show legal destinations
which warranted the ship's proceeding in the same general direction
as the contemplated illegal voyage. Small wherries received coast
cockets entitling them to go from one port of the island to another
and, when stopped by His Majesty's ships off the English coast,
claimed that they were blown there by unfavorable winds. On dark
and stormy nights, winds, which "put it out of the Power of the
King's Vessels to stir," often favored the smuggler's craft, which
were further safeguarded by danger signals from confederates on
shore and by "Numberless Creeks" in which to hide.[14] The same
natural advantages aided illegal exportation. The authorities complained that ships wishing to land debenture tobacco on the Isle
illegally, cleared from an English port for some foreign port that
would "necessarily and unavoidably" cause them to "go close to
the Island" in a normal journey, and that "if they were met in close
with the Island by a King's Ship . . . they answer they are standing
their proper Course for their Nominal Ports, but when it is dark
they directly stand for the Island and get into some small Neck or
Creek and then discharge, it being impossible for a King's Ship to
prevent them."[15]

The history of the Manxmen shows both a natural and an acquired
tendency toward illicit trade. As far back as Irish, Norse, and Saxon
days, they were engaged in piracy. During the sixteenth century, the
restrictive regulations governing trade with the Isle encouraged
smuggling; in the seventeenth century, increases in the English customs duties offered new and highly profitable opportunities. A historian of the Isle tells us that about the year 1670 "a company of

[13] BM Add MSS 38462, f. 89; HMC *Kenyon*, pp. 73-74.
[14] BM Add MSS 38462, ff. 22-24r, 76, 187-88.
[15] *Ibid.*, ff. 22-23r.

adventurers, from Liverpool, settled at Douglas [in the Isle of Man], for the avowed purpose of carrying on a contraband trade."[16] Statistics of the loss to the English customs caused by this den of smugglers vary, but all estimates agree that it was considerable.[17] One of the principal forms of illicit trade was the exportation, for the sake of drawback, of duty-paid tobacco to the Isle of Man, whence it was run into England again.[18] A letter of March 29, 1711, estimates that 70 hogsheads of tobacco were sufficient to supply the 22,000 men, women, and children inhabiting the island, but claims that about 500 hogsheads were carried there and later entered into an illegal trade, "whereby there was a yearly loss of about £16,000 to this Revenue, according to the Estimate of Mr. Williams the Officer appointed to reside at the Island." Two former merchants and customs farmers of the Isle stated in 1725 that they were "informed that if the customs and trade of the Isle were under the collection and inspection of officers appointed by his Majesty, the Customs of Great Britain would be increased at least £100,000 per annum."[19] In 1727 another writer stated that the English government's endeavors to prevent illegal trade cost £2,008 8s. 8d. per annum for officers and cruisers, but that there was still much illegal trade.[20] Charles Lutwidge, writing in 1764, said that he had seen estimates that the loss to the revenue (including that of Ireland) amounted to £300,000 per annum. He believed that he himself could show that the loss was at least £200,000 yearly.[21]

English efforts to frustrate the trade were as persistent as they were futile. As early as 1673, the Lord Treasurer thought that an agent should be sent into the Isle of Man as well as to Ireland, "to prevent abuses in the Plantation Trade."[22] In the same year, and at

---

[16] Train, *An Historical and Statistical Account of the Isle of Man*, II, 306; Walpole, *Land of Home Rule*, pp. 202-5.

[17] In considering the contemporary estimates, it should be noted that in themselves they do not establish the real extent of smuggling (*infra*, pp. 247-49), and as far as the Isle of Man is concerned there is no need for attempting to do so here. The tales of Manx frauds are recounted not as proof of actual conditions, but to indicate the similarity of English and colonial conditions and of the offenses charged.

[18] BM Add MSS 38462, ff. 20-29, 97-98; CSPC (1710-11), No. 40; Walpole, *Land of Home Rule*, p. 208.

[19] BM Add MSS 38462, pp. 97-98; CTP (1720-28), pp. 374-75.

[20] *Ibid.*, pp. 482-83.   [22] CTB IV, 144.

[21] BM Add MSS 38462, ff. 75-76.

various times thereafter, it was proposed that the English government itself should farm the customs of the Isle so as to control their administration, but the plans failed, principally because of inability to agree upon the price that the proprietor should receive for relinquishing his charter rights.[23] However, in 1682, after consulting with the Customs Commissioners, the Treasury appointed one Christopher Eyans as surveyor, waiter, and searcher in the Isle. Its fraudulent practices had "become a mere nuisance."[24]

Charter rights were destined to make much trouble for Eyans and his successors. Eyans got into difficulties as soon as he accused the Earl of Derby's water bailiff of having been "privy to some indirect courses very injurious to his Majesty in his customs." The latter appealed to the governor, who summoned Eyans before him, but Eyans denied the governor's jurisdiction, declaring that he would report directly to the English Lords of the Treasury and would follow their directions. Thereupon the governor informed Lord Derby how much these practices tended "to the breach of your Honor's prerogative . . . that your officers or any other of your tenants here shall . . . be called to any Court of England for trial of misdemeanours committed here," and of "that which is far worse," the hindrance of commerce and trade "as also the great prejudice to your Honor in your customs," by having "such an officer placed amongst us."[25]

Eyans was replaced,[26] but another official, Benjamin Dewey, soon ran afoul of the ninth Earl of Derby, an ardent advocate of the prerogatives granted by the charter, who instructed his governor "to have particular regard" to Dewey and others sent by the Customs Commissioners, "their demeanours and actings." Although they were to receive the governor's aid "whilst they behave themselves according to law for their Majesties service," when they did other-

[23] HMC *Ormonde*, n.s., III, 327; CTB VII, 734, 742.
[24] CTB VII, 449, 452, 716. Eyans is often referred to as "J'ans" in the Treasury Books.
[25] HMC *Ormonde*, n.s., VII, 44-45.
[26] He was succeeded by Roger Henly, May 26, 1684 (CTB VII, 1135), who gave way in Aug. 23, 1689 to Benjamin Dewey (CTB IX, 230), who in time was replaced by J. Prescott on Dec. 21, 1691 (BM Add MSS 38462, f. 97; CTB IX, 1418-19). Meanwhile another officer, Joseph Sheere (CTB VIII, 1045), was appointed Dec. 6, 1686, and replaced on July 2, 1689, by John Copley (CTB IX, 175).

wise he was to enforce the law against them "with care and without timerity." Dewey's reports show that the Earl's officers were loyal to their master. He declared that when he learned of some goods imported without cocket, the local officers entered them in another man's name "to baffle the said Dewey in this business," and thus enabled them to be landed and to disappear before Dewey could discover them. He quoted the governor as having alleged that "the King had nothing to do in the said Island, the laws of England was nothing there, neither had the said Dewey any power there," a view in which, if Dewey's word can be trusted, the Earl agreed heartily: " 'I will humble you,' said his Lordship, 'I will make you know yourself, I will lay you by the heels, get you gone out of the room.' " Nor was the Earl's opposition confined to words. Dewey and his associate, Antrobus, were actually imprisoned. Upon their release Dewey was sent back to England, and Antrobus, although permitted to remain, was instructed not to send any letters to his superiors without first showing them to the governor, nor to meddle with anything before advising him of it.[27]

The Customs Commissioners endeavored to conciliate the Earl by appointing another official. As they explained in a very deferential letter, their end was not "so much to Vindicate the Behaviour of any Particular Officer whether discreet or not, as to obtain those Helps from Your Lordship and your Agents" which best aided them in securing the revenue.[28] Their attempts failed, and early in 1692, regardless of orders which had been sent by the Privy Council, the Earl refused to admit any more officers or any commission to the island. He gave way only when hints from friends high in power convinced him that, charter or no charter, he could not carry his pretensions so far.[29]

The setback did not end struggles with the customs authorities. In the second year of George III's reign, the Duke of Athole, who had succeeded to the Earl of Derby's rights, maintained that "the King himself cannot, in any Particular, derogate from the Extent of his Grant, nor by any Commission make Seizures in the Ports, or

[27] HMC *Kenyon*, pp. 252-53, 258-62.
[28] BM Add MSS 38462, ff. 8-9; CTB IX, 1418-19.
[29] HMC *Kenyon*, pp. 265, 266; CTB IX, 1961.

affect the Imports or Exports." The Duke also denied the authority of the English courts, declaring that

> no Writs, or Process of the Courts of *England*, run there. No Offences, committed there, can be tried in England . . . and the Courts of Judicature in the neighboring Kingdoms have frequently, upon Application, refused to intermeddle from Want of Jurisdiction.[30]

His contention about the exclusive jurisdiction of his courts was not well founded. Early in the reign of Charles II, in the case of William Christian, the Privy Council had declared its right to hear appeals from the island, although its action was of scant aid to Christian, who had been hanged while the decision was being reached.[31] In 1764 two attorneys reported that when ships were seized in the island they could be tried in any court of record in Westminster or, if the suits were tried in the Isle of Man, appeal could finally be had to the King and Council. The point was somewhat academic, because the attorneys doubted whether the Customs Commissioners could empower vessels "to enter the Isle" and seize ships and goods carried there contrary to statute. Although they thought that any subject, including a Commissioners' appointee, could make a seizure as an informer, they confessed that no seizures had been made in ports of the Isle of Man and advised that, owing to the difficulty of "making any effectual Use as the Law now stands, of any right of Seizure," the commanders "ought to be extremely cautious . . . and if possible avoid Bloodshed."[32]

Throughout the period, it was obvious that once the barrier set up by the charter was removed, smuggling could be minimized, if not eliminated. One John Baldwin undertook to suppress all smuggling in and out, "on pain of forfeiting my Post, my Honour, and my Ears." He pointed out that if the charter were forfeited or purchased, a few diligent officers stationed at the four principal ports would be sufficient to prevent illegal trade. Additional precautions could be taken by placing a watchman with a good spyglass on the lofty hill over Peel, and another on the eastern side. In addition, coopers could be prevented from making small casks of the type in

---

[30] BM Add MSS 38462, f. 90.
[31] HMC *Kenyon*, pp. 69, 70, 73-75; Manx Society, *Publications*, XXVI, 57.
[32] BM Add MSS 38462, ff. 78-81.

which it had been the custom to smuggle spirituous liquors.[33] Even the Duke of Athole agreed that the remedy was simple. As he said,

the Design of preventing Smuggling has been taken up at different Times— The Method was obvious, and occurred to every Person in the same Light —An Extension of the Revenue Laws of *England* to the *Isle of Man*, and drawing the Merits of every Seizure made there to an *English* Jurisdiction—. . . . But the exclusive Privileges granted by the Charter . . . stood in the Way.[34]

It has been charged that the dukes were responsible for smuggling and forced it upon their unwilling subjects. Certainly they did little to prevent it, and their revenues from import duties rose with the increasing popularity of the Isle as an entrepôt for illicit traders.[35] When Parliament eventually heeded the reformers' pleas, in 1765, and canceled the charter, the then Lord of the Isle received compensation for being deprived of his right to maintain a den of smugglers—and his son protested bitterly that he did not receive more. Such was the sanctity of private property in his day that there were those who sympathized with him.[36]

The struggle between orderly administration and vested interest in the Isle of Man should be kept in mind when studying colonial enforcement. It demonstrates that claims of charter rights, even in a colony as insistent as Massachusetts, were nothing exceptional, to be explained by virtue of American conditions or Puritan perversity. The colonists merely recognized the convenience of charters as a peg upon which to hang arguments for exemption from the operation of undesired regulation within the locality. The existence of charter barriers only interposed another element of friction in the orderly conduct of business. The phenomenon was not localized; it was not peculiar to the colonies. It was inherent in the nature of the situation.

In discussing colonial enforcement, it will be necessary to abstract the characteristic factors of the problem rather than to narrate those peculiar to any colony. The success of the effort will depend upon how closely we adhere to the problem with which we started. Our concern is not with the virtues or vices of mercantilism or of the

[33] BM Lans. MSS 707, ff. 55r-56.   [35] *Ibid.*, ff. 25r-26, 49-66.
[34] BM Add MSS 38462, f. 89r.
[36] 5 Geo. III, c. 26; BM Add MSS 38462, ff. 89-90; Walpole, *Land of Home Rule*, pp. 220-21.

colonists, nor in justifying the American Revolution. Our interest lies in investigating the operation of a system of regulatory jurisprudence, in the society it was designed to mold to its will. Certainly enough has been said to illustrate the point that, if the colonists violated the laws, the explanation need not be sought in frontier influence; sufficient reason can be found in the fact that the colonists were Englishmen.

XIV

TRANSFERENCE OF ADMINISTRATIVE TECHNIQUE

IN PROVIDING for colonial enforcement, there was no comprehensively planned transference of the technique learned in England. The Act of 1651 did nothing to insure enforcement except to encourage informers by sharing proceeds of seizures with them.[1] In 1660, however, Parliament employed the bonding device to regulate exportations from the colonies,[2] and in 1663 made use of entry requirements to restrict importations.[3] A staff of imperial officials was provided in 1673,[4] but until 1696 they were not supplied with the powers and administrative aids furnished English officers.[5] The needless repetition in the colonies of errors that had been made in the mother country encourages pessimists to deny mankind's ability to profit by experience. Yet optimists need not despair. Colonial administrative mechanisms developed within a comparatively few decades, whereas centuries had been required for the evolution of the English machinery of enforcement. Although colonial administrators may have made the same errors, they were more quickly corrected.

For enforcement purposes the laws governing exportation were written not as much in terms of substantive rights and duties as of requirements for bonds and certificates. Shipmasters trading in the colonies had to give bond that if they should lade any enumerated commodity, like tobacco or sugar, they would prove that such goods were carried to a legal destination. Customs certificates established that proper bonds had been given. Other certificates demonstrated the legal landing of the goods, and permitted the bonds to be dis-

---

[1] *Acts and Ordinances of the Interregnum,* II, 559.
[2] 12 Car. II, c. 18, xix.
[3] 15 Car. II, c. 7, vi.
[4] 25 Car. II, c. 7, v-vi.
[5] 7 & 8 Gul. III, c. 22.

charged. If the master did not thus demonstrate his compliance with the law, his bond was forfeit. Consequently, officials escaped the burden of proving illicit landing abroad and could restrict their activities to finding enumerated commodities aboard a ship unprotected by a certificate.[6]

It is no easy task to understand the law of colonial bonds. The Act of 1660 provided that ships sailing from England or Ireland had to give bond, before leaving, to carry such enumerated goods as they might lade in the colonies to some English or Irish port, and that ships sailing to the colonies from elsewhere could give bond in the colonies to carry the enumerated goods to England, Ireland, *or to any of the plantations.* If the provision were construed strictly, no ship which came from England or Ireland could carry enumerated products from one colony to another, since its bond restricted the carriage to England or Ireland. Also, if a ship came from England or Ireland which had failed to give bond there, it could not carry the enumerated goods anywhere, because the governor's authority to take bonds extended only to ships coming from other places.[7] Nevertheless, common sense rather than technical construction seems to have prevailed, and ships were permitted to trade whether they gave bond in England or in the colonies.[8]

Much confusion arose with respect to bonds for the Irish-plantation trade. As has been seen, the Act of 1660 provided for bonds permitting the carriage of the enumerated goods to either England or Ireland, but Parliament soon repented of its generosity. In 1663 it attempted to exclude Ireland from the plantation trade, by providing that any customs official in England should forfeit his post if he permitted any of the enumerated goods to be carried to another country before they were landed in England.[9] The attempt was obviously futile, since nothing prevented ships from sailing between Ireland and the colonies without regard to customs officials in England. Parliament tried again in 1671, and this time accomplished its

[6] 12 Car. II, c. 18, xix.
[7] *Idem.* To simplify the narrative here and elsewhere, Wales and Berwick on Tweed have not been mentioned in the text, although the statute listed them with England.
[8] See naval office lists, e.g., CO 5/848, *passim*; cf. Beer, *Old Colonial System,* I, 73-75.
[9] 15 Car. II, c. 7, vii, ix.

purpose by providing that until 1680 the word "Ireland" should be left out of all bonds.[10]

In 1673 Parliament provided for the collection in the plantations of certain specified duties on the enumerated commodities, unless bond was given to take them to England "and to noe other place."[11] At the time, no difficulties arose. Because of the 1671 amendment, the only bonds recognized by law were bonds to carry goods to England or to England and the plantations. But in 1680 the amendment expired, and, until it was reënacted, the only bonds provided for by law were those mentioned in the Act of 1660, which permitted the enumerated goods to be carried to England *or Ireland*. Technically speaking, all ships ought to have paid the plantation duties, because no provision was made for giving bond to go to England "and to noe other place." But the Privy Council took the common-sense view and in 1681 authorized the customs officials to accept bonds mentioning England alone.[12]

In the instances already mentioned, technical interpretations were ignored, but they did not always give way—as Lord Baltimore learned to his cost, when he failed to anticipate how the English authorities would interpret the Act of 1673. Parliament's intent in levying the duties had undoubtedly been to tax enumerated goods going from plantation to plantation, and the duties were popularly known as the "plantation duties." When the law was enacted, Parliament made no mention of Ireland, since none of the enumerated goods could then be carried there, but when the Act of 1671 expired, the question arose whether the plantation duties should be collected on enumerated goods shipped to Ireland. Which was to prevail, the intent of Parliament as generally understood, or a strict construction of the wording, which specified that the duties should be collected from all ships that had not given bond to go to England only? With what seems to have been perfect honesty, Lord Baltimore accepted the popular understanding and ordered the Maryland collector not to assess duty on goods going to Ireland. The English authorities, however, followed the literal wording and fined Lord

[10] 22 & 23 Car. II, c. 26, vi.   [11] 25 Car. II, c. 7, v.
[12] APC Col. II, No. 26; CSPC (1681-85), No. 19; Beer, *Old Colonial System*, I, 98.

Baltimore £2,500 for failing to divine that on this occasion they would rule that Parliament meant what it had said.[13]

The New Englanders also misinterpreted the Act of 1673, but their mistake was probably not so innocent. They claimed that if the plantation duties were paid in the colonies, no bond had to be given, as required by the Act of 1660, to carry the enumerated goods to England, and that consequently goods on which such duties had been paid could be carried to any foreign market in Europe without first going to England. As a matter of construction, their position was doubtful.[14] Certainly it was not the intent of Parliament, and the Act of 1696 emphatically declared that, despite the payment of the plantation duties, security must be given to carry the enumerated goods to England or some other plantation as often as any of the goods were reshipped or reladen in the plantations.[15]

Additional problems arose in enforcing the bonding requirement.[16] The Act of 1696 indicates both the procedure followed in administering the rules and the evils which had to be combated. Section twelve explained that many times the sureties in the bonds had been nonresidents, "of uncertaine and unknowne abodes"; and in order that the bonds might not prove "ineffectual to the good purposes intended," it provided that, in all bonds thereafter taken in the colonies, none except persons of known residence and ability to pay should be accepted as sureties. To facilitate bringing suit upon defaulted bonds, attested copies were to be accepted in court "as if the original were produced." Section ten undertook to remedy the "great Frauds and Abuses" committed "by Scotch men and others" in presenting false certificates that bonds had been given or goods landed. When "reasonable ground of Suspicion" existed, a certificate believed to be

---

[13] CSPC (1681-85), Nos. 120, 129, 166, 317, 321, 403, 406, 507, 532; Beer, *Old Colonial System,* I, 98-100. CTB VII, 1454, indicates that three years had elapsed (1681-84) with no payment of the fine, and there is some question as to its ever having been paid.

[14] CSPC (1675-76), Nos. 695, 721, 787, 788, 797, 798, 814, 881, 898; Toppan, *Randolph,* III, 58; Osgood, *American Colonies in the Seventeenth Century,* III, 220-23; Beer, *Old Colonial System,* II, 257.

[15] 7 & 8 Gul. III, c. 22, vii.

[16] Originally the bonds were entered with the governor's deputy, who was known as the naval officer, but in 1682 orders were given that all shipmasters enter their ships with the collector of the plantation duties (PC 2/70, pp. 73-74; CSPC [1681-85], No. 1402).

counterfeit might be disregarded until the truth of the matter could be ascertained from the English Customs Commissioners. Any person falsifying "any Cocket, Certificate, Return or Permit," or knowingly making use thereof, was to forfeit £500, and the document "soe counterfeited, rased or falsified" was to be "invalid, and of noe effect."[17]

The task of comparing bonds and certificates and of bringing suit upon those in default was no mere detail. In 1683 the English authorities wrote to remind the governor of Barbados that "upwards of 2000 bonds delivered to you and your predecessors" had been uncertified, and ordered that in the future all bonds were to be prosecuted "for which certificates are not returned within a convenient time."[18] No definition of a "convenient time" was provided by law, until the Act of 1696 set a limit of eighteen months. Often the practice appears to have been to refrain from suing upon the bond, unless reports or rumors aroused suspicion that the law had been violated. Then suit would be brought, usually upon the order of the governor and council, and the defendant would be obliged to prove that the rumor was false.[19] Precipitate action would often have been unfair, because special circumstances might warrant mitigating the rigor of the law, as was the case when the master's mate of the pink, "Hannah and Elizabeth," forgot to obtain a certificate in Boston. He secured English forgiveness after repairing his neglect, although technically he had incurred the "penalty of said bonds and the forfeiture of the pink."[20]

Just as the bonding requirement was the mainstay in restricting exportations, so were entry regulations the chief reliance in controlling importations. The Act of 1663 required importers, before unlading, to give "a true and perfect inventory or invoice" of the ship's cargo that would show where the goods had been shipped. In addition, the commander was to inform the governor of his vessel's arrival, her name, the name of her master or commander, her owners, where she was built, and how she was navigated.[21] Anyone who

[17] 7 & 8 Gul. III, c. 22.   [18] CTB IX, 811.
[19] VEJ I, 362; Morriss, *Colonial Trade of Maryland*, pp. 123-27.
[20] CTB VIII, 443-44.   [21] 15 Car. II, c. 7, vi.

failed to subject himself to customs inspection was, for that reason alone, guilty of an offense. The scheme was good, but it was not carried far enough. No punishment could be inflicted until the goods were actually landed, no matter how guilty the shipmaster's intent might have been. Thus when the "Rebecca" was seized at New York before it had actually landed its prohibited cargo of European goods, the master saved his vessel by pleading that it had been blown off its course—more than a thousand miles—from Dutch Curaçao to Danish St. Thomas.[22] Even a flimsier excuse would have sufficed, since he had not set his goods ashore. Repeated rulings of English authorities had firmly established that however ample the grounds for suspicion might be, the Act of 1663 justified seizure only when an overt act of trading had been committed.[23]

Supplementary laws were required to prevent such situations from arising. In England the Act of Frauds of 1662 served the purpose, but it was highly debatable whether that measure applied in the colonies. The King's collector argued that it did, but Massachusetts held that it did not.[24] In so ruling, Massachusetts was not impudently defying imperial control. Judging from the phraseology of the Act, Parliament had not intended it to apply in the colonies. Many of its clauses about hovering specifically referred to the coasts of England, to loitering while sailing up the Thames, or to similar matters of obviously local concern. Moreover, there was ample precedent for holding that English acts did not apply in the colonies until they were extended there by action of the proper English authority. Various English legal authorities had ruled that certain English admiralty statutes did not extend to Jamaica.[25] Dr. Lloyd of the Admiralty announced on July 4, 1676, exactly one hundred years before the continental colonies severed the tie binding them to the mother country, that those statutes "being made for England are not law in Jamaica, except his Majesty has declared them so to be."[26]

[22] CO 5/1038, No. 94; CO 5/1039, No. 10; CSPC (1693-96), Nos. 1546, 2033, 2275-76.
[23] *Infra*, pp. 193-94.   [24] CO 1/50, No. 85.   [26] CSPC (1675-76), No. 972.
[25] CSPD (1675-76), No. 987. The case was somewhat exceptional since Jamaica was conquered territory, but the general rule was that English statutes passed after the colonies were founded did not extend there unless Parliament so provided. The whole subject is discussed in Sioussat, *English Statutes in Maryland*, pp. 17-30.

The Privy Council itself held that the privileges of the English Habeas Corpus Act did not apply in the colonies and refused to confirm a colonial statute extending them there.[27] The necessary supplementary rules had to be found in colonial legislation,[28] until the Act of 1696 provided an imperial Act of Frauds. The colonies sometimes refused direct requests for aid, as did Virginia and Maryland when they declined to prohibit shipments of tobacco in bulk;[29] but local regulations, which in their origin and conception had no reference to parliamentary measures, often helped to prevent evasions of the English Acts. Although primarily intended to prevent the escape of fugitives, the Barbadian rule that no person could embark from the island without a ticket, and the Virginian prohibition against persons boarding ships before the masters had reported ashore, discouraged the planters from inspecting smuggled goods on vessels that might lie off the coast.[30] Legislation intended to encourage the building of larger ships[31] hurt illegal traders, who used small vessels for purposes of rapid movement and easy entry into the smaller creeks and inlets. War-time requirements that ships sail under convoy, or in fleets, for their mutual protection,[32] deprived smugglers of the advantages of the speed and secrecy obtained by sailing alone. Import and export duties of colonies such as Virginia, Maryland, and New York,[33] quarantine regulations,[34] various acts to prevent engrossing and forestalling,[35] and West Indian demands that every ship give a true account of its cargo "in order to

[27] PC 2/76, p. 252; CSPC (1693-96), No. 1874.

[28] In secondary discussions, see Giesecke, *American Commercial Legislation before 1789, passim;* Hunter, *How England Got Its Merchant Marine,* p. 109 *et seq.*

[29] CSPC (1685-88), Nos. 1396, 1397, 1461, 1729, 1748, 1760, 1900; (1689-92), Nos. 2140, 2209, 2348, 2349; (1693-96), Nos. 615, 623, 1229, 1290, 1338, 1784, 1897, 2113; CTB VIII, 1521-22; CTP (1557-1696), p. 471.

[30] CSPC (1681-85), No. 1495; (1689-92), No. 1290.

[31] PC 2/70, p. 144; CSPC (1681-85), Nos. 513, 1570, 1576, 1600, 1602, 1858; CTB VII, 1086.

[32] CSPC (1669-74), Nos. 684, 780, 781; (1689-92), Nos. 924, 995, 1128, 1349, 2535; (1693-96), No. 432; Labaree, *Royal Instructions,* I, 461-62.

[33] CO 5/1306, No. 3; CSPC (1677-80), No. 660; (1685-88), No. 2130; (1689-92), Nos. 1030, 1526; (1693-96), No. 1832; CTB IX, 1775-77; CTP (1557-1696), p. 7.

[34] *South Carolina Statutes,* III, 127, 771; IV, 78; *North Carolina State Records,* XXIII, 651, 677, 827, 956; XXV, 328; *New York Colonial Laws,* III, 1071-73, 1141-43.

[35] Such acts were generally disallowed by the English authorities as discouraging trade (CSPC [1669-74], No. 1004; [1681-85], No. 1626; CTB X, 1245).

ensure payment of the one pound of powder per ton,"[36] all placed
additional hazards in the way of would-be evaders of the Navigation Acts.

Yet the aid offered by these colonial measures must not be overemphasized. They themselves were the subject of controversy, and
inherent or extraneous complications sometimes interfered with their
effectiveness. The war-time requirement that ships sail in fleets
broke down because some groups feared that others might obtain an
undue advantage by sailing first, thus preëmpting the market. In
Barbados there was conflict between merchants and masters as to
the date of sailing;[37] in the Chesapeake the element of intercolonial
rivalry between Virginia and Maryland proved troublesome.[38] More
serious difficulties arose in striking a proper balance between the
strictness of regulation desired for enforcement and the liberality
needed to encourage trade, with the result that England sometimes
felt obliged to annul colonial legislation which might have served as
a valuable supplement to the English Acts.

When Massachusetts passed a Naval Office Act, her reputation
caused her motives to be questioned. The local collector of customs,
Jahleel Brenton, complained that the Act permitted coasting vessels
to go from port to port without entering or clearing, even when
they carried some of the enumerated commodities. He contended
that, since "more than 100 sloops and small craft are employed
in the coasting trade at Boston," they would be able to unload foreign ships "as is already much practiced," and, following his report,
the English authorities annulled the law.[39] The enactment, however,
was not unprecedented; Nevis, for example, had passed a Naval
Office Act "in obedience to an Act of Parliament."[40] Moreover, the
little settlements scattered along the New England coast needed the
exception in favor of the coasting trade. Their small craft could not

[36] E.g., St. Christopher, CSPC (1681-85), No. 1438. See also Labaree, *Royal Instructions*, I, 416-20.
[37] CSPC (1693-96), Nos. 450, 1129.
[38] CSPC (1689-92), No. 2137.
[39] This and other measures of the same type were disallowed as too lenient (CSPC
[1693-96], Nos. 1947, 2202, 2216; CTB X, 1252; CTP [1557-1696], p. 333).
[40] CSPC (1675-76), No. 354. A similar act was proposed by the Council of St.
Christopher, forbidding the export of sugar, indigo, and tobacco except to His
Majesty's dominions (CSPC [1677-80], No. 790).

bear the expense of making entry with officials who might be stationed hundreds of miles away. Samuel Mulford, a New York merchant, showed why frontier conditions necessitated modifying requirements that had been successfully applied in more compact England. Referring to a colonial revenue law which required entry at the port of New York, he explained how the residents of Long Island were seriously injured. They were "not suffered to load and unload, except they went to New York to Enter and Clear," and when three vessels coming from Boston to New York made entry as required, they were detained thirteen days. Another sloop, which "presumed to take Mr. Nathaniel Silvester's Family and Household Goods on Board his Sloop, and Carry them to Rhoad-Island the Fall before," was seized and "its poor owner destroyed because he did not go 120 miles for a Permit, to carry him and his 60 miles."[41]

On other occasions the English government itself opposed regulations that were too stringent. The Virginian Assembly attempted to develop port towns by establishing legal wharves and quays at places where there were "no warehouses or accommodation for receiving goods, nor, indeed, any inhabitants." The law was annulled, however, on the report of the Customs Commissioners that if it had been enforced, "the traders would be aggrieved and driven to smuggling."[42] As the Customs Commissioners observed on another occasion, when requesting that a Jamaican act against engrossing and forestalling be annulled, legislation should not go so far as to obstruct trade and discourage merchants.[43]

Careless as Parliament had been in providing the necessary administrative mechanisms, it was even more negligent in creating the necessary staff of enforcement. As has been said, the first and only reliance of the Act of 1651 was the soon-to-be-discredited informer

[41] His complaint was voiced in a speech to the Assembly of New York, on April 2, 1714 (LCB 102).
[42] CSPC (1681-85), Nos. 318, 1063. Such legislation by one colony could not be effectively carried out, without coöperation from its neighboring colonies. A conflict arose between New York and East New Jersey when the governor of New York, who had power "to declare that certain places shall be free ports," did not include Perth Amboy in his list (PC 2/72, p. 471; CSPC [1685-88], No. 1837; CTB VIII, 2057). Note also the governor's instruction that New Jersey duties should equal those of New York (Labaree, *Royal Instructions*, II, 661).
[43] CSPC (1681-85), No. 1626. On the general subject of colonial regulations, see also Labaree, *Royal Instructions*, I, 143-47.

system.[44] Although retained in one form or another by subsequent measures, the scheme of enlisting individual cupidity met with even less success in the colonies than it had in England. In only three of some seventy-seven cases examined (in which it is now possible to determine who lodged the information)[45] was the suit begun by common informers not called upon to act by virtue of their offices, and only one offered a true example of the moiety system's effectiveness, both of the others having been made for reasons extraneous to the mercantile code.[46]

The duties of enforcement, placed by the Act of 1660 upon the governor, were customarily entrusted to an agent known as the "naval officer,"[47] who, by all canons of administrative responsibility, should have been appointed by the governor. In theory, the Act of 1663 entrusted him with such powers of appointment, and the Act of 1696 made him answerable for any offenses, neglects, or misdemeanors of the naval officers until they gave security and were approved by the Customs Commissioners.[48] Nevertheless, in practice, the appointments for many colonies came to be made in England.[49]

[44] *Acts and Ordinances of the Interregnum,* II, 559.

[45] The sources from which the figures were compiled are too varied to cite, but the general accuracy of the result can be confirmed by reference to the records of the Mayor's Court of New York. Of the 34 suits listed in Morris, *Select Cases* (pp. 566-648), 30 were brought by customs officers. The remaining 4 cases do not disclose the identity of the informer, but other sources show that at least one was an official.

[46] In the case of the "Crane" of Dartmouth, the owner was permitted to bring the suit so that he might minimize the penalty by obtaining the informer's reward (*infra,* pp. 211-12); and the information lodged against the "St. Thomas" at Jamaica resulted from opposition to the Assiento trade rather than interest in enforcing the Navigation Acts (CO 1/54, No. 97; CO 140/4, ff. 36d-39d; CSPC [1681-85], Nos. 1673, 1682, 1716, 1759, 1840, 1842, 1990, 1998, 1999, 2027, 2031). The only real example found of a proceeding instituted by an informer was in Rhode Island in 1761 (Towle, *Records of the Vice-Admiralty Court of Rhode Island,* pp. 573-74), although it is possible that, as in England (*supra,* p. 138), some of the suits brought by customs officials may have been the result of information supplied by private persons whose names do not appear in the record. Another objection to the informer system was that the testimony of those financially interested in the seizure was apparently either inadmissible or greatly discounted in the trial (Labaree, *Royal Instructions,* II, 898-900).

[47] 12 Car. II, c. 18, ii; CSPC (1689-92), No. 2561; Beer, *Old Colonial System,* I, 267 *et seq.*

[48] 15 Car. II, c. 7, vi; 7 & 8 Gul. III, c. 22, v.

[49] CSPC (1689-92), No. 1621. In the continental colonies, the power of appointment seems to have remained in colonial hands throughout the seventeenth century, but by the middle of the eighteenth century all such posts in the royal colonies were in the gift of the Secretary of State in England (Beer, *Old Colonial System,* I, 269).

English efforts to maintain administrative continuity in Barbados and in Jamaica played a part in upsetting the theory, as did Sir Jonathan Atkin's tactless refusal, as governor of Barbados, to accept a royal appointee.[50] But undoubtedly the most powerful influence was the desire, so common to seventeenth-century officialdom, to find new sources of patronage. For example, as soon as the Commissioners of the Admiralty heard, in 1692, that a grant was being made of the "naval office" in Jamaica, they demanded that no one be given the post without notice to them—before they had time to learn that the office had no concern with His Majesty's fleet.[51]

The original plan of entrusting enforcement to the governors, or their deputies, did not prove satisfactory. Local machinery did not function efficiently with respect to essentially imperial interests. The Customs Farmers knew that their financial interests would be affected by lax administration. In 1664 they sought and received permission to appoint an acceptable agent in each plantation to see that the law was obeyed, but apparently nothing was done until 1669, when they were commanded by the Privy Council to act—at their own expense.[52] When the Customs Commissioners assumed control, they retained the services of the Farmers' representatives, until a new administrative organization was provided by Parliament.[53]

The Act of 1673 provided that the plantation duties should be collected by officers appointed by the English Commissioners.[54] The staff thus created consisted of the collectors, surveyors (appointed "that there may be a check over the action of the Collectors"),[55] and

---

[50] See *infra*, p. 207. In Jamaica Reginald Wilson, who had inspected "all bills of lading and coquets" under Governor Lynch, and had served as Naval Officer under Governor Vaughan, appealed to England when Governor Carlisle dismissed him, and, because of the English desire for continuity, received a royal patent as Naval Officer (CSPC [1677-80], No. 622; [1681-85], Nos. 213, 308-10, 732; Beer, *Old Colonial System*, I, 270-72).

[51] PC 2/75, pp. 44, 49; APC Col. II, No. 479.

[52] These persons were also to administer the oath to the governor. In addition to Digges in Virginia, Mr. Delavel seems to have represented the Farmers in New York (PC 2/57, p. 79; PC 2/61, p. 179; APC Col. I, Nos. 618, 827; NYCD III, 48-50; CSPC [1661-68], Nos. 597, 605, 644, 649; [1669-74], No. 104; *Va. Mag. Hist.*, XIX, 350, 351, 354).

[53] Digges was given orders to approve the bonds taken in the colonies, and to send copies of them and detailed lists of shipping to England (CTB III, 1126).

[54] 25 Car. II, c. 7, vi.   [55] CTB IV, 126.

surveyors general who traveled from colony to colony.[56] At first the
actual work of searching ships and guarding the water front was
done by deputies, but later the English authorities provided other
officers, such as searchers for Virginia[57] and a boat and two watermen in New England, "for boarding of waiters on ships coming
to Boston," to prevent their delivering prohibited goods before they
came under the guns of the town.[58] Meanwhile, the necessary workers were hired by the deputies' deputies or by the Commissioners' appointees, as occasion demanded, and expenditures for such services
appear as deductible items upon their accounts.[59] Save for this
important distinction, that tenure of office was usually held at the
Treasury's pleasure, the colonial customs service was still in the
"patent stage" of English customs evolution. Gentlemen still held
the posts, pocketed the fees, and left the actual work to hirelings.[60]

Evidence concerning the value of such offices is conflicting. The
£250 paid Digges in Virginia was the exception, rather than the
rule. At first the practice was to allow from one-eighth to one-half
of the collections for salaries.[61] Although the percentage was soon
increased, the amount received was never large.[62] Yet applicants for
office confidently expected to make their fortunes.[63] Some may have
hoped for bribes, but others could find a more legitimate basis for
their expectations in the fees and perquisites granted seventeenth-
century officials.[64] Parliament in 1673 had probably intended colonial officers to take the same fees as were exacted in England, but
it did not say so distinctly, and customs officers hesitated to take
such fees without definite support from their superiors, because the
colonists were "ready to complain against all officers that take even

[56] CO 140/4, f. 32; Beer, *Old Colonial System*, I, 281-86.
[57] Flippin, *Financial Administration of Virginia*, pp. 36-37.
[58] CTB VIII, 341, 362.
[59] See the declared accounts of colonial collectors for the years 1678, 1682, and 1686 (AO 3/305, books 1-3).
[60] CTB III, 948, 1126. Fox has written a biography of one such official, *Caleb Heathcote, Gentleman Colonist.*
[61] BM Add MSS 28089, ff. 30-32.
[62] Beer, *Old Colonial System*, I, 284-85; CTB XI, 312-13.
[63] *Infra*, p. 180.
[64] The Lords Proprietors of Carolina realized how important the fees and perquisites were in obtaining the services of able officials, and ordered that no laws be passed diminishing the fees of the secretary, surveyor, or register (CSPC [1681-85], Nos. 1283, 1542).

what is their right and severely punish the taking what is not so."[65]
Complaints of "exorbitant extortion" led to the fixing of fees, sometimes by statute, but usually by the governor and council.[66]

In addition, there were a host of officers who, in one way or another, came in contact with commerce and thus formed a corps of
potential allies of those directly entrusted with safeguarding the
laws of trade. In Virginia, for example, in addition to the naval
officers and the Customs Commissioners' appointees, there were collectors for the duties on skins and fees, for those on liquors, on
slaves and servants, as well as tobacco inspectors and officially appointed pilots.[67] In Maryland the English Commissioners' deputies
collected the plantation duties; the local officers, the provincial
duties; and Lord Baltimore's representative, certain other dues to
which his proprietary rights entitled him.[68] Most were appointees
either of English or provincial authorities, but there were also
farmers of the excise in New York, and of the 4.5 percent duty in the
West Indies, as well as the representatives of the Royal African
Company in the slave colonies.[69] The similarity of names and
the possibility of confusion in titles demand that care be taken
to distinguish such officials from the deputies of the English Commissioners, the deputies' deputies, and the naval officers. Some, like
His Majesty's surveyor, dealt with the royal woods or the survey of
lands, and had no relationship with the customs surveyor except in
name. Others, like the collector and receiver of His Majesty's revenue in New York, might be required to collect the provincial customs revenue, thus coming into very close contact with commerce.[70]

[65] CTB VIII, 506.
[66] CSPC (1675-76), No. 1027; (1689-92), No. 1087; Labaree, *Royal Instructions*,
I, 371-76.
[67] For an account of such officials and their duties, see Flippin, *Financial Administration of Virginia*, pp. 21-54.   [68] CTB IX, 1442-43.
[69] New York excise farm, CSPC (1693-96), No. 350; 4.5 percent duty, CSPC
(1669-74), No. 1237; (1675-76), No. 727, 775; CTB IV, 576; VII, 960; VIII,
1088, 1716; Beer, *Old Colonial System*, I, 186-90; African Company factors as informers, PC 2/65, p. 379; CO 1/36, No. 38; CO 153/3, p. 336; CSPC (1675-76), Nos. 860,
863, 1148, 1149; (1685-88), No. 1679. The size of the revenue establishments can be
judged by that collecting the 4.5 percent duty in Barbados in 1684: "Two commissioners with one clerk each, five receivers, one person to examine the accounts and
transmit them to England, two searchers, four waiters, six watermen and one good
sloop" (CTB VII, 1115, 1120).
[70] CTB VIII, 1663; IX, 1442-43; X, 1221; NYCD III, 500, 501-3.

The effectiveness of these overlapping cordons of officialdom was not so great as suggested by the number and variety of posts, since it was minimized by the tendency to vest two or more offices in the same individual. Edward Randolph, for example, was surveyor of the woods for the Admiralty; collector of customs for the English Commissioners; deputy of the postmaster and of Blathwayt, the auditor general of the revenue; secretary, first of the colony of Massachusetts and later of the Dominion of New England; councilor; and judge. And in addition, he once acted as agent for an English merchant in the sale of a consignment of hats.[71] Moreover, the multiplicity of officials possibly did more harm than good. It unduly increased the nuisance burden of fees and official interferences borne by the law-abiding merchant, while it enabled the unfair trader to play one official against another.

A keen rivalry developed between the naval officers and the Commissioners' deputies, stimulated in part by competition for fees and the share of forfeitures given informers. The governors generally supported their deputies, the naval officers, in their demands that entry be made with them. As Lord Baltimore said, the Acts "absolutely command all masters to present themselves to the Governor within twenty-four hours of their arrival in any Government, and require them further to give the Governor an account of their ship, its crew and cargo."[72] In Virginia, Governor Berkeley ruled that entry need not be made with the Commissioners' collector, and engaged in a vehement quarrel with Giles Bland, who held that office.[73] Bacon's Rebellion postponed a final determination of the relative rights of the two officers, and thereafter a decision was postponed by appointing the same individual to both posts. The Customs Commissioners wanted other colonies to follow the Virginian practice of selecting their deputies as naval officers, because they were "the fittest persons to be imployed under the Govern[rs]," but they "very

[71] Toppan, *Randolph*, I, 265-66, 279, 286-87; II, 287; III, 326; IV, 38-39, 58, 59, 67-68, 71, 191.

[72] CSPC (1681-85), No. 151. His statement was a part of a complaint against the Maryland collectors, who made a practice of demanding that the masters of vessels "pay their duty" to them before going to the naval officer (*ibid.*, No. 328).

[73] CSPC (1675-76), Nos. 698, 897, 906, 922; CTB V, 67, 308; Beer, *Old Colonial System*, I, 288-90; Osgood, *American Colonies in the Seventeenth Century*, III, 217-18.

rarely prevailed therein."[74] The general rule was to have a ship's papers examined by both the collector and the naval officer.[75] Quarrels might and did arise between the two, but the duplication of effort afforded some slight compensations. Theoretically, the advantage lay in the provision of two complete accounts of imports, exports, and shipping, which might serve as mutual checks.[76] Practically, however, such comparisons were not feasible, but the duplication of labor proved useful when one official failed to provide any list at all, or when the governor's secretary lost what had already been prepared.[77]

Parliamentary draftsmanship must bear part of the blame for the troubles which faced the Commissioners' deputies. Parliament undoubtedly intended, in 1673, to entrust the administration of all the Navigation Acts to the Customs Commissioners, but the section giving them powers of supervision mentioned only the collection of duties *"imposed by this act,"* or "the several duties hereby imposed," thus restricting their legal powers to the so-called plantation duties. When they ordered their deputies to enforce other measures than the Act of 1673, to seize illegal importations of European goods or exportations of tobacco, they could not grant any special authority. They themselves had none to give. They could only empower their deputies to board ships and enter warehouses to search for offenses against the Act of 1673.[78] If, while thus engaged, a deputy should detect violations of other parts of the mercantile code, he could make the seizure, because anyone was entitled to do so. But in court he would have no legal position other than that of a common informer, a circumstance which appears never to have been understood by some of the officials, but which was apparent to their superiors, the Commissioners.[79] Thus the English-appointed col-

[74] BM Add MSS 22617, ff. 141-42. For instances in which the same individual was both collector and naval officer, see CTB IX, 486, 687, 854; X, 1124. See also VEJ I, 364, 379, 393, 449-50. After 1698 the Virginia and Maryland governors were instructed not to vest the two offices in one person (Labaree, *Royal Instructions*, II, 657).

[75] CO 5/904, ff. 330-32; CSPC (1681-85), Nos. 1200, 1402, 1455; Labaree, *Royal Instructions*, II, 761-62, 767-69, 773-74, 777, 796.

[76] CTB VIII, 935.

[77] CSPC (1681-85), Nos. 137, 159, 172.

[78] 25 Car. II, c. 7, vi.

[79] CSPC (1681-85), Nos. 211, 457; Goodrick, *Randolph*, VI, 99.

lectors found themselves greatly handicapped, even in a royal colony like Barbados, with a sympathetic governor who was ready to give them "all assistance," and who had in their presence ordered the clerk of the naval office to join with them "in giving certificates for ships." When they endeavored to prevent unlawful trade in European commodities, they ordered the merchants and planters to make entry at their offices and to land goods only in the presence of their officers. They were soon advised that that was "a thing never yet there done nor enjoyned by any law with penalty for not doing it." Consequently, they wrote their superiors that they feared "little obedience will be yielded" to their orders, "where we cannot punish for not complying."[80]

It was not until 1696 that the colonial officials received adequate administrative powers and rights, and that shipping and traders were subjected to the necessary control. Parliament then provided that ships coming into or going out of port and lading or unlading any goods or commodities, whether His Majesty's men-of-war or merchant ships, and the masters and their cargoes, were to be liable to "the same rules, visitations, searchers, penalties, and forfeitures" as were imposed in English ports by the Act of Frauds. The customs officers in the plantations "were given the same power and authorities, for visiting and searching of ships, and taking their entries, and for seizing and securing or bringing on shore" prohibited or dutiable goods as the English Act of Frauds gave to English customs officials. They were to receive "like assistance in the execution of their offices" and also were to be subject to the same penalties "for any corruptions, frauds, connivances, or concealments." If "sued or molested for anything done in the execution of their office," they could "plead the general issue" and give "this or other custom acts in evidence," and have the same privileges and advantages as allowed in England. Moreover, it was provided that when seizure was made, the burden of proof should be upon the owner or claimer.[81] The Act could not prevent questions from arising, but Parliament had done its best to secure the Commissioners' collectors a chance to present their side of the case.

[80] CTB VIII, 506.   [81] 7 & 8 Gul. III, c. 22, vi.

On the sea the navy played its part in enforcing the laws.[82] Ships of frigate size, which might also defend against foreign enemies, subdue pirates, prevent local uprisings, and keep peace in the merchant fleet, were often employed.[83] Smaller vessels were also used "for the good of the King's Customs,"[84] a yacht and a wherry in Barbados,[85] and sloops in Virginia and New England.[86] The Privy Council ruled in 1669 that even merchant vessels which had given proper security might seize vessels trading illegally,[87] but no evidence has been found of such seizures.[88] The geographic conditions in the tobacco colonies were such that a ship cruising between the two capes of the Chesapeake could do much to minimize smuggling there,[89] and in the West Indies the assistance that His Majesty's ships could offer in checking illicit trade was obvious. One vessel, which was unlawfully landing Negroes, disregarded the governor's orders to depart, since it was common knowledge that he had no vessel with which to enforce obedience, and fired upon the customs

[82] Its use dated from Venables' expedition to Jamaica in 1655 (CSPC [1685-88], No. 1971).

[83] The Council of Montserrat asked "for a good frigate or two in time of peace and for a squadron in time of war" (CSPC [1677-80], No. 1442); Lieutenant Governor Nicholson asked for a frigate to protect Virginia and Maryland during King William's War (CSPC [1689-92], No. 1164); Lord Howard requested a frigate to prevent insurrection in Virginia, as well as to "give countenance to his Majesty's Authority," secure the customs, and oppose pirates (PC 2/70, p. 53; APC Col. II, No. 130; CSPC [1681-85], No. 1273); and Randolph suggested that a man-of-war might prevent mutiny in the merchant fleet (CSPC [1693-96], No. 2198). Lord Craven wrote that protection against pirates was needed lest they "should seize upon some place and make it a second Algiers" (CSPC [1681-85], No. 1707), and the use of men-of-war to suppress piracy is indicated in a Jamaica reference (CSPC [1675-76], No. 822), and in the orders to Captains Talbot and Sprag (CSPC [1685-88], No. 1041).

[84] CSPC (1681-85), No. 1335. Smaller boats were often specifically requested, as preferable for revenue and enforcement purposes. In 1695 it was stated that "the former commanders of the King's ships were too unskilful . . . and the ships themselves of too heavy draught" (CSPC [1693-96]), No. 1005).

[85] CSPC (1669-74), No. 481; CTB VII, 981.

[86] CSPC (1693-96), No. 1881; CTB IX, 714. There is even record of a fifty-oared galley being built for use against piracy (CSPC [1681-85], No. 963).

[87] PC 2/61, p. 187.

[88] Merchant vessels received royal commissions during war time, but presumably they were used only against the enemy (CSPC [1689-92], No. 71; [1693-96], No. 2107).

[89] Captains Crofts and Allen of the Royal Navy were so strict in enforcing the laws in the Chesapeake as to arouse the anger and active opposition of the Virginia merchants and Governor Howard (CSPC [1681-85], No. 1760; [1685-88], Nos. 1218, 1264, 1436, 1507, 1617, 1627, 1774; Beer, *Old Colonial System*, I, 310-14; II, 162-67).

officer when he approached in a rowboat. But when H. M. S. "Foresight" and another of the King's ships arrived upon the scene, it "sailed immediately."[90]

The right of the navy to make seizures under the authority of the Navigation Laws was—as the reader should have come to expect—subject to dispute, in view of the ambiguities in the statutes. The Act of 1660 specifically authorized and commanded His Majesty's ships to make seizures. The Acts of 1663 and 1673 did not. The New Englanders thereupon asserted that the officers should make seizures only for a breach of the Act of 1660, unless they had specific warrants from England for the seizure made.[91] In the West Indies, the authority of the navy to seize violators of the Navigation Acts or interlopers infringing on the African Company's privileges was similarly questioned.[92] The Customs Commissioners, however, said that deputations from them, by virtue of Treasury warrants, were sufficient authority to seize under all the laws.[93]

The human element also hindered effective naval coöperation. Financial irritations arose because the Act of 1660 provided that if seizures were made by one of His Majesty's men-of-war, the forfeiture was divided, one-half to the ship and one-half to the King, whereas otherwise the proceeds were divided into thirds, one of which was granted the governor.[94] Moreover, naval captains probably came to their stations with reluctance. Captain Fairfax complained that the assignment put him "much out of the way of promotion" and that no naval commander "was ever used with common civility" in the colonies.[95] When at her Virginian station, the log of the "Quaker Ketch" showed a dismal succession of entries noting wind and rain;[96] in the West Indies, storms, hurricanes, and earthquakes were a frequent if not constant danger, to say nothing

[90] CSPC (1675-76), No. 670; see also CSPC (1681-85), No. 306.
[91] CTB VIII, 1082.
[92] The Royal African Company wrote that the governor of Barbados would willingly assist them, but lacks "effectual orders to do all he would" (CSPC [1681-85], No. 306).
[93] CTB VIII, 1082.
[94] 12 Car. II, c. 18; CSPC (1669-74), Nos. 567, 567i, 567ii. Note also dispute between Randolph and Captain George (Toppan, *Randolph*, IV, 92-93).
[95] CSPC (1693-96), No. 42.   [96] Adm. 51/3947.

of the perils of reefs and shoals; in New England, the godly Puritans demanded that the officers keep their seamen from swearing.[97]

Many of the seventeenth-century captains were gentlemen only in the sense of class consciousness; their manners and actions more closely resembled those of the freebooters whom they were supposed to subdue.[98] Captain Billop appears clearly guilty of many crimes;[99] Captain Jennings was unduly contemptuous of colonial courts;[100] and Captain Crofts was accused of extorting gifts from masters of merchant ships.[101] Even an honest and energetic officer like Captain St. Loe, of H. M. S. "Dartmouth," had most annoying faults. His record of colonial seizures attests his industry, and his reports vouch for his comprehension of conditions,[102] but his impetuous nature caused trouble. In England, when detailed to guard a lighthouse, he had sailed off to engage in a near-by battle and returned to discover that the enemy had captured the lighthouse workers and the architect.[103] Similarly, in New England he refused to appear before the council, and in the West Indies he disregarded orders of the governor and council of Nevis, did as he pleased in disposing of the ships he had seized, and was charged with insolence and abuses that exceeded Governor Russell's powers of description.[104]

The character of the officials ashore also left much to be desired.[105] While some officials, like George Muschamp and Chidley Brookes,

[97] CSPC (1685-88), No. 2153.
[98] In England the conflicts between officers of the navy and the customs service were often accompanied by physical violence, threats, beatings, and "foul assaults" (CTB III, 1001-2, 1163; VIII, 853-54, 1155; IX, 1015-16; X, 469; CTP I, 119, 233-34).
[99] PC 2/69, p. 552; CSPC (1681-85), Nos. 545, 572, 573, 660, 684, 716, 752, 762, 854, 860, 1078; (1685-88), No. 489.
[100] CSPC (1689-92), Nos. 1452, 1520, 1934.
[101] The activities of Crofts in enforcing the laws may cause this testimony to be somewhat discredited (CSPC [1685-88], No. 1436). See also *ibid.*, Nos. 1627, 1774.
[102] PC 2/72, pp. 458, 466; CSPC (1685-88), Nos. 677, 1232, 1356; CTB VIII, 1530.
[103] DNB, article on St. Loe.
[104] CSPC (1685-88), Nos. 1094, 1111, 2152.
[105] The Treasury attempted quite successfully to prevent absenteeism by means of giving leaves when necessary, and by removing officers absent without leave (CTB V, 347; VIII, 691; X, 711; CTP [1557-1696], p. 135). It was less successful in preventing officials from engaging in private trading activities. Although the receiver of the revenue was forbidden to trade directly or indirectly, various merchants held the similar post of collector of the plantation duties (CTB VIII, 1504, 1521, 1541). Even Randolph acted as factor for an English merchant on at least one occasion (*supra*, p. 174).

had had previous customs experience,[106] appointments often seem to have been based on family connections[107] or on services and sufferings for the Crown.[108] Colonial service attracted many men, irrespective of their qualifications. A letter written in 1713 by Thomas Eyre, an unsuccessful West Indian merchant, indicates the condition that aspirants for office thought to exist. Eyre suggested that his brother-in-law should seek the favor of Lord Bolingbroke or offer "my Lady Massam" a piece of gold plate "of 100 or 150 guineas," so that Eyre might be appointed to one of the surveyorships in America, a post in which he was so confident that one might "make a handsome fortune in 7 or 8 years" that he pledged himself to get a fortune in it or to die in the country without being of further expense to his more prosperous relative.[109]

Many of the customs officials possessed that busy zealousness apt to develop friction. Randolph and Quary managed to stir up resentments throughout their careers. Naturally quarrelsome dispositions and participation in the various colonial controversies and local uprisings caused trouble for others and cost Giles Bland, in Virginia, and Rousby and Payne, in Maryland, their lives.[110] Yet it is often difficult to know what to believe when reading through the maze of charges and countercharges and the confusion of contradictory rulings. Quary, dismissed from office in the Carolinas on suspicion of entertaining pirates, was appointed to the post of vice-admiralty judge in Pennsylvania.[111] Dyer was ejected from his office in New York because the colonists believed that he was exacting too many

---

[106] CTB VIII, 288, 307; IX, 210. Edward Cranfield not only had had experience in the colonial administration in which he sought office, but also had been bred in the colony where he wished a post (CTB VIII, 1084, 1155).

[107] This charge was made against the collector of customs at Bermuda (CSPC [1689-92], No. 1843).

[108] CTB VIII, 1504.

[109] NYPL, *Papers relating to America, Jamaica, etc.,* 955A.

[110] For Randolph, Toppan, *Randolph, passim;* for Quary, *Pennsylvania Provincial Council Minutes,* I, 541-46; Penn, *Correspondence, passim,* especially I, 24-39, 162-63; II, 309; for Bland, CSPC (1669-74), No. 1390; (1675-76), Nos. 698, 897, 922; (1677-80), No. 433; *Va. Mag. Hist.,* XX, 238, 239, 242; Beer, *Old Colonial System,* I, 288-90; for Rousby, PC 2/69, pp. 311, 456-57; PC 2/71, p. 18; APC Col. II, Nos. 37, 64, 173; *infra,* pp. 213, 218-19; for Payne, PC 2/73, p. 429; CSPC (1689-92), Nos. 707, 785, 1426, iv; *Maryland Archives,* VIII, 241-62; Osgood, *American Colonies in the Seventeenth Century,* III, 502-6.

[111] Carroll, *Historical Collections of South Carolina,* I, 86; CSPC (1685-88), No. 1165.

taxes, and his successor, Santen, was removed because he collected too few.[112]

Undoubtedly quarrels of the cantankerous loom too large. Those who went quietly about their business were briefly commended as being "very consistant with the Duty of their other Imployments,"[113] whereas records of controversies assume a disproportionate bulk. In Maryland, during the eighties, Lord Baltimore was involved in successive quarrels with the customs officials, Badcock, Rousby, and Blackiston, in the order named. Badcock died a natural death, Rousby was murdered, and Blackiston lived to quarrel with others after the Calverts had temporarily lost their province.[114] The space devoted in colonial correspondence to these contentions might lead one to assume that the laws failed to operate. Nevertheless, when Patrick Mein, the surveyor general and an officer whose ability and integrity is well attested, made his inspection shortly after the murder of Rousby, he reported that, "Though I find the King's interest here has suffered by Mr. Rousby's death and the defference that ensued upon it betwixt the King's officers and my Lord Baltimore, and that severull Bonds have been taken to goe for England or Ireland, yet I must say I never saw any Merch[ts] Bookes kept in better Order than the accounts are here, and there have been coppies of all Bonds and Certificates sent into England every year, severall Bonds put in suit, and all of them bear a Condition to return Certificat within 12 months."[115] In other words, even in cases where local bickerings reached their peak in murder, the business of the customs went on.

[112] CSPC (1681-85), Nos. 155, 590, 591, 718, 1415; NYCD III, 401-5; Beer, *Old Colonial System*, II, 352-54; Osgood, *American Colonies in the Seventeenth Century*, III, 365-67.

[113] BM Add MSS 22617, ff. 141-42.

[114] CSPC (1681-85), Nos. 325, 1952, 1963, 2064; CTB VIII, 182; Toppan, *Randolph*, IV, 4-5; Beer, *Old Colonial System*, II, 170-75; Osgood, *American Colonies in the Seventeenth Century*, III, 225-28, 496, 499, 505.

[115] Beer, *Old Colonial System*, II, 176.

XV

COLONIAL COURTS

U NLIKE England, the colonies had no Court of Exchequer with centuries of experience in trying offenses against the mercantile code. Frontier jurisprudence was still in the formative stage. With increasing experience the colonial courts improved their procedure, but we must remember not to answer questions raised during earlier stages of their growth in the light of later developments. Although as a matter of legal theory the ultimate answers may relate back to the controversy's origin, the significant fact, historically, is that the questions were unsettled during the time they were debated.

The prevalent attitude was decidedly unfriendly to the legal profession. According to Locke's "Fundamental Constitutions" of Carolina, it was "a base and vile thing to plead for money or reward."[1] In 1671 the judges in Jamaica were instructed to "discourage lawyers, attorneys, solicitors, and such like, who stir up differences and suits amongst his Majesty's subjects" and to allow them no fees.[2] Similar hostility existed in New England, Pennsylvania, Maryland, and elsewhere. Even as late as 1762, a New York merchant complained that "the subject is tore to pieces by Robbers, Lawyers and all sorts of Vermin."[3] Whether as a result of these prejudices or not, there were very few legal specialists. In Bermuda, Governor Cony besought the King to send over "some able lawyer to sit as judge, and two more to plead the country's causes."[4] Governor Russell of Barbados said that only one of the local judges had been bred as a lawyer, the rest being

[1] Carroll, *Historical Collections of South Carolina*, II, 379. For a similar prohibition in Virginia, see Chitwood, *Justice in Colonial Virginia*, pp. 116-17.

[2] CSPC (1669-74), No. 604.

[3] Letter of John Watts (quoted in Morris, *Studies in the History of American Law*, p. 42). [4] CSPC (1685-88), No. 396.

COLONIAL COURTS 183

merchants, planters, and militia officers.[5] Sir Henry Morgan, who tried some cases in Jamaica as Judge Admiral, confessed that "I left the schools too young to be a great proficient in either that or other laws, and have been much more used to the pike than the book."[6]

At the hearings, informality sometimes ran riot. Captain Jennings of Their Majesties' good ship "Experiment" claimed that the justices of Lower Norfolk County, Virginia, when holding court, "were Sitting about a table drinking strong Drinke," and witnesses alleged that the captain himself had added little to decorum when he had taken hold of a certain John Porter "by the hinde part of his hair of his head, and threw him backwards upon the flore."[7] An early eighteenth-century poem contended that Maryland judges did

gravely meet,
Some to get drink, and some to eat
A swinging Share of County Treat.[8]

There was often a lack of procedural uniformity. In the Leeward Islands, the governor, Sir Nathaniel Johnson, reported that the courts, customs, and methods of procedure differed not only in the several islands but even in the precincts of any one; "that in another Island (nay Sometimes in the Court of another Division in the same Island)" the different courts might give different decisions; and "that as farr as I have yet observed the lawes of England and the Customes or pretended Customs of the several Islands according to the fancy of the Judge take place by turns without any more fixed or Certain Rule than that of Chance."[9]

Judging from English experience, one would expect exchequer courts to carry the burden of enforcement. At various times, and in colonies as far apart as Barbados and Virginia, officials contended that the erection of such courts was necessary, "otherwise it is useless to seize ships and put their bonds to suit."[10] Courts of exchequer

[5] CSPC (1693-96), No. 1930.
[6] CSPC (1677-80), No. 1304. Even as late as the American Revolution the judges were not required to have had specialized legal training (Towle, *Records of the Vice-Admiralty Court of Rhode Island*, pp. 90-91). [7] VEJ I, 179-80.
[8] Morris, *Studies in the History of American Law*, p. 43.
[9] CO 153/3, p. 302.
[10] CSPC (1681-85), No. 221; (1689-92), No. 2295. Randolph also suggested that such a court be erected in Maryland, and was supported in this by Lieutenant Governor Nicholson (CSPC [1693-96], Nos. 1896, 2303; Goodrick, *Randolph*, VII, 352, 370).

were actually provided for in Barbados, the Leeward Islands, Bermuda, and New York, if not elsewhere.[11] The method of procedure in the Leeward Islands (which was probably typical) was to commission "the Lt. Govr. and Councill, or any 3 of them, of which Lt. Govr. is to be always one, to be a Ct. of Exchequer."[12] Yet the courts do not seem to have been successful. Sir Nathaniel Johnson disgustedly reported that the council of St. Christopher "was backward and scrupelous" in acting as a court of exchequer and "not to be prevailed with unless maintained [paid] while in service," and attributed its attitude largely to the obstreperous actions of certain councilors, supposed to be engaged in illegal trade.[13] The truer reason was probably given by the council itself when it professed its ignorance of how to sit as a court of exchequer.[14] Practice before the Exchequer in England was so closely monopolized as eventually to stifle the existence of the court even there.[15] Another impediment lay in the cost of maintaining such an establishment for the trial of cases that arose only occasionally. Other colonial courts could deal with most matters handled by the Court of Exchequer in England. Even in revenue causes, there was no need for such intensity of specialization.

The admiralty courts offered most of the advantages to be obtained from courts of exchequer and obviated many difficulties.[16] They were

[11] The court at Barbados was created by an ordinance of the president and council of 1673, which invested the Judge "and his four assistants of St. Michael's" with the powers of a court of exchequer in royal revenue cases (CSPC [1669-74], No. 1179). It was revived in 1681 (CSPC [1681-85], Nos. 357, 463). CO 153/3, p. 221, and CSPC (1685-88), No. 1020 mention the Leeward Islands court, and NYDH I, 199, that of New York. Goodrick (*Randolph*, VII, 585), shows that Bermuda had a court of exchequer in 1699. By the end of the century, the governors of most colonies were instructed to call such courts when necessary (Labaree, *Royal Instructions*, I, 313). However, they do not always seem to have been established, despite agitation for them (Labaree, *op. cit.*, II, 864-65; *South Carolina Historical Society Collections*, II, 146, 188).

[12] CO 153/3, pp. 315-16.

[13] CO 153/3, pp. 330-31; CSPC (1685-88), Nos. 1706, 1773.

[14] CSPC (1685-88), No. 1706.

[15] Until the Act of 1 Gul. IV, c. 70, practice before the court was limited to four "sworn attorneys." The liberalization of its practice, however, did not occur soon enough, and the court was abolished by the Judicature Act of 1873.

[16] Crump, *Colonial Admiralty Jurisdiction*, *passim*. The determination of the authorities to make the admiralty courts the mainstay of the judicial phase of enforcement is shown in 7 & 8 Gul. III, c. 22.

accustomed to the process of condemning seizures, because of their familiarity with the condemnation of prizes;[17] and the rules of civil law which they followed permitted the use of the proceedings *in rem* against an offending ship or smuggled merchandise, which were so often necessary when punishing offenses. Admiralty judges were more apt than others to understand maritime practices. The admiralty practice of taking testimony by depositions, with written questions and answers, was well adapted to cases involving seafaring witnesses who might be available one day and gone the next. Administrators who feared local prejudice in favor of defendants were attracted by the admiralty practice of sitting without a jury (except for a time in certain of the jurisdictions), an advantage not afforded by the common law courts, even in the Exchequer. Moreover, the courts did not have to be created especially for enforcement purposes. Experience had shown the various colonies the need for special treatment of cases involving maritime practices and the usefulness of an admiralty jurisdiction. In New England maritime commerce hastened its development. In Virginia and Newfoundland, local interest in the fisheries furnished the incentive; in Bermuda, it was the problem of wrecks; in Jamaica, piracy.[18]

Despite local approval when first created, the admiralty courts soon became unpopular. Their activities in enforcing the restrictions on the slave trade and the Navigation Acts were not the only reason. Some colonists complained that the expenses of admiralty proceedings were greater than those of the common law courts.[19] Others allowed grudges originating in constitutional controversies to affect their views about legal jurisdictions. Chief Justice Coke, champion of the parliamentary cause, had contended for the common law's claims; his supporters tended to oppose what he had opposed, espe-

[17] The governors tended to refer to cases which properly were seizures, as prizes. For example, see the case of the "James" of Belfast (CSPC [1669-74], No. 567).

[18] Crump, *Colonial Admiralty Jurisdiction*, pp. 26-29, 37-39, 47, 48, 52-53, 58-59, 61, 83-87, 104, 125-26. See also the Introductions by Andrews and by Towle to Towle, *Records of the Vice-Admiralty Court of Rhode Island*, pp. 1-100. Pages 91-95 give a good summary of the procedure of the court.

[19] Crump, *Colonial Admiralty Jurisdiction*, pp. 159, 164. For costs of suits before the vice-admiralty and common law courts, see CO 1/53, No. 33; CO 1/60, No. 61; CO 1/61, No. 64, iv; CO 5/1405, p. 680; CO 1/51, No. 70, i. See also Hough, *Reports of Cases*, pp. 21, 283-84; Towle, *Records of the Vice-Admiralty Court of Rhode Island*, pp. 16 n., 60, 95, 574-75; Morris, *Select Cases*, pp. 40, 169-71.

cially since the pretensions of the maritime jurisdiction had been represented by Sir Julius Caesar, a prominent defender of King James I's rights.[20] The greatest and most justifiable cause of irritation was the belief that the courts were not disinterested. If either the governor, who might receive one-third of the forfeiture, or someone dependent upon him for the office, heard the case, there was always the chance of judgments being biased. It is true, of course, that in the eyes of the law the governor as governor was one entity, and the governor sitting as a judge another, but disgruntled defendants were not convinced that the dual personality had not confused its identities, and that the judicial rulings of one had not been warped by the pecuniary interests of the other.[21]

In providing for the trial of seizures in the colonies, Parliament once again failed to make its meaning entirely clear. There was no doubt about the right to bring proceedings in the common law courts, since they were "courts of record" and, as such, were mentioned in most of the provisions. But there was considerable dispute whether the admiralty courts were "courts of record" and whether cases could

---

[20] Crump, *Colonial Admiralty Jurisdiction*, pp. 20-22.

[21] E.g., the Hanson-Dutton controversy over the "Berkshire" (1682), CO 1/51, No. 93; CO 1/52, No. 92; CO 1/53, Nos. 51, 53; CSPC (1681-85), Nos. 797, 935, 1040, 1043-46, 1290, 1316, 1334, 1368, 1403, 1409, 1435, 1565, 1646, 1671; CTB VIII, 1024-27. Complaints about the partiality of the courts are numerous. For examples, see the case of the condemnation of the "Margaret" in Maryland (CO 5/713, No. 101 x); that of the "James" of Belfast, in which the governor swore he would have her as prize, "give she were the Duke of York's own," even after the Council had declared the ship free (CO 1/28, No. 46, 46 i; CSPC [1669-74], No. 813); and that of the "Abercorne" (CTB VIII, 910). English accounts bear out these complaints of the injured. Sir Thomas Exton, of the English Admiralty, recommended that appeals be allowed from colonial decisions, such as that against the "O'Brien," as he had himself seen unjust colonial judgments (CO 153/3, p. 231; CSPC [1685-88], No. 931). Andrews (Introduction to Towle, *Records of the Vice-Admiralty Court of Rhode Island*, pp. 17-18) points out that after 1697 the governors had less to do with the vice-admiralty courts, but even if independent, the judges were not necessarily disinterested. Secretary of Admiralty Corbett claimed that "having no Salaries" the colonial admiralty judges consult "nothing but their Fees, and prostitute the dignity of the courts for the sake of gain" (Crump, *Colonial Admiralty Jurisdiction*, p. 159). Quary combined the activities of a customs officer with those of a judge (Andrews, *op cit.*, p. 46; Root, *Relations of Pennsylvania with the British Government*, p. 112); and Lockman, a Rhode Island judge, also sought to obtain the post of naval officer (Towle, *op. cit.*, p. 88). However, Andrews (*op. cit.*, p. 60) states that he has yet to find a well-established instance of manifest partisanship or injustice on the part of a judge, and Hough (*Reports of Cases*, p. 215) cites an instance of a judge who testified on behalf of the claimant in a seizure proceeding.

be brought before them unless the particular statute involved specially provided for trials in admiralty courts.²² Parliament tried to clarify the matter in 1696 by providing that suit to recover "all the Penalties and Forfeitures before mentioned" might be brought in vice-admiralty courts "att the Pleasure of the Officer or Informer," but problems continued to arise. Did the provision quoted refer to all penalties arising under all the Navigation Acts or only to those provided for in the Act of 1696? What was the extent of the admiralty jurisdiction in the charter colonies; must juries be used in vice-admiralty trials; and how were appeals to be carried to England?²³

Another jurisdictional question arose from the age-old conflict between the common law and the admiralty courts as to the relative extent of their authority, the chief issue being which court had jurisdiction over such bodies of water as creeks, bays, and harbors that were "within the arms of the land." In England the common law courts prevailed by virtue of certain statutes of Richard II and Henry IV,²⁴ but the English authorities refused to extend the English rule to colonial conditions after the Jamaican admiralty court released the ship "St. George." It had been seized less than three-quarters of a mile from Old Harbour at Jamaica and "within all the Kays," and a local statute had declared that part of the harbor to be a part of the parish of St. Dorothy and outside the admiralty jurisdiction. The case was carefully considered on appeal by the Lords of Trade, the Lord Chancellor, the King's Counsel, and Dr. Lloyd of the Admiralty, who concluded that the admiralty court had jurisdiction, since no Jamaican statute could make the high seas part of a parish, much less "take away or lessen the Admiralty's jurisdiction granted to his Royal Highness by patent."²⁵ When the question next arose, in Barbados, Governor Russell, having heard

²² See discussion in Beer, *Old Colonial System*, I, 292-93; Crump, *Colonial Admiralty Jurisdiction*, pp. 129-32; Root, *Relations of Pennsylvania with the British Government*, pp. 110-11. It must be remembered, however, that the admiralty court was used (Crump, *op. cit.*, pp. 129-46).

²³ 7 & 8 Gul. III, c. 22, i; Andrews, Introduction to Towle, *Records of the Vice-Admiralty Court of Rhode Island*, pp. 5-18, 20-23, 63-79; Root, *Relations of Pennsylvania with the British Government*, pp. 92-107.

²⁴ 13 Ric. II, stat. I, c. 5; 15 Ric. II, c. 3; 2 Hen. IV, c. 11.

²⁵ PC 2/65, pp. 99-100; CSPC (1675-76), Nos. 958, 972, 976, 987.

188   COLONIAL COURTS

of the Jamaican episode, took pains to insure that the judge in his province would uphold the royal prerogative,[26] but the issue was to be revived from time to time in other colonies, even after the Act of 1696.[27]

The same question was raised, in converse form, when common law courts assumed jurisdiction over seizures that had been made upon the high seas. In a Bermuda case involving the concealment of goods from a wreck, transfer of the trial from the council sitting as a court of admiralty to the courts of common law was denied on the grounds that the *Lex Mercatoria* of Malynes stated that such actions should be tried in the admiralty, but the case was probably exceptional, as the common law courts often succeeded in encroaching upon the admiralty preserves.[28] Similarly, in trying Navigation Act seizures, comparatively little objection was raised to the trial in common law courts of seizures made on the high seas, especially when, as in the case of the "James" of Belfast, the vessel was condemned.[29]

Sir Nathaniel Johnson, when governor of the Leeward Islands, permitted sixty Negroes, landed from the "Betty" of Bristol, to be condemned in the admiralty court, despite the fact that they had been seized upon land. He argued that since the ship had traded within the prohibited regions in Africa, she and all her lading "became subject and liable to confiscation before her arrival at Montserrat," and that that fact "made the cause maritime and entitled the admiralty to a jurisdiction thereof, although the seizure of the slaves was made on shore." Possible doubts as to the validity of his ruling led him to conclude his report by stating, "if I have been mistaken in this I hope, my Lords, 'tis a pardonable error." However, he does not seem to have been reproved, although he had warned the English authorities that his action was one "which I shall upon any future occasions be apt to Repeat if I receive not yor Lo^ps

[26] CO 28/2, No. 102, i-iii; CSPC (1693-96), No. 1930.
[27] Andrews, Introduction to Towle, *Records of the Vice-Admiralty Court of Rhode Island*, pp. 63-75; Hough, *Reports of Cases*, pp. 82-83; Root, *Relations of Pennsylvania with the British Government*, pp. 97-127.
[28] Lefroy, *Memorials of the Bermudas*, II, 332, 333, cited in Crump, *Colonial Admiralty Jurisdiction*, pp. 87-88; Morris, *Select Cases*, pp. 12, 38-40, 63, 648-736.
[29] CSPC (1669-74), No. 567.

directions to the Contrary."[30] In this respect, as in others, the mother country was more interested in enforcing the laws than in establishing nice lines of demarcation between jurisdictions as a matter of form.

Even when the question was answered as to which of the two jurisdictions should try the seizure, there still remained the problem of determining the geographical jurisdiction in which the trial was to be held. Could an offense committed in one colony be tried in another? One of His Majesty's captains declared that he could try his seizure "in any Court of Record convenient for his voyage,"[31] and his view was apparently confirmed by instructions to the governors "not to hinder captains of the King's ships if they carry pirates or illicit traders to some other place for trial."[32] In another case, however, Sir Robert Sawyer, His Majesty's Attorney General, reported that the "seizure being in New England the trial must be there," unless the ship were brought to England for trial.[33] The Act of 1696, however, made it clear that trials held in the vice-admiralty courts in the plantations should be held in the plantation "where such Offense shall be committed," but the earlier rule still remained in effect, that both ships and goods might be removed to England for trial before "any of His Majesty's Courts att Westminster."[34]

Further questions concerned the legal warrant for establishing many of the colonial admiralty courts.[35] Could the governor create vice-admiralty courts by virtue of his vice-regal powers, without any specific warrant in his commission? Must he have special authority to do so, and also a commission as vice-admiral from the Lord High Admiral in England? When the "James" of Belfast was seized in Nevis Road as a lawful prize under the Navigation Act, Sir Charles Wheler supposed that as governor of the Leeward Isles he had the

[30] CO 153/3, pp. 336-37; CSPC (1685-88), No. 1773; CTB VIII, 2049.
[31] In the case of the "James" of Belfast. CSPC (1669-74), No. 567.
[32] CSPC (1685-88), No. 1817.
[33] The case of the "Swallow," which imported Canary wines into New England (CTB VIII, 957-58).
[34] 7 & 8 Gul. III, c. 22, vii; CSPC (1661-68), No. 84. The Dutch-built "John" of Topsham was seized in Newfoundland and tried before the Admiralty Court in England (PC 2/56, pp. 199, 206; APC Col. I, Nos. 578, 580).
[35] On the whole subject, especially after 1696, see Introductions by Andrews and Towle to Towle, *Records of the Vice-Admiralty Court of Rhode Island*, pp. 8-20, 82-90.

power to erect a court of admiralty, since he had been granted authority to erect "all sorts of courts." He worried, however, because he also had been appointed vice-admiral, and in that capacity was bound by "such instructions as he shall receive from H.R.H." He thought that the limitation applied only when at sea, but to insure his walking "the surest path" he tried the ship in a court of record.[36] In another case, Colonel Kendall believed that, since the then Commissioners of the Admiralty had no power to grant a commission of vice-admiralty, it might be had directly from the King himself.[37] When Andros received his patent as governor of New York, no mention was made of powers as vice-admiral until 1678; he nevertheless considered himself vice-admiral, as deputy of the man who was Lord High Admiral.[38] The inherent authority of the governor and the general grants of power in his commission were relied upon by the Virginia county courts when assuming admiralty jurisdiction.[39] Massachusetts, Maryland, and Bermuda acted by virtue of their charters. Appointments by the English Admiralty were spasmodic[40] until after the Act of 1696. Then the entire question was taken up in a thoroughgoing manner for all the colonies, charter as well as royal, care being taken that even if one vice-admiral should die, another would be ready to take his place.[41]

Technical considerations such as these seem absurd to the average reader. They appear especially objectionable when, as in the case of the Venables expedition, lack of a duly constituted court to condemn seizures transformed properly seized prizes from rewards of achievement to sources of friction and temptations to embezzle-

[36] CSPC (1669-74), No. 567.

[37] CSPC (1689-92), No. 411.

[38] Crump, *Colonial Admiralty Jurisdiction*, p. 121.

[39] *Ibid.*, pp. 56-78. The first grant from the Admiralty was given to Thomas, Lord Culpeper, on Oct. 26, 1679 (*Virginia Statutes-at-Large*, I, 466, 537).

[40] Commissions were issued as early as 1622, but a fairly continuous sequence of appointees can be found only in Maryland and Jamaica. Even in Jamaica there was a break in 1692 (PC 2/74, p. 504; APC Col. II, No. 466). Movements toward more continuous appointments were made in 1677 (PC 2/66, pp. 60, 64; APC Col. I, No. 1148), and again in 1692 and 1693. The manuscript of Miss Helen Crump's work on the colonial admiralty jurisdiction at the Institute of Historical Research in London includes a list of vice-admirals and vice-admiralty officers in the colonies during the seventeenth century.

[41] PC 2/76, pp. 480, 514, 526, 532, 540, 549.

ment.[42] But before demanding action and the elimination of red tape, the reader must remember that the whole scheme of private property is based upon habits which depend in part upon regular observance of rules. Chaos would result if anyone who chose should undertake to award property rights. Few, if any, English naval captains in the seventeenth century could have been trusted to render objective judgments on questions involving their own self-interest. There were seamen of that era who decided questions of property rights for themselves, but they were known as pirates. The line of demarcation between piracy and privateering was at times rather fine and rested upon technical differentiations at best, but it was none the less real, and civilization profited by maintaining its existence.

Whatever may have been their lack of legal training, the attorneys of the day did not fail to take advantage of the loopholes which legal technicalities offered to offenders. When the ship "St. Jago de la Victoria" was tried in Jamaica, the captain's counsel took exception to the jurisdiction of the court because some of the legal processes had been signed by only one of the judges, whereas the commission authorizing the trial to be held was directed to any three of the judges. The argument was overruled, but later the same attorney contended that the case should be dismissed because his client had had to wait five hours for the informer's witness.[43] In a trial in Maryland, the defendant demurred to the information which was based on the Act of 1663. Among other arguments, he contended that the information was insufficient because it stated that the Parliament passing the law began in the fifteenth year of Charles II's reign, whereas in fact it was a Parliament which began in the twelfth year and was adjourned and prorogued.[44] Any facts were seized upon which offered an opportunity to distinguish the case at issue from the general rule. In the Carolinas, it was argued that the charter exempted the inhabitants from the necessity of complying with the Act of 1660, because the charter had been granted subsequent to the passage of the Act and made no mention of it.[45]

[42] Crump, *Colonial Admiralty Jurisdiction*, pp. 95-97. For a later case involving similar procedural niceties, see the case of a French ship seized in Maryland (CSPC [1693-96], No. 1167).   [43] CO 137/44, No. 1, i.
[44] The trial of the "Margaret" (CO 5/713, No. 101, viii, ix).
[45] CSPC (1685-88), Nos. 1204, 1417, 1457; CTB VIII, 1438.

More important than these questions of procedural nicety were the practical problems. Who was to appoint the judge, marshal, and registrars of the admiralty courts? Should the power rest in the hands of the English authorities, or should it be vested in the colonial vice admiral or governor?[46] How could undue complications, in the form of countersuits and interference of one court with another, be prevented? Who was to pay the costs of seizure proceedings? Colonial answers to these and other questions have sometimes led to unfair accusations against the colonists. For example, Randolph's vehement objections to paying the costs of special courts[47] have helped to popularize the belief that Massachusetts was unduly contemptuous of English authority. Yet someone had to pay for the proceedings. Logically, if Randolph lost his suit, it was a judicial determination that the suit should not have been brought. If he won, the Navigation Acts entitled him to profit, to the extent of one-third or one-half of the seizure. In either case, who was more properly chargeable with the costs than the party who either caused unwarranted litigation or else reaped the fruits of a justified procedure? In looking to the informer for payment, Massachusetts merely followed the English practice.[48]

The problem of proving the offense in court was made relatively simple by the Acts. Ships and goods could be and were condemned by establishing facts within the personal knowledge of the informer, or others residing where the trial was held. The customs records would determine whether or not the proper certificates had been given or received. The build of ships, the nationality of crews, the origin of goods—these were all matters about which expert testimony could be offered by those familiar with trade and commerce. Otherwise enforcement of the laws would have been well-nigh impossible. It would have been highly unpractical to procure evidence

[46] The power rested for a while with the colonial admirals, but English authorities soon secured it for themselves. From 1691, the power was vested variously in colonial officials such as Beeston, Richier, Russell, Nicholson, and Codrington, and in the Admiralty in England. Provision was made for emergency appointments by the governors (Crump, *Colonial Admiralty Jurisdiction*, pp. 105, 152-54). See also *supra*, pp. 189-90.

[47] CSPC (1681-85), No. 122; Toppan, *Randolph*, I, 175.

[48] *Supra*, pp. 117-18. In successful suits the costs appear to have been deducted before the division of the forfeiture was made (Hough, *Reports of Cases*, p. 21).

as to illegal actions abroad. The master could not be expected to testify against himself, and it was likewise to the crew's self-interest to remain silent concerning any illicit trade. If the ship were forfeited, they were likely to lose their wages.[49] A reward to a single sailor might offset his individual loss, but it seldom succeeded in persuading him to incur the ill will of his fellows.[50]

The comparative simplicity of proving offenses against the laws of trade may be shown by the case of the "Orange" of New York. This ship, which had traded with Hispaniola during war time, was seized on its return to New York for violating the Navigation Acts by importing European goods, and the master was also prosecuted for assisting the King's enemies. The master was acquitted, because he had "so disposed of the seamen with him that no evidence for the King could be had which the Grand Jury thought sufficient." But the European goods brought to New York spoke for themselves, and a jury condemned the ship for violating the Navigation Act.[51]

Nevertheless, there is a distinction between what one has been informed and believes to be true, and what can be proved as a fact in court. To meet even the simple requirements of proof under the Navigation Laws, it was necessary to establish certain facts as facts, and not merely as moral certainties. When imprisoned in the common gaol of Boston, Randolph might have had cause to suspect that illicit trade was being carried on in the harbor,[52] but his suspicions, however strong, were not proof. The reputation of the master, however

---

[49] In the case of the "Catherine," the Council of Virginia stated that "noe Wages [were] to be paid them by T M Govt. or Informer" (CO 5/1405, pp. 753-54; CSPC [1689-92], No. 2388). In New York in 1717 the court took under advisement the question whether a libel for mariners' wages should be allowed against a condemned sloop, but we do not have the record of its decision (Hough, *Reports of Cases*, pp. 4-5) In Philadelphia in 1735, although Judge Read expressed the opinion that the practice might open the door to fraud, he stated that it was customary for neighboring judges "to insert a saving clause in their decrees of condemnation for mariners wages" and that the law was "favorable and tender to mariners." Yet when his order was carried out that the wages should come out of the sale, with costs to be paid by the mariners, the wages were cut almost in half (Andrews, Introduction to Towle, *Records of the Vice-Admiralty Court of Rhode Island*, pp. 26-27).

[50] The case of the "Catherine" is one of the few exceptions where members of the crew testified against the ship (*supra*, n. 49).

[51] CO 5/1038, Nos. 94, 94 i-iv; CO 5/1039, No. 10; CSPC (1693-96), Nos. 1546, 1891, 1967, 2033, 2275, 2276.

[52] See his reports on the point in Toppan, *Randolph*, IV, 280, 283, 300; V, 39-44.

notorious, and his illegal intention, no matter how clearly established, could not serve as a substitute for factual proof of the actual offense, the landing of European goods. After the "Esther" of Dublin had been seized on the high seas en route from Ireland to Nevis with European goods, the master pleaded that his ship had committed no offense; "when the Act is broke, it is time Enough then to prosecute the Same," and "upon debate" by the court whether he had broken the Act of 1663, before the goods had been imported, it was decided that he had not.[53] Under our system of jurisprudence, the decision was undoubtedly correct. Except for the school of thought which would imprison those with criminal tendencies before they have committed a crime, jurists recognize a distinction between the evil intent and the overt act.

Any discussion of the problems of proof necessarily raises the question whether or not those who tried the cases could be convinced by the clearest possible demonstration of the facts.[54] English authorities often remarked that colonial juries were so prejudiced that they refused to punish offenders, regardless of the facts of the case.[55] Randolph's views on the subject are well known and relate not only to the colonies of New England, but also to Pennsylvania and New York. A governor in the Leeward Islands declared that in cases involving interlopers, "juries would not be satisfied with any evidence." Nicholson complained from Maryland that a Scottish smuggler had had his vessel tried "twice for breach of the Acts of Trade and Navigation, and was as often cleared by juries." And in Jamaica, Sir Henry Morgan wrote that in the trial of an Irish ship seized for importing Irish soap and acquitted by the jury, "one witness swore that soap was victuals and that one might live upon

[53] CO 1/59, No. 51. See also CO 153/3, pp. 230-33; CO 391/6, pp. 19-27; CSPC (1685-88), Nos. 621, 910, 911, 929, 931, 947, 1329 (ship "O'Brien"); CO 5/1038, No. 94; CO 5/1039, No. 10; CSPC (1693-96), Nos. 1546, 2033 (ship "Rebecca"); CTB VIII, 956-58 (ship "Swallow").

[54] Both Nicholson and Edward Randolph wished to revive an old English practice of making juries personally responsible for their verdicts by the process of attaint, so that in the event one jury released a ship and another determined that the ship should have been condemned, the informer might sue the first jury for damages (CO 5/725, pp. 2, 19, 94; CSPC [1693-96], No. 2303).

[55] In addition to the following examples of complaints, see those collected by Andrews, Introduction to Towle, *Records of the Vice-Admiralty Court of Rhode Island*, pp. 11 n., 50, 74.

it for a month, which the jury readily believed and found the aforesaid verdict."[56]

It is difficult to determine to what extent juries were recalcitrant,
but the evidence available indicates that their opposition has been
very much exaggerated. While the complaints quoted confirm the
natural assumption that the offender at the dock might be acquitted
by a jury of smugglers as a matter of professional courtesy, one
must remember that the community was not composed entirely of
smugglers, and that any legitimate trader who found himself on
such a jury would have a personal interest in punishing illegitimate
competition.[57] Moreover, the available statistics indicate that juries
did convict. Investigation has disclosed information regarding 46
jury trials which took place in various colonies, and the records show
that 25 trials, or 54.4 percent, resulted in convictions. The proportion of convictions becomes 69.6 percent, if the Randolph seizures
in New England are omitted because of the peculiar circumstances
surrounding them.[58]

That one might expect a certain percentage of acquittals is apparent from the nature of a number of seizures. George Muschamp,
an officer of the customs in the Carolinas, reported that he was not
surprised at an unfavorable verdict, because his evidence had been

[56] Leeward Islands: CSPC (1685-88), No. 1773; Maryland: CSPC (1693-96), No.
2303; Jamaica: CSPC (1677-80), No. 1304. Sir Henry Morgan's complaint in the
Irish soap case makes interesting reading, but the Jamaica jury was right in releasing
the ship. The Acts permitted provisions to come from Ireland, and commercially, soap
was classed among provisions (New York naval office lists, CO 5/1222-1229).

[57] *Infra*, p. 270.

[58] The details are as follows: In the West Indies, 7 condemnations out of 9
trials; in New York, 3 out of 6; in Pennsylvania, none out of one; in Maryland,
4 out of 5; in Virginia, 5 out of 6; and in New England, 6 out of 19. The low
percentage of condemnations in New England is due to the inclusion in that group
of all of the Randolph jury trials of which we know the result. He secured only
2 convictions in 13 jury trials, or only 15.4 percent. If, as seems probable, the 18
cases in which the results were unknown were also unfavorable and they were added
to the total, the percentage for both New England and the colonies as a whole
would be considerably lower. However, the uniformity of the result, when the Randolph figures are excluded, suggests that we should disregard the cases in which he
was involved because of his tendency to fail to produce the evidence required to
sustain a verdict. Excluding the Randolph cases, but including all other trials of
which we know the result, whether held before juries or not, 103, or 72 percent,
were condemned and 39, or 28 percent, were not. The sources are too numerous to
cite but can be found scattered among the manuscripts and books listed in the
Bibliography.

weak.[59] In other cases it is likely that the jury exercised that equity which is the virtue of the jury system, and refused to convict ships for technical offenses if the laws of Parliament were being "strained to deprive honest men of their ship and goods."[60] The percentage of acquittals, however, does not seem excessively high. Inspection of the results of trials in the Supreme Court of Judicature of New York, for offenses in no way connected with trade or navigation, shows that the percentage of convictions for such offenses was no greater than that for Navigation Act cases tried before juries.[61]

Problems of procedure and of proof were not the only ones to be met. The substantive law offered as many puzzles of construction, in its relation to the colonies, as existed in its European provisions. Answers might vary, as strict or liberal rules of statutory construction prevailed. Since the Act of 1663 provided that European manufactures could be taken to the colonies only from England, and other laws prohibited certain European manufactures from being imported into England, we would expect to conclude, by the usual methods of syllogistic reasoning, that such European goods could not be carried to the colonies—but the authorities determined otherwise.[62] In the case of English-owned, foreign-built ships, the general rule was that such ships importing goods to England were not subject to seizure, and that they were subject to the payment of alien duties only if the goods imported were among those listed as so dutiable. Tobacco was not listed, but the practice with regard to English-owned, foreign-built ships importing tobacco was either to seize the vessel or to assess alien duties on the cargo.[63]

The English authorities probably had good reasons for reaching the conclusions they did, if considerations other than logic deter-

[59] CSPC (1685-88), No. 1204.

[60] The words quoted are from a commendation by the Lords Proprietors of South Carolina of a governor, for his actions in preventing a seizure for a mere technical violation (CSPC [1693-96], Nos. 2255-56).

[61] The verdicts in the trial of crimes ranging from riot to murder are not always easy to determine, but it is clear that the number of convictions was nearer 33.33 percent than 50 percent (NYHS Col. XLV, 41-214).

[62] BM Add MSS 36109, f. 169; CTB I, 159-60, 289, 453, 620-21; IV, 808; VIII, 1483.

[63] BM Hargrave MSS 141, ff. 35r-36; CO 324/4, p. 142; APC Col. II, Nos. 182, 192.

mined the issue, but how were the laymen in the colonies to know what the eventual answer would be? It was hard enough to solve the conundrums which depended merely upon applying the proper legal theory. A Scotsman living in England could serve as master on a ship trading to the colonies, but not if he lived in Scotland.[64] Was his ship subject to seizure if he lived in Ireland? An alien naturalized by the law of Virginia could not sail a ship to the Leeward Isles,[65] but a French Protestant in the Carolinas, who had been made a denizen by His Majesty's order, could.[66] What decision should be reached when an alien-born Jew, who had paid scot and lot as a burgher of the city of New York, attempted to trade in Jamaica?[67]

The case of the pink, "Swallow," discloses the varied complications which could arise in the course of a single suit, and how considerations, ranging from international rivalry to administrative convenience, might influence the decision and render it difficult for a governor to anticipate the eventual ruling of his superiors. The questions of fact were few. The "Swallow" was a ship which had previously been condemned in a colonial court as a foreign bottom. It had brought logwood, an enumerated commodity, from Honduras Bay without giving bond to carry it to England. The seizure was made in the harbor of Port Royal, by Captain Talbot of His Majesty's ship "Faulcon," and was tried in the vice-admiralty court of Jamaica.[68]

The shipowners argued that it was unnecessary for them to give bond to carry logwood to England from Honduras Bay; that "they were not within the compass of the Act, as the Bay of Honduras, where logwood is shipped," was not an English colony; and that bonds were required for enumerated goods only when shipped in English colonies. Lieutenant Governor Molesworth quickly replied,

then you are robbers, for how can you pretend to cut logwood unless you take the country for an English settlement? You had better call it an

[64] BM Add MSS 36109, ff. 188r-89.
[65] PC 2/69, p. 541; CSPC (1681-85), Nos. 415, 447, 542, 544, 586.
[66] CSPC (1693-96), No. 2255.
[67] The case of Rabba Couty, CSPC (1669-74), Nos. 968, 999. Scot and lot was a customary contribution laid upon all subjects according to their ability, and in New York its payment carried with it the rights of a freeman.
[68] CO 1/60, No. 64; CO 1/63, No. 93; CSPC (1685-88), Nos. 900, 965.

English colony, and bring yourselves within the Act, or you may find yourselves in worse circumstances.[69]

His ingenuity, however, proved embarrassing to the English authorities. They accepted the defendant's contention that bonds need only be given when the enumerated goods were the growth, produce, or manufacture of the English plantations. Honduras was not then an English plantation, and the traders had no right to cut logwood there, but that was a point the English authorities preferred to ignore. They did not wish English vessels to be discouraged from cutting Honduras logwood;[70] long-continued practice might—and later did —give rise to the assertion of an English claim to jurisdiction.

The lawyers had a chance to renew the age-old controversy between the admiralty and the common law courts, because suit had been brought in the admiralty court, while the "Swallow" had been seized within the harbor *infra corpus comitatus*. Although, as has been seen, English authority was to decide that the admiralty jurisdiction extended to the harbor, the local court thought otherwise and ruled that the libel should be dismissed, since neither the information nor the facts showed the seizure to have been made at sea.[71] Captain Talbot appealed the verdict, and his case was considered by the King in Council. But the question had, for all practical purposes, been settled by the court of first instance, because the very night that judgment was given, the defendants unloaded their ship, "so that if a fresh trial should be ordered no one could tell where to find ship or goods."[72]

Another question arose because the "Swallow" was a foreign-built vessel. Did the fact that it had previously been condemned, and the King's part of the condemnation paid, make it free thereafter, in accordance with the "old custom all over the Indies"? The Customs Commissioners took a firm stand against the usage and complained that it had been "a frequent practice in the Colonies for the owners and proprietors of foreign-built ships to procure the condemnation of such ships on very cheap and easy terms by compounding with the Governors for their share of the forfeitures and paying no more

[69] CSPC (1685-88), No. 1066.   [70] *Ibid.*, No. 1580.
[71] CO 1/60, No. 64; CSPC (1685-88), No. 1066.
[72] PC 2/72, p. 456; CSPC (1685-88), Nos. 1212, 1238.

than the King's third part of the appraised value, themselves being the informers and prosecutors." According to their information, "there are twenty sail more of foreign-built ships like the one under consideration, which trade as free ships under such certificates, and carry logwood direct to Holland or Hamburg without paying duty."[73]

Satisfactory administration of the legal system demanded appeals to England, since uniformity obviously could not be expected in the rough-and-ready decisions of the colonial courts. Randolph demanded appeals, to reverse verdicts in favor of defendants.[74] Exton, of the English High Court of Admiralty, believed them necessary to correct arbitrary rulings in favor of informers.[75] Appeals within the hierarchy of local courts did not suffice to overcome such elements of prejudice as might have crept into the original decisions. Too often colonial appellate courts consisted mainly of judges who had presided in the first instance, together with the informer or the governor, each of whom had a direct financial interest in one-third of the seizures.[76] The master of the "St. Jago de la Victoria," for

[73] CSPC (1685-88), No. 1221. See also CO 1/63, No. 93; CSPC (1685-88), Nos. 1212, 1222, 1226, 1580. A common-sense view of the matter would suggest that a condemnation should make a vessel free. The belief that such was the case had long been held, and such ships as the "Prince of Orange" and the "Recovery" (formerly the "Alexander" of Inverness) and one bought by Lieutenant Colonel Devereux in Montserrat, had been purchased on the assumption that condemnation proceedings had made them free to trade (CO 5/1233, No. 4; CSPC [1669-74], No. 726; [1689-92], No. 821; CTB VIII, 106, 212, 314, 1009). Governor Molesworth of Jamaica stated that the general practice in the West Indies was to allow ships once condemned, upon which the King's part of the forfeiture had been paid, to trade as if free (CSPC [1685-88], Nos. 965, 1212). Penn, in Pennsylvania, and Bernard Randolph, in New England, acted on the same principle (CO 1/53, No. 76; CTB VII, 1455; VIII, 106, 212, 244, 1009).   [74] CSPC (1681-85), No. 92.

[75] CO 153/3, p. 231; CSPC (1685-88), No. 931.

[76] In New York, the Court of Chancery and Court of Judicature, which decided disputes in regard to land, were the governor and council (CSPC [1685-88], No. 1160); in the Leeward Islands, equity cases and the general sessions were held before the governor and council (CSPC [1675-76], No. 1152); in Jamaica, the governor was Ordinary and Judge of the Prerogative Court (CSPC [1681-85], No. 1260); in Barbados, in 1690, the fines imposed by the Grand Sessions appear to have been set by the governor and council rather than, as formerly, by the whole court (CSPC [1689-92], No. 1034); in Bermuda, the governor and council formed the Admiralty Court (Crump, Colonial Admiralty Jurisdiction, pp. 89-90). The surveyor general of the customs was also a councillor extraordinary in the eighteenth century (Labaree, Royal Instructions, I, 14-16, 18-19, 31). See also Chitwood, Justice in Colonial Virginia, pp. 26-28, 56-57. Those directly concerned in the outcome might not take part in the decision, but their known financial interests might very well affect the outcome.

example, declared that if he appealed to the highest Jamaican court
he would only double his expense, "since the Judges of that Court
were all of them Judges of the Supreme Court out of wch they must
Sue that Writt of Error and that if afterwards They should proceed
to bring it before the Governor and Councell, they were all the Same
persons or Interested."[77]

Many difficulties of legal engineering arose in devising a remedy
which would not do more harm than good. Although imperial officials
complained when appeals were not allowed, both the Attorney General
and Solicitor General agreed that, while the right to appeal undoubtedly existed, due rules and regulations must be provided under
which the remedy could be applied.[78] Practical reasons stood in the
way of allowing appeals, except in important causes. It was difficult
to examine witnesses or to hold a hearing before a tribunal three
thousand miles removed from the origin of the case. If the cost of
justice became too great, suitors might find themselves in the embarrassing position of having a theoretical right without a practical
remedy. Unscrupulous persons had to be prevented from utilizing
appeals for merely dilatory and vexatious purposes. Moreover, speed
was required as well as accuracy of judgment. Cargoes of wine might
spoil while a decision was being reached, and there was always the
element of demurrage to be considered. In Barbados, Captain Hesketh Holman pleaded with the council for a speedy examination of
his case, "it being a time when hurricanes might be expected and
delays prove dangerous."[79]

Various practical expedients were utilized to minimize the procedural difficulties. Ships and goods were often released upon bail,
pending the issue's determination.[80] In the case of the "Crown,"

[77] CO 137/44, No. 1, i. In a few instances the governors' instructions tended to
remedy the evil by forbidding councillors to be judges, but the policy was not con-
sistently pursued (Labaree, *Royal Instructions*, I, 328, 369-70).
[78] CSPC (1681-85), Nos. 92, 122. The discussion which follows primarily cites
seventeenth-century illustrations, but the same uncertainties concerning procedure, as
well as high costs and long delays, continued thereafter. See Introductions by Andrews and Towle to Towle, *Records of the Vice-Admiralty Court of Rhode Island*,
pp. 20-24, 94; Jameson, *Privateering and Piracy*, pp. 453-56, 461; Labaree, *Royal
Instructions*, I, 318-29; II, 897-98; *North Carolina Colonial Records*, II, 157-63.
[79] CO 31/5, Nos. 61-62.
[80] In the case of the ship "Agnes" (CTB IX, 1579-80; CTP [1557-1696], p. 224).
However, the "Joana" was not released on bail until after a petition had been made

the colonial authorities delayed bringing the matter to an issue until they had had an opportunity to receive a ruling from England on a troublesome point of law.[81] On another occasion judgment was suspended until word could be had from England whether the certificate presented by the master was authentic or a forgery.[82] In Virginia, special verdicts were used to good effect. In the case of the "Katharine and Anne," seized for having an illegal crew, the jury found that the crew consisted of eight men and one boy; that two men and the boy were French; that the boy claimed to be a passenger, since he was only working for his passage. If he were within the statute, the verdict was guilty; if not, not guilty.[83]

The most obvious fact concerning seventeenth-century appeals was that the proceedings were not yet systematized. Exton declared in 1686 that there "was no regular channel of appeal from a colonial [admiralty] court," although he believed that there should be.[84] Technically, there was no basis for review of colonial decisions by the High Court of Admiralty in England before 1691, the date of its first patent to the colonial courts.[85] However, according to Edward Ward and Charles Hedges, an appeal could be had "before the Lord Justices in Councell" from colonial admiralty courts, held by virtue of the governor's authority, independent of the Admiralty in England.[86] Inferentially, the Council should not have heard the appeal if the governor had had his commission from the "office of the Lord High Admiral in England, Ireland and the Foreign Plantations," but such a deduction is ill-founded. Regardless of verbiage in legal

to the Privy Council, alleging that the cargo of wine was spoiling (PC 2/72, pp. 545, 585; APC Col. II, No. 246; CSPC [1685-88], No. 1560; CTB VIII, 1711).

[81] CO 28/2, No. 102, i-iii; CSPC (1693-96), Nos. 1807, 1930.

[82] CO 5/1306, No. 17.

[83] Idem; CSPC (1689-92), Nos. 1438, 1564; VEJ I, 173-75. See the case of the "Biscay Merchant" for another special verdict. The jury declined to decide, and the ship was released upon giving a £1,000 bond to answer in England (PC 2/75, p. 149; CO 5/1306, No. 60; CSPC [1689-92], Nos. 1856, 2403; [1693-96], Nos. 120, 312, 327; CTB IX, 1774; VEJ I, 204-5).

[84] CO 153/3, p. 231; CSPC (1685-88), No. 931.

[85] The situation was different in Ireland, which was under England. Appeal went from the vice-admiralty court of Connaught, for example, to Dublin, to the English Admiralty Court, and finally to the King's Court of Delegates (Crump, Colonial Admiralty Jurisdiction, p. 161).

[86] CO 29/5, p. 206; CSPC (1693-96), No. 1862.

opinions, the Council's jurisdiction rested upon the fact that it represented the King, the ultimate source of all justice.[87]

When the Council believed that injustice had been done, it admitted appeals which were usually acted upon through the Lords of Trade and Plantations, with the aid of legal opinions from the law officers of the Crown and the judges of the Admiralty. Sometimes the case was reversed on the basis of the evidence presented at the trial, in the manner usually associated with our notions of appeal.[88] At other times the Council went outside the record as prepared in the colonial court, and retried the case itself.[89] In the case of the "St. Jago de la Victoria," it did neither. It ordered that the appeal be heard by the governor and council, although the master of the vessel had originally declined the right of an appeal to them when it was offered by the trial court.[90]

The fact that the King was sovereign explains much that would otherwise be incomprehensible. In the case of the ketch "Salisbury,"[91] a New England jury had found as its verdict that certain European goods unladen in Boston had not been brought from England as required by law. Ordinarily, the findings of a jury determine questions of fact, unless the appellate court finds that they are contrary to the evidence that the record shows to have been brought out at the trial. In this case, inquiry concerning the facts was made through the Commissioners of the Customs in England and showed that the goods had in reality come from England. The Council thereupon ordered that justice be done and that the bond given by the petitioner be released. One has no fault to find with the manifestly proper result; the query is, how was it accom-

[87] For instance, Sir Richard Raines, of the English Admiralty, saw no way of remedying the injustice he felt had been done to the "Good Intention" "except by the royal prerogative" (CSPC [1685-88], No. 1280). In this case appeal was permitted to the Privy Council, but the decision was not reversed, as it was shown that French wines had been carried to the English West Indies from Ireland (PC 2/72, pp. 433, 453; APC Col. II, No. 221; CO 153/3, pp. 266-69, 276; CO 1/62, No. 69; CSPC [1685-88], Nos. 1292, 1293, 1294, 1301, 1303, 1313, 1350).

[88] APC Col. II, No. 586.

[89] The case of the "Salisbury," (immediately hereafter) is a good example.

[90] PC 2/74, p. 274; CO 137/2, Nos. 7, 8; CSPC (1689-92), Nos. 50, 179, 233, 235, 236, 258, 925, 974, 979, 1909.

[91] PC 2/74, pp. 219, 319; CTB IX, 1309, 1382-83, 1426; CTP (1557-1696), pp. 197, 205.

plished? The action taken was more executive than judicial. As the Privy Council commented, the petitioner "ought properly to have appealed" to the Lords Commissioners of the Treasury. But appeals, in the correct sense of the word, do not lie from a court to an executive department. It might be argued that the action taken was in reality a pardon granted by the Crown, when investigation showed that a manifest injustice had been done. If so, there was still an error in the proceedings. The order made no reservation of the share in the seizure to which the informer was entitled unless the condemnation was judicially reversed. The explanation probably was that the Council, which was both the fountain of justice and the font of mercy, became confused by the plenitude of its powers.

No harm was done by the failure to differentiate between the diverse functions of the Crown in the case of the "Salisbury," but there were situations in which the actions of the Council as a judicial entity appear to have been colored by its prejudices as a political administrator or its apprehensions as the head of the diplomatic staff. When it considered the case of the "St. Jago de la Victoria," the Council had before it complaints concerning the political conduct of the judges of the colonial court and protests from the Dutch ambassador against the seizure.[92] Such considerations, rather than the evidence in the case, as far as one can judge today, determined the eventual ruling. Thus it seems unnecessary to attempt any analysis of the niceties of procedure in seventeenth-century appeals before the Privy Council. When issues were presented to it, the Council would act and, when convenient to do so, it would not hesitate to employ all its powers, hybrid though the authority thus exercised might be. Whether justice was done depended in part upon the facts and law presented by counsel and in part upon considerations extraneous to the record.

[92] CO 137/44, No. 1, i; CSPC (1689-92), Nos. 50, 179, 233.

XVI

GOVERNORS AND THEIR HANDICAPS

THE conflicts which arise in any administrative machine require means of coördinating the operation of the various parts with the minimum of friction. The problem of devising the mechanism of colonial control was complicated by the necessity of determining whether authority should be vested in a colonial official, or should be reserved for an English committee or board. In enforcing the Navigation Acts, and imperial authority generally, both methods were used and each had its defects.

The governor was selected as the colonial coördinator, and his duties with relation to the Acts of Trade were set forth in his instructions, which at first were simple in form. Those given in 1663 to Lord Willoughby of Parham, governor of the Leeward Islands, ordered him "to put [the] Act of Parliament in Execution," although exceptions were permitted in the case of subjects of countries in amity with His Majesty, who might obtain wood and ship's provisions, and the King of Spain's subjects, who might trade for European commodities and slaves, brought in English bottoms, if they did not take away any West Indian commodities such as ginger, sugar, indigo, tobacco, or dyewood.[1]

As the years passed, the forms became more and more elaborate. The increasing complexity of administration necessitated many new instructions and, once added, they usually remained long after the problem which had called them into existence had been solved. Fear that the omission of any of them might, in some unforeseen way, be detrimental led draftsmen to include them all in subsequent instructions, unless their inclusion was positively harmful.[2] Lists of ships

[1] PC 2/56, pp. 436-37; APC Col. I, No. 598; CO 389/4, pp. 27-30.
[2] Labaree, *Royal Instructions*, II, 752-97. See also *ibid.*, I, 143-47; II, 650-79, 696-98. For examples of the survival of instructions after the occasion for their existence had passed, see *ibid.*, II, 862, 872, 884.

and their lading were to be sent to England, so that bonds which were violated could be put in suit.[3] Goods which came without a certificate, or failed to give bond, were to be debarred.[4] The deputies and under officers of the Customs Commissioners were to be encouraged and assisted in the performance of their duties.[5] It was, of course, impossible to provide specifically for all situations which might arise, and catchall clauses were used to advantage. A letter of 1675 requested the governors of all the colonies except New England to inform the Customs Commissioners of any findings which "may be for the advantage of the King's Customs."[6] In the general revision in 1685 of instructions concerning the Navigation Acts, the governors were ordered first to study the Acts themselves and then to see that the provisions concerning ships, crews, and cargoes were observed. If proof of conformity to the laws was lacking, the penalties were to be exacted.[7] But however detailed the orders might be, they could add nothing to those given Lord Willoughby, "to put [the] Act of Parliament in Execution."

Usually the governor acted in conjunction with the colonial council, which made administrative regulations; supervised officials; held trials; determined whether the laws had been violated, and, if so, whether unusual circumstances might not warrant a dispensation.[8] Yet whatever the council did, legal responsibility rested upon the governor. As the Lords Proprietors of Carolina told Governor Joseph Moreton when he sought to excuse himself by pleading that the council had concurred in an alleged violation of the Acts:

What had the Council to do with that? What right had they to allow or prohibit the entering of any ship? It is the Governor who is to suffer the penalty if ships are allowed to trade contrary to law, and the consent or advice of the Council will not help him to escape it.[9]

The penalty referred to was provided by the laws themselves. The Act of 1660 provided that those "willingly and wittingly negligent in doing their duty" should lose their office, but did not make clear how far the penalty applied.[10] Although the third clause required

[3] CTB IV, 852.
[4] CTB II, 201-2.
[5] CSPC (1685-88), No. 312.
[6] CTB IV, 852.
[7] CSPC (1685-88), No. 312.
[8] CSPC (1693-96), Nos. 2104, 2152, 2169.
[9] CSPC (1685-88), No. 639.
[10] 12 Car. II, c. 18, ii.

governors to swear to do their utmost that "the aforementioned clauses, and all the matters and things therein contained, shall be punctually and bona fide observed," the important provisions making England an entrepôt for certain colonial produce did not appear in the "aforementioned clauses," but in sections eighteen and nineteen, an oversight that remained uncorrected until an all-inclusive oath was inserted in the Act of 1696.[11] Intervening acts, however, included oaths to observe their own clauses, and added a £1,000 fine to the penalty of removal from office.[12] The fine appeared more formidable upon the statute books than in action,[13] although we cannot, of course, determine how many were deterred from wrongdoing by the possibility of its being exacted. The penalty of loss of office probably caused governors more concern. His Majesty's displeasure sufficed to remove from office, and the records show few ways whereby that displeasure was more certainly incurred than by laxness in enforcing the laws of trade.[14]

Exhortations to the governor, however, were not accompanied by the necessary authority to act. Although granted an imposing array of titles, the governor possessed the shadow more often than the substance of power. His vice-regal character as the colonial embodiment of the King gave a historical background for attempts of colonial assemblies to coerce him by means of the power of the purse, but it did not provide him with a salary.[15] The complications ensuing are so well known that they need not be discussed, but there were two other handicaps, of equal importance in enforcing the laws, to which comparatively little attention has been paid. The governor neither possessed the supremacy over his assistants which is so much to be desired in an administrative hierarchy, nor the power to preserve the law by dispensing with it when exceptional circumstances demanded.[16]

[11] 7 & 8 Gul. III, c. 22, iv.   [12] 15 Car. II, c. 7, viii; 22 & 23 Car. II, c. 26, xii.
[13] The only assessment of a fine in the seventeenth century of which record has been discovered was that against Lord Baltimore, and it was apparently unjustly levied. Even in that case, it is not certain whether the £2,500 fine was imposed upon him in his capacity of governor, or in lieu of proceedings to forfeit his charter as proprietor. See *supra*, pp. 163-64.   [14] Beer, *Old Colonial System*, II, 354.
[15] See Greene, *The Provincial Governor, passim;* Labaree, *Royal Government in America, passim.*
[16] In addition to the following discussion, see Labaree, *Royal Instructions*, I, 377-86; II, 904.

The failure to grant the necessary administrative supremacy was caused partly by historical accident, partly by administrative considerations, and largely by continuous pressure brought to bear upon the government at home by English aspirants for office. Although at the beginning of the Restoration era the governor was the chief link between the colonies and the Crown, by the late seventies royal patronage had begun to encroach upon the governor's power of appointment. Offices intimately related to the governor, such as the colonial marshalship and the post of secretary, were sometimes filled by royal grant.[17] In Barbados, Sir Jonathan Atkins was defending his powers of appointment as governor with what seemed to be good hopes of success. The Lords of Trade appeared to be aware of the merits of his contentions. Just at the wrong moment, however, Atkins tactlessly refused to admit one Abraham Langford to the post of naval officer, regardless of the fact that Langford's appointment had been made by the King under the Great Seal.[18] The affront to imperial majesty was too much for the King. He had had troubles enough enforcing imperial policies in New England, the Channel Islands, and the Isle of Man, jurisdictions where rights granted by custom or by charter interfered with administrative efficiency. He resolved to let the colonists in the royal colonies, at least, know that "they are not to govern themselves, but be governed."[19] As the Secretary of State wrote, there was a "rush into the other extreme"; governors were deprived "of the authority which it was necessary for them to maintain by disposal of offices within their Government." These places were filled by His Majesty, "through private solicitation of persons in no way concerned with the Plantations, without the knowledge or approbation of the Governors."[20]

Whatever the cause for patent appointments, the results were to be deplored. The comments of the governors were both sarcastic and bitter. Sir Jonathan Atkins declared,

Not withstanding the King's Patent and a law of the country that all offices of trust shall be disposed of by the Governor, there is not the smallest office, though not worth the expense of obtaining, but is under a

[17] CSPC (1685-88), No. 2049.
[18] CSPC (1677-80), Nos. 482, 493.
[19] BM Add MSS 25120, f. 120; Beer, *Old Colonial System*, I, 271.
[20] CSPC (1677-80), No. 1182.

Patent. . . . The last Patent was brought me by one Mr. Binkes who is deputy's deputy to two persons whom I never heard of before.[21]

Governor Kendall wrote from Barbados in 1691 that

every office of profit now is no sooner vacant than it is begged for by some one or other in England. . . . The best of the offices are granted to non-residents and enjoyed by three, four and even five farmers and sub-farmers. It must be mere chance if they are executed by qualified men.[22]

Upon his arrival in 1690, the Earl of Inchiquin found that Jamaica was suffering from administrative upheavals because of exactions of officeholders in England, who "screw up their deputies here to give such prices for the offices as the posts cannot bear; and it is very displeasing to people here to see their money go to the making of estates for patentees in England, few of whom they have ever heard of, and none of whom have ever done them service."[23]

The situation thus created was detrimental to the governor's interests and interfered with enforcement of the laws. Being obviously unable to perform the detailed duties required for efficient administration, the governor had to act by means of an agent, either the naval officer or his own secretary. He was solely responsible for the results attained, and "subject to great penalties for any miscarriage." As Atkins complained, when a royal appointee was forced upon him in place of the officer of his choice: "The Governor forfeits £1,000 and is declared incapable of serving the King, yet still this man is imposed on me, and I have no security from him or his deputy."[24] Moreover, such appointees presumed upon their royal appointment. They considered themselves colleagues and not subordinates of the governor. Governor Kendall complained that he could not choose his own secretary and that he was at the mercy of the naval officer.[25] The results which might ensue are indicated by Sir Thomas Modyford's report of what did occur in the case of his secretary and his marshal, who had places for life and by patent, and who "ought to be always in attendance on the Governor, but being appointed under the same seal . . . think themselves as good as

he is, and so become 'proud, careless, and indiligent in their work.'"
The secretary would not "even keep his office in the town where
the Governor lived"; he almost refused to copy dispatches, and the
marshal did refuse to accompany the governor to church and on
journeys.[26]

In Virginia, Sir William Berkeley probably expended more energy
in his quarrel with the Customs Commissioners' deputy, Giles Bland,
than in any other activity in connection with the Navigation Acts.
Bland wished to prevent all illegal trade, and Berkeley contended
that Bland should restrict his activities to collecting the plantation
duties of 1673 only, that enforcement of the Acts of 1660 and 1663
was entrusted to the governor, and that it was the governor's bond
which was forfeited if the Acts were not obeyed. Although Sir William did not believe in the laws and did not hesitate to voice his
opposition to them, it must not be assumed that he was trying to
nullify them. The record of seizures shows that however bitterly
he might contest procedural points with Bland, he endeavored to do
his duty.[27]

Relations between the governor and the commanders of His
Majesty's navy suffered from the same decentralization of authority.
The King's captains were instructed to follow the directions of the
customs officers and the superior commands of the governor, for
"the Advancing of H. M. service in his Customs in those colonies
and the Trade and Navigation of the Kingdom."[28] But the governor
did not have complete authority. He could only suspend them "for
disobedience or neglect of orders,"[29] and an order of the King in
Council in 1683 instructed governors not to hold courts-martial in
case of misbehavior, but to take depositions and send them back to
England.[30] The governor was also ordered "not to hinder captains

---

[26] CSPC (1685-88), No. 2049.
[27] Beer, *Old Colonial System*, I, 288-90; II, 112-14; Bruce, *Economic History of
Virginia*, I, 356-60, 400; Osgood, *American Colonies in the Seventeenth Century*,
III, 217-18; Wertenbaker, *Planters of Colonial Virginia*, pp. 94-96. For enforcement
activities under Berkeley, see VCGC, pp. 212, 214, 216, 287, 435, and *passim*; CO
1/51, No. 17; CSPD (1671), p. 218. Wertenbaker (*op. cit.*, p. 95) infers that Berkeley enforced the laws; but cf. Osgood, *op. cit.*, III, 218, 245.
[28] CO 1/53, No. 111; CSPC (1681-85), No. 1492.
[29] CSPC (1689-92), No. 2097.
[30] CSPC (1681-85), Nos. 789, 792, 894.

of the King's ships if they carry pirates or illicit traders to some other place for trial."[31]

Another serious defect in the governor's position was his lack of power to dispense with the laws or even to pardon individual offenses. The instructions given Lord Carlisle in 1680, as Governor of Jamaica, were typical. Although he might suspend their payment, he was not to remit fines or forfeitures "above the value of £10 without first reporting the matter to the Commissioners of the Treasury."[32] Undoubtedly lack of confidence in the governor was one reason for the rule, but the explanation given another governor was the necessity "to bring our revenue arising in America into a more certain method of account."[33] Whatever the cause, the rule led to awkward situations. Lieutenant Governor Molesworth, of Jamaica, had been instructed to suppress piracy by granting a pardon to former freebooters. He told two of these very troublesome individuals, Yankey and Jacob, that he would receive them and their men "in all friendliness, nor shall you be troubled on account of any accusation of piracy, for which you shall receive the royal pardon." But he went on to say that, by reason of the Act of Navigation, "you must positively break up your ships, for, being foreign built, they cannot be used for trade here." Yankey and Jacob listened to the governor's requirement, looked at the ships which had served them so well in their adventurous career, and sailed away, leaving the King's pardon and respectability behind them.[34]

The case of John Alleway, of Bristol, shows how the exigencies of honest mariners might likewise require a judicious bending of the laws. When bound from Barbados to the Cape Verde Islands, his vessel had been taken from him by pirates, who fortunately did not prove to be of the walk-the-plank variety. They put him and his ship's company on board a foreign-built vessel, which, when it afterwards came to Barbados, was condemned as a prize. Alleway

[31] CSPC (1685-88), No. 1817. An attempt was made to avoid unnecessary friction by supplying the captains with copies of the governors' instructions, and the governors with copies of the captains' orders (ibid., Nos. 1041, 1693, 1838, 1988). For later relationships, see Labaree, Royal Instructions, I, 443-44.
[32] CSPC (1677-80), No. 1571. See also ibid., No. 1477; CTB VII, 125; VIII, 93-94; Labaree, Royal Instructions, I, 330; II, 904.
[33] CTB VII, 125.
[34] CSPC (1685-88), Nos. 1449, 1476.

purchased the ship from the governor and loaded it with sugar and tobacco, but on his return to England as the laws required, the ship was stopped. The authorities had questioned whether his new vessel should pass as a free ship, because in adjudging her a prize it had not been expressly stated that she was taken by letters of marque and reprisal.[35] The records do not show the fate of Alleway, but unless he was granted relief almost immediately, he undoubtedly entertained bitter thoughts on the relative rewards to be obtained from a career of crime and the life of an honest mariner. He might not have turned to piracy as a livelihood, but the chances were that thereafter he would make no efforts to comply with administrative rules and regulations. He would prefer such protection—and profits —as might be offered by chicanery and the corruption or avoidance of revenue officials. If there developed an embittered corps of deliberate smugglers, who felt no confidence in the treatment the well-intentioned would receive, it would have been difficult, if not impossible, to enforce the laws in a country with as long a coast line as America.

Of course no system could render able and honest men entirely impotent. In cases of necessity, the governor could, and would, act in violation of the laws and thereafter seek the royal pardon. When no provisions and supplies were to be obtained from other sources, the Leeward Islanders procured them from foreigners and minimized the dangers of imperial wrath by duly reporting the emergency and seeking pardon, which was granted.[36] Even in lesser matters, such as relieving an individual claimant, the severity of the law could be mitigated by a governor who possessed sufficient ingenuity of mind. The case of the "Crane" of Dartmouth is one in point. The vessel ran aground in Virginia, and during the illness of the master the seamen removed some of the goods and put them in a sloop in order to preserve the ship. No fraud was intended, but the judgment of the court was that "it being contrary to the Letter of the Law the said Vessel are Condemned." The sympathies of the authorities, however, were with the owner, Mr. Thomas Cock, who was permitted to act as informer against his own vessel, in order that he might

[35] CTB VIII, 951.
[36] CSPC (1661-68), Nos. 1631, 1694, 1880, 1881.

receive the informer's third of the forfeiture. The lieutenant governor thereupon gave up his share to the unfortunate Mr. Cock, and the vessel was returned after he had given bond to pay the part of the forfeiture still due, if he could not produce a release from England within eighteen months. Eventually the King's share was remitted, and thus Cock saved his vessel by the paradoxical process of obtaining its forfeiture.[37]

As is so often the case, success varied with the character of the official concerned. A strong and honest governor could do much good, and a weak one even more harm. To do complete justice to his tasks under the conditions which existed, the governor would have had to be an individual with the patience of Job, the wisdom of Solomon, and the honesty of the man whom Diogenes never found. It is obvious that such officials were not to be had, but it is extremely difficult to determine the merits of those who did serve His Majesty.

Evaluating character has never been an easy task, and lack of reliable information often intensifies the difficulties in the case of governors. One can understand why the English government spent £77 to remove Lord Culpeper from office,[38] after reading a letter in which he asked "what the wit of man can expect from a Governor beyond peace and quiet, and large crop of tobacco."[39] Sir Charles Wheler's habits of self-glorification and excessive protestations of zeal[40] prepare us for John Evelyn's statement that he had been "complain'd of for many indiscreete managements,"[41] and we are not surprised to learn of his recall a year after his appointment.[42] The forthrightness, balanced judgment, energy and common sense exhibited by both Colonel William Stapleton and Sir Thomas Lynch[43] explain why the Leeward Islanders petitioned that Stapleton's successor be another like him,[44] and how Lynch obtained a revenue grant for

[37] CO 5/1405, Nos. 677-80; CTB X, 6.
[38] AO 1/2312, Roll 9.
[39] CSPC (1681-85), No. 1258.
[40] CSPC (1669-74), Nos. 748, 775.
[41] Evelyn, Diary, II, 265, 271.
[42] CSPC (1669-74), Nos. 393, 758. Higham, (Development of the Leeward Islands, pp. 76-80) paints Wheler in a more favorable light.
[43] For documents illustrating Stapleton's abilities, see CSPC (1677-80), Nos. 563, 1063, 1418. In the case of Lynch, see CSPC (1669-74), No. 921; (1681-85), No. 668.
[44] CSPC (1681-85), Nos. 1526, 1539, 1665.

twenty-one years from a hitherto reluctant Jamaican legislature.[45] Yet the difficulty, for the contemporary superiors as well as for today's historians, was to determine the abilities of the great majority who were neither remarkably meritorious nor notoriously ineffectual. Was Governor Atkins honest as well as tactless? Did Sir Henry Morgan leave his freebooting instincts behind him when he left Panama? Had Governor Codrington committed all the mercantile sins with which he was charged?[46]

The contestants in the numerous squabbles attacked their opponents with vigor and vehemence, and their charges make interesting reading but not very convincing evidence. In the Rousby-Baltimore dispute, for example, Baltimore spoke of Rousby as "this pernicious person," who, besides being guilty of "knavery in his transactions with the shipping," was "the most lewd, debauched, swearing and profane fellow in the whole Government, and, indeed, not fit to be admitted to civil society . . . a rogue in his heart towards the King . . . impudent enough to publish hatred of Kingly Government aboard all ships." Rousby replied that Lord Baltimore "hopes that by casting much dirt, some will stick,"[47] but destroyed the favorable impression that such temperance might convey, when he referred to one Vincent Lowe as "that treacherous, false, lying, swearing, deceitful man," because Lowe had signed a "false, forward, foolish affidavit" that Rousby had made traitorous and indiscreet utterances.[48]

Even when the contestants avoided vituperation, it is difficult to ascertain the facts. In the controversy between Governor Dongan and Collector Santen, the careful abstracts prepared by the Council's clerks of charges and answers and supporting evidence still leave the truth concealed amid a maze of charge and countercharge.[49] Dongan, for example, alleged that Santen "employed his own Servants in such offices as should have been a cheque upon him," and

[45] CSPC (1681-85), Nos. 745, 1275, 1317; Beer, *Old Colonial System*, I, 219.
[46] CSPC (1689-92), Nos. 1608, 1609, 1613. See also Beer, *Old Colonial System*, for references to Atkins and Morgan.
[47] CSPC (1681-85), Nos. 151, 328.
[48] *Ibid.*, No. 312. For the affidavit which Lowe had signed, see *ibid.*, No. 128; for Rousby's answering affidavit, saying "that if Lowe made any such statement he must have been drunk, which was nothing unusual with him," see *ibid.*, No. 328.
[49] CTB VIII, 1626-29.

Santen replied "that the Officers were approved by the Governor and most of them recommended by him." The accusation that, contrary to law, Santen "has trusted sevl. psons for Custom," was met by the counter "that the Governor desired him to Give [trust] to one Drano and severall others who threatened to carry their Goods to East Jersey."[50] The Council itself was perplexed; at the time it decided in favor of Dongan, but it later appears to have changed its mind—at least, it gave Santen another position.[51]

The controversy that arose in New England between fiery Sir William Phips and Collector Jahleel Brenton shows that even sworn testimony might afford no certainty that the whole truth was told. Phips had been summoned home, and the Council of Massachusetts had been appointed a commission to take the evidence in support of Brenton's charges that the governor had been engaged in illicit trade and had threatened to break all of the collector's bones and commit him to prison if he did not give up a ship he had seized. Although the Council met to hear testimony at various times from July to October, 1694, Brenton complained that "Phips did all that he could to hinder the proof thereof, threatening the witnesses that they ought to have their ears cut off, and even barring some of them from swearing." He also complained that the Council "publicly declared themselves parties in the cause, as the Collector had complained against them all," and that "they also refused to let many of the Collector's witnesses be sworn, and did their best to trap and baffle such as were sworn."[52]

Moreover, a governor's merits could not be determined by the single standard of success in enforcing the mercantile code. That task was only one of many. International warfare, Indian alliances, boundary disputes, the suppression of piracy, and questions of political and religious control occupied more of the governor's time.[53]

---

[50] NYCD III, 495-96.
[51] CTB VIII, 1504, 1626-29; IX, 1526; CTP (1557-1696), p. 223.
[52] CSPC (1693-96), Nos. 689, 708, 718-19, 791, 862, 879, 1150, 1222, 1285, 1417, 1432, 1507.
[53] Governor Dongan, of New York, furnishes an interesting example of a governor whose energies had to be expended among various tasks. See Kennedy, *Thomas Dongan, passim*. For his attempts to promote the enforcement of trade laws by means of a tax on goods imported from any colony where they were not produced and by centralizing control of the trade of New York, Connecticut, the Jerseys,

He also had to avoid personal entanglements, maintain his political alliances, and frustrate his opponents' maneuvers. Francis Nicholson's activities in bringing suit upon bonds and enforcing the Acts in the Chesapeake, praiseworthy as they were from the English point of view, could not furnish complete protection against other failings. For a time, his alliance with the Randolph and Quary group, and the Earl of Bridgewater's friendship, enabled him to continue, despite William Penn's enmity, which he had incurred because of complaints about that royal favorite's colony. But quarrels on other subjects with Coode, in Maryland, and the Blair faction, in Virginia, as well as his indiscretions in an unsuccessful love affair with Lucy Burwell, that was characterized by indecorous behavior and "Billingsgate language," led to his transfer elsewhere.[54]

Contemporary complaints alone do not afford a sufficient basis for judgment; the stronger the man the more resentment he was likely to arouse. Sir Thomas Lynch was, as far as can be determined, one of the ablest of the lot, but the charges brought against him were of such nature that at one time he was recalled from his post.[55] Historians differ in their judgments concerning individuals, as well as in their evaluation of the governors as a group. Labaree has successfully met the earlier charges that the governorship was reserved for broken-down politicians, by showing, among other considerations, that the governors were held in esteem in official circles of the day.[56] Yet the question still remains whether the standards of seventeenth- and eighteenth-century officialdom met the requirements of the governor's post.

and Delaware, see NYCD III, 361, 391-93; NYDH I, 97-118. See also Kennedy, *op. cit.*, and Channing, "Colonel Thomas Dongan, Governor of New York," *Am. Antiq. Soc. Proceedings*, XVIII, 336-45.

[54] CSPC (1704-5), Nos. 247, 279, 284, 371, 924; "Proceedings of the Council of Maryland," *Maryland Archives*, VIII, 442; XXIII, 159-60, 282, 293, 333-34, 479-88, 493, 519, 521, 525; XXV, 570-76, 585-86; Huntington Library, Elsmere MSS 9594, 9595, 9598, 9722, 9729, 9729a, 9733; Jacobsen, *Blathwayt*, pp. 305-9; Labaree, *Royal Government in America*, p. 41 n.; Morriss, *Colonial Trade of Maryland*, pp. 123-25; Osgood, *American Colonies in the Eighteenth Century*, I, 377-81; Perry, *Historical Collections relating to the American Colonial Church*, I, 69-75, 80-81, 87-112, 125.

[55] CSPC (1669-74), Nos. 1066, 1129, 1130, 1250, 1251, 1301, 1302, 1374.

[56] "The Early Careers of the Royal Governors," *Essays in Colonial History*, pp. 145-68.

XVII

THE DIFFICULTIES OF REMOTE CONTROL

WHEN the English authorities centered the control of colonial enforcement in London and did not allow the governors to make the necessary adjustments in the machinery of enforcement, they were really choosing between two evils. If the ultimate decision had been left to the governors, matters might have been settled more quickly, but there might also have been as many answers to debated questions as there were colonies. The retention of power in England avoided the evils of decentralization, but it involved many technical difficulties of remote control—at a time when the English government had not yet perfected its technique for coping with the exigencies of empire.

The Atlantic Ocean presented many problems to administrators in days before science had reduced physical barriers to a negligible minimum. Quick dispatch of business was impossible when the mere crossing of the ocean might require two and one-half months, and even greater delays might occur in outfitting ships, finding convoys, or waiting for favorable winds.[1] Moreover, once begun, there was no certainty that a voyage would end at its intended destination. The Atlantic Ocean was stormy and infested with pirates and privateers. For example, Seth Sothell set out for his post in the Carolinas, but was captured and held for ransom; other officials met a watery grave.[2] Papers were customarily sent in duplicate or triplicate by different vessels; yet there were occasions when all of the copies dispatched failed to arrive. At one time in the seventies, Stapleton had not heard from Europe for over two years,[3] and in 1690 Governor Sir Robert Robinson reported that it had been eighteen months

[1] CSPC (1681-85), No. 172; (1689-92), No. 1617; Toppan, *Randolph*, I, 52; Wertenbaker, *The First Americans*, pp. 3-4.
[2] CSPC (1677-80), Nos. 885, 1490; CTB VIII, 1084, 1155.
[3] CSPC (1675-76), No. 405.

since his colony had heard from Whitehall.[4] The relation of the distance to the time factor was officially recognized in the procedure regulating bonds. Whereas only six months were allowed to return certificates in the English coasting trade, eighteen months were granted for similar purposes in the case of colonial bonds.[5]

Even more important than the direct consequences of the Atlantic's breadth were those indirectly resulting from it. There can be no true understanding of the problems of imperial engineering without recognition of the correlation that exists between the geographic realities of distance and the psychological bases of thought.

Administration of the Navigation Acts in the colonies was handicapped by the fact that colonial affairs were at the periphery of administrative consciousness. More pressing problems in England were at the center, and were sometimes solved without thought of the embarrassment which might later be caused in the plantations. Thus in 1719 Parliament undertook to better conditions in England by decreeing that armed smugglers should be transported to the colonies[6]—and forgot that such lawless offenders might teach the colonists some tricks of their trade that had not yet been known in the New World.

The idea of a self-sufficient empire, with the interests of the different sections nicely balanced, was a beautiful dream which it was difficult for those making the adjustments to attain. Even if we assume that legislative and executive officials in England were what neither they nor any similar officials ever have been, absolutely unprejudiced and impartial, they could only decide questions on the basis of the facts brought before them. The Board of Trade, for example, when newly appointed in 1696, made earnest efforts to learn all that it could about the colonies. Whenever it heard of anyone who had recently returned from the plantations, it summoned him to appear before it. Yet these persons were for the most part English officers or traders. Whether consciously or not, the bias of English interest crept into their testimony and thus colored the

[4] CSPC (1689-92), No. 1188. See also Dickerson, *American Colonial Government,* pp. 133-41.
[5] 7 & 8 Gul. III, c. 23, xiii. Morriss (*Colonial Trade of Maryland,* p. 123) cites an instance where bonds were put in suit after a lapse of twelve months.
[6] 4 Geo. I, c. 11 (1717); 6 Geo. I, c. 21 (1719); 8 Geo. I, c. 18 (1721).

Board's decisions. The existing conditions arose from no prejudice for or against colonial interests; they were an inescapable element of the problem.[7]

The possibility of obtaining information from reports or depositions did not equalize conditions. Entirely apart from the difficulties and delays in getting it, such evidence was not a satisfactory substitute for personal testimony. When witnesses appear personally, the investigators can direct the testimony along such lines as they desire and can bring out whatever facts they may think important. When submitting a case in writing, the petitioner must determine at his peril what point of view those in authority will take, what propositions they will accept, and what must be argued at length. It is inadvisable to cover all conceivable questions that may arise; the sheer bulk of such a presentation would discourage attention to any of the arguments.

The colonists might appoint agents, but were not thereby accorded parity with those who might themselves appear in England. If a colonial agent were selected by the governor, as such agents often were, his views were likely to have an imperial tinge.[8] Even when the agent was selected by the Assembly, he would often be handicapped by lack of authority to give binding answers, and by lack of detailed information on the questions presented. If he had his case carefully prepared in advance, new developments might take him by surprise. The London opponents of the colonists were present in person and could adjust their tactics to suit the occasion. The colonial agent would be forced to wait both for the information upon which to base his reply and for the authority to make one.[9] Necessary as such delays might be, they gave an appearance of vacillation and evasion that was apt to make an unfavorable impression and to prejudice the colonial case.

Moreover, imperial questions were not always settled by an impartial weighing of the pros and cons of argument. A letter of Rousby, collector in Maryland, explains the advantage it was to him to be

---

[7] *Journals of the Board of Trade* (PHST), *passim;* Penson, "London West India Interest," *Eng. Hist. Rev.*, XXXVI, 373-92; Gray, *History of Agriculture in the Southern United States*, I, 431-32.

[8] Penson, *Colonial Agents*, pp. 94, 148, 162.

[9] *Ibid.*, pp. 54-56, 76-77.

in London at the time of his controversy with that colony's proprietor, Lord Baltimore. He wrote, "It has cost me much money, but I would not for twice the sum have remained in ignorance of what I now know, or have wanted the interest I have now gained." Interest at court is never without value, and undoubtedly was of the utmost importance in the seventeenth century, especially when it consisted, as did Rousby's, of "several unexpected friends, some not of the meanest rank."[10] One of the secrets of the Earl of Derby's success in retaining the Isle of Man as a den of smugglers lay in the presence of powerful friends in England. Their warnings prevented the Earl at least twice from unduly straining the patience of those in whom final power rested.[11] Lack of similar advice probably explains why certain other lords proprietors lost their charters for less heinous offenses.

The complexity of the tasks involved in imperial administration called for the ablest efforts of government, but unfortunately the colonial machinery of control was still in an experimental stage. Without the centuries of experience from which the English customs service had profited, imperial administration was proceeding by a process of trial and error, illustrated by the multiplicity of committees and councils created for trade and plantations.[12] Worse still, the very terms of their appointment destined such organs of control primarily to deliberate rather than to act.[13] The limitation was in line with contemporary unwillingness to delegate power; the result was none the less to stultify initiative and to reduce the committees' efforts toward bold reforms of policy to mere suggestions for perfecting routine technique.[14]

Moreover, the carelessness with which power was distributed among the successive committees, the Secretaries of State, the Lords of the Treasury, and the Commissioners of the Customs, left it uncertain which body was ultimately to determine questions and what

[10] CSPC (1681-85), Nos. 312, 325.

[11] HMC *Ormonde*, n.s., VII, 48-49; HMC *Kenyon*, p. 266.

[12] For the early experiments, see Andrews, *Committees and Councils*; Bieber, *Lords of Trade*; Dickerson, *American Colonial Government*.

[13] BM Egerton MSS 2395, f. 276; Andrews, *Committees and Councils*, p. 112; Bieber, *Lords of Trade*, p. 82.

[14] Basye, *Lords Commissioners of Trade*, p. 14.

the decisions would be. One familiar with seventeenth-century revenue administration in England can anticipate with reasonable accuracy what the eventual solution of a problem will be, before tracing through the records to its eventual conclusion. If the result does not accord with anticipation, the records usually disclose a rational explanation for the variation. But this power of prophecy disappears in the field of colonial administration. For example, in discussing whether a gentleman by the name of Byndloss should be granted the posts of Clerk of the Crown and Peace and Clerk of Markets and Fairs, objection was made that the offices were to be given for life, granted in plurality, and were all to be exercised by deputy.[15] The Secretary of State recommended that the grant be denied.[16] Nevertheless, Byndloss next emerges in the colonies with a patent for fourteen or fifteen offices, which he had "obtained by surprise" and through the device of dividing the posts between the deputy governor's brother and himself "for their lives."[17]

Decentralization interfered with the relations between the mechanisms of control and the public, by causing colonial business to be referred hither and thither unnecessarily. In 1733 reference of plantation business brought before the Crown to a Committee of the Council, thence to the Board of Trade, and back again to the Council, was routine procedure; special circumstances might occasion further references to other groups. As a consequence, one memorialist declared that persons with proper requests were deterred from "making any application at all rather than have the trouble of attending so many different offices," and that those who proceeded to violate the intent, if not the letter, of the law assumed that their acts would not be "for a long time examined into from the unavoidable delays of the different offices."[18] The colonists, especially, suffered from such defects of administrative organization. Since the tendency for administrators, as for others, is to defer considering those matters which can be set aside for those that are more pressing, colonial petitions, unless represented by an insistent solicitor, were likely

[15] CSPC (1677-80), No. 1182.
[16] His recommendation was endorsed by the Lords of Trade and Plantations and by the Privy Council, and was approved by His Majesty (*ibid.*, No. 1223).
[17] CSPC (1681-85), Nos. 46, 1176, 1759.
[18] CO 5/5, f. 316; Basye, *Lords Commissioners of Trade*, pp. 28-29.

to remain neglected upon some officer's desk until that official could free himself from the importunities of Londoners and others who could appear in person. The perils of the pigeonhole may well have caused more delay than storms at sea.

The successive committees and councils dealing with the plantations were in part composed of merchants and men familiar with the conditions of trade, but primarily their members belonged to the class hitherto referred to as "My Lords."[19] Summary evaluations of officials' abilities are of dubious accuracy, but the impression gained after studying the work of "My Lords" and that of the Commissioners of the Customs, decidedly favors the latter. The Commissioners were trained administrators, practical men of affairs; the Lords of Trade may have been men of parts and of brilliant attainments, but they were without a solid background of factual knowledge and for the most part had too much to do, or too little interest, to attend the meetings.[20]

The Lords of Trade and the Privy Council lacked the wariness of experience usually exhibited by the trained administrator. Reference has already been made to the difficulties caused by their precipitate action in granting New England a dispensation from the Acts.[21] On another occasion the Council wrote to Massachusetts that His Majesty expected that colony to "take care that our officers are able to prosecute offenders under those Acts without charge, as in England."[22] But if they had taken the trouble to make even a casual inspection of the Treasury Solicitor's records, they would have learned that English officials had to incur very considerable expense in prosecuting offenses. These instances contrast sharply with the Commissioners of the Customs' caution when some Virginians, who wished to establish a fishery, requested the right of importing salt direct from Europe. The Commissioners looked "upon it [the project] as a very desirable undertaking" and had "nothing to object to the making an experiment thereof for one voyage." But they sug-

[19] Andrews, *Committees and Councils*, pp. 65-68. For still further information concerning these men, see works cited *supra*, p. 219, nn. 12, 14.

[20] Andrews, *Committees and Councils*, pp. 107-8; Basye, *Lords Commissioners of Trade*, p. 24.

[21] *Supra*, p. 129. See also PC 2/55, p. 126; CSPC (1661-68), No. 28; CTB I, 206-7; APC Col. I, No. 504.

[22] CSPC (1681-85), No. 264.

gested, "because so great art and industry is used and so much deceit practised in the Plantation trade to the prejudice of your Majesty's revenue in this Kingdom," that the shippers be put "under a certain regulation and security, so that under pretence of lading salt they may not take in nor convey to any of the King's Plantations any other European goods except salt for the said fishery."[23]

My Lords also compared unfavorably with the Commissioners in that they sometimes suffered from delusions of grandeur, an affliction which their more humble contemporaries escaped. When the Leeward Islanders praised Stapleton and petitioned for another governor like him, they were reproved for their "too great forwardness . . . in meddling with the King's intentions as to the appointment of a new Governor."[24] At an earlier date, in denying a petition of Barbados against the Navigation Acts, the Lords of Trade reported to the King "of what evill Consequence it is, that any of your Subjects should presume to petition your Majesty against Acts of Parliament (which are the Laws they must live under) and call them Grievances."[25] Lord Howard of Effingham, Governor of Virginia, was under no misunderstanding as to the attitude of My Lords in England when he forwarded an address from the Burgesses respecting the additional duty on tobacco:

I hope it is so humble and submissive that the King will not be offended at it, or I should not have suffered it to pass. Their importunity and insistence on their privilege prevailed with me to permit it, but the Council and I are not otherwise concerned in it.[26]

These instances of prerogative peevishness boded ill for a matter-of-fact consideration of questions upon their merits.

Extraneous interruptions added to other difficulties. The frequent

[23] CTB VIII, 1565, 1612-13, 1639.
[24] CSPC (1681-85), No. 1665. See also the statement made by the Council of Barbados when contemplating a petition to the King against the patent officers: "They believe the King will dissent to any law made against the patents, the Assembly is desired to consider that it will be extremely ill-taken by his Majesty if they should go about to restrain his Majesty from the power of gratifying such of his subjects with offices as he shall think have merited them of him" (CSPC [1669-74], No. 1261).
[25] APC Col. I, No. 1100; CO 1/38, No. 31; CSPC (1675-76), No. 1116.
[26] CSPC (1685-88), Nos. 458-59.

reorganizations of the machinery of control tended in themselves to give a spasmodic character to its activities. The journals of the various committees are full of entreaties that show how often new problems arose to demand attention and to force postponement of the matters then being considered. News received from abroad or at home of customs frauds in the colonies would turn attention from more fundamental reforms to drafting orders for plugging a particular loophole in the revenue administration.[27] The death of a king would bring business to a halt, while new commissions were being prepared for colonial officials.[28] The flight of James II, and the war with France that followed, kept the Lords of Trade and Plantations busy for seven months to the exclusion of other matters.[29] The concluding of peace produced almost as many distractions as war; after hostilities ceased in 1713, the business of preparing new treaties occupied more than its share of the Board of Trade's attention, undoubtedly to the detriment of efficiency in colonial administration.[30]

In so far as the various difficulties which confronted the imperial authorities were overcome, they appear to have been surmounted by the acquisition of experience and the establishment of a procedural routine. The first pages of the journal of each committee were characterized by efforts to discover the facts concerning the colonies. Maps and books were ordered; those who had returned from the plantations were summoned to tell the latest news; inquiries were dispatched to the governors concerning all matters, from the physical dimensions of their colony to the welfare of the inhabitants' souls.[31] However irritating it may have been to the colonial governors to receive a new set of inquiries from the Council of 1672, almost before they had had an opportunity to reply to the questions asked by the Council of 1670, historians owe much of their knowledge of the colonies to the spurt of enthusiasm with which each newly appointed committee set about educating itself for its task.[32]

[27] CTB VII, 1180; IX, 1115.
[28] Feb., 1684/5, LTJ V, 25-39 (PHST).
[29] Oct., 1688, to June, 1689, LTJ VI, 185-226 (PHST).
[30] Dickerson, *American Colonial Government*, pp. 61-66.
[31] Andrews, *Committees and Councils*, p. 131.
[32] Andrews discusses the two Councils and gives a list of the heads of business (*ibid.*, pp. 133-51).

When sophistication, and the depressing knowledge of the comparative futility which was to crown most efforts, diminished the zeal with which tasks were undertaken, the salvation of the colonial office lay in a large measure in the systematization of its activities. Uniformity of action thus became a matter of precedent and, as procedural details were reduced to a routine, more careful consideration could be given to matters of policy. The Journals of the Lords of Trade show that in the preparation of commissions and instructions, careful attention was paid to the forms which previous correspondence supplied.[33] Circular letters simplified the task,[34] but tended toward the crystallization of forms; and, as the Customs Commissioners were obliged to explain on one occasion, differing circumstances, both economic and legal, kept the form of instructions prepared for tobacco-producing Virginia and Maryland from serving as a model for New England, which obtained that commodity only by way of trade.[35]

Closely akin to the establishment of a routine was the development of a secretarial staff. The word "staff" is used advisedly; a secretary would not have sufficed. The list of secretaries of the Committees of Trade and Plantations is an imposing one.[36] The intellectual abilities of at least two are attested by their scientific attainments. The reliance which their superiors placed on their ability to prepare such business as was to come before the Committees is shown by the Committees' Journals. The digest of correspondence and other documents are a testimonial to their care.[37] Yet there is one quality which these men lacked. They lacked the long-continued experience which is so essential to the avoidance of errors in procedure. William Blathwayt was acquiring it, as had Sansom, the secretary of the Customs Commissioners, in the subordinate position

---

[33] Bieber, *Lords of Trade*, pp. 81-82.

[34] Government instructions were sent out in that way as early as 1667 (CTB II, 201-2).

[35] CSPC (1685-88), No. 917; CTB VIII, 944.

[36] Dickerson (*American Colonial Government*, p. 77 n.) has a list of the secretaries of the Board of Trade. Smith (*Board of Trade*, pp. 271-72) gives an incomplete list, which includes those for the earlier period. See also Andrews, *Committees and Councils, passim*, especially pp. 93, 98, 107.

[37] Basye, *Lords Commissioners of Trade*, pp. 13-14.

of clerk,[38] but the tradition of long service did not really become established until the next century.

Another method of insuring against errors was to refer proposed actions or drafts of documents to experts in the field most concerned, which in the case of our investigations would, of course, be the customs authorities. The fact that the Farmers of the Customs were obliged in 1669 to request a copy of the draft, "if not perfected," of a letter to the governors, "blaming them for their neglect, and enjoining a strict observance of the laws," indicates that the habit of reference had not yet been established.[39] But in preparing the draft of instructions for a new governor, the advice of the Commissioners was sought, at least as early as 1684, on the matter of trade and navigation.[40] From that time on, the general rule seems to have been to submit drafts to them for inspection, although there were probably always oversights, such as occurred in 1686 when they did not have opportunity to see the instructions proposed for Andros until signed by the King.[41] Sometimes such questions went directly to the Treasury and the Customs Commissioners without passing through the hands of the Lords of Trade, but, generally speaking, the practice was to have all three authorities consider questions. The procedure was commendable in that it was likely to secure greater wisdom of judgment, and was subject to criticism by reason of the likelihood of delays.

The recurrence of the word "delay" may be as wearisome to the reader as the actual fact was to persons having business with the colonial office, but no study of the machinery of control at work can ignore the significance of delays in administering even the least complex provisions of the Navigation Laws. The requirement that the governor take an oath to obey and to enforce the laws of trade would appear to have been merely an administrative detail, but the history of its enforcement affords a ludicrous illustration of executive inertia, as well as a striking example of the labor involved in

---

[38] Jacobsen, Blathwayt, p. 66 et seq. Clarke ("The Board of Trade at Work," Am. Hist. Rev., XVII, 17-43) gives an excellent account of the eighteenth-century establishment and routine.

[39] CSPC (1669-74), No. 6.

[40] CSPC (1681-85), No. 1956; CTB VII, 1409.

[41] CSPC (1685-88), No. 316; CTB VIII, 305, 941.

enforcing so simple a requirement. Although it had been placed upon the statute books in 1660,[42] no organized steps were taken to enforce the requirement until 1668, when pressure was brought to bear upon the government by the Farmers of the English customs, who wished to tighten colonial enforcement so that the enumerated products would come to England and the revenue increase. The governors were ordered to take the oath before the officer appointed by the Farmers and authorized by His Majesty to administer the oath.[43] Apparently no systematic action was taken for some years, although in 1672 the House of Commons requested the King to see that the oaths were taken, and in 1675 the Commissioners made a similar request.[44]

When finally the problem was taken up by the Lords of Trade, they commenced by referring it back to the Customs Commissioners for information as to the oaths already taken, and were told what they should have known without inquiry, that the Commissioners had no information as the matter "does not come within their cognizance." Inquiries were then made of the Secretary of State.[45] At last, on January 21, 1676, Their Lordships considered a draft of an oath for the execution of the Acts of Trade and directed their subordinates to inspect "the Governor's Commission and instructions on that point."[46] Three months (less one day) later, the Attorney General was requested to draw a commission for administering oaths to the governors "to do their utmost that the Acts of Trade and Navigation be punctually observed in their respective Governments."[47] The Attorney General acted promptly. Eight days later the commission he had prepared was approved by the Council, but that body was obliged to refer the matter back to him again, with the request that he also attend to the preparation of the very important item which had been overlooked by the Lords of Trade, the oath itself.[48] In five days more it too was approved by the Privy

[42] 12 Car. II, c. 18, ii.
[43] PC 2/61, p. 182; APC Col. I, No. 828.
[44] CJ IX, 244; CSPC (1675-76), No. 556; Beer, *Old Colonial System*, I, 266.
[45] CO 324/4, pp. 22-25; CSPC (1675-76), Nos. 568, 679, 694, 728, 747; CSPD (1675-76), p. 505.
[46] CSPC (1675-76), No. 790.
[47] *Ibid.*, No. 894.
[48] PC 2/65, p. 203; APC Col. I, No. 1078; CSPC (1675-76), No. 905.

Council.[49] Meanwhile, apparently, those most interested in the whole matter, and the greatest authorities on the problems involved, were not consulted; the Commissioners of the Customs had, on their own initiative, prepared another draft.[50] Conflicts of opinion or other causes delayed further action until October, 1677, when a revised form was approved by the Council.[51] But it was not until January 9, 1678, that a commission was sent to several gentlemen of the Leeward Islands and of Barbados to administer the oath to Governors Stapleton and Atkins, respectively, and that Stapleton was commissioned to administer the oath to the deputy governors under him.[52] An entry of 1694, however, indicates that in the last decade of the century a much simpler method of administering the oath was being followed. It was ordered that Governor Nicholson of Maryland, be sworn in Council "as has been usual."[53] Thereafter, under the new form required by the Act of 1696,[54] the matter became more nearly one of administrative routine.

The episode of the governor's oath is significant, not merely because almost a half century was required to devise a satisfactory method of administering the oath, but because eventually a method was devised. Any real understanding of the old colonial system, of which the Navigation Acts formed an important part, must take into consideration not only that the system was slow to work, but that ultimately it did work. Historians have sometimes tended to forget the truth of the last half of the proposition, because of the revolution which occurred when the government of George III overlooked the truth of the first half and attempted to accomplish too much in too short a time.

[49] PC 2/65, p. 207; APC Col. I, No. 1080; CSPC (1675-76), Nos. 914, 931.
[50] CTB V, 227.
[51] CSPC (1677-80), Nos. 195, 451, 454, 466.
[52] *Ibid.*, Nos. 567, 568.
[53] CSPC (1693-96), No. 926.
[54] 7 & 8 Gul. III, c. 22, iv.

PART FOUR

RESULTS

XVIII

STANDARDS OF JUDGMENT

POSSIBLY the most difficult problem of social engineering is to determine its results. It does not matter whether the investigator is a mercantilist, trying to evaluate his efforts, or a historian, seeking to ascertain the efficacy of governmental regulations. In either case he will encounter much the same difficulties in deciding upon standards of judgment and in finding data with which to apply them.

Seventeenth-century statesmen sought to solve their problem by gazing in that "Globe of glasse, The Ballance of Trade,"[1] when they were called upon to determine which trades were worthy of encouragement and which were injurious. The most highly esteemed were those in which exports exceeded imports, since it was assumed that international balances would be remitted in the much-desired bullion. But merchants interested in trades which failed to pass this test began to challenge its validity. They pointed out the difficulty of procuring adequate statistical data, and showed that the customs receipts afforded no satisfactory criterion, because imported foreign goods paid greater duties than exported native products. They called attention to the complexities of commerce, and argued that goods received from one country in payment for English products might be exchanged in another, to the eventual profit of England. The calculations of values made from the Custom House books were not altogether satisfactory. They often represented arbitrary rather than real values, and they never recorded smuggled merchandise, freight charges received by English shipowners or paid to foreigners, money transferred by bills of exchange, profits gained by fortunate accidents causing goods "to be extraordinarily advanced

[1] The term was Misselden's (*Circle of Commerce*, p. 142).

in sale abroad," or losses resulting from shipwreck, bad markets, confiscation, or seizure.[2]

Efforts to find other tests than the balance of trade were not markedly successful. An attempt was made to use the rate of exchange, but critics soon pointed out that there was often "no settled course of exchange"; drafts on one country might be used to pay bills in another; "a Vintage, a great Mart, or some Publick sale" might cause a seasonal fluctuation, and accidental variations might result from "emergencies of state and war."[3] Some sought to determine the nation's wealth by ascertaining the amount of coin and bullion actually present within the kingdom, but again the facts eluded discovery. As Child explained, "money seems to vulgar observers most plentiful, when there is least occasion for it; and, on the contrary, more scarce, as the occasions for the employment thereof are more numerous and advantageous."[4] Child, for purposes of his own, advocated taking what might be called the long-time view. He claimed that the truest test of a merchant's success was that of the continued prosperity of father and after him of son. Arguing by analogy, he maintained that:

The best and most certain discovery . . . is to be made from the increase or diminution of our trade and shipping in general; for, if our trade and shipping diminish, whatever profit particular men may make, the nation undoubtedly loseth; and, on the contrary, if our trade and shipping increase, how small or low soever the profits are to private men, it is an infallible indication that the nation in general thrives; for I dare affirm, and that categorically in all parts of the whole world, wherever trade is great, and continues so and grows daily more great, and increaseth in shipping, and that for a succession not of a few years, but of ages, that trade must be nationally profitable.[5]

Child's proposal really confessed defeat. No economic statesman could apply a yardstick which required "a succession not of a few

[2] Child, *New Discourse*, pp. 142-52; Cary, *An Essay towards Regulating the Trade*, pp. 84-85; Davenant, *Works*, V, 443-44; Gee, *Trade and Navigation of Great Britain*, p. 117; Malynes, *The Center of the Circle of Commerce*, pp. 58-59, 68-69; Misselden, *Circle of Commerce*, p. 124; Robinson, *England's Safety in Trades Encrease*, p. 50. See also *infra*, pp. 420-23.
[3] Child, *New Discourse*, pp. 151-52; Barbon, *Discourse concerning Coining*, p. 39; see also Cary, *An Essay on the State of England*, pp. 137-40.
[4] Child, *New Discourse*, p. 155.
[5] *Ibid.*, pp. 152-53.

years, but of ages." It did not permit the generations affected by conscious social control to evaluate the schemes to which they were subjected. No mercantilist could rely upon it; he had to act upon faith, using as best he might his defective "Globe of glasse," and let future historians judge his success.

Historians have the advantage of being able to take the long-time view, but they too have been unable to reach a common con-clusion. In passing upon the merits of the Navigation Acts, the views expressed in the fourth edition of one well-known work disagree with those set forth in the second.[6] If we hope to attain any greater certainty in our conclusions, the experience of others warns us to proceed warily and to be most careful in examining our standards of judgment and the data we use.

We must remember that we are studying the Navigation Acts as an experiment in social engineering. They were a means to an end, and we are concerned with the efficacy of the means rather than the value of the end. England had decided upon the path of empire and of power. Our task is merely to determine whether or not the Naviga-tion Acts aided her in reaching that goal. We can dismiss considera-tions of ultimate happiness, as did the "unfeigned and hearty lover of England," when replying to arguments for the "good old ways" of trade:

I shall not now dispute, whether the World might not have been happier by its continuance under Confinement and stak'd down to Agriculture, and those Mechanick Arts that are needful to the Conveniences of Life, (without purveying for our Pride and Sensuality) than it is by launching out into that Measure and degree of Mercantile Commerce which has excited our Lusts as well as fed them, and given Provocation to Vice by yielding Fewel to it. But some Nations having departed from the ancient simplicity of Living contented with Productions of their own Countries and having by Navigation and Trade, raised themselves to Wealth, Power and Increase of inhabitants; it thereupon grew necessary for other Nations to fall into like Methods, lest otherwise they should have been a Prey, as well as a Derision to them whom trade hath rendered Mighty and Opu-lent.[7]

The question at issue is not whether the Navigation Acts em-

[6] Cunningham, *English Industry and Commerce*, II, 210 n.; see also *ibid.*, II, 212-13, 359-61.
[7] "C. K.," *Some Seasonable and Modest Thoughts*, pp. 3-4.

bodied the highest ideals of a perfect world. They did not. Economic discriminations never have promoted international peace. The nations of Europe failed to accept Charles Davenant's doctrine[8] that trade was *"Fere Nature et primi occupaulis* [sic],"* a derelict which "the first approacher" might legally acquire whenever its former possessor neglected it. The attempts of one nation to engross foreign business, to its neighbors' prejudice, continued to serve as a ground for quarrels, and traders who found that their rivals out-traded them were likely "in process of time . . . under pretence of ascertaining the Merchants' Rights [to] blow up a War."[9] The laws were merely in keeping with the temper of the times, with the belligerent attitude which caused one writer to plead for stout men-of-war, "being readier to offend, then to take affronts at Sea";[10] and with Andrew Burrell's adjectives when he advocated that England build new ships (in his own yards) to recover the naval supremacy she was losing to the "insulting Dutch, the Mungrell Dunkirk, the mercilesse Turks; nay, the contemptible Irish, the scorne of men, especially at Sea."[11] Mankind failed to heed the admonition that war "hath seldom been composed with a Peace but the Merchant goeth by the worst, and the People . . . seldom bettered, or the Trade advanced."[12] The choice was not between international harmony and friction, but between open warfare and the economic competition which Andrew Yarranton declared to be "the best and justest way to subdue our Enemies."[13]

Our task is to learn whether the laws helped England to prepare for war and to hold her own in the economic competition which preceded it. We need not worry whether England's legislation led to foreign retaliation, except in so far as the number of English ships was diminished. The existence of England's Navigation Acts undoubtedly embarrassed her diplomats when they complained about foreign laws discriminating against English subjects, but it would be a mistake to ascribe foreign regulations solely to England's ex-

[8] Davenant, *Works*, V, 458.
[9] Yarranton, *England's Improvement*, Epistle to the Reader.
[10] Violet, *Mysteries and Secrets of Trade*, p. 6
[11] *The Humble Remonstrance of Andrewes Burrell, Gent.*, p. 8.
[12] Yarranton, *England's Improvement*, Epistle to the Reader.
[13] *Idem.*

ample.[14] Regulations of commerce were so common that no English model was necessary to teach others the trick; in fact, England may have patterned some of her measures upon those of other countries.[15] No nation of the seventeenth century was restrained by any nicety of commercial ethics from following policies to its advantage. The accepted international version of the Golden Rule was that of the Yankee horse trader: "Do unto the other feller the way he'd like to do unto you—an' do it fust."

Although the chief aim of the Acts was to increase England's naval strength, it is not proper to judge their merits by the success of England's fleets. The fortunes of war were influenced by too many other factors, such as the genius of naval commanders, the credit of the royal exchequer, and the state of national morale. The achievement of victory in a single battle, or even in a war, is an easier accomplishment than the continued maintenance of maritime power. England had often attained glorious victories, only thereafter to rest upon her laurels until necessity awoke her to the fact that her naval strength had declined.

The correlation between the Navigation Acts and England's maritime power must be sought in the development of her merchant marine. Although the day had passed when England's victories at sea were won by converted merchantmen,[16] the navy still required sailors to man its fleets and shipwrights to build and repair them. England's finances did not yet permit her to maintain permanent crews and, if they were to be available for service in times of war, they had to be trained in commercial pursuits during the years of peace. Thus the test of the Acts' success should be sought in the part they played in helping England to foster English shipping, to train English sailors, and to employ English shipwrights.

[14] E.g., when complaining against Swedish discriminations. CO 388/1, entry of 1679; CO 388/6, B66, B67; *infra*, p. 318.

[15] The Aragonese, Portuguese, and Sicilians had all adopted protective measures long before the reign of Richard II (Schanz, *Englische Handelspolitik*, I, 358-59; Heckscher, *Mercantilism*, II, 35-36; Shillington and Chapman, *Commercial Relations of England and Portugal*, p. 50).

[16] Oppenheim, *Administration of the Royal Navy*, p. 342. Corbett (*England in the Mediterranean*, II, 1) dates the transition by the rule of Cromwell. Even as early as 1626, Captain Pennington had complained that fifteen merchantmen were not a match for two regular men-of-war (Clowes, *Royal Navy*, II, 22). Cf., Albion, *Forests and Sea Power*, p. 76.

The measure of success was necessarily relative. As a matter of national defense, it was more important to have the greatest share of the world's ships than a larger number and a smaller proportion. Specifically, it was most important that England keep pace with, if not outstrip, her greatest rival, Holland. As we have seen, the Dutch had established an entrepôt where good merchandise might be purchased cheaply. Dutch shipyards were models of efficiency, and Dutch shipwrights specialized in building large flyboats which, although lightly armed, were easily managed and economically navigated.[17] It is important to discover what aid the laws gave the more heavily armed and staunchly built, but more expensive, English ships in this competition. Did they improve the ratio of England's participation in her own carrying trade? Or was their tendency merely to stifle the trade which the legislators would have controlled?

No answer will be satisfactory which depends primarily upon the opinions of contemporaries. It does not suffice merely to tally their views, to learn that Child, Brewster, and Davenant hailed the laws as beneficial,[18] while Roger Coke and the despondent author of *Britannia Languens* declared them to be harmful.[19] The testimony of all individuals suffers from the fact that it is individual testimony. Statements concerning the prosperity of trade and shipping and the factors upon which it rests are necessarily conclusions the value of which varies directly with their author's breadth of experience, and inversely with his credulity, carelessness, interests, and prejudices. Such opinions are entitled to consideration, but they form only a portion of the evidence.

As far as possible we must rest our conclusions upon contemporary statistics. No individual could attain the objectivity of treatment and the comprehensiveness of view supplied by records based upon actual entries and clearances of merchandise and vessels. The customs officials at the waterside watched the entries day by day as they occurred. Clerks in London tabulated the returns from all parts of

---

[17] For a comparison of the build of English and Dutch shipping, see Barbour, "Dutch and English Merchant Shipping," *Econ. Hist. Rev.*, II, 275 *et seq.*

[18] Child, *New Discourse*, p. xxv, "Concerning the Act of Navigation"; Brewster, *Essays on Trade and Navigation*, pp. 75-109; Davenant, *Works*, I, 16-17.

[19] Coke, *England's Improvements*, "Petitions"; *Britannia Languens*, pp. 64-69.

England, for nearly all her trades.[20] There were also official surveys of shipping and seamen, made at the various ports by persons in a position to know the conditions there. When we must rely upon estimates, those which have been compiled as a result of official or semiofficial investigations are, generally speaking, more reliable than the guesses of pamphleteers, who too often had axes of their own to grind.[21]

Unfortunately, even contemporary statistics have their defects. As mercantile critics pointed out, the basis of computation was not always the same; merchants might connive with officials to minimize the customs, and smugglers might evade them altogether. Moreover, the surviving statistics are more varied than complete. We cannot have them compiled to order. We are dependent upon the chance that some mercantilist collected the material desired, and that an unkind fate did not store it close to a stove and an indolent fireman.[22] But since we cannot have what we might want, we must make the best of what we have. If we search carefully for material and examine it critically, we discover that it is possible to reconstruct a reasonably complete statistical picture and that even the factor of illicit trade is not wholly indeterminable.

Although our interest will center upon the effects of the laws, we must remember that they were not the only factor influencing England's maritime development. War hurts the shipping of belligerents, benefits that of neutrals, and generally diminishes trade. Under all circumstances, shipping depends upon trade, which in turn may rest upon as variable a factor as the public taste. The English fishing industry, for example, definitely suffered because of the change in religious beliefs which permitted many to omit fish from their diet on Fridays. Inventive genius, maritime skill, diplomatic success,

---

[20] Unfortunately the compilations were completed only for certain years in the seventeenth century, as mentioned hereafter. For information concerning the preparation of the records, see *supra*, p. 91; BM Harl. MSS 6836, ff. 60-65; CTB VI, 794; VIII, 857-59; Clark, *Guide to English Commercial Statistics; infra*, pp. 420-23.

[21] The data used by the abler writers were usually more accurate. Davenant based his arguments upon the Custom House books, and such later writers as Sheffield and Chalmers made general use of available statistics. In his *New Discourse* (p. xxxi) Child had no statistics to quote, but referred skeptics to "Mr. Dickins, surveyor of his Majesty's customs."

[22] There is reason to suspect that some of the early Treasury Papers were thus lost (CTP [1557-1696], p. xviii).

national self-confidence, individual character, and geographic conditions—all aided or hindered commercial success. So did great pestilences or famines, and the more prosaic but none-the-less important matters of freight rates, insurance conditions, the availability of credit, and the soundness of the currency.

The multiplicity of factors involved makes it difficult to demonstrate the influence of the Acts, but does not render it impossible. Our first task is to establish a positive correlation between the laws and maritime prosperity whenever we can. In case we cannot, we should be able to show that some other, more powerful factor intervened. Since other causes may lead to maritime prosperity in any particular instance, we must examine the condition of shipping under as many different circumstances as possible. The natural diversity of commercial conditions will then enable us at one time or another to observe the effectiveness of the Acts in the absence of most of the other factors, and we can estimate the allowance to be made for such constant factors as the geographic location of the British Isles, by studying their effect upon shipping when the laws were not in force.

Such reliance upon the comparative method requires that we broaden the scope of our inquiry. The microscopic examination of conditions from 1660 to 1696, which proved so useful in studying administrative problems, will no longer suffice. We must take such a panoramic view of England's maritime history as will disclose not only the position of shipping under the laws, but also the conditions which preceded their enactment and those which followed their repeal. We can best begin by analyzing the commerce which gave employment to English shipping, continent by continent and trade by trade. Thereafter we may attempt to trace the development of English navigation throughout the centuries and to formulate hypotheses about what might have happened if the laws had never been enacted.

XIX

ASIA, AFRICA, AND AMERICA

THE "far trades" to Asia, Africa, and America were the special concern of the Navigation Acts. Their longer voyages were reserved exclusively for English vessels, but during the life of the laws only the plantation trade with America was destined to be a material factor in developing English navigation.

There is little evidence of any significant relationship between the East India trade, the Navigation Acts, and the development of English shipping. Although it had experimented at different times with the use of Dutch-built ships, the East India Company had already found English-built vessels more satisfactory,[1] as had the Dutch, at least upon one occasion.[2] The chief advantage gained by the company came from the clause requiring all Asian products to be imported directly from ports south and east of the Cape of Good Hope, since it gave the company a protection, which its charter did not provide, against the importation of East India goods from Europe.[3] Yet that advantage must not be overstressed since the English reëxported a large part of most of the East India commodities in which they dealt.[4] In the case of spices, which constituted the

[1] CSPC (1625-29), Nos. 231, 241, 262; *Cal. Ct. Min. East India Co.* (1640-43), pp. 281, 282-83, 292, 297; (1644-49), p. 384; (1650-54), pp. 66, 140; (1660-63), pp. 115-16; (1668-70), pp. 83, 85, 89-90, 110.

[2] CSPC (1513-1616), No. 258. It appears, however, that the native merchants preferred Dutch vessels, "findeing there much better accomodacion and noe less safety" (*English Factories in India* [1642-45], p. 142; [1646-50], pp. 42, 205).

[3] The company's charter gave a monopoly of all trade by Englishmen beyond the Cape of Good Hope, but not of all East India commodities (Birdwood, *Register of Letters*, p. 174). However, owing to a continuously flooded pepper market, a proclamation was issued in Nov., 1609, prohibiting the importation of pepper except by the company, and thereby preventing in effect the indirect importation of that commodity (T & SP No. 1087). The complete text of the proclamation may be found in Corney, *Voyage of Sir Henry Middleton*, Appendix XV.

[4] The coarse spice, pepper, was exported from England in large quantities: nine-tenths of that imported by the company in 1624 (CSPC [1622-24], No. 540), and

principal exception, the English had to rely upon importations from Holland, the Navigation Acts to the contrary notwithstanding. The Dutch, rather than the English, controlled the Spice Islands. Under the Commonwealth most of the importations were probably smuggled,[5] but, beginning in 1662, a series of dispensations by King or Parliament legitimatized a spice trade with Holland.[6]

Trade with India was destined to be of great importance to English shipping after the repeal of the laws in 1850, especially after the Suez Canal was completed,[7] but it played a comparatively unimportant part from 1660 to 1850. Although the size and number of the ships increased, the tonnage entered in 1719 was only 1.5 percent of the total, in 1771 only 2.1 percent, and in 1785 only 2.3 percent.[8]

Similarly, the Acts appear to have had no great effect upon the trade with Africa. Isolated individuals and companies of merchants had previously ventured to its coasts, and the English-built ships proved to be so well adapted to the trade that even the Portuguese sought to use them there.[9] The clause of the Acts prohibiting the indirect importation of African products had in effect been anticipated in 1630, in the charter given to "The Company of Merchants Trading to Guinea," which forbade the importation of African prod-

---

£180,000 of the £208,000 worth imported in 1627 (Khan, *East India Trade*, p. 51). Of the other commodities, "calicoes" in particular were exported in large quantities (*English Factories in India* [1624-29], p. xxxvi). The company reported in 1624 that it reëxported three-fourths of all its East India goods (CSPC [1622-24], No. 439).

[5] The commodities seized in sixty-one of the seventy-two seizures of East India goods imported contrary to the Navigation Act in the years 1652, 1653, 1655, 1656, and 1659 (Exchequer, KR Memo. Rolls) were fine spices, and 76 percent of all the cases involved ships coming from the Dutch Netherlands.

[6] T & SP No. 3374; *Cal. Ct. Min. East India Co.* (1660-63), pp. 271, 284; 6 & 7 Gul. & Mar., c. 7, ii.

[7] Lindsay, *Merchant Shipping*, IV, 426-46, 643.

[8] For 1719, CO 390/5, No. 45; for 1771 and 1785, BT 6/185. In value, East India goods formed a much larger proportion of all imports, being 7.6 percent of all imports in 1698, 10.2 percent in 1719, and 14.6 percent in 1771 (Whitworth, *State of Trade*, pp. 1, 22, 75).

[9] Rymer, *Foedera*, orig. ed. XX, 522-27, cited in *Cambridge History of the British Empire*, I, 230. For information on these early ventures, see *Cambridge History of the British Empire*, I, 41-50, 65, 73, 437-40; Macpherson, *Annals of Commerce*, II, 72, 80, 115, 153, 189, 193, 200, 292, 369-70, 420; Scott, *Joint-Stock Companies*, II, 1-16; Zook, *Company of Royal Adventurers Trading into Africa*, pp. 1-7.

ucts except by the patentees.[10] The factors governing commerce were England's relations with the Barbary pirates; her occupation of Tangier; the conflicts between the interlopers and the chartered companies; and the success of the slave trade, which gave rise to a great triangular traffic from England to Africa, to America, and back again to England, which was far more important than the direct trade to and from Africa.[11] Although only 16 percent of the £629,904 profit realized by the Royal African Company between 1697 and 1708 came directly from Africa, the trade was one to delight mercantilists, since England's exports to Africa greatly exceeded her imports of beeswax, goatskins, gums, dates, "Estredg ffeathers," almonds, elephants' teeth, "Guiny Graines," redwood, senna, gold bullion, and other African products.[12] Similarly, the tonnage clearing for Africa was from two and one-half to ten times greater than that entering from it, but throughout the seventeenth and eighteenth centuries even the outward shipping formed only a small fraction of England's total.[13]

The rules governing commerce in the Americas varied with the political status of the area involved, but only those concerning the trade of the English colonies with the mother country need long detain us. Goods coming to England from other parts of America were subject to much the same regulations as those coming from Asia and Africa, the principal exceptions being granted in favor of goods brought from the Spanish and Portuguese colonies by way of Spain and Portugal; but until after the American Revolution the trade was negligible. Likewise trade between the plantations of the

[10] Macpherson, *Annals of Commerce*, II, 369-70; Scott, *Joint-Stock Companies*, II, 14. This provision may have lapsed, as the company became practically inactive in six or seven years.

[11] See Davenant, *Works*, II, 37-39; V, 73-343; *Cambridge History of the British Empire*, I, 440-59; Macpherson, *Annals of Commerce*, II, 508, 517, 568-69; Routh, *Tangier*, pp. 18-21, 55, 82, 147-52; Scott, *Joint-Stock Companies*, I, 362; II, 16-35; Zook, *Company of Royal Adventurers Trading into Africa, passim*.

[12] Davenant, *Works*, V, 302. The exports listed in BM Add MSS 36785, which indicate that goods exported to Africa were 3.5 times in value those imported from it in 1663, and 7 times those imported in 1669.

[13] Ships leaving for Africa comprised 1.4 percent of English tonnage outwards in 1718, 0.8 percent in 1719, and 1.7 percent in 1785 (CO 390/5, No. 45; BT 6/185). The tonnage clearing for Africa was 2.4 times greater than that entering in 1719 and 2.2 times greater in 1785 (CO 390/5, No. 45; BT 6/185).

various colonial powers is only of incidental importance as far as the Navigation Acts are concerned. As compared with the strict regulations of all the other mother countries except the Dutch, the English laws were quite liberal until 1733, permitting English vessels to trade freely in all but European imports and enumerated exports.[14] Although the Molasses Act of that year was designed to limit the trade of the continental colonies with the foreign West Indies, we need not here attempt to determine whether its provisions were enforced. They were not an essential part of the Acts of Trade, and the evidence clearly shows that both officials and merchants distinguished between them and other parts of the mercantile code.[15]

The main concern of Parliament was to reserve the plantation trade for English shipping, to give England a monopoly of certain colonial products, and to help her in retaining the colonial market. In discussing the parliamentary efforts it is unnecessary for our present purposes to show how the laws affected colonial social and economic development, interesting and important as the study might be.[16] The laws were English measures designed for English ends, and we should concentrate our attention upon determining whether they contributed to England's commercial and maritime development. The point is one which has long been debated by historians. Some argue that the laws were superfluous because England would have received the colonial trade in any case, and others contend that they were ineffectual because not enforced.[17]

[14] For accounts of the colonial regulations of the European powers and the evasions of them, see Haring, *Trade and Navigation between Spain and the Indies;* Mims, *Colbert's West India Policy;* Pares, *War and Trade in the West Indies;* Westergaard, *Danish West Indies.* The English were pledged by treaty to refrain from violating the trading regulations of France and of Spain. Although the attention of the governors was called to the former obligation, no mention was made of the latter (Andrews, Introduction to Towle, *Records of the Vice-Admiralty Court of Rhode Island,* p. 58; Labaree, *Royal Instructions,* II, 717-19, 723; Pitman, *The Development of the British West Indies,* pp. 223, 280-85).

[15] 6 Geo. II, c. 13; 26 Geo. II, c. 32; 4 Geo. III, c. 15; *Letter Book of John Watts,* p. 212; Ashley, *Surveys, Historic and Economic,* p. 337; Harrington, *The New York Merchant,* p. 319; Pitman, *The Development of the British West Indies,* pp. 271-333; Schlesinger, *The Colonial Merchants,* pp. 42-49; Wiener, "Rhode Island Merchants and the Sugar Act," *New Eng. Quar.,* III, 471.

[16] The shipping and trade statistics for such studies are now being prepared in film-book form by a W.P.A. project under the writer's direction. Also an essay on the subject is included in *The Era of the American Revolution.*

[17] Ashley (*Surveys, Historic and Economic,* pp. 336-60) opposed the earlier view

The theory that the colonies would have traded with England in the absence of legislation, rests for the most part upon the assumption that the American Revolution caused no particular change in the course of trade.[18] But the conclusion would not follow from the premise, even if the assumption were true. The Britain of 1783 was not the England of 1660. At the earlier date, English interest rates were notoriously high; credit and long-term accommodations were most readily available in Holland.[19] Evidence from both English and colonial sources shows that during the seventeenth century manufactured goods could be obtained for a third less in Holland, and an even greater saving could be made by freighting Dutch vessels.[20] One hundred years later Dutch financiers had lost their preëminence; Britain had a more flourishing marine and was fast becoming the manufacturing center of Europe.[21] Moreover, one must not disregard the possibility that sixscore years of regulation may have been responsible for developing commercial habits, business connections, and credit relations which rendered the colonies dependent upon England and minimized the likelihood of any sudden change.

According to laissez-faire doctrines, trade, if let alone, will follow the channels of least resistance and most profit. When the colonies

that the laws were disregarded by contending that the colonists had no reason to violate them. Later writers have been more inclined to believe that the Acts were effective.

[18] The early writers stressed the need of the Americans for English manufactures, and the ability of the England of their day to provide general cargoes and to give long credits (Sheffield, *Observations,* pp. 248-52; Ashley, *Surveys, Historic and Economic,* pp. 316-17, 354-56).

[19] In 1696 the Customs Commissioners stated that the bond of the East India Company was 20 percent worse than ready money (CTB XI, 63), and the Treasury was asked to give a discount of 26 or 27.5 percent on money advanced (CTB XI, 359). Sir Josiah Child stated ("A Small Treatise against Usury," p. 204) that money would receive 10 percent interest, and explained (*A Short Reply to a Treatise, Entitled Interest of Money Mistaken,* p. 22) that the lower rate of interest in Holland was the reason that the Dutch could buy Barbados sugars in London, pay the second freight and charges to Holland, and still prosper more than the English sugar brokers.

[20] Beer, *Origins,* pp. 209, 389, 392. *The Advocate* (p. 4) said in 1651 that the Dutch could undersell the English "as much percent in all places, and upon all Trades; yea, sometimes in our own Commodities." For hardships suffered by the colonists because of lack of English shipping, see Kaye, *English Colonial Administration under Lord Clarendon,* pp. 15-17, 147.

[21] Cunningham, *English Industry and Commerce,* II, 673-74.

were forming their commercial habits, these channels did not lead
to England. The early sugar plantations in the English West Indies
had close connections with Holland. They were said to have been
started by Dutch capital.[22] Certainly Dutch ships were doing a
thriving business there, until the Navigation Acts restrained their
activities.[23] The Dutch were also ready and willing to act as dis-
tributors of tobacco from the continental colonies, and the business
connections they made in the Chesapeake between 1640 and 1664
show that they were not unwelcome there.[24] European manufactures
found a good market in the colonies, whether peddled by Dutch
vessels before 1664 or imported by way of England thereafter.[25]

The invalidity of the argument that England was a natural
entrepôt, through which America's trade with Europe would pass
in any event, is easily shown. After independence freed the United
States from mercantile restrictions, England's reëxport trade in
tobacco materially declined, despite earnest efforts to retain it.[26]
Thanks to former commercial connections, English factors temporarily continued to supply Virginia and Maryland with European
manufactures, but the northern states soon began to throw off the
English yoke and to make their continental purchases directly in
Europe.[27] There naturally were certain mixed-cargo shipments as-
sembled in England, but the statistics of American imports after

[22] Harlow, *Barbados*, pp. 37-43, 65-68, 84-93.
[23] Both Sir George Ayscue and Venables found and seized Dutch ships trading
with the English West Indies (Crump, *Colonial Admiralty Jurisdiction*, pp. 94-95).
The Advocate (p. 6) stated in 1651, "in our Plantations they had three, if not four
Sail of Ship, for our one." See also Higham, *Development of the Leeward Islands*,
pp. 37, 143; Newton, *Colonising Activities*, pp. 261-62; *supra*, n. 22.
[24] *Maryland Archives*, XLIX, 299, 323-24, 341-42, 388, 391-93; NYCD XIV, 127;
Brodhead, *History of the State of New York*, I, 725, 735; II, 13; Andrews, *The
Colonial Period*, II, 263-64; Wertenbaker, *Planters of Colonial Virginia*, pp. 68-69.
[25] For values of European goods shipped via England, see *infra*, p. 266, n. 111.
[26] Great Britain, *Report on Trade with the United States;* Sheffield, *Observations*,
pp. 101-3; Gray, *History of Agriculture in the Southern United States*, II, 600, 760.
Of course other factors such as the Napoleonic Wars contributed to the British loss,
but their chief effect was probably to help in breaking old commercial habits. If the
natural entrepôt theory is to be maintained, Britain should have regained her position after peace was restored.
[27] The Chesapeake region received about one-half of all the non-British goods imported by the United States from England in 1789, whereas in 1773 by far the
greater share of such goods had gone to the northern states and only about one-
seventh to the Chesapeake (Customs 17/12; Customs 3/73).

1790 refute the theory that England was a natural entrepôt for America, and they make it clear that for the most part the goods obtained in England were those produced there, and that the great bulk of European goods came direct from the country of production.[28]

The laws requiring colonial trade to pass through England were a real burden, much greater than a casual reading of the statutes would indicate.[29] Administrative regulations required that vessels land their entire cargo when in England.[30] Although most, if not all, of the duty was returned on goods that were reëxported,[31] the entire amount was due upon importation. Consequently, the colonists either had to have more ready cash than frontiersmen are accustomed to possess, or they had to have English factors ready and able to give bond for the payment.[32] There were also fees to waiters, searchers, collectors, and comptrollers; and wharfage, lighterage, and porterage charges, to say nothing of lighthouse and other dues.[33] According to a statement rendered to some Maryland planters, factorage and other charges amounted to 32 percent of the original value of a shipment of tobacco—more than the freight charges across the Atlantic.[34] In 1774 it cost the ship "Friendship" almost 5 percent of the freight she had earned carrying 1,759 quarters of wheat from

[28] U. S. Congress, *American State Papers*, class 4, I (1790), 64-102; II (1821), 529-53; Seybert, *Statistical Annals*, pp. 172-222; *infra*, p. 266, n. 112.

[29] Exceptions must be made, of course, for articles like indigo which were given bounties, and for those like sugar which (in the eighteenth century at least) found their best market within the British Empire (*infra*, p. 263).

[30] Yarmouth Letter Book, pp. 71-73, (MS in the London Custom House).

[31] After 9 Geo. I, c. 21, vi, the entire duty on tobacco was repaid on exportation if the necessary conditions were complied with; before then all but one-half penny was returned (12 Car. II, c. 4).

[32] There was not enough money in Bristol to pay the duty on the tobacco imported there in 1662 (CTB I, 392). Lindsay (*Merchant Shipping*, II, 410) quotes McCulloch about the difficulty in finding sureties for bonds, and tells (*ibid.*, II, 411) of Walpole's attempts to establish a bonded warehouse and thus to avoid the necessity of paying the duties.

[33] Lacy (*Observations on the Nature, Use and Trade of Tobacco*, p. 2) noted with apparent approval that the tobacco trade led to the payment to Englishmen of about 15s. per hogshead for "Custom-house Fees, Cooperage, Lighterage, Wharfage, Porterage, Cartage, Warehouse Rent, Brokerage, and other incident Charges." Langham (*The Nett Duties and Drawbacks*) describes the many fees which might be levied. Lindsay (*Merchant Shipping*, II, 412-13) indicates that a considerable amount of pilfering occurred when vessels were discharged, at least in the port of London.

[34] For 1786, Hill Papers, Shipping Accounts, 1737 to 1793 (Md. HS).

Maryland, to enter and clear at Bristol for pilotage, mayor's dues, reporting and clearing at the custom house, lights, anchorage and moorage, surveyors, etc., to say nothing of an additional 2-percent commission for the English factor.[35] Moreover, there was the very important element of delay. Favorable winds might shift when a vessel stopped in compliance with the laws, and leave it stranded in port. As the Irish pointed out, when complaining because tobacco destined for Ireland had to be shipped via England, the duty assessed was only one of many objections to the requirement.[36]

The resistance which the Acts encountered provides additional evidence that they were directing commercial activities into new channels. In addition to the protests from Ireland, long and vigorous complaints came from many sources: from the West Indies, as well as the American continent; and from governors like Berkeley in Virginia, noted for loyalty to the crown, as well as from colonial assemblies.[37] Smuggling itself affords further proof of the point. Why should anyone go to the trouble of carrying on an illicit trade, attended by risk and the obvious inconveniences imposed by stealth

[35] Guttridge, *The American Correspondence of a Bristol Merchant, 1766-1776,* pp. 36-37. Gray (*History of Agriculture in the Southern United States,* I, 424-45) cites an instance in which the charges for the sale of a hogshead of tobacco exceeded the selling price and left the planter owing the factor on the transaction. It was estimated in 1720 that English factors alone received from £12,500 to £15,000 (Nettels, *Money Supply of the American Colonies,* p. 51). In 1776 a revolutionary agitator asserted Virginia's commercial losses arising from dependence upon Great Britain to be £5,987,500 currency. See Schlesinger, *The Colonial Merchants,* pp. 596-602.

[36] CSPC (1685-88), Nos. 567, 599, 638. The English Commissioners' reply did not deny that the cost of unloading in England might be ½d. a pound (*ibid.,* Nos. 613, 670), and eighteenth-century figures indicate that it was fully that much (Gray, *History of Agriculture in the Southern United States,* I, 224).

[37] From Barbados: PC 2/65, pp. 499-500; CSPC (1675-76), Nos. 707, 862, 973; (1689-92), No. 1923; Collins, "Studies in the Colonial Policy of England," Am. Hist. Assoc. *Annual Report,* 1900, I, 142-46, 149. From St. Kitts: CSPC (1677-80), No. 1441. From North Carolina: *North Carolina Colonial Records,* V, 146; VI, 1022. From Virginia: CSPC (1675-76), No. 923; *Va. Mag. Hist.,* II, 170; III, 38; Bruce, *Economic History of Virginia,* I, 401-7; Wertenbaker, *Planters of Colonial Virginia,* pp. 94-96; Beer, *Old Colonial System,* II, 112-14; Bassett, "Virginia Planter," Am. Hist. Assoc. *Annual Report,* 1901, I, 574. From Maryland: CSPC (1677-80), No. 633; Morriss, *Colonial Trade of Maryland,* p. 127. From Pennsylvania: *Pennsylvania Archives,* 1st series, I, 149-50. From New York: NYCD I, 61; IV, 789. From Massachusetts: CSPC (1677-80), pp. 269, 530; *Am. Antiq. Soc. Trans. and Col.,* III, 130; *Mass. Col. Soc. Trans.,* XIX, 168-70, 379-80; Johnson, "Mercantilism in the Massachusetts-Bay," *New Eng. Quar.,* I, 375-77.

and concealment, unless it offered greater profits than the commerce duly authorized by law?

The task of showing that the rules prescribed by the Navigation Acts ran counter to natural tendencies, however, is easy, compared to that of proving that they were enforced. There is no simple formula by which to measure illicit trade. Smugglers' correspondence, account books, or ships' logs may conclusively establish the existence of smuggling, but they do not establish its extent. Similar documents show that legitimate trade continued.[38] It does not suffice to compare the number of both types, since we have no guarantee that they survived in the right proportions.[39] Administrative accounts of riotous interference with the officials suggest a complete breakdown of authority—until we note that instances occurred when conditions were abnormal, and that there were many more cases of enforcement without violence.[40] Nor do court records afford much

[38] *Commerce of Rhode Island*, MHSC, 7th series, IX; Guttridge, *American Correspondence of a Bristol Merchant, 1766-1776*; Hill Papers, Shipping Accounts, 1737 to 1793 (Md. HS); Wendell Family Papers, 1682-1794 (NYPL); Letter Book of Thomas Moffatt of Boston, 1715-16 (NYPL); De Peyster Papers, 1695-1710 (NYHS); Jacobus Van Cortlandt Shipping Book, 1699-1702 (NYHS); *Letter Book of John Watts, 1762-1765*; *Letters and Diary of John Rowe*, 1759-62, 1764-79; *The Letter Book of James Browne*, 1735-1738. See also Harrington, *The New York Merchant, passim*, especially pp. 42-44, 197-200, 350; Weeden, *Economic and Social History of New England, passim*.

[39] Weeden cites various examples of fraud as showing how the laws were flouted (*Economic and Social History of New England*, II, 607-36, 658), while Ashley marvels at the comparatively small number of illicit transactions, their petty nature, and the caution exhibited to avoid detection (*Surveys, Historic and Economic*, pp. 341-42).

[40] For examples of customs riots or violence in the colonies, see Ashe, *History of North Carolina*, I, 117 (1677); *New Hampshire Hist. Soc. Col.*, VIII, 159-60 (1683); Guttridge, *The Colonial Policy of William III*, pp. 129, 169-70 (1699); Andrews, *Guide*, II, 30 (1729); Hutchinson, *Diary and Letters*, I, 67 (1765); *Conn. Hist. Soc. Col.*, XIX, 181-82 (1769); *Mass. Hist. Soc. Col.*, 4th series, X, 611-17 (1769); *Rhode Island Colonial Records*, VI, 593-96 (1769); *New Jersey Documents*, X, 205-6 (1770); *Maryland Hist. Mag.*, II, 335-38. See also *infra*, p. 267.

For discussions of illicit trade in general the following bibliography is introductory rather than complete. Useful secondary accounts of smuggling and smuggling methods in the colonies are to be found in Andrews, Introduction to Towle, *Records of the Vice-Admiralty Court of Rhode Island*, pp. 43-44, 48-54; Beer, *British Colonial Policy, 1754-1765*, pp. 228-48, and *Old Colonial System*, II, 160-62, 255-61; Guttridge, *op. cit.*, pp. 156-68; Harrington, *The New York Merchant*, pp. 197-200, 222, 250-75; Higham, *Development of the Leeward Islands*, pp. 195-210; Johnson, "Commercial Legislation of England," *Econ. Jour.*, X, 96-103; McClellan, *Smuggling in the American Colonies, passim;* Morriss, *Colonial Trade of Maryland*, pp. 116-22; Pitman, *The Development of the British West Indies*, pp. 190, 193-94, 206-15, 271-334;

aid. A large number of seizures might merely suggest the many offenses which occurred and remained undetected, or it might demonstrate effective enforcement.

In utilizing accounts of frauds it is important to remember that many concerned marginal cases involving highly debatable points of law. Trade with Jersey, the importation of wines from the Canaries, and the direct exportation of tobacco to Ireland, unlike the clearly prohibited trade with Holland and France, were all possibly permissible activities until the imperial authorities ultimately decided against them. Evidence that the colonists engaged in such activities is fully as much an indication that they were attempting to conform as it is that they were deliberately violating the law. Moreover, in drawing conclusions about illicit trade we must always remember that the laws were tricky.[41] The fact that the colonists were openly shipping to Europe articles on the enumerated list does not necessarily prove fraud. The restrictions applied only to the enumerated commodities grown in the English colonies and similar articles of foreign origin could be carried anywhere.[42]

Great care must be exercised in evaluating the statements of individuals. Nearly all had some personal ax to grind. Governors who were charged with enforcing the laws tended to find that they were obeyed,[43] and professional investigators, whose advancement

---

Root, *Relations of Pennsylvania with the British Government*, pp. 61-76; Weeden, *Economic and Social History of New England*, I, 239-41; II, 658-63, 762. See also *supra*, pp. 161-227. Interesting original sources in addition to those cited *supra*, n. 38, include Labaree, *Royal Instructions*, II, 886-88, 898-900; NYCD, III, 43; IV, 791-93; NYHS *Col.*, IX, 27, 102, 195-96, 259; X, 133-34, 370-72; *North Carolina Colonial Records*, I, 244-46, 265, 439-42; *Pennsylvania Archives*, 1st series, I, 131-32; *Pennsylvania Hist. Soc. Memoirs*, IX, 24, 31-32; *South Carolina Hist. Soc. Col.*, I, 195-96, 203-8; "Letters of Alexander Spotswood," *Virginia Historical Society Collections*, n.s., I, 29-30, 108; Toppan and Goodrick, *Randolph, passim*.

[41] Governor Glen of South Carolina, when commenting on his trade instructions, said that he first undertook to study the Acts, "and I was soon convinced that this Task . . . would prove a very tedious one for those laws are far from being so clear as he that runs may read them, on the contrary, they are dark and difficult, they have been made at different times, and Penned by different Persons, who seem not to have had the same view of things, and when their sense may have been the same, they have expressed it in a very different words" (cited in Labaree, *Royal Instructions*, II, 885-86).

[42] *Infra*, p. 397.

[43] McClellan, *Smuggling in the American Colonies*, p. 84; Beer, *British Colonial Policy, 1754-1765*, pp. 234-46. There were, of course, exceptions, such as Colden in

might depend upon the amount of fraud reported, managed to find conditions deplorable. It is not safe to reject the evidence of the former and to discount that of the latter, arguing that where there is smoke there must be some fire. Investigators who wish to call attention to themselves may raise dense clouds of smoke from what in fact are merely dying embers.

The point should be borne in mind when considering the voluminous correspondence of Edward Randolph, whose indefatigable zeal and widespread experience would otherwise warrant respectful attention for his views. Randolph undoubtedly realized that superiors have to be reminded of their subordinates' abilities. His seventeen voyages across the Atlantic[44] may not have been required by His Majesty's service so much as by Randolph's desire that the authorities in London should keep him in mind. When not present in person, his letters served as reminders of his worth. Usually they suggested that Randolph was the sole reliance of the Crown, and sometimes they were obviously unfair to his fellow officials. When he himself was making seizures in New England, Randolph was convinced that juries would never convict, no matter how clear the evidence.[45] Yet when his successor compounded with an offender to avoid the risks of a trial, Randolph suspected his good faith in compounding, and was certain that the jury would have condemned the merchandise.[46] His continual complaints apparently wearied even his superiors, and at the end of his life he wrote rather pitifully to his friend, Blathwayt, "I have no friend but God and you to stand by me."[47]

Like many of his contemporaries, Randolph was ready to accept tales of fraud upon hearsay evidence. While confined in the "nasty Gaol" of Boston, following the uprising in 1689, he wrote emphatic accounts of the illicit trade which he declared was then being car-

New York (NYHS Col. X, 370) and Glen in South Carolina (Labaree, *Royal Instructions*, II, 887, 892). But most of those who acknowledged the existence of illicit trade reported what they were doing to overcome it ("Letters of Alexander Spotswood," *Virginia Historical Society Collections*, n.s., I, 87; Arnold, *History of Rhode Island*, I, 494), or that another colony was at fault (*North Carolina Colonial Records*, V, 590).
[44] Toppan, *Randolph*, II, 181.
[45] Goodrick, *Randolph*, VI, 85, 105, 172.
[46] *Ibid.*, VII, 422.
[47] *Ibid.*, VII, 641.

ried on at the waterfront.[48] He lacked the good sense to overlook merely technical offenses, as when he seized a ship as foreign-built because its rigging and sails were of foreign manufacture.[49] He never seemed to realize that, on close questions of law, a mercantile community might be just as honest in adopting an interpretation which favored it as he was in adopting one conducive to his own advantage. Moreover, his views were obviously colored by self-interest. One of his grievances against juries which brought in verdicts of acquittal was that he lost a share in the forfeiture of the goods he had seized.[50] When seizures were made by officers of the navy, he did not rejoice that others were doing their bit for more effective enforcement. He complained that he had "lost £500 by not having liberty to prosecute according to my office."[51]

The fact is that individual testimony affords an unreliable guide to the amount of smuggling. In so far as they were not mere conjecture the statements of contemporaries had to be based upon their own, necessarily limited, experience, whether they were planters, merchants, administrators, or smugglers. Since we must rely upon conjecture, it seems wisest to form our own. Those of the time vary too radically. In 1676 and 1677 the London mercers and silkweavers charged New England with depriving the King of £60,000 a year,[52] but Governor Bradstreet declared that "on the strictest inquiry it is found that there has never been £5,000 irregularly traded,"[53] and at about the same time Petty noted that the total value of the commodities which New England imported from England was only £40,000 or £50,000 yearly.[54]

Circumstantial evidence furnishes the best basis for forming our own estimates of the amount of illicit trade. The objections raised against the use of contemporary testimony with respect to the volume of smuggling do not apply with respect to accounts of its nature. Individuals who could not supply quantitative figures could give

[48] Toppan, *Randolph*, IV, 270; V, 23-24; Goodrick, *Randolph*, VI, 302-32.
[49] CO 1/50, No. 105; Toppan, *Randolph*, III, 345.
[50] Toppan, *Randolph*, III, 212.
[51] *Ibid.*, I, 295.
[52] Andrews, *Colonial Self-Government*, p. 259.
[53] Hart, *Commonwealth History of Massachusetts*, I, 457.
[54] *The Petty Papers*, II, 107.

qualitative descriptions which help us greatly when considered in connection with the commercial situation as a whole. Moreover, when we proceed on this basis we can even find statistical data with which to work. Although we obviously have no statistics of smuggling itself, we can do much by drawing conclusions from the figures of legal trade. Despite their defects for other purposes,[55] the Inspector General's Accounts furnish a reasonably accurate statement of the quantity of duty-paid goods passing through England. Customs officers, willing as they might have been to issue false certificates of landing European goods or to engage in other fraudulent activities, would not report a greater quantity of merchandise for which they had to render an accounting than that which had actually passed through their hands and paid duty. The English figures may not tell the whole truth, or even nothing but the truth, but they furnish a basic stratum of truth upon which to rely.

The circumstantial approach, however, encounters complications of its own. The difficulty is to prevent our study of the law's enforcement from becoming unduly confused by quarrels over charter rights in Massachusetts and elsewhere, by resistance to the royal timber policy in New England, by opposition to the Bermuda Company's rules in Bermuda, by the unpopularity of the 4.5-percent duties in Barbados and the Leeward Islands, by hostility to the Assiento in Jamaica, by opposition to the Royal African Company monopoly in the slave colonies generally, and by the activities of pirates almost everywhere, not to mention the revolutions, murders, and innumerable personal or political quarrels and other episodes which enlivened colonial history.[56]

In Massachusetts, for example, the efforts of the Puritan leaders to maintain their charter rights have caused their opposition to the

[55] The values given in the Inspector General's Accounts were calculated arbitrarily for customs purposes, on the values of 1696, and consequently do not necessarily show the real values for any subsequent period. See *infra*, pp. 422-23.

[56] Palfrey, *Compendious History of New England*, III, 364-94; IV, 411-12; Scott, *Joint-Stock Companies*, I, 311; Pitman, *The Development of the British West Indies*, pp. 79-81, 170-71, 175-76, 251; Lipson, *Economic History*, II, 355; Beer, *Old Colonial System*, I, 121-27. It is important to remember how many of the most flagrant instances of violent resistance (in addition to that of Puritan Massachusetts) occurred in times of political upheaval, and may have been a manifestation of general unrest rather than of confirmed opposition to the laws (*supra*, p. 247, n. 40).

laws to be greatly overemphasized. Like the Earl of Derby in the Isle of Man, they were claiming full executive, legislative, and judicial powers by virtue of a charter grant.[57] They feared that if they were too ready to accept the royal collector of customs, to allow appeals in matters of navigation offenses, or to acknowledge the local authority of English laws unless duly confirmed or acknowledged by their own General Court, unfortunate precedents might be established that would impair the autonomy which they claimed under their charter. They knew that the Navigation Acts were dear to the English,[58] and the Puritan government did much more to enforce them than it has received credit for, although Puritan traders, like many other traders, violated the laws when they thought it would be profitable. The governor in Massachusetts did what many governors elsewhere had never done. He took the oath to enforce the Acts,[59] and as early as 1664 Massachusetts exacted bonds from ships lading there.[60] The constables were ordered to assist Randolph, and actually did so.[61] Randolph's own brother reported that his deputies, who encountered resistance in searching a sloop, were aided by a constable who "had his staff taken out of his hands; [and] his head broke therewith."[62] And the naval office, to which Randolph objected so vehemently, does not appear to have been a device to frustrate the law, but rather a means of enforcing it in a way consistent with the charter claims of the colony.[63] The attitude of the Massachusetts General Court clearly appears in 1677. It was willing to, and did, order that the Acts of Navigation be observed under penalty of forfeiture, and that the governor and other officers "be required to see to the strict observance of the said acts." At the same session, the same body showed its attitude concerning charter

[57] For the situation in the Isle of Man, see *supra*, pp. 153-59. For Massachusetts charter controversies, see Palfrey, as cited *supra*, p. 251, n. 56.

[58] Downing had advised Governor Bradstreet that "matters relating to trade be so settled, as there be no farther just Complaints upon that account" (Hutchinson, *History of Massachusetts*, I, 300).

[59] Toppan, *Randolph*, I, 134, 288 n.; *supra*, pp. 226-27.

[60] Beer, *Old Colonial System*, II, 247. Apparently bonds were given even as early as 1661. See note in *New England Historical and Genealogical Register*, XXXI, 331, citing *Mass. Archives*, IX, 33.

[61] Toppan, *Randolph*, III, 122.

[62] Palfrey, *Compendious History of New England*, III, 375.

[63] *Supra*, pp. 168-69.

rights. It failed to abolish the "indecent oath" of fidelity to the colony which, the King complained, placed fealty to Massachusetts above that due His Majesty. Instead, the oath was to be "revived and put in practice through this jurisdiction."[64]

If we endeavored to consider every ramification of the subject, our study would lose all semblance of unity. Each phase of the Acts presents different conundrums. Chronologically, one problem exists before the English conquest of New Netherland and another thereafter. After 1733 one wonders whether the contempt for the Molasses Act proved contagious and whether its tacit nullification affected the older laws; and the disturbances occasioned by the reforms from 1764 to 1776 are a separate story in themselves. Geographically, each economic group of plantations, if not each colony, offers problems peculiar to itself.

Fortunately we do not have to demonstrate that the laws were perfectly enforced at all times. Unless there had been some resistance to the laws they would not have been regulating conduct, but would only have been declaratory of established habits. The test of their vitality is not one of perfect enforcement; their effectiveness was a matter of degree. We may assume that extraneous complications increased colonial disobedience, and that violations occurred with varying frequency at different times and different places, and still establish that the laws succeeded, if we can show that in the long run they assisted England in attaining her three great goals. Thus the problem is to discover whether the laws eliminated foreign shipping in the colonies, helped England to control the enumerated exports, and strengthened her hold over the colonial market.

For all practical purposes it seems safe to conclude that after 1664 foreign shipping was excluded at least from trade with the continental colonies. The large Dutch vessels, which might have made violations profitable, were too valuable to expose to the very real dangers of detection encountered by coming openly into port. Obvious differences of nationality and speech would, and did, lead

[64] *Massachusetts Bay Company Records*, V, 154-55. Randolph complained, however, that the Massachusetts Naval Office Act was not properly proclaimed, and that it ignored the Acts of 1662 and 1673, and hindered rather than helped him (Toppan, *Randolph*, III, 123-26, 133-40; Goodrick, *Randolph*, VI, 105; Beer, *Old Colonial System*, II, 291, 297-99).

to seizure. Informations were brought, even against English vessels, merely because of the French denizens among their crews.[65] And in addition to the argument from silence, there are the deductions to be drawn from colonial self-interest. Colonial smugglers would naturally prefer to use their own vessels rather than to share their illicit profits with foreigners. Despite the possible readiness of planters to deal with whoever quoted the most favorable prices, any encouragement they might be willing to give foreigners would be more than offset by the antagonism of the mercantile element of the community which had more incentive and better opportunities to oppose them.[66]

The complete story of what England accomplished by requiring that certain colonial products be shipped to England can only be told in terms of commodities, times, and places; but an analysis of the policy's achievements in restricting shipments of tobacco will illustrate its success. Tobacco was a major crop, one which employed much shipping, and the requirement that it all go to England forced by far the greater part to follow an unnatural route before it could reach its eventual market on the Continent.[67] Moreover, it was sufficiently valuable to warrant a smuggler's serious consideration.

In approaching the problem of smuggling the first step would seem to be to study the activities of smugglers themselves. Their very desire for concealment suggests how to study their actions. Illicit traders would naturally avoid as many hazards as possible, and thus it appears reasonable to assume that we can learn much about what they did by analyzing the barriers they had to avoid.

Just as risks of detection tended to keep foreign vessels from coming openly into port, so did circumstances discourage both English and colonial vessels from carrying tobacco directly from the plantations to Europe. The first hindrance was that bond had to be given to obey the law. Surreptitious lading was not a sufficient safeguard in itself. Vessels without certificates that they had given bond were

---

[65] CTB IX, 1579-80; CTP (1557-1696), p. 224.

[66] In any event such surreptitious dealings between planters and foreign smugglers would be conducted on a barter basis and would be much less extensive than mercantile transactions conducted on credit.

[67] *Infra*, p. 255, n. 70.

subject to seizure wherever found by His Majesty's men-of-war.[68]
They might also be condemned if driven to England by contrary
winds.[69] These risks were very real in the case of tobacco, since the
bulk of it was consumed in northern Europe, especially in Holland
and Germany.[70] The wind blew where it listed, and seventeenth-
century vessels sailed accordingly. Even if the winds were favorable, the conformation of the English Channel made it easy to
patrol.[71] Furthermore, there were the English consuls in the principal markets in Europe to follow the latest developments of commerce and to report the arrival of vessels.[72] If they were bribed to
overlook their duty, there still remained the factors of English merchants, who would presumably be aware of any illicit importations
of sufficient bulk to affect the local market price.[73]

There are, of course, the possibilities of forgery to be considered,
but such evasions were also subject to definite limitations. Bribery,
unaccompanied by falsification of documents, was probably seldom
resorted to. There were too many officials who had to be corrupted
to make it worth while. A false certificate that bond had been given

[68] See *supra*, pp. 161-62.

[69] A Danish ship having been seized and condemned at Dartmouth, was driven by
contrary winds to Plymouth and again seized (CTB XII, 346-47). Coal frauds on
the East Coast were detected when weather drove the colliers into Hull (CTB XI,
249); and storms led to another seizure in the Downs, of pepper destined for Jersey
(PC 2/73, p. 371; CTB XI, 400).

[70] The following table (compiled from Customs 3/1 for 1698 and from Sheffield,
Observations, Appendix for 1773) shows the disposition of tobacco passing through
England:

	1698		1773	
	Pounds	*Percent*	*Pounds*	*Percent*
Flanders	830,786	3.6	7,150,737	12.7
Holland	4,922,862	21.3	14,371,835	25.7
Germany	1,833,165	8.0	11,953,577	21.4
Denmark and Norway	239,622	1.0	2,573,284	4.6
East Country	1,450,115	6.3	265,019	.5
Other Countries	7,868,090	34.1	14,072,473	25.2
Retained in England	5,919,594	25.7	5,542,032	9.9
Total	23,064,234	100.0	55,928,957	100.0

[71] See Beer, *Origins*, pp. 199-201, for examples of the use of the navy in regulating
the carriage of colonial products through the Channel, 1634-37.

[72] *Supra*, pp. 93-95. CTB V, 1000; VIII, 971. If a vessel was not detained abroad, it
might, however, be seized later when in England on another voyage (CTB XI,
165-66, 381; XII, 156).

[73] There also were private informers seeking official favor (*supra*, pp. 95-96).

in the colonies might protect a ship en route to its illegal destination; but when the vessel reached the Continent, its master could not prove, if any questions were raised, that it had gone to England. The more effective technique of evasion was to give a bond and to bribe an English official to certify that the merchandise had been landed in England. The false certificate would both cancel the bond and minimize detection abroad. Smugglers unwilling to share their profits with corrupt officials might forge their own documents; but even then such forgeries, to be successful, required a knowledge of English forms and conditions likely to be possessed only by those in the mother country.[74] And Englishmen had little incentive to use their knowledge to violate the Navigation Acts. The lawless could make greater illicit gains by smuggling tobacco into England and collecting drawback on its exportation, than by carrying it direct from America to Europe.[75]

Illicit trade which centered in the New World, however, was another matter. Although English vessels would have had little or no motive in disposing of their tobacco illegally before recrossing the Atlantic, American vessels might have found it profitable to smuggle in their own waters by going from the English plantations to some foreign settlement in America. The loss involved in case of capture could be minimized by using small vessels. After the smuggler's vessel was laden by connivance or stealth, false documents might help to lessen the danger of seizure, and in any event the peril decreased as the distance lessened.

Thus geographical considerations offer an opportunity for deductions concerning the extent to which tobacco was illegally exported, at least after the capture of New Netherland. Until then, the Dutch settlement had afforded an entrepôt so convenient as to render enforcement almost impossible.[76] Thereafter, the nearest foreign settlements where tobacco might be transshipped were in Newfoundland and the Caribbean, more than a thousand miles from the

---

[74] The theory that colonial vessels did little smuggling direct to Europe is supported by the comparatively small number of vessels seized in Europe on that charge. See for example, *infra*, p. 261, n. 91.

[75] Harper, *The Smugglers, passim*, especially pp. 230-32, 243.

[76] Beer, *Old Colonial System*, I, 272-73; for the presence of Virginia tobacco in New Netherland, see Stokes, *Iconography of Manhattan*, IV, 214, 250. See also Bruce, *Economic History of Virginia*, II, 296-315.

tobacco-producing centers of the Chesapeake.[77] A certain amount of transshipment from small colonial coasters to Dutch flyboats occurred, but various factors limited the practice. The Chesapeake Bay did not offer the opportunities that its numerous rivers would suggest were available. The region was somewhat too well settled, and the bottle-neck of the bay enabled His Majesty's frigates, by riding at anchor or slowly cruising back and forth, to diminish smuggling.[78] Consequently, illicit traders concentrated their activities on the Eastern Shores of Maryland and Virginia.[79] Some tobacco was carried overland from Maryland to Delaware Bay. Long Island Sound, to the north, would appear to have offered a sheltered haven for foreign vessels, but in the seventeenth century, at least, that area was not relied upon in the illegal exportation of tobacco. The favorite meeting place for foreign vessels was the sheltered and unfrequented waters of Albemarle and Pamlico Sounds, whence small boats made their way down the coast from the Eastern Shore of Virginia. But even here, smuggling activities existed under handicaps. The region was also a center for pirates, who, if no other victims were at hand, might prey upon the lesser wrongdoers who visited the same waters.[80]

There were, of course, other methods of evading the laws. Masters might enter part of their cargo, receive a certificate showing that they were bound for another plantation, and then take more tobacco aboard.[81] Tobacco might also be carried to the Dutch West Indies concealed in casks of flour and bread which were presumably

[77] Florida and parts of Canada were, of course, nearer, but the offenses there occurred rather in supplying the enemy with provisions in times of war than in exporting enumerated articles. See, for example, Harrington, *The New York Merchant*, pp. 238-40. The Spanish colonies, however, did carry on an illicit trade with South Carolina (*North Carolina Colonial Records*, V, xliv).

[78] *Supra*, p. 177, n. 89.

[79] Bruce, *Economic History of Virginia*, II, 312, 328-29; Wise, *Ye Kingdome of Accawmacke*, pp. 237-39, 296-301. The Eastern Shore, however, was not the greatest tobacco-producing area, and early showed a tendency to shift to other activities (Gray, *History of Agriculture in the Southern United States*, I, 167, 232-33; Wise, *op. cit.*, pp. 237, 239).

[80] Hughson, *The Carolina Pirates*, *passim*. Moreover, the region was notoriously dangerous to navigate (Crittenden, *Commerce of North Carolina*, pp. 1-20).

[81] *Virginia Statutes-at-Large*, II, 297-98. As early as 1672, Virginia passed a law providing that when ships cleared without being fully laden, the collectors should require a bond that all tobacco laden after clearance would be entered under oath (*ibid.*, II, 297-98).

destined for the English West Indies.[82] But instances of such schemes and methods of concealment do not demonstrate that smugglers nullified the law. They illustrate the risks and expenses attending evasion. The true significance of the tobacco hidden in the flour does not lie in the fraud; it lies in the fact that the fraud was measured in terms of casks and not by shiploads.

It is essential to remember the enormous bulk of tobacco which moved in legal channels. At the end of the seventeenth century there were over 200 ships engaged in the trade. The annual average clearing from England for Virginia and Maryland for the three years 1715-17 was 149, totaling 21,550 tons. At the later time the number clearing for all the colonies was 580, totaling 66,688 tons, and it was destined to increase steadily.[83] The very fact that so great a traffic was able to follow legal channels is in itself an indication that smuggling remained under control, at least to the extent that the dangers of detection and costs of concealment offset expenses incurred by law-abiding merchants.[84] If smugglers had been able to act with

[82] CSPC (1693-96), Nos. 1897, 1916.

[83] NYCD V, 615. The seventeenth-century estimate has been calculated by taking the Maryland figures as one-third of the total (Morriss, *Colonial Trade of Maryland,* pp. 85-87). The statistics for the shipping employed are not so full as those for the tobacco carried, but a rough estimate may be formed by correlating one with the other. According to Holmes (*Tobacco Crop,* pp. 6-7) the exports of tobacco rose from 30,765,903 pounds in 1698 to 36,000,000 in 1730, and to an annual average of 101,035,091 pounds from 1770 to 1772. See also Jacobstein, *Tobacco Industry,* pp. 21-24; Scharf, *History of Maryland,* I, 520. Champion (*Considerations on Great Britain and the United States,* p. 27) states that before the Revolution 195,000 tons were employed in the trade of the Thirteen Colonies with Europe and 146,000 tons in the coast and West India trade.

[84] The argument that if legal trade continued to flourish, illegal trade must be kept at a reasonable minimum, frequently recurs. Quary stated that he had been discouraged by "an infamous illegal trade" (Root, *Relations of Pennsylvania with the British Government,* p. 113). Governor Colden expected the conflict between the smugglers and the legal merchants to defeat the Association (NYHS Col., X, 373). In England certain shopkeepers claimed that they were being ruined by unfair competition of peddlers who sold smuggled goods (GLB 335). Another contended "Clandestine trade is so great that Parliament must help fair traders" (*The Case of the Fair Traders,* GLB 284). It also appears from the same document that when an excessive duty of 1s. 6d. per pound was laid on pepper, smuggling flourished, and the customs receipts fell from £9,000 or £10,000 to £20. Cf. GLB 138 on the same subject, but quoting different figures. Note also that in the import trade from France, which was burdened with excessive duties and was generally conceded to be a most profitable field for smugglers, the legal imports were comparatively few (Chalmers, *Estimate,* p. 63).

impunity, their lower operating costs would have driven from business those who followed the roundabout route via England.

Moreover, the colonists did not own sufficient tonnage to offer serious competition. The New Englanders probably possessed more vessels than all the other colonies combined, but in 1674 they owned only about 14,000 tons of ships and boats according to Petty's notes,[85] and as late as 1715 to 1717, only 415 vessels of 20,929 tons, including repeated voyages, cleared from Boston harbor, on an average each year.[86] None of the figures are as accurate as we would like, but they suffice to show that if the New Englanders had merely specialized in smuggling tobacco (instead of everything, as charged) every New England ship would have had to make at least one illegal voyage. But by far the greater part of colonial shipping is accounted for. The West Indies supplied a brisk demand for foodstuffs, lumber, and other commodities, which could be carried at a profit without the risks involved in violating the law.[87] Peddling activities gave employment for many others along the North American coast, and the fisheries employed whole fleets in supplying the Catholic countries of southern Europe with cod.[88] The few ships which might have had

[85] *The Petty Papers*, II, 100-1. Randolph's figures for 1676 were about 50 percent higher (Toppan, *Randolph*, II, 250), but he was making a case against Massachusetts and may have exaggerated to show the harm it could do. Bellomont in 1700 and Dudley in 1709 both returned smaller estimates than that of Randolph (NYCD IV, 790; Weeden, *Economic and Social History of New England*, I, 363-64). Nettels summarizes the evidence and concludes that Massachusetts alone probably possessed half the colonial carrying capacity (*Money Supply of the American Colonies*, pp. 101-3). A report of 1681 disposed of the whole matter of smuggling as far as Connecticut was concerned by pointing out that it did not possess "any capacitie so to defraud . . . having only a few small vessels to carry our corne, hoggs, and horses unto our neighbours" (Hinman, *Letters to Connecticut*, pp. 120-21).

[86] NYCD V, 618. It was estimated that the tonnage of vessels owned by permanent inhabitants of the Thirteen Colonies from 1770-72 averaged 58,718 tons engaged in trade between those colonies and Great Britain, the British West Indies, or other British colonies (Great Britain, *Report on Trade with the United States*, pp. 13-21; Seybert, *Statistical Annals*, pp. 290-91). The figure should be corrected, however, by making deductions for repeated voyages and additions for vessels included in the fisheries, the coasting, and other trades.

[87] Bell, "West India Trade before the American Revolution," *Am. Hist. Rev.*, XXII, 272-80; Bell, "British Commercial Policy in the West Indies," *Eng. Hist. Rev.*, XXXI, 429-32; Nettels, *Money Supply of the American Colonies*, pp. 67-127.

[88] Although one should not accept the Naval Office lists as a complete account of the goods imported and exported, there seems to be no reason for doubting the general accuracy of their record of the vessels entering and clearing, which shows the variety and extent of colonial commerce. See "Early Coastwise and Foreign Ship-

time for serious smuggling faced conditions that did not permit their making up in activity what they lacked in numbers. It might take the tobacco fleet as long as five months to complete their ladings in Virginia and Maryland, while in the West Indies illicit as well as legal commerce was unsafe during the hurricane season, and a smuggler who valued his ship would find his period of operations restricted.[89]

Another approach to the problem is to analyze the probable extent of smuggling in those areas which caused most concern to the authorities. We hear much of smuggling in Newfoundland, and some tobacco was undoubtedly transshipped there, but there is no reason for believing that the amount was large. The factional struggles between settlers and fishermen gave rise to prejudices which warrant discounting the charges of fraud, whereas both the indirectness of the route and the bulkiness of fish, the cargo for which ships made their way to the North, afford good reason for minimizing the extent of the illicit trade in tobacco carried on by way of Newfoundland.[90]

ping of Salem," *Essex Inst. Hist. Col.*, LXII, 193-200, 305-20; LXIII, 49-64, 145-60, 349-64; LXVII, 281-88, 409-24; LXVIII, 41-64, 241-56, 337-52; LXIX, 49-64, 155-198; Bradlee, "Colonial Trade and Commerce," *Essex Inst. Hist. Col.*, LXIII, 1-29; Morison, "Commerce of Boston," *Am. Antiq. Soc. Proceedings*, XXXII, 24-51; "Newspaper Extracts," *New Jersey Documents*, XVII, XVIII, XIX, XX, *passim*. They do not record the activities of the fishing fleets of which 300 sail, totaling about 30,000 tons (including English vessels), were said to be annually employed from Newfoundland, New England, and Nova Scotia in 1709 (Weeden, *Economic and Social History of New England*, I, 371-72), a figure which increased to 1,099 vessels of 59,775 tons in the New England fishery alone by the time of the Revolution (Champion, *Considerations on Great Britain and the United States*, p. 27).

[89] In arranging for convoys in 1706, it was planned that the fleet should arrive in the Chesapeake in December and return in May (Morriss, *Colonial Trade of Maryland*, p. 94). In the West Indies, it has been said, "Vessels from North America think nothing of lying four, five or six months" (Bell, "West India Trade before the American Revolution," *Am. Hist. Rev.*, XXII, 286 n.). On the other hand vessels, particularly the small ones, might make two or three voyages a year from the Thirteen Colonies to the West Indies (*ibid.*, 278 n.), and in peace time, at least, vessels sometimes made two voyages a year from England to America (CSPC [1661-68], No. 58; Harrington, *The New York Merchant*, p. 176; Champion, *Considerations on Great Britain and the United States*, pp. 95-97).

[90] See Judah, *North American Fisheries and British Policy;* Lounsbury, *British Fishery at Newfoundland.* Lounsbury is inclined to overemphasize the importance of the smuggling in Newfoundland. Although more European goods were smuggled inward than enumerated products outward, even with respect to smuggling inward it does not seem that the volume was "tremendous" when we study the problem from the broader view of commerce as a whole. If it were, it is difficult to understand why the English government remained comparatively inactive; why we do not

In the case of Ireland for a short time there was undoubtedly considerable resistance to the laws. The trouble arose when Parliament suddenly excluded the Irish from the privileges of a direct trade, which they had previously enjoyed. For a time it continued as before, but vigorous efforts seem to have stamped it out, and more than 100 vessels (mostly Irish or English) were seized in the years 1678 to 1681 alone.[91] By 1697 we find that over 4,000,000 pounds of tobacco went to Ireland by way of England, as the law provided.[92] Since there must have been a 'limit to the Irishman's purchasing power if not to his love of the "weed," we must assume that the smuggled importations were a minor factor. If not, certainly the risks of illegal trade sufficiently increased its cost to permit fair traders to do a very sizable business.

According to the accounts of smuggling into Scotland which appear in reports from the colonies and the north of England at the end of the century, 31 ships were engaged in the trade between 1691 and 1702.[93] Although the detailed accuracy of the accounts boded ill for the continued impunity of the offenders, we need not inquire into their fate. The admission of Scotland to the colonial trade by the Act of Union in 1707 affords an opportunity to compare conditions before and after the removal of legislative restrictions. We learn that within five years after the Scots were permitted to trade freely with the plantations, the total number of Scottish ships increased from 215 to 1,123, over 400 percent. The percentage was even greater in the Clyde ports, which had the best opportunity to benefit from the new liberty to trade with America, and the number of ships they owned rose from 21 to 216.[94] In view of this evidence, smuggling

---

hear greater outcries from English merchants (as contrasted with special agents) as we did in the case of early New England competition; and how the great volume of legal trade managed to continue. See *infra*, pp. 270-71.

[91] HCA, *Instance Papers* 12. Of the 99 vessels which could be identified, 76 were Irish, 20 English, and 3 colonial.

[92] MacInnes, *The Early English Tobacco Trade*, p. 168. In 1698 the importations were 3,370,848 pounds (Customs 15/1).

[93] Morriss, *Colonial Trade of Maryland*, p. 118. Miss Morriss seems to believe that most of the ships were seized or the owners otherwise punished (*ibid.*, pp. 118, 120). See also Keith, *Commercial Relations of England and Scotland*, pp. 118-28.

[94] The total Scottish tonnage rose from 14,485 tons at the time of the Union to 50,232 tons by 1712 (BM Harl. MSS 6269). See also Keith, *Commercial Relations of England and Scotland*, p. 205.

obviously was insignificant when compared to what trade would have been except for the laws.

Another opportunity of estimating the probable extent of smuggling can be obtained by comparing the amount of tobacco sent to Britain before the Revolution with that exported from the United States thereafter. Figures after 1791 from American sources, which there is no particular reason to doubt, show that the quantity then exported barely equaled that which the British records from 1761 to 1775 show to have passed through Britain as the law required.[95] The proof is not conclusive, since we have no assurance that the war may not have ruined the planters or that other sources of supply may not have captured the market during the interim, but it strongly suggests that whatever violations occurred were negligible.

For much the same reasons it seems justifiable to believe that the laws controlled the exportation of nearly all, if not all, of the remaining commodities on the enumerated list.[96] Rice, like tobacco, was a bulky commodity. We know that great quantities passed through England both before and for some time after the Revolution, and that there is a reasonably close correlation between the quantity of rice shipped legally before the Revolution and what was exported thereafter.[97] Moreover, the rules permitting ships to go direct to southern Europe minimized the temptations to evade the law. In the case of sugar it is true that the geographic arguments used with respect to tobacco break down, because the proximity of foreign settle-

---

[95] Pitkin, *Statistical View*, pp. 107-9; Holmes, *Tobacco Crop*, pp. 7-9.

[96] Among the enumerated articles not mentioned in the text there was a greater demand for molasses than the supply could fill. Masts, yards, bowsprits, tar, pitch, hemp, turpentine (3 & 4 Anne, c. 9; 2 Geo. II, c. 35), indigo (21 Geo. II, c. 30), raw silk (9 Geo. III, c. 38), and certain lumber (5 Geo. III, c. 45; 11 Geo. III, c. 50) were drawn to England by a bounty. Whale fins (25 Car. II, c. 7) and coffee (5 Geo. II, c. 24) were favored by preferential tariffs, and potash and pearlash were admitted duty free (24 Geo. II, c. 51). Comparisons of exports of deerskins and iron before and after the Revolution do not suggest that much had been exported illegally; the quantity of furs, beaver skins, raw silk, copper ore, and cotton was negligible; and fustic, logwood and other dyewoods, cocoa, ginger, pimento, and coffee were primarily Caribbean products (Pitkin, *Statistical View*, pp. 21-23, 110-11. Seybert *Statistical Annals*, pp. 94-109). See also Gray, *History of Agriculture in the Southern United States*, I, 102, 152-59, 290-97; II, 1019, 1024.

[97] Gray, *History of Agriculture in the Southern United States*, II, 1020-23, 1030. On the whole subject of colonial rice, see McCrady, *History of South Carolina, 1670-1719* and *1719-1776*; and the references cited in Schlesinger, *The Colonial Merchants*, p. 33 n.

ments to the centers of English production made it possible for planters to send their produce to Dutch ships lying off the coast, or else make their way in small sloops and barques to a foreign entrepôt.[98] But economic factors were changing the direction of illicit trade. England was consuming nearly all of the sugar imported, and smugglers' efforts were soon directed to bringing that commodity from the foreign West Indies to the English islands, whence it might be shipped to England at the lower rates accorded the produce of English plantations.[99] Although such activity was illegal, it was a fraud upon the English revenue, rather than a violation of the Navigation Acts.

In short, it seems clear, as far as restrictions on exportations are concerned, that illicit trade constituted only a small fraction of the legitimate commerce. Although the lurid accounts of frauds contained in administrative reports and court records make interesting reading, they must not be allowed to confuse us as to the extent of illegal activities. The evidence concerning the nature of the traffic and the circumstances under which smugglers operated is more convincing.

It is a harder task to determine the cause and extent of illicit importations of European commodities.[100] Geographical considerations afford little help. The opportunities for illegal trade were too varied, and the factors complicating the problem of enforcement too numerous. French settlements in the North, the fisheries in Newfoundland, or the foreign West Indies offered convenient emporiums for procuring European goods, which might also be laden in innumerable ports in Europe itself. When America was reached, the merchandise might be surreptitiously passed to an "experienced coaster," whereupon the smuggler might openly enter the harbor and declare the rest of his cargo.[101] Sheltered sounds and bays would permit

[98] PC 2/72, pp. 458, 466; CSPC (1685-88), Nos. 1232, 1356; CTB VIII, 1530; Beer, Old Colonial System, II, 43-44.

[99] GL MSS 78, p. 48, tells of trade centering in the Dutch islands and the Danish colony of St. Thomas. For methods of smuggling sugar from the French West Indies to England by reshipment, see Pitman, Development of the British West Indies, p. 231; Ragatz, The Fall of the Planter Class, pp. 102-4.

[100] The disposal of pirates' goods might very well constitute a violation of the Navigation Acts, but it is a topic better considered in a study of piracy or of colonial trade as a whole.

[101] Henry Lloyd, writing from Boston to Aaron Lopez, May 3, 1756, said he could

transshipment; numerous coves, inlets, and rivers offered opportunities for its landing, and, even if the small coaster was detected, its forfeiture value was slight when compared with that of an ocean-going ship.[102] Moreover, the comparatively small size of the cargo eliminates the opportunity of drawing conclusions based upon the bulk of the cargo, while the relatively great value increases the presumption that some would be tempted to smuggle.

These are the considerations of greatest probative force. It is comparatively immaterial that we find smugglers declaring that it was easy to import goods illegally. Boastfulness is a well-recognized element in criminal psychology. Moreover, we find other traders either cautioning their correspondents against smuggling or else taking great precautions when evading the law.[103] Such instances establish the fact, which could be assumed, that smuggling occurred, but they do not establish the extent, which is the point in doubt. The fact that in certain instances violations were openly winked at proves nothing. Exceptional circumstances often justify waiving technical offenses. In England, minor transgressions could be, and were, excused by order of the Lords of the Treasury.[104] In the colonies, such mitigation of the rules often rested in the hands of officers at the waterside, who, if truly wise, would close their eyes to offenses of little importance.[105] A ship coming from Spain or Portugal with a legal cargo of salt would naturally bring a few boxes of oranges or lemons, although as a matter of law such merchandise should come only from England. It is no reflection upon the honesty or diligence of the customs officials that they failed to observe the fruit, no mat-

---

"by no means advise to sending any tea without a proper Clearance," but that if any were sent it should be "a chest or two at a time by experienced Coasters" (*Commerce of Rhode Island*, MHSC, 7th series, IX, 67).

[102] The technique of smuggling inward was well perfected by the New Yorkers and has been clearly portrayed by Miss Harrington in *The New York Merchant*, pp. 249-76.

[103] See *supra*, p. 247, n. 38.

[104] *Supra*, pp. 102-3. It was well for Robert Quary that the English authorities did so. He sent a shipment of prize sugar to England, which arrived before the papers which should have accompanied it. By the time he reached England, it had been condemned, but he received the King's share of the forfeiture (CTB XII, 298, 312).

[105] A letter from William Penn shows how much inconvenience and hardship might result from small mistakes, however innocent, if the officials did not ignore them (*Pennsylvania Archives*, 1st series, I, 149).

ter how much of it they and their wives might later enjoy at the master's table. Such careful distinction between what was seen and what was tasted is no proof of moral turpitude; it merely testifies to the officials' common sense and decent neighborliness. Even mercantilists understood the maxim, *de minimis non curat lex*.[106]

There are, however, certain other points to consider which throw light upon the problem. Support for the view that the restrictions upon European importations were effective can be found in the colonists' taste in wines. For the most part they drank Madeira, which could be imported legally direct from the Wine Islands. Their fondness for that beverage was not inherited from England. The English preferred French, Rhenish, Spanish, and Italian wines, and, after the Methuen Treaty with Portugal, port.[107] The argument that the colonists' appetite was affected by the laws would seem to be rebutted by evidence that cargoes of Madeira were imported before 1660,[108] but its persuasiveness is at least somewhat restored when we discover that the colonists turned to other vintages after they procured their independence.[109]

It is interesting to compare the importations of European goods

[106] Moreover, the official mind managed to find a legal excuse for the practice. Governor Bernard wrote of the "Indulgence time out of mind allowed in a trifling but necessary article, . . . the permitting Lisbon Lemons & wine in small quantities to pass as Ships Stores," a practice which also existed in Virginia (Schlesinger, *The Colonial Merchants*, p. 42). A somewhat similar practice, followed at Boston, was to import small quantities of foreign wines for family use, which was justified on the ground that the wine was not for sale (Andrews, Introduction to Towle, *Records of the Vice-Admiralty Court of Rhode Island*, p. 51).

[107] For American consumption of Madeira wine, see references collected by Ashley (*Surveys, Historic and Economic*, pp. 351-52). Wines from the Canary Islands, another favorite, were sometimes challenged, but more often allowed as imports from Africa (Andrews, *The Colonial Period*, IV, 110-13). England's imports of wine from Madeira were normally less than one-half of one percent of the value of those from Spain and Portugal, and never exceeded $10,000 a year; its early preference for French wines, whenever they could be had, is shown by the import figures for 1682 to 1689 (Customs 3; *British Merchant*, I, 302).

[108] Josselyn in his "Account of Two Voyages to New England" tells of finding "a Barke of 300 Tuns, laden with Island Wine" bound there in 1638 (*Mass. Hist. Soc. Col.*, 3d series, III, 41; Andrews, *The Colonial Period*, I, 515, 517).

[109] In 1790 American imports included 321,369 gallons of Madeira wine and 818,976 gallons of other wines. By 1800 the figures were 280,262 gallons of "Malmsey, Madeira, Lond. part. [and] all other Madeira" and 2,438,164 gallons of Burgundy, Champagne, Sherry, St. Lucar, and all other wines (Seybert, *Statistical Annals*, pp. 158, 164, 168).

known to have been made under the Acts with those made before and after that time, but unfortunately the comparison is not conclusive. We have no statistics for the period before 1660, although the evidence of contemporaries and the presence of the Dutch in New York leave little doubt that many European manufactures were imported.[110] Figures for the legal trade after 1696 show that the regulated European commodities usually constituted about 25 percent of the English and European goods shipped to the Thirteen Colonies,[111] and that after independence was achieved the amount of such European goods increased to 39 percent.[112] But the discrep-

[110] *Supra*, p. 244.

[111] The following table has been compiled from the Inspector General's Accounts (Customs 3) to show the percentage of the goods going to the Thirteen Colonies from England which were not English (or Scottish) products:

Years	Average Total	Average Reëxports	Percentage
1697–99	£ 333,946	£ 98,843	29.6
1720–22	358,778	118,023	32.9
1730–32	534,793	196,363	36.7
1740–42	839,475	247,885	29.5
1750–52	1,231,792	358,850	29.1
1760–62	1,880,667	273,569	14.5
1770–72	3,046,892	468,227	15.4

In considering them, however, allowance should be made for the fact that they include East India goods, which comprised 15 percent of the reëxports from 1715 to 1717 (NYCD V, 617) and either two-fifths or three-fifths from 1767 to 1770 (Sheffield, *Observations*, p. 51 states that the fraction was two-fifths, but according to his own figures there were £211,581 of East India goods exported to America out of a total of £344,006 of reëxports, or 61.5 percent). In New York, the non-English manufactures varied from 35 to 10 percent (Harrington, *The New York Merchant*, pp. 173, 354-55). Since the only statistics cited are those for England's trade, the percentages will vary slightly if Scotland's exportations to the plantations did not maintain the same ratio between English and foreign goods.

[112] In estimating the percentage, imports from the Wine Islands were not included in the European total, since they had been exempted by the Act of 1663. No attempt was made to exclude salt for the fisheries, or horses and provisions from Ireland, from the total of the regulated trade, although they had been permitted to go freely to the colonies, but the resultant error is negligible. On this basis the percentage of the imports in question coming directly was 34.8 percent for 1795-97 and 37.8 percent in 1821 (Seybert, *Statistical Annals*, pp. 266-69; U. S. Congress, *American State Papers*, class 4, II, 554). An addition must be made for the European goods brought indirectly by way of England or Scotland. Reëxported goods (including a few goods from Asia, Africa, and America) constituted 6.7 percent of American imports from England and Scotland during the years 1791 to 1794 (Bemis, *Jay's Treaty*, p. 34); 2.8 percent from 1806 to 1808 (Pitkin, *Statistical View*, p. 223); 1.5 percent in 1821 (Great Britain, *House of Commons Sessional Papers* [1822], XXI, No. 274); and 4.4 percent in 1828 (Great Britain, *House of Commons Sessional Papers* [1830], XXVII, No. 292).

ancy cannot be used to measure the amount of smuggling, since conditions did not remain the same during the different periods. On the one hand the development of manufacturing, especially after the bounty given the linen industry, tended to increase the English imports,[113] and on the other, the greater diversification of American commerce which followed independence tended to increase the imports from Europe.[114]

If we judge solely by the discrepancy test, smuggling increased during the Revolutionary period. From 1770 to 1772 only 6 percent of the goods imported by the Thirteen Colonies from England were regulated European commodities.[115] On that basis the colonists smuggled almost £700,000 of European merchandise each year. Although the estimate agrees with that made in 1765 by the author of *The Regulations Lately Made*,[116] the vigor with which the navy and customs authorities were tackling the problem of enforcement suggests that the figure is greatly exaggerated,[117] and both Channing and Morison, who studied the evidence more closely, concluded that the laws were reasonably well enforced during the Revolutionary period, if never before.[118] In any event, conditions were not typical. The economic depression which followed the French and Indian War made the traders "poor, cross, and desperate," non-importation agreements disturbed normal economic activities, and opposition to

[113] Sheffield, *Observations*, pp. 36-40; Macpherson, *Annals of Commerce*, III, 182, 228; Ashley, *Surveys, Historic and Economic*, pp. 349-50; Clark, *History of Manufactures in the United States*, I, 121.

[114] The importance of the restraining influence of the Navigation Acts on diversified commerce can readily be seen by comparing Sheffield's account (*supra*, p. 266, n. 111) of the large quantity of East India goods which was imported by way of England before the Revolution with the insignificant amount thus imported after 1783 (Seybert, *Statistical Annals*, pp. 227, 244-45, 289). See also Morison, *Maritime History of Massachusetts*.

[115] *Supra*, p. 266, n. 111.

[116] Beer, *British Colonial Policy, 1754-1765*, p. 245.

[117] Channing (*History of the United States*, III, 35-150) gives a good summary of the measures taken while describing the "riot, rebellion, and revolution" to which they led. They would have borne very severely on the merchants, if strictly enforced, but apparently were mitigated in practice (Andrews, "Boston Merchants and the Non-Importation Movement," Colonial Society of Massachusetts, *Transactions*, XIX, 170-80; Morison, "Commerce of Boston on the Eve of the Revolution," *Am. Antiq. Soc. Proceedings*, XXXII, 48-50).

[118] Channing, *History of the United States*, III, 88-91; Morison, "Commerce of Boston on the Eve of the Revolution," *Am. Antiq. Soc. Proceedings*, XXXII, 24-51. Cf. Harrington, *The New York Merchant*, pp. 267-76.

the reforming zeal of the English government from 1764 to 1776 stimulated resistance to laws which might otherwise have been respected.[119]

The main support of the hypothesis that the inward trade was reasonably law-abiding comes from the correlation which exists between exports and imports. The large shipments of tobacco, rice, and sugar to England called for return cargoes from England. The planters received credit, not cash, for their produce. They naturally made their purchases in England, where their factors could debit their accounts.[120] With a view to obtaining a two-way freight, owners of shipping reduced the rates charged for the voyage to America,[121] and either sought cargoes of Old-World goods which could be sent to the sugar and tobacco plantations, thence to be distributed among the other colonies, or laded their vessels as best they could for the commercial colonies, whence they returned by way of the planting areas,[122] all of which tended to keep trade passing through England.

If we could ascertain the balance of trade as far as the legal commerce of the colonies was concerned, the existence of a cash balance or its absence should throw light upon the amount of smuggling, but the figures available are unsatisfactory. Most of the statistics do not cover the whole field of colonial commerce, but relate only to the trade with England. Even the English figures are based upon

[119] Watts, quoted in Harrington, *The New York Merchant*, p. 317. See also *supra*, p. 247, n. 40.

[120] Bruce, *Economic History of Virginia*, II, 366-67; Gray, *History of Agriculture in the Southern United States*, I, 409-19.

[121] The freight rate to the colonies appears to have remained at about £3 per ton, and that on tobacco from the colonies varied from £3 to £10, or even £15 (*Virginia Company of London Proceedings*, I, 172; Weeden, *Economic and Social History of New England*, I, 126, 261, 369). Roberts (*Merchants Mappe of Commerce*, p. 62) said that freight rates from Barbados ranged from £3 when ships were plentiful, to £6 or £7 when scarce. See also Bruce, *Economic History of Virginia*, I, 450-52; II, 348.

[122] Byerly's account for March 25 to June 24, 1704 (NYPL MSS), indicates that the dry goods coming from Virginia paid 16 percent of the New York duty on such manufactures and those from Jamaica and Nevis, 39 percent. See also the instruction given to James Hudson in 1744 to purchase European goods in the West Indies (Hudson-Rogers Papers, NYPL MSS). At other times, however, the commercial centers, such as Boston and New York, appear to have distributed European goods to the producing centers rather than acquired them there (Nettels, *Money Supply of the American Colonies*, pp. 111, 114, 119). In 1735, at least, some vessels entered New York from England and cleared for New Jersey presumably en route to the Chesapeake (CO 5/1225).

fixed rather than market values and require adjustment to allow for various intangible items, such as freight, insurance, and factor's charges.

Although we cannot speak in terms of exact figures or percentages, the difficulty which historians have in ascertaining how the Americans paid for what they were known to have obtained in England suggests that they had little opportunity to purchase smuggled goods. In the early years, when the official balance of trade with England favored the colonies, intangible items like freight were sufficiently unfavorable to leave a net indebtedness. Subsequent improvement in the colonial position in these respects appears to have been more than offset by an increasingly greater indebtedness to England, which was too large to be explained away by discrepancies between the real and the official values.[123] It was met in part by profits from the West Indian trade and other sources, but in so far as the colonists were using pieces of eight or foreign bills of exchange to help settle their English balances—as both circumstantial and documentary evidence show that they were—their vessels were not carrying contraband goods.[124]

It is true that this consideration only sets an upper limit on the volume of illicit trade and does not enable us to determine to what extent the law was violated with respect to particular commodities. It is not improbable that some inward trades may have been dominated by smugglers, such as the trade with New York in tea, especially just before the Revolution.[125] The answer in each case de-

---

[123] Pitkin, *Statistical View*, pp. 19-20; Sheffield, *Observations*, Appendix No. IX, 23; Moreau, *Chronological Records*, pp. 13, 15, 17-18, 23; Johnson, *History of Domestic and Foreign Commerce*, I, 120-21; Nettels, *Money Supply of the American Colonies*, pp. 56, 72, 94 n., 198.

[124] John Watts, a "fair trader," said "The good folks at Home are quite overshooting the Mark about Trade here, little do they think, the Mother Country will pay for it all at last . . . the rigirous Execution of the Sugar Act is injurious, like Nine pins says Hudibrass, One Merchant Knocks down another, the King Pinns that fall heavyest will fall at Home & Manufactorys feel the Weight of 'em" (*Letter Book of John Watts*, p. 212). See also Nettels, *Money Supply of the American Colonies*, *passim*; Harrington, *The New York Merchant*, pp. 104-7.

[125] The greatest amount of tea officially entered in any one year prior to the Revolution was in 1768, when duties were collected on 877,193½ pounds. Thereafter the amount was never half as great (Channing, *History of the United States*, III, 128). The annual average of tea imported from 1790 to 1798 (exclusive of that reëxported) was over 2,000,000 pounds (Seybert, *Statistical Annals*, p. 259). The figures, how-

270   *ASIA, AFRICA, AND AMERICA*

pends upon the degree of temptation offered by the savings in duties and the effectiveness of enforcement on any particular occasion, and must be given article by article, period by period.[126] The questions are of great importance in understanding colonial commerce and the effect of the laws upon the plantations, but they would carry us too far afield and to find their answers would require a more detailed knowledge of colonial commerce as a whole than we now possess.[127]

In any event, it is important to observe that the English merchant and producer did not lose all his advantages each time a smuggler succeeded in landing a cargo. The inconvenience of concealment, the indirect routes, the bribes paid officials, the risk of capture—all served as an element of protection against European competition. We must recognize that the danger of detection cannot be lightly dismissed. The colonists were not a unit in violating the laws. There were gentlemen engaged in "fair trade," who, contemporary correspondence shows, were likely to be the smuggler's most determined opponents.[128] In view of the burdens placed upon trade going indirectly through England, it is improbable that the fair traders could have remained in business if the illegal traders had carried on their

ever, cannot be used to measure the amount of smuggling, since one must allow for an increase in population between 1768 and 1798 and for possible changes in the public's taste for tea. (Beer, *British Colonial Policy, 1754-1765,* pp. 245-46 n.). See Greene and Harrington, *American Population,* for early population figures.

[126] One of the chief factors in raising the temptation point was the amount of drawback paid in England (see Beer, *British Colonial Policy, 1754-1765,* pp. 40, 194-95, 281-82). Hence the removal by 4 Geo. III, c. 15 and 7 Geo. III, c. 46 of part of the drawbacks hitherto granted in England should have increased the amount of smuggling thereafter, unless countered by better enforcement.

[127] For an excellent outline of the problems involved see Andrews, "Colonial Commerce," *Am. Hist. Rev.,* XX, 43-63. See also *supra,* p. 242, n. 16.

[128] James Browne wrote from Providence in March, 1736, "it is ticklish times here my Neighbours threaten to informe against us" (*The Letter Book of James Browne,* p. 21). Thomas Cushing wrote from Boston in November, 1763, "It's well known our Merchants in general dislike the Trade to Holland and France as hurtfull to our Mother Country and like good subjects have always discountenanced it. A number of them went so far some years ago as publickly to advertise they woud inform against all Persons carrying on such trade to Holland" (*Jasper Mauduit,* pp. 136-37). Henry Lloyd wrote from Boston, April 3, 1766, to Aaron Lopez about the great dangers of importing Bohea tea illegally, "the gentlemen here in fair Trade are determined to prevent the importation of Hollands goods at all adventures, and tis probable may employ people to be on the look out" (*Commerce of Rhode Island,* MHSC, 7th series, IX, 66).

operations with complete impunity.[129] The point can be illustrated most readily in the case of that smuggler's favorite, the importation of tea. When the burden charged on legal trade was reduced to 3*d.* per pound, the smaller margin for illegal operations caused the smugglers to foresee their ruin.[130]

Conceding that the evidence concerning enforcement of the laws in the case of European imports is not as convincing as that with respect to foreign shipping and the enumerated exports, it is none the less persuasive. In any event it seems clear that the hazards of evasion increased the cost of smuggled products and in that way, if in no other, helped the English merchants to dispose of their wares in the colonial market.

Whatever differences of opinion may exist concerning the effectiveness of the different provisions of the Acts, there can be no doubt about the importance of the plantation trade as a whole to the development of England's commerce and navigation. Although colonial trade unquestionably benefited more from the spread of settlements and the natural increase of population than from any legal code, England profited only from that portion in which she shared, and the Navigation Acts deserve credit in so far as they helped to divert it to her shores.[131] English statistics show that imports from America increased from 12 percent of London's total in 1663 and 14.4 percent in 1669 to 36.5 percent in 1773. According to the shipping figures for 1719, the trade employed 19 percent of the total tonnage entering England at that time, and 24.3 percent by 1773, a figure which was to decline to 20.3 percent in 1785. Even these figures fail to do full justice to the trade's importance in employing English ships. They are based upon the total shipping, English and foreign, which entered port. Calculated on the basis of English ton-

---

[129] *Supra*, p. 258, n. 84.

[130] Harrington, *The New York Merchant*, pp. 249, 344; Schlesinger, *The Colonial Merchants*, pp. 262-67. The Tea Act removed the greatest handicap to England's tea trade with America by eliminating the English middleman. Thereafter the English and Dutch were supposed to have been on a basis of equality as to price, but the Dutch probably still held an advantage, since after 1783, of the comparatively small amount of tea purchased outside the Orient, the Americans obtained more from Holland than from Britain (Sheffield, *Observations*, p. 50; U. S. Congress, *American State Papers*, class 4, I, 39).

[131] See discussion, *supra*, pp. 243-47.

nage only, the figures are 20.6 percent for 1719, 28 percent for 1773, and 22.3 percent for 1785.[132] But entry figures include repeated voyages, and give disproportionate importance to vessels engaged in voyages to Ireland, France, and Holland, or in similar short trades. When proper allowances are made, it appears that commerce between England and America employed more than one-third of the English shipping engaged in over-sea trade.

In addition, there were indirect benefits. In 1717 one official calculated that "near half as much Shipping" was engaged in transporting plantation products from England to their ultimate destination in Germany, Holland, and other foreign countries, as was employed in carrying them directly from the plantations.[133] There were also many ships engaged in carrying goods from one colony to another, or in transporting the nonenumerated commodities to their destinations in Europe.[134]

Possibly the greatest advantage of the plantation trade was the refuge it afforded English shipowners in time of war. Although the tonnage trading with the colonies decreased during war time, it did not drop as precipitously as did that to the neighboring countries of Europe. Furthermore, peace was more likely to offer a compensating increase in the plantation trade than in others. In the European trades, foreign needs had usually been met from other than English sources, but the Navigation Acts forbade the colonists to trade elsewhere. English broadcloths and Holland linens had been wearing out; tobacco had been grown and sugar crushed, even though insufficient shipping was available. Hence, as soon as peace was declared, there was a boom in the plantation trade, which undoubtedly helped to ease postwar readjustments for shipowners.

The maintenance of English maritime prosperity after the American Revolution does not demonstrate that colonial trade was never a requisite for this prosperity. The Revolution did not cause as great a disturbance in trade and navigation as might have been expected. After all, there could have been no very great loss to English shipping. During the postwar boom in trade, the problem was merely

[132] BM Add MSS 36,785; CO 390/5, No. 45; BT 6/185.
[133] NYCD V, 615-16. A large percentage of colonial reëxports, however, were carried in foreign ships. See, for example, Customs 3/72.
[134] NYCD V, 618.

one of adjustment in the routes of existing carriers. Thus, although the English tonnage entering England from America declined from 28 percent of England's total in 1773 to 22.3 percent in 1785,[135] many English vessels found employment in American trades without leaving a record of their activities at the English Custom House. Some carried tobacco and staple products from America to Europe directly. Others replaced the ships of the former thirteen colonies, which had previously supplied the West Indies but were now barred as foreign carriers.[136] Military disturbances during the Revolution, and unsettled political conditions thereafter, handicapped American competition until the establishment of a stable government in 1787. And shortly thereafter the wars with France presented English shipowners with new problems and new opportunities.[137]

When we credit the Navigation Laws with reserving the plantation trade for England, we must remember that their effects were not altogether beneficial. The logical outcome of the mercantile limitations imposed upon Virginia planters was an indebtedness to England that prepared the way for a revolutionary activity in which cancellation of obligations was one of the hoped-for outcomes.[138] Other irritants arose in New England because of the general restrictions on commerce, most especially from the limitations on trade with the West Indies.[139] Yet defenders of the laws may well ask

[135] BT 6/185. Considering the North American trade alone the decline was greater. In 1771 trade with North America occupied 15.7 percent of the tonnage entering England and 12.7 of that clearing; in 1785 it employed only 7.6 percent of the tonnage entering and 8.4 percent of the tonnage clearing. At the later date, tonnage coming from the United States constituted only 4.4 percent of the total entering and 4 percent of the total clearing. Trade with the West Indies increased from 12.9 percent of the tonnage entering and 9.8 percent of that clearing in 1771 to 14.7 percent of the tonnage entering and 11 percent of that clearing in 1785.

[136] In 1784 Mr. Irving, the former Inspector General of Imports and Exports of North America, testified before the Committee of Trade and Plantations that 533 vessels, of 38,544 tons, and 3,339 seamen were engaged in the trade between the West Indies and the continent of North America (BT 5/1, ff. 164-68, a reference for which I am indebted to Mrs. Helen Allen Hunt).

[137] In 1801, 373 English ships, of 93,774 tons, entered England from the islands conquered from France (BT 6/185). Although they were returned to France, the renewed wars led to the opening of the trade with Spanish America.

[138] Harrell, Loyalism in Virginia, pp. 26-28.

[139] Some of the specific causes for grievance were the timber policy (Albion, Forests and Sea Power, pp. 251-72; Palfrey, Compendious History of New England, IV, 411-12), land policy (Alvord, The Mississippi Valley in British Politics, I, 111-12,

whether sufficient causes for revolution did not exist, apart from the Acts. Other colonies than New England and Virginia signed the Declaration of Independence. There is good reason to contend that it was the abruptness with which reforms were attempted by George III that caused the break, rather than any particular measures proposed. And in any case had not the laws accomplished their purpose? More than a hundred years of regulation had formed habits of trade which England continued to enjoy in a measurable degree, after separation had eliminated the expense of contributing to her former colonies' defense.

Whether or not the American Revolution was part of the price of the navigation system, there can be no doubt that the whole scheme of colonial development involved great expense. The acquisition and protection of plantations meant incalculable outlays for fleets and wars, whereas the direct returns from the colonies to the English Exchequer were insignificant.[140] Mercantilists would reply that the chief benefits of the colonies were indirect and consisted of the profits from their trade. This was undoubtedly the opinion of the English merchants, but the merits of the answer depend upon the further question: does a nation, as a whole, benefit sufficiently from the maintenance of business activity to excuse the encouragement of private enterprise at public expense?

Whatever may be the ultimate answer, there appears to have been a correlation between colonial expansion and general business activity in the seventeenth century. One of England's greatest needs was for increased wealth to lower the high rate of interest which was hindering all forms of enterprise. If she were to reap the profits of the tobacco, sugar, and East India trades, under existing international conditions, she needed colonial outposts and mercantile regulations.

183-211, 243, 286, and *passim*), and currency policy (Van Tyne, *Causes of the War of Independence*, pp. 127-30, 144, 195), not to mention the familiar political causes.
[140] Beer, *Old Colonial System*, I, 186-202.

XX

EUROPE AND THE LEVANT

DIFFICULT as was the task of ascertaining the influence of
the laws upon colonial commerce, the problem becomes much
more complex in studying England's relations with Europe, except
in one respect. The element of smuggling may be disregarded in all
but a few instances, best noted when they arise. It was not that
masters engaged in the European trades were any more virtuous.
It was merely that there was little incentive to violate the Navigation
Acts as such. Illegal traders found greater rewards in smuggling
goods that were either virtually excluded by excessive duties or completely prohibited by law than in violating the Navigation Acts.[1]
The advantage to be gained by using foreign ships was that goods
could be carried more cheaply, but when forfeiture of the vessel
was the penalty involved, shipowners and masters would want compensation for the risk they incurred, and would cease offering the
low freight rates which might tempt a shipper to violate the law.[2]
Moreover, the very size of the Dutch flyboats, which made them
more commodious, increased the difficulties of surreptitious unloading, as did the fact that the enumerated commodities were for the
most part bulky goods.[3] It was even more unlikely that ships could
hope to escape detection while coming openly into port. Experts knew
the geographical origin of imports. They could tell where a ship had
been constructed, except in the case of Scandinavian, Eastland, and
German ships, which were often patterned after Dutch designs, if

[1] The clandestine trades complained of in the *Case of the Fair Traders* (GLB 284,
n.d., *post* 1718) were the exportation of wool and bullion, the running in of wine and
brandy from France, wrought silks from France, Holland, and India, and the re-
landing of goods entered for export on which drawback had been allowed.
[2] The desire to escape payment of duties supplied greater incentives, of course, than
a desire to save on freight rates, but such savings accrued to the importer rather
than the shipowner, and resulted from the violation of other laws than the Navigation Acts.
[3] *Infra*, pp. 277-79, 404-8.

not built by Dutch denizens, and even a layman could distinguish between English and foreign sailors.[4]

The elimination of the factor of smuggling from our problem, however, is slight compensation for the other difficulties which confront us. In Europe, shippers faced an intricate maze of restrictions, discriminatory duties, and preferential bounties, which can be understood only after careful study. The regulations embodied in the old charters of the great trading companies continued to favor English shipping, although their influence rapidly decreased. There were also the various town duties, lighthouse dues, and Trinity House exactions, which handicapped foreign carriers until the reciprocity treaties of the eighteen twenties removed most of their discriminatory features.[5] Limitations of space prevent detailed discussion of them, but it is important to note that, although each was comparatively insignificant in itself, all together probably played a part in determining the choice of carriers.

The rules which governed the plantation trade also affected the carriage of commodities in Europe. English factors who were purchasing European goods for correspondents in America would naturally tend to employ their own ships; and the entries of law-abiding colonial masters, whose ships were en route to America with Continental products, helped to swell the English ratio in shipping statistics, although the traffic was primarily American rather than English. It is difficult to determine the amount of shipping thus employed, but from 1715 to 1717 the annual value of the goods averaged £115,516 and comprised 3.5 percent of England's total imports from foreign Europe.[6] Similarly, those colonial vessels which duly entered their cargoes in England in compliance with the law, and then reloaded them for the Continent, helped to increase the English total in the export trade.

[4] See Barbour, "Dutch and English Merchant Shipping," *Econ. Hist. Rev.*, II, 275 *et seq.* Many northern vessels may have at first been Dutch-built and some Dutch-owned (CO 388/12, K 63; Clark, *The Dutch Alliance*, p. 135; Monson, *Naval Tracts*, V, 313-14), but such illegal construction was comparatively unimportant, and Scandinavian records of increased tonnage after 1660 (*infra*, p. 307, n. 34) suggest that few Dutch vessels passed as northern-owned.

[5] For examples of dues payable at London, see Crouch, *Complete View*, pp. 386-408; Champion, *Considerations on Great Britain and the United States*, pp. 60-61; Great Britain, *Report on Trade with the United States*, p. 51.

[6] NYCD, V, 617; BT 6/185.

For our present purposes it will suffice to summarize briefly the regulations governing importations to England from Europe. Certain goods were forbidden to come from the Netherlands or Germany. Even in cases where their importation was permitted, most of those goods and some others, amounting to about one-half the total value of England's European imports, had to be carried in English ships or in ships of the country producing the goods. If brought in such foreign ships, or in English-owned, foreign-built ships, not made free, the goods enumerated were assessed with alien duties. Calculated, as required by law, at 1.25 percent of the value given in the Book of Rates (which might or might not correspond with the real value), the alien duties gave substantial protection in the case of some commodities like wine and brandy, but were merely nominal in the case of others, like wheat.[7] Heavier duties were also assessed upon certain other commodities, like iron, wrought silk, and ostrich wool, when imported in foreign ships.[8]

The effect of protective legislation upon the carriage of goods from England is less generally known, but was none the less real. From 1660 to 1670 beer paid a duty of 2 shillings a ton, if exported in English-built shipping, as against 6 shillings if shipped otherwise.[9] English-caught fish could be exported duty free, if shipped in English vessels, and paid customs, until 1722, if exported in foreign vessels.[10] Similarly, heavy preferential duties gave English shipping a practical monopoly of the outward carriage of Newcastle and Sunderland coal,[11] and the bounties on corn were paid only if the shipments were made in English vessels.[12] In 1698 the shipments to foreign Europe included approximately 285 tuns of beer, 3,700

---

[7] 12 Car. II, c. 4 and c. 18; 14 Car. II, c. 11; Crouch, *Complete View;* for tabular arrangement, see *infra,* pp. 405-6.

[8] *Infra,* pp. 409-14.

[9] 12 Car. II, c. 4; preference removed by 22 & 23 Car. II, c. 13.

[10] By Englishmen, 12 Car. II, c. 4; by aliens, 25 Car. II, c. 6; preference removed, 8 Geo. I, c. 15.

[11] See statutes cited and statistics given in Nef, *British Coal Industry,* II, 222-36, 385; Ashton and Sykes, *Coal Industry of the Eighteenth Century,* pp. 247-48.

[12] The earliest bounty was offered in 1673 (25 Car. II, c. 1, xxxi; Gras, "Corn Bounty Experiment," *Quar. Jour. Econ.,* XXIV, 419-22). The statute lapsed in 1681, but was revived in 1689 (1 Gul. & Mar., c. 12) and continued until 1814 (54 Geo. III, c. 69) except when temporarily suspended. See also Barnes, *History of the English Corn Laws,* pp. 1-151, 296; Gras, *Evolution of the English Corn Market.*

tons of fish, 16,800 tons of corn, and 39,232 tons of coal.[13] Differences between the "ton" as a unit of weight and the "ton" as a measurement of shipping make exact comparisons impractical; but when we remember that English tonnage clearing for foreign Europe that year was about 100,000 tons,[14] it becomes obvious that English shipowners then owed thanks to Parliament for a considerable portion of their cargoes to the Continent. Moreover, the shipments of corn receiving the bounty increased to an annual average of 363,746 quarters from 1697 to 1731, and 675,076 quarters from 1731 to 1766;[15] and exportations of coal rose to 265,000 tons in 1789.[16]

In evaluating the influence of parliamentary legislation, it is not necessary to show that the laws gave English shipping preference in both the inward and the outward carriage. It is elementary business economics that a ship's profits depend upon a two-way freight. If given sufficient protection to control the carriage of goods either inward or outward, a master will cut freight rates on the return trip to meet competition, rather than sail with no cargo at all.[17] For the same reason a practical monopoly in carrying a profitable freight enables a vessel to complete its lading by carrying other goods at rates which it would be unable to afford under completely competitive conditions. Likewise, on a three-legged voyage a vessel may succeed in carrying goods from port to port abroad, in competition with cheaper carriers, so long as the receipts from freight are greater than actual operating costs, and so long as it is possible to pay interest and other overhead charges from profits gained on some other leg of the voyage. Thus, both in the Mediterranean, where natural conditions were favorable, and in the Baltic, where they were not, English vessels succeeded in obtaining a share in the "port-to-port" trade abroad, the gain from which (together with the profits

[13] Customs 3/1. The tonnage equivalents given in the text are necessarily approximations, but should be reasonably accurate.

[14] Chalmers, *Estimate*, table facing p. 37.

[15] Westerfield, *Middlemen in English Business*, p. 164, citing Prothero, *English Farming*, p. 452; see also Barnes, *History of the English Corn Laws*, pp. 12, 16, 297-300.

[16] Ashton and Sykes, *Coal Industry of the Eighteenth Century*, p. 227. However, the estimate probably includes exports elsewhere than to the Continent.

[17] For examples, see the French trade (*infra*, p. 295), and the plantation trade (*supra*, p. 268).

on the turnover of the cargoes carried) was said to have equaled one
percent of the total value of her exports.[18]

Obviously the laws affected the different trades of Europe differ-
ently. English merchants were free to choose whatever carrier they
pleased in many cases, and in most others could use a foreign vessel
if they were willing to lose the bounty or the reduction in duties to
be obtained by employing an English ship. Ample opportunity
remained for the operation of other factors, the natural tendency
of merchants to employ their own ships and to a lesser extent those
of their fellow countrymen, the persistence of habit, the difficulty of
breaking up old commercial connections, the interruptions of war,
and the interference of other nations' regulatory measures, to mention but a few. If we are to keep them all in mind, we cannot survey
the situation as a whole. We must attempt to analyze it port by port
and trade by trade.

An examination of the port books shows that such southern and
western ports as Southampton, Dartmouth, Plymouth, and Bristol
had engaged in the rich and distant trades with Spain, Portugal, the
Mediterranean, and the colonies long before 1651. At no time do
these ports appear to have depended to any great extent upon the
Dutch entrepôt, and during the years examined, Dutch shipping
carried very little of their trade.[19] The principal influences retarding
or stimulating the growth of local shipping appear to have been, on
the one hand, the activities of the Algerine pirates, and to a lesser
extent those of the Dunkirkers; and, on the other, the development
of commerce, especially the Irish coal trade and the plantation trade.

Tonnage statistics for the coal trade with Ireland must be carefully analyzed to avoid overstressing that trade's importance to shipping. At first glance they are most impressive. The quantity of coal

[18] Shaftesbury Papers, GD 24/44. In 1673 merchants told of ships going from Lisbon
and Spain to Venice, and of others from Portugal and Italy to the Levant (CO 388/1),
and the passes issued in 1675/6 show that Eng'ish vessels engaged in a port-to-port
trade, even in the Baltic (SP 29/389, pp. 1-42).

[19] Of a total of 955 ships tabulated, only 44 came from the Netherlands. No Dutch
ships were included in the direct, and very few in the third-party, trades. For citations, see *infra*, pp. 415-16. It should be noted, however, that during the years examined
Holland's ships were being harassed by the Dunkirkers, and it is not unlikely that
at other times Dutch vessels carried a greater percentage of the trade. In 1621 it was
stated in the House of Commons that there were many Western ports which could not
get any masts if the Dutch did not bring them (CJ I, 642).

exported rose from 500 tons in 1600 to 60,000 or 65,000 tons in the nineties, and to an annual average of 205,000 tons for 1771-78.[20] Such exports so swelled Whitehaven's clearance statistics that in 1771 the English tonnage leaving the port exceeded that departing from London.[21] But since, on the average, the same collier made ten voyages a year between Whitehaven and Ireland, London still remained the port which gave employment to the greater tonnage of shipping.[22]

Many factors combined to influence conditions on the East Coast. As on the West Coast, piracy or privateering played an important part at first, although the Dunkirkers rather than the Algerines took the leading rôle.[23] Fundamental changes in trade and industry were also occurring. The North Sea fisheries declined,[24] and the coal trade rose in importance, so much so that by the end of Elizabeth's reign the tonnage of vessels clearing with coal for ports abroad (exclusive of the coastwise coal traffic) came close to equaling that of the total tonnage required to carry all of London's importations of foreign commodities.[25] Even in the coal trade, however, English ships could not hold their own without protection. The coastwise carriage had been reserved for English vessels as early as 1563,[26] and, beginning in 1620, a series of preferential duties favored exportation in English ships.[27] Although the preferential duties caused a loss in the volume of trade when foreigners went to Scotland and to other regions which imposed no similar duties, the action enabled English vessels, which in 1616 had carried only 75 of the 686 cargoes shipped,

[20] Nef, *British Coal Industry*, I, 71 n., 90-91; Ashton and Sykes, *The Coal Industry of the Eighteenth Century*, p. 228.

[21] Chalmers, *Estimate*, table facing p. 46; Sheffield, *Observations*, p. v.

[22] Nef, *British Coal Industry*, I, 394 n.

[23] Oppenheim, *Administration of the Royal Navy*, pp. 198, 252, 272, 274-76.

[24] *Infra*, pp. 329-32.

[25] Nef, *British Coal Industry*, I, 239 n.

[26] 5 Eliz., c. 5, vi. A proposal of 1592 suggests that the prohibition may not have been very effectively enforced. If its estimate that a tax of 1s. per chaldron on all coal brought to London by strangers would raise £500 a year was accurate, about 10,000 out of a total of 25,000 or 30,000 London chaldrons were carried in foreign vessels (Nef, *British Coal Industry*, II, 24 n.).

[27] CSPD (1619-23), p. 174. As early as 1552, it had been proposed to benefit English shipping by making a staple in Kent to which no ships except English might transport coal from Newcastle. In the last years of Elizabeth's reign, John Keymer would have limited the exportation to English vessels. Nef (*British Coal Industry*, II, 211-38) gives an account of these and other early proposals, as well as the later history of the legislation.

to command the traffic in 1661, and to carry 158 of the 190 cargoes clearing from Newcastle.[28]

Marked evidences of Dutch influence appear in the port books before 1651. During the Twelve Years' Truce and before the preferential coal duties, a majority of the ships entering the ports of Newcastle, Hull, Ipswich, Lynn, and Yarmouth were foreign vessels, most of which belonged to Holland. The English ratio improved in the thirties and forties, but fell considerably short of the heights which it attained after the laws' enactment. There also appears to have been a shift in the course of trade on the East Coast, since entries from the Netherlands declined from 44.3 percent before the passage of the Acts to 38.6 percent thereafter.[29] It would be reckless to draw too positive conclusions from the evidence available, but it seems safe to assert that legislative enactments were not the least of the influences affecting East Coast shipping.

There was a more decided shift in the course of trade at London.[30] In 1602, 48 percent of the ships came from the Netherlands and 26 percent of the tonnage,[31] but by 1719 the percentages had decreased to 13.3 and 8.1 respectively.[32] Although we do not have statistics showing the value of the goods imported before 1660, the figures thereafter indicate that Dutch imports were declining in importance. They constituted 12.2 percent of London's total in 1663, 12 percent in 1669, 10.7 percent in 1698, 8.5 percent in 1701, 8 percent in 1715, 4.7 percent in 1750, and only 3.9 percent in 1775.[33] In short, whether because of, or despite the Navigation Acts, London grew, between the glorious days of the Armada and the reign of George III, from a town trading with its immediate neighbors to a world market specializing in goods brought from afar.[34]

[28] Nef, *British Coal Industry*, II, 24-25. In 1594, 260 cargoes out of 852 had been carried in English vessels; in 1633, 124 cargoes out of 534. By 1710-14, the tonnage carried in English ships was about 4 times as great as that taken in foreign ships (*idem;* CO 388/18, No. 22).

[29] For citations, see *infra*, pp. 415-16. In 1719 entries from Holland constituted only 14.4 percent of the ships and 15.6 percent of the tonnage at the outports. For other figures concerning the kingdom as a whole, see *infra*, pp. 304-6.

[30] See also pp. 345-48.

[31] Miller, "New Evidence," *Quar. Jour. Econ.*, XLI, 752. For 1609, see BM Lans. MSS 142, f. 304.

[32] CO 390/5, No. 45.

[33] BM Add MSS 36785; Customs 3.

[34] Nevertheless, as Smith ("The World Entrepôt," *Jour. Pol. Econ.*, XVIII, 702)

Discussion of the tonnage employed in London's trade can best
be deferred, but the accusation, sometimes voiced, that the Navigation Acts resulted from the selfish designs of London merchants[35]
gives interest to a comparative study of the Acts' effects upon London and England's other ports. As far as we can determine, the
accusation originated in outport jealousy and merely echoed other
charges against London.[36] By Charles I's reign, London possessed
one-third of the kingdom's ships, and after 1660 did no more than
maintain the same relative position.[37] Statistics of trade likewise
indicate no great· change, but they are less useful because they
varied radically from year to year,[38] and because the marked gains

warns, we must not overemphasize the importance of London's entrepôt trade. It was
always subsidiary to commerce that was essentially English in origin or destination.
[35] BM Add MSS 11579. f. 92.
[36] For similar charges about other matters, see THT (1609-25), f. 14; "Thomas
Roe's Speech," *Harl. Misc.*, IV, 436; Lipson, *Economic History*, II, 250-57, 322-23.
[37] After 1582 the proportion remains about the same whatever test is used. In the
following data the 1582 figures for seamen include masters and fishermen and exclude
London's watermen, while those for 1628 exclude fishermen also. The London figures
for 1700 are compiled from returns of the Surveyor of the Navigation Act concerning
ships visited from Sept., 1700 to Jan., 1701, for the purpose of giving Algerine passes.

Year	England	London	Source of Data
1582	68,433 tons	12,297 tons	SP12/146
1582	177 ships over 100 tons	62 ships over 100 tons	Oppenheim, *Administration of the Royal Navy*, p. 175
1582	15,326 seamen	1,329 seamen	*Ibid.*, p. 176
1628	350 vessels over 100 tons	132 vessels over 100 tons	*Ibid.*, p. 271
1629	10,379 seamen	3,422 seamen	*Ibid.*, p. 244
1700	261,222 tons	84,882 tons	CO 388/9, F19
1700	27,076 men	10,605 men	*Idem*
1792	101,060 seamen	31,552 seamen	BM Add MSS 38432, section 5
1793	1,206,778 tons	378,787 tons	GL MSS 230

[38] A table of the average yield of the customs revenue for the five years ending
Michaelmas, 43 Elizabeth (Hall, *Custom-Revenue*, II, 245) shows that London
paid 6.7 times as much as the outports. According to an estimate of 1602 (CSPD
[1601-3], p. 267; Lipson, *Economic History*, II, 250) the ratio was 3.9 to 1. In
1604 Sandys showed that it was 6.5 to 1 (CJ I, 218-21; Miller, "New Evidence,"
Quar. Jour. Econ., XLI, 743). The ratio for imports, not including silk, wine,
Venice gold, and silver, was said to be 3.7 to 1 in 1613, and 3.1 to 1 in 1614, although the export ratio was slightly more favorable to the outports (BM Lans. MSS
152 ff., 177-78; Anderson, *Origin of Commerce*, II, 260). The ratio for all duties was
3.7 to 1 in 1649-50 and in 1677 (Hall, *Custom-Revenue*, II, 247; Davenant, *Works*,
V, 352), 2.1 to 1 in 1698 (Customs 3/1), and 6 to 1 in 1699-1701 (CTB XI-XVII,
Introduction, ccccxlii-ccccclxxxviii). The value of London's imports was 2.6 times that
of the outports in 1698, 2.7 in 1773, and 2.1 in 1775 (Customs 3/1, 3/73, 3/75).

which outport trade was making in America and foreign Europe under the Acts are minimized by the growth of East India trade which Company control brought exclusively to London.[39] Although estimates of population growth show that London gained at the expense of the remainder of the kingdom, its encroachments were more rapid before 1651 than thereafter.[40] Thus, even if the Londoners' motives had been selfish when they urged the law's enactment, the outports gained proportionately as much or more than the metropolis.

Ireland had a peculiar status under the Navigation Acts. Although for customs purposes Ireland was considered a foreign country, the Act of 1660 treated the trade between England and Ireland as a coast trade and limited it to English and Irish ships. It also subjected goods entering Ireland to the same restrictions as those destined for England. Irish ships were treated as if English-owned and built, and Irish seamen were considered to be English. But the jealousy of English merchants led to increasing discriminations against the Irish in the plantation trade.[41]

Ireland's merchant marine apparently had a greater share of its own trade in the sixteenth century than ever thereafter,[42] but with the advent of the flyboat, the Dutch took over most of it.[43] Strafford admitted in 1634 that "it is true, that in a manner most of the Trade of this Kingdom passeth to and fro in Dutch Bottoms, and it is a necessary Devil that we must bear with for a Time."[44] The condition of Irish shipping improved markedly thereafter, but Irish shipping was never destined to attain any great tonnage. In 1698, of the 120,728 tons estimated to be employed in Ireland's trade, 21,532

[39] Customs 3/1, 3/73. Output trade rose from 24.5 percent in 1698 to 30 percent in 1773 with America, from 23.6 percent to 36.9 percent with foreign Europe outside the Mediterranean, and from 1.8 percent to 7.9 percent within the Mediterranean where London benefited from the Levant Company's control of most of the trade. East India imports constituted 7.6 percent of England's total in 1698 and 16.9 percent in 1773. See also *supra*, p. 240, n. 8.

[40] Lipson, *Economic History*, II, 249-50.

[41] *Infra*, pp. 388, n. 1; 397, n. 35. It should be noted that the prohibitions in the Act of 1662 relating to goods from Holland and Germany did not extend to Ireland.

[42] Longfield, *Anglo-Irish Trade*, pp. 128, 143, 164, 211, Appendix, and *passim*. Of the 163 ships trading at Bridgewater, 1560-61, 103 were Irish-owned.

[43] O'Brien, *Economic History of Ireland in the Seventeenth Century*, p. 67.

[44] Strafford's *Letters*, I, 233.

tons were Irish, 76,044 English, and the rest, including 4,205
Scottish, were foreign.[45] As far as the course of trade was concerned,
the bulk was always with England, although it was seriously impaired by various restraints on Ireland's industry and commerce,
particularly the exclusion of Irish cattle from England, which
drove the Irish to develop their trade with other countries,[46] to
England's detriment.

Scotland, however, was a foreign country from 1660 to 1707, so
far as the Navigation Acts were concerned, despite the fact that
neither the first two Stuarts nor the Commonwealth had discriminated against the Scots. The most likely reason for the change in
policy was that Scottish merchants, who had a reputation for "parsi-
mony in apparrell and dyet and . . . exceeding industriousness and
diligence," had proved themselves to be formidable competitors.[47]
The close political and commercial connections which Scotland had
formed with France during Elizabeth's reign had given the Scots
privileges, many of which were retained even after 1603, when
James I became King of both England and Scotland. Their ships,
although smaller, were cheaper to operate than English vessels, and
their seamen were content with lower wages and cheaper victuals.[48]
Records of their activities appear in the port books, especially in
the importation of French wines, throughout the first half of the
century.[49] Bristol complained in 1620 that Scottish competition left
its shipmasters "few and poore," and during the Bishops' War there

[45] Customs 15/1. As late as 1792, Ireland owned only 69,567 tons of shipping, or
less than one-twentieth of the total possessed in His Majesty's dominions (BM Add
MSS 38432).

[46] Sheffield, *On Ireland, passim;* Cunningham, *English Industry and Commerce,*
II, 373, 376, 378-79, 582-83, 586, 588-91; Lipson, *Economic History,* III, 128, 197-
206; Murray, *Commercial Relations between England and Ireland,* pp. 31-35; O'Brien,
Economic History of Ireland in the Seventeenth Century, pp. 153, 160-63.

[47] Keith, *Commercial Relations of England and Scotland,* p. 3.

[48] *Ibid.,* pp. 3-5, 13, 47-50.

[49] For citations, see *infra,* pp. 415-16. Apparently they also participated in the Baltic
trade. In 1651 the English Eastland merchants at Danzig declared that "Divers of
the Scottish Nation" were "Great Traders for London," though in 1615 the Scottish
Privy Council had reserved only the southern and western trades to native shipping,
because native ships were not fit to carry the much-needed commodities of the
"easterlyne" trade (Keith, *Commercial Relations of England and Scotland,* pp. 34-
35, 69).

were more than fifty Scottish ships arrested in English harbors or seized on the way to foreign ports.[50]

English jealousy had shown itself in discriminatory fees and other customs hindrances placed in the way of the Scots in certain ports, especially on the East Coast,[51] but London Trinity House did not seem to fear Scottish competition. When consulted about the matter after the Restoration, it advised, "with submission to better Judgments," that "the Scotch Nation have liberty to bring forreigne goods in their owne built shipps," so that "the generallity of that Nation" would continue to buy their foreign goods in London instead of in Holland, and Scottish seamen be available for the King's fleet in time of war, instead of being constrained to serve the Dutch. It did not believe that the competition of the Scots would be particularly harmful, since the commodities they carried consisted chiefly of French wines and were "inconsiderable in respect to the quantity."[52]

Other advisers of the English government, however, had different ideas, and the Act of 1660 denied both Scottish merchants and Scottish shipping the rights accorded their English rivals. The fact made no great difference in the European trade, since special exemptions were made for Scottish corn, salt, and fish, imported in Scottish-built vessels.[53] Moreover, Scotland could and did retaliate with a navigation act of her own, and the percentage of Scottish ships in the trade between England and Scotland increased.[54] The greatest hindrance from which Scotland suffered was her exclusion from the English plantation trade, as is shown by the fact that Scottish ship-

[50] *Ibid.*, p. 39. The principal English ports visited by the Scots were London and Newcastle, but they also visited Plymouth and other harbors in Devonshire and the West. In London the average annual value of Scottish imports for the seven years from 1597 to 1603 was £2,125 (calculating the value of the wares as twenty times that of the customs paid). By 1663 and 1669, it had become £20,012 and £20,999 respectively (*ibid.*, p. 8; BM Add MSS 36785).

[51] Keith, *Commercial Relations of England and Scotland*, p. 36.

[52] THCM (1661-65), p. 156. Similarly, when the Scottish Privy Council attempted to confine Scottish trade to native shipping, it accorded English ships native privileges (Keith, *Commercial Relations of England and Scotland*, p. 35).

[53] 12 Car. II, c. 18, xvi. Other commodities which were important in the trade from Scotland to London in 1663 and 1669 were, in the order of value, linen, linen yarn, coal, skins, and tallow (BM Add MSS 36785).

[54] Keith, *Commercial Relations of England and Scotland*, p. 90.

ping doubled or trebled within five years after the restraint was removed.[55]

The early trade of England with the Mediterranean was conducted chiefly by the Italians, first the Florentines, then the Genoese, and finally the Venetians.[56] When English merchants began to take part, they did not confine their shipments to English vessels, but employed "sundry strangers also . . . Candiots, Raguseans, Sicilians, Genouezes, Venetian galliasses, Spanish and Portugale ships."[57] When merchants asked that companies be organized to control the trade, much was heard of the employment to be given "great and tall ships." Although the charters did not require the use of English ships, the Levant Company, at least, appears to have confined its trade to English vessels, of which they owned some and hired others. It is not safe, however, to declare that the Mediterranean trade was monopolized by English ships, because English interlopers might trade in defiance of the company's rights, and the charter did not prevent aliens from trading. Also the company's jurisdiction did not include most of Italy nor any part of France or of Spain, even though within the Straits.[58]

The evidence is conflicting as to whether or not English shipping needed protection against Dutch carriers within the Strait of Gibraltar. English vessels had a natural advantage in that the voyage was dangerous and the trades were rich. The high value of the cargoes prompted the use of the more staunchly constructed and heavily armed English ships, rather than the Dutch flyboats, despite their lower freight rates. According to a statement of the Levant Company in 1648, even the Dutch themselves preferred to ship their merchandise in English vessels;[59] and in 1693, a war year, less than one-seventh of the total importations of Florentine wine came in foreign ships, despite the fact that it could be imported on equal

---

[55] At the time of union, in 1707, Scotland owned 215 ships, of 14,485 tons. Five years later, she had 1,123 ships, of 50,232 tons (BM Harl. MSS 6269).

[56] Epstein, *The Levant Company*, pp. 1-3.

[57] Hakluyt, *Voyages*, V, 63; Lindsay, *Merchant Shipping*, II, 53.

[58] Epstein, *The Levant Company*, pp. 17, 35, 38-39, 42-47, 50-51, 64, 109, 113-16, 135, 138, 140-144, 149, 153-210, 224, 242, 245. Under the charter of 1661, the company might lay double duties on the goods of aliens (*ibid.*, p. 65).

[59] SP 105/112, p. 69.

terms in either English or Italian vessels.[60] On the other hand, the English trading to the Levant recognized the threat of the Dutch flyboat as early as 1595.[61] Efforts were made to stop importation "in strange bottoms" in 1615 and again in the sixteen forties, and the Levant Company obviously failed to hold its own under free competition in the export of fish from Yarmouth.[62]

Moreover, there appears to have been danger of rivalry from the entrepôts in the Netherlands. In 1617 one of the Merchant Adventurers, a Mr. Flowers, imported some currants from his company's jurisdiction and caused loud outcries from the Levant Company, which contended that its charter rights were violated. As a matter of fact, although some words in the charter might be construed to give the company control over all trade *in Turkey commodities*, the more accurate interpretation gave the company jurisdiction only over trade *with the Levant*.[63] Nevertheless, at the suggestion of the Privy Council, the matter was compromised. Mr. Flowers kept his currants, and members of both companies agreed thereafter not to import currants from Germany or Flanders.[64] Yet apparently the indirect trade continued or was revived, because, as we have seen, it was one of the causes for passing the Act of 1651.[65]

The laws probably exerted their greatest control over the import trade. Imports from Turkey had to come in English-built shipping or pay alien duties. The Italian wrought silk, which paid lower duties when brought in English-built ships, and the goods enumerated in the Act of 1660 comprised 55 percent in value and about two-thirds in weight of the goods coming from Italy.[66] On the outward

[60] One hundred thirteen and one-half tuns came in free ships and 20 1/3 tuns in unfree ships (CO 388/6, B47-51).

[61] Rowland, *England and Turkey*, p. 138.

[62] Monson (*Naval Tracts*, III, 432) tells of "two great Holland ships," of 300 or 400 tons each, which came to London from the Levant, "laden with currants and cotton-wool upon the account of Holland merchants to sell here," causing so much apprehension that the merchants appealed to the King and obtained the proclamation of 1615 (APC [1615-16], p. 98; Epstein, *The Levant Company*, p. 151; and *supra*, p. 31).

[63] See charter of 1605, printed in Epstein, *The Levant Company*, pp. 153-210.

[64] *Ibid.*, pp. 110-12.

[65] *Supra*, pp. 44-45.

[66] BM Add MSS 36785. Percentages are calculated on the basis of London figures for 1663 and 1669. The percentage by weight is necessarily an estimate, since not all

voyage, English ships did not benefit materially from the preferential duties on coal and corn, since the quantities going to either Turkey or Italy were small; but the exports of fish may have helped the English outward ratio until 1722, when foreign vessels as well as English were permitted to carry shipments duty-free.[67]

As far as we can discover from the available statistics, English shipping in the Mediterranean fared well under the laws. Except during war years, it dominated England's trade there,[68] and contemporaries were generally agreed as to the beneficial effects of the Acts. Even that vociferous opponent of shipping regulations, Roger Coke, approved limiting the Turkey trade to English-built shipping[69] and, from its first advocacy of the original measure of 1651, the Levant Company never wavered in its support of parliamentary protection. In the troublesome days of the eighteenth century, its plea was for more, rather than for less legislation.[70]

The statistics also show that, although the absolute value of importations from the Mediterranean did not diminish, they were to play a relatively decreasing part in English commerce. Their value fell from 16.3 percent in 1663, and 18.3 percent in 1669, to an annual average of 6.9 percent from 1770 to 1780.[71] Restated in terms of the

---

the quantities were measured by weight, and it was necessary to approximate the weight of items listed by dozens, barrels, etc.

[67] Customs 3/1, 3/72.

[68] The figures in BT 6/185 show that shipping between England and the Straits was almost exclusively English. Below is the percentage of English tonnage in England's trade with Italy and Turkey:

	INWARD		OUTWARD	
YEAR	Total Tonnage	Percent English Tonnage	Total Tonnage	Percent English Tonnage
1719	1,550	100.0	2,133	100.0
1771	12,968	100.0	23,113	99.5
1775	17,948	100.0	25,702	99.1
1779	7,975	12.7	20,242	1.6
1785	18,291	95.2	19,138	92.3

[69] Coke, *How the Navigation of England May Be Increased*, pp. 91-92; *supra*, p. 236.

[70] CO 388/9, H1; SP 105/144, pp. 282-86; SP 105/151, p. 350. See also *supra*, pp. 44-45.

[71] The figures in BM Add MSS 36785, for London in 1663 and 1669, and the annual averages from 1700 for all England in Sheffield, *Observations*, Appendix IX, illustrate

employment of English shipping, Miller's figures show that the Italian and Levant trades employed 1,870 tons of English shipping, or 11.9 percent of the total English tonnage entering London in 1602, and that 509 tons more came from Barbary.[72] Other evidence indicates that the ratio for the whole kingdom at that time was probably the same.[73] But by 1771, although the same trades employed 12,968 tons, that tonnage constituted only 2.1 percent of the English total entering England.[74]

Blame for the decline should not be placed upon the Navigation Acts. There were other causes. The Duke of Tuscany and the Doge of Venice were discriminating against the English. There were complaints of high duties in Zante and of corrupt governors who tempted sailors to buy small parcels in violation of the law, and then seized the ship unless bribes were forthcoming.[75] During the frequent years of war, English shipping had to navigate between Scylla and Charybdis—Algerine pirates on one coast and French privateers on the other. The Levant Company confronted the rivalry of interlopers and competition from its fellows, the East India and the Russia Companies.[76] Even more important than these factors, since they had existed long before the decline commenced, was the rise of other trades and the competition with the French. When France improved

---

in detail the declining importance of England's Mediterranean trade in relation to her total commerce:

Year	Italy and Venice	Percent of Total	Levant	Percent of Total	Straits	Percent of Total	Total Mediterranean	Percent of Total
1663	£284,332	7.0	£373,595	9.3			£657,927	16.3
1669	303,463	7.2	466,703	11.1			770,166	18.3
1700-10	248,298	5.4	252,942	5.5	£3,455	0.07	504,695	11.0
1750-60	583,852	6.8	157,380	1.8	96,769	1.1	838,001	9.7
1770-80	677,903	5.7	135,842	1.2	3,525	0.02	817,270	6.9

The inclusion of the trade with Barbary, or Africa as it was listed in later years, would make only a fractional change: 0.39 percent for 1663; 0.18 percent for 1669; 0.3 percent for 1700-10; 0.43 percent for 1750-60; and 0.58 percent for 1770-80.

[72] Miller, "New Evidence," *Quar. Jour. Econ.*, XLI, 743, 752, 757-58.

[73] In 1581 the Venetian Company alone used 14 ships, 2,550 tons, and 510 men. In 1600 the Levant Company owned or freighted 29 ships, of 5,290 tons, with 1,189 men. A document dated July 8, 1605, listed 31 ships totaling 5,810 tons (Epstein, *The Levant Company*, pp. 24, 224-27).

[74] BT 6/185.

[75] Tuscany: CO 388/8, C7, C16, C19, C28, D22, E4; Venice and Zante: CO 388/1, Jan. 23, 1673/4; Epstein, *The Levant Company*, pp. 21-23, 27, 41, 51-52, 262-70.

[76] Epstein, *The Levant Company*, pp. 109-16, 142; Lipson, *Economic History*, II, 348-52.

her woolen manufactures and seriously undertook to gain the Turkish trade, her obviously more favorable geographic location gave her traders great advantages over the English, who failed to hold their own.[77]

England's trade with the Iberian peninsula had long been of considerable importance commercially. Early in the sixteenth century, Portugal's control of the African route to the East made her a rich commercial nation, exporting the jewels, spices, drugs, sugar, and other products of Africa and of the Indies, besides her own salt, wine, oil, and fruit.[78] In 1580 King Philip's ambassador declared that the Spanish trade was the most profitable trade the English possessed, and that it made "them almost the masters of commerce in other parts as well."[79] More than a century later, mercantilists looked with pleasure upon the excess of exports over imports, and described the trade as "the best Flower in our Garden, that took off more of our Woollen Manufactures, and made us greater Returns of Money than any other Trade."[80] Of the two, the trade with Portugal was at first decidedly the less important. Roughly speaking, it was about one-fifth of that with Spain in 1584[81] and even somewhat less in 1663 and 1669. Its relative importance increased, however, and after the Methuen Treaty, it usually approximated that of Spain and sometimes even exceeded it.[82]

Together, the trades employed 100 ships and 2,000 mariners, or about 15.1 percent of England's over-sea shipping, at the beginning

[77] *British Merchant*, II, 81-85, 156, 280-90. In a letter to Godolphin, Charles Davenant said that the French were perfecting their woolen manufactures so rapidly that they "must soon supplant us in the Levant" (GL MSS 210, ff. 7-8). For additional information concerning the trade, see Lipson, *Economic History*, II, 335-52; Ambrose, "English Traders at Aleppo (1658-1756)," *Econ. Hist. Rev.*, III, 246-67.

[78] Shillington and Chapman, *Commercial Relations of England and Portugal*, pp. 108, 130, 133.

[79] CSP Spanish (1580-86), p. 8; Lipson, *Economic History*, III, 211-12.

[80] *British Merchant*, III, 198; Whitworth, *State of Trade*, p. 31.

[81] Shillington and Chapman, *Commercial Relations of England and Portugal*, p. 147.

[82] The value of imports from Spain and Portugal bore the following relation to England's total imports:

YEAR	SPAIN		PORTUGAL		SOURCE OF DATA
	Value	Percent	Value	Percent	
1663	£558,437	13.9	£86,691	2.1	Figures through 1669 for London
1669	448,819	10.6	67,692	1.6	only, from BM Add MSS
1700-10	225,090	4.9	243,900	5.3	36785. Annual averages after
1750-60	413,065	4.8	267,656	3.1	1700 from Sheffield, *Observa-*
1770-80	456,597	3.8	375,485	3.1	*tions*, App. IX.

of the seventeenth century.[83] Thereafter, the number and tonnage of ships employed increased, but the relative importance of the traffic declined to 9.3 percent in 1719 and to only 5.9 percent in 1785.[84]

In so far as the parliamentary measures affected the shipping engaged in the Iberian trade, they exerted their influence over shipments inward. Despite a favorable balance of trade, England's exports to Spain were not bulky and, except for corn, included few of the commodities in the carriage of which the laws favored English ships. Two-thirds to three-fourths of English imports from Spain and an even greater proportion of those from Portugal were enumerated, thus virtually excluding third-party carriers.[85] Moreover, the alien duties were sufficiently high to afford real protection against competition from either the Spanish or the Portuguese.

In estimating the value of the laws, the exclusion of third-party carriers seems to have been of greater importance than the granting of protection against Iberian competition.[86] England was supposed to have gained a "monopoly of the shipping" in her Spanish trade by Queen Elizabeth's day. The English had deferred to the Portuguese and had even employed Portuguese shipbuilders as late as Henry VIII's reign, but the situation had been reversed before the time of Cromwell. By 1644 the Portuguese ambassador acknowledged that Portuguese merchant ships ordinarily did not come to England, and in 1649 English vessels were said to have been required even for Portugal's Brazil fleet.[87]

The natural advantages of English vessels, as compared with the Dutch, were fewer in the case of the Iberian trade than they had been in the trades within the Straits. Although the Iberian peninsula's proximity to the dens of the Algerine pirates introduced an element of danger which favored the English, the bulky character of the commodities helped the Dutch. By the middle of the century, Spain

[83] BM Lans. MSS 142, f. 304.

[84] CO 390/5, No. 45 (1719); BT 6/185 (1785).

[85] By value, for London only, 1663, 1669 (BM Add MSS 36785). The percentage by weight was slightly lower.

[86] The port books examined before 1660 show that 88.4 percent of the ships in England's trade with Spain and Portugal were English, the remainder being third-party carriers (three Dutch, two Hamburg, one Lübeck, seven Scottish, and one unidentified).

[87] CSP Spanish (1580-86), p. 8; Lipson, *Economic History*, III, 211-12; Shillington and Chapman, *Commercial Relations of England and Portugal*, pp. 54, 131, 193-94.

and Portugal had lost their earlier control of the rich wares of the East and West Indies, and their stock in trade consisted chiefly of salt, fruit, and wines, products which could best be carried in Dutch-built flyboats. Evidence of Dutch competition in carrying merchandise to and from England before 1648 is limited because of the war between the two countries, but the Dutch rivalry was keen in the comparatively few years of peace. During the Twelve Years' Truce, English shipowners complained that the Dutch had cut the rates for carrying wine from 70s. to 25s. 6d., or even to 20s., per ton;[88] and after 1648 there was another series of complaints concerning the ruin which faced English shipowners. Conditions had not, however, become desperate, and Trinity House still believed that English ships could manage the trade if the import of "Spanish Biskey [and] Portugall" commodities was reserved for them.[89] Events proved the shipowners to be true prophets, and thereafter English vessels carried from 90 to 100 percent of England's trade with Spain and Portugal, unless political or commercial conditions were abnormal.[90]

The Act of Frauds also rendered English shipping a real service. In earlier years, a considerable part of England's trade with Portugal had passed through Middelburg and Antwerp and, if Parliament had not intervened,[91] Holland would undoubtedly have attempted to continue as middleman, at least for England's East Coast ports. By forbidding the importation of the principal Iberian products from Holland or Germany, the Act of Frauds eliminated the possibility of obtaining them from the entrepôts there and made the longer voyage to the south necessary.

The French trade was not popular with mercantilists. They complained that, since it was conducted during the perilous months of September, October, November, and December, it was harmful to ships and seamen, and that it was a "consumptive trade," in which the English, instead of drinking the health of the King of England,

[88] BM Lans. MSS 142, ff. 294-95, 302.
[89] THT (1613-61), pp. 48-49.
[90] CO 388/18, No. 22; CO 390/5, No. 45; BT 6/185.
[91] Shillington and Chapman, *Commercial Relations of England and Portugal*, pp. 133, 141-42.

drank "sickness to ourselves and wealth to the French King."[92] Partly as a result of their opposition and partly because of political and economic differences, Parliament prohibited the importation of French commodities from 1678 to 1685, 1689 to 1697, and 1703 to 1713, and at other times burdened it with most oppressive duties.[93] Meanwhile France was endeavoring to develop her own shipping, industry, and trade, and enacted measures which English merchants thought were unreasonable.[94]

As one might expect in the face of these legislative discouragements, French trade declined in importance. In 1602 the greatest tonnage entering London came from France, 28.4 percent of the whole.[95] But by the last quarter of the eighteenth century, the trade occupied less than 3 percent of the tonnage entering the kingdom.[96] The statistics of goods imported show that those from France declined in importance from 16 percent in 1663 to about 0.4 percent prior to the French Revolution.[97] Although the trade was one in which smuggling flourished, despite the dictates of patriotism and the combined efforts of the revenue officers, the army, and the navy,[98]

[92] Coke, *Discourse of Trade*, pp. 38-39. A broadside of the same period (GLB 38, n.d.) also charged that "Handcraftsmen of kingdom, some hundreds of thousands of people, are generally grown exceeding poor," owing to the import of foreign manufactures, especially from France, "for however slight, defective, and old fashioned, the said foreign Goods are, yet being here, and term'd A la mode de France, are greatly used."

[93] 29 & 30 Car. II, c. 1, prohibited the importation of an extensive list of French commodities during the French war and was repealed by 1 Jac. II, c. 6. All trade with France was prohibited by 1 Gul. & Mar., c. 34 (continued by 4 Gul. & Mar., c. 25) to the end of the war. 3 & 4 Anne, c. 13, imposed a similar war-time prohibition until amended by 9 Anne, c. 8, permitting the importation of French wines. For the high duties, see 7 & 8 Gul. III, c. 20, and 11 Geo. I, c. 7.

[94] For examples, see CO 388/8, D45 (1701); CO 388/11, I65 (1708); CO 388/12, K13, K14, K18 (1709).

[95] Miller, "New Evidence," *Quar. Jour. Econ.*, XLI, 752. It is to be noted that the number of ships coming from France was smaller than that from the Netherlands.

[96] BT 6/185.

[97] The following table shows the representative importations from France in their relation to England's entire trade:

Year	Value	Percent	Source of Data
1663	£643,706	16.03	Figures through 1669 for London only,
1669	541,583	12.91	from BM Add MSS 36785. Annual
1700–10	19,941	0.44	averages after 1700 from Sheffield,
1750–60	30,704	0.36	*Observations*, App. IX.
1770–80	45,572	0.39	

[98] *Supra*, p. 92. Some estimates held that smuggled goods from France amounted to a third of the value of legitimate trade (Shaftesbury Papers, GD 24/44; *British Merchant*, I, 279). It would seem that the commodities most often smuggled were not the

the amount of the decline, as well as a review of the evidence as a whole, suggests that it was not altogether offset by smuggling.[99] Conceding that the narrowness of the Channel permitted small boats to attempt the crossing, that a double profit awaited the illicit trader who could run a boatload of English wool to France and return with a cargo of heavily taxed or prohibited French silks, brandies, and wines, and that many succeeded whose activities never appeared in official statistics, the development of English silk manufactures during the exclusion of French silk suggests that the laws had had a real effect.[100] It is also important to remember that when French wines were excluded, the importation of wines from other countries rose.[101] Although some of such foreign wines may merely have been French vintages in disguise,[102] the fact still remains that, subsequent to the restrictive legislation, port replaced French wines upon many English tables.

In considering the relation of the Navigation Acts to the French trade, the most significant provision appears at first glance to be clause seventeen of the Act of 1660, which imposed a duty of five shillings a ton on French shipping coming to England. But it was merely a retaliatory measure against the 50 sous per ton which France levied on English shipping going to France,[103] and was withdrawn in 1713 when France agreed to remove her duty.[104] Certain Exeter merchants had contended that the five-shilling duty was not an adequate retaliation,[105] and entry figures for the Channel ports suggest that English vessels there did not succeed so well as they

---

enumerated articles, but others, such as linen and silk manufactures, paper, kidskins, "all manner of toys for women and children, fans, laces, embroidered cloths and beds" ("A Scheme of the Trade as It Is at Present Carried on between England and France," GLB 20).

[99] Cf. Lipson, *Economic History*, III, 104-11.

[100] Lipson notes the increase of silk manufacture, but denies any correlation with the Acts (*Economic History*, II, 101). *The British Merchant* (I, 12-13), however, claimed that removal of the discrimination against French silk manufactures would be ruinous to the English industry.

[101] See tables of wine imports (*British Merchant*) I, 302; Shillington and Chapman, *Commercial Relations of England and Portugal*, pp. 334-36).

[102] *British Merchant*, II, 144.

[103] Lipson, *Economic History*, III, 102.

[104] Chalmers, *Collection of Treaties*, I, 390-424.

[105] CO 388/12, K18. The duty seems to have been collected in a mitigated form (CTB VII, 154; VIII, 1817). See also *supra*, p. 79.

had before 1660. But there were ninety-six English entries for every two French entries on the East Coast, and even at the Channel ports the ratio was four to one.[106] Thus it seems reasonable to conclude that however it may have succeeded as compared with earlier years, English shipping more than held its own from 1660 to 1713, always assuming that the amount of smuggling did not render the official statistics meaningless.[107]

During most of the seventeenth century, the volume of French goods coming to England greatly exceeded that of goods being shipped to France. According to *The British Merchant*, whose calculations rested upon the Custom House figures for 1686, the ratio was 30,000 tons to 13,000 tons.[108] As a result, masters shipped freight from England gratis, or at very low rates, for the promise of the back carriage.[109] The era of prohibitions and high duties, however, almost terminated the legitimate trade in wines and bran-

[106] The port books examined (*infra*, pp. 415-16) do not afford the most satisfactory basis for examining the influence of the conflicting French and English duties. Conditions on the East Coast were also affected by the discriminatory duty on exports of coal after 1620 (*supra*, p. 35), and those in the Channel after 1631 by France's entry into the Thirty Years' War. The following figures, showing the percentages of English, French, and third-party ships entering from France, should be used with these reservations in mind, but even so they should be helpful:

| | BEFORE 1651 | | | | AFTER 1660 | | | |
| | Ships | Percent | | | Ships | Percent | | |
	Entering	E	F	T	Entering	E	F	T
East Coast	170	57.6	26.5	15.9	103	96.12	1.94	1.94
Channel Ports	262	81.3	6.5	12.2	163	71.2	17.8	11.0
Bristol	0				39	100.0		
Total	432	72.0	14.3	13.7	305	83.3	10.2	6.5

In 1660 London Trinity House declared that "the trade with Shipping from France into his Mats. Dominions is very little, Compared with the English Shipping trading into France" and that their ships were "very few & of smaller burthens" (THT [1613-61], p. 167). A memorandum in the Shaftesbury Papers (Supplementary, Bundle VII, No. 602, cited by Barbour, "Dutch and English Merchant Shipping," *Econ. Hist. Rev.*, II, 262) shows that, omitting those in ballast, 106 English ships, averaging 54.2 tons, cleared from London in 1670; and that including those in ballast, 802 English ships, averaging 36.5 tons, cleared from the outports for France.

[107] There was considerable smuggling, much of which was probably done in French vessels (Great Britain, *House of Lords MSS*, n.s. II, 194-95; Clark, *The Dutch Alliance*, p. 67), but most of it did not occur until after 1678, and the calculations in the text are based upon figures for years before that date.

[108] *British Merchant*, I, 250, 323.

[109] *Ibid.*, I, 240-41, 248, 327-28. The freight on the return voyage was said seldom to exceed 20s. a ton (BM Lans. MSS 142, f. 294 r.).

dies, and thereafter the outward entries exceeded those inward.[110]

The shifts in the course of legitimate trade, of course, altered the operation of the protective measures. During the eighteenth century, the preferential duties on coal, and to a lesser extent the bounties on corn, exerted the chief pressure brought to bear upon merchants to use English-owned ships. Earlier, the Act of 1660 had had the greater influence. It had enumerated most of the bulky French imports like wines, brandies, salt, and prunes, which constituted about one-half of the total value and three-quarters of the weight,[111] thereby excluding England's most dangerous competitors, the Dutch and the Scots, from the most valuable part of the traffic. Moreover, many of the alien duties assessed when the enumerated commodities came in French ships were substantial and, together with the duty of five shillings a ton on such vessels, gave the English real protection against competition from French carriers.[112]

Nevertheless, one must not overstress the significance either of the laws to the French trade, or of that trade to the maintenance of English navigation. The carriage of French wines had long been legally reserved for English vessels, by laws which had been enforced at least spasmodically.[113] Such changes as can be traced in the trade were occasioned by other measures than the Navigation Acts *per se*. And in any event, entry and clearance figures give an exaggerated idea of the importance of the trade to English shipping. Vessels engaged in traffic with France usually made four voyages a year,[114] and consequently the Custom House figures never truly represented the number of vessels or seamen employed. Moreover, the vessels diminished in size as the wine trade decreased. The average size of the English vessels entering London from France in 1602 was 60.3 tons, but in 1719 it was only 33.7 tons.[115]

---

[110] *British Merchant*, I, 301-2.

[111] For London in 1663 and 1669, BM Add MSS 36785; for the kingdom as a whole, 1686, *British Merchant*, I, 254-77. The *British Merchant* (I, 250, 287-89, 296-302, 321-23) estimated that more than half of the 30,000 tons entering from France in 1686 was devoted to shipments of wine and that the cargoes of the estimated 13,000 tons clearing for that country included 2,631 tons of corn, 3,658 tons of coal, and 360 tons of plantation goods. Figures for early eighteenth-century shipments of coal are given in Nef, *British Coal Industry*, II, 386; and for both coal and corn, in Customs 3.

[112] See *infra*, pp. 405-6. [113] See *supra*, pp. 21-28, 34-37. [114] *British Merchant*, I, 249.

[115] Miller, "New Evidence," *Quar. Jour. Econ.*, XLI, 752; CO 390/5, No. 45. English entries in the outports ranged from 30 to 78 tons during the thirties and forties (*infra*,

In England's trade with France, as in her trade with the Iberian and Mediterranean countries, the principal achievement of the Navigation Acts consisted in holding what she had already acquired. The original victory had been won, in part because of her natural advantages and her merchants' enterprise, and in part because of effective statutory and corporate regulations. All that the Navigation Acts can properly be credited with is meeting the temporary emergency caused by the French tonnage tax, and helping to forestall the more serious challenge of Dutch competition. It is only when we turn to England's trades with the entrepôt towns and with the timber lands of the North that we have a chance to discover whether the Acts were able to create new opportunities for English shipping in Europe.

---

pp. 415-16). In 1670 the English ships clearing for France averaged 54.2 tons from London and 36.5 tons from the outports (*supra,* p. 295, n. 106). Even as late as 1771-73, the average for the kingdom as a whole was only 46.2 tons for English vessels entering and 55.5 tons for those clearing (BT 6/185).

ENTREPÔT TOWNS AND TIMBER LANDS

CONTEMPORARY accounts of England's trade and navigation leave no doubt that the Flemish, Dutch, and Germans offered formidable competition, but the seriousness of the threat and the part that the Navigation Acts played in repelling it varied in each case.

As far as Flanders is concerned, the story is one of past glories. The towns of Flanders had once been the commercial center of Europe. Antwerp had been the principal station of the Hanseatic League in the first half of the sixteenth century, the favorite center of the Portuguese for distributing their spices and other wares, and the chief entrepôt for England's trade with the Continent.[1] Dunkirk had served as the base for Spanish privateers for almost a century.[2] Even as late as 1675, Englishmen spoke of their commercial competitors as "Flemings," though at this time it was the "Dutch" to whom they referred.[3] Flanders had fallen to a decidedly subordinate position by 1660. The wars of the Reformation had seriously injured the commerce of Antwerp, and the closing of the Scheldt completed its ruin. Also Dunkirk had passed into the hands of the English, who were shortly thereafter to transfer it to France.

The laws appear to have had little influence on England's post-Restoration trade with Flanders. The imports consisted almost exclusively of linens, laces, threads, tapestries, rags, and beeswax, none of which were enumerated in the Act of 1660.[4] Similarly, the laws brought little pressure to bear upon the outward trade, since

[1] Shillington and Chapman, *Commercial Relations of England and Portugal*, pp. 130, 133.
[2] From 1559 to 1658.
[3] CSPD (1595-97), pp. 301, 350; Child, *New Discourse*, p. 113.
[4] BM Add MSS 36785; Customs 3/73. In 1663 the imports of enumerated commodities to London constituted 0.97 percent of the total value, and in 1669, 1.4 percent.

the exports of coal to Flanders were not great.[5] The statistics show that the tonnage of ships clearing for Flanders from England was usually much greater than that of those entering, and that the English ordinarily managed to control about 90 percent of the inward trade and 85 percent of that outward.[6] Their success may possibly be explained by the fact that the principal competition came from third-party carriers, since the absence of seaports stifled Flemish rivalry; or it may have been that English shipping could hold its own in carrying the comparatively light and valuable merchandise coming from Flanders, or that the difference in freight rates was not so great that merchants wished to use other than their own ships. In any event, on the outward voyage English ships carried the greater part of the valuable woolen manufactures and, thanks to preferential duties, nearly all the coal. But foreign vessels gained a large share of the carriage of such bulky commodities as alum, wrought brass, colors for paints, copperas, glue, wrought iron, lead and shot, train oil, vitriol, tin and tin plate, oysters, and salt, in the case of which the law had failed to favor English shipping.[7]

The part that hostility to the Dutch had played in the enactment of the laws gives special importance to inquiries about their effect upon commercial and shipping relations between England and Holland. Yet a preliminary word of caution is necessary. We must not allow conclusions about the short-lived Act of 1651 to distort our judgments concerning its more permanent successor, the Act of 1660. And we must remember that the legislation sought two great ends: to keep Dutch ships from dominating England's carrying trade, and to break English traders of the habit of depending upon Dutch

[5] In 1729 the exports of coal to Flanders were 668 tons (Nef, *British Coal Industry*, II, 386). In 1773 they amounted to 6,645 tons (Customs 3/73). The exports of corn were negligible, about 500 tons in 1698 and none in 1773 (Customs 3/1, 3/73).

[6] Some illustrative statistics from BT 6/185 showing the shipping engaged in England's trade with Flanders are given below:

| | INWARD | | OUTWARD | |
YEAR	Total Tonnage	Percent E	Total Tonnage	Percent E
1771	14,412	92.2	24,767	86.3
1773	15,144	94.8	30,086	91.3
1775	15,566	93.7	24,666	85.3
1779	11,260	44.5	22,910	25.1
1785	35,338	91.1	47,146	87.2

[7] Customs 3/73.

entrepôts. Thus we need to ascertain the effect of the laws upon Dutch activity as third-party carriers in England's trade with countries other than Holland, upon the share enjoyed by English ships in the Anglo-Dutch trade, and upon the English habit of resorting to the entrepôt markets in Holland for their imports rather than going directly to the source of supply.

It is clear that the Acts had a real effect in restraining the Dutch from serving as third-party carriers. Although it is impossible to measure statistically the extent of their earlier activity, the available evidence makes it clear that it was considerable. English shipowners complained in 1609 of "the lamentable state" into which English navigation had fallen as a result "of the Flemings that are daily employed by our English merchants," and throughout the first half of the seventeenth century repeated evidence of their activities crops up—in the carriage of fish from Yarmouth to the Mediterranean, and in the Norway, Eastland, French, Spanish, Irish, and colonial trades.[8] After the Act of 1660 enumerated nearly all the goods which Dutch vessels could carry most profitably, mention of Dutch vessels coming from elsewhere than Holland is seldom encountered.[9] The mere absence of such Dutch entries after 1660 proves nothing, since we cannot expect officials to confess a knowledge of illegal actions. But the evidence in the English port books is corroborated by the Danish records of ships passing the Sound. The decline in Dutch entries is accompanied by an increase in England's ships and in those of the other countries with which she traded.[10]

[8] BM Lans. MSS 142, ff. 294-96, 302, 306; *supra*, pp. 31, 244, 256-57, 263, 283, 291-92, 295-97, 365. Nef (*British Coal Industry*, II, 29) states that Flemish vessels were carrying coal to France during James I's reign. Dutch activities probably diminished for a time thereafter, but they were renewed again after 1648. See Yarmouth port book for 1649 (E 190/492/11) and *infra*, pp. 301, 314-16, 349-50.

[9] For port books cited, see *infra*, pp. 415-16.

[10] See *infra*, pp. 311-16. Professor Johnsen in "L'Acte de Navigation Anglais" (*Revue d'histoire moderne*, n.s., III, 5-15), an article to which my attention was kindly called by Professor C. M. Andrews, argues that Dutch participation in English commerce before 1651 has been greatly exaggerated. He contends that if the English had depended upon Dutch carriers before 1651, English commerce would have been crippled after the Dutch were excluded. He cites English port-book figures showing a very marked development in English navigation during the seventeenth century and few, if any, Dutch entries in 1640 or thereabouts, and also points out that Dutch records contain comparatively few charter parties showing England as the destination between 1625 and 1650.

The argument that English ships could not suddenly have replaced Dutch vessels

The evidence also leaves no doubt that English ships gained materially in the direct trade between England and Holland, after the Restoration navigation code became effective. Practically all London's imports from the Netherlands had been carried in Dutch ships. In 1602 only five London ships totaling 290 tons, out of 343 ships totaling 8,391 tons, entered from that region.[11] A writer in King James I's reign stated that the Hamburgers, Emdeners, and Hollanders "had a continual Trade into this Kingdom with five or six hundred Ships yearly, with Merchandises of other Countries and Kingdoms . . . and we trade not with fifty Ships into their Country in a Year."[12] The Merchant Adventurers claimed in 1618 that they could find no English ships in Holland.[13] In 1650 Trinity House hoped for nothing more than that English and Dutch ships be laden by turns when sailing for Amsterdam, and was willing to grant complete freedom to import and export all manner of goods in strangers' bottoms to Holland and the provinces adjacent.[14]

English shipping definitely improved its position in the trade after 1660. Although England's share in the carriage of exports from the outports rose only from 90.6 percent during the first half of the seventeenth century to 93.7 in the second, data from the port books indicate that her participation in the inward carriage increased from 56.6 percent prior to 1651 to 91.9 percent after 1660, the

---

in any great numbers loses much of its force because the Act of 1651 did not require English ships to be English-built. English merchants could have met their needs and have satisfied the law by buying Dutch vessels during the transitional period. As far as the Dutch records are concerned, Professor Johnsen himself points out that they are too scanty to warrant any general conclusion. And the English port books he examined for the period after Elizabeth's reign were, with two exceptions, all for the thirties and forties, years when the threat of Dunkirk privateers caused neutrals to avoid Dutch shipping (see *infra*, p. 349, n. 74).

It is undoubtedly true that English navigation was improving during the thirties and the forties, and that English commerce was not solely dependent upon Dutch carriers. But one must not go too far and conclude that the Dutch were not threatening English commerce after 1648 or that English shipping required no governmental aid. The Yarmouth port books for 1648 and 1649 and the figures of ships passing the Sound show that the Dutch were active again. In any event we must remember that the preferential coal duties and other assistance offered shipping by the early Stuarts did not leave English owners completely without protection (*supra*, pp. 34-38).

[11] Miller, "New Evidence," *Quar. Jour. Econ.*, XLI, 745, 752, 754.
[12] "Observations touching Trade" in Raleigh's *Works*, II, 118.
[13] *Supra*, p. 33.
[14] THT (1613-61), p. 49.

change being most pronounced in the case of such East Coast ports as Newcastle, Hull, Ipswich, Lynn, and Yarmouth.[15] The statistics for 1710-14 show that at the height of the war period, Dutch participation in England's total trade exceeded that of the English. But it did not retain its supremacy even until peace was signed. Thereafter English shipping controlled the trade, usually maintaining a greater predominance in the outward than in the inward trade.[16] Equally important, the English vessels were not merely cross-Channel craft such as engaged in the trade with France and had once dominated the Anglo-Dutch trade. The average size of the English vessels entering England was 89.2 tons and that of those clearing was 130.4 tons, in both instances greater than that of their foreign competitors.[17]

[15] For port books examined, see *infra*, pp. 415-16. The figures showing the relationship of English to foreign shipping in the Anglo-Dutch trade are as follows:

| | SHIPS BEFORE 1651 | | | | SHIPS AFTER 1660 | | | |
| | Inward | | Outward | | Inward | | Outward | |
	E	F	E	F	E	F	E	F
Newcastle	78	69	115	1	76	9	191	10
Hull	76	44	82	4	64	7	82	14
Lynn	18	14	17		78	6	143	10
Yarmouth	223	192	67	24	47	1	85	
Ipswich	29	38	18	2	11		13	
Southampton	5		1	1	1			
Dartmouth	20		9		23	1		
Plymouth	16	1			2	3		
Bristol	2				6			
Total	467	358	309	32	308	27	514	34
Percent	56.6	43.4	90.6	9.4	91.9	8.1	93.8	6.2

[16] As was the case prior to the Navigation Acts, the figures for 1710-14 show that in the Anglo-Dutch trade English shipping fared better in the outports than in London. The English proportion at London dropped in 1711 to 36 percent of the ships and 36.8 percent of the tonnage clearing (CO 388/18, No. 22). By 1719 it had risen to 85.4 percent of the ships and 85.4 percent of the tonnage clearing and was 89 percent of the ships and 90 percent of the tonnage entering port (CO 390/5, No. 45). The following table taken from the same source for 1719 and from BT 6/185 thereafter gives the statistics for the kingdom as a whole:

| | INWARD | | | | OUTWARD | | | |
YEAR	Total Ships	Percent English	Total Tons	Percent English	Total Ships	Percent English	Total Tons	Percent English
1719	633	95.1	42,411	92.0	1,482	94.5	107,172	96.0
1771	605	65.3	50,991	68.9	525	74.7	107,578	90.8
1775	926	60.8	76,541	73.2	1,039	88.6	103,220	91.3
1779	1,215	43.7	107,691	63.5	822	66.9	81,770	78.4
1785	1,069	67.7	113,575	80.2	1,107	86.8	123,696	91.4

[17] The averages are those for 1771-73; averages for later years are even greater

The correlation of these statistics with the legislation is simple enough in the case of ships leaving England for Holland. The preferential duties granted English ships carrying out coal, and the Restoration bounties granted on corn when shipped in English vessels, did much to support the English ratio in the clearance statistics, since the great bulk of English shipments to Holland consisted of coal and of corn.[18] The same fact explains why English shipping in the outports made so little gain in the carriage of goods outward. The protection afforded English ships in the case of coal exports was of pre-Cromwellian origin and had made its effect felt long before 1660.

It is, however, more difficult to explain how the laws affected ships carrying goods to England from Holland. The alien duties prescribed by the Act of 1660 applied to only 14 percent (in value) of the articles imported in 1663 and 1669 at London from Holland, and even in the instances where they applied, were often merely nominal.[19] The increased English percentage may be explained in part by the fact that colonial ships stopping at England, as the Act of 1663 required, when en route from Holland to America, would be entered as English, but a more probable explanation lies in the workings of the Act of Frauds. Thanks to it, cargoes in the Anglo-Dutch trade did not include such bulky articles as French wines and salt and Baltic naval stores, which Dutch vessels could carry most economically. The English had a good opportunity to compete for the carriage of the remaining traffic, which consisted chiefly of rich wares like linens and other goods produced in Holland, espe-

---

(BT 6/185). For French trade averages see Miller, "New Evidence," *Quar. Jour. Econ.*, XLI, 747, 754.

[18] Lipson, *Economic History*, II, 453, 459-60. In 1698, 14,106 tons of corn, and 23,746 tons of coal were exported from England to Holland. It should also be noted that the exports included 2,197 tons of tobacco and 4,845 tons of sugar (Customs 3/1). In 1773 the exports included 48,857 tons of coal, 12,135 tons of rice, and 6,416 tons of tobacco, of which all the coal, more than nine-tenths of the rice, and three-quarters of the tobacco were carried in English ships (Customs 3/73).

[19] BM Add MSS 36785. It is impossible to make an exact calculation of the percentage of enumerated commodities by weight, because most of the nonenumerated entries were not measured by weight, cloth being the most important example. However, a fair approximation is that they constituted from 25 to 30 percent by weight of the imports from Holland to London. With the exception of Rhenish wines, the principal enumerated commodities, hemp, flax, pitch, potash, barley, and wheat, paid comparatively low alien duties; see *infra*, pp. 405-6.

cially since they had received protection on the voyage from England to Holland.

Another important change was the decrease in the relative importance of the Dutch trade to England. The records of vessels entering London and various East Coast ports, which show that from one-fourth to one-half of the ships entering came from Holland before 1651, also indicate that the percentage declined thereafter, especially in the eighteenth century.[20] All accounts of England's trade in the first half of the seventeenth century agree that a goodly percentage was with the Netherlands,[21] and an overwhelming preponderance with the commercial centers grouped there and in Germany.[22] During the forties, the Eastland and Levant Companies complained that goods from the regions covered by their monopolies were coming to England from Holland,[23] and the record of seizures under the Act of 1651 shows that the greatest resistance occurred in stopping goods not the growth of Holland from being brought from there.[24] After 1660, Dutch imports declined.[25] London led at first in

[20] In addition to references cited *supra*, pp. 280-81, the figures for 1609 (BM Lans. MSS 142, f. 304) show that about 200 English ships out of a total of 666 were supposed to be engaged in trade with Holland. The following table shows the part Anglo-Dutch trade played in England's commerce. The percentages have been calculated from figures in CO 390/5, No. 45 for 1719, and in BT 6/185 for 1771-85:

| | | PERCENTAGE INWARD | | | | | PERCENTAGE OUTWARD | | |
| | | *English and Foreign Ships* | | *English and Foreign Tonnage* | | | *English and Foreign Ships* | | *English and Foreign Tonnage* |
YEAR	*English Ships*	*Foreign Ships*	*English Tonnage*	*Foreign Tonnage*		*English Ships*	*Foreign Ships*	*English Tonnage*	*Foreign Tonnage*
1719	13.8	13.7	11.3	11.7		23.8	24.0	24.0	24.1
1771	6.8	8.8	5.6	6.8		4.9	6.1	12.6	12.9
1775	7.6	10.8	6.9	8.1		11.3	11.9	12.0	12.2
1779	12.3	19.0	13.3	14.5		9.4	11.7	11.2	11.5
1785	9.4	11.7	10.3	10.5		9.8	10.3	11.9	11.7

[21] In 1550 the English Merchant Adventurers were said to have employed at least 20,000 persons in Antwerp and 30,000 more in other parts of the Netherlands. Although later driven from Antwerp by the Duke of Alva, they flourished elsewhere, and in 1639 their chief mart town was Rotterdam (*Newcastle Merchant Adventurers*, I, xxxvi).

[22] CSPD (1595-97), p. 353; "Observations touching Trade," in Raleigh's *Works*, II, 116-18; *Newcastle Merchant Adventurers*, I, p. xxxvi; Hume, *History of England*, IV, 365; Lipson, *Economic History*, II, 197, 228.

[23] SP 105/143, pp. 326, 368, 412; SP 105/144, pp. 21-22, 55-56; CSPD (1649-50), p. 12; (1651), p. 273. For further complaints by the Levant Company in 1650, see SP 105/151, pp. 96, 98.

[24] The following table, showing grounds of seizure under the Act of 1651, has been compiled from the Exchequer, KR Memo Rolls. The years began at Easter Term and extended to the succeeding Easter Term. War with Holland, 1652-54, and with Spain

freeing itself from the Dutch yoke, but by 1715 the outports were even more successful in that regard.[26] Best of all from the mercantile point of view, while England's imports from Holland were decreasing, her exports to Holland increased.[27] As far as other countries were concerned, Holland was still a distributing center; but the English, who had formerly been retail purchasers at the Dutch emporium, had now become wholesalers who supplied the entrepôt.[28]

The Navigation Acts must receive much credit for bringing about

thereafter, probably accounts for the variations in seizures of commodities illegally exported from the Spanish Netherlands.

ILLEGAL IMPORTATIONS

Year	Of Fish	From Holland, Zeeland	From Spanish Netherlands	From Other Places	Other Offenses	Total Seizures
1652	2	13	22	2	6	45
1653	2		14	5	12	33
1655	2	59	2	6	8	77
1656	6	54		7	15	82
1658	24	28			5	59

[25] Exact comparisons for the periods before and after 1660 are difficult because of the failure of the earlier records to distinguish at times between trade with Holland and with Flanders, but the following figures from BM Add MSS 36785 show that the combined trades would not attain the earlier percentages:

	1663		1669	
	Exports	*Imports*	*Exports*	*Imports*
All Countries	£2,022,812	£4,016,019	£2,063,274	£4,196,139
Flanders	108,632	245,079	189,404	260,347
Holland	105,212	491,376	178,044	501,674

[26] The point is best made clear by comparing the percentages of imports from Holland already given for London (*supra*, p. 281) with those given in BT 6/185 for the kingdom as a whole:

Year	Percent London	Percent England	Year	Percent London	Percent England
1663–69	12.1		1715	8.0	7.7
1698	10.7	13.7	1750	4.7	4.2
1701	8.5	8.9	1773	3.9	3.6

[27] This was true to such an extent that Davenant (*Works*, V, 435-36) complained that England was losing profits by allowing her products to be distributed by the Dutch.

[28] The development of world commerce, of course, helped to diminish the importance of England's trade with Holland, but that trade also declined in relation to England's European commerce. As compared with 25 to 50 percent in the early seventeenth century (*supra*, p. 281), by 1719 trade with Holland furnished only 17.2 percent of the number of ships and 11.1 percent of the tonnage entering London from Europe, and 16.4 percent of the ships and 15 percent of the tonnage entering the kingdom as a whole (CO 390/5, No. 45). In 1775 the proportion was even smaller, being only 13.6 percent of the ships entering England from Europe and 11.3 per cent of the tonnage (BT 6/185).

the change. Although the Acts of 1660 and 1662, unlike the Cromwellian measure of 1651, did not ruthlessly interfere with general trade, they prevented the Dutch from supplying England with such articles as colonial produce, naval stores, and groceries, which then comprised more than 50 percent of London's total imports.[29] The tendency of merchants to refrain from importing articles about which any question might be raised indicates that the rules were being enforced, as do Dutch complaints about the Acts of 1651, 1660, and 1662.[30] Logical arguments, based upon the profits of smuggling, and administrative and court records suggest that most illicit trade was in spices, dyewoods, or other rich non-European commodities. Except in the case of spices (the importation of which was permitted for many years by dispensation),[31] there is no evidence that the quantity of importations in violation of the Navigation Acts was large, and the Exchequer records, especially during the Protectorate, show that such smuggling must have been fraught with perils, since seizures were being made with regularity.[32]

It is difficult to estimate how much the Acts did to bring about Holland's decline as a commercial and maritime power. There were many other factors at work, such as the exhausting effects of her wars with Louis XIV, her lack of sufficient natural resources, her mounting burdens of taxation, the breakdown of political centralization, and the increasing interest of other countries in industry and commerce.[33] But even so, one must not ignore the effects of the Acts. They did more than break the Dutch hold upon England's carrying trade and keep Holland from sharing in the profits of England's colonies. They tended to stimulate the commercial activities of other countries and, by dividing competition, to weaken Holland's posi-

[29] In 1663 and 1669 (BM Add MSS 36785). The prohibited goods comprised only about 40 percent of the kingdom's total imports in 1698 (Customs 3/1), but the increase in trade with Asia, Africa, and America caused them to amount to considerably more than 50 percent by 1773 (Customs 3/73).

[30] CSP Venetian (1653-54), pp. 103, 225; Cal. Ct. Min. East India Co. (1660-63), Foster's Introduction, p. xxiv; Thurloe, State Papers, I, 236, 373-74; Gardiner, Letters and Papers relating to the First Dutch War, I, 48; Macpherson, Annals of Commerce, II, 530-31; Clark, "The Navigation Act of 1651," History, n.s., VII, 282-83.

[31] Supra, p. 240.

[32] Supra, pp. 304-5, n. 24.

[33] Ricardo, Anatomy of the Navigation Laws, pp. 31-32; Schmoller, Mercantile System, p. 53; Knight, Barnes and Flügel, Economic History of Europe, pp. 282-83; Cunningham, English Industry and Commerce, II, 675 n., 676 n.

tion. England's willingness to allow ships of other nations to bring her their own produce at first encouraged them to try to replace the Dutch as carriers to England, and eventually stimulated them to extend their navigation with other countries.[34] Moreover, the requirement that English ships, and ships of other countries entitled to carry the enumerated goods to England, be locally built, hit directly at Holland's shipbuilding and indirectly at her timber trade.[35]

Lying geographically between Holland and the northern powers, the Hanse towns combined the trading features characteristic of both. In so far as they were entrepôt towns like those of Holland, the policy of the Navigation Acts was to prevent the importation from Germany of goods enumerated in the Act of Frauds. In so far as they were the natural ports of shipment for timber or other naval stores, the best interests of England required that such products be permitted to enter freely. Much that is otherwise difficult to understand in the application of the Acts to the trade of these towns may find its explanation in this twofold nature of their commerce.

The records now available are not altogether clear as to whether the law on the statute books was really the law which in practice governed the importation of goods from the towns, either within or without the Sound. If enforced, the Act of 1651 would have restricted each town to carrying goods of its own hinterland in its own ships, but the necessities of war with the Dutch led to an exemption for naval stores.[36] As a Hamburg memorial was later to explain, Hamburg, at least, had "an infinite store of . . . necessaries for a quick and ready equipping of a fleet, specially when the passage of the Sound is stopt, or dangerous." The memorialist declared that the Act was never put in execution against Hamburg,[37] but corroborative evidence is lacking to support his statement. We do know, however, that Charles II granted dispensations to the other towns, even despite the opposition of certain English interests.[38] It is also in-

[34] This appears clearly in the case of Norway and Sweden. See Kiaer, "Historical Sketch of the Development of Scandinavian Shipping," *Jour. Pol. Econ.*, I, 330-64, especially 332.

[35] See evidence of Dutch decline in the Baltic, *infra*, pp. 311, 315-16. Cf. *supra*, p. 276, n. 4.

[36] CSPD (1652-53), p. 442.

[37] SP 82/10, ff. 37-114.

[38] *Supra*, p. 69, n. 23. For a general survey of Anglo-German relations at this time,

teresting to note the persistence and earnestness with which the Hanse towns sought exemptions. Their assumption that, unless exceptions were duly authorized, the law could and would be enforced throws an interesting sidelight on contemporary opinion as to the laws' effectiveness.

Studies of the laws' effects upon the Hanse towns and other regions north and east of them also encounter difficulty because of the lack of consistency in statistical classifications. Sometimes the figures are given by countries or towns, and at other times are grouped as trade to Germany, the Baltic, or the Eastland, without specifying what places the groupings included, and the groupings seem to have changed almost as rapidly as the political geography of the region. The difficulty cannot be solved by going back to the original charters of the Merchant Adventurers and the Eastland Company, because their jurisdictions overlapped, just as do the terms "Germany" and the "Eastland." In 1609, when the merchants and shipowners spoke of Germany, apparently they referred only to the region outside the Sound and designated that within as the "East Countries."[39] The term "East Countries" in 1663 and 1669 seems, however, to have referred to Denmark and Norway, Sweden and Poland, and presumably the entry for Germany included the towns both within and without the Sound.[40] The account of imports and exports after 1696 provides separate classifications for Denmark and Norway, Sweden, Russia, the Eastland, and Germany, and as far as one can judge from Whitworth's introduction, the term "Sweden" referred only to its Scandinavian possessions, "Germany" at least primarily to the Hanse cities outside the Sound, and "East Country" to such cities as Elbing, Danzig, Riga, and Königsberg.[41]

---

see articles by Brinkman, "England and the Hanse under Charles II," *Eng. Hist. Rev.*, XXIII, 683-708, and "The Relations between England and Germany, 1660-1688," *ibid.*, XXIV, 448-69.

[39] BM Lans. MSS 142, f. 304.

[40] BM Add MSS 36785.

[41] Customs 3; Whitworth, *State of Trade*, p. xx. According to Chance ("England and Sweden in the Time of William III and Anne," *Eng. Hist. Rev.*, XVI, 676-77), Sweden and Finland were one unit, Denmark and Norway another, for English commercial purposes. Hamburg was the center for almost all the trade with northern Germany; Russian trade passed through Archangel, St. Petersburg, and Narva; and according to the delimitation of Eastland Company privileges in 1672, the region known as the East Country was restricted to the provinces between the Oder and the

Despite the prohibitions of the Act of Frauds, there does not appear to be any well-marked correlation between the Navigation Acts and the volume of England's trade with Germany. The lack of correlation cannot be blamed entirely upon defects in our statistical knowledge, because even when we have comparable figures, we find variations in the German trade which suggest that other factors than the Navigation Acts were active in determining its volume at any particular time.[42]

As far as the carriage of the trade was concerned, the pre-Cromwellian measures had apparently functioned only where the Merchant Adventurers were able to make their control effective. Most of the ships entering London in 1602 from Stade, where the company had its staple, were owned by Londoners, but most of the ships from Emden were foreign-owned.[43] Similar conditions apparently continued, because in 1649 and 1650 Trinity House thought "it fittinge to give tolleracon" for goods in strangers' ships from Emden, although it was willing to throw open only the grain trade with Hamburg.[44] According to the figures taken from the outport books, English shipping improved its position after 1660:[45]

	Before 1651	*After 1660*
Inward	48.6 percent	75.0 percent
Outward	56.5 percent	70.5 percent

Statistics for the kingdom as a whole, from 1771 to 1785 inclusive, show that the annual average of the foreign entries equaled the foreign clearances, but that the English tonnage leaving port generally was almost half again as great as that entering. During peace time, English shipping controlled both the inward and outward traffic,

---

Gulf of Finland, half of which belonged to Sweden and the other half to Prussia or to Poland.

[42] The figures for 1602 (Miller, "New Evidence," *Quar. Jour. Econ.*, XLI, 743, 756) show that 2.9 percent of the ships and 4.6 percent of the tonnage entering London came from Germany (exclusive of the Eastland). The figures for 1609 (BM Lans. MSS 142, f. 304) indicate that 6 percent of the vessels England owned, traded there. The trade occupied 6.1 percent of the ships entering England and 5.3 percent of the tonnage in 1719 (CO 390/5, No. 45), but only 2.5 percent of the ships and 2.9 percent of the tonnage in 1771. The imports from Germany constituted 4.9 percent of London's total for 1663-69, 13.5 percent of the kingdom's total in 1719 and 6 percent in 1771 (BT 6/185).

[43] Miller, "New Evidence," *Quar. Jour. Econ.*, XLI, 755-56.

[44] THT (1613-61), pp. 9, 49.

[45] For citations, see *infra*, pp. 415-16.

but during war years foreign vessels gained the greater portion both inward and outward, although the coal trade assured a certain minimum employment for English vessels.[46]

The laws after 1660 exerted pressure for the employment of English vessels on the outward rather than the inward trade. Of the goods imported at London in 1663 and 1669 from Germany, only 5 percent were among those which the Act of 1660 required to be brought in English ships or ships of the country producing them.[47] The alien duties on even this small fraction were negligible. Grain, for example, which comprised more than one-fifth of the total imports enumerated, paid only fourpence per ton extra when imported in German vessels.[48] Yet when we turn to the outward shipments, we find that the laws exercised a real control through the preferential duties on coal. In 1773, 9,604 tons of that commodity were shipped to Germany, all but 139 tons of which went in English vessels.[49] Since the total English tonnage clearing for Germany that year was only 20,695 tons, English shipowners seem to have been indebted to the laws for almost one-half of their outward cargoes.[50]

When we turn to a study of conditions in Scandinavia and the Baltic, we are dealing with a situation which has led to many charges against the Navigation Acts. Since they have been accused not only of being ineffectual but also of being positively harmful, we must analyze the problem carefully and consider the Acts' effects upon trade as well as upon shipping.

Accusations to the contrary notwithstanding, the Navigation Acts did not stifle England's trade to the eastward, for the benefit of her

[46] The tonnage in the Anglo-German trade (BT 6/185) was as follows:

Year	Inward		Outward	
	E	F	E	F
1771	12,459	9,426	17,573	9,295
1775	19,519	10,708	28,156	10,084
1779	4,990	14,756	5,666	18,904
1785	19,652	9,205	33,129	11,114

[47] BM Add MSS 36785. The percentage increased in 1775 to 25 percent, because of the scarcity of grain in England in that year; but except for grain, less than 3.5 percent of the imports were enumerated (Customs 3/75).
[48] Crouch, *Complete View*, pp. 102-6; *infra*, pp. 405-6.
[49] Customs 3/73.
[50] BT 6/185. The exports to Germany also included 762 tons of rice and 5,336 tons of tobacco, but approximately one-quarter of the rice and three-quarters of the tobacco were carried in foreign ships (Customs 3/73; Sheffield, *Observations*, Appendix I).

other commerce. Responsibility for whatever shift occurred must be placed elsewhere. The decline of Hanseatic supremacy, the development of world trades, the rise of Holland and of France to commercial greatness, each tended to decrease the volume of trade. England, who had imported considerable quantities of corn from the Baltic in 1597, had become more than self-sustaining in that regard by the second half of the next century.[51] Also, England's export trade had been declining.[52] As early as 1620, the sale of cloth was said to have decreased from £200,000 to £70,000 or £80,000 per annum; and the English lost still more during the distractions of the Civil War, which kept them from supplying the Polish market as fully as usual, and enabled Dutch manufacturers to gain at their expense. Also the Eastland Company suffered from internal dissension and the opposition of interlopers.[53] Compared to these factors, the effect of the Navigation Acts on the volume of trade was negligible. The most that can be said against them is that they may have increased inward freight rates, but it was the export trade, which they affected only indirectly, if at all, that suffered the most.

Moreover, there is cause to doubt that the total volume of traffic really declined. Although the exports diminished,[54] the imports did not. In the second half of the seventeenth century, England's imports from her eastern neighbors increased considerably in value, and formed a greater percentage of England's total trade than they had in the first. In the eighteenth century, England began importing

[51] Deardorff, *English Trade in the Baltic*, p. 228; Customs 3/1 *et seq.*

[52] Coke (*England's Improvements*, pp. 32-33) states that as a result of English dissenters settling in Holland and teaching the Dutch how to manufacture woolens, and of the Silesians weaving the fine Polish wools to supply Poland, English exports to the Eastland fell from 20,000 broadcloths, 60,000 kerseys, and 40,000 doubles to less than 4,000, 5,000 and 2,000 respectively.

[53] CSPD (1619-23), pp. 157, 211; Lipson, *Economic History*, II, 320-26.

[54] The following table, compiled from Bang, *Tables, 1497-1660*, and from Bang and Korst, *Tables, 1661-1783*, shows the increase in English vessels entering the Sound in ballast, and indicates the decrease before 1700 of Dutch vessels going in ballast.

| | ENGLISH ENTRIES | | | DUTCH ENTRIES | | |
Year	Laden	In Ballast	Percent in Ballast	Laden	In Ballast	Percent in Ballast
1557-1600	2,271	851	27.3	16,259	32,474	66.6
1601-50	2,912	1,640	36.0	28,852	30,232	51.2
1651-57	206	34	14.2	1,715	1,854	51.9
1661-1700	3,419	3,209	48.4	14,342	13,807	49.2
1701-50	6,934	3,439	44.0	14,761	18,377	55.3
1751-83	7,594	13,141	64.5	10,665	21,076	66.4

from the Baltic ports of Russia many of the products earlier obtained from Norway, Denmark, Sweden, and other East countries. But the net result was merely a shift in the course of trade within the Baltic itself, and the proportion of England's imports coming from that region remained about the same,[55] the variations being governed chiefly by the presence or absence of war-time demands for naval stores. England's statesmen would not have been averse to lessening the volume of her commerce with her eastern neighbors, since it showed an unfavorable balance of trade; but try as she might, England could not lose her dependence upon their supplies of timber and naval stores so long as she had to build ships of wood.[56]

Trade with Scandinavia and the Baltic had been regulated long before Cromwell's day. The charter of 1579 gave the Eastland merchants the right to control trade with Norway, Sweden, Poland, and other Baltic regions, except Narva.[57] But it is not clear how far the company's authority was limited to Englishmen and how far it extended over aliens.[58] Nor is it certain whether the company's con-

[55] Imports from the Baltic, and their relation to the total imports of England, may be summarized as follows:

Year	From Denmark, Norway, Sweden, and East Countries		From Russia		Combined	
	Value	Percent	Value	Percent	Value	Percent
1613*	£120,000	5.6				
1663†‡	219,992	5.5	£17,785	0.4	£237,777	5.9
1698‡¶	331,103	9.7	56,443	1.7	387,546	11.4
1698¶	507,926	10.7	74,738	1.6	582,664	12.3
1700–10§	403,146	8.8	123,752	2.7	526,898	11.5
1710–20	344,283	6.5	181,587	3.4	525,870	9.9
1720–30	465,570	6.7	191,124	2.7	656,694	9.4
1730–40	502,645	6.6	282,834	3.7	785,479	10.3
1740–50	525,082	7.1	341,468	4.6	866,550	11.7
1750–60	536,379	6.2	526,504	6.1	1,062,883	12.3
1760–70	482,552	4.3	660,279	6.0	1,142,831	10.3
1770–80	568,820	4.8	1,084,539	9.2	1,653,359	14.0

* Eastland imports in SP 14/72, No. 70; Acts and Ordinances of the Eastland Company, p. liii. The total imports for that year were taken from Misselden, Circle of Commerce, p. 122.
† BM Add MSS 36785.   ‡ London only.
¶ Customs 3/1.
§ Annual averages computed by Sheffield (Observations, Appendix IX).

[56] Albion, Forests and Sea Power, pp. 344-45, 361, 399, 402-3; Chance, "England and Sweden in the Time of William III and Anne," Eng. Hist. Rev., XVI, 684. For attempts to find other sources of supply, see Albion, op. cit., especially Chaps. VI-IX.

[57] Acts and Ordinances of the Eastland Company, pp. 142-51. For limitation of jurisdiction in 1672, see supra, p. 308, n. 41. After May 1, 1673, the trade with Sweden, Denmark, and Norway was opened to all persons, "native or forraigne" (ibid., pp. 93-94).

[58] The charter referred only to the King's subjects (ibid., pp. 142-51), but the proclamation of 1629 enforcing it, made no distinction between natives and aliens (ibid., pp. 153-55). The same proclamation removed all restraints upon the importa-

trol extended to the indirect importation of Baltic and Scandinavian commodities from Holland. The charter referred only to goods *coming from the Eastland*, but the proclamation of 1629, calling for the observance of the company's rights, forbade the importation of certain *specified Eastland commodities*, regardless of the region from which they came. Similarly, the brethren of the company agreed in 1622 to import Eastland commodities only from the Eastland,[59] but such goods apparently continued to come indirectly from Amsterdam and other places.[60]

As far as shipping was concerned, the company was originally subject to no restrictions except the general laws; but in 1615 the Privy Council forbade its using foreign vessels,[61] and one of the company's rules of 1617 provided that except in war time no brother should employ any person in transporting goods, who was not an Englishman "free or capeable to bee free of" the company.[62] Another rule, concerning toll bills to be given masters, implies that goods might be shipped on foreign as well as on English vessels.[63] In 1622 a royal proclamation, which demanded obedience to the company's charter, also reminded the company of its duty to obey the kingdom's navigation laws.[64] The company thereupon provided for a penalty of one-sixth part of all Eastland commodities imported in foreign ships, except that any brother might "importe all sortes of victualls & Gunpowder or Saltepeter for the service of this kingdome as other his Majest⁸ subjects are permitted by Lawe to doe."[65] And in 1629 another proclamation provided that only English ships might import the commodities specified, "upon the paines in the said Statutes contained and upon paine of Our high indignation and displeasure."[66]

---

tion of corn and grain, and the company itself conceded the right of others to trade with the Eastland if they exported "Coales, beere or other things not prohibited" and brought the proceeds home "in money, corne, etc." (*ibid.*, p. 67).

[59] *Ibid.*, pp. 59-60.
[60] *Ibid.*, p. 67.
[61] APC (1615-16), p. 142.
[62] *Acts and Ordinances of the Eastland Company*, pp. 28-29.
[63] *Ibid.*, pp. 43-46.
[64] *Ibid.*, pp. 151-52.
[65] *Ibid.*, pp. 59-60.
[66] *Ibid.*, p. 154. For the Eastland Company's attitude toward early regulations, see *supra*, pp. 36, 44.

It is unnecessary for our present purposes to attempt to reconcile all the different rules, or to determine if they were enforced. Whether because of evasions or because of loopholes, it is clear that the regulations did not prevent English navigation in these regions from declining materially with the rise of the Dutch flyboats at the end of the sixteenth century. Although more than 50 English ships had visited Danzig in two months of 1557, and it had been estimated in 1582 that from 60 to 100 ships might be found within the Sound at any one time during the summer,[67] by 1602 the London figures indicate that English ships then controlled the trade only at the Eastland Company's staple port at Elbing, and that Dutch ships dominated at Danzig.[68] According to the shipmasters, the Dutch could carry goods more cheaply, and they worked their way into the carrying trade by offering loans, to be repaid in England after the merchant had sold his goods.[69] They succeeded so well that in 1620, 200 Dutch ships were supposed to have been employed in the English trade with Scandinavia and the Baltic.[70] In 1659 the English Eastland Company claimed that it employed 200 ships,[71] but its statement either demonstrated the beneficial effects of the Act of 1651 or was a gross misrepresentation of the facts. Trinity House had in 1650 abandoned hope of holding the trade with Norway and the Sound when it confessed "that a Tolleracon was Conceived necessary for these Places, for Exportinge and Ymportinge all manner of Goods in Strangers bottomes."[72]

These facts show that Roger Coke was wrong when he blamed the Navigation Acts for the loss of the eastward trades.[73] For a trade to have been lost by reason of parliamentary measures, it must have

---

[67] Deardorff, *English Trade in the Baltic*, pp. 245, 246. Bang's tables show that fifty-seven English ships entered the Sound in 1557 and ninety-six in 1582.

[68] Miller, "New Evidence," *Quar. Jour. Econ.*, XLI, 755.

[69] BM Lans. MSS 142, f. 302 (1609).

[70] CSPD (1619-23), pp. 152, 211; Lipson, *Economic History*, II, 320. Even in 1601-2, the Dutch carried the bulk of the imports. Miller's figures ("New Evidence," *Quar. Jour. Econ.*, XLI, 745, 757) show that twenty-two ships entered London from Norway and Denmark, but only one London ship came in from that area, and the majority were Dutch.

[71] *Acts and Ordinances of the Eastland Company*, p. lii.

[72] THT (1613-61), p. 49.

[73] Coke, *Treatise concerning Coyn*, p. 27. See also CO 388/6, A13; Brewster, *Essays on Trade and Navigation*, p. 99; and Lipson, *Economic History*, III, 130-36.

been possessed before the legislators acted. In so far as we can judge from a comparison of conditions of navigation before and after the laws' enactment, their effect tended to be beneficial rather than detrimental. According to the port books examined, England's vessels increased their percentage in the carriage of goods from the Eastland towns from 62.3 percent before 1651 to 64.4 percent thereafter, and their share in England's commerce with the Scandinavian countries likewise rose from 32 percent to 38.8 percent.[74] The figures of ships entering and leaving the Sound during the seventeenth century show that from 1601 to 1650 the English annual average was only 182 but that from 1660 to 1700 it increased to 332. Restated in relation to the total number of ships passing the Sound, the English percentage rose from 4.7 percent to 10.3 percent.[75]

Even more significant from the mercantile point of view was the fact that the Dutch were driven from the field. According to the port books, the third-party carriers from the Eastland, most of which were Dutch, constituted 74.2 percent of the foreign ships entering England's ports before 1651, and declined to 12.5 percent after 1660.[76] The only Sound figures showing foreign participation in England's trade are those for ships leaving England. They prove that, before 1660, the overwhelming percentage of foreign vessels belonged to the Netherlands or to the Hanse towns, Lübeck and Danzig, and that thereafter Swedish ships took the lead among foreign competitors and Dutch vessels were few in number.[77] The east-

[74] The foreign percentages were materially higher during the Twelve Years' Truce and from 1648 to 1651, when Dutch competition was not handicapped by war. For port books examined, see *infra*, pp. 415-16.

[75] The calculations are based upon Bang, *Tables, 1497-1660*, and Bang and Korst, *Tables, 1661-1783*. The corresponding English annual averages and percentages for other periods were 141 ships and 3.6 percent from 1557 to 1600; 69 ships and 2.4 percent from 1651 to 1657; 493 ships and 14.8 percent from 1701 to 1750; and 1,252 ships and 18.3 percent from 1751 to 1783. It is possible that the figures are distorted by a diversion of trade from Archangel to St. Petersburg, and the great rise of English commerce there after 1715; but even with the St. Petersburg figures eliminated, English ships constituted more than 13 percent of the total from 1701 to 1750 and more than 15 percent from 1751 to 1783.

[76] Third-party carriers entering the outports from Norway and Sweden, comprised 26.7 percent of the foreign total before 1651, and 6.6 percent after 1660. For citations, see *infra*, pp. 415-16.

[77] The following table, compiled from Bang, *Tables, 1497-1660*, and Bang and

316   ENTREPÔT TOWNS AND TIMBER LANDS

ward figures, however, do not give an adequate indication of the earlier activities of the Dutch, since the most natural route of trade was from Holland to the Eastland to England and back again to Holland. We get a better idea of how the English were gaining upon the Dutch when we compare the proportion of the trade enjoyed by each. Dutch ships entering the Sound outnumbered English ships by 16 to 1 from 1557 to 1600, and by 13 to 1 from 1601 to 1650. Their numbers were even more overwhelming when Holland was at peace, being 18 times those of the English during the Twelve Years' Truce, and 20 times greater from 1648 to 1650. After the passage of the laws, however, this ratio dropped to 4 to 1 from 1661 to 1700, to 2.7 to 1 from 1701 to 1750, and to only 1.5 to 1 from 1751 to 1783.[78]

The fact that England's eastern neighbors obtained a greater share in their countries' trade with England should not be charged against the laws. Preferential duties on the carriage of exports could have little effect, because the Baltic and Scandinavian countries purchased comparatively little from England. Although the Act of 1660 and the Act of Frauds eliminated Dutch competition,[79] Parliament was handicapped in meeting the competition of the country of origin. The goods imported consisted chiefly of essential naval stores, and whatever aid might have been given to the shipowner in the form of high alien duties would necessarily be at the expense of the shipping of the realm as a whole. Thus the more cheaply built Norwegian vessels dominated the carriage of masts. The protection afforded by the alien duties was more apparent than real, since the preferential advantage accorded an English ship carrying an average

---

Korst, *Tables, 1661-1783*, shows the home ports of ships leaving England for the Sound from 1557 to 1783:

Year	Total Ships	Percent English	Percent Dutch	Percent Lübeck	Percent Danzig	Percent Swedish	Percent Norwegian and Danish	Percent Other Ports
1557-1600	3,951	74.82	5.26	1.92	6.99	0.10	3.65	7.26
1601-50	6,393	68.59	11.36	7.09	4.39	0.22	4.68	3.67
1651-57	524	42.37	9.92	15.84	10.50	3.63	3.43	14.31
1661-1700	6,879	74.04	0.67	0.48	3.27	9.80	2.47	9.27
1701-50	12,160	84.66	0.54	0.17	2.07	3.24	2.53	6.79
1751-83	24,031	78.95	0.96	0.03	4.97	1.82	1.27	12.00

[78] *Supra*, p. 311, n. 54. Decimals are omitted for figures before 1701.

[79] Of the commodities imported from the Eastland at London in 1663 and 1669, more than two-thirds in value and still more in weight were enumerated (BM Add MSS 36785).

cargo of fifty great masts was only 12s. 6d.[80] In other trades, such as the carriage of Swedish iron or Eastland pitch, where the differential was more substantial, the protective features of the laws had practical effect, and English shipping gained a respectable proportion of the traffic.[81] Despite frequent assertions to the contrary, the Navigation Acts did not handicap English shipowners by forbidding them to use foreign-built ships in the trade. Until 1786 such ships enjoyed the same legal rights in the eastern trades as their foreign-owned competitors.[82] Both could trade if they paid alien duties. In so far as the opponents of protection have any justified complaint against the Acts in this regard, it is merely that the laws failed to offer protection to English-owned, foreign-built vessels.[83]

[80] Albion, *Forests and Sea Power,* p. 149; *infra,* pp. 405-6. A report of 1668 states that strangers' customs on all wood products did not exceed £7 for a 250-ton ship, £3 on balks, spars, and masts in a similar ship, and £12 on a cargo of deals (CO 388/1, 349-50). In 1696 the freight rate on a 200-ton ship, carrying timber from Norway, was said to be £150, or about one-third the value of the cargo (CO 388/6, A11).

[81] The chief imports from Norway were timber, masts, and deals; from Sweden, iron, hemp, flax, timber, masts, pitch, and tar; from the Eastland, timber, flax, pitch, and tar (Customs 3/1; BM Add MSS 36785; Whitworth, *State of Trade,* pp. xix, xx, xxxvii). In the Swedish trade, English vessels received considerably greater protection, since the alien duties of 1.25 percent were calculated on cargoes worth about £3,000 per ship, but the average cargo in the Norwegian trade was valued at only £450. As a result of this difference, 193 English and 317 foreign ships came from Sweden from 1692 to 1695, and only 39 English and 857 foreign ships from Norway (CO 388/6, A11). Apparently conditions were even worse in the Norway trade the next year, see Chance, "England and Sweden in the Time of William III and Anne" (*Eng. Hist. Rev.,* XVI, 679). The entry figures for 1719 (CO 390/5, No. 45) are very much out of line, since the Baltic powers were at war among themselves and English vessels took over the trade, even with Norway, but the percentages for the later part of the century (BT 6/185) return to normal. The correlation between the success of English shipping and the duties charged on the products of the various Baltic regions can be seen by studying the alien duties (*infra,* pp. 405-6, 408-13), in connection with the following table of tonnage entering England from the countries indicated:

YEAR	NORWAY		SWEDEN		THE EASTLAND	
	Total	Percent E	Total	Percent E	Total	Percent E
1719	99,524	97.8	16,105	100.0	10,780	85.7
1771	82,530	21.1	20,427	66.8	66,121	63.5
1775	99,618	37.5	38,369	70.8	99,129	83.5
1779	70,741	3.4	45,532	37.3	74,083	52.9
1785	108,120	31.7	30,087	58.4	107,244	78.4

[82] In 1786, 26 Geo. III, c. 60 required that all English ships be English-built.

[83] It is true that before then foreign-built ships were handicapped, in that they were not free to engage in all trades, but until 1685, the coastwise trade was open to them, and until 1786, trade with Germany and Flanders (*supra,* pp. 59, 298, 310). Also,

The countries with which England traded were affected by none of the inhibitions which checked the English Parliament in granting preferences to English ships coming from the East. Instead, they deliberately undertook to promote their own interests on the seas. Sweden was referred to as "the Northern Engrosser and Encroacher upon Navigation" because the Swedish King was granting Swedish shipping special favors and had extorted preferential treatment at the Sound when Sweden defeated Denmark.[84] Denmark's control of the Sound enabled her to grant her own shipping favorable tolls, and to harass competitors who traded in the Baltic with what the English claimed were troublesome inspection regulations and unfair restrictions.[85] Norway was said to have laid a duty of 14 percent on strangers' ships, while the alien duty which England collected on Norwegian goods imported in foreign shipping did not exceed one-eightieth of the value.[86] Moreover, it was alleged that in England the Danes and Norwegians were helped by their countrymen in making sales, but that in Norway the English were obliged to sell at wholesale to Danish subjects, and only during three six-hour days each week.[87] Under the circumstances, it is not difficult to understand why English commerce languished. The validity of the regulative principle, however, was not impaired. Its application was, from the English point of view, merely misdirected.

Under these circumstances, blame for England's failure to dominate the trade to the eastward, especially that to Norway, must be found in the fact that these trades were not "rich trades" which would bear high freight rates. Although in case of necessity England could take over the carrying trade, as she did when the northern powers were engaged in wars among themselves,[88] ordinarily only the older English vessels were employed in a "poor" trade such as

in naturalizing vessels for the Norway trade only, the government apparently did not think that a vessel thus limited would be hopelessly handicapped (CO 388/1, pp. 349-50, 353-55; CO 388/6, A13; Clark, *The Dutch Alliance*, p. 135).

[84] Mr. Gregg, at Copenhagen, 1696 (CO 388/6, B66, B67). Swedish restrictive measures are summarized in Chance, "England and Sweden in the Time of William III and Anne" (*Eng. Hist. Rev.*, XVI, 682-84).

[85] CO 388/1, pp. 353-55.

[86] CO 388/6, A11.

[87] CO 388/6, A13.

[88] See figures for 1719, *supra*, p. 317, n. 81.

that to Norway.[89] English investors sought and found more profitable fields for their capital elsewhere.

The comparatively low ratio that English vessels maintained in the entry and clearance statistics, however, should not blind us to the fact that the Navigation Acts had substantial contributions to offer England, even in the regions to the eastward. Their chief purpose had been to insure a supply of naval stores free from the dominance of her greatest naval and commercial rival, Holland. From England's point of view, it had been folly to permit the Dutch to act as carriers of necessary naval supplies, and even worse to depend upon procuring them through Holland.[90] To this extent at least, the Navigation Acts succeeded. It was relatively immaterial that when England was escaping from possible Dutch dominance, Norway, and to a lesser extent Sweden, saw the opportunity that their abundant forests offered them and developed their own merchant marine. Distasteful as it probably was to England to have others make use of her exigencies, the annoyance was not serious. As a contemporary observed, no one feared that the fleets of either Norway or Sweden could ever compete with the English navy.[91]

Little need be said concerning the trade to Russia. From the year, 1566, when a second charter was granted to the Muscovy Company, the carriage of goods was confined to English ships.[92] Even in 1650 Trinity House listed the importation of commodities from Greenland and Muscovy in the group of trades to be reserved for English vessels.[93] Unless there was considerable smuggling, which the bulky nature of Russian cargoes would have made unlikely, the customs statistics prove that the trade was almost exclusively in the hands of the English. The volume of the trade appears to have been little affected by the Navigation Acts. The predominating factors were attempts to establish a market for tobacco and a new

[89] Albion, *Forests and Sea Power*, p. 150.

[90] *The Advocate* says (at page 5) that England by its practices had been giving the Dutch "still the greater opportunitie to make themselves the Mart and Masters over us, of all Commodities belonging to the building or furnishing of Shipping." He argues (at page 13) that for national success England must "buy at the first or best hand . . . [and] fetch Commodities at the Immediate places of their Production, or Growth."

[91] William Wood, April, 1675, in BM Add MSS 28079, ff. 7-8.

[92] *Supra*, p. 32, n. 54. Cf. the official title *supra* and the popular title here.

[93] THT (1613-61), p. 49.

source of supply for naval stores, the development of credit facilities, struggles over company control, and interruptions caused by war.[94] Lack of comparable statistics here, as elsewhere in the North and East, makes it impossible to recount the ups and downs of the trade, but as to its rise, century by century, there is no doubt. The figures for 1609 show 12 ships out of 666 to have been engaged in it;[95] the statistics for 1719 give 42 ships from Archangel alone; and the total number in the Russian trade gradually mounted to 452 English vessels in 1771.[96] Stated in relative terms, the increase was from 1 percent to more than 9 percent of the total English entries.

In short, the record of English shipping in the regions to the east and north of France does not support the charges which have been brought against the Acts. Conceding that maritime conditions in Europe were controlled by many factors, it still appears that the laws in many respects did manage to benefit English navigation.

[94] See arguments of Micajah Perry and other Virginia merchants in 1698 (CO 388/6, B69).

[95] BM Lans. MSS 142, f. 304.

[96] Chance ("England and Sweden in the Time of William III and Anne," *Eng. Hist. Rev.*, XVI, 678) cites BM Add MSS 15898, f. 141 as showing that the number of ships clearing for Russia was 78 in 1703-4. CO 390/5, No. 45 gives the ships entering for 1719, and BT 6/185 gives similar information for later years as follows:

Year	English Ships from Russia	Total English Entries	Percent from Russia
1719	42	4,377	1.0
1771	452	5,801	7.8
1775	341	7,452	4.6
1779	397	4,321	9.2
1785	359	7,687	4.7

XXII

SHIPS AND SEAMEN

ILLUMINATING as it may be in other respects, the preceding analysis of maritime conditions in the various trades is not the most direct approach to the problems of the laws' success. It merely furnishes a background which we can use to advantage when attempting to answer the question, how did they affect the number of English seamen, the total tonnage of English shipping, and the development of English shipyards.

It is apparently impossible to study the effects of the laws upon the number of English seamen, apart from a study of the total tonnage of English shipping. Although various attempts were made to register seamen, fear of impressment caused many to conceal their identity.[1] On the other hand, estimates of the numbers to be raised for naval service during war time have caused the statistics to be exaggerated, because sufficient allowance has not been made for the fact that the estimates included soldiers, servants, and others whose primary occupation could not properly be classified as maritime.[2] Surveys made of seamen at the various ports offer some aid, but the best method of estimating the number of seamen is to correlate it with the tonnage of shipping owned in England.[3] The problem is fairly simple for 1660 and thereafter, since, in peace time at least,

[1] After the American Revolution the number of seamen who had paid the Greenwich Hospital duty was only 55,013; the Register General estimated that Great Britain's shipping required 118,286 seamen (BM Add MSS 38432, ff. 31, 36-37).

[2] Monson (*Naval Tracts*, IV, 61) reported that the various ships' officers "have many people under them in their rooms, not able upon any occasion to tackle the ship, or do any other work more than they are bred to," who should be "put to the use and practice of the musket, or to the labour in hauling and doing other helps to the gunner."

[3] In 1582 one man served 4.5 tons (*infra*, p. 322). According to the pass figures for 1661-68 (which represented foreign trade for the most part), he then served 7 tons (Adm. 7/630), a figure which increased to 11 tons by 1773 (*infra*, p. 329, n. 28). The ratio also varied with the size of the ship (BM Add MSS 38432, Section 5) and with the trade in which it was employed (*infra*, p. 323, n. 10).

the practice was for masters to leave England with crews which were 99 percent English, despite the fact that the legal requirements were more lenient.[4] The correlation for years before that date is less accurate because of the greater possibility of aliens forming part of the crew.[5]

The task of determining the tonnage of English shipping resembles that of solving a cross-word puzzle. We have many fragmentary leads. From time to time there are official surveys of ships and of seamen owned in the kingdom, statistics of entries or clearances in the various ports which can be supplemented by reports concerning the fisheries and the coal trade, by accounts of contemporary writers, and by our general knowledge of maritime and commercial conditions. Sometimes the relationships which exist between the different elements of the problem are too fluctuating to enable us to fill in the gaps in our knowledge with any degree of certainty, but in other instances we can proceed with assurance. The first step is to obtain the best estimates available of England's total tonnage. The next is to learn what we can about the four great divisions of English navigation: the fisheries, the collier trade from Newcastle, other coasting trade, and foreign trade. If each of the figures obtained is consistent with all the others, as well as with the known facts of England's commercial history, the element of error should be reduced to a minimum.

The pre-Armada muster roll of ships and seamen in 1582 gives us a good point of departure. England then possessed a total of 1,642 ships, 68,433 tons, 15,270 seamen, and 957 London watermen.[6]

[4] The failure of masters to make greater use of their opportunity to employ foreigners probably arose from the numerous hazards, such as accident, desertion, plague, and the press gang, which might befall the English sailors and lower the English percentage below the required three-quarters (E134, 22 Car. II, Mich. 43; Adm. 7/75, 7/630).

[5] In 1582 (SP 12/146, No. 45) the reports from the outports averaging one English seaman for every 4 tons indicate that they dominated the coasting and fishing trades, and unless the return from London was more inaccurate than those for the outports, the comparatively small number of English seamen (one for every 9.3 tons) suggests that London owners were accustomed to rely in part upon foreigners until the Act of 1660 put an end to the practice.

[6] SP 12/146, No. 45; Monson, *Naval Tracts*, III, 188-92; Oppenheim, *Administration of the Royal Navy*, p. 176. The totals in the different accounts vary slightly, and in a few instances the contemporary totals are not the exact sum of the items listed, but such errors are negligible. The more important element of possible error

But by 1602 Trinity House declared to the Lord High Admiral that "the shipping and seamen had decayed . . . one third part" since 1581.[7] Judging from the shipowners' complaints of 1609, conditions had not then improved,[8] and the comments of Brewster and the anonymous author of *The Trade's Increase* about conditions in 1615 are couched in similar terms of gloom and lament.[9] As far as we can determine from their estimates and other available evidence, the pessimism arose from conditions in foreign trade. Growth of the coastwise coal trade increased the total to approximately 101,566 tons of shipping.[10]

lies in the failure to include a return for South Wales, which in 1628 reported 753 seamen, or 4.9 percent of an estimated total of 15,417 men (Oppenheim, *op. cit.,* p. 244; *infra,* pp. 332-33, n. 39). For present purposes, however, it has seemed wisest, both here and elsewhere in this volume, to accept the totals as given without making additions for South Wales.

[7] Quoted in Chalmers, *Estimate,* p. 38.

[8] BM Lans. MSS 142, ff. 302-6.

[9] Brewster, *Essays on Trade and Navigation,* pp. 75-76; "The Trade's Increase," *Harl. Misc.,* IV, 212-31.

[10] In estimating the total, the tonnages for the Greenland (2,083 tons), Newfoundland (11,229 tons), and other fisheries (14,409 tons), the collier trade (28,223 tons), and other coastwise traffic (15,743 tons) were computed as described *infra,* pp. 329-39. The tonnage going to the East Indies (2,203 tons) was computed from the figures given in Bal Krishna (*Commercial Relations between India and England,* pp. 334-35) by determining the annual average tonnage employed during the eight years, 1608-9 to 1615-16 inclusive. When more than one burden was given for the same ship, the different estimates were averaged, and the tonnage of the "Speedwell," which was not given at all in the entry for 1614-15, was assumed to equal the average of the other vessels in the same fleet. There are no contemporary tonnage figures for the remaining trades, but there are estimates of the number of ships and of the number of seamen employed in them. Such estimates have been converted into tonnage figures by multiplying the number of ships by their average tonnage and the number of seamen by the average number of tons which each served. When more than one estimate for a trade was available, all were averaged. The failure of a source to mention a trade was not considered a denial of its existence, but merely an inadvertence.

The basic figures used for ships and seamen were those given in BM Lans. MSS 142, f. 304; Brewster, *Essays on Trade and Navigation,* pp. 75-76, and "The Trade's Increase," (*Harl. Misc.,* IV, 214-17, 220-23), except that the 1609 seamen figures were disregarded as being completely out of line, and for the same reason the estimate of the number of ships in the Dutch trade given in "Observations Touching Trade" (Raleigh, *Works,* II, 118) was substituted for the one given in the Lansdowne manuscript. In the case of "The Trade's Increase" the figures were used, even though a trade was described as lost. All estimates of the tonnage trading with the Mediterranean countries and the Iberian peninsula were averaged together, as that procedure provided a common denominator of the different groupings which contemporaries made.

The average size of the ships in the several trades was assumed to be that given

It is difficult to estimate the condition of English shipping in the years which followed. There is ample evidence of a marked increase in English carriers of coal, both coastwise and foreign. The establishment of direct trade with the Levant and the East Indies, the great migration to New England, the development of tobacco in the Chesapeake plantations, and the planting of colonies in the West Indies offered opportunities for English ships in foreign commerce. But the frequent recurrence of complaints suggests that whatever advantages may have been acquired in the new fields were offset by losses in the older trades. In 1618 the Newcastle Merchant Adventurers found a lack of English shipping in the Netherlands, and two years later the shipowners of Hull complained that the merchants did not use English ships when they were available, but laded Dutch ships in the Eastland and Scottish ships in the trade to and from Bordeaux. A London petition declared in November, 1626, that owing to unfriendly relations with France, English merchants were shipping their goods in foreign vessels under the names of Frenchmen, and that 800 tons had been shipped in twelve strangers' bottoms since the preceding April 20, while only one English ship

---

for English ships entering London in 1602 (Miller, "New Evidence," *Quar. Jour. Econ.,* XLI, 745): those trading with France, 69.8 tons; with the Netherlands, 58 tons; with Germany, 109.4 tons; with Russia, 146 tons. In default of other data, the Denmark-Norway figure of 80 tons was used for the Eastland (including "Dantzick, Melvin, and Quinsburgh . . . Norway and the Sound"). Although for the purpose of averaging contemporary estimates, trade with the Mediterranean and the Iberian countries was grouped together, for the present purpose of converting ships to tons the average burdens of ships were used as given in Miller: for Spain and Portugal, 47.5 tons; for Barbary, 72.7 tons; for Italy, 103 tons; and for the Levant or any other Mediterranean designation or grouping, 125 tons. The average number of tons which each seaman could serve was deemed to be 4.4 tons in vessels going south of Cape Finisterre (the average served in the Levant trade in 1600, according to Epstein, *The Levant Company,* pp. 224-25) and 6.7 tons in the remaining trades ("Observations Touching Trade," *op. cit.,* II, 114).

On this basis the Mediterranean and the Iberian trades employed 9,314 tons; the French, 5,737 tons; the Dutch, 2,900 tons; the German, 4,068 tons; the Eastland (including Danzig, Norway, and the Sound), 2,840 tons; the Russian, 2,817 tons. Although doubtless none of the figures are entirely accurate, since the various bases are merely estimates, the errors should offset one another so that the total should be substantially correct. Despite the different bases for calculation, each gave approximately the same tonnage, except that the figures for 1609 tended to be higher than those for 1615. See also *infra,* p. 341, n. 60, for a discussion of data compiled by Marsden ("English Ships in the Reign of James I," RHS *Trans.,* n.s., XIX, 309-42).

had been employed.[11] Trinity House reported in 1633 that 6,000 tons of shipping lay idle in the Thames, and the following year "a great number of Poor Mariners" declared that they had "fallen into much decay and poverty," since the laws had been neglected and French and Dutch ships, upon discharging their cargoes in England, had been permitted to "relade back again at under rates for far less than petitioners can live by, because they go but with four men and a boy, when petitioners cannot go under fourteen."[12] Throughout the period, the government was exhorting merchants to freight English vessels, and shipowners were trying (usually without success) to prevent foreign vessels from serving as carriers for the export of fish.[13]

Sometime during the next decade shipping conditions improved materially and continued prosperous until the outbreak of civil war. Peace with Spain and France in 1630 undoubtedly helped, and so did the activities of the ship-money fleet, which diminished the depredations of the Dunkirk and Algerine pirates. At the same time Dutch shipping was being harried by the Dunkirk raiders, and its competition in England may also have been restrained by more stringent enforcement of royal decrees during the period of personal government.[14] Whatever the cause, English shipping passing the Sound rose, during the years 1631-40, from an average of 151 ships and 4.4 percent for the preceding decade to an average of 256 ships and 7.3 percent of those entering and clearing.[15] Official concern decreased, and for some years after 1634 English mariners ceased their complaints, even about the export of fish by foreign carriers. In fact, the Masters of Trinity House declared in 1639 that English shipping had increased tenfold within the preceding thirty years.[16] The statement undoubtedly was exaggerated, as the Masters

[11] For Newcastle Merchant Adventures, see THT (1609-25), f. 49; for Hull shipowners, see HMC VIII, App., 239; for London merchants, see THT (1609-25), f. 946; HMC VIII, App. 242-43.

[12] THT (1613-61), p. 30; CSPD (1634-35), pp. 23-24, 498.

[13] *Supra*, pp. 31, 34-37.

[14] Blok, *History of the Netherlands*, IV, 40-43, 70-71; Oppenheim, *Administration of the Royal Navy*, pp. 276-78; *infra*, p. 349, n. 74.

[15] Bang, *Tables, 1497-1660*. The statistics for 1631 to 1640 are based upon only eight years, since figures for 1632 and 1634 are missing.

[16] HMC III, 79. Monson, writing in the same decade, declared that English maritime

of Trinity House were asking for an appropriation from the government, but it does indicate that conditions fluctuated radically between the nadir and the zenith of early Stuart navigation.

In any event, English over-sea shipping probably attained its greatest pre-Restoration growth during the late thirties. By 1643 it was again declared that "trade is decayed, the merchant ships are at anchor,"[17] and by 1649 Trinity House was ready to permit "straungers bottomes" to import most Dutch and Eastland commodities.[18] Undoubtedly English shipping suffered from the Civil War, which caused one Englishman to prey upon another, at the same time that Dutch vessels were freed from the fear of Spanish corsairs by the acknowledgment of Dutch independence in 1648.[19] The English captured between 1,000 and 1,700 prizes during the First Dutch War, but the gains were probably offset during the war with Spain, when they were supposed to have lost from 1,000 to 1,800 ships.[20]

Unfortunately, we have no thoroughly satisfactory figures for conditions at the date when the Navigation Acts became effective. There was a survey of English shipping in 1652, but the returns have been lost. A register of passes for 1662-68 gives us our first opportunity to judge post-Restoration conditions.[21] Although the passes were issued to give protection against the Algerine pirates, entries in the port books show that they were received by ships in the Norwegian, French, Dutch, American, and East Indian trades. We know, however, that the list was not complete. An official report states that the shipmasters were negligent in obtaining passes;[22] the comparative absence of small craft indicates that the fishing boats

strength had trebled since 1604, but his statement should also be discounted (see *infra,* p. 342, n. 60).

[17] T & SP No. 2359.
[18] THT (1613-61), p. 9.
[19] *Infra,* p. 349, n. 74.
[20] For gains during the Dutch War, Shaftesbury Papers, GD 29/2, No. 58; Clowes, *Royal Navy,* II, 155; for losses in war with Spain, BM Harl. MSS 6287, f. 1; "The World's Mistake in Oliver Cromwell," *Harl. Misc.* I, 291; CSPD (1657-58), p. 245. Coke (*Discourse of Trade,* Preface) declared the war with Spain "was a folly never to be forgiven in his [Cromwell's] politicks nor the losses this nation sustained thereby, ever again to be repaired."
[21] Adm. 7/630; Oppenheim, *Administration of the Royal Navy,* p. 343.
[22] CSPD (1663-64), p. 326.

and little coasters were usually not included; and the preponderance of London ships shows that the outports were not adequately represented.

Under the circumstances, the best procedure seems to be to concentrate upon the London figures, which are most nearly complete. We shall come closest to the tonnage owned in 1660 by using the passes from June, 1662 to June, 1664 only, when the great bulk were issued. As far as they disclose, there were then 350 ships, averaging 128 tons each, or 44,800 tons in all. Since the pass records extended over a period of two years, a deduction of at least 10 percent should be made to cover vessels which might be lost during that time.[23] Another deduction of 15 percent should be made to allow for the extraordinary number of ships purchased abroad early in 1662, just

[23] The first accurate figures available concerning the destruction of shipping are those for the nineteenth century, and they show that the United Kingdom lost 4.4 percent of its tonnage annually from 1840 to 1842, and the British Empire, 4.3 percent from 1861 to 1863 and 4.5 percent from 1871 to 1873 (Lindsay, *Merchant Shipping*, III, 467-69). The percentage lost in the seventeenth century was doubtless higher. Lynn reported that in one storm it lost 10 or 12 ships (HMC *Pepys*, p. 190), and 393 were said to have been lost by wreck between 1625 and 1628 (Oppenheim, *Administration of the Royal Navy*, p. 272). A comparison of Lindsay's list of East Indiamen lost by shipwreck from 1702 to 1708 (*op. cit.*, II, 572) with the list of ships employed in the East India trade given by Bal Krishna (*Commercial Relations between India and England*, pp. 358-59) indicates that the annual loss averaged about 10 percent. In addition there were the ships intentionally broken up because of old age, which probably equaled the tonnage lost accidentally. Monson (*Naval Tracts*, V, 239) wrote in Charles I's reign of the ordinary life of a fishing bus being 20 years, and in 1792 the Inspector General of Imports and Exports estimated that 17,000 tons of new construction annually was required to maintain a total of 210,000 tons (CJ XLVII, 356-57). During the early seventeenth century, there were also the depredations of pirates. According to R. Playfair (*The Scourge of Christendom*, p. 34) the pirates seized 466 of Britain's vessels between 1609 and 1616, and war-time losses from privateersmen were even greater (Oppenheim, *op. cit.*, pp. 271-72, 274-78; *supra*, p. 326). The contemporary business man's estimate of the probable longevity of vessels is reflected in the insurance rates which, during the seventeenth century, might be 3 percent for a voyage to Leghorn, 4 to 5 percent to the Levant, and 6 percent to the East Indies in peace time and many times more in war time (Barbour, "Marine Risks and Insurance in the Seventeenth Century," *Jour. Econ. and Bus. Hist.*, I, 589-90). Figured on a twelve-month instead of the voyage basis given above, the rate would have been nearer 10 percent in peace time, and figures for the eighteenth century suggest that in war time it might have amounted to as much as 110 percent (Harrington, *The New York Merchant*, pp. 155-56, 312). Thus it would seem that the annual turnover of vessels was nearer 10 percent a year than 10 percent for two years, but the more conservative estimate was used in lieu of making a special arbitrary allowance for possible omissions in the pass figures.

before the Act of Frauds went into effect.[24] Additions should, of course, be made to the 34,272 tons thus estimated for vessels which did not obtain passes, but in London's case the number in foreign trade or in the Greenland and the Newfoundland fisheries was probably small. Her varied commerce should have taken the vessels at least once within the two years into a region infested by pirates, where the advantages of a pass would have outweighed the trouble of procuring it. Assuming that the pass figures represented only tonnage in foreign trade (including, as did contemporaries, the Greenland and the Newfoundland fisheries) and adding thereto London's share of the tonnage in the other trades, we should come close to having a true estimate of London's total tonnage.[25] Some of the vessels engaged in the coastwise traffic or in fishing may have obtained passes, but such duplications can serve as an allowance for undetected omissions. If, as seems probable, the total tonnage thus calculated for London bore the same proportion to the kingdom's total in 1660 as it did in 1702, England owned 161,619 tons of shipping in 1660.[26]

[24] In 1662 Lynn purchased 20 foreign-built ships totaling more than 700 tons (E 190/436, No. 1) or 15 percent of an estimated 4,708 tons. This figure was calculated by assuming (in default of better evidence) that the 67 ships owned in 1626 (Oppenheim, *Administration of the Royal Navy*, p. 270) were of the same average size as the 86 ships which totaled 5,702 tons in 1702 (Adm. 1/3863, Bundle for 1702) and by determining (after excluding the extraordinary increase of 700 tons in 1662) what average annual increase should be allowed for in order to reach a figure for 1662.

[25] In 1702 London possessed 16.5 percent of the colliers, and 20.2 percent of other coastwise craft (*infra*, p. 329, n. 27). Although the probabilities are that London had no fishing boats in 1702 (other than Newfoundland and Greenland vessels which would be accounted for in the foreign total), it seems wiser to assume that in 1660 she had the same proportion of fishers as she had in 1628, or 8 percent (Oppenheim, *Administration of the Royal Navy*, p. 244; *infra*, p. 333, n. 39). The tonnages of the fishers, the colliers, and other boats carrying goods coastwise were calculated as described *infra*, pp. 329-39. Although in each case the percentage used was based upon the most closely comparable data available, the additions are probably overestimated. London's colliers had constituted only 5.7 percent of the total in 1612 (Nef, *British Coal Industry*, II, 26), and by 1751 London possessed neither fishing boats nor coastwise craft of any sort (BM Add MSS 11255).

[26] The calculation is complicated by the fact that the tonnage of the coastwise craft can be determined only after we have the total tonnage owned in the kingdom, which is the unknown we are seeking. Since we know that London's share of the kingdom's total tonnage in 1702 was 31.7 percent (*infra*, p. 329, n. 27), we can solve the problem by letting x equal the kingdom's total tonnage in the following formula: $.317x$ (London's share of the kingdom's tonnage) $= 34,272$ (London's tonnage in foreign trade, as shown by the pass figures, after making necessary deductions) $+.08 \times 3,159$

Calculations for the eighteenth century rest upon a more solid foundation of factual data. A survey of 1702 shows that England then possessed 3,504 ships, totaling 267,444 tons[27] and that by 1773 England possessed more than twice as many ships, their total burden being 581,000 tons.[28]

Our task does not end, however, with this general chronological review. For our purposes it becomes necessary to learn the relative parts played by the different activities in which English shipping was employed. They may be grouped under four different headings: the fisheries, the coastwise trade in coal, the coastwise carriage of other commodities, and the over-sea or foreign trade.

According to some writers, the most important branch of English navigation lay in the "great and glorious trade of fishing," and

----

(the fishing fleet tonnage, *infra*, p. 332) + .165 × 70,899 (the colliery tonnage, *infra*, p. 336) + .202 × •155x (the formula for arriving at other coastwise craft, *infra*, p. 337).

[27] CO 388/9, F19 (copied in Macpherson, *Annals of Commerce*, II, 719) gives 560 ships, 84,882 tons, and 10,605 men for London, but as its returns from the outports were incomplete, the report of 2,944 ships and 182,562 tons found in Adm. 1/3863 was used instead. CO 388/9, F19 makes it clear that it did not include reports for the local fisheries. Adm. 1/3863 did not report the number of fishermen, but as there is the possibility that it included the tonnage of their boats, the total tonnage given in the manuscript, together with the London total, is assumed to be the total of the entire kingdom, including the local fisheries.

By distributing the outport tonnage among the several trades (fishing 4.8, coastwise 53.9, and foreign 41.3) in accordance with the proportion which existed in 1709 (BM Add MSS 11255) and by utilizing figures obtained on other bases for the kingdom's total tonnage in the collier and other coastwise trades (*infra*, pp. 336-37), together with the percentage showing London's share of the collier fleet (Brand, *History and Antiquities of Newcastle*, II, 677; Westerfield, *Middlemen in English Business*, p. 229; *infra*, p. 337, n. 51), we can complete the analysis of English navigation at the turn of the century. The following table (in which Newfoundland and Greenland tonnages are included as foreign) shows how the remaining data has been supplied, the figures in italics representing the results of the calculation:

Trades	Outport Tonnage	Outport Percentage	London Tonnage	London Percentage	Total
Fisheries	8,763	100.0			*8,763*
Foreign	75,398	54.2	*63,617*	*45.8*	*139,015*
Coastwise	98,401	82.2	*21,265*	*17.8*	*119,666*
Coal	65,307	83.5	*12,905*	*16.5*	*78,212*
Other	33,094	79.8	*8,360*	*20.2*	*41,454*
Total	182,562	68.3	84,882	31.7	*267,444*

[28] According to BM Add MSS 11255, the outports had 206,728 tons engaged in foreign trade, 214,977 tons in the coasting trade (including colliers), and 23,646 in fishing. London possessed 135,649 tons, all engaged in foreign trade. Sheffield's figures (*Observations*, p. 160) differ slightly, giving a total of 7,619 ships of 580,579 tons and 52,789 seamen.

it sought and received much governmental encouragement.[29] But the naval experts did not share the pamphleteers' enthusiasm. Although Admiral Boteler conceded that fishermen had acquired "sea legs and sea stomachs," the more representative feeling of the service was probably expressed by one of His Majesty's captains when he wrote to the Admiralty, "since going ashore I have tried to get men, but not a seaman to be had; only poor fishermen, who are no use."[30] Yet it should be remembered that there was more than one type of seaman. Those who stayed close to shore might deserve the contempt heaped upon them, but many sailed out into the North or Irish Seas out of sight of land, and the most venturesome made their way to Iceland, Greenland, and Newfoundland.[31]

As nearly as we can judge, boats in the Iceland fleet attained the size usually ascribed by contemporary writers to fishing busses. If so, they averaged about 70 tons' burden, and each man served 3.4 tons.[32] We are told that 140 vessels sailed for Iceland in 1528 and only 43 in Edward VI's reign. Parliament complained in 1581 that the Iceland fleet had "decayed" from 200 sail, but does not state when the process had commenced or how far it had gone. The trade was undoubtedly depressed because the King of Denmark had commenced in 1580 to exact a license fee, but it was not destroyed, because complaints are heard from Suffolk in 1584 that Scottish pirates lay in wait "for the Iceland ships," and a year later an Order in Council offered redresses for wrongs done to the King of Denmark's subjects in Iceland "by the Englishmen that fish there."[33] In default of more

[29] For typical claims for fisheries, see Barbon, *Discourse of Trade*, p. 5; Davenant, *Works*, I, 429; V, 462; Misselden, *Circle of Commerce*, p. 41; Monson, *Naval Tracts*, V, 249; "S.E.," *Touchstone of Mony and Commerce*, p. 653.

[30] CSPD (1652-53), p. 302.

[31] "Boteler's Dialogues," Navy Records Society *Publications*, LXV, 47-48.

[32] On the basis of an entry of Henry VIII's reign, showing that vessels going to Iceland with a few exceptions ranged in size from 35 tons to 95 tons (Great Britain, *Letters and Papers, Henry VIII* [1533], No. 1380; Williamson, *Maritime Enterprise*, p. 202), and others in 1677 and 1678 mentioning Iceland fishing boats of 50 and of 60 tons (CTB V, 745, 870), it seems likely that such vessels averaged 70 tons like the busses about which pamphleteers were usually so enthusiastic. Although the busses employed one man for each 4.6 tons, English boats were generally conceded to require more men, and the better estimate seems to be that calculated from the figures in "The Trade's Increase," of one man for each 3.4 tons (*Harl. Misc.*, IV, 217, 221; Monson, *Naval Tracts*, V, 238, 240; Elder, *Royal Fishery Companies*, pp. 124-31).

[33] 23 Eliz., c. 7; CSPD (1581-90), pp. 186, 252; Judah, *North American Fisheries and British Policy*, p. 30; Williamson, *Maritime Enterprise*, p. 202.

accurate statistics, we can only average those we have for 1528 and for Edward VI's reign, and assume that there were 92 vessels in 1582. Subsequently we find mention of 123 vessels in 1615, 160 in 1628, and 50 in 1659.[34] Thereafter, separate mention of the Iceland fleet is seldom found except as part of the general statistics for fishermen or fishing boats.

The vessels fishing off Britain's coasts averaged 16 tons in size and employed one man for each 2.5 tons.[35] Comparatively little is known about the pilchard and other fisheries in the Channel, but their tonnage can be roughly estimated on the basis of reports from the southern ports, which indicate that they supplied 20.7 percent of all the fishers other than those at Newfoundland and Greenland.[36] Eng-

[34] For 1615: an average of the figures in Tobias Gentleman, "England's Way to Win Wealth," *Harl. Misc.*, III, 400-4, and "The Trade's Increase," *Harl. Misc.*, IV, 217; for 1628: CSPD (1627-28), p. 512; for 1659: CSPD (1658-59), pp. 551, 560. An entry of 1661 speaks of only 15 Iceland barks (CSPD [1661-62], p. 91).

[35] When referring to fishing busses of 60 to 80 tons (e.g., Elder, *Royal Fishery Companies*, pp. 120-31; Monson, *Naval Tracts*, V, 236-49), except in the Iceland trade, writers were describing what ought to have been, rather than what was. The fishing towns which declared that the statute of 5 Eliz., c. 5 had increased the "Sea fisher bottes and Barkes" by 140 sail, said that the burden ranged from 10 to 30 tons (*Tudor Economic Documents*, II, 122), and the same report was given for the fishing fleet in Charles I's reign (Elder, *op. cit.*, p. 26), facts which suggest that the 16-ton average given by Sheffield (*On Ireland*, p. 123) prevailed throughout Tudor and Stuart days. In fact as late as 1773 it had risen only to 17.6 tons (Sheffield, *Observations*, p. 160). On the basis of a 16-ton average, each fisherman would serve 2.5 tons, according to the figures for 1609-15 (averaging calculations based upon ships and men as given in BM Lans. MSS 142, f. 304, and "England's Way to Win Wealth," *Harl. Misc.*, III, 402), a ratio which probably remained true throughout the century. Even in 1773, when the number of men reported was probably materially under the true figure, the ratio was only 3.7 tons per man (Sheffield, *op. cit.*, p. 160).

[36] Only ports west of the Cinque Ports (from Southampton to Gweek) were included as Channel ports. The percentage is the average of the following: 22.9 percent in 1628 (*infra*, p. 333, n. 39; Oppenheim, *Administration of the Royal Navy*, p. 244); 17.6 percent in 1709; 16.7 percent in 1744; and 25.4 percent in 1774 (BM Add MSS 11255). Except in 1628, when the number of fishermen was used as a base, the percentages were calculated upon the number of tons reported. No attempt was made to calculate a percentage for 1582 because of the failure of that year's figures to distinguish between fishermen and mariners in the return for Cornwall (SP 12/146, No. 45). The percentages given may exaggerate the importance of the Channel fisheries, because some of the fishermen from the ports there probably engaged in the North Sea and Iceland fisheries, as did those from the Cinque Ports "and all the rest of the West-countrymen of England, as far as Bridport and Lime in Dorsetshire." But on the other hand, the element of error may be somewhat offset by fishermen from other ports participating in the Channel fisheries—and by failure to enumerate some of the smaller boats in the North Sea (CSPD [1627-28], p. 512; Tobias Gentleman, "England's Way to Win Wealth," *Harl. Misc.*, III, 402, 404; Oppenheim, *op. cit.*, p. 276).

lish interest centered in the fleets which began the season's labors in search of cod and ling off the coast of Ireland and ended by casting nets for herring upon the banks of Yarmouth. Yet despite repeated exhortations of the pamphleteers to English fishermen, the Dutch gained a predominating position in the North Sea fisheries, except for red herring, best cured at Yarmouth.[37]

English figures for fishing boats and fishermen apparently refer solely to men and boats operating in the waters off Britain and Iceland, and relegate vessels going to Greenland and Newfoundland to the statistics of foreign trade.[38] Thus interpreted, the list of 1582 indicates that there were then some 3,772 fishermen, or a fishing fleet of 11,316 tons. As far as we can estimate, the tonnage fluctuated thereafter, being 14,409 tons for the period 1609-15; 11,343 tons in 1628; 3,159 tons at the Restoration; 8,763 tons in 1702; and 23,646 tons in 1773.[39]

[37] Elder, *Royal Fishery Companies*, pp. 26-27; Monson, *Naval Tracts*, V, 269.
[38] See, for example, CO 388/18, No. 22; BT 6/185.
[39] Three different methods of calculation have been utilized in forming the estimates given in the text. For 1582 and 1628 they have been based upon the number of fishermen in the various ports multiplied by 3, the average of the 2.5 tons and 3.4 tons served by fishermen in the North Seas and Iceland fleets respectively (*supra*, pp. 330-31). For 1609-15 and 1660 the estimates are calculated from reports of the fishing fleets, and for 1702 and 1773 they are taken from contemporary statistics. In almost every instance, however, other complications require further explanation.

The report of 1582 made a distinction between fishermen (2,243) and masters and mariners (6,851) only for 9,094 of the 15,270 "mariners of all sorts" (exclusive of London watermen). Consequently the total number of fishermen was calculated as being 3,772, on the basis of the ratio disclosed for counties which made more specific reports (SP 12/146, No. 45. Monson, *Naval Tracts*, III, 188-92 differs slightly). The smaller estimates given by Oppenheim (*Administration of the Royal Navy*, p. 177) for 1582 and by BM Harl. MSS 4228 (f. 45r) for 1583 appear to have overlooked the unsegregated entries, which included counties like Norfolk, Suffolk, and Cornwall, noted for their fisheries. The segregation of seamen and fishermen in 1628 (Oppenheim, *op. cit.*, p. 244) appears to be reasonably adequate, but the returns make no mention of Sussex, Gloucester, York, Chester, or Lancaster, which in 1582 had supplied 18.2 percent of the fishermen and 10.8 percent of the other seamen (as computed above). When additions have been made to the returns for the unlisted counties, the total is 3,781 fishermen and 11,636 other seamen, the figures used here.

In 1609-15 the tonnage of the North Sea fleet was calculated by averaging the 120 vessels reported by BM Lans. MSS 142, f. 304 and the 231 reported by Tobias Gentleman ("England's Way to Win Wealth," *Harl. Misc.*, III, 400-4) and multiplying by 16 tons (*supra*, p. 331, n. 35), and by adding thereto the tonnage for the Iceland and Channel fisheries, computed as described (*supra*, pp. 330-31). Estimates of seamen employed in the North Sea and Iceland fleets as given in BM Lans. MSS 142, f. 304, and "The Trade's Increase" (*Harl. Misc.*, IV, 221) were disregarded, but if the calculation

Ships in the Greenland trade appear to have averaged 139 tons in 1615, about 250 tons by the middle of the century and thereafter, and to have employed one man for each 5.2 tons.[40] Although the English did not begin to participate in the trade until 1597, it employed 2,083 tons by 1615, and 2,600 tons under the Commonwealth. It declined for some years after the Restoration, and was listed by

was based upon the number of seamen instead of ships, the total would have been reduced only 10.3 percent.

In the figures for 1660, the North Sea fisheries were assumed to employ 40 vessels (or 640 tons), which was the average of the 50 vessels reported to have been at sea in 1659 (CSPD [1658-59], p. 560) and the 30 vessels reported in 1660 (CSPD [1660-61], p. 40). Adding the Iceland and Channel tonnages on the basis already described (*supra*, pp. 330-31), the total was 5,221 tons. As it was computed from reports of fleets at sea, an allowance was made for possible duplication of activity, as was probably done by contemporaries in the other estimates. Only 60.5 percent of the 5,221 tons was considered to be exclusively employed in the fisheries, that being the relationship which calculations show to have existed in 1628 when contemporary data for the number of men supposed to be employed in the fisheries and the number of vessels at sea were both available. Compare the 18,764 tons calculated on the foregoing basis from the 230 North Sea fishers and 160 Iceland boats in 1628 (CSPD [1627-28], p. 512) with the 11,343 tons calculated on the basis of 3 tons for each of the 3,781 fishermen in the several ports. Although it is questionable whether such a reduction in the total should be made, French fishing vessels in 1552 were said to have carried coal from Newcastle "as soon as theyr fishing is don" (*Tudor Economic Documents*, II, 99), and in the late eighteenth century English officials recognized that fishing boats might also engage in the coasting trade (BM Add MSS 11256, f. 42). Comparatively speaking, the fishing tonnage in 1660 seems out of line, but the Ostend men-of-war were said to have destroyed most of the Northern fishery (CSPD [1660-61], p. 174). In any event an underestimate of the fishing tonnage in 1660 will increase the tonnage employed in foreign trade when the Navigation Acts were passed, and thereby tend to minimize rather than to exaggerate their effects.

The fishing tonnage given for 1702 is the percentage of the outport total tonnage, which the statistics for 1709 (BM Add MSS 11255; *supra*, p. 329, n. 27) indicate was devoted to fishing. No similar figures exist for London at that date, but it seems reasonable to assume that even if London was not then without fishing boats, as it was in 1751 (when statistics are next available), the tonnage was negligible and may be disregarded. The figure for 1773 was taken from BM Add MSS 11255 and differs slightly from the 1,441 vessels, 6,774 men, and 25,339 tons given by Sheffield (*Observations*, p. 160).

Additional data concerning the fishing fleets can be found in an unpublished thesis by Margaret W. Clark, "English Fisheries and the Mercantilistic Schemes of the Seventeenth Century," in the University of California Library, which directed attention to many of the basic figures used here for the North Sea and Iceland fleets.

[40] The "Rosetta stone" used in the case of the Greenland fisheries was an entry in 1654 referring to 12 ships, of 3,000 tons, employing 580 men (CSPD [1653-54], p. 421). An undated manuscript in the British Museum (BM Add MSS 35898, f. 291) gives a ratio of 3.8 tons per man, but it apparently refers to the French whale fisheries. The average tonnage for 1615 was calculated at 5.2 tons per man, from the figures reported by "The Trade's Increase," (*Harl. Misc.*, IV, 223) of 15 sail and 400 men. The average shown by entry figures for 1773 was 255 tons (BT 6/185).

Coke among the "lost trades." Child declared in 1675 that England had sent but one vessel that year and none the year before, but the trade revived somewhat by the end of the century, when the Greenland Company was allowed to send 7 vessels, presumably totaling 1,750 tons; and by 1773 the fleet totaled 14,790 tons.[41]

Although Newfoundland was not the only American fishery visited by Englishmen, it was the most important during the seventeenth century, and for present purposes we must assume that the English tonnage engaged elsewhere in American waters was offset by colonial or other vessels reported as part of the Newfoundland fleets. Ships going to Newfoundland, especially in later years, were divided between "sack boats," which desired primarily to transport the fish purchased from the inhabitants, and those vessels which planned to catch and dry their own fish, but for present purposes we may disregard this distinction. The ratios of ships, men, and tons varied from year to year, but an average of 80 tons in burden and 2.6 tons per man should afford a working basis for estimating tonnage.[42] Thus calculated, the tonnages at the periods we are studying were 6,000 tons in 1582; 11,229 tons for 1609-15; 17,730 tons in 1660; 14,407 tons in 1702; and 23,795 tons in 1773.[43]

[41] For 1597: Whitworth, *State of Trade*, p. liv; for 1615: "The Trade's Increase," *Harl. Misc.*, IV, 223; for the Commonwealth: CSPD (1653-54), pp. 377, 421; for the Restoration: Child, *New Discourse*, p. xvii, Coke, *Discourse of Trade*, Preface; for 1695: CTB X, 968; for 1773, the entry figures given in BT 6/185.

[42] The average of 80 tons per ship was based upon the following contemporary figures: 80 tons for 1644 (Judah, *North American Fisheries and British Policy*, p. 90); 76 tons for 1675 (CSPC [1675-76], No. 666); 89 tons for 1710-14 (CO 388/18, No. 22); 75, for 1729-63 (Lounsbury, *British Fishery at Newfoundland*, p. 314). The ratio of 2.6 tons per man likewise represented an average of the ratios calculated from contemporary data: 2.5 for 1634 (Lounsbury, *op. cit.*, p. 69); 2.0 for 1644 (Judah, *op. cit.*, p. 90); 3.0 for 1675 (CSPC [675-76], No. 666); 2.7 for 1736-39 (Lounsbury, *op. cit.*, p. 311-12); 3.1 for 1738-41 (*ibid.*, p. 312); 2.6 for 1743 (*idem*); and 2.5 for 1753 (*ibid.*, p. 313). Neither average is exact, but errors in one tend to offset those in the other.

[43] The tonnage given for 1582 is an average of that of the 50 ships listed in 1578 (Judah, *North American Fisheries and British Policy*, p. 28) and the 100 noted for 1594 (*ibid.*, p. 32). The figure for 1609-15 has been obtained by converting the various estimates of ships and of men to tons at the ratios given *supra*, n. 42, and averaging the tonnages thus computed. The estimates used were those given for 1609 in BM Lans. MSS 142, f. 304; for 1614 in Judah, *op. cit.*, p. 72; and for 1615 in "The Trade's Increase," *Harl. Misc.*, IV, 217, 221, and in Judah, *op. cit.*, p. 58. The estimate for 1660 was obtained by averaging figures of shipping and seamen for both 1653 (CSPD [1652-53], p. 107; Judah, *op. cit.*, p. 96) and 1668 (CSPC [1661-68], No. 1731). The estimate for 1702 was based upon similar data for 1699, 1700, and

The coal trade was another mercantile favorite and was highly praised as a "nursery for seamen."[44] The masters of colliers, as the coal ships were called, were usually willing to take a green hand or two,[45] and the arduous voyage from Newcastle to London offered excellent training for seamen "near at hand." The availability of the colliermen for His Majesty's fleet, however, was somewhat exaggerated, since the winters were as cold in war time as during peaceful years. London continued to need Newcastle coal, and the seamen required for the traffic were usually promised freedom from impressment, although in cases of emergency the promises could be and were forgotten.[46]

The researches of Nef and of others have greatly simplified the correlation of the various statistics available. As the average size of the collier increased throughout the century from 56 tons in 1592, to 73 tons by 1606, 83 tons by 1615, 139 tons by 1638, and 248 tons by 1701,[47] the number of seamen employed per 100 tons decreased. In 1587 it required 10 hands to man a 100-ton, coal-carrying bark, but the same number of men could man 247 tons of

---

1701, as being more representative of conditions at the end of the century than the figure of 41 ships and 441 seamen reported for the war year, 1702 (CO 390/6, p. 3). No figures for 1773 were at hand, and the estimate rests upon Prowse's statement that in 1765 there were 9,152 fishermen in Newfoundland, exclusive of the inhabitants (*History of Newfoundland*, p. 325). It should be noted, however, that there were considerably more fishermen (16,873) in 1773 in the English fisheries in the Gulf of St. Lawrence (MacGregor, *Commercial Statistics of America*, p. 476).

For data on which to base estimates for other years, see Judah, *op. cit.*, pp. 42, 43, 58, 123, 157; Lounsbury, *British Fishery at Newfoundland*, pp. 63, 111, 120, 162-64, 169. The tonnage fluctuated rather radically in the seventeenth century from a high of 36,800 tons in 1640 to a low of 3,960 tons in 1653. During the first half of the eighteenth century the figure remained fairly constant at about 25,000 tons.

[44] "The Trade's Increase," *Harl. Misc.*, IV, 220-21; Houghton, *Husbandry and Trade Improv'd*, IV, 400; see also Ashton and Sykes, *Coal Industry of the Eighteenth Century*, p. 201 n.; Lipson, *Economic History*, II, 117; Nef, *British Coal Industry*, I, 238-39.

[45] "The Trade's Increase," *Harl. Misc.*, IV, 220-21.

[46] T & SP No. 4069; Ashton and Sykes, *Coal Industry of the Eighteenth Century*, p. 201; Nef, *British Coal Industry*, I, 391; II, 93-94, 263-66.

[47] Nef, *British Coal Industry*, I, 390-91. Ashton and Sykes (*Coal Industry of the Eighteenth Century*, p. 199) state that the average capacity in 1702 was estimated at 140 tons. The average cargo from Sunderland was about 60 tons; the largest was less than 150 tons, as late as 1685 (Nef, *op. cit.*, I, 31). Many of the Newcastle colliers built after 1625 were designed to carry from 200 to 300 tons of coal. The maximum efficiency appears to have been reached with vessels of 500 tons, and as years passed the number of small colliers decreased (*ibid.*, I, 391-92).

shipping in 1665, and 296 tons by 1703.[48] Since the seventeenth-century practice was to employ a ton of shipping to transport a ton of coal,[49] we can calculate the tonnage of the shipping entering in the coastwise coal trade from the statistics of coal carried; and if we are correct in assuming that the average Newcastle and Sunderland collier made eight trips a year,[50] we can estimate the tonnage of the collier fleet employed in this activity. In the early years it rose rapidly: 7,618 tons in 1582; 28,223 in 1609-15; and 70,899 in 1660. After the Restoration its growth was less rapid, and the trade employed only 78,212 tons in 1702 and 125,346 tons in 1773.[51]

[48] Nef, *British Coal Industry*, I, 390-91. These figures probably represent the minimum number required, as they were prepared for war-time needs.

[49] An example given by Oppenheim (*Administration of the Royal Navy*, pp. 266-67) shows that, as calculated in the seventeenth century, when fully laden a collier's cargo equaled her burden. Nef (*British Coal Industry*, I, 390 n.) says that when seventeenth-century traders and customs officials spoke of the burden of a collier, they meant the weight of a full cargo of coal. In calculating the duties of 1685, Trinity House counted a chaldron of coal as a ton of burden, although they declared the method favored the shipowner (THL [1689-1709], pp. 9, 16, 36) as it doubtless did, since a London chaldron equaled a ton and a third (Nef, *op. cit.*, II, 367-68).

[50] Nef, *British Coal Industry*, I, 394, 396; II, 389. See also Ashton and Sykes, *Coal Industry of the Eighteenth Century*, p. 200. It is somewhat difficult to ascertain the average number of trips. Some could make from 12 to 14 trips each year, but Nef concludes that since there were four months during which sailings were practically suspended until the latter part of the eighteenth century, a collier averaged from 5 to 9 round trips between London and Newcastle during a year of normal trade. Although on this basis the average would be 7, an estimate of 8 trips seems more reliable. It allows for the extra voyages of the small percentage which did make winter voyages, and takes account of the fact that some of the coastwise voyages would be shorter than the trip from Newcastle to London (e.g., from Sunderland to London, or from the Tyne or Wear to other coast ports). It also provides a margin of error to cover the possibility that foreign vessels might have engaged in the trade despite the laws (*supra*, p. 280, n. 26). In addition, calculations based upon 8 trips a year are more in line with other estimates than those based upon 7 trips.

[51] Except for 1773, when the collier tonnage was calculated by deducting the non-collier tonnage from the total coastwise (BM Add MSS 11255, f. 8; BM Add MSS 11256, f. 51), the tonnages are based upon the carriage of coal coastwise from Newcastle and Sunderland as given in Nef, *British Coal Industry*, II, Table facing p. 380. Gaps in the statistics force us to estimate the figures in which we are interested from those given for the nearest comparable dates when both Newcastle and Sunderland records are available. In each case the total tonnage has been divided by 8 to allow for repeated voyages of the same ship (*supra*, n. 50). The estimate for 1582 was calculated as being two-thirds of the shipments from Newcastle in 1592, assuming that Sunderland as yet had none of any importance. Although exact percentages are not available, the record of entries at London makes it clear that the trade had increased at least that much during the decade (Nef, *op. cit.*, II, 381). The estimate for 1609-15 rests upon an average of the figures for the years 1609 to 1612, and that for 1660 upon an average of those for 1658-59 and 1659-60. For 1702 the Newcastle statistics

It is much more difficult to calculate the tonnage of other coastwise shipping, but we should be able to make a fairly close approximation. An average of contemporary figures shows that coasting vessels other than colliers constituted 15.5 percent of the kingdom's total from 1772 to 1781.[52] For want of a better method of calculation, we must assume that such craft comprised the same percentage throughout the two centuries with which we are concerned. On that basis, the tonnage ranged from 10,607 tons in 1582, 15,743 tons in 1609-15, 25,051 tons in 1660, 41,454 tons in 1702, to 89,631 tons in 1773.[53]

were obtained by averaging those for 1706-9, a period which included two poor years and two good years. No figures for Sunderland were available for that period, but calculations disclosed what percentage its tonnage constituted of the Newcastle tonnage in 1685 and in 1733 (the two closest dates for which figures are available), and the percentage for 1702 was assumed to be the same as the average of the percentages for those two years. The failure of the collier tonnage in 1773 to be as large as one would expect may be due to the collier's sailing in winter as well as in summer (*supra*, p. 336, n. 50) or to underestimates in recording their size (*infra*, p. 423). If, as charged, one-third of the tonnage in 1592 was foreign (CSPD 1591-94, pp. 195-96; Nef, *op. cit.*, II, 24 n.) early collier figures are exaggerated, but the mere charge is insufficient to warrant altering our figures.

The accuracy of our method of ascertaining the collier tonnage can be attested by comparing the results obtained by it with calculations made on different bases. When we convert contemporary estimates of the number of colliers and seamen into tons, at 83 tons per ship and 10 tons per man (*supra*, pp. 335-36), we find that the tonnage computed on the basis of the coal shipments for 1609-15 is only 310 tons less than the average of the calculations based upon the contemporary figures (BM Lans. MSS 142, f. 304; Brewster, *Essays on Trade and Navigation*, pp. 75-76; "The Trade's Increase," *Harl. Misc.*, IV, 216, 221; Nef, *op. cit.*, II, 95). If we multiply the 300 colliers estimated by the Navy Commissioners in 1626 (CSPD [1625-26], p. 221) by 111 tons (the average of the burdens in 1615 and 1638, *supra*, p. 335), the resulting estimate is only 8.7 percent lower, and the 80,000 tons estimated by Petty (*Economic Writings*, I, 304) in 1671 is but 1.9 percent greater than the tonnage calculated, as described above, on the basis of the coal carried coastwise from Newcastle and Sunderland for the years 1626 and 1671 respectively (Nef, *op. cit.*, II, table facing p. 380 [26.4 percent was added to the 1671 Newcastle figure to allow for the Sunderland tonnage, that being the relationship which existed in 1674, the nearest year for which figures are available]). The estimates of seamen in the collier fleet at the end of the century are mere guesses, obviously too great to refer only to the coastwise traffic from Newcastle and Sunderland (Nef, *op. cit.*, II, 141; *supra*, p. 329). The figures in Brand (*History and Antiquities of Newcastle*, II, 677; see also Westerfield, *Middlemen in English Business*, p. 229) indicating that there were 1,277 ships "using the Coale Trade at Newcastle in the yeares 1702, 1703, and 1704" merely mean that that number of vessels at one time or another made entry at Newcastle during the three years specified. At 248 tons per vessel (*supra*, p. 335), 1,277 ships would equal 316,696 tons, more than England's total tonnage in 1702 and more than twice the collier tonnage in 1773.

[52] BM Add MSS 11255, 11256.
[53] The figures have been calculated on the basis of the totals given *infra*, p. 339,

Although arbitrarily made, the assumption does not seem unreasonable, in view of the enumeration in both 1582 and 1792 of many small vessels which could easily sail up rivers and into small harbors.[54]

In determining the amount of shipping engaged in foreign trade, we can use contemporary estimates for 1609 and 1615 and official figures for 1773,[55] but otherwise we must proceed by deduction. If we subtract the tonnage of vessels devoted to the fisheries, the coal trade, and other coastwise trade, from the total English tonnage, we should have the tonnage of the vessels engaged in foreign trade. There is, of course, the possibility that the same ship might have engaged in more than one trade; but, as has been explained, our method of calculation has been such that the duplications should cancel one another, except in the case of the Newfoundland and the Greenland fisheries. The Greenland whaling vessels may possibly have engaged in other activities, but it does not seem very probable. In any event, their number was not great except in 1773, and the element of error will not seriously affect our conclusions. Lewes Roberts stated that the Newfoundland fishermen settled down to agricultural pursuits when not off the Banks, but we know that many of the boats went to France and Spain for salt and carried fish direct to Southern Europe, whence they presumably returned to England with cargoes.[56] Thus it may well be that part of the Newfoundland tonnage should be credited to foreign trade, but for present purposes we can disregard that possibility. Such foreign trade would be subsidiary to the Newfoundland fisheries, a field in which the Dutch, safely en-

---

except for 1773 when the contemporary figure for that year was used (BM Add MSS 11256, f. 51).

[54] For 1582, SP 12/146, No. 45; Monson, *Naval Tracts*, III, 188-92; for 1792, BM Add MSS 38432, Section 5. Usher ("Growth of English Shipping," *Quar. Jour. Econ.*, XLII, 475) notes that while 27.4 percent of England's tonnage was under 40 tons in 1582, only 5.6 percent was below that size in 1788. This fact does not necessarily demonstrate that the proportion of coasters was greater in 1582, because at that date many vessels under 40 tons in burden engaged in foreign trade (*infra*, p. 339, n. 57).

[55] For 1609, BM Lans. MSS 142, ff. 302-6; for 1615, Brewster, *Essays on Trade and Navigation*, pp. 75-76; "The Trade's Increase," *Harl. Misc.*, IV, 212-31; for 1773, Sheffield, *Observations*, p. 160.

[56] *Merchant's Mappe of Commerce*, pp. 57-58; Prowse, *History of Newfoundland*, pp. 107, 163; Lounsbury, *British Fishery at Newfoundland*, pp. 37, 315; Judah, *North American Fisheries and British Policy*, p. 73.

trenched in the herring fisheries, did not provide really serious competition. Our inquiry has not attempted to analyze England's effort to encourage fishermen, either at home or in America, and to be consistent, we should concentrate upon the foreign trade in which English merchant vessels had to hold their own against Dutch competition. The following tabulation discloses the tonnage thus employed:

DISTRIBUTION OF ENGLISH TONNAGE

Year	Total Tonnage	Collier Trade	Other Coast- wise Trade	Newfound- land and Greenland Fisheries	Other Fish- eries	Foreign Trade
1582	68,433	7,618	10,607	6,000	11,316	32,892
1609–15	101,566	28,223	15,743	13,312	14,409	29,879
1660	161,619	70,899	25,051	20,330	3,159	42,180
1702	267,444	78,212	41,454	16,157	8,763	122,858
1773	581,000	125,346	89,631	38,585	23,646	303,792

The elimination method of ascertaining the tonnage in foreign trade is confirmed by contemporary apportionments which exist for 1609-15, 1702, and 1773; it is weakest for 1582 and 1660, but there is independent evidence supporting the accuracy of the estimates even for those dates. The very size of the vessels in 1582 suggests that foreign trade employed fully as many tons as have been credited to it,[57] and there are two alternative methods of checking the estimate for 1660. We can calculate the kingdom's tonnage in foreign trade

[57] Vessels engaged in the non-collier coast trade and the North Sea and Channel fisheries were mostly small craft under 30 tons. Examination of the list for 1582 (SP 12/146, No. 45) shows that there were about 13,000 tons of such vessels, whereas the apportionment credited their activities with 15,483 tons (*supra*, pp. 330-32, 337). The discrepancy is most probably accounted for at the expense of the tonnage in foreign trade, since the allowances for other maritime activities err, if anything, on the side of generosity. Although a few of the larger vessels undoubtedly participated in local fisheries and the non-collier coastwise trade, their number was probably offset by the smaller vessels engaging in other trades. In 1580, for example, 29 ships between 20 and 30 tons, totaling 716 tons, entered London (SP 12/148, ff. 124-28); and the number unquestionably was much larger in the outports, because as late as 1670 the average size of English vessels in the outport trade with France was only 36.5 tons (*supra*, p. 295, n. 106). At the beginning of Elizabeth's reign, corn was said often to have been transported to Spain and Portugal in vessels under 30 tons' burden (Shillington and Chapman, *Commercial Relations of England and Portugal*, p. 163), and legislation had been required to keep the small boats known as hoyes and plates from engaging in foreign trade (*supra*, p. 26).

directly from the figure we have for London's share, arriving at an estimate of 54,500 tons;[58] or we can follow an entirely different process of deduction based upon the statistics of tonnage entering London, leading to the conclusion that England devoted 53,919 tons to foreign trade.[59] Neither of these methods provides as many safeguards against error as that already described, but both are useful for corroborative purposes.

If the apportionment made of English tonnage is even approximately correct, certain facts stand out clearly. Those mercantile favorites, the North Sea and the Iceland fisheries, rendered their greatest service to England's navigation during the reigns of Elizabeth and James I, and became less important thereafter, the tonnage

[58] The accuracy of the method depends upon the truth of the assumption that the kingdom's tonnage in foreign trade (including Newfoundland and Greenland) was divided in 1660 as in 1702. We arrive at London's share for 1660 as we did in the elimination process (*supra*, pp. 327-28). On the basis of its 34,272 tons being only 45.8 percent of the total (*supra*, p. 329, n. 27), the estimate is 74,830 tons from which we deduct the 20,330 tons devoted to the Newfoundland and the Greenland fisheries.
[59] The basic figure used in this estimate is 95,266, sometimes given as the total of English entries in all the kingdom in 1660, but which is more probably the English tonnage entering London in the years 1663-69 (*infra*, p. 346, n. 67). The first step is to allow for the increase in English shipping prior to the effective date of the Act of Frauds (*supra*, pp. 327-28) by deducting 15 percent. Judging from the figures for 1693-96 (CO 388/6, A 16), the English entries in London constituted 57.4 percent of the total English entries for the kingdom, which thus computed is 141,073 tons. Since that figure includes repeated voyages, it is necessary to ascertain the average number of times the same vessel might enter port in one year. In default of other figures, we must compute the tonnage entering the kingdom by assuming that London's entries constituted 57.4 percent of the total English entries as it did in 1693-96. In thus calculating the entry figures, it will be wisest to use as our base figures for the year of prosperity, 1700, rather than those for the war year, 1702 (Adm. 1/3863), despite the fact that the ownership figures for the tonnage devoted to foreign trade are for 1702 (*supra*, p. 329, n. 27). Proceeding on that basis, we discover that each vessel on the average entered port 1.9 times a year. Assuming that the same condition prevailed in 1660, the 141,073 tons estimated to have entered the kingdom at that time represented an ownership of only 74,249 tons, from which we must deduct the 20,330 tons engaged in the Newfoundland and Greenland fisheries (*supra*, p. 339) to ascertain the tonnage in foreign trade proper. Questions can be raised as to the accuracy of the basic figure of 95,266 tons and as to the justification for deducting 15 percent when calculating the tonnage for 1660. Also there is no guarantee that the entry statistics for London maintained substantially the same relationship with those for the outports in 1660 that they did in 1693-96, or that on the average a vessel made the same number of repeated voyages in 1660 as in 1701 and 1702. But judging from the statistics for 1773, the element of error was not great. English entries at London then constituted 46.5 percent of the total, and figures for the kingdom show that each vessel made two voyages a year (BM Add MSS 11255; BT 6/185). Moreover, the possible errors often offset each other.

employed decreasing from 16.5 percent in 1582 to 4.1 percent in 1773. During the first half of the seventeenth century, the most marked development was the phenomenal rise of the coastwise trade in coal, which, together with the Newfoundland fisheries, served as a refuge for English ships and seamen while the Dutch were dominating the trade of Europe. Thereafter, although the coastwise coal trade continued to increase, the burden of sustaining and developing English navigation came to rest upon over-sea shipping. Obviously Parliament chose wisely in 1651 and in 1660, when it looked to foreign trade for the salvation of English shipping, and whether we take the largest or the smallest estimate for 1660, it is apparent that English over-sea shipping increased more rapidly after the legislature acted than before.[60]

[60] The estimates of the growth of English shipping by Usher ("Growth of English Shipping," *Quar. Jour. Econ.*, XLII, 465-78) and by Vogel ("Zur Grösse der europäischen Handelsflotten," *Forschungen und Versuche zur Geschichte des Mittelalters und der Neuzeit*, p. 322), although computed on different bases, likewise indicate that English shipping increased more rapidly after the Restoration than before. Sombart's estimates are given for dates which do not throw any direct light on our problem, but his figures are not inconsistent with the same conclusion (*Der moderne Kapitalismus*, II, 301). Nor does Marsden's list ("English Ships in the Reign of James I," *RHS Trans.*, n.s., XIX, 309-42) of 1,200 to 1,400 ships indicate any great increase in English tonnage prior to 1625. His list includes 50 ships of the royal navy and some 185 Irish, Scottish, Jersey, Guernsey, and foreign vessels, none of which was part of England's merchant shipping. It also does not distinguish between ships in foreign trade, in the collier fleet, or in other activities. Even more important, extending as it does over a period of 22 years, it does not indicate the number of ships lost during any one year, which during James I's reign was probably 10 percent or more (*supra*, p. 327, n. 23). Thus corrected, the list is reduced to 400 or less, a figure so obviously incomplete as to throw no light on the condition of shipping. Similarly, records showing that during the first thirteen years of Charles I's reign an annual average of 26 new ships was built (Oppenheim, *Administration of the Royal Navy*, p. 269) do not prove that England's merchant marine was increasing. It required 6,800 tons of new shipping each year merely to maintain the pre-Armada standard (*supra*, p. 322).
The conclusions of contemporaries vary and cannot all be reconciled with the known facts and with one another. "Experienced merchants" generally agreed that English shipping doubled between 1660 and 1688 (Davenant, *Works*, I, 363; Chalmers, *Estimate*, p. 39). Child stated in 1675 (*New Discourse*, p. 106) that without the Navigation Act "we had not now been owners of one half the shipping or trade . . . that we do at present." A statement made by Petty between 1671 and 1676 (*Economic Writings*, I, 235, 304), that "his Majesties Navy is now triple, or quadruple, to what it was forty years since" throws no light upon our problem. He mentions the navy, but his reference to the Newcastle, Guinea, American, and wine trades suggests that he really has merchant shipping in mind. In any event, he gives us no clue as to how much English tonnage in foreign trade increased before and how much after the laws went into force. Attention has already been called to the obvious overstatement—that shipping had increased tenfold within the preceding thirty years—which the Masters

Yet the fact is not in itself sufficient to demonstrate the efficacy of Parliament's activity; it remains necessary to inquire whether or not the result was due to a natural growth of commerce, regardless of mercantile planning. Statistics of trade, like those for shipping, leave much to be desired on the score of accuracy and completeness. The customs duties do not provide a fixed standard for comparison, since they increased from time to time. Similarly, too great emphasis should not be laid upon the statistics for importations, since the unit valuations were not always the same. Nevertheless, such figures do furnish a rough-and-ready index concerning the state of trade, which shows that trade developed rapidly before 1660, when shipping lagged, and that thereafter the rôles were reversed.[61]

---

of Trinity House made when asking for an appropriation in 1639 (HMC III, 79; *supra*, pp. 325-26). Monson said that English shipping trebled between 1604 and 1635 (*Naval Tracts*, II, 288-92; III, 204-5, 430-33), but Oppenheim, his editor, frequently calls attention to his inaccuracy. His estimate was probably influenced by the increase in the number of vessels of 100 tons or more, which rose from 177 in 1588 to more than 350 in 1629, rather than by the total tonnage (Oppenheim, *Administration of the Royal Navy*, pp. 270-71). In this connection it is important to remember that owing to the great growth in the collier trade and the fisheries before 1660, England's total tonnage would increase much more rapidly than her tonnage in foreign trade, whereas after 1660, if the total tonnage were to double, the tonnage in foreign trade had to treble or quadruple. The uncertainty as to just what tonnage contemporaries were referring to deprives their statements of much of their value for comparative purposes.

Although the statistics given in the text are doubtless erroneous in detail, it is important to note that the most probable errors—the decision not to make an allowance for foreign vessels in the coasting trade in 1582 (*supra*, p. 337, n. 51) or additions for vessels not reported from Wales that year (*supra*, p. 323, n. 6), and the deductions made for the local fisheries in 1702 (*supra*, p. 329, n. 27)—tend to underestimate the tonnage in foreign trade at those dates, thus exaggerating the growth of shipping before 1660 and minimizing its development thereafter.

[61] The figures for English tonnage in foreign trade (as calculated *supra*, p. 339) have been repeated here to facilitate comparisons. It has been impossible to correct or adjust all the figures so as to obtain entire accuracy in the indices of trade, but the effect of errors should be reduced to a minimum because of the opportunity to check one's conclusions with data computed on a different basis. In any event, the figures will have to suffice until someone undertakes to prepare a systematic study of seventeenth-century trade statistics.

The statistics of duties collected upon importations at London given for the reign of Elizabeth are for the last five years (Hall, *Custom-Revenue*, II, 245), and those for James I are an average of the annual receipts for 1605-11, 1613, and 1623 (Friis, *Alderman Cockayne's Project*, p. 213; Misselden, *Circle of Commerce*, pp. 122, 129). Similar figures for the Restoration have been calculated by increasing the receipts for 1649-50 by 40.2 percent, the percentage by which the kingdom's average annual total in 1660-62 exceeded that for 1649-50 (Hall, *op. cit.*, II, 247; CTB II, Shaw's Introduction, p. xvi). The figures for the reign of William III are the average of the receipts of Shaw and Wolstenholme, the collectors of the "Old Subsidy" of customs

RATE OF GROWTH OF SHIPPING AND TRADE

Period	English Tonnage in Foreign Trade Tons	London Customs Inwards £	Kingdom's Customs Receipts £	Value Kingdom's Imports £
Elizabeth	32,892	29,825	99,400	...
James I	29,879	55,750	146,075	2,141,151
Restoration	42,180	257,819	386,088	5,474,773
William III	122,858	564,905	667,122	5,849,150
George III	303,792	...	...	11,406,841

A comparison of commercial conditions before and after the Restoration confirms the view that the development of shipping after the adoption of the Navigation Acts did not merely follow the growth of trade. The Turkey trade, which was only in the formative stage

and poundage (referred to in the accounts after December 25, 1699, as the "growing customs"), on the various commodities imported at London (CTB XI-XVII, Introduction, ccccxlii, cccclvii, ccccx, cccclxx, cccclxxx). The figures here, as elsewhere, however, do not furnish an ideal basis for comparison, because it is necessary sometimes to compare net duties with gross duties. Also the receipts for the last five years of the reign of Elizabeth, for 1613, 1623, and 1649-50, exclude, while those for 1605-11, 1660-62, and 1699-1701 include the wine duties, which amounted to 3.7 percent of the total duties inwards in 1613 and 1622, according to Misselden (*op. cit.*, pp. 122, 129) and 19 percent in 1649-50 (Hall, *op. cit.*, II, 247).

The customs receipts for the entire kingdom were based for Elizabeth's reign on the average of the net receipts paid into the Exchequer, 1594-1603 (Dietz, "Elizabethan Customs," *Eng. Hist. Rev.*, XLV, 56 n.); for the reign of James I on an average of the figures given for 1605, 1611, 1613, and 1622 (Hall, *op. cit.*, II, 246; Misselden, *op. cit.*, pp. 121-22, 127-29); for the Restoration on an average of the gross receipts for 1660-62 (CTB II, Shaw's Introduction, pp. xvi); and for the reign of William III upon an average of the gross receipts from the subsidy of tonnage and poundage for 1699-1701 (CTB XI-XVII, Introduction, ccccxlii-iii, cccclvii-viii, ccccx-xi, cccclxx, cccclxxx). By using only the figures for the subsidy of tonnage and poundage, rather than the total receipts, which included many additional duties, it was possible to keep the figures on a comparable basis with those for 1660-62 (CTB XI-XVII, Introduction, v). No such uniformity can be assured for the earlier figures, but the increase in the valuation in the Book of Rates throughout the years has probably been more than offset by the decrease in the duties charged on exports after the Restoration, by the inclusion in the figures for the earlier years of other impositions than the subsidy of tonnage and poundage, and by the fact that the Elizabethan estimate is for 1594-1603 instead of 1582, especially since Atton and Holland state that an account for thirteen earlier years of Elizabeth's reign gives an average of only about £70,000 (*The King's Customs*, I, 70).

The import valuation given for James I's reign is Misselden's estimate for 1613 (*op. cit.*, p. 122); that for the Restoration has been calculated by adding one-third to the London figures for 1663-69 (BM Add MSS 36785), which was the allowance made by contemporaries (Davenant, *Works*, V, 351-52); and the values for William III and George III have been taken from the Inspector General's Accounts for 1699-

in 1582, and the East India and plantation trades, which did not even exist at that time, had by 1663-69 grown so large that together they furnished 33.5 percent of London's imports, but they did not continue their rapid rise, and by the end of the century comprised only 36.5 percent of the imports for the kingdom as a whole.[62] In the older trades the importation of wines at London probably furnishes as good a guide as any. It shows an increase of 140.7 percent between the last twenty years of Henry VIII's reign and 1663-69, and only 33.5 percent between that time and the end of the century.[63] Some of

1701 and 1773 respectively (Whitworth, *State of Trade*), the three-year average from 1699-1701 being used as more representative of commercial conditions at the end of the century than the war year, 1702. In making the estimate for 1613, Misselden multiplied the customs receipts (which were 5 percent of the value given in the Book of Rates) by 20, and made additions for undervaluation. He declared it to be his aim to ascertain "the value of the Goods as they cost with charges, and not as they are worth to be sold" (*op. cit.*, pp. 120-29). The figures for 1663-69 were based upon the value in England, including freight, customs charges, and merchants' gains (Davenant, *op. cit.*, V, 366-68). The values used by the Inspector General were based upon the current prices abroad (*ibid.*, V, 350). Although the unit values upon which they were based vary slightly, and do not always correspond to the market value, they afford a reasonably stable basis for comparisons after that date (Schumpeter, "English Prices and Public Finance, 1660-1822," *Review of Economic Statistics*, XX, 21, 32; Moreau, *Chronological Records*, pp. 13, 15, 17, 18, 23). It is also reassuring that despite the different bases of calculation, a comparison of the unit values of items constituting about one-half of the total imports in 1663-69 show that the 1663-69 values were only about 5 percent higher than they would have been if calculated upon the values used by the Inspector General at the end of the century, the decrease in the valuation for plantation and East India goods being for the most part offset by the increase in the value of many European goods.

Use has been made of values for imports rather than for exports because the London figures for 1663-69 do not include re-exported goods (Davenant, *op. cit.*, V, 351), thus undervaluing the exports by about one-half, if we can judge by the figures for France in 1685-86 (*British Merchant*, I, 263-77) and by the ratio of exports of English manufactures from London to the total of all exports from England in 1698 (Customs 3/1). For other defects in the export figures, see Davenant, *op. cit.*, V, 443-49; Lipson, *Economic History*, III, 94; *infra*, pp. 422-23.

[62] BM Add MSS 36785; Whitworth, *State of Trade*. The percentage was based upon the three years, 1699-1701.

[63] The annual average of wine imports was 5,769 tons for the last twenty years of Henry VIII's reign (Schanz, *Englische Handelspolitik*, II, 128-29); 13,884 tons for 1663-69 (BM Add MSS 36785); and 18,541 tons for 1701 (Shillington and Chapman, *Commercial Relations of England and Portugal*, pp. 335-36). The last 20 years of Henry VIII's reign are, of course, not ideal for purposes of comparison, but are the latest for which figures have been computed. There are figures showing that importations by aliens were even smaller in 1611 than in Henry VIII's reign (APC [1615-16], pp. 479-81; Schanz, *op. cit.*, II, 128-29), but they throw little light on the problem because English merchants should have been gaining at the expense of foreigners. A better method of estimating conditions at the time of the Armada is to assume that importations increased at a uniform rate. On that basis, it appears that wine imports

the trades, like that with Dunkirk and the export of cloth to the Eastland, probably decreased, but their decline was more than offset by the increase in other trades. The annual value of Eastland imports rose from about £120,000 for the kingdom as a whole in 1613 to £261,218 in 1663-69 for London alone; and imports from the Iberian peninsula to London totaled £580,820 in 1663-69, as compared with £84,000 in 1584 for London, Bristol, and Southampton.[64]

The conclusions which we have reached by studying the ownership statistics can be corroborated by analyzing the record of entries and clearances. Although statistics are lacking for the kingdom as a whole during most of the seventeenth century, those available for London serve as a satisfactory index to general conditions. We have a record of the total English entries at London in 1580-81, and figures for various months in 1596-97, which give us an opportunity to gain some idea of shipping conditions at that time.[65] By adding one-third to the figures obtained by Miller in his study of the London port book for nine months of 1602, we can reconstruct the situation for that year.[66] No figures are available to show conditions in London

---

increased 61.4 percent from 1582 to 1663-69, as contrasted with 33.6 percent thereafter. Since the rate of increase most probably became greater as England gained more wealth from the East India, Levant, and plantation trades, it seems safe to conclude that the wine trade developed at least twice as fast between 1582 and 1663-69 as between 1663-69 and the end of the century.

[64] BM Add MSS 36785; *Acts and Ordinances of the Eastland Company*, pp. li-liii; Shillington and Chapman, *Commercial Relations of England and Portugal*, pp. 147-48; Durham, "Relations of the Crown to Trade under James I," RHS *Trans.*, n.s., XIII, 211 n. See also, *supra*, p. 311.

[65] For 1580-81, see CSPD (1581-90), p. 12. The number of ships entering in Aug., 1596, was 61 (BM Lans. MSS 81, No. 45); from Nov. 1 to 20, there were 98 (*ibid.*, No. 48), or presumably 147 for the month; in May, 70 (*ibid.*, No. 50); in Jan., 1597, 107 (CSPD [1595-97], p. 353); and in June, 1597, 143 (CSPD [1595-97], p. 432), or on a twelve-month basis, 1,267 ships. During the year ending Sept., 1596, 646 foreign ships entered London (BM Lans. MSS 81, No. 81; Oppenheim, *Administration of the Royal Navy*, p. 176). Assuming that conditions were approximately the same throughout the two-year period, there would have been 621 English ships. Recalculating our figures on the basis of the tonnage averages for English and foreign ships, as found by Miller for 1602 ("New Evidence," *Quar. Jour. Econ.*, XLI, 743), the figures would be 46,823 tons for English ships, and 20,930 tons for foreign ships.

[66] Miller, "New Evidence," *Quar. Jour. Econ.*, XLI, 740-60. In raising the money promised for an expedition against the Algerine pirates, the London Trinity House calculated the rates to be charged on the estimate of tonnage entering in 1616 and 1618. If the calculations are reversed, it appears that 44,207 tons entered in 1616, not including ships in the East India trade, and 43,000 tons in 1618, including them (THT [1609-25], ff. 46, 54b). It is not certain whether the reference was to the total entries,

immediately prior to the Act of 1651, but we should be able to calculate them with a fair degree of accuracy from those available for 1663-69. Since the total tonnage entering (both English and foreign) should vary in proportion to the volume of trade as represented by the customs receipts, it is simply a matter of elementary algebra. The only unknown is the entry figure for 1649-50. Thus the formula reads: the customs receipts in 1649-50 are to the customs receipts in 1663-69 as the unknown entry total in 1649-50 is to the known entry total in 1663-69.[67] It is still necessary to differentiate between the English and the foreign tonnage, but the Trinity House recommendations in 1650 indicate rather clearly that one-half of the tonnage entering was foreign.[68] The figures for 1663-69 are usually

both English and foreign, or to the English entries only, but the probabilities are that the tonnage referred to included that of aliens, because the practice appears to have been to allow the companies pledging funds to raise them by assessments upon nonmembers as well (APC [1618-19], pp. 371, 376, 380, 408, 414, 449-50; [1619-21], pp. 70-71). According to Johnsen's tally (*"L'Acte de navigation anglais," Revue d'histoire moderne,* n.s. III, 9) there were 733 London vessels and 102 other English vessels engaged in carrying London's exports in 1640, but he gives no figures for the foreign tonnage.

[67] Atton and Holland declare (*The King's Customs,* I, 113) that the customs rates were practically the same at the Restoration as under the Commonwealth. The figure used as receipts for the Restoration period was based upon the annual average for 1660-62, because after 1662 the customs were farmed at a specific rate, and the returns were affected from 1665 to 1667 by war, plague, and the Great Fire. Customs returns for 1649-50, Hall, *Custom-Revenue,* II, 247; for 1660-62, CTB II, Shaw's Introduction, pp. xvi-xvii. The tonnage figures are given variously, as inward for the kingdom as a whole for 1660 (BM Add MSS 38432, f. 32), outward for the kingdom as a whole for 1663-69 (Chalmers, *Estimate,* table facing p. 37; Cunningham, *English Industry and Commerce,* II, 932; Usher, "Growth of English Shipping," *Quar. Jour. Econ.,* XLII, 467), and outward for London for 1663-69 (Lipson, *Economic History,* III, 139). A comparison with statistics for other dates, however, suggests that the figures are for London only unless shipping conditions in 1663-69 were much worse than contemporary reports or trade conditions warrant our believing. Since the most inclusive figures for 1663 and 1669 were those inward, it seems most likely that the shipping tonnage would have been calculated on the inward entries.

[68] THT (1613-61), pp. 48-49; *supra,* pp. 42-43. The recommendations made no effort to exclude foreigners from the trades to Holland, Scandinavia, and the Baltic, and consequently it seems only reasonable to assume that foreigners already had complete control of such trades. It also appears probable that the foreign tonnage averaged one-fourth of the total in the trades from which the Masters of Trinity House urged that they be excluded, since the proposals were designed to improve the lot of English shipping. If so, all that remains is to estimate the relative importance of the several trades, which has been done by reference to shipping. The relative importance of the several trades has been estimated by reference to the tonnage entering London in 1602 (Miller, "New Evidence," *Quar. Jour. Econ.,* XLI, 752) and that entering the kingdom

cited for the kingdom as a whole, but the probabilities are that they were compiled at the same time as the trade figures, and are for London only.[69] The figures for 1688 arouse suspicion, because they so closely correlate with those for 1663-69. The total tonnage entering is exactly twice that given for the earlier date, and so is that for both English and foreign entries, but it is the best we have and is given for what it may be worth. Thereafter we have available statistics contemporarily compiled at frequent intervals.

When we compare the data, it becomes apparent that the entry figures fluctuated much more wildly than those for the ships owned and employed in foreign trade:[70]

YEAR	ENGLISH		FOREIGN	
	Ships	*Tonnage*	*Ships*	*Tonnage*
1580–81	413	30,881	. . .	. . .
1596–97	621	46,814	646	20,930
1602	276	20,801	676	21,932
1649–50	. . .	50,957	. . .	50,957
1663–69	. . .	95,266	. . .	47,634
1688	. . .	190,533	. . .	95,267
1692–96	417	46,760	578	72,250
1699–1701	1,343	136,750	312	40,530
1702	882	81,945	506	85,575
1719	1,646	187,149	122	11,175
1751	. . .	198,023	. . .	36,346
1758	. . .	125,086	. . .	69,060
1772	. . .	305,481	. . .	76,867
1779	. . .	234,974	. . .	122,064

Obviously other factors than the laws played a part in determining the carriage of commodities. The poor English showing from 1692 to 1696, for example, was directly due to the war-time conditions. England lacked sufficient seamen for both merchant and naval needs, and Parliament at first refused to allow the temporary employment of foreigners. Since the fleet had to be manned, embargoes were

---

in 1718 (CO 390/5, No. 45), the two closest dates for which we have the necessary figures.

[69] *Supra,* n. 67.

[70] Citations for the years 1581-1688, *supra,* pp. 345-47; for 1692-96, CO 388/6, A16; for 1699-1701 and for 1702, Adm. 1/3863, Bundle for 1702; for 1719, CO 390/5, No. 45; for 1751, 1758, 1772, 1779, BM Add MSS 11256.

enforced to keep English merchant shipping in port,[71] and foreign shipping profited. Conditions improved somewhat during the war year, 1702, but for a representative picture of conditions at that period, one should look to the peace-time figures for 1699-1701, or to those for 1719. With the one exception of 1692-96, it is apparent that the English tonnage entering London had increased under the laws and that the rate of increase was much greater after 1651 than before.

The effectiveness of the laws can also be tested by comparing the share of English and foreign shipping at different dates.[72] The method helps to overcome the greatest defect of the chronological surveys we have been considering. In both the ownership and entry calculations, the validity of the conclusion depends largely upon the accuracy of the pivotal figures, and those for both 1651 and 1660 involve the greatest conjectural elements. Moreover, as we have seen, other factors than commercial conditions affect maritime development, and they may have kept the figures for those dates from being representative of the period. By investigating what changes, if any, occurred in the percentages of English and foreign vessels entering England's ports before 1651 and after 1660, we need not rest the validity of our conclusions upon the accuracy of any one set of figures. Although the method presents difficulties of its own, each percentage stands alone, and, by combining the results of a number of samples taken from various ports at different dates, we should minimize the effect of individual mistakes and broaden our basis of judgment.

The London figures indicate that the percentage of English shipping there was markedly higher after the Navigation Acts went into effect. In so far as it is possible to ascertain percentages for London before 1651, the most favorable was that of 1596-97, when the English tonnage entering was 69.1 percent of the total; and the least

[71] PC 2/73, p. 358; CTB X, 358, 387, 429, 831, 834, 1212.

[72] Sheffield (Observations, p. 161) asked if it were necessary to add more to induce Englishmen to support the "inestimable" Navigation Act than to show that, although at the time of establishing the Act the foreign tonnage clearing outward was equal to one-half the English tonnage, it had dropped to considerably less than one-fifth in 1700 and to slightly more than one-nineteenth about 1725. In 1750 it was rather more than a twelfth and in 1774 considerably less.

favorable, that of 1602, when the English tonnage was only 48.7 percent. In 1663 and in 1669, English vessels carried 66.7 percent of the
traffic. Although their share fell to 39.3 percent during the war with
France from 1692 to 1696, it rose again as soon as the temporary
use of foreign seamen was permitted in the merchant service while
Englishmen were being impressed into the navy. It reached a high
of 94.4 percent in 1719, and thereafter did not fall below 64.4 percent,
even in war years.[73]

Figures compiled for representative outports show that the percentage of foreign participation dropped from 30.1 percent before
1651 to 19.1 percent in the sixties and seventies, and to 2.5 percent
in 1718. Foreign ships carrying goods of another country decreased
from 7.1 percent before the laws were enacted to 2.6 percent thereafter.[74]

The improvement in the English ratio tends to confirm the view
that the laws were beneficial, but again we must remember the multiplicity of factors involved, that *post hoc* does not always mean
propter hoc. It can be argued that the difficulties confronting English
shipping before 1651 were only temporary, and would have adjusted
themselves without legislation. When we eliminate the port-book
figures for the years of depression from 1609 to 1621 and from 1648

---

[73] *Supra*, p. 347; 2 & 3 Anne, c. 13, viii. There is no way of determining the
exact ratio of English to foreign vessels in 1609. All indications point to a very low
English percentage. On the other hand, conditions were probably considerably better
from 1631 to 1642 (*supra*, p. 325).

[74] For 1718, CO 390/5, No. 45; for other years, see citations *infra*, pp. 415-16. The conclusions drawn here from an examination of the port books differ radically from those
reached by Professor Johnsen in "L'Acte de navigation anglais" (*Revue d'histoire
moderne*, n.s., III, 5-15). The differing results arise from the difference in the years
examined. As previously explained (*supra*, p. 300, n. 10) Professor Jóhnsen examined the
port books of the thirties and forties, but according to Blok (*History of the Netherlands*, IV, 40-43, 70-71) those were the years when the Dunkirk privateers were harry-
ing the Dutch. From the end of the Twelve Years' Truce until 1645 at least, their
swiftly moving ships "robbed the richly laden merchantmen, plundered and murdered the fishermen on the Scottish coasts, and sailed into the rivers for booty. Their
spoils were ten times as great as those of the Zeelanders and Hollanders. Even war-
ships were captured by them, hundreds of ordinary merchant vessels fell into their
hands, and Enkhuizen lost a hundred fishing boats in one year." Despite efforts at
reform, "Maassluis alone, from 1631 to 1637, mourned the loss of two hundred fishing
vessels, and hundreds of fishermen and sailors met death in the North Sea or languished
in Flemish prisons. Not a village by the sea but had to complain of heavy losses, and
Dunkirk flourished by its millions in spoils." Under such circumstances, it is only
natural that other nations would not be inclined to entrust their goods to the Dutch.

to 1651, the figures for the prosperous thirties and the early forties show that English vessels imported 77.6 percent of England's inward trade, a percentage which compares favorably with that from 1660 to 1680.

Yet it must be recognized that the pre-Restoration years of English maritime prosperity were abnormal rather than typical. England succeeded when fear of capture by the Dunkirkers restricted the activities of the Dutch flyboat. When Dutch competition was unhampered by war, England carried only 35.6 percent of her trade, and 11.6 percent was carried by ships of some country other than that producing the goods. These were the percentages under comparable conditions, when both nations were at peace. Advocates of the laws can contend that such conditions merely foreboded the horrible fate in store for English shipping, unless it had been provided a "fortress of retreat."

Fortunately, in our analysis of the laws' effects, we are not entirely limited to comparing conditions in the poorly documented seventeenth century. We can, at least for the moment, turn from these speculations concerning "what might have been" to a study of what actually happened in the nineteenth century, the century when the laws were repealed.

Except for the changes wrought by the successful revolt of the United States, the Acts continued to govern English commerce during the first quarter of the century. Until 1815, war-time conditions probably did more to control the course of shipping than parliamentary statutes, but after peace was restored, the laws again had an opportunity to make their influence felt. During the long depression after the Napoleonic Wars, English shipping declined less than 12 percent, whereas shipping of other European countries, such as Norway, diminished about 25 percent.[75]

From 1824 to 1850, Huskisson's reciprocity policy dominated English maritime history. A series of treaties with those countries which agreed to reciprocate removed the preferential duties, tolls, and bounties that had discriminated against foreign shipping. Yet it is important to note that the treaties only modified the law, country

[75] Kiaer, "Historical Sketch of the Development of Scandinavian Shipping," *Jour. Pol. Econ.*, I, 340-41; Page, *Commerce and Industry*, II, 155.

by country, thus compartmenting competition.[76] The Acts still stood in the way of any general assault on English ships by their most dangerous competitors.

Post-reciprocity statistics have frequently been misused by opponents of protection. J. L. Ricardo, for example, was guilty of two errors. In speaking of the trades governed by the reciprocity policy as "unprotected," he ignored the fact that the Acts still continued to divide competition. He also used the wrong statistical base in making his comparisons. He compared the increase of English shipping in the fully protected trades with those he described as "unprotected"—and discovered that English shipping in the "protected" trades had increased only 842,827 tons, or 94 percent, between 1824 and 1846, while English shipping in the so-called "unprotected" trades had increased 1,654,586 tons, or 183 percent.[77] He makes much of the larger absolute increase of English shipping between 1820 and 1846 and neglects to point out that relatively the English were losing ground.[78]

In order to determine how successfully English shipping could meet more nearly competitive conditions, we must think in comparative terms, and base our conclusions upon annual averages for the periods compared, rather than upon certain selected years. Proceeding in this fashion, we learn that, although the yearly average of English tonnage entering the United Kingdom during reciprocity increased 76.6 percent, as compared with the average for the eight preceding years, the corresponding increase in foreign entries was 131 percent.[79] Obviously, these figures do not show that reciprocity was a policy upon which England could have relied to attain mari-

[76] For the text of some typical conventions, see Hertslet, *Collection of Treaties*, III, 226-31, 353-55, 433-39. See also *infra*, pp. 396, 408, 413-14.

[77] Ricardo, *Anatomy of the Navigation Laws*, p. 40.

[78] Calculations on the basis of his own figures show an English gain of 157 percent and a foreign gain of 304 percent (*ibid.*, p. 42).

[79] Page, *Commerce and Industry*, II, 162. The following table compiled from the same source illustrates in another way the decline of English shipping as compared with foreign by showing the percentages of English and foreign entries during the two periods.

| | ANNUAL AVERAGE TONNAGE ENTERING | | | PERCENTAGE | |
	All Vessels	*English*	*Foreign*	*English*	*Foreign*
1816-23	2,179,375	1,676,000	503,125	76.9	23.0
1824-49	4,123,307	2,960,384	1,162,846	71.8	28.2

time supremacy or even to retain the position gained under protection.

When we investigate the share that English shipping retained in the trades with different countries, we find that reciprocity did little to disturb the proportions in the trade with France, Holland, and Russia.[80] For one reason or another, these three nations were as handicapped as England. France had to import much of her timber from northern Europe or America.[81] Russia had the supplies with which to build ships, but lacked shipwrights and seamen.[82] Holland never had enjoyed natural advantages, and by this time had lost the financial supremacy and the numerous well-equipped dockyards upon which her earlier success had rested.[83] Since the Navigation Acts still required these countries to carry the enumerated goods in ships owned, built, and manned by nationals, English shipping could continue to hold its own in competition with them.[84]

A very different situation resulted in the trades with the maritime countries of Sweden, Norway, Denmark, and Prussia. Although in each instance the total number of ships in the traffic increased, the

[80] The percentage of trade held by English ships is shown below:

	ENTERING THE UNITED KINGDOM		CLEARING FROM THE UNITED KINGDOM	
	Prereciprocity	Reciprocity	Prereciprocity	Reciprocity
France	53.9	56.4	61.3	59.5
The Netherlands	61.8	61.9	61.3	63.8
Russia	85.2	86.5	83.6	84.1

The periods studied were: for France, 1816-25, 1826-49; for the Netherlands, 1832-37, 1838-49; for Russia, 1835-42, 1843-49. The percentages are based on the annual number of ships, as given in Great Britain, House of Commons, *Sessional Papers,* VIII, App. III, "Report of the Select Committee on British Shipping, 1844"; Great Britain, House of Commons, *Sessional Papers,* "Tables of the Revenue, Population, Commerce, etc. of the United Kingdom and its Dependencies." No effort has been made to analyze the effect of steam navigation upon these trades.

For texts of the three treaties, see Hertslet, *Collection of Treaties,* III, 123-28; V, 338-42; VI, 762-70. The treaty with France was signed Jan. 26, 1826; that with the Netherlands, Oct. 27, 1837; that with Russia, Jan. 11, 1843. The French and the Dutch treaties provided for reciprocity only in the direct trade; the Russian treaty applied only to goods imported directly, but to all goods exported.

[81] See American consular reports, U.S. 34th Cong., 1st sess., *Senate Ex. Doc.* No. 107, IV, 34, 42, 57, 70, 84, 96.

[82] *Ibid.,* 14, 15, 16, 22, 26.

[83] *Ibid.,* 244, 246, 262, 263.

[84] One-quarter of the crew could be of some other country. A special exception was made in the case of the Hanseatic cities of Lübeck, Bremen, and Hamburg. See Hertslet, *Collection of Treaties,* III, 228-29.

English percentage dropped markedly.[85] In the trade with Norway, even the absolute number of English ships decreased from a yearly average of 191 ships before reciprocity to 54 ships thereafter.[86]

The effect of reciprocity upon the American trade is more difficult to analyze. The first reciprocity treaty was made in 1815. Comparison of conditions thereafter with the years immediately preceding shows a drop in the American share of the traffic; but the comparison is misleading, because the long-drawn-out wars in Europe had caused the earlier American percentage to be abnormally high. If we go back to 1787-89, when the English Navigation Acts had had a chance to make their effects felt, we discover that English ships had then controlled about 66 percent of the traffic, as compared with 26 percent from 1821 to 1830.[87]

The matter becomes even more complicated after the second reciprocity agreement of 1830. The earlier arrangement had provided for reciprocity between the two countries in the direct carriage of their own products.[88] Although American shipping flourished, the Americans were dissatisfied, and kept trying to obtain freedom to trade with the English West Indies.[89] They gained their end in 1830,[90] but the victory was costly. The West Indian trade steadily decreased in importance,[91] and the agreement which had opened it

---

[85] See chart, *infra*, p. 356, n. 102.

[86] The average number of English ships clearing decreased from 154 to 50. In the case of Sweden, the average number of English ships entering decreased from 118 to 83, but those clearing rose from 51 to 74 (Great Britain, House of Commons, *Sessional Papers*, VIII, App. III, "Report of the Select Committee on British Shipping, 1844"; Great Britain, House of Commons, *Sessional Papers*, "Tables of the Revenue, Population, Commerce, etc. of the United Kingdom and Its Dependencies").

[87] The percentage for 1787-89 was calculated on entries and clearances in Great Britain (Great Britain, *Report on Trade with the United States*, pp. 14-15). American competition may have still suffered somewhat from the earlier lack of a strong central government, but even from 1789-92 foreign ships (the greater part of which were English) carried more than 40 percent of the United States' commerce (Pitkin, *Statistical View*, pp. 405-7; Seybert, *Statistical Annals*, pp. 318-19). The percentage for 1821-30 is based on an average of the tonnages entering and clearing from the United States for ten years, 1821-30; the entrances were 71.1 percent American and 28.8 percent English, the clearances, 75.5 percent American and 24.5 percent English (based on U. S. *Commerce and Navigation*).

[88] Hertslet, *Collection of Treaties*, II, 386-91.

[89] See Benns, *British West India Carrying Trade, passim*.

[90] Hertslet, *Collection of Treaties*, IV, 514-19.

[91] U. S., 31st Cong., 2d sess., *Senate Ex. Doc.* No. 23, p. 9.

to the Americans contained concessions which detrimentally affected American activity in the trade between the United Kingdom and the United States.[92]

The agreement of 1830 permitted both the Americans and the English to trade between the United States and England's American colonies, but only the English could carry goods between those colonies and the British Isles.[93] English ships could and did utilize the colonies as pivots in a triangular trade from which their American competitors were excluded. Products destined for the English colonies in the West Indies and Guiana provided westward cargoes for a considerable tonnage, which returned to the United Kingdom by way of the United States, loaded with southern cotton. Other English vessels sailed directly to the United States and found their return cargoes of timber and grain in Canada. With the English monopolizing these protected triangular trades, it is easy to understand why their share of the traffic between the United States and the British Isles rose to 42.1 percent of the tonnage entering the United States and to 36.2 percent of that leaving for the British Isles. If we correct the statistics by eliminating the vessels relying upon these protected triangular trades, the English inward percentage declines to 36.7 percent and that outward to 34.3 percent.[94] Then we must remember that there were various other pivots in America and in Europe which

[92] *Ibid.*, pp. 8-9; U. S., *Commerce and Navigation, 1864*, p. 17; Bennis, *British West India Carrying Trade*, pp. 35, 186.

[93] Moreover, American vessels were confined to trade in a limited number of British colonial ports, and the method by which duties were assessed upon goods imported to the British colonies from the United States discriminated against American shipping (U. S., 31st Cong. 2d sess., *Senate Ex. Doc.* No. 23, pp. 7-13; Benns, *British West India Carrying Trade*, pp. 185-86).

[94] The tonnage which relied upon the West India pivot has been assumed to equal the difference between the English tonnage entering the United States from the West Indies and Guiana and that leaving for those regions. Similarly, the tonnage dependent upon the Canadian pivot has been assumed to equal the difference between the English tonnage leaving the United States for the English North American colonies (including Newfoundland) and that entering from them. The basic statistics can be found in U. S., *Commerce and Navigation*. The percentage given in the text is based upon figures for the years 1832-34, 1841-49. The year 1831 was eliminated, to give time for shipping to adjust itself to new conditions; the years 1835-40, because the statistics did not distinguish the nationalities of foreign vessels. If we use the figures for the entire period, 1832-49 (assuming that all foreign vessels in the trades discussed were English), the percentage would have been even less favorable to English shipping.

might have enabled English vessels to obtain an element of protection upon some part of the voyage.[95]

Another difficulty in making comparisons arises from the fact that by 1830 England's colonies in North America were building an increasing number of vessels which were entered as English in the statistics of the Anglo-American trade. Such vessels were built in naturally favored yards, and their inclusion prevents the figures from being a fair measure of the ability of English shipping (as distinguished from colonial) to compete on equal terms with that of the United States.[96] Moreover, improvement in the English position, especially during the latter part of the period, was more apt to result from changed methods of navigation than from England's ability to compete without protection under the conditions which the Navigation Acts were designed to meet.[97]

The effect of repeal upon the state of trade and shipping strengthens the conclusion that English sailing ships had really required protection. The point can best be shown by a comparative study of entry statistics:[98]

[95] A number of English ships entered from or cleared to the Mediterranean and South America. See detailed reports in U. S., *Commerce and Navigation.* England had reciprocity treaties with a number of the South American countries, which were very advantageous, since these countries had few ships and other foreign tonnage could not carry their produce to England.

[96] U. S., 31st Cong., 2d sess., *Senate Ex. Doc.* No. 23, pp. 7-8, 25. On the other hand, Clapham suggests ("The Last Years of the Navigation Acts," *Eng. Hist. Rev.,* XXV, 688) that English ships were handicapped, since goods not the produce of the United Kingdom could not enter the United States in English bottoms, and hence American ships had almost a monopoly of the carriage of reëxports. But the reëxports formed only a small fraction of the Anglo-American trade (*supra,* p. 266, n. 112).

[97] Commissioner of Navigation Chamberlain (citing Fry, *History of North Atlantic Steam Navigation*) states that the change from sail to steam began in 1833, and that from wooden to iron hulls in 1843. He also suggests that a better test of the effect of reciprocity could be found in the ports of the United Kingdom, where American entries and clearances increased from 11 to 13 percent, while those of English vessels declined from 70 to 58 percent (U. S. Merchant Marine Commission, *Report,* III, 1768-69).

[98] The chart is based on statistics in Page, *Commerce and Industry,* II, 162-67. The prereciprocity period taken for Great Britain is 1816-23; it varies for the other countries, beginning in 1816 (except for the Netherlands, which starts with 1834, the first year in which Dutch tonnage is distinguished from Belgian in the statistics), and coming down to the year in which the reciprocity treaty in each case was concluded. There is no prereciprocity period indicated for the United States, because the reciprocity treaty was signed in 1815 and the Napoleonic Wars had caused conditions to be abnormal before then. The percentage for Russia during repeal is based on

RELATIVE PERCENTAGE OF SHIPS ENTERING THE UNITED KINGDOM

Nationality of Ship	Prereciprocity	Reciprocity	Repeal (1850–61)
English	76.9	71.8	59.6
American	...	7.3	11.6
Norwegian	3.8	2.7	5.0
Swedish	0.9	1.2	1.5
Danish	0.6	1.8	2.5
German	4.2	6.0	8.0
Russian	1.3	1.2	2.5
Dutch	1.7	1.6	2.5
French	2.2	3.5	3.9

It is true that, thanks to the world-wide boom in trade, the tonnage of ships owned in the United Kingdom did increase after repeal; but English shipping failed to maintain its relative position, just as it had failed under reciprocity. The total English tonnage owned in 1861 was 52.2 percent greater than it had been in 1849, but the American total had almost doubled.[99] The advance of Norway, England's most dangerous rival in Europe, was just as marked. Her total tonnage jumped from 281,377 tons in 1850 to 558,928 tons in 1860, and by 1870 it had climbed to 1,022,515 tons, only 13,715 of which were steam.[100]

The fact that the yearly average of English tonnage which entered and cleared from the United Kingdom during the first twelve years after repeal increased 102.7 percent, as compared with the corresponding average from 1824 to 1849, means nothing. The foreign gain was 252.9 percent.[101] It was most pronounced in the Scandinavian and Baltic trades.[102] In the American trade, an increase in

figures for 1850-53, because the Crimean War cut off Russian shipping, which did not again reach the level of 1852 until 1864.

[99] The English percentages are based on statistics in U. S. Bureau of Navigation, *Annual Report*, 1901, pp. 480-81; the American percentages are based on U. S., *Merchant Marine Statistics, 1932*, pp. 27-29.

[100] Lindsay, *Merchant Shipping*, IV, 646. For a detailed discussion of Norwegian shipping, see Kiaer, "Historical Sketch of the Development of Scandinavian Shipping" (*Jour. Pol. Econ.*, I, 346-52).

[101] Based on statistics in Page, *Commerce and Industry*, II, 162-67.

[102] The percentage of trade held by English ships is shown below:

TRADING WITH:	ENTERING THE UNITED KINGDOM			CLEARING FROM THE UNITED KINGDOM		
	Prereciprocity (1816–23)	Reciprocity (1824–49)	Repeal (1851–60)	Prereciprocity (1816–23)	Reciprocity (1824–49)	Repeal (1851–60)
Sweden	52.2	24.1	16.2	39.2	27.3	20.0
Norway	27.9	6.9	4.5	28.3	6.2	4.0
Denmark	40.6	9.2	11.9	60.6	22.5	10.7
Prussia	61.7	41.1	31.3	54.4	39.3	32.7

the number of English subsidized steamships bolstered up the English share of the total trade, but only 21.5 percent of the sailing ships entering the United Kingdom from the United States, and 24.7 percent of those leaving for it, were under the English flag.[103]

Even more significant was the increase of third-party carriers. As early as 1853, 443 foreign vessels, of 225,753 tons, entered the United Kingdom from her North American colonies. By 1860, third-party carriers were making large inroads in all trades. In that year, those entering with cargo totaled more than 1,600,000 tons; those clearing, 1,732,000 tons.[104]

English shipping was destined to survive, but its salvation lay in changing conditions. After 1861, it benefited greatly from the merely fortuitous circumstance that a civil war removed its leading rival. By 1865, the United States had sold over 750,000 tons of shipping to her foreign competitors,[105] and American participation in the English carrying trade had decreased 1,328,000 tons.[106] By the time England's European competitors had a chance to substitute for America, the opening of the Suez Canal, the development of trade with India, Australia, and New Zealand, and later that with Africa, offered new opportunities for English shipping. Favorable mail contracts, which acted as a subsidy, also helped; but the most important factor in the revival of English shipping was the change in the

---

The percentages are based on the annual number of ships; they would differ somewhat if calculated on the basis of tonnage figures, notably for Denmark in the repeal period, when the large number of English steamships in that trade, with greater average tonnage than the sailing vessels, gives Britain a much higher percentage of the tonnage than of the ships, but for our purposes the ratio by ships is more significant (Great Britain, House of Commons, *Sessional Papers*, VIII, App. III, "Report of the Select Committee on British Shipping, 1844"; Great Britain, House of Commons, *Sessional Papers*, "Tables of the Revenue, Population, Commerce, etc. of the United Kingdom and Its Dependencies").

[103] These percentages are averages for the years 1851-60, based on the annual tonnage figures for sailing ships given in Great Britain, House of Commons, *Sessional Papers*, "Tables of the Revenue, Population, Commerce, etc. of the United Kingdom and Its Dependencies." Of all tonnage, steam as well as sail, English ships held an average of 27.7 percent of entrances into the United Kingdom from the United States, and 29.2 percent of clearances (or 31.7 percent and 35 percent, respectively, on the basis of United States statistics, 1850-60).

[104] Great Britain, House of Commons, *Sessional Papers*, "Tables of the Revenue, Population, Commerce, etc. of the United Kingdom and Its Dependencies."

[105] Keiler, *American Shipping*, p. 78; U. S., 41st Cong., 2d sess., *House Report*, No. 28, p. ix.

[106] Page, *Commerce and Industry*, II, 166.

methods of ship construction, which enabled English builders to do without protection.[107]

The reason why English shipwrights had needed protection is obvious enough. They could not construct wooden sailing ships as cheaply as their principal competitors. England lacked the abundant supply of raw materials possessed by her Scandinavian, Baltic, and American competitors. When the laws were enacted, she lacked the low interest rate which permitted the Dutch to find compensation for natural disadvantages in adequate reserves and efficient plants.[108]

A positive correlation between the Navigation Acts and the development of English shipbuilding can be clearly established. Patriotic scruples had not been sufficient to restrain Englishmen from using foreign-built ships before 1662.[109] Although figures concerning the build of merchant ships before the Restoration are generally lacking, those available for the period immediately thereafter show how large a proportion had been constructed abroad. An Admiralty register of passes for 1662-68 shows that 35 percent of the vessels under 200 tons, and 50 percent of the larger ships listed, were foreign-built.[110]

[107] On mail subsidies, see Bates, *American Marine*, p. 147; Lindsay, *Merchant Shipping*, IV, 180-85, 261-62, 264-69, 292-302, 320-21, etc.

[108] Barbour, "Dutch and English Merchant Shipping," *Econ. Hist. Rev.*, II, 270-71.

[109] Monson, writing about 1635 (*Naval Tracts*, IV, 181), said that "till of late, which perhaps few will believe, the greatest part of our ships of burthen was either bought or built out of the east country, who likewise enjoyed the greatest trade of our merchants in their own vessels." The mayor of Plymouth stated that most of the fishermen's vessels were Dutch-built (Judah, *North American Fisheries and British Policy*, p. 77), and in 1642 the Dutch Resident at Elsinore, in the Sound, reported that although the English used to come in English-built ships, most were coming in Netherland ships bought at Dunkirk, and that from 80 to 90 such ships had entered the Sound during the spring (Barbour, "Dutch and English Merchant Shipping," *Econ. Hist. Rev.*, II, 288). Even the East India Company had experimented with the use of Dutch-built vessels, but it found that they were not as convenient for its purposes (*Cal. Ct. Min. East India Co.* [1650-54], pp. 66, 140; [1668-70], pp. 83, 89, 110).

[110] Adm. 7/630. Prizes captured during the Anglo-Dutch War, 1652-54 (*supra*, p. 326) may have increased the percentage of Dutch-built vessels somewhat, but the importance of that factor should not be exaggerated. Dutch ships did not have a very good reputation for longevity (Barbour, "Dutch and English Merchant Shipping," *Econ. Hist. Rev.*, II, 274-76), and shipwreck and obsolescence, as well as the numbers captured by the enemy during the war with Spain from 1656 to 1659, should have caused the loss of more than 10 percent a year (*supra*, p. 326). The more important factor in swelling the foreign-built percentage was probably the last-minute rush to acquire foreign-built ships before the Act of Frauds discriminated against them. See

The victory of English shipyards over their foreign competitors was achieved gradually. The fortunes of war gave England many prizes,[111] and for one reason or another Stuart dispensations naturalized more than 790 foreign-built ships.[112] In addition, there were the foreign-built ships which Englishmen had purchased abroad, but which had never been made free as if English-built. At Bristol, 21 percent of the English vessels which entered port in 1671 were foreign-built, and the percentage in the plantation trade was even greater.[113] In 1675, 28 percent of the vessels belonging to Yarmouth, and 5 of the 7 over 200 tons, were foreign-built.[114] A register of Baltic passes for the next year shows that more than 50 percent of the vessels engaged in that trade had not been built in England.[115]

Nevertheless, there are definite evidences of improvement. Less than 10 percent of the ships receiving passes in 1684-88 were foreign-built,[116] as compared with over 40 percent in 1662. Somewhat more than a century later, 96.2 percent of all English ships were English-built, and 3.4 percent were prizes of war.[117] It is also significant to note, in view of the earlier difficulties of English yards when competing in the construction of larger ships, especially for the Baltic trades, that their success no longer varied with the size of the ships, and

---

supra, pp. 327-28. Even after making liberal allowances for such factors, it would seem that at least one-quarter of the English tonnage was probably Dutch-built.

[111] *Supra,* p. 326, gives the estimates of prizes taken during the First Dutch War. More than 522 prizes were taken during the Second Dutch War (BM Egerton MSS 861), the East India prizes being apparently not included in this number. Seven hundred and eight enemy and neutral ships were captured during King William's War, of which 483 vessels were sold (Clark, *The Dutch Alliance,* p. 61).

[112] Barbour, "Dutch and English Merchant Shipping," *Econ. Hist. Rev.,* II, 289.

[113] E 190/1137, Nos. 2-3.

[114] Yarmouth Letter Book (a MS in the London Custom House).

[115] The register of passes for the Baltic Sea, April-Aug. 2, 1676 (SP 29/389, pp. 1-42) gives the following figures:

	Ships	Tons	Average Tonnage
Total	43	8,190	190.5
Foreign-built Made Free	23	5,480	238.2
English-built	20	2,710	135.5

[116] Adm. 7/75, 7/76. The war with Holland from 1672 to 1674 may have swelled the Dutch percentage somewhat, but for the reasons explained (*supra,* p. 327, n. 23), most of the Dutch prizes then acquired had probably been lost before 1684.

[117] In 1792. BM Add MSS 38432, p. 31. See also *infra,* p. 361, nn. 127, 128.

that even in the Baltic the percentage of foreign-built ships was negligible.[118]

Although it had required time for English yards to gain supremacy, the very gradualness of the transition reflects the legislative influence. Parliament had moved slowly in requiring the use of English-built ships. Except for the grant of bounties, such shipping had received few favors before 1660.[119] Even then the Turkey trade was the only one reserved for it.[120] In 1663 the exportation of goods to the colonies was similarly limited, and in 1696, all colonial trade.[121] But until 1786,[122] English-owned ships of foreign build, not made free, could compete on equal terms for the carriage of nearly all the linens, satins, and other manufactures, totaling more than one-half the value of England's imports from Europe.[123] Except in the cases mentioned, Parliament chose to encourage, rather than to command, the use of English-built ships. Until after 1786, English shipbuilders had to be content with the protection afforded by the customs practice of assessing a 5-percent duty on foreign vessels when first purchased,[124] and with various bounties and preferential duties, the most important being those in the Act of 1662, which imposed alien duties upon certain goods imported in English-owned but foreign-built ships not made free, and those in the Act of 1685, which levied a duty of five shillings per ton on similar craft trading coastwise.[125]

[118] *Idem.* Of the English ships entering Memel in 1785 and 1787, about 80 percent were English-built, 4 percent were American-built, 6 percent were prizes, and 10 percent were foreign-built (CO 390/5).

[119] *Supra,* pp. 31-32. A bill, which failed to pass in 1614, proposed to confine all English shipments to English-built vessels (CJ I, 474, HMC IV, App., 119. See also *supra,* pp. 34-35).

[120] 12 Car. II, c. 18, xii. See also *supra,* p. 56, n. 22.

[121] 15 Car. II, c. 7, vi; 7 & 8 Gul. III, c. 22, i.

[122] By 26 Geo. III, c. 60, all English ships had to be English-built.

[123] Customs 3/77; BM Add MSS 36785. See also pp. 388-90.

[124] It was the practice of the Custom House to demand this 5-percent ad valorem duty on all foreign ships, bought abroad or taken as prizes, as is evident from the port-book figures for the year 1662, at Lynn (E 190/436, No. 1). Sir William Jones, in an opinion of 1676, declared the collection of duty on foreign ships bought abroad and brought home, illegal. He also believed that no duties should be collected on ships brought to England and sold there, but since it was the customs practice to collect them, he recommended that the question be brought to trial (BM Add MSS 36109, ff. 37-38).

[125] 14 Car. II, c. 11, v; 1 Jac. II, c. 18, ii. In addition to other preferences (noted *infra,* pp. 408-14), only English-built ships could be used by the Postmaster General in

Shipbuilders in England had to face competition from other centers of construction within the empire, especially during the eighteenth and nineteenth centuries. Building cost less in America, and colonial competition was keen. By 1724 the shipwrights in the Thames complained of it,[126] and by 1775 more than one-third of England's tonnage was supposed to have been American-built. At the same time, the shipyards of northern Britain were outstripping those of the south, the ratio being almost 2 to 1.[127] With the outbreak of the Revolution, the percentage of colonial-built ships fell off markedly. Foreign-built vessels temporarily took their place, but by 1790, at least, English-built ships dominated the scene.[128] In the nineteenth century, the more cheaply built Canadian vessels began to gain, at the expense of the English. By 1847 colonial-built shipping comprised one-sixth of the tonnage owned in the United Kingdom.[129] Despite a system of bounties and preferential tariffs which drew timber and naval stores from America to England, the tonnage constructed in the plantations was considerable, and in 1847 and again in 1849 actually exceeded that produced in the mother country. Mercantilists might have wished that a greater share were built in England, but they could have no serious objection. On whichever side of the Atlantic they had been constructed, the ships had been made by His Majesty's subjects.

carrying mail from England (12 Car. II, c. 35; 9 Anne, c. 11), and certain "ships of force" received rebates in the customs duties (*supra*, pp. 58-59).

[126] Weeden, *Economic and Social History of New England*, II, 573.

[127] Lloyd's *Register*, 1764-66, 1775-76; CJ XLVII, 353-55; Macpherson, *Annals of Commerce*, III, 570; IV, 11; Albion, *Forests and Sea Power*, pp. 115, 246. Champion states that of the 7,694 ships employed in England's commerce at the beginning of the war, 2,419 were built in the northern parts of Britain, 1,311 in the southern, 199 in Ireland, 2,342 in the thirteen colonies, 163 in other colonies, and 1,260 in foreign countries (*Considerations on Great Britain and the United States*, p. 14).

[128] In 1784 2,892 of a total of 7,580 ships were said to have been built in foreign countries, 2,226 in north Britain, 1,088 in south Britain, 144 in Ireland, 104 in her American colonies, and 1,126 in her former American colonies (Champion, *Considerations on Great Britain and the United States*, pp. 14-15). An "Account of the Ships Entered at London, 1786-1800," in the London Custom House, shows that only one-eighth of the English-built ships entering that port had been built in the Thirteen Colonies, and by 1790 there remained in British registry only 424 of the ships which had been built in the Thirteen Colonies, totaling 67,346 tons, as contrasted with 14,204 ships, totaling 1,329,180 tons, which were English-built (CJ XLVII [1792], 354).

[129] U. S., 31st Cong. 2d sess., *Senate Ex. Doc.* No. 23, pp. 23-25; U. S. Bureau of Navigation, *Annual Report*, 1901, p. 471.

English shipbuilding should have suffered severely after the removal of the laws' protection, if our theory is correct that the English were operating under a handicap. But we find no great evidence of suffering after 1850.[130] Consequently, we must either revise our hypothesis, or explain how the English yards managed to survive under fully competitive conditions.

The explanation for the success of the English builder during the years immediately following repeal lies partly in the extraordinary demand for shipping, which exceeded the supply throughout the world and caused prices of vessels to rise so high that the yards of all nations were kept busy. Free trade should be given part of the credit for the expansion of commerce which caused the demand, but only part. After the long depression which followed the Napoleonic Wars, the time was ripe for increased commercial activity. The opening of new gold fields in California and Australia had a worldwide inflationary effect. In England's case, the demand for ships was further increased by the Crimean War, which meant not only that ships were required for military purposes, but that those vessels which normally brought grain supplies from Russia must take the longer voyage to America.[131]

Moreover, the English builder continued to reap the advantages of established position. Well-equipped dry docks (built during protection) helped him to retain much of the repair work. The preference for English oak, which had persisted for generations, and the interlocking interests of builders, owners, and merchants, helped to keep new construction at home. Lloyd's command of insurance rates also served as a form of protection, since Lloyd's system of classifying vessels discriminated, at least for a time, against foreign builders.[132]

Important as these elements were during the period of transition, the permanent solution of the English shipbuilders' problem lay in the changing methods of ship construction. During the era of wood and sail, they had been forced to scour the world for masts and ship

[130] For statistics on shipbuilding, see U. S. Bureau of Navigation, *Annual Report, 1901*, pp. 473-74.
[131] Bates, *American Marine*, p. 133; Keiler, *American Shipping*, pp. 60-61; Lindsay, *Merchant Shipping*, III, 352-55.
[132] Bates, *American Navigation*, pp. 300-12; Keiler, *American Shipping*, p. 61.

timber, and to depend upon foreigners for pitch, tar, hemp, and other naval stores;[133] but, with the advent of steel and steam, they enjoyed a natural advantage for the first time. Thanks to the Industrial Revolution, the English were familiar with the problem of utilizing steam. Moreover, nature had placed abundant supplies of both coal and iron close to the water's edge, as if to reward them for their perseverance in the face of previous difficulties. Foreigners recognized the English advantages; even the Norwegians had steamboats constructed in England; and by 1889 Great Britain was building a total of 182,331 tons of iron or steel merchant vessels for foreign account—but only 2 wooden sailing ships, totaling 167 tons.[134]

The rapidity with which the English changed their methods suggests how unpleasant former conditions must have been.[135] As early as 1865, the United Kingdom had stopped building enough new sailing ships to replace those lost or sold.[136] By 1870 more steamships than sailing vessels were being constructed, and twelve years later the tonnage of steam in the foreign trade exceeded that of sail.[137] Moreover, iron was replacing wood, even in the hulls of sailing ships.[138] By 1890, 95 percent of the tonnage owned in the United Kingdom was of iron or steel, although more than half of the rest of the world's shipping was still of the old type of construction.[139]

In the final analysis, the matter of ship construction resolves itself into a question of comparative advantages. The English could build iron or steel vessels as well as or better than any one else. Foreigners were more efficient in building sailing vessels of wood. But England wanted to build her own ships during the earlier era of construction. She could not afford to rely solely upon the normal

[133] Albion, *Forests and Sea Power, passim.*
[134] Great Britain, Board of Trade, *Navigation and Shipping, 1889,* p. 288.
[135] There might have been agitation for a new navigation act had it not been for the American Civil War and the change to iron and steam (Clapham, "The Last Years of the Navigation Acts," *Eng. Hist. Rev.,* XXV, 705-6).
[136] U. S. Bureau of Navigation, *Annual Report, 1901,* pp. 476-78.
[137] *Ibid.,* pp. 474-82.
[138] In 1874, 65,548 tons of iron sailing ships were launched on the Clyde alone. In 1889, only 9,092 tons of 117,481 tons of new sailing ships were built of wood, and the small size of such craft, which averaged only 47.6 tons, suggests that they were merely yachts or fishing craft (Lindsay, *Merchant Shipping,* IV, 593; Great Britain, Board of Trade, *Navigation and Shipping, 1889,* pp. 286-87).
[139] U. S. Bureau of Navigation, *Annual Report, 1901,* pp. 129-30.

operation of economic forces. The logic of the free traders themselves shows that she would have been disappointed. English capital and enterprise would have turned to other fields, where natural advantages brought greater profits—if Parliament had not intervened by providing protection.

XXIII

WEIGHING THE EVIDENCE

A SURVEY of commercial and maritime conditions, even if anno-
tated with critical comments, does not answer all questions
concerning the success of the Navigation Acts. Differences of opinion
remain which do not concern the facts so much as their significance
and the inferences to be drawn from them. Before concluding, it
will be necessary to review the evidence and weigh it in the light of
the arguments both pro and con.

Our researches do not show that the laws materially affected
England's maritime relations with Asia and Africa, but they do
establish that regulation definitely benefited English shipping in
America. Before the laws went into effect, Dutch vessels were busy
in the colonies. Thereafter their activities materially declined. Fleets
of English ships found employment transporting staple colonial
products, like tobacco and sugar, to England and carrying European
goods from England to America. These changes took place despite
the fact that English vessels cost more to operate and that the natural
route of traffic was not by way of England. Discussions of smuggling
merely raise questions concerning the colonists' mercantile morality.
In the continental colonies, at least, there can be no doubt as to the
fact of the laws' success after the capture of New Netherland, or at
the latest, after the appointment of a corps of enforcement under the
Act of 1673.

The laws left definite traces of their influence on European commerce. English vessels fared worst in trades like those with Denmark
and Norway, in which they received the least actual protection, and
best in trades like those with Russia and the Mediterranean, in which
they received the most. The multiplicity of factors involved in navigation might justify the explanation that such correlations were

accidental, but the frequency of their occurrence suggests a causal relationship rather than mere coincidence.

Some free traders, like Ricardo, contended that the participation of English vessels in the port-to-port trade on the Continent shows that English shipping could hold its own without protection,[1] but the argument is fallacious. Any country with far-flung commercial connections is certain to gain a portion of the port-to-port traffic abroad. In the examples cited by Ricardo, the English shipping which entered Trieste from elsewhere than the United Kingdom came chiefly from South and Central America,[2] and was probably engaged in a triangular trade in which it had protection from England to America and from the Mediterranean to England. In the Russian trade, English shipowners were hard put to find cargoes on the outward voyage, since the balance of trade was very unfavorable to England.[3] They probably figured that low freights were better than none at all, and sought cargoes on the Continent, relying for their profits upon the protected voyage homeward. And even in Russia, where conditions were so favorable to English port-to-port shipping, the record of English activities as third-party carriers was comparatively unimpressive. In 1845 less than 10 percent of the English ships entering St. Petersburg had come from foreign ports,[4] whereas in 1860 some 38 percent of the foreign shipping entering Great Britain came from third-party ports.[5]

In ascertaining the laws' effects upon seamen, the greatest difficulty comes in determining whether their number increased because of the laws, or regardless of their enactment. The free traders contend that the natural preference of English masters for English crews would have sufficed to secure their employment in any case.[6]

[1] Ricardo, *Anatomy of the Navigation Laws*, pp. 207-9.
[2] *Idem.*
[3] *Hansard's Parliamentary Debates*, Third Series, XII, 1306, 1307; Page, *Commerce and Industry*, II, 106-7.
[4] A rough estimate, based upon Ricardo's list of 42 English ships entering St. Petersburg in 1845 (*Anatomy of the Navigation Laws*, pp. 208-9) and American consular reports showing 684 English ships entered at Cronstadt, the port through which St. Petersburg's commerce passed, in 1853 (U. S., 34th Cong., 1st sess., *House Ex. Doc.* No. 47, p. 104).
[5] Great Britain, House of Commons, *Sessional Papers*, "Tables of the Revenue, Population, Commerce, etc., of the United Kingdom and Its Dependencies."
[6] Ricardo, *Anatomy of the Navigation Laws*, pp. 101-5.

The large percentage of English seamen found in the crews of English ships after the laws were repealed[7] seems to lend statistical support to the theory, until we remember that conditions affecting seamen after repeal were not really comparable to those existing when the laws were in force. During the greater part of that time seamen were exposed to the horrors of the press gang. Wars were frequent, and the treatment of seamen aboard His Majesty's fleet was notoriously bad. Seamen complained that the "gentlemen commanders" were more distinguished for corruption and brutality than for tactical skill or personal bravery, and that as the likelihood of harsh treatment increased, the chances of glory and prize money declined.[8] Moreover, the government was far in arrears in paying wages. When it issued a call for seamen in 1692, it did not even pretend to offer prompt payment for services to be rendered. It only promised to make a *partial* payment of wages *already overdue*.[9] The brutalizing impressment system certainly merited attack; yet the responsibility for it did not rest upon the Navigation Acts, but upon the precarious condition of English finances, which for so long stood in the way of the ultimate solution—a professional corps of well-paid seamen.

The change in naval conditions throughout the centuries intensifies the difficulty of determining what might have happened if the laws had not been in force; but in considering what did happen, two points stand out. In the first place, the natural consequence of giving English seamen a monopoly of English shipping was to raise seamen's wages, and so far as we can judge, that was the result.[10]

[7] In 1889, of the total number of seamen employed on sailing and steam merchant vessels, 80 percent were English, 12 percent were foreigners, and 8 percent Lascars (Great Britain, Board of Trade, *Navigation and Shipping, 1889*, p. 264).

[8] Lindsay, *Merchant Shipping*, III, 184 n.; Hutchinson, *The Press-Gang Afloat and Ashore*. For pamphlet and broadside literature, which by vehemence of language illustrates the hardships confronting seamen of the fleet, see Hodges, *Ruin to Ruin after Misery to Misery*, and *Humble Proposals for Relief . . . of Seamen;* Dennis, *An Essay on the Navy, or England's Advantage and Safety;* Slush, *The Navy Royal: Or a Sea Cook Turn'd Projector*. The faults of the system led to its abandonment after the Napoleonic Wars, although continuous service for seamen in the royal navy did not begin until 1853 (Clowes, *Royal Navy*, VI, 207).

[9] T & SP No. 4106.

[10] By the time of the Third Dutch War, seamen were said to receive 40-45s. per month (Barbour, "Dutch and English Merchant Shipping," *Econ. Hist. Rev.*, II, 283), as compared with a maximum of 30s. and a probable average of 20s. in the first half of the century (Oppenheim, *Administration of the Royal Navy*, pp. 225, 232, 314). Petty (*Economic Writings*, I, 259) said that the husbandman earned only 4s. per

Although no one can conclusively determine whether higher wages were required to offset the sailors' fear of impressment, they certainly gave added incentives to landsmen who felt the call of the sea. And in the second place, it is undisputed that, in so far as the Acts led to an increase in the number of English ships, they increased the number of English seamen.

The difficulty is to determine how much English shipping increased and what share of the credit belongs to the Navigation Acts. Comparisons between pre-Cromwellian conditions and those after the Restoration cannot be conclusive, because of insufficient statistical data. Also they permit us to study only the reaction of English shipping to different forms of regulation, and we must wait until after 1850 for statistical evidence concerning its ability to compete without protection.

Nevertheless, the evidence available has a cumulative force. Whether we study the tonnage owned by Englishmen and engaged in foreign trade, the number of English entries at London, the ratio of English participation in entry and clearance figures, or the number of English ships passing the Sound, we reach the same conclusions—that English shipping developed more rapidly under the Navigation Acts than it had before the days of Cromwell, and that the development did not follow, but outstripped, the growth of commerce. After the laws were repealed, we find that English shipping suffered from the lack of protection until a change occurred in the methods of ship construction.

Critics of the laws complain that the percentage of English vessels entering English ports continued to fluctuate after 1660 as it had before, but that fact does not prove that the laws were ineffectual.[11] Before 1660, the English percentage rose when the Dutch were em-

---

week, whereas "the seamen have as good as 12s. in Wages, Victuals (and as it were housing) with other accommodations." Lindsay, however (*Merchant Shipping*, II, 244-45), declares that wages remained high after the repeal of the Acts.

[11] Here as elsewhere in discussing criticism of the laws, the charges will be summarized without citing references for the specific complaints mentioned. For some contemporary criticisms, see Coke, *Discourse of Trade, England's Improvements,* and *How the Navigation of England May Be Encreased, passim; Britannia Languens;* Decker, *Essay on the Causes of the Decline of Foreign Trade,* pp. 53-54; Ricardo, *Anatomy of the Navigation Laws.* For recent criticism, see Lipson, *Economic History,* III, 128-40; Andrews, *The Colonial Period,* IV, 39-49, 131-42.

369 WEIGHING THE EVIDENCE

barrassed by war and fell when they again enjoyed peace. England's success depended upon her rival's handicaps, rather than upon her own strength. After 1660, it was only when England herself was at war that the English percentage dropped materially. Such decline did not show that the laws failed to protect English shipping, but merely that they possessed a flexibility which insured their long-continued success. Military and naval needs made extraordinary demands upon English shipping and seamen, and the neutral vessels which found their way into England's European trades helped to meet the temporary situation.[12]

The times when a declining percentage in entry and clearance figures would have been harmful to English shipping were during the postwar readjustments, but it was at such periods of stress that the laws rendered their greatest service. Wars tended to cause a shipping inflation, and England seldom fought a war in which she did not have more ships after it ended than before it began.[13] Thanks to the laws, these ships did not have to face cutthroat competition from neutral shipping, which had also overexpanded. In the European trades, the scheme of preferential duties, which had been elastic enough to permit the use of neutral vessels during war time, again operated to bring pressure to bear upon merchants to use English vessels. In the transatlantic traffic, the cargoes which had been awaiting carriers proved a godsend to many other shipowners and seamen, however painful the total exclusion of foreigners may have been to the American planters when English vessels were not available during the war. Thus English shipping managed to attain a comparative stability, contrasting markedly with the extremes of prosperity and depression that characterized its history under the

[12] *Supra*, pp. 347-48. Merchants using neutral shipping had to pay alien duties in some cases, but they benefited by minimizing the dangers of capture by the enemy.

[13] The war with Spain was probably the outstanding exception (*supra*, p. 326), but note the number of prizes captured during the Dutch wars (*supra*, p. 359, n. 111) and evidence of increased shipbuilding under Charles I during the strife with Spain and France (Oppenheim, *Administration of the Royal Navy*, p. 269). Also the British possessed 627,616 tons more after the Peace of Amiens than before the French Revolution, an average yearly gain of about 62,000 as compared with a similar average of less than 35,000 tons during the 37 years of peace from 1815 to 1852. The total tonnage of the entire empire was only 2,167,861 in 1803, and that of the United Kingdom alone was 2,478,000 in 1815 (Pitkin, *Statistical View*, App. II, Tables 14, 19; Page, *Commerce and Industry*, II, 155).

early Stuarts, and testifying to the beneficial effects of the laws upon English shipping.[14]

Of all the questions raised by the Navigation Acts, the easiest to answer concerns their effect on English shipbuilding. Conditions in the unprotected periods confirm the testimony of contemporaries that England was handicapped in the matter of ship construction as long as ships were built of wood. The case for the laws need not be overstated. Patriotic pride in local activity and the interrelations between merchants, owners, and builders would have somewhat offset foreign advantages. English-built ships were better adapted for some trades. They may also have lasted longer than vessels built elsewhere, although this is a point which is disputed.[15] Nevertheless, cheaper-built ships obtained the greater bulk of the carriage when the laws permitted them to compete. Without committing oneself to a Gresham's law for shipping, it seems reasonable to conclude that as far as England was concerned, greater costs of construction would have inhibited the development of English shipyards if the laws had not acted as an equalizing influence.

The fact that many dispensations were granted to foreign-built ships during the early years does not prove that the legislation was inoperative. The dispensations are rather a true illustration of the proverbial wisdom that exceptions prove the rule. Neither ships nor yards are built in a day, whatever legislators may decree. If the laws were intended to develop shipbuilding rather than merely to perpetuate existing conditions, dispensations were required for commerce to continue during the period of transition. That period may, as the Commissioners of the Customs claimed, have been unnecessarily extended,[16] but the persistence with which the unprivileged

[14] Following the Napoleonic Wars, Scandinavian and Baltic tonnage declined about one-quarter from 1816 to 1826, while that of Great Britain did not decrease more than one-seventh (Kiaer, "Historical Sketch of the Development of Scandinavian Shipping," *Jour. Pol. Econ.*, I, 341-42). Compare conditions before 1651 (*supra*, pp. 322-26, 349-50).

[15] Concerning the durability of English-built vessels, see Albion, *Forests and Sea Power*, pp. 14, 16, 19-20; Barbour, "Dutch and English Merchant Shipping," *Econ. Hist. Rev.*, II, 269-70, 275-76; Ricardo, *Anatomy of the Navigation Laws*, pp. 167-204. Bates (*American Marine*, pp. 216-18; *American Navigation*, pp. 304, 306), however, denied their superiority to American-built ships.

[16] CTB VIII, 447.

sought to overcome the legal barriers testifies to the protection which was afforded English shipbuilders.

The survival of English shipbuilding after 1850 offers no ground for believing that the English yards of 1651 could have successfully challenged the then supreme Dutch without parliamentary aid. The concerns established during protection naturally continued to operate for a time, but the conditions were scarcely such as to attract new capital, and the rapidity with which English yards turned to new construction after repeal suggests that they had been handicapped when building ships of wood.[17]

The Navigation Acts have been blamed for the high cost of ship construction in England, but they were not responsible. Certainly they cannot be blamed for the limitations of England's supply of oak and her lack of masts, pitch, tar, and hemp. When the Baltic and Scandinavian countries raised the price of their supplies, they relied upon the practical monopoly which had been granted them by nature, rather than on any advantages given them by the English Parliament.[18] The Acts permitted purchases from any country which *produced* the necessary materials. The prohibition in the Act of Frauds of importations from Holland may have prevented English builders from buying in what was then the cheapest market, but the insistence that they develop their own direct connections with the source of supply cut out a middleman's profit. Moreover, the laws, by stimulating construction in England, caused her to keep greater stocks on hand and eventually to enjoy the economies of quantity production which had hitherto been one of Holland's greatest advantages.

The benefits conferred upon shipbuilding more than offset any ill effects from increased freight rates or customs duties. Although the exclusion of Dutch carriers from competition may have enabled the Scandinavians to raise the rates, there were limits to what they could

[17] *Supra*, p. 363.
[18] The figures gathered by Albion (*Forests and Sea Power*, pp. 91-93) show that the most marked rises in the price of oak occurred between the reign of Henry VIII and the Restoration, and that for eighty years thereafter the rise in prices was gradual. It should also be remembered that the Danes began to use their control of the Sound to their own advantage before 1660 (*ibid.*, pp. 164-76; Hill, *The Danish Sound Dues*, especially Chapter V).

charge. If the freight rates rose too high, the English could purchase foreign-built flyboats and take over the carriage themselves. As we have seen, the alien duties assessed on foreign ships or English-owned foreign-built ships were negligible.[19] In fact, all the duties charged were a relatively unimportant addition to shipbuilding costs. One observer calculated that in building a ship of 800 tons, the duties upon the Danzig oak, Norway fir, New England masts and Swedish iron, Russian tar, Italian brimstone, and other imports which went into its construction amounted to only 2.6 percent of the total cost of £11,600.[20] Certainly such an amount was a small premium to pay for protection which enabled the English-built ship to overcome a 30 percent greater operating cost,[21] and the shipping interests recognized the fact by refusing to be swayed from their protectionist position in the decade preceding repeal, when the free traders sought to eliminate all duties on ship materials, as well as to repeal the Navigation Acts.[22]

The theory that the invigorating influence of competition would have stimulated English shipwrights to greater efficiency, if they had not been stupefied by protection, has little to support it. Those who cite the victories of the "Thermopylae" and of the "Sir Lancelot" in the clipper races for the China trade as proof of English ability under the spur of necessity, forget that those victories had more dramatic appeal than economic significance, that both ships were of composite construction with metal frames, masts, and rigging, that wood was used only in the planking, and that even it was Indian

---

[19] *Supra*, pp. 316-17.

[20] An eighteenth-century calculation (BM Add MSS 38387, f. 84). By the nineteenth century, duties added 7 percent to the cost (Lindsay, *Merchant Shipping*, II, 286). Child, however, (*New Discourse*, pp. 111-12) stated in the seventeenth century that the Danes, Swedes, or Easterlings could construct a flyboat of 300 tons for £1,300 or £1,400, which in England would cost £2,200 to £2,400. In 1846 English ships for long voyages cost on an average £17 10s. per ton, while Norway could build ships for £11 10s. a ton, Hamburg for £11, and Finland for £8 10s. a ton (Ricardo, *Anatomy of the Navigation Laws*, pp. 184, 188, 194). See also Lindsay, *op. cit.*, III, 141.

[21] Thirty percent was the minimum difference in costs generally accepted by contemporaries (Broadside [BM 816 m11-108]; BM Lans. MSS 142, ff. 292, 294-96, 302, 306; CSPD [1676-77], p. 130; CSP Foreign [1564-65], p. 529; *The Advocate*, pp. 3-4; "Observations touching Trade," in Raleigh's *Works*, II, 114; Barbour, "Dutch and English Merchant Shipping," *Econ. Hist. Rev.*, II, 282-86).

[22] *Hansard's Parliamentary Debates*, Third Series, LXXXIX, 1031-32; Lindsay, *Merchant Shipping*, III, 141-53.

teak rather than English oak.[23] English shipwrights had had opportunities in the seventeenth century to rise to the occasion, but they failed to do so in the Scandinavian trades, where the laws gave them insufficient protection, and in the Newcastle trade, where before 1685 it gave them none at all.[24] When special types of vessels were required for fishing or for carrying the mails, Dutch vessels had had to be sought.[25] English ingenuity eventually asserted itself in all fields of construction when steam and iron became the order of the day, but it is merely wishful thinking to assume that such or similar developments would have occurred two centuries earlier if English shipwrights had not been protected.

Another criticism was that, except for the laws, the English would have purchased ships abroad and that, by forcing the English to build their own ships, the laws reduced the supply of English oak available for the navy and thus endangered the nation's security. But the charges can all be refuted.

In the first place, the critics assume that England's merchant marine would have been as great if built abroad as it was when built at home, whereas there is much to be said for the theory that a nation's maritime success depends upon possessing its own shipyards.[26] At least in England's case, her shipping fared worst when English owners were free to buy foreign-built ships, and best during the periods when either the Navigation Acts fostered the building of wooden ships or natural advantages enabled England to take the lead in constructing iron vessels.

In the second place, England's forests would probably have been impoverished, even if no merchantmen had ever been built in England. The process had begun before 1660, and the demands of the iron industry for charcoal, the competition of farmers for corn lands, the desire of landowners for profit, and the almost inconceivable

---

[23] Lindsay, *Merchant Shipping*, III, 414-19. *Ibid.*, III, 417, 418 n.; Lubbock, *China Clippers*, pp. 214, 237; Cornewall-Jones, *British Merchant Service*, p. 234; Clark, *Clipper Ship Era*, pp. 322-23.

[24] *Supra*, pp. 59, 316-17, 360.

[25] Fishing, PC 2/70, pp. 116, 241; CTB VII, 1371-72; mails, PC 2/62, pp. 219, 429; CSPD (1671), p. 203.

[26] Bates, *American Marine*, pp. 50-55.

374 WEIGHING THE EVIDENCE

stupidity of naval boards in permitting wastage were potent factors, each in itself sufficient to create a timber shortage.[27]

In the third place, and most important of all, the critics are wrong in believing that the building of merchant ships endangered the national security. They wanted England to build her own men-of-war and not to rely even in part—as Henry VIII had done[28]—upon buying them abroad, but they forgot that flourishing private yards were a means of attaining national self-sufficiency. Mercantile needs could and did lead to the establishment of sources of supply, business connections, and facilities of transportation, which were valuable in meeting naval requirements.[29] Foreign timber and deals were useful as supplements to the preferred English oak; imported masts were a necessity.[30] Moreover, the building of ships demanded an art and experience which could not be obtained the instant that national danger demanded; Shipwright's Hall maintained that it took six or seven years "to breed a shipwright."[31] Even the stubbornness of the English shipwright in adhering to traditional models had its advantages. While Dutch shipwrights concentrated upon cargo capacity and the Americans developed speed of line, the English continued to emphasize strength of hull and defensibility, qualities which tended to reduce the competitive efficiency of the vessels as peace-time

[27] Albion, *Forests and Sea Power*, especially Chapters II and III.

[28] Oppenheim, *Administration of the Royal Navy*, pp. 52, 87.

[29] According to Tench, Elizabeth was forced to buy naval stores from foreigners "at their owne rates . . . they being strangers not regarding the Interest of the Nation, and Her own Subjects, being as then but little Traders" (quoted in *Acts and Ordinances of the Eastland Company*, p. xxxvii). By the Restoration, at least, practically all the timber used by the navy was procured by contract, a system which, had it not been perverted, should have been ideal from the standpoint of the navy. If the navy was to be able to select the best timbers, private yards were needed to use the remainder. Also, experience showed the need for well-organized trade, and when the navy sought to use timber from America, it found that it was to its interest to stimulate lumbering in general there (Albion, *Forests and Sea Power*, pp. 39, 41, 55-56, 152-53, 234, 332).

[30] Albion, *Forests and Sea Power*, pp. 140-41, 152-55, 206.

[31] BM Add MSS 22183, f. 14. Albion states (*Forests and Sea Power*, pp. 88, 90) that the royal dockyards were not equal to the entire task of building and repairing for the navy; that the insistence upon English-built shipping was justified by these reserve yards, with their thousands of trained shipwrights; and that private yards were essential to the navy. "In most of the later wars, many of the capital ships and nearly all of the smaller ones were built by contract, while the fleets which won several of the greatest victories contained a majority of the ships of the line built in the merchant yards."

carriers, but better fitted the shipwrights to build men-of-war and the ships to serve as training grounds for His Majesty's fleet.[32]

The most serious charge against the Acts, however, still remains to be considered. It does not relate to the details of seamen, shipping, or shipbuilding, but concerns the factor upon which they all depend —the volume of trade.

Free traders argue that commerce flourishes best when free, and that by restraining it the Navigation Acts defeated the very ends they were designed to foster. The argument finds statistical support in the marked expansion of European trade which occurred after the laws' repeal. It is also strong from the purely theoretical point of view. Artificial stimulation of activities is always expensive. The laws gave certain advantages to the various groups interested in shipping—shipwrights, seamen, and shipowners—but the benefits derived by each were gained at the expense of the others. Even if they all shifted the burden to the merchant, and he to the consumer, it would eventually be borne by commerce, in so far as increased prices might decrease sales.

The weakness of the free-trade argument, however, is that it merely leads to the conclusion that the total volume of trade decreased, and does not establish that England's commerce suffered as compared with that of her rivals. Advocates of economic plenty would dismiss the distinction as immaterial, but seventeenth-century statesmen were interested in England's power. They believed that it did not depend upon the total volume of commerce so much as upon the percentage which she controlled. They were not merely deluded by mercantile fallacies; their views represented stern reality in an age of international strife.

There are good reasons for believing that the Navigation Acts tended to increase rather than diminish England's share of the world's trade. Although many other factors were involved, the Acts helped her to make the most of her opportunities. With the opening of an era of world trade, England's fine ports enjoyed a central position, but it was an advantage which she shared with her rivals

---

[32] In this connection it is interesting to note that the Dutch admirals protested against the flimsy, lightly manned flyboats, which offered such low freight rates as to discourage the building of more warlike craft (Barbour, "Dutch and English Merchant Shipping," *Econ. Hist. Rev.*, II, 281; see also pp. 264, 280).

in Holland and Germany.[33] The English Navigation Acts did much
to develop England as an entrepôt. If merchants established themselves in Holland or Germany, the Acts forbade them to send any
Asian, African, or American products and many European goods to
England, but if they used England as their base of operations they
could distribute such products in all three countries. Also the Navigation Acts gave the English merchant a monopoly of certain colonial
products. Although England owed her control of these products
primarily to English daring, enterprise, and colonizing ability, it was
the Acts which required the goods to pass through England, and
which helped to maintain the naval strength so essential for the
acquisition and retention of colonies.

There is no way of measuring what the volume of trade might
have been in the absence of legislative restraints, but it is possible
to demonstrate that, relatively speaking, England improved her position. Her foreign trade increased under the laws faster than her
population,[34] and it is obvious that she was gaining in international
competition. In 1651 Holland was the greatest commercial and
maritime power. After two centuries of protection, England had
taken her place.[35] If Ricardo was right when he declared that the

[33] Germany's advantages as an entrepôt are illustrated by the fact that Bremen became
the center for hogshead tobacco when its exportation from America was no longer constrained by the Navigation Acts (Smith, "The World Entrepôt," *Jour. Pol. Econ.*,
XVIII, 709), and Holland's advantages by the hold she retained over the distribution
on the Continent of Asian, African, and American products, even though she had to
acquire them in England (Davenant, *Works*, V, 434-36; *supra*, p. 305).

[34] For statistics of the increase of trade, see *supra*, pp. 342-45. Estimates of population
vary rather radically, but all agree that population failed to keep pace with the
growth of commerce and industry during the century following the Restoration.
According to Chalmers' calculations (*Estimate*, pp. 150, 176), there were 4,688,000
people in 1575, 6,596,075 or 7,123,761 in 1690, and 8,023,729 in 1774. Another tabulation
gives England's population as only 5,512,900 in 1700, 6,523,300 in 1750, and 9,165,900
in 1801 (Fussell, "English Countryside and Population," *Econ. Geog.*, XII, 426). See
also Jones and Judges, "London Population," *Econ. Hist. Rev.*, VI, 45-63; Lipson,
Economic History, III, 165; Usher, "Growth of English Shipping," *Quar. Jour. Econ.*,
XLII, 473-74, and references cited therein.

[35] The decline of Holland and the rise of England as a trading center between 1651
and 1850 is too well known to require documentation. For our purposes, however,
it is interesting to compare estimates of the relative maritime strength of Holland
and England at different periods. Although it is obvious that the estimates were usually
mere guesses, they throw light upon the opinion of contemporaries. The "Observations
Touching Trade and Commerce" (Raleigh, *Works*, II, 123) presented to James I
declared that "the Low Countries have as many Ships and Vessels as eleven Kingdoms
of Christendom have, let England be one." Colbert estimated Europe's merchant

Navigation Acts had deranged half the trade of the world, it would seems that they had deranged it to England's advantage.[36]

It cannot be denied, and nothing that has been said should be construed as denying, that a price had to be paid for England's maritime supremacy. Whether or not we charge the Navigation Acts with responsibility for the American Revolution, the bill of costs was a large one. There was the expense of colonial development already discussed. Account must also be taken of the sacrifice of plenty for power, and of the human suffering which accompanies international rivalry, to say nothing of the bloodshed which so often results.

But for the purposes of this study, we should not attempt to determine whether the benefits derived from the laws were worth the price which was paid. To do so, we should have to consider the fundamental philosophy and value of mercantilism and to solve the question of ultimate happiness. The task we have set for ourselves is a humbler one, to study the laws as an experiment in social engineering. Our interest lies in determining whether a consciously planned policy would produce results.

The Navigation Acts should be judged as we would judge any physical mechanism—with relation to the end it is designed to accomplish. Judged by this standard, the Acts were successful. When entrusted with the task of developing England's maritime power, they were called upon to foster English shipping, to aid in

---

marine as comprising 20,000 ships, of which England possessed 3,000 or 4,000 and Holland 15,000 or 16,000 (Lavisse, *Histoire de France*, VII, 170; Higham, *Leeward Islands*, p. 99). About 1676, Petty believed that England had two-ninths of the world's trade and two-sevenths of its shipping (*Works*, I, 297). An estimate made for 1771 credited England and Holland each with having 30 percent of Europe's shipping (Moreau, *Chronological Records*, p. 22). By 1850, England and the United States each possessed about one-third of the world's total tonnage, whereas Holland's tonnage was less than one-twelfth that of England. By 1870, the United States also had fallen behind and England possessed more than 40 percent of the world's tonnage (U. S. Bureau of Navigation, *Annual Report*, 1901, pp. 125-26, 560-63). In so far as the reports can be credited, they show that England's maritime success owed much to the development of her trade, especially after the Industrial Revolution, but they also show that even then England's position was threatened by the more naturally favored United States until a new era of navigation gave her the advantage. Such evidence is perfectly consistent with the belief that governmental protection helped England's merchant marine to hold its own and even to improve its position, despite the handicaps under which it had previously labored.

[36] Ricardo, *Anatomy of the Navigation Laws*, p. 167.

training English seamen, to develop English shipbuilding, and to preserve English trade. The evidence demonstrates that they benefited England's shipping, seamen, and shipbuilding. Her trade prospered and even gained, in comparison with that of her rivals. Different measures might have proved to be of greater benefit in advancing any one, but the secret of the Navigation Acts' success was the degree to which they protected all the elements of maritime greatness.

CONCLUSION

XXIV

POINTS TO REMEMBER

IF OUR analysis is to help in understanding the process of social engineering, we must restate our conclusions in terms of abstract relationships which may facilitate comparisons with similar investigations. Stripped of the accidental characteristic that our study happened to concern an English attempt to develop shipping, the essential nature of the problem stands out in clearer relief.

It is worth remembering that although the experiment we have studied was made possible because contemporaries generally believed in governmental regulation, their unanimity of opinion did not extend to the particular measures to be adopted. Each group wished to attain the ultimate goal by the path which most favored its particular interests. Yet the fact that the initiative was taken by interested groups did not prevent the measures enacted from serving a great national purpose. More difficulty arose from the popular tendency to assume that everything could be "well fixt by a good law," without inquiring into the means by which the end was to be accomplished.

The legislative history of the laws shows that good intentions are not enough. The first statute did more harm than good, because the legislators failed to anticipate its obvious consequences, and even though centuries of experience improved Parliament's technique, it still had to learn that the logical statement of a good idea does not suffice. Success was attained only when Parliament supplied a network of provisions which, however awkwardly combined from the standpoint of good draftsmanship, had the inestimable advantages of making allowance for the complexities of commerce and of possessing a flexibility which permitted adjustments to changing conditions.

It is also important to note that none of the laws stood alone.

Their success depended upon how much support they received from the mercantile code. Again and again we find officials relying not upon the laws themselves, but upon other measures, passed at other times, for other occasions. Often it was administrative action rather than parliamentary legislation which bent or strengthened the laws as exigency demanded. But it is also significant that administrators modified the law more often when the dispensing power justified their doing so openly, than when they had to accomplish their end by more subtle administrative means.

In enforcing the laws, it did no good to decide how men ought to act; it was necessary to consider how they would act, and to provide ways and means of checking those activities which did not conform to the prescribed pattern. The most useful devices were those which put the burden of obedience upon the individuals being regulated, but regardless of the excellence of administrative machinery, there was no substitute for capable and honest officials. Little was accomplished when the government tried to rely upon the informer system. Most was achieved after the creation of an administrative staff, especially if it fitted into the existing cordon of officials. Efficiency suffered whenever anything barred the free flow of authority, whether it was the interference of charter grants or merely the vested interests of officeholders. Achievement was delayed by the interjection of extraneous elements, such as financial exigencies, political upheavals, and international strife. Yet it is important to remember that eventually an administrative machine was evolved by making a few additions here and a few subtractions there, the additions being much more easily made than the subtractions.

Success depended upon finding the proper answer to the conundrums of social mechanics. How rapidly could changes be made without inviting disaster? What short cuts were feasible in determining individual cases, without conflicting with previous decisions? When did routine cease being beneficial and become red tape? Was it possible to adapt existing local machinery to imperial concerns? To what extent should authority be centralized and how far could the discretion of subordinates be trusted? Could balanced judgments be formed so as to protect the interests of those who resided at a distance, or were those near the center of authority destined to receive an advantage?

The variety of factors involved in social engineering requires that before passing judgment on an experiment, one look at the process as a whole and not merely some of its phases. It is no easy task to change commercial habits, and those who think only of the initial energy required to overcome inertia are apt to question the value of the effort. Yet once commerce is started running in the desired direction, it may flow so smoothly that those who note the development are inclined to believe that it would have occurred without legislation. Moreover, achievement often depends upon circumstances, and even a sound scheme may fail through no defect of its own, just as a well-built dam will prove useless if an unprecedented drought should deplete the water supply it was intended to conserve.

Let no one complain that the points emphasized are obvious. They are—when attention is called to them. Yet hardly a day passes when we do not show our need for the reminder. We know that it takes time for worth-while projects to become effective, but critics continue to demand immediate results. Despite the dangers of short-time views, both proponents and opponents of the government pass confident judgments, and both select bits of evidence which suit their purpose, without worrying about the completeness of their analysis. There are many who complain that proposed reforms work in different directions, forgetting that any nation has many groups to consider and that its duty does not consist in furthering the desires of any one as fully as might be possible, but in advancing the interests of all together. Our experts have increased their technical knowledge, especially in the field of administration, but we still have much to learn about the process as a whole, and we yet have to formulate adequate standards of judgment and to procure their acceptance by the public.

If historical studies of social engineering do nothing else, they can at least remind us of what we should already know. Despite man's vaunted intelligence, he usually proceeds by the method of trial and error, of blundering and correcting the blunder. The advances of society are at times painfully slow and its mistakes often foolish, but even so England's experiment holds forth hope that, by repeated efforts and sheer persistence, we can help to regulate our own destinies. And it suggests that we shall succeed more rapidly if we remember that it is not sufficient to determine what we want to do, that we must also consider how we are to accomplish it.

APPENDICES

I

BRIEF SUMMARY OF THE LAWS OF TRADE AND NAVIGATION

A COMPLETE statement of the law of navigation throughout its history would require a book many times the size of this. The summary here is necessarily much abridged, and the reader should remember that there are many things which it does not attempt to do. It makes no pretence to survey all the law which governed trade and commerce. The various foreign countries had restrictions of their own applying in both the Old and the New Worlds. England herself had many other regulations immediately relevant to maritime prosperity, such as those relating to the encouragement of seamen by apprentice laws and the monopolies granted the chartered companies, discussion of which has to be omitted for lack of space.

Even with respect to the measures usually referred to as Navigation Acts much has been omitted. No mention has been made of various penalties for violation of the Acts or for failure to enforce them; regulations pertaining to fisheries have been expressly omitted; regulations governing the crew of an English vessel have not been given in detail; nor have the temporary but sometimes extensive variations for war time and emergencies been described, nor all the continuing statutes which made no significant changes. It should also be remembered that the substantive provisions recited in the statutes might have little practical effect if the administrative regulations under which they could be exercised were too burdensome, as in the case of the privilege granted His Majesty's West Indies to export sugar direct to Europe.

No attempt has been made to untangle the confusion which surrounded the status of England's European possessions. Suffice it to say that the following discussion refers to England, Wales, and Berwick, and to Scotland after 1707, with occasional notes concerning other areas. One interested in the status of Ireland, the Channel Isles, or the Isle of Man should carefully study the relevant laws cited.[1]

---

[1] As far as the basic laws were concerned, Scotland was a foreign country until the Act of Union in 1707 (6 Anne, c. 11). Thereafter, both the privileges and the restrictions were extended to all Great Britain, and for purposes of this summary, references to "England" or "English" after that date should be read as if "Britain" or "British" (see *supra*, p. xi). Except for being required to obtain its East India

Considerable effort, however, has been taken to make the summary as accurate as possible. Although originally compiled from the statutes themselves, it has been compared with various contemporary handbooks, such as Abbott, *Treatise of Law Relative to Merchant Ships* (1850); *Abstract of the New Navigation Act* (1822); Baldwin, *A Survey of the British Customs* (1770); Boyd, *British Tariff* (1822); Carkesse, *The Act of Tonnage and Poundage* (1726); Clements, *Customs Guide* (1844); Crouch, *Complete View of the British Customs* (1730); Earnshaw, *Digest of the Laws* (1818); Ellis, *The British Tariff* (1829) and *The Laws Connected with Commerce* (1844); *Index Vectigalium* (1670); Reeves, *History of the Law of Shipping and Navigation* (1792); Ricardo, *Anatomy of the Navigation Laws* (1847); Saxby, *The British Customs* (1757); Score, *A Guide to the Customers* (1699); Sims and Frewin, *Rates of Merchandise* (1782); Walford, *Laws of the Customs* (1846); and also with more recent analyses in Clapham, "The Last Years of the Navigation Acts," *English Historical Review*, XXV, 480-501, 687-707; and McGovney, "The Navigation Act as Applied to European Trade," *American Historical Review*, IX, 725-34.

The reader should not attempt to rely solely upon this summary as a statement of every detail. The laws are tricky and have caused so many to misinterpret them, at least in part, that the present writer does not hope to be an exception. Moreover, the necessities of condensation may cause distortion of details which will be misleading unless one checks by reference to the statutes cited. But with these reservations, the work should present an adequate general picture, and serve as a point of departure for more extended investigations by those interested.

ENGLISH SHIPS

The chief classifications of shipping under the navigation laws were ships English-built and English-owned, ships foreign-built and English-owned, and foreign-owned ships of either foreign or English build; but there were numerous other types recognized by the laws.[2] The qualifications to which

---

goods from England (7 Geo. I, c. 21, ix), the Isle of Man was not governed by the laws until 1765, and even thereafter was not treated like England for all purposes (7 Geo. III, c. 45; see also 12 Geo. I, c. 28). The Channel Islands were specifically included in the regulations concerning the coast trade, and importations from foreign Asia, Africa, and America. They were not granted the privileges of the plantation trade nor the right to receive goods direct from East India, but they were not restricted by the clauses governing the European trade and imposing a duty of five shillings per ton upon French vessels. Until Jan. 1, 1801, when the Act of Union (40 Geo. III, c. 67) placed Ireland upon the same footing as England with respect to navigation and trade, Ireland was treated like England with respect to her ships, seamen, the coasting trade, and importations from foreign Asia, Africa, America, and Europe (except for goods coming from Holland and Germany), but her status with respect to the plantations varied (see *infra*, n. 35).

[2] *Supra*, pp. 64-65. Prizes legally condemned were recognized by law as entitled to privileges of English-built ships. Some ships were made free by letters patent before

a ship had to conform in order to enjoy the privileges of an English ship varied at different periods and in different trades.

The term "English shipping" should always be read as including ships owned by the people of England, Ireland, Wales or Berwick.[3] After the Act of Union in 1707, ships owned by Scottish subjects were also deemed English. Colonial-owned ships were specifically authorized by the Act of 1660 to engage in the Asia-Africa-America trade, and colonial-owned, colonial-built ships in the plantation trade. No mention was made of colonial ships with respect to the carriage of enumerated European commodities, but in practice they seem to have enjoyed this and other privileges on the assumption that in nearly every instance when it referred to "English shipping" Parliament intended to include colonial vessels. In order to qualify as an English ship, the master and three-fourths of the crew had to be Englishmen.[4]

An English-built ship was defined by the Act of 1660 as a ship built in England, Ireland, Wales, Guernsey, Jersey, Berwick, or English possessions in Asia, Africa or America. English build was required only for the Turkey and currant trades, for exceptional privileges in the Levant and East India trade, and for certain preferential duties.[5] The Act of Frauds, 1662, provided that only ships built in His Majesty's dominions, except ships bought before October, 1662, or ships condemned as lawful prizes, should enjoy the privileges of ships belonging to England or Ireland; all other ships were deemed alien ships. Under this law it was held that for-

---

1688 and by private acts of Parliament thereafter. Foreign ships which had undergone extensive repairs in England were considered English-built by customhouse practice (Reeves, *Law of Shipping and Navigation*, pp. 259-67). For some of the more important later statutes dealing with the status of ships, see 15 Geo. II, c. 31; 13 Geo. III, c. 26; 26 Geo. III, c. 60; 27 Geo. III, c. 19; 42 Geo. III, c. 61, xvi-xxiv; 48 Geo. III, c. 70; 49 Geo. III, c. 41; 54 Geo. III, c. 59; 6 Geo. IV, c. 110; 3 & 4 Gul. IV, c. 54 and 55; 8 & 9 Vict., c. 89.

[3] The status of ships owned in the Channel Islands is not defined, but the omission was probably an oversight, because ships built there were declared to be English-built.

[4] This requirement as to manning was not removed until 1853 (16 & 17 Vict., c. 131, xxxi). The modifications other than those in war time (*infra*, n. 6) were minor, such as permitting the use of Negroes in America, Lascars and other natives east of the Cape of Good Hope, classing as English, foreigners who had served aboard English vessels in war time, and deeming vessels to be properly navigated if navigated by one English seaman for every twenty tons. For other regulations concerning crews, see Reeves, *Law of Shipping and Navigation*, pp. 257, 267-70; 14 Car. II, c. 11, v; 6 Anne, c. 64; 13 Geo. II, c. 3; 28 Geo. II, c. 16; 19 Geo. III, c. 11, c. 14; 33 Geo. III, c. 26; 34 Geo. III, c. 68; 42 Geo. III, c. 61; 43 Geo. III, c. 64; 4 Geo. IV, c. 80, xx-xxviii; 6 Geo. IV, c. 109; 7 Geo. IV, c. 48; 7 & 8 Geo. IV, c. 56; 3 & 4 Gul. IV, c. 54, xvi; 8 & 9 Vict., c. 88, xviii.

[5] *Infra*, pp. 409-10.

eign-built ships were not excluded from trades where they were hitherto legally employed, but merely were subject to all duties to which alien ships were liable.

The Staple Act of 1663 provided that European goods destined for the colonies must be laden in English-built shipping; and 7 & 8 Gul. III, c. 22, in 1696, confined all the colonial trade to English-built ships.

Foreign-built ships were further restricted by 26 Geo. III, c. 60, which provided that after August 1, 1786, "no ship or vessel foreign-built . . . shall be any longer entitled to any of the privileges or advantages of a British-built ship or of a ship owned by British Subjects," except that foreign-built ships already owned by Englishmen could continue to enjoy privileges hitherto enjoyed.

During war time the regulations governing English ships were frequently relaxed. A larger percentage of foreign seamen, up to three-fourths of the crew, was permitted; and licenses were granted to purchase foreign ships for privateering, these afterward to have the privileges of English-built ships. Trades ordinarily restricted to English ships were opened to foreign carriage, and discriminatory duties usually imposed on alien or English foreign-built ships were sometimes removed.[6]

COASTING TRADE

The trade between England, Ireland, Wales, Guernsey, Jersey or Berwick, and along the coasts of those areas, was limited by the Act of 1660 to English-owned ships with master and three-fourths of the mariners Englishmen. Foreign-built ships were in effect excluded from the port-to-port trade of England, Wales and Berwick by 1 Jac. II, c. 18, which subjected them to an additional duty of five shillings per ton for every voyage. This statute also placed a duty of twelve-pence per ton on those foreign-built ships already employed in the trade. After 1794 coastwise crews had to be wholly English (34 Geo. III, c. 68, iv; 42 Geo. III, c. 61, iv). The coastwise trade was not opened to foreigners until 1854 (17 & 18 Vict., c. 5), although in 1849 the remainder of the laws had been repealed, except in so far as foreign discrimination might require retaliatory measures (12 & 13 Vict., c. 29, x-xii).

[6] For example, see Reeves, *Law of Shipping and Navigation*, pp. 214-15, 257-58, for Orders in Council during war with Holland in the reign of Charles II; 6 Anne, c. 64, during the War of the Spanish Succession; 13 Geo. II, c. 3 and 17 Geo. II, c. 36, during the War of the Austrian Succession; 29 Geo. II, c. 34, xix, during the Seven Years' War; 19 Geo. III, c. 28; 20 Geo. III, c. 45; 21 Geo. III, c. 27; 22 Geo. III, c. 38; and 23 Geo. III, c. 1, during the War of American Independence; 35 Geo. III, c. 15, c. 80, and c. 115; 36 Geo. III, c. 76; 39 Geo. III, c. 95, c. 98, c. 111, and c. 112; 42 Geo. III, c. 80; 43 Geo. III, c. 153; 46 Geo. III, c. 111; 49 Geo. III, c. 60, and continuing acts during the subsequent wars with France.

IMPORTATIONS FROM ASIA, AFRICA AND AMERICA

Goods of Asia, Africa and America had to be imported in English shipping directly from the country of growth or port of usual first shipment. At first, products might be brought from Europe after manufacture there; but beginning June 24, 1779, the importation of any articles manufactured from goods of Asia, Africa or America in any foreign country other than that of their growth or first shipment was prohibited (19 Geo. III, c. 48).

A few exceptions to the principle of direct shipment were made by the Act of 1660, and a considerable number of a permanent or continuous nature were later added. Temporary exceptions were frequently made during periods of emergency or warfare. Similarly, the English shipping monopoly was relaxed in opening the trade to foreign ships in the case of certain specified articles and for limited periods during emergencies or war time.[7] The following table indicates the goods affected by exceptions of a permanent nature, the ports other than those of origin from which they might be sent, the type of ship permitted to carry them, and the date on which the exception became effective.[8]

Exceptions to Rule Requiring Direct Shipment

Commodity	Ship	Date	Statute
Goods from within the Straits laden at usual ports[9]	English-built	Dec. 1, 1660	12 Car. II, c. 18, xii
East India goods laden at usual ports south and east of Cape of Good Hope	English-built	Dec. 1, 1660	12 Car. II, c. 18, xiii
Spanish or Portuguese colonial goods from mother country (including Azores, Madeira and Canaries)	English	Dec. 1, 1660	12 Car. II, c. 18, xiv
Prize goods	English	Dec. 1, 1660	12 Car. II, c. 18, xv

[7] See *supra*, n. 6. On the other hand, importations were also often regulated by the charters of the great trading companies such as the East India, the Royal African, and the Hudson's Bay companies.

[8] For the repeal of many of these exceptions in 1822, see 3 Geo. IV, c. 41, 42, 43; for further repeals in 1825, see 6 Geo. IV, c. 105.

[9] Trieste, Venice, Genoa, and Leghorn "are now considered as ports which, by usage, are entitled to this privilege for the export of Asiatic goods from the Levant" (Reeves, *Law of Shipping and Navigation*, p. 113). After Sept. 29, 1720, Asiatic raw silk and mohair yarn coming from within the Straits could be imported only from Turkish ports (6 Geo. I, c. 14).

EXCEPTIONS TO RULE REQUIRING DIRECT SHIPMENT (*Continued*)

Commodity	Ship	Date	Statute
Bullion	English and foreign[10]	Dec. 1, 1660	12 Car. II, c. 18, xv
Certain spices[11]	English-built	May 1, 1695	6 & 7 Gul. & Mar., c. 7, ii
American drugs from English colonies in America	English	June 24, 1709	7 Anne, c. 31, xii
Cochineal[12]	English and foreign[10]	May 20, 1727	13 Geo. I, c. 25
Precious stones	English and foreign[10]	April 10, 1733	6 Geo. II, c. 7
Indigo[12]	English and foreign[10]	June 24, 1734	7 Geo. II, c. 18
Persian goods brought from Russia by Russian Company	English-built	June 24, 1741	14 Geo. II, c. 36
Tea from Europe[13]	English	June 24, 1745	18 Geo. II, c. 26, x, xi
Gum senegal from Europe	English-built	April 10, 1752	25 Geo. II, c. 32
Calicoes and certain other East India goods[14]	English	June 1, 1765	5 Geo. III, c. 30
Cotton wool	English-built	July 1, 1766	6 Geo. III, c. 52, xx
Goatskins[15]	English-built	June 20, 1775	15 Geo. III, c. 35
Morocco goods from Gibraltar	English-built[16]	July 1, 1787	27 Geo. III, c. 19, xi
Black-oak bark, if not from Europe	English-built	July 5, 1792	32 Geo. III, c. 49
Any goods from Ireland	English-built	June 17, 1793	33 Geo. III, c. 63
Tobacco[17]	English and foreign	March 30, 1809	49 Geo. III, c. 25
Ivory from Portuguese dominions	English-built and Portuguese	May 31, 1811	51 Geo. III, c. 47, iv

[10] The exceptions for cochineal and indigo referred to English ships or ships of a friendly foreign country. In the case of precious stones the statute read "any ship whatsoever," and the all-inclusive exception in favor of bullion was so worded as to avoid the necessity of specifying the vessels which should carry it.

[11] Nutmeg, cinnamon, cloves, and mace, but license had to be obtained. The permission was continued and further regulated by 3 & 4 Anne, c. 18, vii; 8 Anne, c. 12, xiii (made perpetual by 6 Geo. I, c. 4); and 6 Geo. I, c. 21, xiv. See also p. 240.

[12] For a limited time, but renewed by the act of 7 Geo. II, c. 18, when indigo was added, and extended by continuing acts. Earlier relaxations had allowed cochineal to be brought from Spain (6 Anne, c. 60, made perpetual by 12 Anne, c. 18).

[13] License was required; for similar permission between 1695 and 1721, see 6 & 7 Gul. & Mar., c. 7, ii; 3 & 4 Anne, c. 18, ii; and 7 Geo. I, c. 21, xii.

[14] Principally coarse printed calicoes and other goods prohibited for use in England. They had to be imported by the East India Company from Europe for the African trade.

[15] For a limited time, but made perpetual by 31 Geo. III, c. 43.

[16] Or ships owned by English subjects before May 1, 1786.

[17] From any port in a foreign state or from Malta and Gibraltar, by an English ship or a ship of a country in amity. The act was continued until 59 Geo. III, c. 74 (1819), which required that tobacco come from the place of origin, but permitted it to be carried in ships of that place.

EXCEPTIONS TO RULE REQUIRING DIRECT SHIPMENT (*Continued*)

Commodity	Ship	Date	Statute
Goods of the Straits from Malta[18]	English-built	March 23, 1815	55 Geo. III, c. 29, x
Raw silk or mohair yarn brought by Turkey Company from Malta[18]	English-built	March 23, 1815	55 Geo. III, c. 29, xi
Italian thrown silk from Malta[18]	English-built	March 23, 1815	55 Geo. III, c. 29, xii
East India goods from Malta and Gibraltar[19]	English-built[20]	June 20, 1817	57 Geo. III, c. 36

The exceptions which permitted goods of foreign territories in America to be shipped from His Majesty's American colonies constituted a special group of relaxations in keeping with the tendency to interpret broadly the "country of growth or port of usual first shipment," and also with the inclination of the English government to encourage the trade between Spanish America and the English colonies. These exceptions were largely made by customhouse practice,[21] but they were embodied in statute by the free-port acts, beginning with 6 Geo. III, c. 49 (1765).[22]

After the American Revolution special concessions were made to the ships of the United States so that they might bring goods of their country to the United Kingdom. At first this trade was regulated by Orders in Council under the authorization of 23 Geo. III, c. 39 and continuing acts. The orders varied as to the rates of duty to be charged but in general permitted the direct importation, in English or American vessels, of goods grown or produced in the United States. By the treaty of 1794 it was definitely established that ships of the United States might import produce of their own land, although subject to a discriminating duty until the reciprocity treaty of 1815.[23] A similar exception was granted to Portuguese

[18] And from Gibraltar after March 4, 1817 (57 Geo. III, c. 4).

[19] All goods from territory within the limits of the East India Company charter, including the Cape of Good Hope but excluding China. The statute, however, limited the importation of tea to the East India Company or its licensees.

[20] Not specified in the Act; but the trade was with an English possession.

[21] Reeves, *Law of Shipping and Navigation*, pp. 145-47, 189.

[22] See *infra*, n. 30; and also 29 Geo. III, c. 68, xv, permitting United States tobacco to be brought from the English West Indies; and 30 Geo. III, c. 29, permitting United States goods to be imported from Quebec.

[23] Reeves, *Law of Shipping and Navigation*, pp. 285-96, 417, Appendix, No. I. In 1792 all goods grown or produced in the United States could be imported at the lowest rate imposed upon goods coming from countries not under England's dominion, except snuff, which paid the same duties as if it were manufactured in Europe, and except tobacco, pig iron, bar iron, pitch, tar, turpentine, rosin, potash, pearlash, indigo, masts, yards, bowsprits, and all unmanufactured goods (except fish oil, blubber, whale fins, and spermaceti) which paid the same duties as if they had come from the English

possessions in South America by 48 Geo. III, c. 11 (March 11, 1808),[24] and to Spanish colonies or former colonies in America by 3 Geo. IV, c. 43 (June 24, 1822).

In the legislation of 1822 (3 Geo. IV, c. 43) and 1825 (6 Geo. IV, c. 109), the rules governing the trade with Asia, Africa, and America were considerably revised. By the Act of 1825 goods of the three continents might be imported in English-built ships from any place other than Europe, and from Europe in the case of Moroccan goods; goods of Asia or Africa from within the Straits;[25] goods from the East India Company's territory, brought to Gibraltar or Malta in English ships; prize goods, bullion or precious stones; and all goods brought for reëxport.[26] All manufactured goods were deemed the produce of the country of manufacture. Ships of the country of which the goods were the produce and from which they were imported were permitted to carry goods from Asia, Africa or America into the United Kingdom.[27] At the time of repeal the carriage of these goods, except for reëxport, was still closed to third-party carriers.

TRADE OF THE COLONIES

The laws regulating the trade of the colonies in Asia, Africa, and America[28] dealt chiefly with (1) the ships carrying the goods, (2) the

---

colonies in America. See also 37 Geo. III, c. 97; 41 Geo. III, c. 95; 48 Geo. III, c. 6 and c. 85; 49 Geo. III, c. 59; 56 Geo. III, c. 15; 57 Geo. III, c. 58; 59 Geo. III, c. 54; Hertslet, *Commercial Treaties*, II, 386-91.

[24] With equal duties in Portuguese ships by 51 Geo. III, c. 47.

[25] Amended by 7 Geo. IV, c. 48, xxi (1826), to require that such goods should not have been brought within the Straits via the Atlantic Ocean.

[26] The legislation of 1822 varied slightly (3 Geo. IV, c. 43). For acts repealed at that time, see 3 Geo. IV, c. 41, 42; for those repealed in 1825, see 6 Geo. IV, c. 105.

[27] Special permission was given to Turkey ships to carry Asiatic raw silk and mohair yarn from Turkish ports and to carry goods of the Grand Seignior's territory in Asia from Turkish European ports. 1 & 2 Vict., c. 113, xxx authorized treaties permitting goods from within the Straits to come in foreign ships of the country from whose port the goods were shipped.

The revisions of 1833 and of 1845 continued the regulations of 1825 (3 & 4 Gul. IV, c. 54 and 8 & 9 Vict., c. 88).

[28] There was considerable doubt about the status of Newfoundland for many years, but by 1764, at least, it was determined to be a colony (Lounsbury, *British Fishery at Newfoundland*, pp. 199, 202, 257, 275; Reeves, *Law of Shipping and Navigation*, pp. 98-100). Despite the presence of English logwood cutters, Honduras was considered not to be a colony (Reeves, *op. cit.*, pp. 100-1). Beginning in 1816, Demerara, Berbice, and Essequibo were (with minor exceptions) subjected to the same regulations and given the same privileges as His Majesty's West Indies (56 Geo. III, c. 91). None of the territory within the limits of the charter of the East India Company was considered to be restricted by the Acts, although the exemption was a matter of practice rather than of statute until 57 Geo. III, c. 95 (July 10, 1817). In this connection, see also 37 Geo. III, c. 117; 56 Geo. III, c. 51; 59 Geo. III, c. 54, vi, and note the discretionary power left to the king in Council for regulating the Cape of Good

places to which colonial goods might be exported, and (3) the places from which goods might be imported.

(1) English shipping alone was permitted to trade with the colonies by the Act of 1660, and only a few relaxations of this rule were subsequently permitted. Chief among these were the privileges allowed foreign ships in the trade, particularly in Negroes, between His Majesty's West Indies and Spanish America, privileges which the free-port acts eventually regularized and extended.[29] By the first of these statutes, in 1765, foreign one-deck vessels were permitted to bring certain produce of foreign American colonies into two ports of Dominica and five of Jamaica, and to carry back most goods legally imported into these ports. Later, vessels of more than one deck were admitted, and a number of additional ports (both in the West Indies and North America) were included in the list of free ports.[30]

The ships of the United States did not even enjoy the freedom permitted other foreign American vessels in the free ports until 1822 (except for limited rights in Nova Scotia, New Brunswick, and Bermuda and during war time). The English West Indies and Newfoundland were again closed to ships of the United States from December, 1826, until November, 1830, when an agreement opened the direct trade on a permanent reciprocal basis.[31]

Other exceptions to the English shipping monopoly included the export of salt from Turks Island by the United States ships arriving in ballast after April 4, 1788 (28 Geo. III, c. 6) and from specified ports in the Bahamas after August 1, 1804 (44 Geo. III, c. 101; 59 Geo. III, c. 18); trade with the East Indies by ships of the United States after the treaty of 1794 and

Hope and territory to the eastward, except for the privileges of the Company (46 Geo. III, c. 30; 49 Geo. III, c. 17; 57 Geo. III, c. 95; 6 Geo. IV, c. 114, lxxiii; 3 & 4 Gul. IV, c. 59, 1, lxxxi; 8 & 9 Vict., c. 93, xv). For special regulations for Mauritius (usually treated like the West Indies) see 6 Geo. IV, c. 114, xliv; and for Hong Kong, see 6 & 7 Vict., c. 84, xix; 8 & 9 Vict., c. 88, xii.

[29] Reeves, *Law of Shipping and Navigation*, pp. 64, 84; Nettels, *The Money Supply of the American Colonies*, pp. 25-27.

[30] The most important statutes were 6 Geo. III, c. 49 (1765); 27 Geo. III, c. 27 (1787); 45 Geo. III, c. 57 (1805); 3 Geo. IV, c. 44 (1822). Others included 13 Geo. III, c. 73; 14 Geo. III, c. 41; 21 Geo. III, c. 29; 30 Geo. III, c. 29; 31 Geo. III, c. 38; 32 Geo. III, c. 37 and c. 43; 33 Geo. III, c. 50; 38 Geo. III, c. 39; 41 Geo. III, c. 23 (1800); 42 Geo. III, c. 102; 43 Geo. III, c. 133; 46 Geo. III, c. 72; 47 Geo. III, sess. 2, c. 34; 48 Geo. III, c. 125; 49 Geo. III, c. 22; 50 Geo. III, c. 21; 52 Geo. III, c. 20, c. 99, and c. 100; 54 Geo. III, c. 48; 57 Geo. III, c. 29 and c. 74; 58 Geo. III, c. 27; 1 Geo. IV, c. 12 and c. 32. See also *infra*, n. 31.

[31] *Supra*, n. 30; 3 Geo. IV, c. 44; 6 Geo. IV, c. 73 and c. 114; Hertslet, *Commercial Treaties*, III, 529-35; IV, 517-19; Benns, *British West India Carrying-Trade, passim;* and *infra*, p. 404. For war-time exception (1806) see 46 Geo. III, c. 111; for Nova Scotia and New Brunswick, 47 Geo. III, sess. 2, c. 38; 49 Geo. III, c. 49; 58 Geo. III, c. 19; 1 & 2 Geo. IV, c. 7; for Bermuda, 52 Geo. III, c. 79; 53 Geo. III, c. 50; 57 Geo. III, c. 28; 59 Geo. III, c. 55.

by ships of other friendly countries after 1797 under the regulations of the East India Company, as authorized by 37 Geo. III, c. 117; and Holland's trade with New York for a short time after its conquest (*infra*, n. 45) and with her former colonies in South America after June 17, 1814 (54 Geo. III, c. 72 and 56 Geo. III, c. 91).

The legislation of 1825 modified the English monopoly by permitting goods to be imported by foreign ships of the country which produced the goods and from which they were brought, and by allowing foreign vessels to carry exports to any place outside the Empire, provided the countries of the foreign vessels gave similar privileges to English ships.[32] The colonial ports were opened on these conditions to ships of the following countries, by Orders in Council of the dates indicated:[33]

RECIPROCITY TREATIES RELATING TO COLONIAL TRADE

Country[34]	Date
Prussia	May 3, 1826
Hanover	July 16, 1827
Sweden and Norway	July 16, 1827
Oldenburgh	July 16, 1827
Lübeck, Bremen, and Hamburg	July 16, 1827
Colombia	July 16, 1827
Rio de la Plata	July 16, 1827
Mexico	July 16, 1827
Russia	July 16, 1827
Austria	April 7, 1830
United States	Nov. 5, 1830
Denmark	April 1, 1835
German Customs Union	Aug. 11, 1841
Chile	Aug. 11, 1841
Portugal	Nov. 2, 1842
Mecklenburg-Schwerin	Sept. 3, 1844
Mecklenburg-Strelitz	Sept. 3, 1844
Dominican Republic	May 1, 1849

(2) By the Act of 1660 colonial produce might be exported from the colonies freely, except certain enumerated articles which had to be sent

[32] 6 Geo. IV, c. 73 and c. 114. In 1843 authority was given Her Majesty to allow foreign ships to bring articles of other countries to the colonies for reëxport (6 & 7 Vict., c. 84, xx).

[33] For Orders, see Hertslet, *Commercial Treaties*, III, 360-61; IV, 8-10, 94-95, 184-92, 517-19; VI, 209-10, 711-13, 759-61; VII, 812-13; VIII, 170-71.

[34] In addition, beginning July 16, 1827, French ships were permitted to carry certain specified French goods to the English possessions in the West Indies and America, and to export goods thence to any foreign country, and beginning April 28, 1828, Spanish ships were permitted to carry Spanish colonial goods from Spanish colonies to the English colonies, and to export goods thence to any foreign country (Hertslet, *Commercial Treaties*, iv, 184-92, 412-14).

to England or an English colony.[35] This act listed seven such articles, and later statutes extended the regulation to a number of other commodities. In 1673 (25 Car. II, c. 7) a duty was placed upon the originally enumerated articles, if sent to another colony without bond being given that they would be carried to England. The following tables show the articles enumerated, the date on which the restriction took effect, and the duties payable on the originally enumerated goods if shipped to another colony. The enumeration includes products of all His Majesty's plantations in Asia, Africa, and America, unless specially marked to indicate that it was limited to products of the region mentioned. The restrictions did not apply to products from foreign colonies.[36]

[35] Scotland was not admitted on a basis of equality with England until the Act of Union in 1707 (6 Anne, c. 11). Ireland was included under the Act of 1660, along with England, Wales, and Berwick, as a place to which the enumerated colonial goods might be sent directly. Parliament intended to exclude Ireland in 1663 (15 Car. II, c. 7), but the clause was ambiguous and was much disputed until the Act of 22 & 23 Car. II, c. 26 (1671) definitely excluded Ireland. This statute lapsed at the end of nine years, but was revived in 1685 (1 Jac. II, c. 17). The Act of 7 & 8 Gul. III, c. 22 (1696) was construed to prevent the importation of nonenumerated colonial goods directly into Ireland, but except for hops (and specklewood—see *infra*, n. 36), nonenumerated goods were allowed to be imported again after 1731 (4 Geo. II, c. 15; 5 Geo. II, c. 9; 7 Geo. III, c. 2). Beginning in 1765, iron and lumber were allowed to go directly to Ireland (5 Geo. III, c. 45, xxii); and in 1780 Ireland was admitted to equality with England in the trade with the West Indies, continental America, and Africa (20 Geo. III, c. 10), and the Act of Union (40 Geo. III, c. 67) provided that on and after January 1, 1801, Ireland should be "on the same footing . . . generally in respect of trade and navigation in all ports and places in the United Kingdom and its dependencies." For further discussion see Reeves, *Law of Shipping and Navigation*, pp. 73-91.

[36] The wording of 22 & 23 Car. II, c. 26, vii, caused some doubts as to whether the colonists might not be obliged to carry to England the commodities listed in 1660, whatever their origin; but it was eventually decided that if they were not plantation produce, they were not enumerated (Add MSS 8832, pp. 198-200) and consequently not regulated until the free-port acts imposed certain other limitations (for citations, see *supra*, n. 30). Specklewood was not enumerated in the Act of 1660 nor in most of the statutes, but was listed in 15 Car. II, c. 7 (relating to the goods which English customs officials should require to be landed in England) and in 4 Geo. II, c. 7 (concerning goods which could not go directly to Ireland). 10 Gul. III, c. 16 prohibited the exportation to any place whatsoever of any wool or woolen goods of the English plantations in America from and after December 1, 1699, although beginning March 22, 1806, wool produced in the plantations could be sent to the United Kingdom (46 Geo. III, c. 17). Exportation of hats or felts was forbidden from September 29, 1732, to July, 1823 (5 Geo. II, c. 22), and commencing September 29, 1765, rum and other spirits could be shipped from the American colonies only on condition that they would not be carried to the Isle of Man (5 Geo. III, c. 39, v). Other acts prohibited the erection of any slitting or rolling mill, tilt-hammer forge, or steel furnace after June 24, 1750, but also freed pig and bar iron made in America from import duties in England (23 Geo. II, c. 29; 30 Geo. II, c. 16). See also Bining, *British Regulation of Colonial Iron Industry*.

COLONIAL EXPORTS

SEVENTEENTH-CENTURY LIMITATIONS UPON COLONIAL EXPORTS

Commodity	Date	Statute	Plantation Duty
Cotton wool	April 1, 1661	12 Car. II, c. 18, xviii	½d., lb.[37]
Dyewoods	April 1, 1661	12 Car. II, c. 18, xviii	6d., cwt.[38]
Fustic	April 1, 1661	12 Car. II, c. 18, xviii	6d., cwt.
Ginger	April 1, 1661	12 Car. II, c. 18, xviii	1s. 0d., cwt.
Indigo	April 1, 1661	12 Car. II, c. 18, xviii	2d., lb.
Logwood[38]	April 1, 1661	12 Car. II, c. 18, xviii	5s. 0d., cwt.[38]
Sugar, white	April 1, 1661	12 Car. II, c. 18, xviii	5s. 0d., cwt.[39]
Sugar, brown	April 1, 1661	12 Car. II, c. 18, xviii	1s. 6d., cwt.[39]
Tobacco	April 1, 1661	12 Car. II, c. 18, xviii	1d., lb.

EIGHTEENTH-CENTURY ADDITIONS TO LIMITATIONS UPON COLONIAL EXPORTS

Commodity	Date	Statute
East India goods*[40]	Sept. 29, 1698	9 Gul. III, c. 44, lix
Rice	Sept. 29, 1705	3 & 4 Anne, c. 3, xii
Molasses	Sept. 29, 1705	3 & 4 Anne, c. 3, xii
Naval stores†[41]	Jan. 1, 1706	3 & 4 Anne, c. 9
Beaver skins and furs	March 25, 1722	8 Geo. I, c. 15, xxiv
Copper ore	Sept. 29, 1722	8 Geo. I, c. 18, xxii

* East India products only.   † American products only.

[37] Repealed by 6 Geo. III, c. 52, xix, from and after Nov. 1, 1766.

[38] Logwood was not specifically named under the Act of 1660 but was included under dyewoods. 25 Car. II, c. 7 specified that the logwood duty should be £5 per hundredweight, but Earnshaw (*Digest of the Laws*, p. 414 n.) declares that the customs authorities considered that only 5s. per hundredweight was intended.

[39] The duty on sugar exported from His Majesty's plantations in America was repealed beginning November 1, 1766, but a duty of 1d. per gallon was placed upon molasses or syrups brought into the same plantations (6 Geo. III, c. 52, i, iv).

[40] The required bond allowed goods to be taken only to England. September 29, 1698 has been given as the date when the regulation became effective, but an exception was made in favor of vessels which had cleared from England before July 1, 1698. Other exceptions were made by 6 Anne, c. 37 (1707) for necessaries landed at St. Helena; by 13 Geo. I, c. 8 (for six years beginning in 1727) for Negroes delivered at Buenos Aires; by the treaty of 1794 for vessels of the United States, and by 37 Geo. III, c. 117 (1797) for vessels of friendly foreign nations; by 5 Geo. IV, c. 88 (1824) for shipments to His Majesty's possessions in America from China, by the East India Company or its licensees, of any goods produced within the limits of the Company's charter; by 6 Geo. IV, c. 114, lxxiv (beginning Jan. 5, 1826) for shipments to such possessions by the Company of any goods from within the limits of its charter, or by its licensees of any goods from China, or of tea from within the limits of the Company's charter. Note also the authority given to regulate such trade by Orders in Council (*supra*, n. 28).

[41] The Act of 3 & 4 Anne, c. 9 (1706), continued by 12 Anne, c. 9 (1713) for eleven years and to the end of the next Parliament, enumerated tar, pitch, rosin, or turpentine, hemp, masts, yards, and bowsprits. The enumeration was allowed to lapse, but was revived by 2 Geo. II, c. 35 (1729), except with respect to rosin and hemp.

EIGHTEENTH-CENTURY ADDITIONS TO LIMITATIONS UPON COLONIAL
EXPORTS (*Continued*)

Commodity	Date	Statute
Pimento†[42]	Sept. 29, 1764	4 Geo. III, c. 15, xxvii
Coffee†[42]	Sept. 29, 1764	4 Geo. III, c. 15, xxvii
Cocoa nuts†[43]	Sept. 29, 1764	4 Geo. III, c. 15, xxvii
Whale fins†	Sept. 29, 1764	4 Geo. III, c. 15, xxvii
Raw silk†	Sept. 29, 1764	4 Geo. III, c. 15, xxvii
Hides and skins†	Sept. 29, 1764	4 Geo. III, c. 15, xxvii
Pot and pearlashes†	Sept. 29, 1764	4 Geo. III, c. 15, xxvii
Iron, to Europe†	Sept. 29, 1764	4 Geo. III, c. 15, xxviii
Lumber, to Europe†	Sept. 29, 1764	4 Geo. III, c. 15, xxviii
Gum senegal[44]‡	June 24, 1765	5 Geo. III, c. 37, iv
All nonenumerated goods to Europe north of Cape Finisterre	Jan. 1, 1767	6 Geo. III, c. 52, xxx

† American products only.   ‡ African products only.

Except for the permission granted to ship various enumerated commodities to the United States and the privilege given Dutch inhabitants of Holland's former colonies to ship the produce of their estates to Holland,[45] the principal relaxations granted before 1815 affected sugar, rice, coffee, cocoa, and lumber.[46] In that year permission was granted to export directly to Malta (and in 1817 to Gibraltar) all produce of the North American colonies and rum, molasses, pimento, indigo, fustic, and ginger

[42] Beginning Sept. 29, 1764, a duty of 7s. was placed upon every hundredweight of coffee and ½d. upon every pound of pimento produced in His Majesty's plantations in America and exported from there to another plantation (4 Geo. III, c. 15, ii, iii). It was replaced Nov. 1, 1766, by a similar duty charged upon importation rather than upon exportation (6 Geo. III, c. 52, i, iv).

[43] The "cocoa nuts" were cacao nuts. They had had to pay a plantation duty of 1d. per pound since 1673 (25 Car. II, c. 7).

[44] It could go to the other colonies only by way of England.

[45] For the United States, see 28 Geo. III, c. 6, and citations *infra*, pp. 403-4; for Dutch exemptions, see APC Col. I, Nos. 730, 812; 54 Geo. III, c. 72; 56 Geo. III, c. 91.

[46] If the proper licenses were obtained and requirements were met, rice could be carried to Europe south of Cape Finisterre from Carolina by 3 Geo. II, c. 28 (1730); from Georgia by 8 Geo. II, c. 19 (1735); and from East and West Florida by 11 Geo. III, c. 39 (1770); to any part of America south of Georgia from South Carolina and Georgia by 4 Geo. III, c. 27 (1764); and from North Carolina by 5 Geo. III, c. 45 (1765). Under similar circumstances sugar could be sent from the Sugar Colonies to Europe, after touching at England, or directly to Europe south of Cape Finisterre, from September 29, 1739 until May 9, 1794, although in 1792 it was provided that no licenses should be issued when the price of sugar exceeded certain prescribed rates (12 Geo. II, c. 30; 15 Geo. II, c. 33; 32 Geo. III, c. 43, x; 34 Geo. III, c. 42). Beginning in 1808 sugar together with coffee (and in 1810 cocoa also) could be shipped south of Cape Finisterre (48 Geo. III, c. 69; 50 Geo. III, c. 13; 52 Geo. III, c. 98); and beginning in 1765 lumber was permitted to go to Madeira, the Azores, and Europe south of Cape Finisterre (5 Geo. III, c. 45, xxii). Various exceptions were made for Ireland (see *supra*, n. 35), and beginning in 1768, the Act of 9 Geo. III, c. 28, iii, modified that of 6 Geo. III, c. 52, xxx, by allowing nonenumerated goods (except rum) to be landed in Jersey or Guernsey.

(as well as sugar, coffee, and cocoa) of the Sugar Colonies (55 Geo. III, c. 29, i; 57 Geo. III, c. 4).

The principle of enumerated articles (and the collection of duties upon exportation to another colony) was abandoned beginning in 1822 by the act of that date, which provided that all the produce of the colonies could be exported to any place in Europe, Africa, or America.[47]

(3) Regulations governing imports first appeared in 1663 and became increasingly complex until 1826, when the Act of 6 Geo. IV, c. 114, although allowing importations in America from foreign countries to be made only at the free ports, opened such ports and Mauritius to almost all imports (if shipped as required, *supra*, p. 396)[48] and authorized the regulation of trade in Asia and Africa by Orders in Council, relying thereafter upon preferential import duties for the encouragement of England as an entrepôt. The earlier rules, however, cannot be so readily summarized and must be considered in relation to the continent from which the goods came.

Asian and African products, although subject to the monopolies granted the East India and Royal African Companies, could otherwise be imported freely until 9 Gul. III, c. 44, lix (1698), which required the English plantations in Africa and America to obtain all their East India goods from England. This rule was liberalized in 1824.[49]

---

[47] 3 Geo. IV, c. 44 and c. 45. Shipments had to be made from the free ports, if destined for foreign America, and beginning Jan. 5, 1826, all foreign trade had to be carried on through such ports (6 Geo. IV, c. 114 [1825]; 3 & 4 Gul. IV, c. 59 [1833]; 8 & 9 Vict., c. 93 [1845]).

[48] The goods prohibited were gunpowder, arms, "Ammunitions or Utensils of War," base or counterfeit coin, and books prohibited to be imported into the United Kingdom. Beef, fresh or salted, and pork (except for Newfoundland) could come only from the United Kingdom or from some other English possession; fish, dried or salted (except locally caught herrings from the Isle of Man), train oil, blubber, fins or skins of creatures living in the sea could come only from those places, or from fishing vessels fitted out therein. Tea, unless brought by the East India Company or its licensees, could come only from the United Kingdom or some other English possession in America. Coffee, cocoa nuts, sugar, molasses, and rum could not enter His Majesty's possessions in South America or the West Indies except the Bahama Islands and Bermuda (and even there might be prohibited by Order in Council), if produced abroad or within the limits of the East India Company's charter, unless in Mauritius; and such articles were similarly restricted although produced within His Majesty's plantations, if they had entered those English colonies in America which were open to such foreign products. Beef, pork, and cocoa nuts were omitted from the prohibited list by 3 & 4 Gul. IV, c. 59 (1833), and the same commodities, together with tea, fish, oil, and books, were omitted by 8 & 9 Vict., c. 93 (1845).

[49] *Supra*, n. 40. East India goods legally imported could be shipped from one colony to another until such goods were forbidden to go to other English colonies in America from Dominica by the free-port act of 6 Geo. III, c. 49, xi (1765), or from the other free ports by subsequent acts (*supra*, n. 30).

The importation of European goods into the English colonies in Asia, Africa, and America was governed by the Staple Act of 1663 (15 Car. II, c. 7), which required that such goods be obtained in England[50] with certain exceptions specified in the original act or subsequent amendments, as indicated in the following table:

EXCEPTIONS TO RULES CONCERNING COLONIAL IMPORTATIONS FROM EUROPE

Commodities	To	Date	Statute
Servants and horses from Scotland or Ireland	Any colony	March 25, 1664	15 Car. II, c. 7, v
Scottish victuals from Scotland	Any colony	March 25, 1664	15 Car. II, c. 7, v
Irish victuals from Ireland	Any colony	March 25, 1664	15 Car. II, c. 7, v
Madeira wines from Madeira	Any colony	March 25, 1664	15 Car. II, c. 7, v
Wines of the Western Islands or Azores from there	Any colony	March 25, 1664	15 Car. II, c. 7, v
Salt from Europe	Fisheries of New England and Newfoundland	March 25, 1664	15 Car. II, c. 7, v
Irish linen from Ireland	Any colony	June 24, 1705	3 & 4 Anne, c. 7
Salt from Europe	Fisheries of		
	Pennsylvania	June 24, 1727	13 Geo. I, c. 5
	New York	June 1, 1730	3 Geo. II, c. 12
	Nova Scotia	July 1, 1762	2 Geo. III, c. 24
	Quebec	June 24, 1764	4 Geo. III, c. 19
English goods or victuals from Guernsey and Jersey	Fisheries	1768	9 Geo. III, c. 28
Goods and victuals of England, Jersey or Guernsey, and Irish victuals from Jersey or Guernsey	Fisheries	1768	9 Geo. III, c. 28
Herrings caught and cured in Isle of Man from it	Any colony	June 24, 1772	12 Geo. III, c. 58, iv
English and Irish provisions and equipment from Ireland	Fisheries	Jan. 1, 1776	15 Geo. III, c. 31, v
English and Manx provisions and equipment from Isle of Man	Fisheries	Jan. 1, 1776	15 Geo. III, c. 31, v

[50] Tangier was excepted from the restriction by the Act of 1663, and until 1780 (20 Geo. III, c. 10) Ireland was treated as a foreign country which could export to the plantations only when specific permission was granted. European goods, duly imported into one of the English colonies, might be sent to another colony until 1765. From then until 38 Geo. III, c. 39 (1797), they could not be shipped to another English colony in America from any English island having free ports, except Jamaica (for citations, see *supra*, n. 30; see especially 52 Geo. III, c. 100).

EXCEPTIONS TO RULES CONCERNING COLONIAL IMPORTATIONS
FROM EUROPE (*Continued*)

Commodities	To	Date	Statute
Most Irish or English goods from Ireland[51]	Any colony	June 24, 1778	18 Geo. III, c. 55
All goods from Ireland which could go from England	Any colony	1780	20 Geo. III, c. 10
Fruit from Gibraltar & Malta[52]	North American Colonies	July 21, 1806	46 Geo. III, c. 116
Wine from Malta[52]	North American Colonies	July 21, 1806	46 Geo. III, c. 116
Oil from Malta[52]	North American Colonies	July 21, 1806	46 Geo. III, c. 116
Cork from Malta[52]	North American Colonies	July 21, 1806	46 Geo. III, c. 116
Salt from Malta[52]	North American Colonies	July 21, 1806	46 Geo. III, c. 116
Corn from Europe, south of Cape Finisterre[53]	American Sugar Colonies	June 18, 1808	48 Geo. III, c. 69
Goods from Holland	Former Dutch Plantations[54]	June 17, 1814	54 Geo. III, c. 72
85 articles from Malta[55]	North American and Sugar Colonies	March 23, 1815	55 Geo. III, c. 29
85 articles from Gibraltar[55]	North American and Sugar Colonies	March 4, 1817	57 Geo. III, c. 4
Oranges and lemons from Azores and Madeira	North American Colonies	July 10, 1817	57 Geo. III, c. 89
97 articles from Europe[55]	American Colonies and West Indies	June 24, 1822	3 Geo. IV, c. 45, viii

At first American products could be imported without hindrance, except for the generally disregarded treaties of 1670 and of 1686 with Spain and France, in which England agreed to respect the colonial regulations

[51] All Irish goods except wool, woolen and cotton manufactures, hats, glass, hops, gunpowder, and coal, and all goods of England except woolens and glass. Iron was to pay a specified duty, and all other manufactured goods a tax equal to that assessed on similar goods exported from England.

[52] In return for fish. These articles could come from any port south of Cape Finisterre to St. John's (New Brunswick), St. John's (Newfoundland), Quebec, Sydney, Halifax, Shelburn, and Charlotte Town after May 12, 1809 (49 Geo. III, c. 47). 51 Geo. III, c. 97 (1811) allowed their import by ships bringing certain Canadian produce.

[53] Also from Africa north of 30° latitude, but in both cases only by ships bringing sugar and coffee as permitted by the act. See also 52 Geo. III, c. 98.

[54] Limited to supplies (not for sale) imported from Holland by Dutch proprietors in Demerara, Berbice, and Essequibo, beginning June 26, 1816 (56 Geo. III, c. 91, iii).

[55] The eighty-five articles were mostly Mediterranean products and included fruits, drugs, wines, oils, perfumes, marble, caviar, and macaroni. The ninety-seven included the same articles and biscuit, cattle, fruit, garden seeds, mules, nuts, salt, sausages, sheep, shingles, staves, and wood hoops. They could also come from Africa, Gibraltar, Malta, Guernsey, Jersey, Alderney, and Sark.

of those powers. Beginning in 1733, however, a duty was laid upon molasses and sugar coming into His Majesty's colonies in America from the foreign colonies there (6 Geo. II, c. 13; 4 Geo. III, c. 15 [1764]; 6 Geo. III, c. 52[1765]); beginning in 1735 foreign coffee was required by 5 Geo. II, c. 24, iv, to be imported from England;[56] 4 Geo. III, c. 15, xviii (1764) forbade the importation of rum and spirits of foreign colonies in America into His Majesty's colonies there; and 23 Geo. III, c. 79, viii (1783) required foreign cocoa nuts to be imported from England, unless brought to the free ports for exportation to England (supra, n. 30). The original free-port act, 6 Geo. III, c. 49 (1765), however, prohibited the importation into Dominica or Jamaica of the enumerated products grown in the English colonies in America, or of manufactures of foreign colonies in America, and the shipments from Dominica of any West Indian produce (except cattle) to any other West Indian island; but 27 Geo. III, c. 27 (1787) gave much greater freedom of trade, as did the subsequent acts (supra, n. 30).

During the American Revolution, trade with the rebellious colonies was prohibited (14 Geo. III, c. 19; 15 Geo. III, c. 10; 16 Geo. III, c. 5), and thereafter English policy was dominated by a desire to frustrate American competition and complicated by a need for American provisions, naval stores, and lumber. In 1788 (28 Geo. III, c. 6), after preliminary experimentation by Orders in Council,[57] only certain United States commodities (mostly provisions, naval stores, and lumber) were allowed to enter His Majesty's West Indies (including the Bahamas and Bermuda); most of the same commodities were not allowed to enter from the colonies of foreign Europe except in emergencies;[58] and all importations from the United States to Nova Scotia, New Brunswick, Cape Breton, St. John's, Newfoundland, and Quebec were prohibited, although dispensations might be made in case of necessity, especially with respect to foodstuffs and naval stores.[59]

Exceptions soon crept into the laws regulating imports from America, as they had in the case of imports from Europe (supra, pp. 401-2). The goods of settlers were permitted to enter the Bahamas, Bermuda, or North America from the United States (30 Geo. III, c. 27, i [1790]); the colonies

---

[56] As far as has been discovered, the regulation lapsed at the end of the next session of Parliament after March 25, 1758 (25 Geo. II, c. 35), but beginning Sept. 29, 1764, a duty of £2 19s. 9d. per hundredweight was placed upon foreign coffee imported into the American colonies, unless brought from England (4 Geo. III, c. 15, i), or (beginning in 1805) for exportation into certain free ports (45 Geo. III, c. 57, iv, v; 46 Geo. III, c. 72, i), or (beginning in 1812) into the Bahamas (52 Geo. III, c. 99, i).

[57] 23 Geo. III, c. 39; 24 Geo. III, c. 45; 25 Geo. III, c. 1; 26 Geo. III, c. 1; 27 Geo. III, c. 7; Reeves, Law of Shipping and Navigation, pp. 271-300.

[58] In such case they were not to be reëxported (29 Geo. III, c. 56: 31 Geo. III, c. 38).

[59] 28 Geo. III, c. 6. Not in the case of Quebec until 1789 (29 Geo. III, c. 16; 30 Geo. III, c. 8).

of foreign Europe could ship to His Majesty's West Indies "bully trees" and certain other woods which were needed in the manufacture of sugar but had been excluded by the general prohibition of lumber not brought directly from the United States (33 Geo. III, c. 50, xiii [1793]); and the Portuguese colonies in South America were allowed to send to the same colonies all the articles which could come from the United States (51 Geo. III, c. 47, v, vi [1811]). More important, frequent dispensations by governors and statutory relaxations, especially in war time, allowed certain goods from the United States (mostly provisions) to enter designated ports in North America and to be reëxported from there to His Majesty's possessions in the West Indies and South America, which possessions were also allowed to obtain tobacco, rice, grain, peas, beans, and flour from the colonies of foreign Europe, even if such products had originally come from the United States.[60] In 1822, a list of sixty-five articles[61] was permitted to come from foreign America (including the United States) into the free ports (3 Geo. IV, c. 44), and later in the same year, all the ports of entry in Upper and Lower Canada were opened to American trade (3 Geo. IV, c. 119). Beginning January 5, 1826, the rules were further relaxed, as already described (*supra*, p. 396) by 6 Geo. IV, c. 73 and c. 114, but the United States did not gain as much as would first appear. Some of her products were excluded entirely; duties were laid on many others; and a rebate of ten percent was offered on goods imported by way of the United Kingdom, thus handicapping direct importation from America. Moreover, as explained earlier (*supra*, p. 395), United States vessels were forbidden to trade in the English colonies from December, 1826 to November, 1830, because the United States had not granted most-favored-nation treatment to English vessels.

ENGLISH IMPORTS FROM EUROPE

European goods could be imported in any ship from any place according to the original acts, except that certain enumerated articles had to be imported in English-owned shipping or shipping of the country of growth, and except that (beginning in 1662) a number of articles, mostly the same as those enumerated, could not be imported from the Netherlands or Germany. If the enumerated articles were imported in other than English-built shipping, they were subject to alien duties.

The details of these regulations are shown in the following table:

[60] 29 Geo. III, c. 56 (1789); 31 Geo. III, c. 38 (1791); 33 Geo. III, c. 50, xiv (1793); 46 Geo. III, c. 111 (1806); 47 Geo. III, sess. 2, c. 38 (1807); 48 Geo. III, c. 125 (1808); 49 Geo. III, c. 49 (1809); 52 Geo. III, c. 20, c. 55, and c. 79 (1812); 53 Geo. III, c. 50 (1813); 57 Geo. III, c. 28 (1817); 58 Geo. III, c. 19 (1818); 58 Geo. III, c. 27 (1818); 1 & 2 Geo. IV, c. 7 (1821). See also, Hertslet, *Commercial Treaties*, III, 484-541; IV, 498-533; Benns, *British West India Carrying-Trade, passim*.

[61] The list included various provisions, livestock, drugs, dyestuffs, hides, timber, hoops, staves, cabinet wood, masts, naval stores, and tobacco. A number of the commodities were assessed with duties.

REGULATIONS CONCERNING ENGLISH IMPORTS FROM EUROPE

(1) *Must be imported in English-owned shipping or shipping of country of growth, production, or manufacture:*[62]	(2) *Could not be imported from the Netherlands or Germany upon any pretense whatever:*[63]	(3) *If imported in other than English-built shipping, must pay extra duties, as follows:*[64]
Muscovy goods[65]		Various[65]
Turkey goods[66]		Various[67]
Aqua vitae		1s., hhd.
Brandy wine		3s. 9d. to 7s. 6d., ton
Corn or grain		3/5d. to 6d., quarter[68]
Currants		5s. 3-3/5d., cwt. [69]
Figs		5d., cwt.

[62] 12 Car. II, c. 18, viii, ix (1660).

[63] 14 Car. II, c. 11, xxiii (1662).

[64] The alien duties on enumerated articles other than currants and Turkey goods did not apply to foreign-built English-owned ships until after the Act of Frauds (12 Car. II, c. 18; 14 Car. II, c. 11). For 1787 and thereafter, see *infra*, pp. 411-13.
The difference in rate has been taken from the compilation of Crouch, *A Complete View of the British Customs*. The same figures (with a few insignificant exceptions, the cause for which is unknown) can be obtained by calculating the alien duty for oneself, since it is 1¼ percent of the rated value of the commodities specified, except for wine, on which discriminating duties were placed by the Old Subsidy of tonnage; and except for currants, in the carriage of which English-built and Venetian ships were given added preference by 3 & 4 Anne, c. 3, and 8 Anne, c. 14, xxv.
A "quarter" was equivalent to 1/5 of a long ton; a hundredweight (cwt.) was 112 pounds; a last contained 12 barrels, approximately two tons in the case of pitch and tar; a barrel of potashes weighed 200 pounds; a ton (tun), liquid measure, was 252 gallons; a wey equaled 40 bushels, or in the case of salt 2,000 lbs.

[65] There was considerable debate concerning the exact meaning of the clause referring to the importation of Muscovy commodities (Reeves, *Law of Shipping and Navigation*, pp. 180-83), but as far as can be judged from administrative practice, the general rule was applied. Most of the Muscovy commodities which England imported, at least in 1663 (BM Add MSS 36785), were specifically enumerated. Of the remainder, the greater part were furs of different sorts. These would presumably have paid discriminatory duties, in foreign ships, ranging from 18s. 9d. per hundred sable skins to 6d. per hundred "cat" skins; however, no discrimination appears in Crouch, *A Complete View of the British Customs*.

[66] Turkey commodities were required to be imported in English-built ships properly manned, or in ships of Turkey, or of the port of first shipment, properly built and manned.

[67] The most important Turkey commodity, currants, was listed separately. Other goods such as mohair yarn, cotton wool, cotton yarn, aniseed, and thrown silk presumably paid alien duties, but no discrimination appears in Crouch, *A Complete View of the British Customs*.

[68] The duties assessed on grain were scaled according to the market price, *i.e.*, if the price fell below 28s. per quarter, the duty was much higher than when the price rose above 40s. per quarter. There was no discrimination against foreign ships on the low-priced grains. There were different duties for each grain, but the amount of discrimination varied only from 3/5d. to 1d., except for buckwheat, when the price ranged between 32s. and 44s.

[69] Currants imported in Venetian ships paid an excess of only 1s. 6d.

REGULATIONS CONCERNING ENGLISH IMPORTS FROM EUROPE
(*Continued*)

(1) *Must be imported in English-owned shipping or shipping of country of growth, production, or manufacture:*[62]	(2) *Could not be imported from the Netherlands or Germany upon any pretense whatever:*[63]	(3) *If imported in other than English-built shipping, must pay extra duties, as follows:*[64]
	"Grocery"[70]	
Flax, dressed		3s. 9d., cwt.
Flax, rough		3d., cwt.
Hemp, dressed		2s. 6d., cwt.
Hemp, rough		2d., cwt.
Masts		$\frac{1}{2}d.$ to 3d., each
Olive oils	Olive oils	8s., ton[71]
Pitch	Pitch	8d., last
Potashes	Potashes	3$\frac{3}{4}d.$, barrel
Prunes		2$\frac{1}{4}d.$, cwt.
Raisins		1$\frac{1}{2}d.$ to 6d., cwt.
Rosin	Rosin	1d., cwt.
Salt (except Scottish)	Salt	3d. to 4d., wey
	Spicery[72]	
Sugar, muscovado		1s., cwt.
Sugar, white		1s., 10d., cwt.
Sugar, refined		4s., 3d., cwt.
Tar	Tar	7$\frac{1}{2}d.$, last
Timber or boards[73]	Timber (fir) deal boards	Various[74]
	Tobacco	
Vinegar		No alien duties
Wines[75]	All wines except Rhenish	£4 1s. to £4 8s. 2-2/5d., ton

The additional duty originally amounted to 25 percent more than the duty paid by English-built ships. Broadly speaking, the difference between the rates paid by English ships and those paid by foreign ships remained substantially the same, in terms of pounds and shillings, from 1660 until the general customs revision of 1787.[76] But the difference in rate became

[70] The term "grocery" included currants, figs, prunes, raisins, and sugar, as well as almonds, dates, plums, candy, and spices (Crouch, *A Complete View of the British Customs*, pp. 161-65).

[71] "Sallet oil" had a discriminatory duty of 3/5d. per gallon, or 12s. 7 1/5d. per ton.

[72] However, a proclamation of Dec. 20, 1662, allowed the importation of spices from any place; and statutes later authorized importation by license (T & S P I, No. 3374; 6 & 7 Gul. & Mar., c. 7, ii).

[73] The term "timber or boards" was apparently broadly interpreted so as to include almost all varieties of wood.

[74] For example, on clapboards, 2¼ d. per 120 boards.

[75] All wines were subject to the regulation concerning shipping; but section ix of the Act of 1660, which placed the alien duties on foreign shipping, specifically named the wines of France, Germany, Spain, Canaries, Portugal, Madeira, or Western Islands. Crouch shows the discrimination as applying to all wines, however, except for prisage.

[76] However, there was a change in the discriminating duty on at least one commodity—currants (see *supra*, n. 64); and possibly there were some other special changes, particularly after 1730. The new book of rates issued by Sims and Frewin

much less than 25 percent, since the various new duties added to the basic Old Subsidy did not as a rule provide discriminating rates against foreign shipping.

Changes occurred in the regulations governing the importation of European goods, just as in other branches of the navigation laws.[77] The restriction on imports from the Netherlands or Germany was first affected by the Treaty of Breda (1667), which provided that the Dutch might carry into England in their own ships commodities of the growth, production, or manufacture of Lower or Upper Germany. No statute was passed to carry this stipulation into effect, but the law officers of the Crown acted in accordance with the spirit of the provisions when making their decisions.[78]

Some relaxations were made by statute. German pearlashes could be imported from Germany after May 10, 1699 (10 Gul. III, c. 10, xxvii); Hungary wines could come from Hamburg after 1701 (1 Anne, c. 6, cxxxvi); and English-owned and built ships could carry from Germany fir timber, planks, masts, and deal boards of that country after August 1, 1720 (6 Geo. I, c. 15). In 1782 wines of Hungary, the Austrian dominions, or Germany might come from the Austrian Netherlands (22 Geo. III, c. 78), and from May 10, 1787 to May 10, 1800, French olive oil was permitted to come in English or French ships from any port of the Netherlands belonging to the French king, and French wines from any of his European dominions (27 Geo. III, c. 13, xxii). In 1807 His Majesty was empowered to grant licenses for the importation, in vessels of friendly countries, of naval stores from any port (47 Geo. III, sess. 2, c. 27). In 1816 the import of German prunes was allowed (56 Geo. III, c. 37). The prohibitions against goods from the Netherlands and Germany were removed entirely in 1822 (3 Geo. IV, c. 42, vi).

The qualifications for foreign ships bringing enumerated articles underwent revision. Shipping of the country of production or usual first shipment had originally been required to be owned by that country, built there, and manned with a master and three-quarters crew of the same country.[79] Law officers held that only the territorial limits of 1660 could be recognized as "the country of production."[80] In 1782 the privilege was ex-

---

in 1782 shows some slight variations. For the amount of discrimination after 1787, see below, section on "Other Preferential Duties."

[77] For war-time exceptions and various administrative exceptions, see *supra*, pp. 68-73, 390.

[78] Reeves, *Law of Shipping and Navigation*, pp. 164-65. See decisions of Ward on spruce plank (BM Add MSS 36109, f. 118) and on pitch (*ibid.*, f. 134r).

[79] Although legal decisions on the point were not consistent, for the most part it was held that English-built ships, owned by the country of production, could not carry the enumerated articles (Reeves, *Law of Shipping and Navigation*, pp. 184-89).

[80] BM Add MSS 36109, f. 221r; Reeves, *Law of Shipping and Navigation*, p. 190.

tended to all ships which were the property of subjects under the same sovereign (22 Geo. III, c. 78). Whether intentionally or not, the Act of 1782 did not mention the earlier requirements concerning build and manning, but these were included again in 27 Geo. III, c. 19, which, however, continued the broader interpretation of country. The legislation of 1822 and 1825 (3 Geo. IV, c. 43; 6 Geo. IV, c. 109) retained these requirements, but extended the privilege to like ships of the country from which the goods were imported (even if not the port of first shipment).[81]

The principle of enumeration was further weakened by the reciprocity treaty with Austria in 1838, which allowed Austrian ships to carry goods, including enumerated articles, from Turkish Danubian ports with the same duties as English ships. Similar privileges were extended to other countries under the authorization of 3 & 4 Vict., c. 95 (1840).[82]

The enumerated articles were somewhat changed when relisted in 1822. Tallow and tobacco appeared in the list; Russian goods and Turkey goods[83] were omitted. Potashes, pitch, rosin, sugar, salt, and vinegar were removed in 1827; and barilla, brimstone, cork, clover seed, lemons, linseed, madders, madder root, oranges, oak bark, rapeseed, shumac, and wool were then added. These changes were embodied in the list of 1833 and remained in force until repeal.[84]

OTHER PREFERENTIAL DUTIES

In addition to the laws generally included among the Navigation Acts, there were certain other statutes which gave definite advantages to English shipping by preferential duties or bounties on the import or export of certain commodities.[85] Until the complete revision of the customs duties

[81] To constitute importation from any particular place, goods had to come direct and either be first laden there or actually have been landed and reshipped from there (6 Geo. IV, c. 107, xlvi; 3 & 4 Gul. IV, c. 52, xlviii). 6 Geo. IV, c. 109, xv recognized also, as ships of the country concerned, English-built ships, prizes, and vessels condemned under laws to prevent the slave trade. A number of the reciprocity treaties somewhat broadened the qualifications; for example, according to the treaty of Sept. 29, 1825, with Lübeck, Bremen, and Hamburg, a ship might be built in one of the towns, owned by citizens of another, and manned by a crew drawn from all three (Hertslet, *Commercial Treaties*, III, 226-31).

[82] See Hertslet, *Commercial Treaties*, V, 1-9 (Austria); VI, 517-20 (Hanse towns), 583-87 (Oldenburg), 751-55 (Prussia, and 17 other German states), 762-70 (Russia); VII, 729-35 (Hanover), 803-7 (Mecklenburg-Schwerin).

[83] In effect, however, the regulation was continued as to Turkey goods by another section of the act (3 Geo. IV, c. 43, viii); in 1825 the restrictions on Turkey goods were only on those of Asiatic origin (6 Geo. IV, c. 109). See also *supra*, n. 27.

[84] 7 & 8 Geo. IV, c. 56, xvi; for the revisions of 1833 and 1845, see 3 & 4 Gul. IV, c. 54 and 8 & 9 Vict., c. 88.

[85] A related type of protection was that given in the Act of Frauds, which provided a premium for building stronger vessels by giving a rebate of one-tenth of the customs duties on the first two voyages, a premium which was continued and increased by

in 1787, these provisions, except in the case of the enumerated European goods, were scattered throughout the laws.

The following tables indicate the commodities (in addition to the enumerated articles discussed above) which received preferential advantages before 1787, when carried in English vessels, the statutes which gave the protection, and the amount of extra charges paid by foreign vessels. In the case of those commodities indicated by an asterisk, the ships had to be of English build in order to enjoy the advantage.

EARLY PREFERENTIAL DUTIES ON IMPORTS[86]

Commodity	*Statute*	*Preferential Duty*[87]
Beaver wool, of Russia	2 Gul. & Mar., sess. 2, c. 4	14s. $\frac{3}{4}d$., lb.
Cotton wool*	6 Geo. III, c. 52, xx	4s. 9d., 100 lbs.[88]
Drugs*	12 Car. II, c. 4	English-built ships paid 1/3 duties[89]
Ostrich wool*	12 Car. II, c. 4	5s. 3-3/5d., cwt.[90]
Goatskins*	15 Geo. III, c. 35[91]	3s. 9-9/20d., doz.[92]
Iron*	2 Gul. & Mar., sess. 2, c. 4	9s. 4½d., ton

* If carried in English-built ships.

---

subsequent statutes (14 Car. II, c. 11, xxxiv; 22 & 23 Car. II, c. 11, xii). 5 & 6 Gul. & Mar., c. 24 gave the rebate on the first three voyages. Moreover, privileges granted importers sometimes required that they use English-owned or English-built ships. For example, 7 Geo. III, c. 43, ii (1766) limited the importation of cambric and French lawn into London to English-owned ships; 35 Geo. III, c. 110 (1795) reduced the bounty granted on sugar if it was exported in foreign vessels; 35 Geo. III, c. 117 (1795) allowed English-built ships, when prices reached a prescribed level, to import rapeseed and other seed used to extract oils; 36 Geo. III, c. 113 (1796) allowed English-built vessels to bring linseed and rapeseed cakes duty-free; and 43 Geo. III, c. 68, xxix (1803) provided that Russian and Turkish tobacco should be imported directly in English-built ships.

[86] The distinction in duties made on fish and whale fins was primarily to benefit the English fisheries, and has not been included here (see *infra*, n. 101). For other privileges given English-built ships, see *supra*, p. 360.

[87] The difference in duty is of 1730, taken from Crouch, *A Complete View of the British Customs*, wherever the preference existed at that date. The duty has also been taken from Crouch in the case of cotton wool (imported), goatskins, logwood, and raw linen yarn.

[88] English-built ships might import duty-free; others paid 11 and 2/5 twentieths of a penny per pound of cotton wool.

[89] If they came directly from the place of growth. Beginning July 25, 1782, drugs of Hungary and Germany received the preferential treatment if imported from the Austrian Netherlands or Germany (22 Geo. III, c. 78, i).

[90] 12 Car. II, c. 4 simply provided that ostrich wool should be free, if imported in English-built ships; it was first rated by 11 Geo. I, c. 7 (1724), if imported in foreign-built ships.

[91] Originally temporary, but apparently continued. See Reeves, *Law of Shipping and Navigation*, p. 386.

[92] In the hair; a higher duty existed on tanned skins. Under the statute English-built ships could import goatskins duty free.

EARLY PREFERENTIAL DUTIES ON IMPORTS (*Continued*)

Commodity	Statute	Preferential Duty
Silk, wrought*	12 Car. II, c. 4	
from East Indies, direct		1-2/5*d*., lb.[93]
from Italy, direct		1*s*. 8-3/5*d*., lb.
Spices, except pepper*	12 Car. II, c. 4[94]	English-built ships paid 1/3 duties[94]
Yarn, raw linen	29 Geo. II, c. 15[95]	2¼*d*. to 7½*d*., lb.[96]

EARLY PREFERENTIAL DUTIES ON EXPORTS

Commodity	Statute	Preferential Duty
Coal*	12 Car. II, c. 4	3*s*., ton[97]
Corn	25 Car. II, c. 1, xxxi[98]	2*s*.6*d*. to 5*s*., quarter (bounty to English ships)[99]
Beer*	12 Car. II, c. 4	4*s*., ton[100]
Fish, English-caught	12 Car. II, c. 4, v	Various[101]
Logwood*	7 Geo. III, c. 47	1*s*., cwt.[102]
Cotton wool of colonies*	19 Geo. III, c. 53	£5 10*s*., for £100 value[103]

* If carried in English-built ships.

[93] According to the rating of 12 Car. II, c. 4, the difference in duty paid under the Old Subsidy was 3*d*. a pound for East Indian and 4*d*. a pound for Italian silk. 11 Gul. III, c. 10 prohibited the import of wrought silk of the East Indies, except for reëxport, and removed all duties except the half-subsidy after Sept. 29, 1701. Beginning July 25, 1782, organzined thrown silk of Hungary, or any port subject to the emperor of Germany or to Austria, could be brought from the Austrian Netherlands or Germany at the same rate as like silks imported from Italy (22 Geo. III, c. 78, ii). In 1815 the act of 55 Geo. III, c. 29, xii provided that thrown silk of Italy, Sicily, and Naples, coming from Malta in English-built ships, should pay the same rate as if imported direct; and in 1817 the act of 57 Geo. III, c. 4 extended the same privileges to thrown silk from Gibraltar.

[94] *Supra*, n. 89. See also 9 Gul. III, c. 23; 8 Anne, c. 12, vi; and 8 Geo. I, c. 15.

[95] Continued by 10 Geo. III, c. 38 and 19 Geo. III, c. 27.

[96] The figure given is approximate; the exact duty in 1730 was 2*d*. 5 9/20 twentieths, per pound of Dutch raw linen yarn, and 7*d*. 10 9/20 twentieths, per pound of French raw linen yarn. English-built ships might import the yarn duty-free under the legislation cited.

[97] In 1660 the extra duty was 5*s*. per London chaldron (about 1 1/3 tons) and 8*s*. per Newcastle chaldron (about 2½ tons). There were numerous changes in the coal duties and in the amount of discrimination. For example, see 6 & 7 Gul. & Mar., c. 18; 6 Anne, c. 50; 8 Anne, c. 14; 9 Anne, c. 6; 13 Anne, c. 18, ix; 6 Geo. I, c. 4; also see Nef, *British Coal Industry*, II, 233-36. In the customs revision of 1787 the discrimination was 4*s*. per ton; in 1803, 4*s*. 3*d*.; in 1809, 4*s*. 7*d*.; in 1819 and 1825, 4*s*. 3*d*.; in 1833, 3*s*. 4*d*. An Order in Council of July 29, 1842, directed that the higher duty should not be charged ships of a country with which England had a reciprocity treaty when they exported coal to that country; later Orders allowed such ships to export coal at the low duties to third countries (Clements, *Customs Guide*, pp. 122, 191). In 1845 all duties were removed from coal exported in English ships (8 & 9 Vict., c. 7), but a duty of 4*s*. was continued on coal exported in foreign ships (8 & 9 Vict., c. 90). This did not appear in the customs duties of 1853 (16 & 17 Vict., c. 106). Similarly, a duty and discrimination was placed on culm and cinders.

In 1787 the old system of customs based on fixed valuations or ratings was replaced by specific duties.[104] In the customs tables of that year and the general revisions following in 1803, 1809, and 1819, all goods on which higher duties were assessed when carried in foreign vessels may easily be determined. Most of the originally enumerated European articles were still affected. The following table indicates what articles and what discriminating duties were included in each of the general revisions.[105]

---

[98] This statute lapsed in 1679, but was revived by 1 Gul. & Mar., c. 12 in 1688. Except for temporary suspensions, the bounty remained until abolished in 1814 (54 Geo. III, c. 69). See also 6 Anne, c. 29, xviii; 13 Geo. III, c. 43, xi; 31 Geo. III, c. 30, iii; 33 Geo. III, c. 65, xv; 44 Geo. III, c. 109. For a few war years, half the bounty was granted to foreign ships (20 Geo. III, c. 31 and continuing acts).

[99] The bounties were given only when the price of corn was at or under certain specified amounts. By the legislation of 1688 the bounty was 5s. a quarter for wheat, at 48s. or under; 3s. 6d. for rye at 32s.; 2s. 6d. for barley and malt at 24s. Later acts made changes in the sale-price requirement and added other varieties of grain produce, notably oats, meals, and flours. The bounty remained constant for wheat and barley; after 1773 it dropped to 3s. on rye and appeared at 2s. on oats. After 1791 English build was specified for ships receiving the bounty. For statute references, see *supra*, n. 98; and Barnes, *History of the English Corn Laws.*

[100] The figure given is based on the Old Subsidy of tonnage as given in 12 Car. II, c. 4. The duty was removed by 22 & 23 Car. II, c. 13.

[101] Englishmen exporting in English vessels paid no duty. The duty paid by others was based upon the values in the Book of Rates which listed hake, oysters, pilchards (if exported by strangers), sprats, and various sorts of herring. Despite the provision in 12 Car. II, c. 18, that where any privilege was given to goods imported or exported in English-built shipping the ship be manned as that Act required, it was ruled that a ship did not have to have an English crew to export properly caught fish duty free (BM Add MSS 36109, pp. 18-19, 120-21). However, when aliens were accorded the privilege of exporting English-caught fish duty free in an English ship, it was specified that the master and at least three-fourths of the mariners should be English (25 Car. II, c. 6, iii). The export duty on fish was entirely removed by 8 Geo. I, c. 15, ix. It must be remembered, however, that this discussion does not cover the regulations to develop the fisheries such as the duties (12 Car. II, c. 18, v; 15 Car. II, c. 7, xiv) and the prohibitions (18 & 19 Car. II, c. 2, ii; 10 Gul. III, c. 13, viii; 1 Geo. I, stat. 2, c. 18) regulating the importation of foreign-caught fish; the bounties paid to vessels in the white herring fishery (11 Geo. III, c. 31; 26 Geo. III, c. 81); in the Greenland and whale fisheries (11 Geo. III, c. 38; 16 Geo. III, c. 47; 22 Geo. III, c. 19; 26 Geo. III, c. 41 and c. 50); in Newfoundland (15 Geo. III, c. 31; 26 Geo. III, c. 26); and to those exporting pilchards (25 Geo. III, c. 58).

[102] Logwood could be exported duty free in English-built ships; the duty when carried in foreign ships remained in the customs revisions of 1787, 1803, and 1809 at 1s. 2d., 1s. 4d., and 1s. 8d., respectively.

[103] The figure given is the duty as of 1787 (27 Geo. III, c. 13); English-built ships could export such cotton wool free of duty. No duty appeared in the later customs revisions.

[104] 24 Geo. III, c. 16 (1784) had repealed alien duties so far as they pertained to goods of foreign-born persons, but had specifically retained the discriminating duties upon goods carried in foreign ships.

[105] Of course changes in customs duties were made between the general revisions.

PREFERENTIAL DUTIES ON IMPORTS, 1787 TO 1823

Commodity[106]	1787[107]	1803[108]	1809[109]	1819[110]
Barilla, cwt.[111]			8d.	Various
Brandy, gal.			2d.	2d.
Brimstone, cwt.			8d. to 1s.	8d. to 1s. 3d.
Bristles, 12 lbs.				
Rough	1½d.[112]	2d.[112]	4d.	5d.
Dressed	2d.	2d.	8d.	1s.
Butter, cwt.				5s.
Cheese, cwt.[113]				2s. 6d.
Cork, cwt.			8d.	9d.
Cotton wool, 100 lbs.		8s. 4d.	8s. 7d.	6 percent[114]
Currants, cwt.	1s. 6d.	1s. 8d.	2s. 8d.	3s. 2d.
Down, lb.		1d.[112]	2d.	2d.
Ostrich wool, cwt.	7s. 9d.	5s. 4d.	6s. 8d.	
Feathers, cwt.	1s. 8d.[112]	1s. 10d. [112]	5s. 4d.	6s. 4d.
Figs, cwt.	6d.	5d.	1s. 4d.	1s. 6d.
Flax, cwt.				
Rough	3d.		2d.	3d.
Dressed	2s. 2d.	5s. 3d.	7s. 4d.	9s.
Hemp, cwt.				
Rough	3d.	2d.	1s.	1s. 2d.
Dressed	2s. 9d.	3s. 8d.	4s.	5s.
Hides, each[115]		10d.	1s. 4d.[116]	1s. 8d.

[106] The protection given in the case of fish, fish oil, and whale fins has been omitted because it was primarily to benefit English fishing.

[107] 27 Geo. III, c. 13, effective May 10, 1787.

[108] 43 Geo. III, c. 68, effective July 5, 1803.

[109] The duties given are the war or temporary duties, which were one-third more than the so-called "permanent" duties established by the act, except for (1) wines; (2) fir timber of Norway, more than eight and less than ten inches square, on which no additional war duties were placed; and (3) cotton wool, the war duty on which was the same for English and foreign ships and almost equal to the "permanent" duty for English ships. The "permanent" duties never came into effect, for the war duties were continued (54 Geo. III, c. 64 and 56 Geo. III, c. 29). In fact, further duties, involving increased discrimination, were placed on certain woods (50 Geo. III, c. 77; 51 Geo. III, c. 93; 52 Geo. III, c. 117); and linens (51 Geo. III, c. 44); and in addition an increase of 66 2/3 percent on French goods and 25 percent on other goods (53 Geo. III, c. 33).

[110] 59 Geo. III, c. 52, effective July 5, 1819.

[111] In 1819 listed under alkali.

[112] Of Muscovy only.

[113] Except that of Ireland.

[114] Until Jan. 5, 1820, the discrimination was 8s. 7d. per hundredweight; thereafter, £6 per £100.

[115] Hides were those untanned, and included buffalo, bull, cow, horse, mare, and gelding.

[116] The Crown was authorized to permit, by Order in Council, hides, together with calf and goatskins, to be imported in foreign ships on payment of the same duties as when imported in English-built ships.

PREFERENTIAL DUTIES ON IMPORTS, 1787 TO 1823 (*Continued*)

Commodity	1787	1803	1809	1819
Iron, ton				
Bars	11s.	12s. 7d.	£1 4s.	£1 8s. 4d.
Bars of Muscovy	12s. 11d.	14s. 10d.	£1 4s.[117]	£1 8s. 4d.[117]
Rods			£1 6s. 6d.	£1 10s.
Rods of Muscovy	6s. 6d.	10s.	£1 6s. 6d.[117]	£1 10s.[117]
Kelp, cwt.			8d.	Various
Lemons, 1000			1s.	2s. 6d.
Linen[118]	Various	Various	Various	Various
(*e.g.*, Russian towelling) 120 ells	8d.	9d.	2s. 4d.	3s. 4d.
Masts, each	½d. to 3d.	4d. to 9d.	8d. to 1s. 4d.	1s. 6d. to 3s.
Mats, 100	9d.[112]	9d.[112]	1s.[112]	1s. 3d.
Olive oil, tun	8s. 11d.	9s. 4d.	16s. 8d.	£1
Salad oil, gal.	1d.	1d.	8d.	£1[117]
Oranges, 1000			1s.	2s. 6d.
Pearlashes, cwt.			8d.	10d.
Pitch	8d., last	8d., last	1s. 4d., last	1d., cwt.
Potashes, cwt.			8d.	10d.
Prunes, cwt.			1s.	1s.
Rags, ton			1s. 4d.	2s. to 4s.
Raisins, cwt.	1d. to 5d.	2d. to 5d.	1s.	1s.
Rosin, cwt.	1d.	2d.	8d.	9d.
Salt, wey	4d.	6d.	1s.	duty free, but excise
Silk, wrought Italian, lb.	2s. 4d.			
Skins and furs[119]		Various	Various[116]	Various
(*e.g.*, calves), doz.		3s.	4s. 4d.	5s.
Spirits, Geneva, gal.			2d.	2d.
Stones, emery, cwt.	1d.			
Tallow, cwt.			8d.	10d.
Tar, last	8½d.	9d.	1s. 4d.	1s. 6d.
Tow, cwt.	2d.[112]	3d.[112]	8d.	10d.
Wines, tun[120]	£2 16s. to £4 4s.	£3 3s. to £4 4s.	£3 5s. to £4 6s. 6d.	£3 3s. to £4 4s.
Wood	Various	Various	Various	Various
(*e.g.*, clapboards), 120	2d.	6d.	1s. 4d.	3s.
Yarn, raw linen, cwt.			11s. 10d. to 12s. 6d.	16s. 8d.	19s.

Beginning in 1823 a reciprocity policy was inaugurated, which allowed foreign ships equal import and tonnage duties, drawbacks, bounties,

[117] Not listed separately; included under item above.

[118] There were many varieties of linen, including sailcloth. The 1787 and the 1803 discriminatory duties applied to Russian linens only; those of 1809 and 1819 included other than Russian linens.

[119] Calf, dog, elk, goat, seal (and in 1819 kip also) were the skins listed, with different duties and different amounts of discrimination.

[120] Discriminating duties also appeared on wines entered for prisage, varying in 1787 from £1 16s. 7d. to £2 15s.; in 1803 from £1 13s. 11d. to £2 15s. (most wines £2 3s. 7d. or more); in 1809 £1 15s. 6d. to £2 18s. (most wines £2 5s. or more); in 1819 £3 3s. to £4 4s.

allowances, and pilotage fees, if similar privileges were given English ships in ports of the country concerned;[121] and in the general revision of the Navigation Laws in 1825 no provision was made for continuing the old alien duties on ships carrying enumerated goods. The customs tables after that date omit the old rate distinction. However, a countervailing duty might be levied by Order in Council on any goods imported in ships of a country which levied higher duties on English ships than on national ships, or which had not placed English commerce and navigation on a most-favored-nation basis.[122]

EFFECTIVE DATES

Except in a few instances it has been impractical to state when the different provisions of the several acts went into effect. Certain clauses of the Navigation Act of 1660 (12 Car. II, c. 18) became operative as soon as the measure received the royal assent on September 13, 1660 (Stock, *Proceedings and Debates,* I, 282), but the effective date of others was postponed to October 20, 1660, to December 1, 1660, to April 1, 1661, and even to September 1, 1661. Thus whenever it is important to set the effective date of a regulation within a matter of months, reference should be made to the statute involved for the exact date, except in the few instances when the day as well as the year are specified herein.

Similarly, in the case of repeal, various phases of the navigation code were modified or altered as has been indicated,[123] but the protective system as a whole was not abandoned until the act of 12 & 13 Vict., c. 29, which did not become effective until January 1, 1850, more than six months after its enactment. Even then England reserved the right to retaliate if other countries discriminated against her shipping, continued to require that English ships be English manned until August 20, 1853 (16 & 17 Vict., c. 131, xxxi), and did not open the coasting trade to foreigners until March 23, 1854 (17 & 18 Vict., c. 5).

---

[121] 4 Geo. IV, c. 77. Earlier reciprocity treaties existed with the United States and Portugal; and the law providing for their enforcement (59 Geo. III, c. 54) was specifically extended to the subsequent treaties by 1 & 2 Vict., c. 113, xxvii. For reciprocity treaties see Hertslet, *Commercial Treaties*; Clements, *Customs Guide,* p. 19; Ellis, *British Tariff,* p. 9.

[122] 4 Geo. IV, c. 77, x. The countervailing duty was limited to one-fifth by 6 Geo. IV, c. 104 and c. 111. Similarly, additional duties of tonnage might be charged (5 Geo. IV, c. 1, iii); and foreign ships of less than 60 tons might be exempted from taking pilots (4 Geo. IV, c. 77, v).

[123] In the eighteenth century the habit developed of revising the entire code from time to time, and the citations to measures repealed by such statutes as 3 Geo. IV, c. 41, 42, 44 (1822); 6 Geo. IV, c. 105 (1825); 3 & 4 Gul. IV, c. 50 (1833); and 8 & 9 Vict., c. 84 (1845) may be helpful to those who wish to find references to minor acts which had to be omitted here.

II

PORT BOOKS EXAMINED

In the case of the years marked with an asterisk, the tabulations made distinguished between English ships, third-party carriers, and foreign ships carrying goods to or from their own countries. In other cases distinction was made only between English and foreign vessels.

East Coast Ports

Newcastle
*1616	E190/188/6
*1637	192/
*1674	

Hull
*1614	E190/313/8
1634	317/7
*1640	318/7
1670	320/11

Lynn
*1613	E190/434/1
*1638	435/7
*1662	436/1
1663	436/2

Yarmouth
*1612	E190/484/2
1648	492/11
*1649	492/11
*1662	493/5

Ipswich
*1617	E190/601/2
1639	605/2
1644	605/13
1670	607/13

West Coast Ports

Southampton
*1638	E190/824/8
1644	825/2
*1667	826/13
*1673	828/2

Dartmouth and
  Exeter
      *1638   E190/950/7
       1641   951/8
      *1662   953/6
       1663   953/8

Plymouth
      *1638   E190/1035/10
      *1666   1037/17
      *1672   1039/5

Bristol
       1638   E190/1136/10
       1671   1137/2

BIBLIOGRAPHY

BIBLIOGRAPHY

Manuscript Sources

Since conclusions are determined fully as much by what is left out as by what is put in, the following description is offered of the research methods employed. It does not pretend to be a complete account of the materials available for the various topics studied. Except in so far as the footnotes may suffice, that task has been deferred for the supplementary volumes to which reference was made in the preface.

The Public Record Office supplied the greater part of the material upon which the study rests. Access to the relevant documents was facilitated by a detailed examination of the Calendars of State Papers Domestic, State Papers Colonial, Treasury Books, and Treasury Papers, whenever they were available for the years from 1650 to 1696, and by occasional references to the same sets and to the Calendars of State Papers Foreign for other periods.

The leads so disclosed were supplemented by reference to Giuseppi's *Guide*, to Andrews' *Guide*, and to the official *Lists and Indexes*, and were followed up by personal examination of promising collections. Included in such material were the Privy Council Registers, the Journals of the various committees governing trade and plantations from 1660 to 1696, the naval officer's shipping lists, the Audit Office declared accounts, the pass figures and other shipping statistics of the Admiralty Office, the customs accounts of imports and exports, the port books returned to the Exchequer, its records of trials and seizures and those among the High Court of Admiralty papers, the reports on commercial conditions in the Colonial Office papers, various accounts of frauds and summaries of administrative procedure in the Treasury and Colonial Office collections, the Shaftesbury papers, and other manuscripts too numerous to mention.

Next in order of importance were the manuscripts in the British Museum. Here the *Guide* of Andrews and Davenport gave welcome assistance in finding documents relating to the colonies, but those dealing with England had to be uncovered by the laborious process of scanning the various catalogues, page by page, and checking the references thus obtained with those included in the classified catalogue. The most useful manuscripts were those relating to the work of the Privy Council, and to the customs administration in Ireland, the Isle of Man, and the Channel Isles, the Attorney and Solicitor General's opinions in revenue cases, Plumpton's and Caesar's data about maritime conditions, under Elizabeth and James I, the statistics for London trade in 1663 and 1669, and those of British ships and seamen in the eighteenth century. In the department of printed books, much use was made of the tracts and broadsides, the books of rates and customs guides, the manuals for Exchequer practice, and innumerable other works of all sorts.

Other pamphlet and broadside literature was found in the Goldsmiths' Library, the Library of Congress, the Huntington Library, the Seligman Library at Columbia, and the Guildhall, and, at all but the last two, use was also made of their manuscript collections.

The records of the London Custom House helped to clear up many administrative questions and furnished statistical data of value, and the seventeenth-century volumes remaining at Trinity House proved invaluable in studying the origins of the laws. The library at Lloyds contained valuable material for late eighteenth-century shipping, and the muster rolls retained in the Office of the Registrar General of Shipping and Seamen date back to 1768.

Further assistance was received from the collection of colonial statutes in the Columbia School of Law, the ships' logs (mostly for the late eighteenth century) in the Essex Institute at Salem, and the merchants' accounts, papers, and correspondence, and other documents, in the libraries of the Columbia School of Business, the Maryland Historical Society, the Massachusetts Historical Society, the New York Historical Society, the New York Public Library, and the Pennsylvania Historical Society. The manuscripts in the Virginia State House include a number on the tobacco trade and court trials, while the Massachusetts Archives contain much material, not yet printed, which helps to explain seventeenth-century developments.

Any attempt at a critical discussion of all the manuscripts used would require a volume several times this size. An exception, however, should be made for the statistics of trade for 1663 and 1669. Although relevant points concerning them have already been mentioned in various footnotes, their importance to the study and the frequency with which misconceptions concerning them recur warrant a summary of the reasons for accepting their authenticity and particularly that of the copy upon which we rely, BM Add MSS 36785.

The statistics were compiled as a result of an investigation by a committee of the House of Lords appointed on October 25, 1669, "to consider of the causes and grounds of the fall of rents and decay of trade within these Kingdoms." On November 8 it ordered the Farmers of the Customs to prepare a detailed account of trade for the seven years ending at Michaelmas. On March 3 they were ordered to bring in as much of the account as they had finished. This was delivered two days later and has been described as being "an account of all goods imported and exported for 1663 and 1669."[1] The better view, however, is that it contained only figures for London.

Davenant states that when preparing a report to comply with the order of the Commissioners of Accounts of July 17, 1711, he found a manuscript in the Custom House which contained

. . . an abstract drawn out almost in the same form as the ledgers of my office are now kept, with the then valuations of all the commodities, but it only gives an account of the several goods and merchandizes, of the growth of England, exported out of the city of London, and an account of the several goods and merchandizes that were imported into the said city, from Michaelmas 1662 to Michaelmas 1663, and from Michaelmas 1668 to Michaelmas 1669, but it takes no notice of what we properly call the re-exports, viz. foreign goods and plantation goods carried to other countries by certificate, in time, or out of time, whereof consideration should be had in stating the balance between two kingdoms. It is to be wished the like abstract (which appears to me an authentick copy of what had been offered to the House of Commons, but in what year I cannot find) could be obtained of the out-ports for the said two years, but it is not come to me . . .[2]

Davenant, however, thought that an allowance could be made for the trade of the outports based upon the proportion of the customs paid by London and by the outports, which was £1,268,095 to £346,081, for the year beginning Michaelmas, 1676, or "about 3-4ths, according to which the imports and exports may be computed." For the convenience of the Commissioners he planned to annex a copy of the manuscript to his report. The volume in the British Museum known as Add MSS 36785 is probably this "annexed" copy.[3]

During the discussion concerning a commercial treaty with France at the beginning of the eighteenth century, the Commissioners of the Customs failed to find any record in their office of orders having been given for the compilation of such statistics by their predecessors, and they prepared another set for 1669, which gives different figures.[4] The doubt thus cast upon the authenticity of the earlier set is not serious. As the manuscripts of the House of Lords show, it was the Customs Farmers rather than the Customs Commissioners who ordered the compilation, and the discrepancy between the two sets of figures may have been due to an attempt to include both outport and London statistics in the Commissioners' compilation or merely to mistakes arising from a hasty compilation of data from records which were more than forty years old.

Moreover, ample corroboration can be found for the accuracy of the

[1] HMC VIII, 135.
[2] *Works*, V, 351.
[3] *Works*, V, 351-52. Cf. Clark, *Guide to English Commercial Statistics*, p. xv n.
[4] *British Merchant*, II, 56-57, 300.

figures in BM Add MSS 36785. Except for minor discrepancies, transpositions, and other obvious clerical errors, the quantities given in two papers in the House of Lords Manuscripts,[5] which purport to be "Goods Imported" and "Goods Exported," prove to be the same as the British Museum manuscript figures for London's trade with Holland in 1669. The "Old Scheme" of trade with France in 1674, which was supposed to have been introduced into Parliament "by that worthy Patriot the Famous Mr. Sacheverell," likewise was based upon the statistics for 1669 with respect to quantities, although slight changes were made in the values.[6] A manuscript in the Board of Trade papers gives substantially the same data, except that it gives no values and does not mention that the figures relate only to London.[7] Confirmation of the values as well as quantities can be found in Davenant's Report and in an "Extract of several Calculations taken by Mr. Pollexfen [a member of the Board of Trade] from a Manuscript in the hands of Mr. Blathwayt [then clerk to the Privy Council]" which gives values only and is noted as having been received by the Board on October 28, 1702.[8]

The similarity in values, however, merely indicates that the documents all had the same source and does not establish the correctness of the valuation. The *Mercator* and the *British Merchant* had very different ideas on the subject;[9] Davenant believed that imports were overrated[10] and the Farmers of the Customs themselves had confessed in 1669 that the values were uncertain.[11] But, as has been pointed out, the discrepancy between the values for 1663-1669 and those for 1698 is not as great as one would expect.[12]

Attention should also be called to the criticism of eighteenth-century English statistics in the recent volume by G. N. Clark, *Guide to English Commercial Statistics*. It describes the inaccuracies in the "official values" used in the Inspector General's Accounts[13] and notes that the tonnage figures may have been underestimated by as much as 50 percent. But as Professor Clark well says, such criticisms of the statistics "are merely directions for effective work, not warnings against expecting useful results."

Fortunately, the inaccuracies do not materially affect our conclusions. However detrimental the discrepancy between the official valuation and the real value may be for other purposes, the relative fixity of the official values makes them more useful to us, since we are not interested in the

---

[5] Calendared in HMC VIII, 134-35.
[6] *British Merchant,* I, 156-61; II, 61.
[7] CO 388/2.
[8] CO 388/8 E31; Davenant, *Works,* V, 347-463.
[9] *British Merchant,* I and II, *passim.*
[10] *Works,* V, 366-68.
[11] HMC VIII, 135 n.
[12] *Supra,* p. 344 n. 61.
[13] CO 3, from which the tables in Whitworth, *State of Trade,* were compiled.

balance of trade but in the extent to which the volume of trade increased. It would, of course, be preferable to have completely accurate tonnage statistics, but the underestimation of the tonnage of vessels should not affect the relationship between English and foreign tonnage. If the 50-percent discrepancy extended back from 1773 to 1582, it would not affect the conclusions to be drawn from our chronological survey of English maritime development, since all the statistics would be increased in the same proportion. If, as seems more probable, the underestimation did not become significant until the increase in the number of lighthouses[14] gave shipmasters more incentive for minimizing the tonnages upon which light-house dues were assessed we would have to add to the figures after 1702. Such a correction would not lead to results inconsistent with our other evidence. In fact it would help to eliminate the discrepancy in the collier statistics which fail to increase as rapidly after 1702 as might be expected.[15] As far as foreign trade is concerned, the correction would merely indicate that English shipping had made even greater gains in that field after the Acts were passed than we had previously calculated and that the suggested error in estimating tonnage tended to belittle rather than to exaggerate the influence of the Acts.

Similarly the criticisms which have been directed against another set of our basic statistics, the Sound Toll Registers as tabulated in Nina E. Bang's *Tables*, do not materially affect the conclusions which we have drawn.[16] It is true that the master of an occasional vessel might declare himself or his vessel to be Dutch when entering the Sound, Russian when leaving, and any convenient nationality in time of war, and that for these and other reasons the figures do not warrant conclusions concerning minute points like the distribution of shipping among the several towns of Holland (problems which aroused the criticisms), but the range of error is comparatively narrow, and the *Tables* are an invaluable addition to our knowledge. When studied over a period of decades to discover the general trend of trade, misdescriptions tend to offset each other. At least the *Tables* lead us to general conclusions the same as those derived from the English port books and the Scandinavian records.[17]

Printed Works Cited

The following list makes no pretense to completeness. It is merely a list of titles to supplement the abbreviated forms used in the footnotes. More

---

[14] Adams, *Lighthouses and Lightships*, pp. 289-311.
[15] *Supra*, pp. 336-37.
[16] Brakel, "Schiffsheimat und Schifferheimat in den Sundzollregistern," *Hansische Geschichtsblätter* (1915), pp. 211-28; Brünner, "Die Waarde der Skibsfart-Tabellen," *Bijdragen voor Vaderlandsche Geschiedenis*, 5th series, IX, 269-80.
[17] *Supra*, pp. 307, n. 34, 310-19.

extensive bibliographical material can be found in the *Bibliography of British History*, by Conyers Read for the Tudor period, 1485-1603 (Oxford, 1933), by Godfrey Davies for the Stuart period, 1603-1714 (Oxford, 1928); W. T. Morgan, *A Bibliography of British History, 1700-1715* (Vol. I, *1700-1707*. Indiana University Studies Nos. 94, 95, Bloomington, 1931-32); J. B. Williams, *A Guide to the Printed Materials for English Social and Economic History, 1750-1850* (2 vols., New York, 1926); or in *The Term Catalogues, 1668-1709 and 1711,* ed. by E. Arber (3 vols., London, 1903-6); *Transcript of the Registers of the Stationers' Company, 1640-1708,* ed. by G. E. Briscoe Eyre (3 vols., London, 1913-14); *Catalogue of the Collection of Broadsides in the Goldsmiths' Library* (London, 1930); G. A. R. Callender, *Bibliography of Naval History* (2 vols., Historical Association Leaflets, Nos. 58, 61, London, 1924-25); G. E. Manwaring, *A Bibliography of British Naval History* (London, 1930); E. Channing, A. B. Hart, and F. J. Turner, *Guide to the Study and Reading of American History* (Boston, 1912); G. G. Griffin, *Writings on American History* (New York, 1908-); A. P. C. Griffin, *Bibliography of American Historical Societies* (American Historical Association, *Annual Report, 1905.* Washington, 1907); E. B. Greene and R. B. Morris, *A Guide to the Principal Sources for Early American History (1600-1800) in the City of New York* (New York, 1929); E. G. Swem, *Virginia Historical Index* (2 vols., Roanoke, 1934-36). See also the bibliographies in the following special works, cited hereafter: *Cambridge History of the British Empire;* Albion, *Forests and Sea Power;* Lipson, *Economic History;* Nef, *Rise of the British Coal Industry;* Scott, *Joint-Stock Companies;* and Winsor, *Narrative and Critical History of America.*

Most of the works published in English which are directly relevant to the subject should be found in the list of references or in the bibliographies cited, but that literature was so extensive as to preclude any attempt to cover the foreign material thoroughly. The foreign titles utilized were merely the more important of those to which my attention was called by chance references or by the kindness of friends, especially of Professor Violet Barbour of Vassar College.

Abbott, Charles, A Treatise of the Law Relative to Merchant Ships and Seamen. Boston, 1850.
Acts and Ordinances of the Eastland Company, ed. by Maud Sellers. London, 1906. "Royal Historical Society Publications, Camden Series," 3d series, XI.
Acts and Ordinances of the Interregnum, 1642-1660, ed. by C. H. Firth and R. S. Rait. 3 vols., London, 1911.
Adams, W. H. D., Lighthouses and Lightships; a Descriptive and Historical Account of Their Mode of Constructon and Organization. New York, 1870.
Advocate, The; or, A Narrative of the State and Conditions of Things between the English and Dutch Nation, in Relation to Trade. London,

1651. Probably written by Benjamin Worsley; see Andrews, The Colonial Period, IV, 23 n., 41 n., 60.

Albion, R. G., Forests and Sea Power; The Timber Problem of the Royal Navy, 1652-1862. Cambridge, Mass., 1926. "Harvard Economic Studies," XXIX.

Alvord, C. W., The Mississippi Valley in British Politics. 2 vols., Cleveland, 1917.

Ambrose, Gwilym, "English Traders at Aleppo (1658-1756)." *Economic History Review*, III (1931-32), 246-67.

American Antiquarian Society, Transactions and Collections. 12 vols., Worcester, 1820-1911.

Anderson, Adam, Historical and Chronological Deduction of the Origin of Commerce. 4 vols., London, 1787-89.

Andrews, C. M., "The Boston Merchants and the Non-Importation Movement." Publications of the Colonial Society of Massachusetts. *Transactions*, XIX (1918), 159-259.

—— British Committees, Commissions, and Councils of Trade and Plantations, 1622-1675. Baltimore, 1908. "Johns Hopkins University Studies in Historical and Political Science," XXVI, Nos. 1, 2, 3.

—— "Colonial Commerce." *American Historical Review*, XX (1914), 43-63.

—— The Colonial Period of American History. 4 vols., in progress, New Haven, 1934—.

—— Colonial Self-Government. The American Nation, a History, Vol. V, New York, 1905.

—— Guide to the Materials for American History, to 1783, in the Public Record Office of Great Britain. 2 vols., Washington, 1912-14. "Carnegie Institution of Washington, Publications," No. 90A.

—— and F. G. Davenport, Guide to the Manuscript Materials for the History of the United States to 1783, in the British Museum, in Minor London Archives, and in the Libraries of Oxford and Cambridge. Washington, 1907. "Carnegie Institution of Washington, Publications," No. 90.

Answer to Mr. Cary's Reply . . . , An. London, 1700.

Arnold, S. G., History of the State of Rhode Island and Providence Plantations. 2 vols., New York, 1860.

Ashe, S. A., History of North Carolina. Greensboro, 1908.

Ashley, Sir W. J., Surveys, Historic and Economic. London, 1900.

Ashton, T. S., and Joseph Sykes, The Coal Industry of the Eighteenth Century. Manchester, 1929.

Atton, Henry, and H. H. Holland, The King's Customs; an Account of Maritime Revenue & Contraband Traffic to the Year 1800. 2 vols., London, 1908-10.

"B. W.," Free Ports, the Nature and Necessity of Them Stated. London, 1652.

"B. Y.," The Modern Practice of the Court of Exchequer in Prosecutions relating to His Majesty's Revenue of the Customs . . . to Which Is Prefix'd an Account of the Settlements of the Extent and Limits of the Several Ports in England and Wales. London, 1731. (Ascribed to Francis Hargreave in a note on the British Museum copy.)

Baldwin, Samuel, A Survey of the British Customs. London, 1770.

Bal Krishna, Commercial Relations between India and England, 1601-1757. London, 1924.

Bang, Nina, Tabeller over Skibsfart og Varetransport Gennem Øresund, 1497-1660. Tables de la Navigation et du Transport des Marchandises passant par le Sund, 1497-1660. Copenhagen, 1906.

——— and Knud Korst, Tabeller over Skibsfart og Varetransport Gennem Øresund, 1661-1783, og Gennem Storebaelt, 1701-1748. Tables de la Navigation et du Transport des Marchandises passant par le Sund, 1661-1783, et par le Grand Belt, 1701-1748. Copenhagen, 1930.

Barbon, Nicholas, Discourse concerning Coining the New Money Lighter. London, 1696.

——— A Discourse of Trade. [London, 1690.] Reprints of Economic Tracts, ed. by J. H. Hollander. Baltimore, 1905.

Barbour, Violet, "Dutch and English Merchant Shipping in the Seventeenth Century." *The Economic History Review,* II (1929-30), 261-90.

——— Henry Bennet, Earl of Arlington, Secretary of State to Charles II. Washington, 1914.

——— "Marine Risks and Insurance in the Seventeenth Century." *Journal of Economic and Business History,* I (1929), 561-96.

Barnes, D. G., A History of the English Corn Laws from 1660-1846. London, 1930.

Bassett, J. S., "The Relation between the Virginia Planter and the London Merchant." Washington, 1902. American Historical Association. *Annual Report,* 1901, I, 551-75.

Basye, A. H., The Lords Commissioners of Trade and Plantations Commonly Known as the Board of Trade, 1748-1782. New Haven, 1925. "Yale Historical Publications. Miscellany," XIV.

Bates, W. W., American Marine; the Shipping Question in History and Politics. Boston and New York, 1893.

——— American Navigation; the Political History of Its Rise and Ruin and the Proper Means for Its Encouragement. Boston and New York, 1902.

Battie, John, The Merchants Remonstrance: Published in the Time of the Late Warre, Revived and Enlarged. London, 1648.

Beer, G. L., British Colonial Policy, 1754-1765. New York, 1907.

——— The Old Colonial System, 1660-1754. 2 vols., New York, 1912.

——— The Origins of the British Colonial System, 1578-1660. New York, 1908.

Bell, H. C., "British Commercial Policy in the West Indies, 1783-93." *English Historical Review*, XXXI (1916), 429-41.

—— "The West India Trade before the American Revolution." *American Historical Review*, XXII (1917), 272-87.

Bemis, S. F., Jay's Treaty: A Study in Commerce and Diplomacy. New York, 1923.

Benns, F. L., The American Struggle for the British West India Carrying-Trade, 1815-1830. Bloomington, Indiana, 1923. "Indiana University Studies," X, No. 56.

Beresford, John, The Godfather of Downing Street; Sir George Downing, 1623-1684. London, 1925.

Bieber, R. P., The Lords of Trade and Plantations, 1675-1696. Allentown, Pa., 1919.

Bining, A. C., British Regulation of the Colonial Iron Industry. Philadelphia, 1933.

Birdwood, Sir George, ed., The Register of Letters, etc. of the Governour and Company of Merchants of London Trading into the East Indies, 1600-1619. London, 1893.

Blackstone, Sir William, Commentaries on the Laws of England, ed. by Edward Christian. 4 vols., London, 1809.

Blackwell, John, An Essay towards Carrying on the Present War against France. London, 1695.

Blok, P. J., History of the People of the Netherlands, tr. by O. A. Bierstadt and Ruth Putnam. 5 vols., New York, 1898-1912.

"Boteler's Dialogues," ed. by W. G. Perrin. London, 1929. "Navy Records Society Publications," LXV.

Bouvier, John, A Law Dictionary, ed. by W. E. Baldwin. New York, 1926.

Boyd, Charles, The British Tariff and Commercial Guide. London, 1822.

Bradlee, F. B. C., "Colonial Trade and Commerce, 1733-1774." *The Essex Institute, Historical Collections*, LXIII (1927), 1-29.

Brakel, S. van, "Schiffsheimat und Schifferheimat in den Sundzollregistern." *Hansische Geschichtsblätter* (1915), pp. 211-28.

Brand, John, The History and Antiquities . . . of the Town of Newcastle upon Tyne. 2 vols., London, 1789.

Brewster, Sir Francis, Essays on Trade and Navigation in Five Parts. London, 1695.

Brinkmann, C., "England and the Hanse under Charles II." *English Historical Review*, XXIII (1908), 683-708.

—— "The Relations between England and Germany, 1660-1688." *English Historical Review*, XXIV (1909), 247-77, 448-69.

Britannia Languens; or a Discourse of Trade, Shewing That the Present Management of Trade in England Is the True Reason of the Decay of Our Manufactures. London, 1680. Usually attributed to William Petyt;

see, however, McCulloch's Introduction to reprint, Early English Tracts on Commerce, p. x.

British Merchant, The: A Collection of Papers relating to the Trade and Commerce of Great Britain and Ireland, comp. by Charles King. 3 vols., London, 1743.

Brodhead, J. R., History of the State of New York. 2 vols., New York, 1871-72.

Brown, William, Practice of His Majestie's Court of Exchequer at Westminster. London, 1699.

Browne, James, The Letter Book of James Browne of Providence, Merchant, 1735-38. Providence, 1929.

Bruce, P. A., Economic History of Virginia in the Seventeenth Century. 2 vols., New York and London, 1896.

Brünner, E. C. G., "Die Waarde der Skibsfart-Tabellen van Nina Ellinger Bang voor de kennis der Handelsgeschiedenis van Holland in de 16ᵉ eeuw." *Bijdragen voor Vaderlandsche Geschiedenis en Oudheidkunde,* 5th series, IX (1922), 269-80.

Bryant, Arthur, Samuel Pepys: The Years of Peril. New York, 1935.

Burnet, Gilbert, Bishop of Salisbury, History of My Own Time . . . ed. by Sir Thomas Burnet. 2 vols., London, 1724-34.

Burrell, Andrewes, The Humble Remonstrance of Andrewes Burrell Gent. for a Reformation of England's Navie. London, 1646.

Burton, Philip, Practice of the Office of Pleas in the Court of Exchequer. 2 vols., London, 1791.

Burton, Thomas, Diary of. . . . 4 vols., London, 1828.

"C. K.," Some Seasonable and Modest Thoughts Partly Occasioned by, and Partly Concerning the Scots East-India Company. By an Unfeigned and Hearty Lover of England. Edinburgh, 1696.

Calendar of the Court Minutes of the East India Company, 1635-[79] comp. by E. B. Sainsbury. Introductions and notes by Sir William Foster and W. T. Ottewill. Oxford, 1907—.

Cambridge History of the British Empire, The, ed. by J. H. Rose, A. P. Newton, and E. A. Benians, 6 vols., in progress, Cambridge, Eng., 1929—.

Carkesse, Charles, The Act of Tonnage and Poundage, and Rates of Merchandize. London, 1726.

Carr, C. T., ed., Select Charters of Trading Companies A. D. 1530-1707. London, 1913. "Publications of the Selden Society," XXVIII.

Carroll, B. R., ed., Historical Collections of South Carolina. 2 vols., New York, 1936.

Cary, John, An Essay on the Coyn and Credit of England: As They Stand with Respect to Its Trade. Bristol, 1696.

——— An Essay on the State of England in Relation to Its Trade. Bristol, 1695.

Cary, John, An Essay towards Regulating the Trade and Employing the Poor of This Kingdom. London, 1717.

———— An Essay towards the Settlement of a National Credit in the Kingdom of England. London, 1696.

Chalmers, George, ed., A Collection of Treaties between Great Britain and Other Powers. 2 vols., London, 1790.

———— An Estimate of the Comparative Strength of Britain. London, 1782.

Champion, Richard, Considerations on the Present Situation of Great Britain and the United States of North America. London, 1784.

Chance, J. F., "England and Sweden in the Time of William III and Anne." *English Historical Review,* XVI (1901), 676-711.

Channing, Edward, "Colonel Thomas Dongan, Governor of New York." *American Antiquarian Society Proceedings,* XVIII (1907), 336-45.

———— A History of the United States. 6 vols., New York, 1907-25.

Chapman, George, Ben Jonson, and John Marston, Eastward Hoe. Boston and London, 1905.

Child, Sir Josiah, A New Discourse of Trade. New ed. London, 1775.

———— A Short Reply to a Treatise, Entitled Interest of Money Mistaken, London, n. d.

———— "A Small Treatise against Usury," in A New Discourse of Trade. London, 1775.

Chitwood, O. P., Justice in Colonial Virginia. Baltimore, 1905. Johns Hopkins University Studies in Historical and Political Science, XXIII, Nos. 7-8.

Churchill, E. F., "The Dispensing Power and the Defence of the Realm." *The Law Quarterly Review,* XXXVII (1921), 412-41.

Clapham, J. H., "The Last Years of the Navigation Acts." *English Historical Review,* XXV (1910), 480-501, 687-707.

Clarendon, Edward Hyde, First Earl of, The History of the Rebellion and Civil Wars in England. 7 vols., Oxford, 1839.

Clark, A. H., The Clipper Ship Era, 1843-1869. New York and London, 1911.

Clark, G. N., The Dutch Alliance and the War against French Trade, 1688-1697. Manchester, 1923.

———— Guide to English Commercial Statistics, 1696-1782. London, 1938.

———— "The Navigation Act of 1651." *History,* new series, VII (1923), 282-86.

———— The Seventeenth Century. Oxford, 1929.

Clark, V. S., History of Manufactures in the United States, 1607-1860. 2 vols., Washington, 1916-1928. "Carnegie Institution of Washington, Publications," No. 215B.

Clarke, M. P., "The Board of Trade at Work." *American Historical Review,* XVII (1911-12), 17-43.

Clements, George, Customs Guide . . . London, 1844.

Clowes, W. L., The Royal Navy, a History from the Earliest Times to the Present. 7 vols., London, 1897-1903.

Cobbett, William, ed., Parliamentary History of England . . ., 1066-1803. 36 vols., London, 1806-20.

Coke, Roger, A Discourse of Trade in Two Parts. The First Treats of the Reason of the Decay of the Strength, Wealth, and Trade of England. The Latter of the Growth and Increase of the Dutch Trade above the English. London, 1670.

———— England's Improvements. In Two Parts: In the Former Is Discoursed How the Kingdom of England May Be Improved in Strength, Employment, Wealth, Trade. In the Latter Is Discoursed How the Navigation of England May Be Increased. London, 1675.

———— How the Navigation of England May Be Encreased. London, 1675.

———— A Treatise concerning the Regulation of the Coyn of England & How the East India Trade May Be Preserved and Increased. London, 1696.

Collins, E. D., "Studies in the Colonial Policy of England, 1672-1680: the Plantations, the Royal African Company, and the Slave Trade." American Historical Association. *Annual Report*, I (1900), 139-92.

Commerce of Rhode Island, 1726-1800. 2 vols., Boston, 1914-15. "Collections of the Massachusetts Historical Society," 7th series, IX-X.

Connecticut Historical Society. Collections. Hartford, 1870—.

Considerations Concerning Free Ports. London, n. d.

Corbett, Sir Julian S., England in the Mediterranean . . ., 1603-1713. 2 vols., London, New York, and Bombay, 1904.

Cornewall-Jones, R. J., The British Merchant Service. London, 1898.

Corney, Bolton, ed., The Voyage of Sir Henry Middleton to Bantam and the Maluco Islands. From the edition of 1606. London, 1856. "Hakluyt Society Publications," XIX.

Coxe, Tench, A View of the United States of America, in a Series of Papers Written at Various Times, between the Years 1787 and 1794. Philadelphia, 1794.

Cradocke, Francis, Wealth Discovered or an Essay upon a Late Expedient for Taking Away All Impositions and Raising a Revenue without Taxes. . . . London, 1661.

Crittenden, C. C., The Commerce of North Carolina, 1763-1789. New Haven, 1936. "Yale Historical Publications. Miscellany," XXIX.

Crosfield, Robert, England's Glory Revived. London, 1693.

Crouch, Henry, A Complete View of the British Customs. London, 1730.

Crump, H. J., Colonial Admiralty Jurisdiction in the Seventeenth Century. London, 1931.

Cunningham, William, The Growth of English Industry and Commerce in Modern Times. 4th ed. 2 vols., Cambridge, Eng., 1907.

Davenant, Charles, The Political and Commercial Works of That Cele-
brated Writer, . . ., ed. by Sir Charles Whitworth. 5 vols., London,
1771.

Deardorff, N. R., English Trade in the Baltic during the Reign of Elizabeth. Philadelphia and New York, 1912. "Studies in the History of
English Commerce in the Tudor Period."

Decker, Sir Matthew, An Essay on the Causes of the Decline of the
Foreign Trade, Consequently of the Value of the Lands of Britain
and on the Means to Restore Both. Dublin, 1751.

[Dennis, John], An Essay on the Navy, or England's Advantage and Safety
Prov'd Dependant on a Formidable and Well Disciplined Navy. London,
1702.

Dickerson, O. M., American Colonial Government, 1696-1765; a Study of
the British Board of Trade in Its Relation to the American Colonies.
Cleveland, 1912.

Dictionary of National Biography, The, ed. by Leslie Stephen and Sidney
Lee. 66 vols., London, 1885-1901.

Dietz, F. C., "Elizabethan Customs Administration." *English Historical
Review*, XLV (1930), 35-57.

Durham, F. H., "The Relations of the Crown to Trade under James I."
Royal Historical Society Transactions, New Series, XIII (1899),
199-247.

"Early Coastwise and Foreign Shipping of Salem." *The Essex Institute
Historical Collections*, LXII (1926), 193-200, 305-20; LXIII (1927),
49-64, 145-60, 349-64; LXVII (1931), 281-88, 409-24; LXVIII
(1932), 49-64, 241-56, 337-52; LXIX (1933), 49-64, 155-98.

Earnshaw, William, A Digest of the Laws Relating to Shipping, Navigation, Commerce, and Revenue in the British Colonies. London, 1818.

Elder, J. R., The Royal Fishery Companies of the Seventeenth Century.
Aberdeen, 1912. "Aberdeen University Studies," No. 52.

Ellis, Robert, The British Tariff . . . [London], 1829.

―――― The Laws and Practical Regulations . . . Connected with the
Commerce and Navigation of the British Empire. London, 1844.

English Factories in India, The; a Calendar of Documents in the India
Office, British Museum, and Public Record Office, ed. by William Foster.
13 vols., in progress, Oxford, 1906—.

Epstein, Mordecai, The Early History of the Levant Company. London,
1908.

Era of the American Revolution, The. New York, 1939.

Evans, F. M. G., "Emoluments of the Principal Secretaries of State in
the Seventeenth Century." *English Historical Review*, XXXV (1920),
513-28.

Evelyn, John, Diary . . . Familiar Letters and . . . Private Correspondence, ed. by William Bray. 4 vols., London, 1879.

Fanshaw, Sir Thomas, The Practice of the Exchequer Court. London, 1658.

Flippin, P. S., The Financial Administration of the Colony of Virginia. Baltimore, 1915. "Johns Hopkins University Studies in Historical and Political Science," XXXIII, No. 2.

Forster, Samuel, A Digest of All the Laws relating to the Customs, to Trade, and Navigation. London, 1727.

Fortrey, Samuel, England's Interest and Improvement. Consisting in the Increase of the Store and Trade of This Kingdom. London, 1673.

Fowler, David, Practice of the Court of Exchequer in Proceedings in Equity. 2 vols., London, 1795.

Fox, D. R., Caleb Heathcote, Gentleman Colonist, 1692-1721. New York, 1926.

Friis, Astrid, Alderman Cockayne's Project and the Cloth Trade; the Commercial Policy of England in Its Main Aspects, 1603-1625, tr. by Anne Fausbøll. Copenhagen and London, 1927.

Fry, Henry, The History of North Atlantic Steam Navigation. London, 1896.

Fussell, G. D., "English Countryside and Population in the Eighteenth Century." *Economic Geography,* XII (1936), 294-310, 411-30.

Gardiner, S. R., ed., Letters and Papers relating to the First Dutch War, 1652-1654. 6 vols., London, 1899-1930. "Navy Records Society Publications," XIII, XVII, XXX, XXXVII, XLI, LXVI.

—— ed., Parliamentary Debates in 1610. Edited from the notes of a member of the House of Commons. London, 1862. "Camden Society Publications," LXXXI.

Gee, Joshua, The Trade and Navigation of Great Britain Considered. London, 1731.

Gentleman, Tobias, England's Way to Win Wealth, and to Employ Ships and Mariners . . . [London, 1614]. *Harleian Miscellany,* III, 395-409.

Giesecke, A. A., American Commercial Legislation before 1789. New York, 1910.

Gilbert, Sir Geoffrey, A Treatise on the Court of Exchequer. London, 1758.

Gill, D. M., "The Treasury, 1660-1714." *English Historical Review,* XLVI (1931), 600-22.

Giuseppi, M. S., A Guide to the Manuscripts Preserved in the Public Record Office. 2 vols., London, 1923-24.

Goodrick, A. T. S., ed., Edward Randolph. Vols. VI and VII. See also Toppan, R. N. Boston, 1909. "Prince Society Publications."

Gras, N. S. B., "The Corn Bounty Experiment of Charles II." *Quarterly Journal of Economics,* XXIV (1910), 419-22.

—— The Early English Customs System; a Documentary Study . . . from the Thirteenth to the Sixteenth Century. Cambridge, Mass., 1918. "Harvard Economic Studies," XVIII.

Gras, N. S. B., Evolution of the English Corn Market from the Twelfth to the Eighteenth Century. Cambridge, Mass., 1915. "Harvard Economic Studies," XIII.

Gray, L. C., History of Agriculture in the Southern United States to 1860. 2 vols., Washington, 1933. "Carnegie Institution of Washington, Publications," No. 430.

Great Britain, Board of Trade. Annual Statement of the Navigation and Shipping of the United Kingdom, 1889. London, 1890.

––––––– Journals of the Commissioners for Trade and Plantations, 1704-1782. 14 vols., London, 1920-38.

Great Britain, Historical Manuscripts Commission. Reports on Collections of Manuscripts of Private Families, Corporations and Institutions. London, 1872-1928.

Great Britain, House of Commons. Journals of the House of Commons, 1547-19––. London, 1607[?]-19––.

Great Britain, House of Commons, Sessional Papers, 1822, XXI (274). Official Value of Imports and Exports.

––––––– Sessional Papers, 1830, XXVII (292). Official Value of British and Irish Produce and Manufacturers, and of Foreign and Colonial Produce, Exported from, together with Imports into, Great Britain and Ireland.

––––––– Sessional Papers, 1844, VIII (545). Report of the Select Committee on British Shipping, 1844, App. III, "A Return of Vessels, Entered Inwards and Cleared Outwards in the Ports of the United Kingdom, Year by Year, since the Year 1814, Distinguishing British from Foreign Ships and Sailing Vessels from Steamers; Noting the Countries from and to Which They Have Entered and Cleared Out . . ."

––––––– Sessional Papers. Tables of the Revenue, Population, Commerce . . . of the United Kingdom and Its Dependencies, 1820-1831, ed. by G. R. Porter, London, 1833, supplemented by yearly volumes until 1852. Thereafter continued, as respects tables used herein, by Annual Statement of Trade and Navigation of the United Kingdom with Foreign Countries and British Possessions. For citations *see* General Index . . . House of Commons . . . 1801-1852 (London, 1938), p. 458; General Alphabetical Index . . . House of Commons . . . 1852-1899 (London, 1909), pp. 1387, 1389-90. For similar references in the House of Lords, Sessional Papers *see* General Index . . . House of Lords . . . 1801-1859 (London, 1938), pp. 810, 915; General Index . . . House of Lords . . . 1859-1870 (London, 1872), p. 334.

Great Britain, House of Lords. Journals of the House of Lords, 1509-19––. London, 1578[?]-19––.

Great Britain, Laws. The Statutes at Large . . . of Great Britain. Continued as Statutes of the United Kingdom of Great Britain and Ireland. Vols. 1-46 ed. by D. Pickering, Cambridge, then London, 1762-1869.

Great Britain, The Statutes of the Realm . . . 1101-1713. 11 vols., London, 1810-28.

Great Britain, Privy Council. Acts of the Privy Council of England, 1542-1604, 1613-1626, ed. by J. R. Dasent and others. 41 vols., in progress, London, 1890—.

—— Acts of the Privy Council of England, Colonial Series, 1613-1783, ed. by W. L. Grant and James Munro. 6 vols., Hereford, 1908-12.

—— Report of a Committee of Lords of the Privy Council on the Trade of Great Britain with the United States, January 1791. Washington, 1888.

Great Britain, Public Record Office. Annual Report of the Deputy Keeper of the Public Records, 25th Report, Feb. 18, 1864.

—— Calendar of Letters, Despatches and State Papers Relating to the Negotiations between England and Spain . . ., ed. by G. A. Bergenroth, P. de Gayangos, M. A. S. Hume, Royall Tyler. 11 vols. in 17, London, 1862-1916.

—— Calendar of State Papers and Manuscripts Relating to English Affairs, Existing in the Archives and Collections of Venice . . . 36 vols., in progress, London, 1864—.

—— Calendar of State Papers, Colonial Series, ed. by W. N. Sainsbury, J. W. Fortescue, and Cecil Headlam. 38 vols., in progress, London, 1860—.

—— Calendar of State Papers, Domestic Series, ed. by John Bruce, F. H. Blackburn Daniell, M. A. E. Green, W. D. Hamilton, W. J. Hardy, S. C. Lomas, R. P. Mahaffy. In progress, London, 1856—.

—— Calendar of State Papers, Foreign Series, of the Reign of Elizabeth, ed. by J. Stevenson, A. J. Crosby, A. J. Butler, S. C. Lomas. 22 vols., in progress, London, 1863—.

—— Calendar of Treasury Books, 1660—, ed. by W. A. Shaw. 17 vols., in progress, London, 1904—.

—— Calendar of Treasury Books and Papers, 1729-1745, ed. by W. A. Shaw. 5 vols., London, 1868-1908.

—— Calendar of Treasury Papers, 1557-1728, ed. by Joseph Redington. 6 vols., London, 1868-89.

—— Letters and Papers, Foreign and Domestic, of the Reign of Henry VIII, ed. by J. S. Brewer, James Gairdner, R. H. Brodie. 21 vols., London, 1862-1910.

Greene, E. B., The Provincial Governor in the English Colonies of North America. Cambridge, Mass., 1898. "Harvard Historical Studies," VII.

—— and V. D. Harrington, American Population before the Federal Census of 1790. New York, 1932.

Guttridge, G. H., ed., The American Correspondence of a Bristol Merchant, 1766-1776. Letters of Richard Champion. "University of California Publications in History," XXII, No. 1, 1-72. Berkeley, 1934.

Guttridge, G. H., ed., The Colonial Policy of William III in America and the West Indies. Cambridge, Eng., 1922.

Hagthorpe, John, England's Exchequer, or A Discourse of the Sea and Navigation. London, 1625.

Haines, Richard, The Prevention of Poverty: or, A Discourse of the Causes of the Decay of Trade, Fall of Lands, and Want of Money. London, 1674.

Hakluyt, Richard, ed., The Principal Navigations, Voyages, Traffiques and Discoveries of the English Nation. 12 vols., Glasgow, 1903-05.

Hall, F., The Importance of the British Plantations in America to This Kingdom; with the State of Their Trade, and Methods for Improving It. London, 1731.

Hall, Hubert, A History of the Custom-Revenue in England from the Earliest Times to . . . 1827. 2 vols., London, 1885.

Hansard's Parliamentary Debates. Third Series. 356 vols., London, 1829-91.

Hardy, A. L., ed., Letters Patent Appointing Commissioners, with a Chronological List of Commissioners and Historical Notes. London, 1897.

Haring, C. H., Trade and Navigation between Spain and the Indies in the Time of the Hapsburgs. Cambridge, Mass., 1918. "Harvard Economic Studies," XIX.

Harleian Miscellany, The: A Collection of Scarce, Curious, and Entertaining Pamphlets and Tracts, ed. by John Malham. 10 vols., London, 1808-13.

Harlow, V. T., A History of Barbados, 1625-1685. Oxford, 1926.

Harper, C. G., The Smugglers. Picturesque Chapters in the Story of an Ancient Craft. London, 1909.

Harrell, I. S., Loyalism in Virginia. Philadelphia, 1926.

Harrington, V. D., The New York Merchant on the Eve of the Revolution. New York, 1935. "Columbia University Studies in History, Economics and Public Law," No. 404.

Hart, A. B., ed., Commonwealth History of Massachusetts Colony, Province and State. 5 vols., New York, 1927-30.

Heckscher, E. F., Mercantilism, tr. by Mendel Shapiro. 2 vols., London, 1935.

Hertslet, Lewis, comp., A Collection of Treaties and Conventions between Great Britain and Foreign Powers, and of the Laws, Decrees, Orders in Council, etc., Concerning . . . Commerce and Navigation. . . . 31 vols., London, 1840-1925.

Higham, C. S. S., The Development of the Leeward Islands under the Restoration, 1660-1688. Cambridge, Eng., 1921.

Hill, C. E., The Danish Sound Dues and the Command of the Baltic. Durham, N. C., 1926. "Duke University Publications."

Hinman, R. R., comp., Letters from the English Kings and Queens . . . to the Governors of the Colony of Connecticut, together with Answers Thereto, from 1635 to 1749. Hartford, 1836.

Hodges, William, The Groans of the Poor, the Misery of the Traders, and the Calamity of the Publick for the Spoiling of Our Money, for the Want of Our Money. . . . London, 1696.

—— Humble Proposals for the Relief, Encouragement, Security and Happiness of the . . . Seamen of England. London, 1695.

—— Ruin to Ruin after Misery to Misery. Being the Distressed and Ruined and Perishing State of the Loyal and Faithful Seamen of England. . . . London, 1699.

Holmes, G. K., comp., Tobacco Crop of the United States, 1612-1911. U. S. Department of Agriculture, Bureau of Statistics, Circular No. 33. Washington, 1912.

Hoon, E. E., The Organization of the English Customs System, 1696-1786. New York, 1938.

Hough, C. M., ed., Reports of Cases in the Vice Admiralty of the Province of New York and in the Court of Admiralty of the State of New York, 1715-1788. New Haven, 1925. "Yale Historical Publications Manuscripts and Edited Texts," VIII.

Houghton, John, comp., Husbandry and Trade Improv'd: Being a Collection of Many Valuable Materials. . . . 4 vols., London, 1727-28.

Hughson, S. C., The Carolina Pirates and Colonial Commerce (1670-1740). Baltimore, 1894. "Johns Hopkins University Studies in Historical and Political Science," XII, Nos. 5, 6, 7.

Hume, David, The History of England from the Invasion of Julius Caesar to the Revolution in 1688. 6 vols., New York, 1880.

Hunter, H. C., How England Got Its Merchant Marine, 1066-1776. New York, 1935.

Hutchinson, J. R., The Press-Gang Afloat and Ashore. London, 1913.

Hutchinson, Thomas, The Diary and Letters of His Excellency Thomas Hutchinson . . . Governor-in-Chief of Massachusetts Bay, comp. by P. O. Hutchinson. 2 vols., Boston, 1884-86.

—— The History of Massachusetts, from the First Settlement Thereof in 1628, until the Year 1750. 3d ed. 2 vols., Boston, 1795.

Index Vectigalium, The. Compiled under the Authority of the Farmers and Managers of the Customs. London, 1670. (Listed in the British Museum Catalogue under "England. Laws and Statutes, IV, Collections and Abridgements on Particular Subjects: Customs.")

"J. P., Esq.," Of Trade . . . Also, of Coyn, Bullion. Of Improving Our Woollen Manufacture. . . . London, 1700.

Jacobsen, G. A., William Blathwayt, a Late Seventeenth Century English Administrator. New Haven, 1932. "Yale Historical Publications. Miscellany," XII.

Jacobstein, Meyer, The Tobacco Industry in the United States. New York, 1907. "Columbia University Studies in History, Economics, and Public Law," XXVI, No. 3.

Jameson, J. F., Privateering and Piracy in the Colonial Period. New York, 1923.

Jasper Mauduit, Agent in London for the Province of the Massachusetts-Bay, 1762-1765. Boston, 1918. "Collections of the Massachusetts Historical Society," LXXIV.

Jenver, Thomas, London's Blame If Not Its Shame Manifested by the Great Neglect of the Fishery. London, 1651.

Johnsen, O. A., "L'Acte de navigation anglais du 9 octobre 1651." *Revue d'histoire moderne*, New Series, III (1934), 5-15.

Johnson, A. H., "Professor Ashley on the Commercial Legislation of England." *Economic Journal*, X (1900), 96-103.

Johnson, E. A. J., "Some Evidence of Mercantilism in the Massachusetts-Bay." *New England Quarterly*, I (1928), 371-95.

Johnson, E. R., T. W. Van Metre, G. G. Huebner, and D. S. Hanchett, History of Domestic and Foreign Commerce of the United States. 2 vols., Washington, 1915. "Carnegie Institution of Washington, Publications," No. 215.

Jones, P. E., and A. V. Judges, "London Population in the Late Seventeenth Century." *Economic History Review*, VI (1935), 45-63.

Josselyn, John, An Account of Two Voyages to New England. [1675.] Reprinted in "Collections of the Massachusetts Historical Society," 3d series, III (1833), 211-354.

Judah, C. B., The North American Fisheries and British Policy to 1713. Urbana, 1933. "University of Illinois Studies in the Social Sciences," XVIII, Nos. 3-4.

Kaye, P. L., English Colonial Administration under Lord Clarendon, 1660-1667. Baltimore, 1905. "Johns Hopkins University Studies in Historical and Political Science," XXIII, Nos. 5-6.

Keiler, Hans, American Shipping, Its History and Economic Conditions. Jena, 1913.

Keith, Theodora, Commercial Relations of England and Scotland, 1603-1707. Cambridge, Eng., 1910.

Kennedy, J. H., Thomas Dongan, Governor of New York, 1682-1688. Washington, 1930.

Khan, S. A., The East India Trade in the XVIIth Century in Its Political and Economic Aspects. Oxford, 1923.

Kiaer, A. N., "Historical Sketch of the Development of Scandinavian Shipping." *Journal of Political Economy*, I (1892-93), 329-64.

Kingsbury, S. M., "A Comparison of the Virginia Company with the Other English Trading Companies of the Sixteenth and Seventeenth Centuries." American Historical Association. *Annual Report*, I (1906), 159-76.

Knight, M. M., H. E. Barnes and Felix Flügel, Economic History of Europe. Boston, 1928.

Labaree, L. W., "The Early Careers of the Royal Governors." Essays in Colonial History Presented to Charles McLean Andrews by His Students, New Haven, 1931, pp. 145-68.

———— Royal Government in America; a Study of the British Colonial System before 1783. New Haven, 1930. "Yale Historical Publications. Studies," VI.

———— ed., Royal Instructions to British Colonial Governors, 1670-1776. 2 vols., New York, 1935.

Lacy, Joseph, Observations on the Nature, Use and Trade of Tobacco. London, 1773.

Langham, Thomas, The Nett Duties and Drawbacks Payable on Importation and Exportation of All Sorts of Merchandize. 8th ed., London, 1758.

Lavisse, Ernest, Histoire de France depuis les origines jusqu'à la révolution. 9 vols. in 18, Paris, 1905.

Lefroy, J. H., Memorials of the Discovery and Early Settlement of the Bermudas, 1515-1685. 2 vols., London, 1877-79.

Leftwich, B. R., "The Early London Customs Service." *P. L. A. Monthly*, Sept., 1928, pp. 337-44.

Lewis, Mark, Proposals to Increase Trade and to Advance His Majesties Revenue, without Any Hazard, or Charge to Anybody, and with Apparent Profit to Everybody. London, 1677.

———— Proposals to the King and Parliament, How the Tax . . . May Be Raised . . . London, 1677.

Lindsay, W. S., History of Merchant Shipping and Ancient Commerce. 4 vols., London, 1874-76.

Lipson, Ephraim, The Economic History of England. 3 vols., London, 1931.

Longfield, A. K., Anglo-Irish Trade in the Sixteenth Century. London, 1929.

Lounsbury, R. G., The British Fishery at Newfoundland, 1634-1763. New Haven, 1934. "Yale Historical Publications. Miscellany," XXVII.

Lubbock, A. B., The China Clippers. Glasgow, 1914.

Ludlow, Edmund, The Memoirs of . . ., 1625-1672. 2 vols., Oxford, 1894.

McClellan, W. S., Smuggling in the American Colonies at the Outbreak of the Revolution, with Special Reference to the West Indies Trade. New York, 1912.

McCrady, Edward, The History of South Carolina under the Proprietary Government, 1670-1719. New York, 1897.

———— The History of South Carolina under the Royal Government, 1719-1776. New York, 1899.

McCulloch, J. R., ed., A Select Collection of Early English Tracts on Commerce. London, 1856.

McGovney, D. O., "The Navigation Act as Applied to European Trade." *American Historical Review*, IX (1904), 725-34.

MacGregor, John, Commercial Statistics of America. London [1847].

McIlwain, C. H., The American Revolution: a Constitutional Interpretation. New York, 1923.

MacInnes, C. M., The Early English Tobacco Trade. London, 1926.

Macpherson, David, Annals of Commerce, Manufactures, Fisheries and Navigation. 4 vols., London, 1805.

Malynes, Girard de, The Center of the Circle of Commerce. London, 1623.

Manley, Thomas, Usury at Six Percent Examined and Found Unjustly Charged . . . London, 1669.

Manx Society Publications. 33 vols., Douglas, Isle of Man, 1859-94[?].

Marsden, R. G., "English Ships in the Reign of James I." *Royal Historical Society Transactions*, New Series, XIX (1905), 309-42.

Marvell, Andrew, The Works of . . ., ed. by Capt. Edward Thompson. 3 vols., London, 1776.

Maryland. Archives of Maryland, ed. by W. H. Browne and others. 54 vols., in progress, Baltimore, 1883—.

Maryland Historical Magazine. Baltimore, 1906—.

Massachusetts. Colonial Society, Publications of . . . Transactions and Collections. 32 vols., in progress, Boston, 1892—.

Massachusetts. Records of the Governor and Company of the Massachusetts Bay in New England, ed. by N. B. Shurtleff. 5 vols., Boston, 1853-54.

Massachusetts Historical Society. Collections. Boston, 1795—.

Miller, L. R., "New Evidence of the Shipping and Imports of London, 1601-02." *Quarterly Journal of Economics*, XLI (1927), 740-60.

Mims, S. L., Colbert's West India Policy. New Haven, 1912. "Yale Historical Studies," I.

Misselden, Edward, The Circle of Commerce. Or the Ballance of Trade in Defence of Free Trade. London, 1623.

Monson, Sir William, The Naval Tracts of . . . , ed. by Michael Oppenheim. 5 vols., London, 1902-14. "Navy Records Society Publications," XXII, XXIII, XLIII, XLV, XLVII.

Moreau, César, Chronological Records of the British Royal and Commercial Navy. London, 1827.

Morison, S. E., "The Commerce of Boston on the Eve of the Revolution." *American Antiquarian Society Proceedings*, XXXII (1922), 24-51.

—— The Maritime History of Massachusetts, 1783-1860. Boston, 1921.

Morris, R. B., ed., Select Cases of the Mayor's Court of New York City, 1674-1784. Washington, 1935. "American Legal Records," II.

—— Studies in the History of American Law, with Special Reference to the Seventeenth and Eighteenth Centuries. New York, 1930. "Columbia University Studies in History, Economics, and Public Law," No. 316.

Morriss, M. S., Colonial Trade of Maryland, 1689-1715. Baltimore, 1914. "Johns Hopkins University, Studies in Historical and Political Science," XXXII, No. 3.

Mun, Thomas, England's Treasure by Forraign Trade. London, 1669.

Murray, A. E., The History of the Commercial and Financial Relations between England and Ireland. London, 1903.

Naked Truth, The, in an Essay upon Trade; with Some Proposals for Bringing the Ballance on Our Side, etc. London, 1696.

Nef, J. U., The Rise of the British Coal Industry. 2 vols., London, 1932.

Nettels, C. P., The Money Supply of the American Colonies before 1720. Madison, 1934. "University of Wisconsin Studies in the Social Sciences and History," No. 20.

Newcastle Merchant Adventurers. Extracts from the Records of the Merchant Adventurers of Newcastle-upon-Tyne, ed. by J. R. Doyle and F. W. Dendy. 2 vols., Durham and London, 1895-99. "Surtees Society Publications," XCIII and CI.

New England Historical and Genealogical Register. 89 vols., in progress, Boston, 1847—.

New Hampshire Historical Society. Collections. Concord, 1827—.

New Jersey. Documents relating to the Colonial History of the State of New Jersey, ed., by W. A. Whitehead, F. W. Ricord, William Nelson. 34 vols., Newark and Paterson, 1880-1931. "Archives of the State of New Jersey," first series.

Newton, A. P., The Colonising Activities of the English Puritans. New Haven, 1914. "Yale Historical Publications. Miscellany," I.

———— "The Establishment of the Great Farm of the English Customs." *Royal Historical Society Transactions*, 4th series, I (1918), 129-56.

New York. The Colonial Laws of New York. 5 vols., Albany, 1894-96.

———— The Documentary History of the State of New York, ed. by E. B. O'Callaghan. 4 vols., Albany, 1850-51.

———— Documents relative to the Colonial History of the State of New York, ed. by E. B. O'Callaghan. 15 vols., Albany, 1853-87.

New York Historical Society. Collections. New York, 1868—.

North Carolina. The Colonial Records of North Carolina, ed. by W. L. Saunders. 10 vols., Raleigh, 1886-90. Continued as The State Records of North Carolina.

———— The State Records of North Carolina, ed. by Walter Clark, S. B. Weeks. 20 vols., Raleigh, 1886-1914. Continuation of The Colonial Records.

O'Brien, G. A. T., Economic History of Ireland in the Seventeenth Century. Dublin and London, 1919.

Observations Touching Trade and Commerce with the Hollander (1620). In Raleigh's *Works*, II, 109-36. More recently attributed to John Keymor (Barbour, "Dutch and English Merchant Shipping," *Economic Historical Review*, II, 267; Oppenheim in Monson, Naval Tracts, V, 206).

Ogg, David, England in the Reign of Charles II. 2 vols., Oxford, 1934.

Oppenheim, Michael, A History of the Administration of the Royal Navy and of Merchant Shipping in Relation to the Navy, from MDIX to MDCLX. London, 1896.

Osgood, H. L., The American Colonies in the Seventeenth Century. 3 vols., New York, 1904-7.

——— The American Colonies in the Eighteenth Century. 4 vols., New York, 1924.

Page, William, Commerce and Industry; a Historical Review of the Economic Conditions of the British Empire from 1815 to 1914. 2 vols., London, 1919.

Palfrey, J. G., A Compendious History of New England from the Discovery by Europeans to the First General Congress of the Anglo-American Colonies. 4 vols., Boston, 1883.

Pares, Richard, War and Trade in the West Indies, 1739-1763. Oxford, 1936.

Penn, William, Correspondence between William Penn and James Logan . . ., 1700-1750, ed. by Edward Armstrong. 2 vols., Philadelphia, 1870-72. "Memoirs of the Historical Society of Pennsylvania," IX-X.

Pennsylvania. Memoirs of the Historical Society of Pennsylvania. 14 vols., Philadelphia, 1826-95.

——— Minutes of the Provincial Council of Pennsylvania, from the Organization to the Termination of the Proprietary Government (1683-1775). 10 vols., Philadelphia, 1851-52.

Pennsylvania Archives, 1st series, ed. by Samuel Hazard. 12 vols., Philadelphia, 1825-56.

Penson, L. M., The Colonial Agents of the British West Indies; a Study in Colonial Administration, Mainly in the Eighteenth Century. London, 1924.

——— "The London West India Interest in the Eighteenth Century." *English Historical Review*, XXXVI (1921), 373-92.

Pepys, Samuel, The Diary of . . ., ed. by H. B. Wheatley. 9 vols., London, 1904-10.

Perry, W. S., ed., Historical Collections relating to the American Colonial Church. 5 vols., Hartford, 1870-78.

Petty, Sir William, The Economic Writings of . . ., ed. by C. H. Hull. 2 vols., Cambridge, Eng., 1899.

——— The Petty Papers, ed. by the Marquis of Lansdowne. 2 vols., London, 1927.

Pickering, Danby, ed., The Statutes at Large . . . of Great Britain. 46 vols., Cambridge, Eng., 1762-1807.

Pitkin, Timothy, A Statistical View of the Commerce of the United States of America. Hartford, 1816.

Pitman, F. W., The Development of the British West Indies, 1700-1763. New Haven, 1917. "Yale Historical Publications. Studies," IV.

Playfair, Sir R. L., The Scourge of Christendom: Annals of British Relations with Algiers prior to the French Conquest. London, 1884.

Potter, William, The Key to Wealth. London, 1650.

―――― The Tradesman's Jewel: or, a Safe, Easie, Speedy and Effectual Means for the Incredible Advancement of Trade. London, 1650.

Practice in the Office of Pleas of the Court of the Exchequer, Epitomized. London, 1824.

Price, George, Attorney's Practice in the Exchequer of Pleas. London, 1831.

―――― A Treatise on the Law of the Exchequer. London, 1830.

Prothero, R. E., English Farming, Past and Present. 8 vols., London, 1912.

Prowse, D. W., A History of Newfoundland, from the English, Colonial, and Foreign Records. London, 1896.

Purchas, Samuel, ed., Hakluytus Posthumus or Purchas His Pilgrimes: Contayning a History of the World in Sea Voyages and Lande Travells by Englishmen and Others. 20 vols., Glasgow, 1905-7.

Ragatz, L. J., The Fall of the Planter Class in the British Caribbean, 1763-1833. New York, 1928.

Raleigh, Sir Walter, or Sir Dudley Digges, A Discourse of Seaports; Principally of the Port and Haven of Dover. . . . [London, 1700.] *Harleian Miscellany,* IV, 305-9.

―――― The Works of, . . . Now First Collected. 8 vols., Oxford, 1829.

Reeves, John, History of the Law of Shipping and Navigation. Dublin, 1792.

Rerum britannicarum medii aevi scriptores. 99 vols. in 254, London, 1887-1911.

Reynel, Carew, The True English Interest: or an Account of the Chief National Improvements. . . . London, 1674.

Rhode Island. Records of the Colony of Rhode Island and Providence Plantations in New England. 10 vols., Providence, 1856-65.

Ricardo, J. L., The Anatomy of the Navigation Laws. London, 1847.

Rive, Alfred, "A Brief History of the Regulation and Taxation of Tobacco in England." *William and Mary College Quarterly Historical Magazine,* 2d series, IX (1929), 1-12, 73-87.

―――― "A Short History of Tobacco Smuggling." *Economic History,* I (1926-29), 554-69.

Roberts, Lewes, The Merchants Mappe of Commerce; Wherein the Universal Manner and Matter of Trade, Is Compendiously Handled, etc. London, 1638.

―――― The Treasure of Traffike: Or a Discourse of Forraigne Trade. London, 1641.

Robinson, Henry, Certain Considerations in Order to a More Speedy . . .
Justice. London, 1651.
———— Certain Proposals in Order to the People's Freedom, etc. London,
1652.
———— England's Safety in Trades Encrease. London, 1641.
Roe, Thomas, "Sir Thomas Roe's Speech in Parliament." [London, 1641.]
Harleian Miscellany, IV, 433-37.
Root, W. T., The Relations of Pennsylvania with the British Govern-
ment, 1696-1765. New York, 1912. "University of Pennsylvania Pub-
lications. History."
Routh, E. M. G., Tangier, England's Lost Atlantic Outpost, 1661-1684.
London, 1912.
Rowe, John, Letters and Diary of John Rowe, Boston Merchant, 1759-
1762, 1764-1779, ed. by A. R. Cunningham. Boston, 1903.
Rowland, A. L., England and Turkey. Philadelphia, 1924. "Studies in
English Commerce and Exploration in the Reign of Elizabeth."
Rules and Orders of the Court of the Exchequer relative to the Equity
Court, the Office of Pleas, and the Revenue. London, 1766.
Rymer, Thomas, comp., Foedera. 10 vols., London, 1739-45.
"S. E., A Lover of His Country," The Touchstone of Mony and Com-
merce, or an Expedient for Increase of Trade, Mony and Shiping in
England. . . . London, 1653.
Saxby, Henry, The British Customs, Containing an Historical and
Practical Account of Each Branch of That Revenue. London, 1757.
Schanz, Georg, Englische Handelspolitik. 2 vols., Leipzig, 1881.
Scharf, J. T., History of Maryland, from the Earliest Period to the Present
Day. 3 vols., Baltimore, 1879.
Schlesinger, A. M., The Colonial Merchants and the American Revolu-
tion, 1763-1776. New York, 1918. Columbia University Studies in
History, Economics and Public Law, LXXVIII, No. 182.
Schmoller, Gustav, The Mercantile System and Its Historical Significance.
[London, 1896], tr. by W. J. Ashley. New York, 1931.
Schumpeter, E. B., "English Prices and Public Finance, 1660-1822."
The Review of Economic Statistics, XX (1938), 21-37.
Schuyler, R. L., Parliament and the British Empire; Some Constitutional
Controversies concerning Imperial Legislative Jurisdiction. New York,
1929.
Score, Richard, A Guide to the Customers and Collectors Clerks. London,
1699.
Scott, W. R., The Constitution and Finance of English, Scottish, and Irish
Joint-Stock Companies to 1720. 3 vols., Cambridge, Eng., 1910-12.
Seybert, Adam, Statistical Annals . . . of the United States of America.
Philadelphia, 1818.
Shaw, W. A., "The Beginnings of the National Debt." Historical Essays

by Members of the Owens College, ed. by T. F. Tout and J. Tait. Manchester, 1907, pp. 391-422.

Sheffield, J. B. H., Observations on the Commerce of the American States. 6th ed., London, 1784.

—— Observations on the Manufactures, Trade, and Present State of Ireland. 2d ed., London, 1785.

Sheridan, Thomas, A Discourse of the Rise and Power of Parliaments . . . 1677. Reprinted in Saxe Bannister, Some Revelations in Irish History. London, 1870.

Shillington, V. M., and A. B. W. Chapman, The Commercial Relations of England and Portugal. London, 1907.

Sims, William, and Richard Frewin, Rates of Merchandize as Settled by . . . 12 Car. II, cap. 4 . . . London, 1782.

Sioussat, St. G. L., English Statutes in Maryland. Baltimore, 1903. "Johns Hopkins University Studies in Historical and Political Science," XXI, Nos. XI-XII.

Skeel, C. A. J., "The Canary Company," *English Historical Review*, XXXI (1916), 529-44.

Slush, Barnaby, The Navy Royal: Or, a Sea Cook Turn'd Projector; Containing a Few Thoughts about Manning Our Ships of War with the Best of Sailors, without Violences. . . . London, 1709.

Smith, Adam, An Inquiry into the Nature and Causes of the Wealth of Nations, ed. by J. S. Nicholson. London, 1901.

Smith, Sir Hubert L., The Board of Trade. London, 1928.

Smith, J. R., "The World Entrepôt." *Journal of Political Economy*, XVIII (1910), 697-713.

Sombart, Werner, Der moderne Kapitalismus. 3 vols. in 6, Munich, 1928.

South Carolina. The Statutes at Large of South Carolina, ed. by Thomas Cooper and D. J. McCord. 10 vols., Columbia, 1836-41.

South Carolina Historical Society. Collections. 5 vols., Charleston, 1857-1897.

Spotswood, Alexander, The Official Letters of Alexander Spotswood, Lieutenant-Governor of the Colony of Virginia, 1710-1722 . . . 2 vols., Richmond, 1882-85. "Collections of the Virginia Historical Society," New Series, I-II.

Stock, L. F., ed., Proceedings and Debates of the British Parliaments respecting North America. 4 vols., in progress, Washington, 1924—. "Carnegie Institution of Washington, Publications," No. 338.

S[tockton], W[illiam], The Foreign Excise Considered. London, 1663.

Stokes, I. N. P., comp., The Iconography of Manhattan Island, 1498-1909. Compiled from Original Sources. . . . 6 vols., New York, 1915-28.

Strafford, Thomas Wentworth, Earl of, Letters and Despatches, with an Essay towards His Life by Sir G. Radcliffe, ed. by W. Knowler. 2 vols., London, 1739.

Teignmouth, Lord, and C. G. Harper, The Smugglers. 2 vols., London, 1923.

Thurloe, John, A Collection of the State Papers . . . Containing Authentic Memorials of the English Affairs from the Year 1638, to the Restoration of King Charles II, ed. by Thomas Birch. 7 vols., London, 1742.

Toppan, R. N., Edward Randolph; Including His Letters and Official Papers . . ., 1676-1703. Vols. I-V. Vols. VI-VII ed. by A. T. S. Goodrick. Boston, 1898-1909. "Prince Society Publications."

Towle, D. S., ed., Records of the Vice-Admiralty Court of Rhode Island, 1716-1752. Introduction by C. M. Andrews. Washington, 1936. "American Legal Records," III.

"Trade's Increase, The." [London, 1615.] *Harleian Miscellany*, IV, 212-31. Until recently the author was known only as "J. R.," but on the basis of APC (1615-16), pp. 99, 107-8, it is now attributed to Robert Kayll.

Train, Joseph, An Historical and Statistical Account of the Isle of Man. 2 vols., London, 1845.

Trevers, Joseph, An Essay to the Restoring of Our Decayed Trade, Wherein Is Described the Smugglers, Lawyers, and Officers Frauds, etc. London, 1675.

Tudor and Stuart Proclamations, 1485-1714; Calendared by Robert Steele under the Direction of the Earl of Crawford. . . . 2 vols., Oxford, 1910.

Tudor Economic Documents, ed. by R. H. Tawney and Eileen Power. 3 vols., London, 1924. "University of London Historical Series," IV.

Turner, E. R., The Privy Council of England in the Seventeenth and Eighteenth Centuries, 1603-1784. 2 vols., Baltimore, 1927-28.

United States. Bureau of Navigation: Annual Report of the Commissioner of Navigation, 1901. Washington, 1901.

———— Merchant Marine Statistics, 1932. Washington, 1932.

United States. Commerce and Navigation. Annual Reports of the Register of the Treasury, published separately from 1845 to 1865. Prior to 1845, appear only in House and Senate Executive Documents. 1865-1911, published by Bureau of Statistics; 1911 to date, a publication of the Bureau of Foreign and Domestic Commerce.

United States. Congress. American State Papers. Documents Legislative and Executive of the Congress of the United States. Class IV, *Commerce and Navigation*, Mar. 3, 1789-Mar. 3, 1815. Washington, 1832-34.

———— Thirty-first Congress, Second Session, Senate Executive Document No. 23. "Trade and Commerce of the British American Colonies with the United States and Other Countries since 1829."

———— Thirty-fourth Congress, First Session, House Executive Document No. 47. "Report on the Commercial Relations of the United States with All Foreign Nations."

———— Thirty-fourth Congress, First Session, Senate Executive Document No. 107. "Report on the Commercial Relations of the United States with All Foreign Nations."

United States. Forty-first Congress, Second Session, House Report No. 28. "Causes of the Reduction of American Tonnage and the Decline of Navigation Interests." Washington, 1870.

United States. Merchant Marine Commission. Report of the Merchant Marine Commission, together with Testimony Taken. 3 vols., Washington, 1905.

Usher, A. P., "The Growth of English Shipping, 1572-1922." *Quarterly Journal of Economics*, XLII (1928), 465-78.

Van Tyne, C. H., Causes of the War of Independence. Boston, 1922.

V[ickaris], A., Merchant, An Essay for Regulating of the Coyn. London, 1696.

View of Some Deficiencies in the Aids of Trade, A. London, 1707.

Viner, Jacob, "English Theories of Foreign Trade before Adam Smith." *Journal of Political Economy*, XXXVIII (1930), 249-301, 404-57.

Violet, Thomas, Briefe Observations of Whatte Hath Beene Acted at the Council of Trade 20 Aug. 1650 to Last Dec. 1651. London, 1659.

―――― Mysteries and Secrets of Trade and Mint Affairs. London, 1653.

Virginia. Executive Journals of the Council of Colonial Virginia. 3 vols., Richmond, 1925-28.

―――― Minutes of the Council and General Court of Colonial Virginia, 1622-1632, 1670-1676, ed. by H. R. McIlwaine. Richmond, 1924.

―――― The Statutes-at-Large, Being a Collection of the Laws of Virginia, ed. by W. W. Hening. 13 vols., Richmond, 1819-23.

Virginia Company of London. Abstract of the Proceedings of the Virginia Company of London, 1619-1624, ed. by R. A. Brock. 2 vols., Richmond, 1888-89. "Collections of the Virginia Historical Society," New Series, VII-VIII.

―――― The Records of the Virginia Company of London, ed. by S. M. Kingsbury. 4 vols., Washington, 1906-35.

Virginia Magazine of History and Biography. Richmond, 1893—.

Vogel, Walther, "Zur Grösse der europäischen Handelsflotten im 15., 16. und 17. Jahrhundert," *Forschungen und Versuche zur Geschichte des Mittelalters und der Neuzeit*, Festschrift Dietrich Schafer zum siebsigsten Geburtstag dargebracht von seinen Schülern, pp. 268-333. Jena, 1915.

Walford, J. G., The Laws of the Customs. London, 1846.

Walpole, Sir Spencer, The Land of Home Rule; an Essay on the History and Constitution of the Isle of Man. London, 1893.

Watts, John, Letter Book of John Watts, Merchant and Councillor of New York, January 1, 1762-December 22, 1765, ed. by D. C. Barck. New York, 1928. "Collections of the New York Historical Society," LXI.

Weeden, W. B., Economic and Social History of New England, 1620-1789. 2 vols., Boston, 1890.

Wertenbaker, T. J., The First Americans. New York, 1927. "A History of American Life," II.

—— The Planters of Colonial Virginia. Princeton, 1922.

Westerfield, R. B., Middlemen in English Business, Particularly between 1660 and 1760. New Haven, 1915.

Westergaard, Waldemar, The Danish West Indies under Company Rule (1671-1754). New York, 1917.

Whitworth, Charles, State of the Trade of Great Britain in Its Imports and Exports Progressively from the Year 1697. London, 1776.

Wiener, F. B., "The Rhode Island Merchants and the Sugar Act." *New England Quarterly*, III (1930), 464-500.

Williamson, J. A., Maritime Enterprise, 1485-1558. Oxford, 1913.

Winsor, Justin, Narrative and Critical History of America. 8 vols., Boston and New York, 1884-89.

Wise, J. C., Ye Kingdome of Accawmacke; or the Eastern Shore of Virginia in the Seventeenth Century. Richmond, 1911.

Woodforde, James, The Diary of a Country Parson, ed. by John Beresford. 5 vols., London, 1924-31.

World's Mistake in Oliver Cromwell, The. [London, 1668.] *Harleian Miscellany*, I, 237-96.

Yarranton, Andrew, England's Improvement by Sea and Land to Out-Do the Dutch without Fighting, to Pay Debts without Moneys, to Set at Work All the Poor of England with the Growth of Our Own Lands. . . . London, 1677.

"Z. G.," Excise Anatomiz'd and Trade Epitomiz'd. London, 1659.

Zimmern, Helen, The Hansa Towns. New York, 1889.

Zook, G. F., The Company of Royal Adventurers Trading into Africa. Lancaster, Pa., 1919.

TABLE OF STATUTES CITED

TABLE OF STATUTES CITED

THE FOLLOWING table of statutes has been compiled for the convenience of those who wish to trace the discussion concerning any particular measure and to minimize the confusion which often arises because of the different forms of citing the same law. Cross references appear in the subject index for acts cited by their popular titles, which are included here as an additional means of identification. No attempt has been made to supply the popular titles for all the measures cited; they are given only if mentioned in the text.

Citations for statutes up to and including the reign of Queen Anne are given as they appear in the *Statutes of the Realm* and thereafter as in Pickering's *Statutes at Large*. When the citation in the *Statutes of the Realm* differs from that given in Pickering (or other earlier editions), the Pickering citation is set forth in square brackets. Measures passed during the Interregnum are cited by the date of their enactment, and a parenthetical reference is given to the pages on which they appear in the Firth and Rait edition of such acts.

Another complication which should be explained arises from variations in dating the statutes. An act may have been passed in one year, be given another date in the *Statutes of the Realm*, and still a third by Pickering. Thus one will find the law establishing the plantation duties referred to not only as 25 Car. II, c. 7 (1672), the date given in the two statute compilations, but also as the "Act of 1673," the date of its adoption. In this table the dates used are those given in the *Statutes of the Realm* or in Pickering's *Statutes at Large*, whichever was the source, but in the discussions in the text, reference is made to the date of a law's enactment or to the date it went into effect. Though this method may seem confusing, it does enable one to identify most statutes easily, regardless of the form of the citation sought.

27 Edw. III, stat. 2, c.15 (1353), 86,n.55
28 Edw. III, c.13 (1354), 102,n.21
38 Edw. III, c.8 (1363-64), 102,n.21
42 Edw. III, c.8 (1368), 19,n.1
5 Ric. II, stat. 1, c.2 (1381), 100,n.12
5 Ric. II, stat. 1, c.3 (1381): general provisions of, 19; repeal of, 25, 28; renewed enforcement of, 35,n.3, 36,n.9, 37,n.12; doubts as to interpretation of, 37
6 Ric. II, stat. 1, c.8 (1382), 20,n.2, 37
13 Ric. II, stat. 1, c.5 (1389-90), 187,n.24
14 Ric. II, c.6 (1390), 20,n.3
14 Ric. II, c.7 (1390), 86,n.55
14 Ric. II, c.10 (1390), 81,n.28
15 Ric. II, c.3 (1391), 187,n.24
15 Ric. II, c.8 (1391), 86,n.55
17 Ric. II, c.5 (1393-94), 81,n.28
20 Ric. II, c.4 (1396-97), 102,n.21
21 Ric. II, c.17 (1397-98), 86,n.55
1 Hen. IV, c.13 (1399), 83,n.35
2 Hen. IV, c.11 (1400-1), 187,n.24
4 Hen. IV, c.20 (1402), 83,n.35

INDEX

Customs (*Continued*)
proved by, 170; colonial deputies of,
171-76; administration in colonies, 205;
careless delegation of powers to, 219-
20; governor's instructions prepared
by, 224; concerning governor's oath,
226-27; complained concerning dispensations, 370; statistics of trade for 1669
reported to, 421
farms and farmers of: influenced in passage of Act of 1660, 57, 58; complained
concerning dispensations, 72; under
Charles II, 77-85; before Restoration,
78; numbers of, 78,nn.8,9,10; in minor
branches of revenue, 83-85; power to
inspect all bonds, 121; quarrel with
other officials, 122-24; of 1667, 124;
agents in colonies, 133; advice sought
as experts, 137, 225; early administration of customs staff, 138; quarrel
with colonial proprietors, 156; interested in efficient colonial revenue system, 171, 226; specific rates from, 346,
n.67; relationship to customs statistics,
420-22
officers of, in general: regulation of imports and exports by, 31, 37,n.15, 89-91,
173, 236; seizure and search by, 50, 96,
111, 176; build of vessel determined by,
56; complained of defects in laws, 60-
61; historical background of, 77, 172;
term of office of, 81; powers granted
to, 84,n.47, 163, 175, 176; character
of, 97, 103, 179-81, 237, 251, 264-65,
382; routine of, 102; personnel of,
103-8; salaries of, 106; prosecution by,
114, 170,n.45, 221; efficiency of, 122;
subordinated to Commissioners, 138-39,
140; permanent staff of, 144; problems
in Channel Islands of, 152-53; relations
with other officers, 173-75, 179,n.98;
authority in colonies, 176; quarrels
with colonial proprietors, 181, 209;
plurality of office held by, 186,n.21;
enforcement problems in colonies, 267.
specifically: cashier, 81, cashier general, 106,n.34, 119; Clerk of the Bills or
Tickets, 125; collector: in England, 89,
90, 91, 105-7, 119, 120-21, in outports,
140, in colonies, 166, 168, 171, 173, 175-
76, 245; comptroller, 77, 81, 89, 90, 91,
119, 245; customer, 77, 81, 82,n.34; Inspector General of Exports and Im-

ports (often referred to as Inspector
General of Imports and Exports), 143,
251, 266,n.111, 327,n.23, 344,n.61, 422,
of North America, 273,n.136; Inspector
of Prosecutions, 116-17; "jerquer," 91;
King's waiter, 105; landcarriagemen,
92; landsurveyor, 104; landwaiters, 82,
n.34, 83,n.35, 90, 91, 105, 107-8, 141;
noontenders, 107; patent officers, 82-83,
220; Receiver General, 81, 106,n.34,
140; receiver of London, 119; register
of seizures, 116, 143, 152-53, 172,n.64;
riding surveyor, 153; searcher: at London, 81, 90, 105, 108, in outports, 101-2,
in Virginia, 172, in Barbados, 173,n.69;
solicitor, 113, 116, 123; surveyors: in
England, 81, 89, 90-91, 104, 119, qualifications of, 104, applicants for positions of, 105, in outports, 126, in Channel Islands, 153, in Isle of Man, 156,
in colonies, 171, 172,n.64; surveyor
general: in colonies, 60-61, 172, 181,
199,n.76, in England, 91, 119, 140,n.25;
surveyor of landwaiters, 90-91; Surveyor of Navigation Act, 57, 79,n.10;
surveyor of warehouse, 91; tidesmen,
89-91, 95, 106; tidesurveyor, 90, 91;
tidewaiter, 104; waiter, 77, 81, 105, 106,
n.34, 156, 173,n.69, 245
See also Administration and enforcement; Bond(s); Cargo(es); certifi-
cate(s); Colonies; Court(s); Duty
(ies); Port(s); Revenue; Seizure(s);
Smacks; Smuggling and frauds; Storehouse, King's; Taxes; Toll bills

Danzig: Eastland merchants in, 44, 95,
284,n.49; dispensations granted under
Charles II, 69; relation to Eastland of,
308; Dutch vessels in, 314, 315; Eng-
lish trade with, 314, 324,n.10; duties
on oak of, 372. *See also* Hanse towns
Darien Company, 61
Dartmouth, 38,n.16, 255,n.69, 279, 302,
n.15, 416
"Dartmouth" (ship), 179
Dates, importation of, 241
Davenant, Charles, 10, 234, 236, 237,n.21,
290,n.77, 421, 422
Deals (deale), 55, 317,nn.80,81, 374, 407
Debt(s), 9, 72
Debtor(s), 120, 123
Declaration of Independence, 274

cial relations with, 243-44; early trade with English colonies, 244; seizure of ship trading with, 244,n.23; effect of Acts upon, 365; exceptions allowing trade with former colonies, 396, 399, 402. *See also* commodities by name

Holman, Capt. Hesketh, 200

Honduras, 197-98, 394,n.28. *See also* Logwood

Hong Kong, 395,n.28

Hoops, 402,n.55, 404,n.61

"Hope of Lübeck" (ship), 129,n.23

Hops, 397,n.35, 402,n.51

Horses, 60, 83, 100, 128, 266,n.112, 401

Hosier, Richard, 117

House of Commons, 35,n.2, 45, 46, 61, 226, 279,n.19, 421. *See also* Parliament

House of Lords, 36,n.11, 61-62, 420-23. *See also* Parliament

Hovering, 86, 103-4. *See also* Smuggling and frauds

Howard, Lord Charles, of Effingham, 177, nn.83,89, 222

Hoyes, 26, 339,n.57

Hudson, James, 268,n.122

Hudson's Bay Company, 97, 391,n.7

Hull: John Tavener of, 32; complaints of merchants of, 37; clearings and entries at port of, 38,n.16, 281, 302; coal frauds detected in, 255,n.69; complaint of shipowners of, 324; port books examined, 415

Hundredweight, as unit of weight, 405,n.64

Hungary, 407, 409,n.89, 410,n.93

Huskisson, William, reciprocity policy, 350-51, 352

Hutchinson, Richard, 116

Iberian Peninsula, trade with, 290, 324, n.10, 345. *See also* Portugal; Spain

Iceland, 330-31, 332, 333,n.39, 340-41

Illicit trade, *see* Smuggling and frauds

Imports: exports preferred to, 10, 231; definition of, 64, 408,n.81; procedure for, 90; correlation between exports and, 268, 271; inaccuracy of statistics of, 342. *See also* Customs; Duty(ies); Exports; Smuggling and frauds; commodities and countries by name

Imposts, *see* Duty(ies)

Impressment: of men, 14, 29, 131, 349; of ships, 32; freedom from, 335; fear of, 367-68. *See also* Press gang

Imprisonment, as punishment, 100

Inchiquin, William O'Brien, 2d Earl of, 208; William O'Brien, 3d Earl of, 128, 129

India, *see* East Indies

Indigo: regulations on colonial exportation of, 57, 168,n.40, 204, 398, 399; cocoa entered as, 107; bounty for, 245, n.29, 262,n.96; as exception to direct shipment rule, 392; duties on, 393,n.23. *See also* Dyestuff(s)

Industrial Revolution, the, 363, 377,n.35

Informer(s): provisions encouraging, 26, 51, 161, 169; tribute paid to, 74; forfeitures for, 97, 211-12; complaints against, 98; punished for taking reward, 107; system used by, 113-17; desires to have name withheld, 138; failure of, 169-70, 382; African Company factors as, 173,n.69; in seizure trials, 187, 192-94, 199, 203, 212; seeking favors, 255, n.73. *See also* Forfeiture(s); Penalties; Seizure(s); Smuggling and frauds; Violations

Inspector General of Exports and Imports (often referred to as Inspector General of Imports and Exports): office of, 140,n.25, 143; accounts of, 251, 266,n.111, 422; of North America, 273, n.136; estimate on annual tonnage construction requirements, 327,n.23; values used by, 344,n.61

Inspector of prosecutions, 116-17

Insurance, 12, 86, 238, 269, 327,n.23

Interest rate, 12, 16, 17, 243, 274, 358. *See also* Usury laws

Interlopers, 43, 286, 289, 311. *See also* Slaves and slave trade

Interregnum (Commonwealth): legislative activities of, 34-49; incompleteness of parliamentary records, 39, 58; contributions to Acts of, 50; defects of legislation during, 50-52. For conditions during Interregnum with respect to any topic, *see* that topic

Inverness, "Alexander" (ship), of, 199,n.73

Ipswich, 38,n.16, 281, 302, 415

Ireland: status under Acts with respect to: foreign importations, 38,n.17, 54, 68, 283, 283,n.41, 388,n.1, ships and seamen, 55, 66, 197, 283, 388,n.1, 389, imports from colonies, 162-63, 283,

367,n.10; hazards and hardships of: in East India trade, 14-15, in French trade, 292, in impressment and generally, 100, 322,n.4, 367,n.8; ships to be navigated by English, 25, 32,n.54, 52,n.11, 55, 59, 143, 389-90; failure of Elizabethan fishing legislation to increase, 30; tonnage served by, 35, 321, 330-33, 335, 337,n.51, 389,n.4; scarcity in Russia of, 55, 352; war-time control of, 127; determining nationality of, 192; in intercolonial trade, 273,n.136; Scottish, 285; numbers of, 68, 237, 282,n.37, 321, 322,n.10, 325, 329,nn.27,28; effect of Acts upon, 366-68, 375, 378; attempts to encourage by apprentice laws, 387. *See also* Coal trade; Crews; Fisheries; Impressment; Press Gang; Wages

Searcher(s): post granted by letters patent, 81; relation to exports, 90; in London, 105, 108; in outports, 101-2; in colonies, 172

Search warrant(s), 92

Secretary(ies) of State: connection with Acts of, 131, 137; relationship to colonies, 170,n.49, 207, 219, 220, 226

Seizure(s): of ships and goods in trade with: East Indies, 44,n.35, 240,n.5, Netherlands, 129,n.23, 304, 306, Ireland, 152, 194, 261, colonies, 166, 176-79, 191, n.42, 192-99, 244,n.23, Scotland, 285; during the Interregnum, 50-51, 52,n.10, 304; releases of, 74, 102; form part of officials' salaries, 82,n.32; reasons for, 89; condemnation proceedings for, 109-13, 120, 123; prosecution of, 92, 114-20, 139-40, 192-203, 209, 214; informer system in, 114-16, 161, 169-70, 175, 199, 203; register of, 143; Admiralty jurisdiction over, 185-90; conclusions to be drawn from, 232, 248; by officers of the navy, 250; colonial violations deterred by danger of, 253-56; records of, 419. *See also* Court(s); Penalties; Smuggling and frauds; Violations

Select Council of Trade of 1668, *see* Councils, Committees, etc.

Senegal River, Africa, 69

Senna, 241

Servants, 173, 401

Seth, John Baptist, 95

Settlers, 260

Shaftesbury, Sir Anthony Ashley Cooper, 1st Earl of, 136,n.5

Shallop, 92. *See also* Ships and shipping

Shaw, John, Collector, Customs Farmer, Surveyor of Navigation Act, 57, 78,n.8, 79,n.10, 80,n.22, 82

Sheep, 22, 59, 100-1, 402,n.55

Sheere, Joseph, 156,n.26

Sheffield, J. B. H., 237,n.21, 348,n.72

Shelburne (Shelburn), 402,n.52

Sheriff: trial of seizures by, 92; bail given to, 113; powers of, 120, 121; to assist Customs Commissioners, 140; of London, 142

Shingles, 402,n.55

Shipbuilding (ship construction, shipyards): encouraged by bounties, 31-32, 59, 360; greater protection after 1688, 73; effect of the laws upon, 147, 358-63, 370-75, 378; Dutch, 236; new ships in reign of Charles I, 341,n.60; change in method of, 355,n.97, 357-58, 362-63, 372-73; effect of duties on cost of, 372; costs in various countries of, 372,n.20; as means to national self-sufficiency, 373-74. *See also* Shipwrights

Shipmasters: desire high wages, 12; requirements concerning: pre-Cromwellian, 22, 25, 27-28, 33, Interregnum, 51, post-Restoration, 55, 59, 66, 86, 389; must post notice of intended voyage, 24; members of Trinity House, 31,n.49; petitions of, 42, 52; not expected to determine origin of cargoes, 55; names kept in tidesurveyor's register, 91; must comply with customs requirements, 89, 93, 95; allowed portage bills, 140; bonds given by, 161-62; gifts extorted from, 179; offenses committed by, 193, 257; lacked incentive to trade illegally in Europe, 275; preferred English crews, 366. *See also* Smuggling and frauds; Trinity House

Shipment(s), *see* Trade; commodities by name

Ship-money fleet, 325

Shipowners, 231; not always owners of goods shipped, 11; petitions and complaints: before Interregnum, 20, 31, 34, 35, during Interregnum, 41-42, 52, thereafter, 292, 300, 323; struggles with fishermen, 31; with Merchant Adventurers, 52; played part in enacting Act

Violet, Thomas, 45, 46, 145

Virginia: effect of Acts upon, 40, 60, 129, n.24; administration of trade laws in, 51, 172-74, 177-78, 209; fisheries of, 70, 185, 221-22; price of tobacco of, 115,n.22; colonial regulations in, 167, 169; tobacco trade in, 167, 224, 258; rivalry with Maryland, 168; customs farmers in, 171,n.52; governor of, 174, 175,n.74, 209, 211, 215, 222; courts and trials in, 183, 185, 190, 193,n.49, 195,n.58, 201; trial by naturalization in, 197; used English goods after Revolution, 244; commercial losses of, 246, n.35; illicit trade in, 257; indebtedness of, 273; merchants of, 320,n.94. *See also* Chesapeake Bay Colonies

Vitriol, 299

Vyner, Sir Robert, Customs Farmer, 80, n.22

"Wager in law," 109

Wages: conflict over, 12; relation to prices and trade, 13; insistence upon high, 144; effect of condemnation of ship upon, 193; government in arrears in paying seamen, 367

Waifs, King's title to, 111

Waiters: unnecessary post, 81; in London, 105; salary of, 106,n.34; in Barbados, 173,n.69; fee to, 245

Wales: status under Acts, 21, 65, 162,n.7, 387; Act of 1660 in relation to, 54, 390, 397,n.35; importations from Netherlands and Germany prohibited, 55; Act of 1696 in relation to, 66; imports and exports of, 78; authority of Court of Exchequer in, 110; collection of subsidies and imposts in, 140; seamen in, 323,n.6; ships deemed English, 389

Walker, Dr. Walter, Judge Advocate of the Admiralty, 42

Walpole, Robert, 245,n.32

War, Secretary of, 72,n.40, 142

Ward, Edward, 201

War(s): danger of, 9; importance of money for, 10; convoy regulations during, 12, 167; colonies to serve as a base for, 15; trade freer in time of, 15; between Russia and Sweden, 28,n.35; supply of naval stores in time of, 51,n.2, 69, 307; trade with enemy in time of, 52,n.9, 257,n.77; of pamphlets,

58; dispensations and relaxations in time of, 68, 72, 73, 126, 391, 404; supply of saltpeter during, 73,n.48; privateering in time of, 100, 177,n.83; duties of the Admiralty, 131; colonial trade with Hispaniola during, 193; effect on rate of exchange, 232; futility of, 234; factors influencing, 235; effect on shipping, 237, 326; effect on trade of Napoleonic, 244,n.26; Bishop's, 284; Civil, 326; ships as prizes of, 326,n.20, 359, 369,n.13; effect on customs returns, 346, n.67; shipping inflation because of, 369; duties, 412,n.109. *See also* France; Holland; Spain

Warehouse: record of surveyor of, 91; to be searched by day, 140; King's, in Isle of Jersey, 153; attempt to establish bonded, 245,n.32. *See also* Storehouse, King's

Watchman, 91, 106-7

Waterbailage, officers of the, 96, 156

Waterfront, illicit trade at the, 249-50

Watermen, 96, 126, 172, 173,n.69, 322, 332,n.39

Waterside: law at the, 63; officials at the, 64, 236, 264

Waterways, internal, 12

Watts, John, 182, 269,n.124

Wear River, 336,n.50

Weights, of King, 84

Western Islands, 401, 406,n.75

West Indies, *English:* interest of Thompson and Drax in, 46,n.46; fear of Scottish participation in trade of, 61; duties in, 140, 173; enforcement of Acts in, 167, 177-79, 195,n.58; illicit trade in, 177-78, 202,n.87, 257-58, 260, 263; influence of weather on shipping in, 178, 260, 269-70; treatment of condemned ships in, 199,n.73; wine carriage to, 202,n.87; seizures in, 202,n.87, 244,n.23; in trade with: foreign countries, 204, 244, 354, 395-96, North American colonies, 259, 260,n.89, 269, 403, foreign West Indies, 263, the United States, 273, 353, 393,n.22, 395, 403-4, Ireland, 397, n.35; early sugar plantations in, 243-44; complaints from, 246; reëxports to, 268, n.122, 404; tonnage of, 354,n.94; sugar exports from, 387; trading privileges in, 387, 394,n.28, 395, 400,n.48, 402-4

foreign: wool from, 103; regulation of

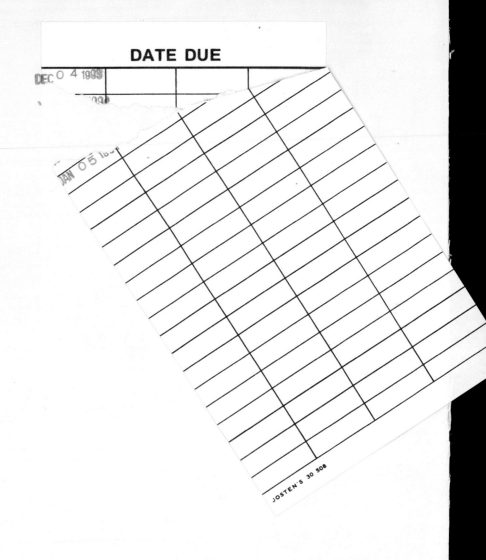